TRIAL
BY JURY

BY
STEVEN BRILL
and the editors and reporters of
The American Lawyer

American Lawyer Books/Touchstone
Published by Simon & Schuster Inc.
New York • London • Toronto • Sydney • Tokyo • Singapore

American Lawyer Books/TOUCHSTONE
Simon & Schuster Building
Rockefeller Center
1230 Avenue of the Americas
New York, New York   10020

Copyright © 1989 by Steven Brill and the editors and
reporters of The American Lawyer

SIMON AND SCHUSTER, TOUCHSTONE *and colophons are*
registered trademarks of Simon & Schuster Inc.

Designed by Irving Perkins Associates
Manufactured in the United States of America

1 3 5 7 9 10 8 6 4 2
1 3 5 7 9 10 8 6 4 2 Pbk.

Library of Congress Cataloging-in-Publication Data

Brill, Steven.
Trial by jury / by Steven Brill and the editors and reporters of
The American Lawyer.
p.   cm.
"American Lawyer Books/Touchstone."
1. Trials—United States. 2. Trial practice—United States.
I. American lawyer. II. Title.
KF220.B7   1989
347.73'7—dc20
[347.3077]   *89-26309*
CIP

ISBN 0-671-67132-4
ISBN 0-671-67133-2 Pbk.

CONTENTS

CONTENTS

CONTENTS

PREFACE

Do jurors *really* think cigarette companies should be held liable when their customers get lung cancer? Do jurors *really* understand libel law? What do they think about "sting" operations? And which lawyers and what types of lawyering *really* impress them?

The best journalism reports on how "the system" works. And in a democracy it is exactly that kind of reporting that provides the ultimate check on our government.

Yet little of that journalism has been focused on one of our three branches of government: the courts. While innumerable books and articles are published analyzing court decisions, far fewer have been written about the decision makers in our legal system: juries and judges.

How and why do they do what they do? What kinds of litigation tactics persuade them? Who really are the most effective trial lawyers? What do judges do that makes juries perform their crucial role the way they are intended to, or that causes juries to fail?

In this collection of articles that appeared in *The American Lawyer* from 1983 to 1988, we look at how judges and juries tackled tough questions in disputes ranging from the *Washington Post* libel trial to the Ivan Boesky insider trading case and the first successful product liability suit against a cigarette company. Although the cases are diverse, they all deal with major issues facing a democratic society: criminal justice, freedom of the press, privileges and obligations of businesses, human rights. How judges and juries attempt to solve these basic problems goes to the heart of how and whether the system works. Reporting on their success—or lack of it—suggests how the system might work better.

Steven Brill

President and
Editor in Chief,
The American Lawyer

FREEDOM OF THE PRESS

A man may publish anything which twelve of his countrymen think not blamable.

—LORD CHIEF JUSTICE LLOYD KENYON, 1789

Tavoulareas
v.
The Washington Post

INSIDE THE JURY ROOM AT THE *WASHINGTON POST* LIBEL TRIAL

BY
STEVEN BRILL

How clever plaintiff's work, the defense lawyer's mistakes, and a stubborn jury foreman decided the case

There was some small talk, even laughter, at 11:25 A.M. on Wednesday, July 28, 1982, when the three-man, three-woman jury went out to decide the libel case of William Tavoulareas, the president of Mobil Oil, and his son Peter versus *The Washington Post* and several of its editors and reporters. Tavoulareas had sued when the *Post* charged in two 1979 articles that he had "set up" his son in an oil-tanker business serving Mobil. Now, as the jurors sat down in the jury room, one of the men remarked, "What's the big deal? We'd all help our sons." Everyone laughed, except Geoffrey Mott, 27, who gruffly noted that it didn't matter if the *Post*'s accusations were true: what mattered was whether the paper had *proved* them.

The only serious business the jury completed before lunch was electing a foreman—Mott. The jurors knew Mott as a tenacious young man with a quasi-legal background. He had told the court at the beginning of the

13

trial that he was a reference librarian in the Library of Congress law library; what he hadn't said—after answering in the negative when U.S. District Court Judge Oliver Gasch asked if he had ever studied law—was that he was enrolled to enter Catholic University law school in September and that he was an ardently aspiring lawyer.

Soon after the first vote was taken. It went 4 to 2 in favor of the *Post* on all counts. The two voting against the *Post* were Western Electric company storekeeper David Ford, 32, and Mott. For the next two days Ford would play a supporting role to Mott's lead in turning the other four jurors around. As we shall see—from accounts provided by five of the six jurors, all of whom asked not to be quoted by name—Mott's argument turned on a wholly incorrect reading of libel law as it applies to any plaintiff and especially to a public figure such as William Tavoulareas.

This case pits the tough, Brooklyn-born, self-made president of the second-largest and most high-profile oil company against the *Post* and its Watergate-famed editors, Ben Bradlee and Bob Woodward. And it matches the Tavoulareases' $2-million legal team from Wall Street's Cadwalader, Wickersham & Taft against the legendary trial lecturer and lawyer Irving Younger, of Washington's Williams & Connolly. Yet it is more than a clash of titans.

It is a story of jury instructions that didn't take hold, flawed defense strategy, and clever, if plodding, plaintiffs' tactics. More than that, it's a story of why the courthouse is a bad place to resolve questions of journalistic fairness, especially when the judge fails to focus issues for the jury and when defense counsel brilliantly masters his case but makes enough mistakes of language and strategy that he performs as if he were lecturing to lawyers rather than to a group of five white- and blue-collar working people and a foreman who thinks he's a lawyer with clients—the Tavoulareases—to acquit.

THE ARTICLES

In 1976 Bob Woodward, back at the *Post* after writing *The Final Days* with Carl Bernstein, received an anonymous note asserting that William Tavoulareas had improperly used Mobil assets to boost his son Peter's shipping business. Woodward called a Mobil official and Peter Tavoulareas and got explanations from both that satisfied him this was not a front-burner story. Nevertheless, according to Woodward's trial testimony, he remained interested and kept a file of his notes.

In July 1979 Woodward, by then editor of the *Post*'s metropolitan section, gave his file on the Tavoulareas tip to one of his newest and most aggressive metropolitan reporters, Patrick Tyler, then 27. About three months later, with Tyler pursuing other oil-company stories but not actively checking this one, Woodward's secretary took a call from Sandy Golden, then a 34-year-old reporter from the *Montgomery Journal* in Rockville, Maryland. Golden claimed he had a great story about an oil-company president; Woodward passed the message on to Tyler.

When Tyler called back, Golden explained that he'd recently had his eyes examined in Baltimore by a Dr. Philip Piro, Jr., and in the course of casual conversation Piro had mentioned that he was the estranged husband of William Tavoulareas's daughter and that he had information about how Tavoularcas had used his position at Mobil to help Peter get started in what had since become a fabulously lucrative oil-shipping business.

Golden also told Tyler that he'd give his information and his source (Piro) to Tyler and the *Post* only if Tyler promised him a byline on the resulting story. Golden needed that kind of byline credit to bootstrap his way into a job at a better paper, perhaps even the *Post*, he explained. Tyler was noncommittal, saying he'd have to meet Piro first to see how good his information was.

On October 26, 1979, Golden, Tyler, and Piro, who would all later be named as defendants in the Tavoulareas suit, met for dinner at the Owl Restaurant in Baltimore. Piro offered a vague tale of the elder Tavoulareas setting up his son in an oil-tanker business called Atlas, which served Mobil exclusively. According to Piro, the father characterized his efforts as having given Peter, who was 24 when Atlas started, "a little nudge" to get his career going.

After the dinner Tyler told Golden he thought Piro's information was too vague to merit Golden a byline. Nevertheless, Tyler pursued the story independently. So did Golden.

Golden, who has a habit of writing postmortem notes of his reporting escapades, detailed the evening's events and his own speculations about Piro's motivations and the *Post*'s ethics. Tyler, he noted, had remarked as they drove to meet Piro that "it's not every day you knock off one of the Seven Sisters [oil companies]." Golden also tape-recorded a series of long and inconsequential phone conversations with Piro—even after he told Piro, on tape, that he wasn't taping him. That exchange, and Golden's stream-of-consciousness notes, were admitted in evidence and would later become some of the plaintiff's most damning evidence of allegedly nefarious motives.

In pursuing the story Tyler soon came across the name George Comnas. Comnas is a longtime oil-shipping executive who had been the key man in establishing Atlas, the company in which Peter Tavoulareas ended up owning a 75-percent equity interest.

When Tyler interviewed Comnas he was told that in 1974 Mobil had begun to fear that Saudi Arabia might take further advantage of its stranglehold on the world oil market by requiring oil companies to use Saudi-owned ships. Thus, Mobil decided that it should form a partnership with a group of Saudis in a shipping company so that Mobil could not be shut out by such a rule. However, having decided to start the shipping company—called Samarco—Mobil also suggested that Samarco should contract with a separate management company to run the ships. That company was Atlas. In short, Samarco would be a nonoperating joint venture that contracted with Atlas.

Comnas told Tyler that William Tavoulareas had asked that Comnas run and part-own Atlas. However, Comnas claimed, Tavoulareas also suggested that his son Peter, then working for Comnas at another, larger Greek shipping company as a $16,500-a-year trainee executive, be brought in as an equity partner. Comnas agreed, he told Tyler, and took in Peter without requiring him to put up any money.

Atlas and an affiliated insurance company prospered, but in 1975, according to Comnas, he was forced out of the company. This left Peter Tavoulareas and a friend of his who also worked there as the sole partners.

Tyler checked Comnas's story, getting additional data on Samarco and Atlas from government shipping records and from others involved in the two companies. He also contacted Peter Tavoulareas. Tyler would later testify that Peter hung up on him after saying only that Mobil had nothing to do with Atlas. (Peter testified that he was a bit more polite and forthcoming than that.) Tyler's requests to interview William Tavoulareas and other Mobil officials were denied, but he was allowed to put questions to Mobil in writing, which a Mobil executive vice president answered in kind.

As Tyler was completing his research, he became worried about Golden getting the story first. In mid-November he got a call from Peter Stockton, a staff aide to Representative John Dingell, who chairs a House investigation subcommittee that oversees agencies such as the SEC. (In 1977 the SEC had briefly looked into the Mobil-Atlas relationship and had found nothing untoward.) Golden had come to Stockton with Piro's charges, Stockton reported. As a result, Stockton told Tyler, he was reopening the investigation and, accordingly, was going to get a statement from Comnas.

Afraid that Golden might scoop him by getting Comnas's information from Stockton and taking it to another paper, Tyler quickly concluded a deal in which Golden would get a credit at the end of the story saying he had helped as a "special correspondent."

On November 30, 1979, Tyler's story ran on the front page, headlined MOBIL CHIEF SETS UP SON IN VENTURE.

The story's lead paragraph stated, "Mobil Oil Corp. president William P. Tavoulareas set up his son five years ago as a partner in a London-based shipping management firm that has since done millions of dollars in business operating Mobil-owned ships under exclusive, no-bid contracts."

Tyler's article, a densely detailed 3,500 words, went on to explain the complicated Mobil-Samarco-Atlas relationship. It charged that "U.S. securities law requires that corporate officials disclose the details of business transactions between companies and relatives of the companies' executives" but that Mobil had not disclosed Peter Tavoulareas's involvement with a Mobil venture until two years after it began, and then only after the press (i.e., Woodward in 1976) had inquired about it. In fact, because Peter was not living in the same household as William, the relationship did *not* have to be disclosed, an inaccuracy hammered away at in the libel trial by the Tavoulareases' lawyers.

The article then quoted Comnas, though not by name, as saying that William Tavoulareas had asked that Comnas take Peter into Atlas, that William had negotiated the Atlas-Samarco deal, that William had been instrumental in forcing Comnas out to his son's benefit and had used Mobil funds to buy Comnas out of his Atlas position, and that after Comnas had been forced out, William Tavoulareas had sent a top Mobil executive to London to help Peter run Atlas.

The story also reported the substance of Mobil's reply to Tyler's written questions—including that Comnas, not William Tavoulareas, had wanted to take Peter into Atlas; that William Tavoulareas had quickly told the Mobil board of the potential conflict and removed himself from final

17

decisions involving Samarco and Atlas, including the dismissal of Comnas and the dispatching of the Mobil executive to replace him; that it was Mobil's fear of a Saudi shipping-preference law, not William's desire to help Peter, that led to the establishment of Samarco; and that the salary of the Mobil executive who had helped run Atlas after Comnas's departure had been shifted to Atlas.

Despite the space given to Mobil's side of the story, it was clear from the headline, the front-page placement, and the tone of the story that the *Post* writer and editors believed Comnas's version of events and generally thought that William Tavoulareas had acted improperly, a point which *Post* editors and Tyler do not now dispute.

This story was followed the next day (December 1, 1979) by a story, also by Tyler, that cast William Tavoulareas in a far more negative light. It reported that Representative Dingell had written the SEC charging that Tavoulareas may have lied when he testified about the Mobil-Samarco-Atlas venture during the 1977 SEC investigation. Dingell's information was based on Stockton's interview with Comnas, which had come after *Post* "special correspondent" Golden had caused the investigation to be reopened by telling Stockton about Piro. Stockton had leaked the Dingell letter to Tyler a week before on the condition that Tyler use it for a follow-up story to his first, November 30, story.

THE COMPLAINT

Beginning with a meeting with *Post* executive editor Ben Bradlee four days after the first story, William Tavoulareas tried to get a retraction. All he got was a brief *Post* story on December 7 acknowledging that Mobil had been repaid by Atlas for the money Mobil paid to buy Comnas out of Atlas.

"For a year," says Tavoulareas, "I tried to get them [the *Post*] to admit their mistakes [such as the misreading of the SEC disclosure requirement]. But they're so damn arrogant. I kept telling them I'd sue. But they said I wouldn't because they'd drag me through the mud in discovery. Well, I know my reputation and my integrity, and I knew they'd get nothing on me. I said, 'You don't know me. I'm gonna sue.'

"I'm not trying to destroy the press," he adds. "I know what a free press means to this country. This suit would not have happened if they'd admitted their mistakes."

Tavoulareas is a plainspoken, appealing man who, indeed, had had an

18

unblemished reputation. Sitting in his office, surrounded by pictures of his family, he pleads guilty to having helped his son—a Columbia business school graduate and, if his trial testimony is any indication, a man who knows quite a bit about the shipping business. Yet William Tavoulareas argues that he helped his son only when an opportunity arose, not that he used Mobil assets to create the opportunity. In short, he asserts, the tone and insinuation of the *Post* stories were wrong and unfair. Whatever one thinks about libel suits as a threat to a free press, it is impossible to understand this case without appreciating Tavoulareas's sense of outrage and his insistence on righting a perceived wrong.

In the fall of 1980 Tavoulareas asked Cadwalader to sue. The firm had done tax work for William and Peter but no work for Mobil. John Walsh, a litigating partner who, by his own estimate, has tried "ten relatively dull cases in the last ten years" and no libel cases, got the assignment.

"You walk into the halls and people you've known for years feel sort of sorry for you. And some are saying, 'Hey, maybe he did something wrong,' " says William Tavoulareas of the days following the *Post* stories. "But the moment I sued, the attitude of everybody changed. . . . Suddenly people started to believe you. My days changed the day I started the suit."

The *Post* turned to Williams & Connolly, where senior partner Edward Bennett Williams has long handled the *Post*'s work and where partner David Kendall tends to day-to-day *Post* matters. It was originally thought that Williams and Kendall would defend against the Tavoulareases. But after Williams fell ill, Younger, who had left academia and the lecture circuit to join the firm in early 1981, took over.

Also sued, for slander, was Dr. Piro, who was defended passively (with only a closing statement) by David Machanic, of Washington's Pierson, Ball & Dowd.

Williams & Connolly made two initial defense mistakes that predate Younger's involvement. The first—not severing its case from that of Piro, the bitter, estranged son-in-law—should have been clear at any point. The second—insisting on a jury trial—is clear at least in retrospect.

Younger, the great lecturer on jury strategy, insists he always prefers a judge to a jury. "As a young criminal defense lawyer I always offered the prosecutor the option of picking a judge, any judge," he says. "I can learn the judge and play to him, whereas a jury, with all its interpersonal by-play and dynamics in the jury room, is unpredictable."

The *Post*, pre-Younger, didn't think a jury would be unpredictable.

19

"We spent several thousand dollars on a poll [by Peter D. Hart Research Associates, Inc.] of people in the District [of Columbia]," says one informed source at the *Post*, "and found that the potential jurors usually liked the *Post* and did not like Mobil. I guess we were associated [through the Watergate stories] with the downfall of Nixon, which in [mostly black] D.C. had to help us."

"In terms of general image and credibility, the *Post* appears to be on much stronger ground than a major oil company like Mobil," the Hart poll found.

"We overreacted to the poll," Woodward says. "I wanted the judge to try it." Woodward, however, was argued down when *Post* general counsel Boisfeuillet Jones, Jr., did a sweep of its clip file and found that the paper had run a slew of uncomplimentary stories about Judge Gasch over the years—including pieces saying that he had "violated the judicial canons" by contributing $500 to John Warner's Virginia senatorial campaign; that he was among the "tax delinquents" on some Virginia real estate; that his afternoon departure for a fishing trip had necessitated that another judge replace him in the middle of a case; and that on at least two occasions Williams, as defense counsel, had criticized Gasch's performance in trials. The judge seemed, in light of the poll, a far less desirable alternative.

Such was the *Post*'s confidence in its Watergate gloss that Younger, in fact, never brought up the backgrounds of his two famous defendants, Woodward and Bradlee, to the jurors (who, as it turned out, were indeed all black, except for foreman Mott). "Irving thought it was better for the jury to do its own detective work—for someone to remind the others who we were," says Woodward, in an account confirmed by Younger. "I suggested he take me through my background, but he said, 'No, let them discover you're Robert Redford [Redford played Woodward in the movie *All the President's Men*] and that Ben is Jason Robards.' "

Of five jurors questioned on this point, none had seen the movie; only one knew of any role Woodward and Bradlee had played in Watergate. And no one brought up any of this in the jury room. ("You mean that's the same Bob Woodward? Oh my God," exclaimed one juror when asked.) What did get mentioned constantly in the jury room was a line of reasoning no judge would have followed—that the paper had to prove that what it said about the Tavoulareases was correct, instead of vice versa.

Younger says that "from the opening statement" of the 19-day trial, "I was sure I had won the case. If the opening clicks, the rest of the case really doesn't matter. And my opening clicked.

"Walsh," Younger adds, "was stumbling. He read everything. That's no way to talk to the jury. I read from no notes. You could tell we had 'em."

Yet while Younger—pacing the floor, gesturing dramatically, tossing off ten minutes of brilliance without a word of notes—may have mesmerized the journalists and the lawyers in the audience, he may have become so used to talking to more trained minds that he talked past his audience of jurors and alternates.

Edwin David Robertson, an intense young Cadwalader partner who assisted Walsh, seems to be exaggerating when he says "the Irving Younger we all saw in the lectures and tapes is the Irving Younger the jury saw, and it was too much." Younger has a different version of his performance: "Dealing with an audience is a matter of physics," he says. "The larger the force, the more of a presence I have to be. With a six-person jury I'm not who I am with an audience of hundreds."

All five jurors interviewed say Younger is a far better lawyer than Walsh. Yet while three described Younger as "charismatic" and two used "exciting" and "fascinating," none used "clear" or anything to that effect; all five used words such as "direct" or "straight" to describe Walsh. Similarly, none of the five could define the phrase "red herring," which Younger used twice at key points in his summation. And when Younger paused in his opening, midway through a breathless, complicated explanation of the Mobil-Samarco-Atlas arrangement to ask, "Have you got it?" none could possibly have answered in the affirmative at that point.

Walsh, on the other hand, was much simpler. He is a man obviously unencumbered by Younger's eloquence or style, and he seemed comfortable about losing the debate contest to Younger as long as his client won the debate.

"Walsh did his work day and might," says Tavoulareas. "But Younger," he adds, "just didn't do his homework the way our group did." As an example, Tavoulareas, a member of the New York bar, cites an instance in which Younger committed a cardinal sin: asking a question to which he obviously did not know the answer. When Mobil public relations vice president Herbert Schmertz was on the stand, he mentioned to Younger that part of his portfolio involved the oil giant's "urban affairs" program. "Tell the jury about that," Younger pressed, for no reason, enabling Schmertz to reply with an example of a program Mobil had recently run at mostly black Howard University in Washington. "The night before my testimony, we had toyed with how I might slip that in,"

Schmertz recalls. "But we decided it would look too obvious if John [Walsh] tried it. Besides, Walsh isn't the kind to do something like that. But Irving did it for us." Adds Tavoulareas, "Here's a guy who's spent [seven] years lecturing about cross-examination, and look what he does with Herb."

Williams & Connolly lawyers say they have examples of Walsh also "shooting himself in the foot," as they put it. My count has Younger shooting far more often.

WALSH MAKES HIS CASE

Walsh decided, as he puts it, with unabashed if unintentional indifference to the law, that "what was on trial here was the raw power of *The Washington Post* to hurt people. When should they be allowed to do that?" The lawful answer is, in the case of a public figure, whenever they want to, as long as they don't publish falsehoods deliberately, or publish falsehoods without caring if they're false *and* if the plaintiff *proves* they're false. But Walsh saw the answer the way the jury ultimately did, with foreman Mott's prodding—that if the paper is abetted in such publishing by a vindictive son-in-law and an ambitious free-lancer who tapes conversations he says he is not taping, the paper should at least pay something if it can't prove the story.

And so the trial proceeded, with Walsh shrewdly stealing the defense's thunder by leading off with two of the defendants—Golden and Tyler—as *his* witnesses. "This allowed me [under the hostile-witness rule] to ask them all kinds of leading questions, to get my case in against them in *my* words with *my* questions," Walsh explains.

Walsh would also have called Bradlee and Woodward for his case if Gasch had not made what Younger calls "an inexplicable ruling" to hold them for the defense's case. "By about the third day," Younger recalls, "I was playing the judge like a violin. I really understood him and how to get to him. So when Walsh tried to call Woodward and Bradlee, I said, 'Judge, you've tried a few cases in your day'—he loved that—'and you know it's all theater. Well, Mr. Walsh is trying to take away my two glamour witnesses.'—you know, Robards and Redford—'It's not fair.' So he [Gasch] told Walsh he couldn't. When I got back to the office and told Ed Williams, he couldn't believe it. 'Gasch has no right to do that,' Williams said."

But Golden and Tyler were enough for Walsh to make his case. Rather

22

than stress inaccuracies in the article, of which there are precious few, Walsh dwelled on the Owl Restaurant meeting. He hit on a suggestion Tyler had made to Piro—recorded in Golden's notes—that it would be great to get someone to "rifle" William Tavoulareas's safe. Tyler testified that it was a joke, and Piro, in a deposition, agreed, but Golden testified that he took it seriously. Walsh also hammered away at a claim made that night by Piro that he had seen Peter Tavoulareas take a briefcase filled with $25,000 in cash to the Bahamas. Of course, there had been no safe-rifling and nothing printed in the *Post* about any briefcase full of cash.

Robertson, the young partner who assisted Walsh, hit away at Golden for his dishonest tape-recording of Piro and his ambition to use this story to boost his career. And he linked Golden to the *Post*, more than either deserved or wanted: Golden because he ended up getting sued for an article he didn't write, and the *Post* because Golden is such an unsavory journalist. Robertson did this by tying Golden to the investigation by Stockton (of the Dingell subcommittee), the existence of which was the focus of the *Post*'s second article. (A journalism ethics class could spend fruitful time focusing on the relationship that allowed Tyler to get Stockton's leak of the Dingell letter on the condition that he save it for headline-making follow-up rather than bury it in the first article. Similarly, Golden's giving information to a congressional investigator yet claiming to be part of a profession that seeks protection under a First Amendment premised on the press's independence from the government is outrageous.)

With Tyler, Walsh dwelled on all kinds of accusations made by Piro and Comnas that Tyler had diligently pursued *but had not printed in the story*. He slammed away at Tyler for having asked customs officials about the $25,000 that had allegedly been removed from the country, thus causing Customs to punch the Tavoulareases into a computerized list of suspects and detain them at various airports. No matter that Tyler was doing his job in checking that story (and in not printing it after it didn't check out) and that if the Tavoulareases had a complaint it was with Customs's lax procedure for identifying suspects.

Gasch allowed all of this testimony, and more. "The judge wasn't inclined to exclude anything," Walsh explains. "He wanted to be fair to everyone and let the jury hear everything."

Walsh also called *Post* copy editor Cass Peterson to the stand. Prior to the publication of Tyler's story, she had written a memo to a national news editor, Peter Milius, questioning its merits. The memo, saved by the *Post*, discovered by the plaintiffs, and admitted into evidence, said in part, "It's impossible to believe that Tavoulareas alone could put together such a scheme for the sake of his son's business career, or that he would want to." Tyler, of course, had been careful to point out in the article that Atlas and Peter's involvement in it were by-products of Mobil's legitimate concern about possible Saudi shipping-preference laws. Yet Younger concedes that "this was the worst single piece of evidence against us because it sounded so bad."

"What Walsh did in his plodding, stumbling way," says Woodward, who sat through most of the trial, "was lay all kinds of land mines that I guess killed us in the jury room."

YOUNGER'S MISDIRECTED DEFENSE

Meanwhile, Younger was trying to prove to the jury that the articles were true.

Unlike Walsh, who used Robertson and senior associate Joseph Artabane to examine some witnesses, Younger did almost everything himself, without notes, always presenting to the jury the figure of a man in total control of his case. In most ways this impressed the jurors, but in at least one respect it backfired. "He was trying to paint a picture of what a bad, arrogant boss [William] Tavoulareas was. But he came off kind of bossy, too, with his snapping his fingers to that young assistant of his," says one juror. What the juror is referring to (and what one other juror mentioned) was Younger's practice of having associate Robert Post hand him exhibits precisely on command.

"We rehearsed that down to the last detail," says Younger, when asked about the jurors' reaction. "We rehearsed how he'd walk up to me and how he'd hand it to me as if I were a surgeon and he were the nurse with the scalpel. That's the impression I wanted to leave. I guess maybe a couple of times the scalpel wasn't there when I put my hand out, and it looked like I was snapping my fingers."

Younger's effort began in earnest with his cross-examination, near the end of Walsh's case, of Mobil chairman Rawleigh Warner, Jr., and William Tavoulareas. He got Warner to concede that Tavoulareas "more than anyone else" was responsible for George Comnas's coming into Atlas. He got Tavoulareas to concede that even if he hadn't asked Comnas to do it, he knew Comnas was taking on his son as an equity partner in Atlas to curry favor with him; that he doted on Peter to the point of speaking with him at least once a day no matter in what part of the world

24

either happened to be; that he had five other relatives working at Mobil; and that his involvement in Samarco and Atlas's affairs was such that after open-heart surgery he'd awakened in a hospital bed and issued an order to Peter concerning a Samarco deal.

Later, Younger had Woodward testify that Tyler's articles were "model" reporting, and he elicited from Bradlee the conclusion that the Tyler stories were a "textbook case of how a responsible newspaper should behave."

In most respects Bradlee is right. Tyler's story was so thoroughly researched that when I asked Walsh to list factual inaccuracies he could find only four:

1. That the SEC does not require, as Tyler wrote, disclosure of transactions between relatives who are not living in the same household. Christopher Little, who was the *Post*'s in-house counsel and is now publisher of a *Post*-owned newspaper in Everett, Washington, read the piece thoroughly prior to publication and should have caught this.

2. That William Tavoulareas had not traveled twice to Saudi Arabia to negotiate the establishment of Atlas with the Arab partners of Samarco. He's right, trivially: Tavoulareas traveled once to Saudi Arabia and once to Geneva.

3. That Tavoulareas's talks on those two occasions were not "negotiations" but discussions he'd inadvertently been dragged into by the Arab partners.

4. That Comnas had asked Peter to join Atlas, and William Tavoulareas had *not* asked Comnas to take Peter in, as Tyler reported. Therefore the term *set up* in the headline and lead to describe whatever William might have done for Peter is inaccurate.

Those last two disputes are, of course, matters of interpretation. Tyler and his editors obviously believed Comnas's claim that William Tavoulareas had "negotiated" and "set up" Peter. And it's that interpretation that Younger insisted on defending.

Had this been an ethics court at a journalism school, Walsh and his clients might have had a good case. (And certainly, a jury there could pillory the *Post* for not knowing to this day who wrote a headline that is arguably biased, depending on one's definition of *set up*. An earlier headline said, FATHER AND SON TIED IN MOBIL VENTURE; no one knows who changed it.) But here, at this trial, the legal standard was: did the *Post* knowingly or recklessly print a proven falsehood?

That's what Younger's summation should have stressed. He should have said the following:

25

• Tyler's story is essentially true: Peter Tavoulareas, whose 1978 tax return as a 28-year-old showed gross annual business income of more than a million dollars four years after Atlas was established versus his $16,500 salary the year before Atlas began, would not have been a partner in Atlas had his name been Peter Jones.

• Tyler was careful to report that the Mobil board had been informed by William Tavoulareas of the possible conflict of interest and careful to report Mobil's written replies to his questions.

• Cass Peterson's memo questioning the story was, in fact, the hallmark of a newspaper that carefully considers its stories; indeed, following Peterson's memo Tyler had clarified several points.

• Nevertheless, there may have been some mistakes in the story; yes, the point about the apparent violation of an SEC regulation was a mistake and, in retrospect, the headline may have been too conclusory. *But none of those mistakes was made recklessly or deliberately*.

Tyler argues that the use of *set up* is justified because he had a right to believe Comnas and his other sources and, moreover, that whether it was Comnas or William Tavoulareas who actually suggested Peter's involvement in Atlas, it was Tavoulareas's position at Mobil that enabled Peter—indisputably with his father's acquiescence and help—to get involved in Atlas. Therefore, Tavoulareas was responsible for his son being "set up" at Atlas, as the headline said.

Woodward, like everyone else at the *Post*, believes Younger did a "fantastic job" and that "it's unfair of us to second-guess him." Yet he does note that "a week before the trial, I got a little concerned about our defense. . . . A month before when I'd first met [Younger], he'd said, 'This case is about a story that's true.' I believed that, but I was wondering if we could win that way. And I told him the real issue is what you can do in journalism. . . . In journalism you have to be able to make judgments based on the best available facts you have. Maybe we should have followed that line more."

Woodward was the only one of the *Post* defendant-witnesses to admit a mistake: that Tyler should have tried to call Mobil for comment one more time before publishing the second story (about Dingell's letter to the SEC). And he was by all juror accounts the most effective defense witness. His view of the issues in the case produced the best *Post* argument at the trial.

"When I took the stand," Woodward recalls, "I quickly realized that the judge was letting witnesses say anything they wanted to." As a result he made this statement during Younger's direct examination of him:

I guess those stories, both of them, fit fully my definition of what I think our job is: the best obtainable version of the truth. It's a version. It's something particularly Pat Tyler worked as intensely as any reporter can work to get at from both sides.

I've heard Mr. Tavoulareas testify that he didn't have time for the George Comnases of the world. I guess in the newspaper business we listen to . . . the Dr. Philip Piros of the world, we listen to everyone. We listen to Peter Tavoulareas, Mr. Tavoulareas—William Tavoulareas, I mean—we listen to the Mobil public relations apparatus. . . . These stories, rather than being something that should be on trial, are a model of digging, thinking, being fair, balancing the story out, and getting at that time what was the best obtainable version of the truth.

And in my opinion Mr. Tyler got it.

A bit later Woodward and Walsh—who made much of the way the story's lead had left out the existence of Samarco as a buffer between Mobil and Atlas—exchanged the following comments:

WALSH: Did you ever suggest to Pat Tyler that he ought to mention Samarco in those opening paragraphs?

WOODWARD: No, sir, I did not, and in fact, as I think I indicated earlier, the problem for us in the story was getting a full, accurate presentation of what was going on in a simple, clear way. I guess everyone who's dealt with this knows it's not very simple and it's complicated.

WALSH: And the best available version of the truth that you gentlemen could put out at that point was to write a story, the lead of which did not mention one of the three companies you were looking at until you got to the sixth paragraph, is that so?

WOODWARD: No, no.

WALSH: Isn't that a fact? It didn't mention Samarco until the sixth paragraph?

WOODWARD: That's a fact and there's a reason for this, and that's what this is all about: you people saying, "Gee, we want you to write the story this way, we want this included, we want that included."

You can write a story a million ways or even more than a million ways. What we do is we process information . . . make it clear. We are trying to be fair and accurate as we were in this story. . . . You're asking a question that hinges on your assumption that you guys [at Mobil] dictate how it's done.

Woodward might have been willing to frame the debate in terms of the *Post*'s having printed its own "best available version of the truth," but Younger never conceded that the article was anything but *the truth*.

"After nineteen days of trial and five thousand pages of testimony, Younger was saying, 'We still wouldn't change a line of the articles,' " says Tavoulareas. "That was the biggest single error he made. All they had to say was, 'At the time, that's what we *believed* was true.' "

"Had Irving [Younger] not had Tyler and the others say, 'We stand on every word in that story,' we might well have lost it," says Walsh. "It would have totally changed the jury's perception of the issues. My only question," Walsh concludes, "is whether the *Post* refused to concede the possibility of some error as a matter of publicity or strategy."

Asked about his decision to argue absolute truth instead of Woodward's "best version" (that is, instead of the law's test of whether the story was published in 'reckless disregard' of the truth), Younger's eyes light up. With all the electricity of his lectures he reaches back to his trial experience as a young defense lawyer and prosecutor in criminal cases in the sixties. The *Post* case, he says, "can kind of be looked at as a criminal case in the sense that the jury's deciding here whether we did something bad. In such a case, where both lawyers are perceived by the jurors to be decent people, the jurors will try to find a compromise. . . . I think, and I've written a treatise on it, that to defend a criminal case on the basis of reasonable doubt—even to use the words *reasonable doubt*—is a mistake, because then you're not giving the jury its room to compromise. You let the judge give them the middle-ground compromise position with his charge to the jury about reasonable doubt.

"Here, the compromise is reckless disregard. So I never mentioned it. I let the judge do it in his instruction."

Thus, Younger concluded in his summation: "Mr. Tavoulareas has been sitting here for the last three or four days, I trust you know, with a Bible. . . . I like to read the Bible, too. . . . The greatest teacher who ever lived, according to John, said, 'For ye shall know the truth and the truth shall make you free.' That's what it says and that, ladies and gentlemen, is what this case is all about."

But first, he noted: "You know [the judge's] words '[the case is now] in your hands,' send a chill down my spine because after three weeks of testimony . . . when it comes time to decide the case, it's in your hands. A group of people chosen at random. . . . I think the law is very wise when it says they, the jury, decide. Because, ladies and gentlemen, jurors can do some things better than lawyers, better even sometimes than judges. Jurors have a wonderful way of being able to put the details to one side, of seeing through the smoke and the fog and getting to what the case is really about.''

Judge Gasch then spent nearly two hours reading instructions that number 37 pages in the trial transcript. He ruled William Tavoulareas a public figure, but not Peter, and he painstakingly explained the burdens of malice and reckless disregard William Tavoulareas therefore had to meet. (The day before, he had also made the absurd declaration that the *Post*'s quoting of the Dingell letter would have been fully protected as neutral reportage of a public official's statement only if Dingell had read his letter to the SEC at a formal press conference or released it officially to the press.)

Then the jury went out.

BEHIND CLOSED DOORS

One of the ironics of Mott's being chosen as foreman during the jury's first pre-lunch deliberation was that he wouldn't have been on the panel at all if an original juror hadn't arrived 15 minutes too late one morning to suit the punctilious Gasch. Mott had been the second alternate, the first having been chosen a few days before, after another juror had National Guard duty. (Both dismissed jurors say they were adamantly in favor of the *Post*.)

Mott was chosen as foreman after Ellie Kelley, a housewife who'd mentioned to the others that she'd had experience on three other juries, declined nomination by David Ford, the Western Electric storekeeper. Kelley would turn out to be the most pro-*Post* juror. Mott, now enrolled at Catholic University law school, works at the Library of Congress law library, where a co-worker describes him as an aspiring lawyer who "is fascinated with the legal process—you know, arguing like a lawyer.''

Just before breaking for lunch the first day, Wednesday, one of the jurors mentioned that a copy of the judge's instructions would be helpful. The idea was quickly seconded. However, Gasch ruled—with Younger and Walsh in agreement—that because the instructions might be read piecemeal instead of taken as a whole, he did not want the jurors to have them. Four jurors would later volunteer to me that, as one put it, "we never understood the instructions and never pretended to.''

When the jurors filed back after lunch, they took seats around the table in the windowless, comfortably air-conditioned room. The two articles in question had been blown up on thick pieces of cardboard about three feet by two feet. They were mounted on an easel at the end of the table, near Ford. Mott asked Ford to read them aloud, which he did, slowly and without emotion.

A vote was then taken on all the confusing multiple counts. (There were two articles, six defendants, including Piro, and two plaintiffs.) "Just the score sheet itself was totally confusing and the subject of some laughter, except to Mott, who was trying to move things along," recalls one juror. Despite the confusion, the vote was 4 to 2 in favor of the defendants on all counts.

Voting with Mott was Ford, who later told the others he'd been persuaded by the fact that the SEC had investigated the Tavoulareases a second time after the publication of the *Post* stories and taken no action. What he didn't know, and what Gasch, in a rare display of restrictiveness, had not allowed into evidence, was the fact that SEC Enforcement Division investigators, with more facts available to them than Tyler, *had* recommended that William be sued, but the commissioners had turned them down. Moreover, Tyler had not charged that anything was illegal except for his mistake about the disclosure role.

Following the first 4 to 2 vote, Mott suggested that the jurors read through whichever of the 160 document exhibits they thought might be helpful. He immediately asked for the memo by Cass Peterson, the copy editor, questioning the first Tyler story. He would cite that exhibit over and over in the next three days. Others traded documents among themselves. No one asked for transcripts of testimony; the group's emphasis on exhibits over testimony would continue unbroken.

Until the judge sent the jurors home at 6 P.M., the jury room resembled a library's silent reading room.

The second day, Thursday, started with more reading, but by 10 A.M., recalls one juror in an account backed by several others, "there was lots of discussion. Mott kept reading the headline and the first paragraph and saying, 'You show me where it proves anywhere else in the articles that Tavoulareas set up his kid.' "

"But he did set him up and we all know that," juror E. Franklin Johnson, an oceanographer for the Department of Commerce, is reported by several jurors to have replied. Whereupon Mott, several recall, said, "I know he did, too. But the article has to prove it. And it doesn't. Even the copy editor said so."

After much back and forth, with juror Ford seconding Mott, the pro-

Post majority seemed to have been backed into Mott's debating arena. Johnson pored through the exhibits trying to prove the "setup." He was joined by Kelley, who argued that the story was essentially true, even if all of it couldn't be proved. But Johnson persevered in trying to meet Mott's test, plowing through the exhibits as the other jurors watched.

When he failed, having been repeatedly cut off and beaten back by Mott, Johnson said, "Let's get off the word *set up*. Let's make believe it's not there, and maybe we can get some progress."

Mott refused. "Just show me where William Tavoulareas set up his son," he yelled.

According to one juror, "After our verdict, one of the alternates who was really swayed by Bob Woodward's speech to Walsh called me and said, 'How could you let that Geoff Mott sway you?' Well, I told [the alternate] that if [the alternate] had been there, [the alternate] would understand. Mott just stuck to his view and wore us down. It was go with him or go and be a stupid, hung jury."

"Mott was like a broken record," recalls one juror. "He kept yelling, 'Where's the setup proved?' " In so seizing the debate, Mott turned Younger's presumptions about the parallel between a criminal trial and a libel trial inside out: it was William Tavoulareas, not the *Post,* who had to be proved guilty. For if he were not proven guilty of the *Post*'s charges, the *Post,* as his prosecutor, would lose.

Had Younger read the Hart report on its opinion poll carefully, he'd have found a harbinger of that turning of the tables. Although one of the questions stated the facts of the suit and found that 75 percent of those polled said they'd be disposed to decide in favor of the *Post,* another question asked which side the respondents would favor if they felt the *Post*'s story was factually inaccurate but that the mistakes were honest mistakes. The results: 40 percent for the *Post* and 40 percent against. Thus, the Hart people reported, if doubts about the story's accuracy were raised, "the *Post* would be in extreme jeopardy because people are not convinced that there is a need to prove malice in order to find the *Post* guilty."

Unguided by Younger, who did not mention reckless disregard in his summation, the jurors fulfilled the pollsters' fears, ignoring the judge's laborious instructions. "The whole thing was," recalls one juror, "that none of us thought big Tavoulareas had *not* set up his son. It's just we couldn't prove it." What if you had just been asked to decide whether the *Post* had been recklessly or deliberately inaccurate or unfair? this juror was asked: "Oh, in that case, there's no way the plaintiff would have won. We all, even Mott, I think, conceded they hadn't done anything careless or on purpose.''

Within Gasch's instructions is this statement:

> It is not the defendants' burden to prove that the articles are true. The burden is upon the plaintiffs to prove to you that they are substantially false. . . .
>
> It is not enough for William Tavoulareas to prove the defendants did not conduct a thorough investigation of the facts or that they were negligent in the way they wrote or edited the articles. To recover, William Tavoulareas must prove the defendants had a high degree of awareness that the articles were false or probably false and that they were recklessly disregarded, whether the articles were false or not. . . .
> If you find the defendants believed the sources of information in the story to be reliable and believed the story to be accurate when published, you must find the defendants have not acted with actual malice as to William Tavoulareas.

Mott and the others operated as if these instructions had not been given. And, ironically, Mott used the article's own balanced treatment to make his case that the headline was not fully accurate, or at least that the *Post* hadn't proved it was. ''Nothing here proves he set up his son,'' he argued, noting that the *Post* article reported both Comnas's assertion that putting Peter into Atlas was William Tavoulareas's idea and William Tavoulareas's assertion that it was Comnas's idea. Mott's point should have rendered the article culpable in a headline-writing contest but totally protected in court, given the judge's instruction that it be read as a whole to determine if it had been defamatory.

Late Thursday another vote was taken. This one went 3 to 3, with publishing assistant Helen Stubbs going over to Mott's side. A reticent woman, she offered little explanation. According to four jurors, a compromise now seemed likely, especially after one juror mentioned that they had to be ''out of here by Friday because the judge is going to go on vacation.'' Gasch had mentioned a planned vacation, and the jurors, mindful of his insistence throughout the trial that court run on schedule, apparently took him a bit too seriously. Another juror recalls that she was concerned by Thursday night that ''we'd be a laughingstock like the Hinckley jurors [who acquitted John Hinckley, Jr., also in Washington] if we let this trial go on for a month and then decided nothing.''

After more arguing, with Mott and, occasionally, Ford pitted against

Kelley and Johnson, another vote was taken on Friday morning. This one went 4 to 2 in favor of the Tavoulareases. The swing vote was Agriculture Department secretary Elease Webb, 33. Webb told the group that the reason she had left Kelley and Johnson and gone over to what was now the pro-Tavoulareas majority was that Younger had not called George Comnas, Tyler's key source and the man behind Atlas, to testify.

Comnas, whose accusations about the ''setup'' were the fulcrum of Tyler's story, seemed a likely *Post* witness, and in his summation Walsh relied on this, repeatedly urging the jury to ask itself, ''Where was George Comnas?'' Younger and *Post* general counsel Bo Jones decline comment on why Comnas was not called, though they argue persuasively that Gasch should not have allowed Walsh to invoke his absence, since, as a non-party living in New York, he was technically beyond the reach of the *Post*'s subpoena power.

Of course Comnas was readily available to the *Post* and willing to testify without subpoena; after all, he, too, is being sued by the Tavoulareases in a separate case. And his deposition testimony had been solidly pro-*Post*. But one source close to the *Post* explains that ''Irving was worried about some less than consistent testimony he'd given the SEC and was afraid it might be used to impeach him. And Irving, you see, was absolutely confident we had it won without him.''

When juror Webb went over to the plaintiffs' side, she suggested a compromise: drop the second article (about the Dingell letter) and lower the damages from the $50 million sought by the two Tavoulareases. In fact, Webb reportedly said, ''Let's give them each a dollar—they don't need the money—and let's go home.'' Mott, Ford, and Stubbs quickly agreed to drop the charges on the second article, but Mott objected to awarding just a dollar. William Tavoulareas was a well-known man whose reputation had been hurt and who'd been humiliated, he argued. One key example, he noted, was the way he'd been detained and searched by airport customs guards, which of course had nothing to do with anything printed in the *Post* articles.

It might be okay to give Peter Tavoulareas only a dollar or even nothing, Mott and Ford continued, because the judge had ruled him a private person with no real reputation to damage. But William Tavoulareas, the judge had said, was a public figure. Therefore, he had a valuable reputation to protect, Mott argued. In short, Mott, whether knowingly or not, had taken the judge's public-figure instruction about William, meant to give the *Post* more latitude in writing about him, and stood it on its head.

33

THE FINAL VOTE

By 1:30, just after lunch on Friday, pro-*Post* holdout Johnson was ready to give in. He was persuaded by Webb's point about Comnas's absence. He suggested as a compromise something on the order of a $250,000 verdict for William Tavoulareas against the *Post,* plus "a five- or six-thousand dollar" verdict for him against Piro, whose case was always discussed as an afterthought. Now even Johnson, along with the others, was urging Ellie Kelley to go along, citing the distance they had come from the demand of $50 million. Several jurors again mentioned the judge's vacation plans and the humiliation of a hung jury. Two jurors also suggested that Bradlee and Woodward—whom all the jurors, especially Kelley, regarded as the most sympathetic defendants and effective witnesses—be exonerated totally.

At 3:30 Kelley relented, after telling the other jurors, several recall, that the pressure was too much for her, that she felt sick, and that this case was why, in her view, there should be 12 jurors as there had been when she'd served on jury panels in the past.

After the jury announced its verdict—$250,000 in compensatory damages for William Tavoulareas from the *Post* defendants (except the exonerated Woodward and Bradlee) and $5,000 from Piro—Gasch immediately held a hearing for the jury to consider punitive damages. With the *Post* conceding its healthy financial condition and William Tavoulareas testifying that his legal bill to Cadwalader would be about $1.8 million (Peter will pay an additional $200,000), the jury quickly decided that $1.8 million was a fair amount.

William Tavoulareas, claiming total vindication for himself, his son, and Mobil, left the courthouse Friday afternoon with a $2.05-million verdict. He is now talking to Simon and Schuster—Bob Woodward's publisher—about writing a book about the trial. He says he'll argue that the law requiring a showing of malice (reckless disregard or deliberate falsehood) should be dropped if a publication refuses to retract mistakes in a story within a month of being informed of them.

Walsh and his colleagues left the courthouse with their first libel victory, a win that would allow Cadwalader managing partner Grant Hering to tout, justifiably, his firm's litigation prowess to the legal press and allow Walsh to hope that "there's always the future" when asked if he anticipates now getting any of Mobil's corporate work.

As for Younger, he says he was "stunned" at the jury's decision but is confident he'll win an appeal because "there's just no evidence to support this verdict."

Both Younger and Walsh have asked the judge to set aside the verdict. Walsh's claim is that if the jury found for William, they had to find for Peter. Gasch is expected to rule on the motions by the end of November.

If Gasch doesn't rule in Younger's favor, the *Post,* in an appeal that Younger and *Post* publisher Donald Graham both say Younger will handle, will have to argue that the jury shouldn't have gotten this case because there was no evidence of reckless disregard upon which they could have reached their verdict.

Another appeal Younger is handling involves the *National Enquirer's* libel loss to Carol Burnett over the groundless article it published saying she'd drunkenly accosted Henry Kissinger in a restaurant. Ironically, Younger may do better in that one, for there, with an unabashedly sleazy client, he'll have no qualms conceding that the article wasn't true and arguing instead that it wasn't deliberately or recklessly false and that the high damage award was unjustified—in short, that absent circumstances even more extreme and odious than the *Enquirer's* garbage journalism, the First Amendment does not countenance the fate of a publication resting in the hands of a jury.

That, in fact, is what Younger should have argued, and should argue now, in the *Post* case. True, no juror recalls any general anti-press or anti-*Post* comments during the deliberations, despite the guesses of several pundits afterward that the verdict for Tavoulareas was the result of a referendum on the press. Except perhaps for Mott, no anti-press bias seems to have been at work here. One shudders to think how complete a farce the process could have been if, for instance, the jurors had been less fair-minded, or if the paper were a less respectable publication or its target a more popular figure. Nonetheless, this case did become a citizen vote on the merits of a story—indeed on the merits of an editorial judgment about a headline and opening paragraph—not a fact-finding inquiry into whether there was *proof* that the *Post* had knowingly or recklessly published damaging falsehoods.

And what should really send a chill down Irving Younger's spine when a jury gets this or any libel case is the prospect of free expression's freedom resting on these kinds of value judgments, in the unguided hands of a Geoffrey Mott, a David Ford, or even an Ellie Kelley.

EPILOGUE

The dispute between William Tavoulareas and *The Washington Post* continued to Ping-Pong its way through the courts after the 1982 trial.

On May 2, 1983, Judge Gasch set aside the jury verdict on the grounds that there had been no actual malice on the part of the *Post*.

But in April 1985 the Court of Appeals for the District of Columbia Circuit reversed Judge Gasch's decision by a 2-to-1 vote.

In a strongly worded opinion written by Judge George MacKinnon, the panel found that *Post* reporter Patrick Tyler had set out to "get" William Tavoulareas "and deliberately slanted, rejected, and ignored evidence contrary to the central premise of the story, generally resolving ambiguities in the light most damaging to Tavoulareas." Judge MacKinnon also suggested that the *Post*'s policy of "sophisticated muckraking" was "relevant to the inquiry of whether a newspaper's employees acted in reckless disregard of whether a statement is false or not." He quoted testimony from Bob Woodward, one of the *Post* editors who had handled the story, and concluded, "A reasonable inference is that Woodward . . . wanted from his reporters the same kind of stories on which he built his own reputation: high-impact investigative stories of wrongdoing."

In his dissent Judge J. Skelly Wright wrote that if "this excessive jury verdict" were upheld, it would have a chilling effect on freedom of expression. "The message to the media will be unmistakable," Wright wrote, "steer clear of unpleasant news stories and comments about interests like Mobil or pay the price."

The *Post* appealed the panel's decision to the full D.C. Circuit Court. And on March 13, 1987, the full court affirmed Judge Gasch's ruling by a 7-to-1 vote, with Judge MacKinnon dissenting. In a majority opinion written by Judge Kenneth Starr and Judge Wright, the appellate court ruled that the *Post* article was "substantially true" and that the paper did not act with actual malice when it ran the front-page story. The appellate court also challenged the plaintiff's use of an internal memo that had been written by *Post* copy editor Cass Peterson and which raised some doubts about Tyler's conclusions. "This will not do," the court said. "Nothing in law or common sense supports saddling a libel defendant with civil liability for a defamatory implication nowhere to be found in the published article itself."

On June 11, 1987, Tavoulareas, still represented by John Walsh of Cadwalader, Wickersham & Taft, filed for certiorari. The *Post*, represented by Kevin Baine, a partner at Williams & Connolly, opposed and on October 5, 1987, the petition was denied.

William Tavoulareas retired as Mobil president in 1985. After the *Post* trial, Tavoulareas became somewhat of a self-styled advocate for libel plaintiffs, giving speeches on the subject and appearing on the PBS show *Anatomy of a Libel*. His book about the suit, *Fighting Back*, was published by Simon and Schuster in 1986.

Peter Tavoulareas is running his shipping business in London and Cadwalader continues to do tax work for some Mobil executives, as well as some franchise litigation, commodities, and bankruptcy work for the corporation.

Since the *Post* trial, Cadwalader's John Walsh has handled two more libel cases. In 1985 he represented Hammer De Roburt, former president of the Republic of Nauru, in a suit against the Gannett company's *Pacific Daily News*. In that case, the jury found that the article in question was false and defamatory, but that there had been no actual malice. De Roburt appealed the decision to the Ninth Circuit Court of Appeals, but Walsh did not represent him. The appeals court affirmed the trial court ruling and the Supreme Court denied certiorari.

Walsh also represented E. F. Hutton as a defendant in a libel suit brought by John Pearce, a former E. F. Hutton Group, Inc., branch manager, in Washington, D.C., federal court against Hutton and former Attorney General Griffin Bell, a partner at Atlanta's King & Spaulding. Hutton had retained Bell in 1985 to identify the employees responsible for a check overdrafting scheme that led to the company's guilty plea to two thousand counts of fraud. In a report to Hutton, Bell concluded that Pearce was heavily involved in the scheme and that his actions were "so aggressive and egregious as to warrant sanctions." Pearce claimed that Bell and Hutton knew those accusations were false. In June 1988 a jury returned a verdict for Bell; the claim against Hutton was transferred to a New York Stock Exchange arbitration panel and was dismissed by agreement in September 1988.

Irving Younger left Williams & Connolly in December 1983 to teach at the University of Minnesota Law School. He died in March 1988.

Westmoreland
v.
CBS

BY
CONNIE BRUCK

THE MEA CULPA DEFENSE

How CBS brought on the Westmoreland suit—and sacrificed one of its own

Last April (1983), Dan Burt, who is representing General William Westmoreland in his $120-million libel suit against CBS, won a crucial discovery battle, gaining access to a confidential CBS report on *The Uncounted Enemy: A Vietnam Deception.* The documentary, which alleged that U.S. military-intelligence officers manipulated estimates of enemy troop strength during the Vietnam War, had aired in January 1982. Four months later, after *TV Guide* ran a cover story entitled "Anatomy of a Smear—How CBS News Broke the Rules and 'Got' General Westmoreland," CBS News president Van Sauter commissioned veteran newsman Burton "Bud" Benjamin to conduct an internal investigation of the *TV Guide* charges.

Burt had been trying to get the Benjamin report ever since he filed the Westmoreland suit in September 1982. Now federal district judge Pierre Leval had ordered CBS—represented by David Boies, a partner at New York's Cravath, Swaine & Moore and a veteran of the marathon IBM litigation—to produce it.

To Burt, it seemed well worth the effort: replete with harsh judgments, the Benjamin report went beyond the *TV Guide* charges, attacking the documentary's substance as well as its procedures and keying mainly on the show's producer, George Crile. Interviewed by *USA Today* following the report's release, Burt proclaimed, ''We are about to see the dismantling of a major news network.''

Burt—who is president of Washington, D.C.'s Capital Legal Foundation, one of several conservative public interest firms that have sprung up in antagonistic counterpoint to the Ralph Nader model—is still buoyant over his victory and maintains that his prophecy of doom is gradually being fulfilled. ''There are terrible morale problems at CBS News, and they are the same kind of morale problems that they had at the White House during Watergate,'' he declares, repeating a favorite analogy: like Richard Nixon, he argues, CBS embodies the arrogance of unbridled power.

For those at CBS who are defendants in this lawsuit—Sauter; Mike Wallace, the show's correspondent; and especially Crile—Dan Burt must be like a bad dream from which they keep expecting to awaken. Seething with an anger that seems peculiarly personal, having as much to do with settling his old scores as his client's, Burt's rhetoric is so much that of a killer lawyer that it is sometimes hard to take him seriously. But the threat that Burt and *Westmoreland* pose to CBS News is serious indeed, and it goes beyond the issues of money and image that a major libel suit usually raises.

As even Westmoreland's lawyer readily concedes, harm to the retired general's reputation is not what this case is about. As Burt puts it, ''The real issue here is not General Westmoreland. It is, will the press police themselves?''

Westmoreland is being represented free of charge. His backers, who have contributed to the Capital Legal Foundation, include such funders of conservative and New Right causes as Richard Mellon Scaife, the Smith Richardson Foundation, the Fluor Foundation, and the Olin Foundation. Leslie Lenkowsky, staff director of the Smith Richardson Foundation, has funded several of what he calls ''media criticism'' projects in the past. He frames the Westmoreland suit as having two potential long-range impacts. First, he believes it may bring about a change in the malice standard of *Times* v. *Sullivan*. ''Westmoreland is a public figure—does that mean CBS can do the kind of job it did to him?'' asks Lenkowsky. ''Should shoddy journalism be the defense, as it presumably will be here? Libel laws in Europe are different. Maybe ours need to be changed.'' And second, Lenkowsky suggests, *Westmoreland* may result in the demise of the CBS Reports division of CBS News, which produced *The Uncounted Enemy* and which since the days of Edward R. Murrow has carried on, more than any other place in broadcast journalism, the hallowed tradition of the hard-hitting documentary.

CBS Reports is a money loser. And, as Lenkowsky points out, although former CBS chairman William Paley is still a director and major shareholder, his era is really over. CBS Inc. is now in the hands of management types like president Thomas Wyman, who came to the network from Pillsbury Foods. Wyman and his colleagues have more feeling for the bottom line than for the news, says Lenkowsky, who claims to have friends "as close to the top of CBS Inc. as you can go."

"CBS Reports doesn't interest them," he continues. "To them, CBS is a diversified entertainment corporation. And when this came along from CBS Reports, their attitude was, who needs this? They would like to get rid of the whole division."

One CBS insider who also has ties to the Westmoreland camp seconds Lenkowsky's assessment. "There's been a sea change here at CBS," he says, pointing to a recent budget fracas in which Sauter reportedly threatened to resign when CBS Broadcast Group president Gene Jankowski demanded $12 million in cuts from a $200 million budget that had suffered a $7 million cut last spring. (Jankowski backed down.) "Encapsulated in this case is the dilemma of broadcasting today," this source says. "Are we going to only make money and always play it safe—and I am talking about a *real chill*—or are we going to provide a public service?"

What makes the *Westmoreland* assault so ominous to many within CBS News is that it seems to spring from so many sources—some who would do away with the malice standard, some who favor a revisionist view of the Vietnam War, some who would like to chill CBS News, some with more grandiose dreams of dismantling it altogether. And within the beleaguered fortress itself—in the upper reaches of CBS Inc.—the support that would have been forthcoming in the last two decades now seems uncertain.

That the stakes are so high in this multifaceted case only makes more stunning the one fact that has been evident from the start: this is one lawsuit that never should have been. It was fueled, if not created, by a series of mistakes made by Sauter, by in-house lawyers Ralph Goldberg and George Vradenburg, and by newsman Bud Benjamin. Because of these CBS officials' respective contributions to the creation and discoverability of the Benjamin report, the press has for the past year been led to focus not on the substance of the show—which Sauter and his executives have belatedly come to believe in—but on the procedures used to produce it. This preoccupation with process has made the case into an unparalleled public relations disaster for CBS—one which Dan Burt, publicist par excellence, has exploited at every turn. Indeed, many at CBS believe that even a victory in court—March 1984 is the scheduled trial date—will not recoup the damage already done.

What emerges from it all is a textbook case of what a news organization should *not* do when threatened with a libel suit. As one CBS insider says ruefully, "This has been a comedy of errors from the start."

The *TV Guide* article could not have come at a worse time. It hit the stands on May 25, 1982, smack in the middle of CBS's annual general affiliates conference, which was being held in San Francisco. The relationship between CBS and its more conservative affiliated stations has historically been fractious, and it was particularly so over CBS's coverage of the Vietnam War and Watergate. So when "Anatomy of a Smear" appeared, it touched an old nerve. Roger Colloff, a CBS News vice president who was at the conference, says of the affiliate reaction, "I wouldn't want to ascribe it a number on the Richter scale, but there was certainly a tremor."

It was Sauter's first affiliates conference as president of CBS News. He had become deputy president in November 1981 and president early in 1982; before that, he had headed CBS Sports for about a year and had been general manager of KNXT, a CBS-owned affiliate in Los Angeles. Some CBS insiders claim Sauter was too much of a novice to realize that he should not be cowed by the affiliates. "Van's concern for satisfying what the public wants comes out of his station-management background," says one associate. "The responsibility of news is *not* to give people what they want, but Van wants to be responsive to all constituencies—in this case, the affiliates."

Sauter immediately convened a meeting in San Francisco attended by two people from CBS Inc.—Gene Mater of CBS Broadcasting Group and Ralph Goldberg, an associate general counsel who has since moved to a nonlegal job—and two from CBS News, vice presidents Robert Chandler and Roger Colloff. (Jankowski was consulted later.) Many options were considered: an inquiry conducted by a newsman supervised by an in-house lawyer; one supervised by outside counsel; one conducted by outside counsel. According to one well-placed source, William Paley suggested retaining Archibald Cox. But Sauter says all these ideas got short shrift. Although he'd seen a lawsuit as a distinct threat since West-

41

moreland's press conference a few days after the broadcast, Sauter asserts that he considered the commissioning of this inquiry to be "a journalistic, not a legalistic judgment.

"CBS News had to know whether we were right or wrong," Sauter declares. "And it wasn't by having some goddamn lawyer from Wall Street come in here to find out. That's what *we're* about."

At the meeting, Sauter adds, "the universal conclusion we reached—including the lawyer [Goldberg] who was with us—was that it should be done within the news division." Goldberg declines comment, except to say, "I had discussions with my superiors." George Vradenburg, a former Cravath associate who joined the CBS legal department in 1980 and became deputy general counsel in the fall of 1981, is one of Goldberg's superiors and has had responsibility for the Westmoreland suit from the start. Asked whether Goldberg checked with him, Vradenburg says, "Later," but he concedes that he concurred with Sauter's decision to conduct the inquiry without a lawyer involved. General counsel and senior vice president James Parker, who for the last year has been occupied with development activities at CBS Inc., was also consulted.

With an inexperienced deputy general counsel and an inexperienced division president whose knowledge of *The Uncounted Enemy* came from a screening several weeks before the broadcast, the decision can be read as one that slipped through the cracks. It was, in any case, wrong, however one looks at it. From a legal perspective, it is hard to fathom how—with a libel suit threatening—CBS officials chose to exclude even an in-house lawyer from participating in Benjamin's inquiry; this would have greatly increased CBS's chance of protecting the report as a legal work product prepared in anticipation of litigation.

Besides, even from a journalistic and administrative viewpoint, which is how Sauter says he saw it, the decision was deficient. As former CBS News president Richard Salant points out, "When you have a report done by somebody, you're delegating—and after that, whatever you get, you're stuck with." What Salant did in 1971—when a far more formidable attack than *TV Guide*'s was launched on CBS by the House Armed Services Committee and the Communications Subcommittee of the House Commerce Committee following a documentary entitled *The Selling of the Pentagon*—was immediately to make a statement in support of the broadcast, and then, behind closed doors, to look into the allegations about procedures himself. (Admittedly Salant had the advantage, which Sauter did not, of having closely followed the documentary's preparation, so he was confident of its substantive soundness.) In his inquiry, which involved extensive review of transcripts, Salant had help, but he never let it out of his hands.

On the third day of the affiliates conference, in his maiden speech as CBS News president, Sauter announced that Benjamin, a senior executive producer, would conduct an investigation of all the charges and report on his findings. There was no statement of support for the documentary.

(Critics claim that rather than reacting immediately to the *TV Guide* attack by announcing an investigation or by expressing support for a show he wasn't familiar with, Sauter should have quickly undertaken an intensive review to satisfy himself that the show was substantively sound—as he is now convinced—then made a public statement of support and later taken more time to examine the procedural allegations.)

Sauter chose Benjamin because of his impeccable reputation for honesty. "With Benjamin doing it," says Vradenburg, "no one could accuse us of a whitewash." But there were other problems with the choice that might have been foreseen. Benjamin, who came to CBS in 1957 and is best known as the executive producer of Walter Cronkite's *Twentieth Century* series and of the evening news during the seventies, has never produced the kind of controversial, ambitious piece that *The Uncounted Enemy* was; his forte is historical documentaries. Even his friends describe him as "purist," "literal-minded," and "fundamentalist." In his loyalty to the institution, Benjamin is also more fervent than most; for him, friends say, CBS is almost a religion. According to John Sharnik, a retired CBS producer who saw Benjamin before he received Sauter's summons, Benjamin was terribly shaken by the *TV Guide* article. "It seemed to impugn a form of journalism he'd devoted much of his life to," says Sharnik.

It is important to note that the person Benjamin set out to investigate—the man with primary responsibility for the show—was not Mike Wallace, but the relatively unknown and infinitely dispensable George Crile. (Although Wallace was chief correspondent in *The Uncounted Enemy*, he had limited responsibility.) Unlike most CBS producers, who start out low in the ranks, pay their dues, and slowly rise, Crile entered at the producer level in 1976 when CBS approached him with a proposal for what became *The CIA: Secret Army*—which Salant, then CBS News president, recalls as "one of the all-time great documentaries." Crile went on to coproduce and report *The Battle for South Africa*, which won a George Foster Peabody Award and an Emmy. Not only did he produce show after show, but he occupied the unusual role of producer and on-air reporter in some efforts, while most people at CBS are either one or the other.

Long before *The Uncounted Enemy,* Crile was a controversial figure, resented not only for his quick prominence but also for what some construed as his arrogance. "George is very bright," says one CBS colleague, "and he doesn't suffer fools gladly. He's a perfectionist: he wants to get the absolute best, he's just at it and at it and at it, and people don't like that. They don't like the fact that often he'd change the things they'd done. He's not a diplomat." Adds a former colleague, "George works more by inspiration than by organization. And he was always more into his craft—totally immersed in what he was doing—than plugged into the bureaucracy."

Crile's shows have been controversial as well. *Gay Power, Gay Politics,* a documentary he coproduced in 1980, caused the San Francisco gay community to file a number of allegations of unfairness with the National News Council, which ultimately concurred in two of them. One was a CBS News Guidelines violation: a sequence had been edited so that applause appeared to come earlier than it actually had.

Crile's propensity for making enemies is apparently what sparked this conflagration. What gave the *TV Guide* article its force was the fact that its authors, Don Kowet and Sally Bedell (now Sally Bedell Smith), had obtained CBS's unedited transcripts of on-camera interviews for *The Uncounted Enemy.* The consensus among at least a dozen people at CBS News—though it is speculative—is that the most likely source of the transcripts was a production person connected with the show who was known to have not gotten along with Crile. (That person denies the stories as "flat, dead wrong.")

Benjamin's assignment was to explore each charge in the *TV Guide* article. Kowet and Bedell dealt only with CBS's procedures; while the implicit message is that any show so biased in its procedures is likely to be factually flawed, the authors explicitly forswear this inference. "We do not know whether Crile and his colleagues were right about General Westmoreland and his military intelligence operation," they state in conclusion. The central theme of *The Uncounted Enemy* was that in the months leading up to the Tet offensive in January 1968, General Westmoreland's command deliberately underestimated enemy strength in reporting to the president and Congress in order to make it seem that America was winning what had come to be called the "war of attrition." Nine retired CIA and military officers supported that claim on camera.

Kowet and Bedell leveled about 20 charges and subcharges. Many come down to judgment calls; three are irrefutable.

Two of the three concern George Allen, a former CIA officer who in the late sixties was an expert on enemy strength. Allen described how he participated in the underestimations for what he understood to be political reasons. According to Crile, since Allen was stiff and somewhat inarticulate in his first interview, Crile interviewed him twice—the first offense. And, before the second interview, Crile showed Allen tapes of other officers describing their own malfeasance. In the first instance, Crile's bias seems obvious: Westmoreland did not wear well in *his* interview, but he didn't get a second chance. The screening, though not a guidelines violation, is widely known to be taboo at CBS.

The third unrefuted charge leveled by *TV Guide* is that Crile failed to interview Phillip Davidson, Jr., the top military intelligence officer in Vietnam. Crile says he believed Davidson was in very poor health, as Wallace said on camera to Westmoreland, who did not contradict him. But Kowet and Bedell located Davidson in good health—and he denied Crile's main thesis.

The charges that have the greatest ring of authority are those made on the basis of the unedited transcripts, which the reader, of course, does not see. The authors repeatedly charge that CBS took statements out of context and distorted the interviewee's point of view, but Crile argues that *TV Guide* committed the same sins by misrepresenting transcripts and other material unseen by their readers. In one instance, Kowet and Bedell argue that Crile in effect ambushed Westmoreland by sending him a letter outlining the subjects to be discussed in his interview in which "the real subject . . . stood fourth on the list." What they fail to mention is that the lead-in paragraph stated explicitly what the interview was about—"How well did we identify and report the intentions and capabilities of the enemy?"—and what followed was a listing of subtopics.

In another instance *TV Guide* makes a great deal of the fact that Walt Rostow, who was national security adviser for President Lyndon Johnson, was interviewed for three hours by Wallace but that his interview was "killed." They state that Rostow "repeatedly denied to Wallace that critical intelligence had been kept from" Johnson and imply that Rostow was not used because he had challenged the theses of the broadcast. In fact, a reading of the Rostow transcript shows that Rostow backs off that denial, arguing that even if numbers were falsified, that would not have seriously affected Johnson's decision making. Moreover, whenever Rostow is confronted with the specific charges made by former military officers, he simply says he doesn't know anything about it. Crile and Wallace maintain that the reason they decided to exclude Rostow was not because he authoritatively countered their premise, but because he was *not* authoritative: on the key issue—the manipulation of enemy troop strength estimates—he continually professed ignorance.

In the other cases in which Kowet and Bedell charge distortion, they seem to be disagreeing with Crile's editorial judgment calls—ones which in some instances were not made by Crile alone but by Wallace, senior producer Andrew Lack, executive producer Howard Stringer, and Roger Colloff, then the CBS News vice president in charge of broadcasting.

Several of the officers Kowet and Bedell charge were misrepresented have sent letters to CBS in support of the broadcast and its fairness. Asked about that, Kowet responds, "Who cares? I don't give a damn whether *they* think they were fairly represented. That's not the issue— they're not journalists." Bedell, now at *The New York Times,* says, "*Times* lawyers have told me not to talk. Their advice is that it's easier to fight a subpoena if you keep your mouth shut."

However thin the *TV Guide* piece looks when held to the light, Benjamin seems to have viewed its allegations through Kowet's and Bedell's eyes. In his report, he supports nearly all their charges and even adds a few of his own—Sam Adams, the former CIA agent who brought the story to CBS, was identified on the air as a consultant; Benjamin maintains that he should have been identified as a *paid* consultant. Benjamin, who editorializes throughout his report, also quotes vituperative comments about Crile from a former film editor, Ira Klein, whom Crile had slighted by bringing in another editor for the second half of the program— and Benjamin does not allow Crile to reply to Klein. In several instances, Benjamin recounts dialogue between himself and Crile, including one exchange which he finishes off with, "Couldn't you have let Carver [a CIA agent he thought Crile should have interviewed] tell his story and let the audience decide—which we often do around here, George."

Most striking, though, is Benjamin's apparent lack of appreciation of the reporting achievements in *The Uncounted Enemy*. Crile had managed to persuade a group of former military intelligence and CIA officers to come on camera not to make charges about someone else's wrongdoing, but to confess their own. As Mike Wallace points out, "These men were not your traditional whistleblowers. They were coming forward more in sorrow than in anger, and they had nothing to gain from it but pain." Benjamin, however, confirms the *TV Guide* charge of "coddling sympathetic witnesses'' and includes a number of excerpts from the transcripts in which Crile or Wallace are either encouraging, mildly flattering, or joking with their subjects.

Benjamin also accepts *TV Guide*'s indictment of the show as unbalanced because it did not present more denials from government or military officials on Westmoreland's side. Counting up the interviewees, Benjamin concludes, ''This is a nine-to-two equation. . . . Measured another way, Westmoreland and Graham [Lieutenant General Daniel Graham appeared to deny charges against him] spoke for five minutes and fifty-nine seconds, [and] Adams and the eight supporters of [his] premise spoke for nineteen minutes and nineteen seconds. The question that should be asked is this. Is this fairness and balance in terms of people or time on the camera?'' Crile's response is that the eight supporters Benjamin cites were *from* Westmoreland's side—members of his own command—a fact to which Benjamin attaches little significance.

Benjamin elevates the CBS News Guidelines—64 almost impenetrable pages—to a position of importance that they have never held before. To him, they are literal, canonical imperatives. Benjamin declares that Crile violated the guideline that interviews be ''spontaneous and unrehearsed'' when he returned to George Allen for a second interview. He also indicts Crile for combining answers from several questions into one answer: ''None of these combined answers distort the meaning of what the interviewees are saying,'' Benjamin writes. ''They do, however, violate the guidelines.''

Interviews with more than a dozen people at CBS News indicate that until the Benjamin report appeared, many news employees had never read the guidelines, but only checked specific points on occasion. Many said they would not have known that the ''spontaneous and unrehearsed'' directive meant that they could not reinterview on the same subject. And several producers said the marrying of answers goes on all the time. In the eyes of most of his colleagues, Crile's only sin was his having screened other officers' interviews for Allen. On that, there was unanimous judgment. Of this action, Crile says, ''It was stupid. I did it on impulse—I wanted him to see that he wasn't alone. I wanted him to see that the real charges were being made not by him but by Westmoreland's own command.''

Unlike *TV Guide*, Benjamin did not stop at procedures. At the start of *The Uncounted Enemy*, Wallace says, ''We're going to present evidence of what we have come to believe was a conscious effort—indeed, a conspiracy at the highest levels of American military intelligence—to suppress and alter critical intelligence on the enemy in the year leading up to the Tet offensive.'' In what has amounted to some crucial spadework for Westmoreland's attorney, Benjamin undertook to decide whether the word *conspiracy* was defensible. He decides against it by what looks like the most uncritical poll-taking: he lists various people's views on the appropriateness of the word and then sides with the majority.

At the close of this report, Benjamin sheds more doubt on the documentary's substance. "Even today, military historians cannot tell you whether or not MACV [Military Assistance Command—Vietnam] 'cooked the books' as the broadcast states,'' he writes. "The flow of definitive information is painfully slow and may never be conclusive.''

That statement not only flies in the face of the evidence compiled by Crile and consultant Adams over a year and a half—military cables, massive chronologies of enemy troop strength estimates, and more than 139 interviews—but it also contradicts the much more accessible conclusions of the House Select Committee on Intelligence. In 1976 that committee determined that "pressure from policy-making officials to produce positive intelligence indicators reinforced erroneous assessments of allied progress and enemy capabilities.'' The committee further stated, "the numbers game not only diverted a direct confrontation with the realities of war in Vietnam, but also prevented the intelligence community, perhaps the President, and certainly members of Congress from judging the real changes in Vietnam over time.''

Put more simply, Benjamin gave Westmoreland an incredible gift. He actually revived the issue of whether Americans were misled about the progress of the war—when most Americans have long since resigned themselves to the obvious fact that the war was never going as swimmingly as the Pentagon assured us it was.

Today many of those at CBS who have dogged their way through the Benjamin report will say that the report is severely skewed—"high school stenography,'' says one—but they will not do so for the record because CBS has yet to disown the report in any way. But David Boies, the Cravath lawyer who has had to contend with it from the time the case was filed in September 1982 and who will ultimately have to explain it away at trial, feels no such constraints: "Benjamin approached this from a very strict, old-line standard that doesn't distinguish between investigative reporting that says that in the middle of the Vietnam War figures were misrepresented for political purposes and reporting that says that a chunk just fell out of the Connecticut turnpike and killed three people. There is a difference between reporting events that have clearly happened and reporting about something that the people involved will naturally tend to deny." Boies adds that he "of course" wishes that the report had been done by a lawyer: not only would its chance of being protected have been greater, but he thinks a lawyer would have done a "more sensible" report. (Benjamin refuses to comment on this point or on other issues raised in this article.)

"This is all very unfortunate, very unfair," says Boies of what has happened to Crile. "Crile is very talented, and he's a journalist who cares about truth with a capital *T*. He told a story that needed to be told, and they've nitpicked him to death. Nobody's work could withstand the kind of scrutiny his has gotten."

Still, Boies points out, Sauter had commissioned the report and promised to announce its conclusions. When he received it, his options were few. "What were they supposed to do with it?" asks Boies. "Eat it?"

What Sauter did was immediately send two copies to Black Rock, as CBS Inc.'s headquarters is known. Jankowski and Mater got the report, but Sauter says he knows Wyman and Paley also saw it. Sauter then drafted a statement for public release. On the night of July 14, after a stormy session that went into the early hours of the morning, Sauter redrafted the release. At the meeting Crile, Wallace, Colloff, and Stringer all attacked Benjamin's conclusions, and Sauter agreed to move his declaration that "CBS News stands by this broadcast" up to the top instead of burying it near the end.

Even the second and final eight-page memorandum reads like a mea culpa. The statement of support is followed by a Benjamin-like litany of procedural sins. And Sauter also concludes—in words that will surely pursue him at trial—that "a judgmental conclusion of conspiracy was inappropriate." Vradenburg and Parker signed off on the memo and it was released on July 15, 1982.

Crile was devastated. The report had fingered him, he felt, by making him out to be not only producer but senior producer, executive producer, correspondent, and vice president in charge of broadcasting, all rolled into one. Not surprisingly, the two most valuable CBS newsmen involved in the broadcast—Wallace and Stringer, who is now producer of the evening news—had escaped virtually unscathed. After the *TV Guide* piece appeared, Crile had been instructed not to talk to the press under any circumstances; Colloff, now a vice president of the broadcast group, and Wallace had told him repeatedly that they were "all in the same boat," and that it would be better to wait and let CBS speak with its powerful voice when the Benjamin report was completed.

Crile believed he could have mounted not only a powerful defense of the broadcast but also a massive counterattack on *TV Guide*. But now, after Sauter's statement, CBS had so diminished Crile's credibility that his statements would have little force. And he was astounded that CBS chose not to utter a word of criticism of the *TV Guide* article.

At the meeting at which Sauter's public statement was redrafted, Crile had argued passionately that they should shift the focus from technical violations to the soundness of the documentary's substance; but to no avail. He felt betrayed, now, by CBS's entire handling of the *TV Guide* charges. Crile had been denied an audience with Sauter until that meeting: by that time Sauter had already digested the Benjamin report, but Crile was seeing it for the first time. Crile had also been denied an internal forum at CBS; he had wanted, during the seven weeks that the Benjamin inquiry was in progress, to defend the broadcast and himself to his colleagues.

Asked about the requirement of silence imposed on Crile up until that time, CBS News senior vice president Robert Chandler says, "We felt that if George had spoken out against *TV Guide* it would have given an image of divisiveness. Crile has had his opportunity to speak his piece." Asked where, Chandler replies, "In deposition." (Burt deposed Crile in May.)

With *TV Guide* and the Benjamin report in hand, Crile looked black indeed. According to Smith Richardson's Lenkowsky—and this is confirmed by CBS sources—the reaction at CBS Inc. to the report was intense. "People said, 'Omigod, this is even worse than we thought,' " says Lenkowsky. "There was a strong urge to get rid of Crile. The only reason they didn't fire him then was because they were afraid of what he might go around saying. They still didn't know whether Westmoreland was going to sue. So they decided it would be better to have Crile in the tent pissing out than outside pissing in."

Westmoreland did not come easily to the decision to sue. In fact, he had been receiving so much advice against going forward that it seems clear that without the *TV Guide* article and CBS's mea culpa response seven weeks later, no suit would have been filed. Clark Clifford of Washington, D.C.'s Clifford & Warnke had advised against it. Edward Bennett Williams had discussed it with Westmoreland and stressed the difficulty he would have, as a public figure, in meeting the malice standard. Stanley Resor, a former secretary of the army and a partner at New York's Debevoise & Plimpton, strongly advised against it. Senators Barry Goldwater and Strom Thurmond also cautioned him against filing. According to Godfrey Schmidt, a partner at the small midtown Manhattan firm of

Schmidt, Aghayan & Associates, when Peter Grace of W. R. Grace & Co. sent Westmoreland to him shortly after the *TV Guide* article appeared, he was the first lawyer to come down in favor of Westmoreland's suit.

Money was a problem, but Schmidt felt certain that Grace would contribute heavily, and Schmidt was willing to work on a contingency basis. His idea was that he would do the papers and have someone like Edward Bennett Williams come in as trial counsel. Meanwhile, however, Burt arrived on the scene. "Westmoreland told me that Burt had solicited him," says Schmidt, "come to him and told him that it wouldn't cost him a dime. Westmoreland said he'd decided to go with Burt because he wanted to be guaranteed that he wasn't stuck with any bills at the end." (In fact, David Henderson, a public relations consultant who organized Westmoreland's press conference and later accompanied him from lawyer to lawyer, says he contacted Burt to see if he would be interested.)

Burt's projected 1983 budget for Capital Legal is $1.5 million, and he estimates that 40 to 50 percent of that will go toward Westmoreland's suit. He insists he is badly pressed, straining to take on the CBS giant. In addition to five staffers, Burt has brought in David Dorsen, a litigator from Sachs, Greenebaum & Tayler in Washington, D.C. While Dorsen made early court appearances and took some depositions, Burt has taken all of the recent depositions and declares he will take "all the important ones" from here on. Burt will not allow Dorsen to be interviewed: "There is only one spokesperson for this case," he states.

For Burt, this case is tailor-made. "If you ever saw where I came from," he explains, "you'd understand what this is all about." Burt grew up in Philadelphia's Rising Sun district, a rough neighborhood of row houses—"No silver spoons for us," he volunteers. "Not even plastic spoons. We ate out of the pot." In 1975, five years after graduating from Yale Law School, he opened a one-man office in Marblehead, Massachusetts, specializing in tax. "Within three years," he boasts, "I had sixteen lawyers and two offices in Saudi Arabia." Burt says he did so well in Saudi Arabia (his major client there was the Fluor Corporation) that he never has to work again. "My taxes are in seven figures," he claims.

In 1980 Burt joined Capital Legal at the invitation of Fluor vice president Leslie Burgess. "I'd always wanted to do policy work," says Burt.

Burt, who refers to himself as "a short, foulmouthed Jew from the streets," takes unmistakable pleasure in the status of his opponents in this case. "This is *Cravath* we're up against—the biggest network and the finest law firm in the country. Do you understand that?'' Burt demands. ''We're just a bunch of crazy little people down here just fiddling around.''

Cravath may be more than an abstract symbol of the establishment to Burt. According to Boies and two others who were present during a break in a recent deposition session, Burt recounted this story: A former Cravath partner, John Barnum, interviewed Burt when he was at Yale but did not make him an offer. Barnum did, however, invite Burt out for drinks, and they went to a bar where the benches were very high. Burt, who is about five foot two, commented on their height. ''Then, Burt said, Barnum said, 'I guess that's the story of your life, Dan—always three inches too short for the table,' '' recalls Boies. ''Burt said, 'I've been waiting to get even for that for the past fifteen years.' '' Burt denies this account: ''I don't recall what I said to Mr. Boies,'' he says.

If the story is true, however, Burt now has a chance of getting his wish. CBS retained Cravath in the Westmoreland suit because, Vradenburg explains, ''I decided not to go the more predictable route—with a First Amendment lawyer from Coudert, say, or Floyd Abrams [Cahill Gordon & Reindel's noted First Amendment specialist]—because we have to face it: more and more of these cases are going to trial. I wanted a lawyer who could try a case before a South Carolina jury [the suit was filed in South Carolina and later moved to New York's Southern District] and not seem like a foreigner. So I picked Boies.'' Vradenburg, a longtime admirer of Boies, had worked for him as an associate at Cravath.

Boies, who scored a brilliant win defending IBM in the CalComp antitrust case, has in the last several years done mainly antitrust and securities work, a great deal of it for CBS. But this is his first libel case, and he is quick to say that he doesn't view it through a First Amendment advocate's prism. ''I'm different from Floyd Abrams,'' Boies declares. ''I'd take a plaintiff's libel case without a moment's hesitation. I'm in no way ideological about this—I just want to win my case.'' If he does, Boies will firmly establish himself as CBS's main contact at Cravath.

But the case Boies undertook to defend in September 1982 did not look much like a winner. The Benjamin report and the Sauter statement were both strikes against CBS. (Judge Leval would later rule that CBS, by releasing the Sauter memorandum, had rendered the Benjamin report clearly discoverable: one could not claim confidentiality for an internal inquiry and at the same time issue a press release based on it, he reasoned.) CBS appeared to have no confidence in its broadcast. Benjamin was the only one not directly involved in its production who had examined the charges against it, and he had called its substance into question. Crile, who would be put to the test of malice or reckless disregard for the truth, had been set up as an easy mark, and within CBS he was perceived not only as a wrongdoer, but as an unrepentant sinner: one who continued to protest his innocence and the show's integrity—and who was somewhat out of control.

Boies apparently wanted to bring Crile and the other defendants under his control, but from the moment the Benjamin report was written, Crile and CBS were at odds. Crile consulted a lawyer who had advised him in the past, John Vardaman of Williams & Connolly. Vardaman told Crile he could not represent him because Westmoreland had consulted Williams about the case, but he advised Crile that there was a clear potential for conflict between him and CBS and that CBS lawyers could not represent him. Crile then turned to Victor Kovner, an experienced First Amendment lawyer from New York's Lankenau Kovner & Bickford. Kovner has been assisted in this case by Harriet Dorsen (the sister-in-law of Burt's co-counsel, David Dorsen).

It took months of arguing before CBS agreed that a possibility for conflict existed and thus, that CBS and its insurer, CNA, should pay for Crile's separate counsel. Boies says it was always his position that Crile "ought to have separate counsel if he wanted separate counsel." Pressed further, he adds that it was a matter of dispute between Crile, CBS, and the insurance company and that his advice "was not really solicited."

Crile and Dorsen recall Boies's position differently. "David's firm position was that there was no conflict and therefore no reason why he could not represent me," says Crile. And, explains Dorsen, if there was no clear conflict, while Crile could of course hire his own counsel, CBS's insurer would not pay for it. "Both Vradenburg and Boies felt it would be very bad for the case if there was separate representation," says Crile. Once CBS and the insurer finally agreed to pay for separate counsel, Boies argued for a time that Kovner should not be "of record" in the case; and he did not become of record until March of 1983.

Today, Boies is extraordinarily confident, even ebullient, about the Westmoreland case. He has reason to be; so far, the litigation has gone well. Against strong odds, he won a change of venue motion, moving the case from Greenville, South Carolina, where the general is something of a folk hero (he recently led a Veterans Day parade), to New York. He lost the arguments over the Benjamin report, though he has the solace of having predicted this defeat: he had urged CBS to turn over the Benjamin report at the outset because he felt it would appear that they were trying

53

to hide something if they did not—and because he thought they would be ordered to produce it anyway. But CBS insisted that the privilege of self-evaluation was something it wanted to fight for.

Boies also says he has taken depositions of key witnesses that "could not be stronger." One, George Godding, was a source that Crile had interviewed but not used in the broadcast. But, according to Crile's notes, Godding, a retired general who had been the military's delegate to a pivotal intelligence-estimates conference with the CIA, told Crile that Westmoreland had ordered him to keep the enemy-strength figure below a certain level. The documentary states that Westmoreland gave such an order, and it is only one of two instances in which Westmoreland is linked by an overt action to the manipulation of enemy-strength estimates; it is thus crucial to CBS's defense. But at Westmoreland's press conference, Godding denied that he'd received such an order. "Godding was turning like a weather vane in a rainstorm," says Boies. By the time of his deposition in April 1983, Godding had turned again, reverting to what Crile says is his original statement that he *had* received orders on the ceiling from Westmoreland. "Whatever they try to do with Godding now will amount to subornation of perjury," Boies insists. (Crile says he did not use Godding on camera because he felt he had the story without him, and Godding was not "an enthusiast.")

Boies points to Westmoreland's depositions, taken in June, as further litigation bonuses. "Westmoreland said he couldn't remember anything the broadcast said about him that was unfavorable, except for the word *conspiracy*—and that wasn't about him," Boies asserts. "He testified, too, that until the program he was wholly unaware that people in his command were making charges that numbers had been suppressed and that he talked to these people afterwards but didn't ask them about the charges to see if they were true or not."

The one litigation tactic that has caused lawyers in the First Amendment bar to mutter about Boies's antitrust background is his decision not to make a motion to dismiss the complaint. Last fall Kovner—who was then not even of record—argued as strongly as he could to Boies and CBS that such a motion should be made. Kovner cited three arguments CBS could have advanced: First, the use of the word *conspiracy* was protected as opinion and, moreover, did not pertain to Westmoreland. Second, many of the statements Westmoreland had charged were defamatory could not be since they had been so well aired in the conclusions of the House committee; in *Harper's* magazine (Crile had edited an article written by his consultant, Sam Adams); and in other publications. And a third possible argument was the seditious libel theory: Westmoreland could not sue for criticism of his official conduct, since as a high government official he was one with the government; his suit would thus be tantamount to the government's suing for criticism. According to Boies, no high government official has ever brought such a libel suit before. "I'm convinced that Westmoreland is libel-proof," Boies declares.

Yet, enamored as he is of the seditious libel theory, Boies didn't want to ask the judge to rule on novel grounds on a bare record. The risk, he says, is that the judge could get locked into a "negative mind-set" early in the case. It would also have been awkward, he adds, for CBS to make a motion to dismiss while it was withholding the Benjamin report. Boies expects to use these three arguments, as well as absence of malice, when he makes a motion for summary judgment early next year. "But the centerpiece of the motion will be truth—enormous unambiguous support for the program," says Boies. He predicts a win on summary judgment.

Despite CBS's successes in litigation, the network's image in the press has been that of a guilty defendant moving toward certain defeat. When the *TV Guide* piece appeared, CBS insiders had taken comfort in muttering that it was an attack from the right, one more sign of Walter Annenberg's much-rumored desire to "get" CBS. But they were aghast when an equally virulent attack came from Hodding Carter in an April 1983 edition of *Inside Story*. Carter mainly illustrated *TV Guide*'s charges, bringing forward several former military and government officials who denied the thesis of *The Uncounted Enemy*.

Carter's star witness was Godding—the only one who flatly contradicted the statements Crile had attributed to him in *The Uncounted Enemy*. Godding denied, as he had at Westmoreland's press conference, that the general had given him orders. In his epilogue, Carter concluded that *The Uncounted Enemy* constituted a "lynching," though, like Bedell and Kowet, he forswore knowing whether the substance of the show was true. But the day before the show aired, Godding had recanted that statement *under oath* in a videotaped deposition. Godding, who had served as the military delegate to an intelligence conference with the CIA on enemy troop strength, explained in the deposition how he arrived at the numbers he presented at the conference. According to transcripts of the deposition, he stated that he was following Westmoreland's instructions and was not allowed to exceed a certain figure without authorization.

Boies says he tried to reach Carter and the show's producers to tell them about the deposition, but that no one returned his calls until late afternoon on the day the show was to air. Associate producer Betsy Stark acknowledges that she returned Boies's call and that he told her about Godding's testimony. Stark, who says several producers have since told her that it might have been possible to change the show, relayed Boies's information to executive producer Ned Schnurman; Carter was out of town. Schnurman refuses to say whether it was possible to alter the program.

Carter, who purports to preside over a program devoted to exploring questions of journalistic ethics and responsibility, claims that the show had been "locked up" three days earlier. "We never got the word before the show was locked up; *I* never got the word at all; but even if I had, it wouldn't have changed the conclusion of the piece," he says.

A week later, CBS was still reeling from *Inside Story* when Leval ruled on the Benjamin report and it made its long-awaited debut in the press. Everyone from *Agronsky & Company* to James Kilpatrick leaped into the fray, savaging CBS with Benjamin's ammunition. Then, in early June, just as the Benjamin report was fading from the public's attention, Burt struck again.

According to Boies, Burt called him on June 10 to say that Ira Klein, the former film editor, had claimed that Crile had taped a conversation with former secretary of defense Robert McNamara and that the tape had at one time been kept in Crile's lower left-hand drawer.

Crile found a tape in the drawer, but it was of a conversation with General Winant Sidle, not McNamara. Although he told Boies that he recalled recording the telephone interview with McNamara, Crile maintained that, months earlier, he had told his attorney, Harriet Dorsen, that he had made the tape and that he believed it had been lost or reused. Dorsen said she had relayed this to Patricia Embry, one of Burt's associates, in April, but Embry denied having been told of the tape, and Burt cried cover-up.

On Sunday, June 12, Burt told *New York Times* reporter Stuart Taylor, Jr., that he would file a letter with the court the next day charging that CBS had surreptitiously taped the off-the-record interview with McNamara, destroyed the tapes, and improperly concealed these facts in pretrial proceedings. Burt added further that he believed at least five other tapes had been destroyed, and that this amounted to "destruction of critical evidence." He demanded sanctions against CBS, and his request is pending.

Boies responded by calling Burt's action a "smoke screen" to divert attention "from the fact that they're concealing documents from us" and further asserted that the McNamara tape had been destroyed or erased in the usual course of business.

Crile, meanwhile, was searching his home for other tapes he might have overlooked in the first sweep he had conducted just after the suit was filed. "I was very excited about having found [the Sidle tape]," he recalls, "because I listened to it and thought it would be great for the case." Over the weekend of July 10, Crile found another cassette which contained part of the conversation with McNamara as well as interviews with George Ball, a former undersecretary of state; Matthew Ridgeway, a former army chief of staff; and Arthur Goldberg, who had served as the U.S. delegate to the United Nations. Crile turned this find over to his lawyers.

What emerged in the press over the next two days was that Crile had not previously told his lawyers of this new cassette, that he had recorded the conversations with Ball, Ridgeway, and Goldberg without their permission, and that in McNamara's case, the conversation had been off the record. Crile says his lawyers had not asked him to identify every interview he had conducted; even if he had been told to identify audiotapes that had been reused or lost, he says he had forgotten that the cassette existed.

"Boies didn't tell me to search for those tapes," Crile says. "I just did. I was furious that Burt was saying I had destroyed tapes and that the lawyers were lying. So I thought it would be great if only I could find them. I rose to Burt's bait."

No one has charged that there is anything compromising in the content of the Sidle and McNamara tapes, but CBS's inability to get its story straight and Crile's surreptitious recording fueled Burt's attacks in the press and in litigation. He spent two days in June deposing Crile on the subject of the tapes, opening the session by demanding to know if Crile was aware of the criminal penalties for perjury and then describing them to him. Burt was playing the prosecutor, posturing and sneering. He also displayed his inexperience as a litigator in his inability to frame questions properly. Crile, in transcripts, appears unflustered; his answers are straightforward and offer little new information.

Asked about the tapes fiasco, Crile seems to maintain that making tapes without a subject's permission is a relatively minor indiscretion. "The person assumes you're taking notes, and this is more accurate," he says, pointing out that it is not illegal in New York State. Moreover, he claims he was unaware that it violated the guidelines.

Of more than a dozen people interviewed at CBS News, most said they were aware of others' taping phone conversations without permission, but had not done so themselves. Several admitted to having made such recordings and claimed it is not an unusual practice. Nonetheless, Sauter insists that taping without permission is *not* a frequent practice in his division. (*The New York Times,* ABC, NBC, and this magazine all maintain policies similar to that expressed in the CBS News Guidelines.)

On June 15, three days after Burt leveled his latest round of charges against CBS, CBS announced that Crile had been suspended with pay. Well-placed sources at CBS News report that Sauter had at first wanted to fire the producer. His own memorandum and the Benjamin report notwithstanding, Sauter had up to this time shown significant support for Crile: he had, against considerable opposition, given Crile a plum assignment—a documentary entitled *The Battle for Nicaragua,* which was to have been aired in August 1983. But, says Sauter, "I'd just reached my tip-over factor on Crile."

Boies, reflecting the oddly dual role he has played vis-à-vis Crile from the start, was the one to announce Crile's suspension to the press—even though at the time he was still Crile's co-counsel. (Kovner's firm is now Crile's sole counsel.) In the interest of the litigation, Boies says he argued against Crile's being fired, and he hopes to keep the fact of his suspension from the jury. (He says, with a straight face, he will argue it is irrelevant.)

The McNamara cassette was turned over to the court and to Burt with McNamara's okay and an understanding that its contents not be made public. Crile argued strenuously that the off-the-record tape should be withheld as confidential, but Boies replies, "It just would have looked too bad. The tape was innocuous, but if we'd tried to withhold it, nobody would have believed that." Sauter followed orders: "Counsel said, 'You gotta turn this over,' " he says.

For the lawyers, this case that never should have been brought has been a windfall. Burt's press bonanza has brought him national renown, and he has achieved far more success in strikes against CBS than should have been possible. Asked about Burt's repeated press coups, Boies responds with what can only be described as singular blindness for a lawyer whose client relies so strongly on public credibility. "These aren't really *litigation* wins," he declares. "The whole tapes issue, for which Crile got suspended, has nothing to do with the case. What Burt has gotten is *publicity.*" But bad publicity—which, with the Benjamin report waiting in the wings, was certainly foreseeable from the start—is all the more reason, one can argue, that a motion to dismiss should have been tried, long shot or not.

Burt, meanwhile, appreciates the irony of what he has achieved. "*I'm* not the press maven," he says with barely concealed glee. "*CBS* is the one who knows how to handle the press." He concedes that his has been an "astonishing performance" but will not be drawn into describing his strategy from here on. "I don't want to do anything to upset the apple-cart," he declares. "I don't want to tempt fate. I just want to fight my case. I don't want to pretend to be anything other than I am—a little gnome. Outgunned, outthought, outfought."

Boies is in the peculiarly lucky position of a lawyer whose case is perceived to be a real loser but who, when the decision comes in from the judge (in summary judgment) or jury, will look like a magic maker. Enraptured with *The Uncounted Enemy* and his chance to defend it, Boies declares that "the irony of this story is that if the case doesn't get thrown out and gets to trial, this show will finally get the attention it always deserved—much more than on that Saturday night back in January. Do you know that it got preempted for a basketball game in Greenville, South Carolina, where they brought the suit?"

Crile is not as upbeat. He recalls what Edward Joyce, executive vice president of CBS News, said as he was suspending Crile: "The irony is that over the past year we have come to have complete confidence in the documentary and believe we will win on a truth defense—but your public credibility has diminished to the point where it is virtually nonexistent. And with the last incident we don't feel we can have you working on any more editorial product." (Joyce confirms this account.)

Crile's public credibility has evaporated at least in part because CBS did not find out at the start what it believes today—that the show is sound. CBS focused on procedures with a mind-set that made journalistic mis-demeanors into capital crimes. While taping without permission is a guideline violation—and Crile admits he shouldn't have done it—he would never have been suspended without Benjamin's earlier judgments. Says Crile, "I feel like the leukemia victim who, with all his resistance gone, dies of a flu."

CBS, no matter what happens at trial, has sustained deep—and self-inflicted—wounds. But the man who triggered this whole mechanism gone haywire insists he would do it all again. "I would still do an internal document," Sauter declares resolutely. "I would still publicly announce its conclusions. And I would still go to Bud Benjamin as the best-qualified person to do it.''

WESTMORELAND TRIAL: A ROCKY START

BY
CONNIE BRUCK

In three weeks of trial, Dan Burt provided little evidence to support the general's case against CBS—but he made some shrewd moves.

When the *Westmoreland* v. *CBS* trial opened in federal district court in Manhattan in mid-October, only trumpets were lacking from the media fanfare. Billed as ''the libel trial of the century'' by *Newsweek,* the case has clearly been prepared as though it were destined for an august place in history. Lawyers on each side—Dan Burt, of the Washington, D.C., Capital Legal Foundation, for Westmoreland, and David Boies, of New York's Cravath, Swaine & Moore, for CBS, with their teams of associates and paralegals—have spent two years, full-time, on a $10 million, 100,000-hour discovery program that has produced 300,000 pages of documents from government agencies and other sources and 12,000 pages of deposition testimony from prospective witnesses interviewed here and abroad. If ever there was a showcase libel trial, *Westmoreland* should be it.

Thus far, however, there have been more pratfalls than polished performances, especially on the part of Dan Burt. And it is on Burt that, for now, the floodlights are fixed, since it is the plaintiff's case that is unfolding. How much Burt's boners will matter when the jury goes out is not clear. But if you're looking to *Westmoreland* as a model of the best in trial practice—look again.

OPENING STATEMENTS: THE BATTLE OF THE OUTTAKES

Watching Burt, one is constantly reminded that he is not a litigator, but a tax lawyer, and that this is his first jury trial. Much of the time, indeed, he looks as if he has wandered into courtroom 317 by mistake. He suffers particularly in comparison to Boies, a securities and antitrust lawyer with about ten jury trials to his credit. While this is Boies's first libel trial, and so in a sense he is a novice too, he seems to consider the courtroom home.

The contrast between the two adversaries was clear from the start. Burt read his opening statement. Interspersed with film clips from the 1982 CBS documentary *The Uncounted Enemy: A Vietnam Deception,* it lasted nearly three hours and seemed longer, because he kept his voice at a monotone and his face almost expressionless. Boies also delivered a three-hour opening, but with no notes. He was relaxed, conversational, occasionally even eloquent, and seemed—as he has through much of the trial thus far—to be having the time of his life.

Nevertheless, Burt's decision to read his statement may have been a wise one. In an effort to keep the jury from getting lost in a maze of numbers, charts, cables, and military acronyms, Judge Pierre Leval has allowed counsel to give interim summations, which are not to total more than two hours. When Burt attempted to proceed with one such extemporaneous summation after Boies had successfully objected to one of his charts, he rambled incoherently for several minutes. Judging from this performance, one cannot suggest that Burt ought *not* to have read his opening.

Burt's statement was, however, well enough crafted to be effective, in spite of his monochromatic and rigid delivery. Its strongest section was built around segments from the broadcast and outtakes (footage not used in the documentary) shown on six television monitors. Burt's pattern was to show a segment from the broadcast and follow it with an outtake—a longer section of the same interview that seemed to give the statement a different context, for example, or footage of another person making a contradictory statement—in order to make the broadcast segment seem distorted.

Burt's opening jibed with the way he has publicized this case from the start: always moving the focus away from the substance of the documentary's charges, to CBS's procedures—which seems intended to leapfrog the case right past the truth of what was broadcast to the question of CBS's "actual malice." (Under *Times* v. *Sullivan,* a public figure must prove that a defamatory statement was made with actual malice, that is, either with knowledge that it was false or with reckless disregard for the truth.) Burt spent far less of his time trying to score points on truth than trying to establish actual malice (or state of mind, to use the phrase that Leval has chosen in order to avoid confusion between everyday malice

61

and *Sullivan*'s actual malice). Of the three individuals who have been sued along with CBS—producer George Crile, correspondent Mike Wallace, and consultant Samuel Adams—Burt made Crile his prime target.

Actual malice is doubtless Burt's strongest suit: if the jurors are persuaded that CBS's procedures were unfair, they may—despite Leval's best efforts—twist the legal meaning of actual malice into a more colloquial meaning having to do with unfairness and unfair use of facts and interviews, all the while ignoring not only the question of whether the broadcast was essentially accurate, but also the fact that determining the fairness of such editorial judgments is not legally the province of jurors.

Boies first responded to Burt's opening by moving for a mistrial during a sidebar conference. Boies charged that Burt had violated the parameters of his own case, and had "repeatedly misstated" and "repeatedly mischaracterized the evidence."

"If I have quoted anything out of context," Burt replied, "Mr. Boies is free to make me a liar." Leval denied Boies's motion.

Caught off guard by Burt's video onslaught, Boies hastily assembled his own assortment of outtakes, which would, he told the jury, prove Burt guilty of the very act of which he was accusing CBS: unfair editing. One of Boies's examples opened with a broadcast segment in which Westmoreland replied to Wallace's query about President Johnson's response to bad news: "Well, Mike, you know as well as I do that people in senior positions love good news. Politicians or leaders in countries are inclined to shoot the messenger that brings the bad news. Certainly he wanted bad news like a hole in his head." Burt had shown the jurors an outtake in which Westmoreland went on to say, "But he was given both the good and the bad." Now Boies showed slightly more of the interview, in which Westmoreland added, "But he was inclined to accentuate the positive. . . . There was a tendency by the President, by Secretary Mc-Namara, by Secretary Rusk, and by those of us in Vietnam, to include myself, to accentuate the positive."

Boies argued that Burt had overreached in his opening, both in his editing of the outtakes, and in promising more than he could deliver. "You may recall that Mr. Burt said you're going to hear a lot of witnesses, many witnesses, come in and testify that CBS knew that the program was false when they put it on the air," Boies reminded the jurors. "That's not so. And one of the things I would like to ask you to do is to keep track as you go through this case, of each witness that testifies about that, because when I get to my closing statement I am going to want to talk about that issue again."

The next morning, Boies resumed with his real opening, the one he had planned before Burt upset his balance. He argued unremittingly that the broadcast was true—buttressing his position with sworn statements from officials, some still high-ranking in the military and CIA, that there had been deception on enemy troop strength, and that they had participated in it. These quotes were printed in giant letters on a chart six feet tall.

PROCEDURAL WRANGLES: BURT TRIES THE JUDGE'S PATIENCE

Prior to calling his first witness, Burt submitted 15 exhibits to be admitted into evidence, handing them to Boies as he did so. Leval had instructed counsel to inform one another of the exhibits they planned to offer, and Boies immediately protested that he had not been notified about the exhibits.

Burt insisted that both sides had already stipulated that the documents were admissible. "Simply untrue," Boies responded. Leval then asked Boies to review the exhibits, but when Boies inquired which ones were being offered for truth and which for state of mind, Burt equivocated. "Some are for truth," he said, "some are for state of mind, in some cases for both. We will so identify them when we use them, your Honor, with the witness."

"It is obviously difficult for me to decide whether I am going to object until I know what they're being offered for, your Honor," Boies complained. Burt then said that the first eight were being offered for truth. Boies objected that there had been "no evidentiary foundation laid for any of these documents," and that many constituted "hearsay."

Finally the judge excused the jury, and the parties spent more than two hours in tortuous argument over the exhibits. Leval has taken the extraordinary step of imposing a precise time limit on this trial—150 hours to each side—and these hours were charged to Burt.

But Burt seemed to be losing more than time, as far as the judge was concerned. "We are not going to get through this trial if we need to have sessions like this in the middle of the day," Leval commented. "What I have been urging since I think a year and a half ago, or maybe longer, was that counsel be getting together with their lists of exhibits and telling each other what the exhibits are offered for . . . and I thought when I got the nods and acquiescence that there was more than just a nod and acquiescence." Finally Leval said to Burt, "You know, there may very well be pieces that, when put together, would make all these admissible. You are starting with a piece at the top of the pyramid, and you just want to put it up there with nothing holding it up, and it ain't going to stay up if nothing is holding it up.''

Of Burt's 15 proffered exhibits, seven of the memos and documents were admitted—only two of them as evidence of the truth of their contents. Most of the others were admitted only as evidence of having been sent and received during the time period examined in the documentary.

If the judge's patience was tested by Burt's ineptness in introducing his exhibits, it was exhausted by what seemed to be his attempt to hide a witness.

Robert Komer, who had been in charge of the pacification effort in Vietnam in the late 1960s, had never been deposed. After his first day of testimony as Burt's second witness, Komer objected to having his deposition taken by CBS in the evening. He stated that he had been available for two years. Moreover, he said, he had returned early from a trip to Europe the previous week, and had told Westmoreland's lawyers then that he was available for CBS to take his deposition.

Boies said he had received no such notice. In fact, he said, he had gotten a letter from Burt—sent on the very night Komer said he had notified a Capital Legal Foundation lawyer of his readiness to be deposed—stating that Komer would not be available until the following week.

Now, under questioning by Leval, Burt said he had had no request from Boies to make Komer available earlier.

''Do you want to say that louder so everyone can hear it?'' Leval asked. ''Do you recall the twenty minutes or so that we spent discussing this issue in courtroom 402,'' the irate judge continued, ''when the defendant was saying, 'We want to depose Mr. Komer, we insist on our right to depose Mr. Komer,' and we talked about the fact that he was going to be abroad and the fact that he wouldn't be available until the fifteenth of October?''

Burt beat a hasty retreat. ''Yes, your Honor,'' he conceded meekly.

Komer's deposition was taken that evening.

''THOSE DAMN DEPOSITIONS'': BURT'S WITNESSES FAIL THE TEST OF CROSS-EXAMINATION

In the first three weeks of trial, several key witnesses for Westmoreland offered strong, helpful testimony on direct questioning. But they were then neutralized—or worse—on cross-examination. While no witness can be made immune to attack, these were so vulnerable they seemed to have been virtually unprepared.

Because he was the crucially important first witness, Walt Rostow, former national security adviser to President Johnson, may have been the most disastrous for Burt. On direct, Rostow was authoritative, full of his own importance, eager to expound on every area—including enemy strength—that had come within his view.

Probably his most compelling testimony focused on an April 1967 meeting in the White House attended by General Westmoreland, President Johnson, and others. In the documentary, correspondent Mike Wallace said Westmoreland told the president at that meeting that "the Viet Cong's army had leveled off at two hundred and eighty-five thousand men. And best of all, he told the president, the long-awaited crossover point had been reached." Wallace continued, paraphrasing what he said was Westmoreland's report to the president, "We were now killing or capturing Viet Cong at a rate faster than they could be put back into the field. We were winning a war of attrition."

Rostow testified that he had attended an April 1967 White House meeting in which Westmoreland discussed with the president and others his need for 200,000 more troops. But he did not recall that Westmoreland made any of the statements reported by CBS: no estimate of the enemy leveling off at 285,000; no crossover point reached; no winning the war of attrition.

On cross-examination, Boies asked Rostow if he recalled Westmoreland's having given the president the figure of 285,000 at this meeting. Rostow stated that he did not.

Boies then pointed to a chart that Burt had been using to display statements from the broadcast. One of them was Wallace's claim that, in the fall of 1967, "instead of being told of an enemy army of more than half a million, the president, the Congress, and the American public were told that there were only two hundred and forty-eight thousand Viet Cong left; that the enemy was running out of men." Boies asked Rostow if he now recalled Westmoreland telling President Johnson that only 248,000 of the enemy were left. Rostow replied again that he did not.

At this point Boies reproduced a memorandum from Rostow to the president, which stated that the total enemy strength was 248,000. Rostow still maintained that he did not recall Westmoreland presenting such a number to the president.

Boies then produced another memorandum written by Rostow, the cover sheet to a chart of enemy troop strength. "Ambassador Bunker and General Westmoreland used these charts to brief the president in November 1967," the memo read. According to the charts, enemy strength had declined from 285,000 in the third quarter of 1966 to 242,000 in the third quarter of 1967. Then Boies introduced a page from the Pentagon Papers that quoted a memorandum written by a Defense Department lawyer; the memo described an April 1967 White House meeting in which Westmoreland told the president what the CBS documentary charged he had said.

At long last, Rostow took the only route left to him—but with far less credibility than if he had done it at the beginning: he stated that he had not been present at the meeting described in this memorandum, and that the meeting he had attended was apparently a different one—even though it seemed from his direct testimony that one of his primary purposes as a witness was to testify about *this* meeting, because it had been highlighted in the broadcast.

Boies's documents could hardly have surprised Burt. All three had been mentioned in CBS briefs, and the one most damaging to Rostow—his own memo about the figures Westmoreland had used to brief President Johnson—had been included in a package of documents related to Boies's opening statement that CBS had given to Burt several days earlier.

When Boies learned that Rostow was to be the first witness, he says, he omitted the Rostow memorandum from his opening, for fear that Burt would use it in preparing Rostow.

Lieutenant General Phillip Davidson, Jr., who was the head of military intelligence in South Vietnam in 1967 and who had not been interviewed for the program, was also an impressive witness on direct testimony. A war hero with the Distinguished Service Medal, the Silver Star, and the French *Croix de Guerre,* Davidson testified that no military officers—including those whose complaints were aired in the CBS documentary—had ever told him about being pressured to reduce estimates of enemy troop strength.

He also responded emphatically to several CBS charges that Westmoreland had specified as libelous: that Westmoreland had placed an arbitrary ceiling of 300,000 on army, or Military Assistance Command—Vietnam, estimates of enemy forces; that he had blocked a report of higher figures; and that he had suppressed high estimates of enemy infiltration into South Vietnam in the months prior to Tet. Davidson denied all these charges. He testified that there had been no ceiling; that the self-defense and secret self-defense troops had been dropped from estimates of enemy troop strength because they were not a military threat, not because Westmoreland feared press reaction to higher numbers; and that there had been no suppression of higher enemy infiltration numbers.

Adamant and coherent in his recollection of events on direct, Davidson suddenly became aphasic on cross-examination. Boies produced a cable from Davidson to Brigadier General George Godding that said, "The figure of about 420,000, which includes all forces including [self-defense] and [secret self-defense], has already surfaced out here. This figure has stunned the embassy and this headquarters [in Saigon] and has resulted in a scream of protests and denials. . . . In view of this reaction and in view of General Westmoreland's conversations, all of which you have heard, I am sure that this headquarters will not accept a figure in excess of the current strength figure carried by the press."

Did Davidson recall what he meant by "a scream of protests and denials"? Did he recall the Westmoreland conversations? Davidson testified that he did not. Nor did he recall how he had formed his view that the self-defense and secret self-defense forces should be removed from enemy strength estimates. Nor did he recall when he had come to hold such a view, nor the name of any individuals who had told him that such a view was valid.

"I have no recollection of having come to that conclusion, other than what I can find in the documents," Davidson testified. During the course of his cross-examination, Davidson said that he could not recall nearly a hundred times.

Brigadier General Godding, the recipient of Davidson's cable, has been, as Boies has said, "turning like a weather vane in a rainstorm" since the start of the litigation. Godding was the military's chief negotiator at a conference held by Military Assistance Command—Vietnam (MACV) and the CIA on the strength of the enemy in South Vietnam, which took place at CIA headquarters in Langley, Virginia, in 1967. Although the documentary did not refer to him by name, Wallace stated that "the head of MACV's delegation told us that General Westmoreland had, in fact, personally instructed him not to allow the total to go over three hundred thousand." CIA analysts at this conference wanted a figure close to 500,000.

At a press conference after the broadcast aired, Godding denied that he had been instructed not to go over 300,000. But in a subsequent deposition he swung back again, saying he had followed Westmoreland's instructions and had not been allowed to exceed a certain figure—about 300,000—without authorization.

On direct questioning at the end of the second week of trial, Godding recanted again, testifying now that the estimates he carried to the conference were not the result of a "ceiling," and that he had told producer Crile they were not. But under a heavy barrage of questions from Boies, who was armed with Godding's deposition, the general admitted that he had been instructed to present and defend an estimate of approximately 297,000 at the Langley conference, and that he had not been authorized to depart from that estimate without getting permission from MACV headquarters.

Not only did Boies take away the advantage Burt had had on direct, but he also gained something new from Godding: testimony that the general had told CBS consultant Sam Adams, and perhaps Crile as well, that he had taken the May estimate of enemy troop strength, roughly 300,000, back from MACV headquarters to defend at Langley.

Boies, in his most successful cross-examinations, has been able to highlight contradictions between the witnesses' direct testimony and their earlier testimony in affidavits or depositions. ("Those damn depositions," murmured Mrs. Westmoreland, a daily observer at the trial, to a friend as Boies once again moved to show a witness his deposition transcript.)

Burt's approach seems to be to ignore the depositions, lead the witness as far as he will go on Westmoreland's behalf in direct testimony, and then hope he can fend for himself on cross. The result has been to expose one witness after another to humiliation and embarrassment, and to questions they cannot possibly answer without seeming to dissemble. (Unlike Boies, Burt declines comment on the trial for this article.)

THE *TIMES*'S COVERAGE: "A LITIGATION CONCERN" FOR CBS

Reporter Myron Farber's coverage of the first two weeks of the trial in *The New York Times* gives no idea how badly Rostow and Davidson were damaged in cross-examination. Farber has produced dense, detailed articles, but they have consistently been devoted to the testimony that has emerged on direct, paying relatively little attention to the conflicts and contradictions that have emerged on cross-examination.

The day after Rostow denied CBS's version of the April 1967 meeting, for example, Farber devoted considerable space to his testimony. There was no reference to what had emerged about the meeting on cross-examination—that is, that Rostow had not been at the key meeting between Westmoreland and President Johnson, although his direct testimony implied that he had been there. And it was not until two days later, in the final paragraph of his piece, that Farber referred back to Rostow's day on the stand, saying, "Mr. Boies also produced notes by a former Defense Department lawyer that appeared to contradict Mr. Rostow's recollection that General Westmoreland in a meeting with the president in April had not said the strength of the enemy was leveling off." Again, Farber never mentioned that Rostow acknowledged on cross-examination that he had apparently not attended the meeting in question.

Farber did cover Godding's cross-examination, but he had little choice: it took nearly an entire day, leaving him no alternative, as he is writing about the trial daily. The consequence of Farber's focus on direct testimony is that anyone relying on the *Times* alone would conclude that CBS was taking a worse beating than it is. Farber declines comment.

By the first week of November, CBS sources were saying that Farber's coverage had become a "litigation concern." The CBS team was worrying that its witnesses, scattered around the country and following the trial in the *Times*, might start feeling queasy. And—perhaps most worrisome to CBS—members of this well-educated jury are probably addicted to their morning *Times* and may not forswear it despite all admonitions. Will they be influenced by accounts that mold these long, difficult sessions into a lucid and compelling form?

Burt says he has "no problem" with the *Times*'s coverage, which he calls "evenhanded, right down the middle." No one suggests that he has influenced Farber by currying his favor. Writing a complex story under constraints of time and space, Farber is obviously reporting it as he sees it. But his coverage is the subject of comment in the press corps. Even one of Burt's teammates admits that it is far better than they had hoped for. "The only downside," says this source close to Burt, "is that Dan [Burt], who tends to get mesmerized by publicity, might start believing that the *Times* version is reality. Then he could be in trouble."

BOIES: WILL TRUTH PROVE A TRAP?

That Boies is more adept in the courtroom than Burt and *looks* like a winner—sure, easy, and dominant—is clear. But his grand strategy—a defense based on truth—may portend problems more decisive, in the end, than all of Burt's blunders.

Most defendants in libel suits brought by public figures seek dismissal on the issue of actual malice; usually they are successful. In his May motion for summary judgment, Boies tried a different tactic. Although he made an argument for dismissal on actual malice and other constitutional grounds, the thrust of his brief—a 378-page document with a 206-page statement of facts—was truth.

In a libel case as complex as *Westmoreland* v. *CBS,* this tactic was a sure loser. Judge Leval dispensed with Boies's truth argument in four sentences: "The principal bulk of defendants' voluminous brief is dedicated to the point that summary judgment should be granted because what was stated in the documentary was true," Leval wrote in denying summary judgment. "To this contention, it is sufficient answer that plaintiff proffers evidence to the contrary." Adding that he was expressing no view on the persuasiveness of proofs offered by either side, Leval went on to recite the kind of hornbook law that second-year law students know: "Summary judgment must be denied if there is conflicting evidence on any substantial issue."

Leval found CBS's actual malice argument "the most forceful," though he still denied a summary judgment on that basis. He also gave CBS leave to renew at the close of trial its seditious libel argument—that Westmoreland should be barred from suing, since as a high government official he was one with the government, and his suing would be tantamount to the government suing to recover for criticism.

Boies must beware of the trap that snared Irving Younger in the *Mobil* v. *Washington Post* trial. Younger built nearly his entire case on the argument that the *Post* article was true, and neglected to impress on the jury that, even if some points were not true, the defendants had believed them to be true at the time of publication. Boies, too, has seemed almost enraptured with the substantial truth of his client's presentation. Some lawyers—noting that Boies's most important previous case was the Cal-Comp antitrust suit—have wondered aloud whether he will try *Westmoreland* as if it were an antitrust suit, immersing himself in documents and numbers, and neglecting to strike home the simple theme that even if

70

some points in the documentary were not true, the defendants had had reason to believe they were.

BURT: CAN HE BUILD A CASE ON HONOR?

In the early weeks of trial, Burt has looked like what he is: an amateur litigator with a cause. Many of his courtroom moves belong in a trial lawyer's compendium of what *not* to do. But it would be a mistake to conclude from this that Burt has no talent for handling this case. From the time he filed the suit, he has exhibited a masterful understanding of its strengths and weaknesses—always veering away from the documentary's substance to CBS's procedures—and an instinct for exploiting CBS's vulnerability at every turn.

Just days before trial, Burt made a move that, while risky, will probably prove to have been tactically smart. He decided not to contest what Boies will repeatedly call the major assertion of the 90-minute documentary—that Westmoreland deceived Congress and the American people about enemy troop strength. Instead he narrowed his complaint, charging only that CBS libeled Westmoreland by saying that the general deceived his superiors—President Johnson and the Joint Chiefs of Staff— about the size and nature of the enemy in the year before the Tet offensive in January 1968.

At a pretrial conference shortly after Burt amended his complaint, Leval spoke about the possibility that the narrowing of the case might require him "to give instructions to the jury at the end of the case that might seem terribly damaging to the plaintiff." The judge went on to offer what he called a "cruder and more exaggerated" analogy: He hypothesized an individual accused in a newspaper article of having contracted for the murder of 33 people. The alleged murderer then sues, claiming that he was libeled by the accusation that he had killed the thirty-third victim. ". . . [I]t seems to me what the judge would have to explain to the jury is: [T]his plaintiff does not in any way contest that the newspaper stated that he arranged for the killing of thirty-two people," said Leval. "And you could not find for the plaintiff unless you found that, given the complete propriety of their stating that he killed thirty-two people, that he was injured in his reputation by the further statement that not only did he kill thirty-two, but he killed thirty-three." (That finding might be possible, Leval added, if victim number 33 was qualitatively different from the other 32—the plaintiff's father, for example.)

The downside of Burt's narrowing of the complaint is clear: if he does not challenge the documentary's major theme, that Westmoreland deceived Congress and the entire American public, how damaging, if at all, can it be to the general's reputation that in a few specific instances he deceived the president and the joint chiefs?

Nevertheless, Burt's tactic may yet play out to his advantage. The reason the documentary's few references to the president and/or the joint chiefs were so narrowly phrased, as both Boies and the show's producer, Crile, acknowledge, is that CBS had been able to gather only comparatively limited evidence of what President Johnson did or did not know about enemy troop strength. Burt, therefore, has succeeded in targeting the documentary's weakest spot. Boies puts it this way: "Burt has shifted the focus of the case away from the focus of the broadcast. We're really fighting on ground that is far removed from the broadcast."

Thus far, Burt has been having the best of both worlds. After he narrowed his case, his opponent argued that aspects of the documentary not relating to what Westmoreland told the president should be excluded. Leval has thus far refused to so rule—which means that Burt must prove his case on truth only on the peripheral charges CBS would least want to defend, yet he is free to explore anything in the documentary that serves his other implicit purpose of showing unfairness.

If Burt is wise, he will spend more time in the wings than on the stage. Although at first he ran the case single-handedly, by the third week both co-counsel—David Dorsen of Washington, D.C.'s Sachs, Greenebaum & Tayler, and Burt's associate Anthony Murry—were examining witnesses. Burt's rigid delivery and his obsequiousness to famous witnesses make him wearing to watch, so this diffusion of responsibility is a good idea. As time goes on, too, Burt's errors in trial practice should become less frequent, especially if he takes the counsel of George Leisure, Jr., veteran litigator at New York's Donovan Leisure Newton & Irvine, who has been in court every day taking copious notes. "I'm advising about trial practices," says Leisure. "Sometimes Dan listens and sometimes he doesn't, but I think I'm useful."

Leisure says he agreed to advise Burt after being introduced to him by jury expert Jay Schulman, who was then working with Burt (but was later fired). Leisure's firm is providing Burt with office space and two associates. All this is being done on a modified contingency basis: if Westmoreland wins, says Leisure, the firm will bill at an hourly rate on which a cap has been established. If the general loses, it's *pro bono*. "William J. Donovan, the founder of this firm, was the head of OSS in World War II," says Leisure, "and I think that if he were alive, this is something he would want us to do."

That kind of sentiment, which drew an experienced litigator to Burt's side, could help win over a jury as well. Respect for the military has resurfaced, and in some circles, at least, the Vietnam War is now viewed as having been an acceptable American endeavor.

Although Burt has done little in the way of building evidence in the first three weeks of the trial, he may have gained something no less significant: a courtroom ambience resonant with the respectability of his client and of the witnesses who have come forward to testify for him. Some of these witnesses have been badly damaged on their cross-examinations, the specifics of their testimony all but obliterated. And yet the impression remains of a staunch parade of men who have served their country in war, risen to high rank, and advised presidents. Ten years ago the more renowned of them were, like Westmoreland, almost exiles in their own land. Today the question is whether Burt can build a case on their honor, and win.

THE SOLDIER TAKES THE STAND

BY
CONNIE BRUCK

Westmoreland as witness: if CBS's lawyer was primed for mortal combat, so was the general.

"My troops did a wonderful job," declared General William Westmoreland, gazing intently at the jurors, his voice ringing with emotion. "A commander could have expected no more than they gave. I was proud of them, they were proud of themselves, and properly so. They did a difficult job. . . . They were doing it magnificently. They never thought— and I got this everywhere I went—they were getting a fair shake from the media."

Near the close of his second day of direct testimony in his $120 million libel suit against CBS, Westmoreland delivered this paean to his troops in the Vietnam War and vented his long-simmering animus for the press. The general's soliloquy must have been well rehearsed with his attorney; indeed, Westmoreland's counsel, Dan Burt, had cleared the way for his client's remarks in a sidebar conference with the trial judge, Pierre Leval. But when it came, the speech did not *seem* staged. It seemed, rather, like a monologue the general had been delivering to himself, silently, at odd moments over the past 18 years, one that had suddenly found voice. That it appeared so spontaneous is a tribute to Westmoreland's considerable force of personality and his ability to project it from the witness stand.

Although the general's direct testimony continued for two more days, this speech was its climax. When Westmoreland finished, Burt asked for a recess. Even after the judge had left the bench, the courtroom remained hushed, many of the spectators not stirring from their seats. "That," said one observer, "was *Masterpiece Theatre*." Escorting Westmoreland from the courtroom, Burt looked unburdened of all angers. He allowed the usual glower to slip from his face and was positively radiant, as though he felt victory within his grasp.

One of Burt's teammates had predicted in the opening weeks of this trial that Westmoreland's case would be won or lost on the general's performance: the kind of personality he projected—how appealing, how credible. Indeed, it is probably true that in a trial such as this—stretching over four months, with hundreds of hours of conflicting testimony about enemy troop strength 18 years ago, with many witnesses testifying that the numbers were imprecise then and their memories are imprecise now— personal impressions made by key witnesses will be, in the end, more vivid in the jurors' minds than the cacophony of statistics and chronologies. Even though the impressions made by the individual defendants— the CBS documentary's correspondent, Mike Wallace; its producer, George Crile; and its consultant, Samuel Adams—will factor into the jurors' equation, particularly on the secondary issue of malice, the credibility of General Westmoreland will be weighed first by the jurors as they deliberate on the primary issue of truth. Moreover, if Westmoreland is a sufficiently compelling and popular witness, the jurors may even ignore *Sullivan* rules—as other jurors have been known to do—and grant Westmoreland full victory, whether or not reckless disregard for truth is proven against CBS.

By the end of Westmoreland's direct testimony, it seemed clear that unless CBS lawyer David Boies inflicted considerable damage during cross-examination, CBS would lose the jury verdict. The interplay between these two, then—the stalwart four-star general and the silky-smooth, practiced Wall Street litigator—became the crucial counterpoint in the case.

In a sense, Westmoreland was Burt's surprise witness. Although the general had been in court every day, seated ever-erect and expressionless at the plaintiff's counsel table, he always departed with quick strides through the courtroom corridors, speaking to no one, except to exchange a few perfunctory greetings with members of the press. Nothing on the record in the case hinted at a star witness. In the outtakes of his interview with Mike Wallace, as Wallace's accusations became more intense, Westmoreland appeared to be dissembling, unable to offer convincing rebuttals, licking his lips constantly in what looked like a telltale sign of guilt. In his depositions, he seemed to have no memory of some of the key events upon which the CBS documentary was based and to be generally uninformed about the information emerging in discovery. At this early stage of the case, he seemed to fit CBS lawyers' characterization of him as no more than a puppet of his attorney and the conservative backers who were funding the case.

Once he took the stand on direct, however, the Westmoreland of the Wallace interview and the depositions vanished. In his place was a strong, confident, knowledgeable, and forthright man. Now, the general did recall, with a great deal of convincing specificity, the events that punctuated the enemy troop strength controversy back in 1967.

And not only did Westmoreland have memory; he had a great deal of personal appeal as well. In fact, he was so well suited to his role in the courthouse that had Burt set out, Pygmalion-like, to create a winning plaintiff, he might well have fashioned an exact duplicate of the man now testifying.

Westmoreland took the stand just a week after President Reagan's landslide victory. Hearing the general testify, one could not escape the similarities between the two men. Both are in their seventies. Both are so talented at projecting personality that, in some contexts at least, they can successfully elevate personality over substance. Both stand for traditional, old-fashioned values—family, country, patriotism, a strong military—which they have always championed, even at times when these values have been sorely questioned. Reagan emerged from the obscurity of the far right to sweep the country in the greatest electoral victory ever;

Westmoreland came back from the Vietnam defeat and antiwar protests to be honored and cheered.

It is no accident that Westmoreland's trial coincides with the national mood of revisionism about the Vietnam war. Ten years ago, an impartial jury would have been difficult to find, and even right-wing backers would have hidden their money from such a lost cause. Today, his cause is so current—he seems so completely *in command,* both inside the courtroom and outside—that one could almost suspect that it was more than a stroke of good fortune that the dedication of the Vietnam War Memorial in Washington, D.C., occurred on the weekend in the middle of his direct testimony. He attended the ceremony, was cheered by thousands, and managed, when he returned to the stand on Monday, to tell the jury an anecdote about having been there and meeting some of his old soldiers. At one point during that day, while Westmoreland was seated in the witness box waiting for the jurors to return to the courtroom, he spotted among the spectators a man with flowing white hair and a lapel button with the lettering WESTY'S WARRIORS against a red, white, and blue background. The man was Bernard Palitz, a former member of the 101st Airborne Division who says he helped raise $94,000 in the last ten months for Westmoreland's battle. Westmoreland saluted Palitz smartly, and Palitz returned the salute.

In his direct testimony, Westmoreland appeared powerful, even dominant, and he struck all the right chords. When his lawyer asked him if he'd ever been disciplined in his 40-year military career, he paused, gazing up at the courtroom's high windows, then confessed that he *had* once been reprimanded for paying a commissary bill late. And one other time, he had lost his driving privileges after going 20 miles an hour in a 10-mile-an-hour zone on his base. It seemed rehearsed, but genuine nevertheless. He looked every inch the straight arrow. He was a man who loved his country, had served it in three wars, and was devoted to his troops.

The background questions concentrated heavily on World War II. The general, a veteran of three wars, testified at great length about the combat he had seen. His career, until Vietnam, had been full of promise. At 42 he had become the youngest active major general in the army, and at 46 the youngest superintendent of the military academy at West Point, with the exception of General Douglas MacArthur.

He also seemed to be a family man. He mentioned bringing his wife (and once, his five-year-old daughter) on visits to the White House when President Johnson summoned him for reports about the war.

Westmoreland's wife, a vivid, smartly dressed blonde, has never missed a day in court, seated always in the third row, just behind the press section. Redolent with charm, "Kitsy," as her friends call her, enlivens that area of the courtroom.

The general has even managed to draw her considerable presence into his corner. During his direct testimony, Burt asked why he had been in the Philippines at a certain time. Westmoreland furrowed his brow in thought.

Burt asked again. The general said he was trying to remember.

"He'd *better*," Mrs. Westmoreland said in a stage whisper.

Westmoreland grinned broadly and announced, "I was there to see my wife."

Burt, who knows talent when he sees it, has indicated that, if the court will permit him to add her to his witness list, she will testify as the last witness, on the issue of her husband's damages.

A final aspect of Westmoreland's character that emerged from his direct testimony was his long-standing hostility toward the press—a popular sentiment, as many recent plaintiffs' libel verdicts have shown.

Westmoreland's sensitivity to the press during the Vietnam War is a major issue in the trial. In its documentary *A Vietnam Deception: The Uncounted Enemy*, CBS charged that Westmoreland's command altered and suppressed estimates of enemy troop strength because he feared that their publication would erode support for the war and show that we were *not* winning the "war of attrition"—contrary to his reports to the president and Congress in 1967.

Much of the trial testimony has focused on the fact that in the fall of 1967 two categories of enemy forces—the self-defense and secret self-defense forces—were deleted from the order of battle, the official record of enemy strength that was prepared by Westmoreland's command. CBS maintains that these forces—composed mainly of old men, women, and children—were responsible for the defense of the villages and hamlets, planting mines and booby traps and sometimes participating in combat. Had the two categories not been taken out, CBS maintains, the estimates of enemy troop strength would have increased dramatically.

On direct, Westmoreland testified repeatedly that he had wanted those categories removed because they included nothing but "old men, women, and young boys . . . who were not a significant military element," and he had wanted to separate the "fighters" from those who "did not fight." He also testified—as cables between him and his officers in that period confirm—that he feared the press would draw a "gloomy" conclusion about the progress of the war if the larger figures were reported. In his grandstand speech, during his second day of testimony, Westmoreland acknowledged that he and his officers had been "sensitive" to press reaction: "We would have been dummoxes if we weren't." He worried, he added, that the press's predictable reaction to higher numbers—despite any caveats about "fighters" and "nonfighters"—would further demoralize his troops, who were already distressed by the negative clips they received from home about the war.

In the outtakes of his interview with Mike Wallace, which were shown to the jury, Westmoreland had made crystal-clear his sentiment that he fought the Vietcong more successfully than he did the media; that the war was lost not militarily but politically. The press, in his view, had roiled the public and thus caused the loss of the political support vital to his military effort.

Giving vent to what doubtless are his deepest feelings toward the CBS reporters, and perhaps toward the media in general, Westmoreland testified about his interview with Wallace, which Crile had also attended: "I realized that I was not participating in a rational interview, that this was an inquisition, and I also realized that I was participating in my own lynching. . . . I realized that he [Wallace] and Mr. Crile had orchestrated a scenario so that they would go for the kill. They wanted to go for my jugular. . . . I realized that I was ambushed."

Boies objected. At sidebar he told the judge he was objecting to this and all the other speeches Westmoreland had been giving, including the one about the Vietnam War Memorial. Not only were they improper, Boies argued, but they clearly had been rehearsed with counsel. Said Burt, "I won't deign to answer this business about rehearsing." Leval, however, said that "a large part" of Boies's objection was "well taken," and cautioned Burt to restrict Westmoreland's testimony. But by that time it was too late. Westmoreland had had his say—not only about CBS, but about his war, his troops, and the destructive role the media had played. He said, too, that his judgments had been right, and history would bear him out. Indeed, one could argue that CBS did Westmoreland a great favor in broadcasting *The Uncounted Enemy;* without it, he never would have had such an opportunity to attempt an adjustment of history.

At the end of the general's direct testimony, Burt showed him a cartoon Westmoreland had been sent after the documentary aired. It was a caricature of Westmoreland, standing with a smoking gun over three dead bodies. The bodies were labeled with the West Point motto: "Honor; Duty; Country."

Asked whether he had looked at the cartoon when he received it, Westmoreland replied, "I most certainly did, and it was an unbelieving experience. It was the most humiliating experience."

Shaking his head, Burt approached the witness, saying, "General Westmoreland, let me take that back," as though the cartoon was too offensive to allow it to remain in Westmoreland's sight.

Burt then asked him whether, in his 40 years in uniform, he had ever lied to one of his superior officers.

"Never," Westmoreland replied. With that, his direct examination ended. Westmoreland left the stand, walked to the side of his wife, who was weeping, and escorted her from the courtroom.

Until Westmoreland took the stand, his case had not looked like a winner. Although one or two of his witnesses had been strong on direct and impervious to Boies's attacks on cross-examination, most were not—and a few were effectively neutralized. During these early weeks of trial, Boies had seemed the image of confidence, sporting a good-natured, even merry air.

During his four days of direct testimony, however, Westmoreland—by sheer force of personality—breathed new life into his case, while Boies became progressively more pale and somber. By the time he rose to face the general on cross-examination, all signs of Boies's habitual gaiety had fled.

Boies began with what would become the major theme in his confrontation with the old general: that Westmoreland had given testimony in his depositions that, in trial, either was proven false by other evidence or was being contradicted by Westmoreland himself. In this instance, Boies directed Westmoreland's attention to a passage in his deposition testimony:

"And did you discuss enemy strength estimates with the president of the United States at any time?" a question in the deposition read.

"Not that I recall," the general had responded. "He was not particularly interested in that. He was usually well briefed by his staff. I don't precisely recall talking to him with respect to specifics."

"Did you discuss with the president of the United States enemy strength estimates in general?"

"I don't recall."

Having read this exchange, Boies now confronted the general with evidence of three occasions on which he *had* discussed enemy strength with the president. Westmoreland, disregarding his statements in deposition, now testified that his recollection had since been "refreshed."

Boies then focused on one of those three meetings, a briefing Westmoreland had given in April 1967. At that time, according to notes of the meeting that Boies read into the record, Westmoreland told President Johnson that enemy strength in South Vietnam totaled 285,000 men and that "it appears that last month we reached the crossover point. In areas excluding the two northern provinces, attrition will be greater than additions to force."

Boies now brought up an intelligence conference that had been held in Honolulu two months earlier, in February 1967. A report issued shortly after the conference stated that "preliminary indications point to a sharp increase in the number of irregulars to be carried in the order of battle." New estimates, prepared by Westmoreland's intelligence chief for release in early May, showed that the irregulars category (which included the secret self-defense and the self-defense forces mentioned above) had nearly doubled in size. Yet in mid-April, when Westmoreland met with the president, he took no notice of the impending increase.

As Boies cross-examined him, Westmoreland now testified that he might not have received a report about the Honolulu conference; he could not recall whether he had been given an oral briefing. Boies showed Westmoreland his direct testimony, where, just days before, he had spoken authoritatively about the purpose of the Honolulu conference and testified that he had "been made cognizant" of what transpired there.

Again and again, Boies hammered home that Westmoreland had introduced the conference in his direct testimony, and spoken with authority about it, but that now—when faced with the fact that the conclusions reached there made the information he had given to the president in April 1967 appear misleading—the general had no recollection of having been briefed about it.

In this first quarter hour of cross-examination, Westmoreland seemed to undergo a metamorphosis, reverting to an earlier self. As Boies continued to challenge him, he began licking his lips. His left hand constantly jerked, in what seemed an involuntary motion, against the arm of the witness chair. Minutes before, the general had seemed wholly forthcoming and full of vivid recollection; now he appeared evasive, cornered by his own earlier statements. By the time he left the stand at the end of the day—after little more than an hour of cross-examination—he seemed a shadow of the witness who had testified on direct.

Walking down the steps of the courthouse, a Cravath, Swaine & Moore associate who had spent the last two years working on CBS's case was almost crowing. "We always *knew* Westmoreland would be our best witness," he declared. "After listening to him at deposition, we were really surprised at how good he was on direct—what obviously happened is that they taught him their version of the story. But it's only a facade. He can't hold up. He's just an actor. The only question now is, how long do we leave him on the stand? If he stays there too long, the jurors may decide he's so stupid that he did whatever he did out of incompetence."

That night Boies took stock of the day's events. For an hour's effort he seemed to have made great gains. He decided, he would later say, that if Westmoreland continued to unravel, he would keep him on the stand for only one more day of cross-examination. There would be no need to undo every point Westmoreland had made, Boies reasoned, because the general himself would be undone.

It is unlikely that Boies shared these thoughts with anyone at the time. Utterly single-minded and self-absorbed (albeit charming if that serves his end), Boies is said by those who know him well to be reclusive in his work. Possessed of a laserlike power of concentration, he does not generally seek out others' ideas. While his colleague Thomas Barr has three partners (and seven associates) assisting him in defending *Time* magazine in the *Sharon* suit two floors below the *Westmoreland* courtroom, Boies has no partner with him. He extols the talents of his cluster of four associates, but none is more than fourth-year, and none has had trial experience. So Boies, unburdened by any peer, charts his own course.

One advantage of this style is clear: Boies, a superb technician, is clearly master of his case. With all the boxes of documents that the Cravath paralegals wheel in and out of court every day, it is clear that there is one central repository for these mountains of data, and Boies is it. A disadvantage, however, according to one source, is that since he does it all himself, much of the work on this case has been eleventh-hour. For example, Boies's key witness, George Crile—the documentary's producer and Burt's chief target—went on the stand as a hostile witness for Burt without having spent any time in preparation with Boies. (Crile testified for only 90 minutes that first day, however, and during the weekend that intervened before Crile's second day on the stand, Boies did prepare him.)

Boies's relative neglect of his key witness may have simply been the product of being so dramatically overextended. But it may also suggest a critical flaw in Boies's insular personality—a tendency to be more the consummate technician than the sensor and orchestrator of a case's dynamic, human elements.

Boies's misjudgment of personality never seemed more marked than when Westmoreland returned to the stand for the second day of cross-examination. After that devastating hour on the previous day, the CBS attorney seemed to assume that a quick show of force would bring capitulation. Nothing could have been further from the truth. Westmoreland, after all, had not risen to command the U.S. armed forces by being a pushover. Within the first minutes of his testimony, Westmoreland made it plain that he was prepared to fight on every point, large or small. His sudden intransigence, his refusal to complete the retreat he had begun the previous afternoon, seemed to infuriate Boies.

Boies again turned to an event in the spring of 1967 that was described in the CBS broadcast and has been the subject of a great deal of court testimony. In May of that year Westmoreland's intelligence chief, General Joseph McChristian, showed Westmoreland a cable he had prepared to send to Washington. The cable, which was never sent, contained among other things the results of a new study of the irregulars category that had been badly underestimated in the past. The new figures were almost double those then in the order of battle.

In the documentary, CBS charged that Westmoreland "blocked" the cable, telling McChristian that it could be a "political bombshell" if it were sent back to Washington and that McChristian should leave it with him.

In his direct testimony, Westmoreland had denied CBS's charges, testifying instead that he had asked McChristian to arrange a briefing on the numbers. The briefing, he said, occurred about one week later at a weekly intelligence session. (This particular meeting, according to Westmoreland, was attended by his military superior, Admiral U. S. Grant Sharp, the commander in chief of the Pacific forces. If Sharp was indeed present for a briefing about the higher numbers, that is significant, because Westmoreland has charged that CBS libeled him in part by saying he deceived his military superiors.)

Boies set out to shake Westmoreland's story. But Westmoreland instantly dug in his heels, rattling Boies by resisting his characterization of McChristian's briefing as a report on "enemy strength." Rather, Westmoreland asserted, it was "enemy organization." He insisted time and time again that the two categories ultimately dropped from the order of battle in the fall of 1967—the self-defense and secret self-defense forces—were dropped not, as CBS charged, to reduce the number of enemy troops shown in the order of battle and thus demonstrate attrition, but because he wanted to separate the fighters from the nonfighters.

Moments after Westmoreland rejected Boies's characterization of the briefing on these categories as a briefing on "enemy strength," Boies referred to "enemy strength" in a new question about McChristian's visit. The judge, as he does fairly often, "sustained" an unmade objection in a manner that suggested he was displeased. Boies asked to approach the bench. Leval, who ordinarily grants this request, said curtly, "I don't think that's necessary."

Stiffening, Boies said in a harsh voice, "I would request it, nevertheless." Leval then assented.

At sidebar, Boies recovered himself sufficiently to apologize for his demeanor, then insisted that his question was proper. Leval, however, pointed out that Boies had rolled into his question a conclusion that the witness had specifically rejected.

Boies returned to the lectern and tried again, this time acknowledging Westmoreland's contention. "You say you take exception to the word 'enemy strength,' " he began, and then asked whether the two categories in question had been included in the order of battle in May 1967.

Throughout his direct testimony, Westmoreland had referred to the "so-called order of battle," thus emphasizing his assertion that it was a "misnomer" until the "nonfighters"—the self-defense and secret self-defense forces—were dropped. Now, Westmoreland replied that "at that time they were included in what was called the order of battle."

"When you say the so-called order of battle, it was so called by MACV, correct, sir?" Boies demanded, his voice rising.

"It was called that at that time," the general responded.

"And you were the commander of MACV, correct, sir?" Boies said, his voice louder still.

"Mr. Boies, you know that," Westmoreland said testily.

"Yes, I do know that," Boies replied, his voice almost a shout, as the judge attempted to restore order, calling, "Mr. Boies, Mr. Boies, Mr. Boies." Heedless of the judge, Boies continued, "What I am wondering is whether you forget it, sir."

Leval finally succeeded in quieting Boies, told the jury to disregard the "argumentative passage," and instructed Boies to resume his questions.

As this second day of cross-examination progressed, Boies continued to hammer away at Westmoreland, but none of his blows seemed to hit home. Even when Boies caught the general in an apparently untenable position, Westmoreland held on to it—solid, strong, unshaken.

At one point, for example, Westmoreland told Boies he had refreshed his memory of the McChristian meeting by looking at "history notes"— notes he had kept for posterity while in Vietnam—and other documents. But Boies showed him there was no mention of the McChristian meeting in his history notes and implied that the absence of any record was part of an overall suppression effort.

Westmoreland countered that the McChristian meeting was insignificant—so insignificant that when he had dictated his history notes, about two weeks after the event, he probably had forgotten it altogether.

Boies then asked the obvious next question: If Westmoreland had had no memory of the meeting two weeks after it occurred, how could he now, 17 years later, be so categorical about the time of the meeting, the discussions that occurred, and the events that followed?

Westmoreland did not lick his lips. His hand did not twitch against the side of the chair. Looking straight at Boies, speaking in a strong, level voice, he offered an explanation he would repeat so often over the next several days that it would become the leitmotif of his testimony. "Since this particular matter has become a cause célèbre by virtue of the CBS program," the general declared, "I have over a period of a couple of years *concentrated,* had my memory refreshed with certain documents. I have tried to put it all together, and I think we have accurately put it together as to times and dates and what happened during that time frame."

When Boies asked who the "we" was, Westmoreland replied, with no evident discomfiture, "My attorneys have done the basic research, yes."

As the day wore on, Westmoreland not only held his own—by projecting the personality that had made him so winning on direct—but also turned some of Boies's own missiles back on him. In one instance, still focusing on the McChristian episode, Boies reminded the general that he had testified on direct examination that he was certain he had not told McChristian—as the CBS documentary said he had—that the cable would be a "political bombshell." *"Bombshell,"* the general had said, was not "part of my lexicon."

Boies now fell headlong into the bog of trying to pin down an insignificant inconsistency. He directed Westmoreland to a page of his deposition and asked him to read a passage from it. " 'The public relations aspect related to an underestimating, underestimization of categories, and the realization that if we did not reorder the numerical representation of the enemy, that it would have been terribly misunderstood, it would have been a real bombshell,' " Westmoreland read.

Then, he quickly added, "Now, there is nothing inconsistent with what

I said. . . . *Bombshell* has been thrown around so much, and I heard it so much during some fourteen days of depositions with you, Mr. Boies, that you just thrust it right into my lexicon.''

That brought down the house. The jurors, as well as others in the courtroom, laughed loud and long. Westmoreland, obviously pleased with himself, grinned broadly.

The jurors' mirth, of course, was at Boies's expense. Hard as it is to read jurors' reactions, it seemed clear at this moment that they had not liked Boies's treatment of Westmoreland. All day, Boies had been angry and indignant, trying to pummel the old man and expose him as a liar. He looked very young and clever and slick as he thrust away at the old-fashioned general from South Carolina. But Westmoreland stood fast and held his temper. His Southern accent, giving rounded edges to his speech, made him seem all the more gentlemanly.

When the laughter subsided, Boies was still unsmiling. He pointed out to the general that his comment about *bombshell* appeared on page 1,642 of his deposition. Would Westmoreland look back in the earlier pages of deposition testimony ''and tell me when you find the page in which I thrust the word *bombshell* into your lexicon?''

''Over 1,642 pages?'' asked Leval incredulously.

Boies persisted. After looking for a brief time, Westmoreland said that he had spent ''hours and hours'' with Boies and had heard it many times. Boies kept on: Why, he asked, had the general never said, either in the interview with Mike Wallace or in his depositions, that he had *not* used the words *political bombshell*?

Finally, Westmoreland said, with a hint of a smile, not defensively, ''I made a mistake. I should have done it. If I thought this was going to be a big issue in this case, I sure as hell *would* have done it.''

All this for the litigation etymology of *bombshell*? Boies seemed to be spending massive amounts of time, effort, and emotion on a piece of trivia. He may have had the facts, but the general had the strength of personality—a mix of authority, conviction, and no small measure of charm—to make Boies's assault seem gnatlike.

Near the end of the day, the general seemed to gain even more stamina. No doubt galvanized by the success of his performance, he seized the opportunity to make speeches again, as he had on direct.

When Boies returned to the topic of whether Westmoreland had been briefed about the self-defense forces prior to meeting with McChristian about the cable, Westmoreland responded, ''I recall no such briefing, and as I traveled that country from north to south and east to west, and I was briefed at every echelon and I talked to sergeants, I talked to privates, I talked to Vietnamese soldiers, I was briefed by province chiefs, I have no recollection of this very nebulous, very inconsequential, relatively inconsequential organization ever being brought up because they were no threat: they were old men and women, they were young boys, they were confined to the hamlets, they were poorly armed, if at all, and nobody paid any attention to them. I mean, it's ridiculous to put such emphasis on an organization like that. I was four and a half years in that country. Nobody knew more about it than I did.''

When Boies asked whether McChristian had told Westmoreland that he believed the self-defense and secret self-defense forces should stay in the order of battle, Westmoreland answered, ''I don't remember whether he did or not, but that's totally immaterial. What he believed is one thing, what I believed was another. And I happened to have the responsibility. I was the commander. I had the responsibility to make judgments, I made those judgments.''

By the time Westmoreland left the stand that day, after almost four hours of cross-examination (the daily limit agreed to by Boies, in consideration of Westmoreland's age), Boies looked utterly spent. And then, talking to reporters outside in the corridor, as he always does, Boies received the coup de grace—not from the plaintiff or opposing counsel, but from his own client. A reporter showed him a story that had just come over the wire, stating that CBS News president Ed Joyce had told a Rotary Club gathering in Ellsworth, Maine, that he expected CBS to lose the *Westmoreland* case before the jury and win on appeal.

The next morning *The New York Times* ran a story about Joyce's remarks, on the same page with Myron Farber's story about the trial. It was Thanksgiving Day, when one may assume the jurors would have been more likely than ever to ignore the judge's admonitions against reading articles about the trial. Joyce was quoted as having said, ''If you follow libel trials in this country, you know that juries tend to award cases to the plaintiff, and in equal proportions they are overturned either by the judge or in the appeals process. We feel very confident that that will be the outcome in the *Westmoreland* case.'' When reached for comment, the *Times* piece continued, Joyce demurred, saying he had not meant to predict that CBS would lose, that he had been ''just speaking in general about libel.'' The article also quoted Joyce saying that CBS had gone ''into this with respect for the general and with some sadness about all of this'' and referring to Westmoreland as ''an honorable man.'' And it mentioned that another CBS executive, Anthony Malara, the president of CBS-TV, had told a group of broadcasters in San Antonio several weeks earlier that CBS expected to win, but not on the jury trial. "After all," Malara was quoted as having said, "Westmoreland is a national hero."

The following week Boies allowed that news of Joyce's remarks had not exactly brightened his Thanksgiving. He agreed it was probably without precedent to have a client declare publicly that he expects to lose a case, while his lawyer is in the middle of trying it to a jury. And finally, asked how he had felt at the moment he heard the news, Boies—who was leaning against the courthouse wall—gave a crooked grin and slumped to the floor.

After the Thanksgiving recess, Boies kept Westmoreland on the stand for three more days of cross-examination. He had decided, he would later say, that he had to continue to try to batter the general until he had stripped away that aura of command that Westmoreland had carried on direct.

If Boies was primed for mortal combat now, however, so was Westmoreland. His spirits must have been lifted by his successful performance on the day before the Thanksgiving recess. When the judged asked Burt on Monday if he had a witness, Mrs. Westmoreland murmured loudly, "Does he have a *witness*." And Westmoreland, on taking the stand, appeared more pugnacious than ever.

Once again, the general was willing to fight over relatively unimportant points. But now he started losing. He insisted numerous times that a 1966 memorandum laying out tactical objectives for enemy attrition that year was an "informal memorandum" rather than a formal one—until Boies showed him his own book, *A Soldier Reports,* in which he referred to it as a "formal memorandum."

Westmoreland also wrote in his book that he was "extremely disappointed" at getting far fewer troops than he had requested in 1967. Now, on cross-examination, he said, "I wouldn't say extremely, no." In the book he stated that the force he had requested was "scaled down sharply, cut almost in half." Now he insisted, time and time again, that this characterization was too strong, that "it was degraded, but not to the extent of cutting it in half."

When Boies asked whether anyone had interpreted the general's request for further troops as evidence that progress was not being made, Westmoreland had answered in the negative. Boies then introduced a 1967 *New York Times* article that quoted a general in Vietnam saying, "Every time Westy makes a speech about how good the South Vietnam army is, I want to ask him why he keeps calling for more Americans. His need for reinforcements is a measure of our failure with the Vietnamese.'' When Westmoreland testified that he did not recall ever seeing this article, Boies introduced a blistering intramilitary cable from Westmoreland about the article and the reporter who had written it. The general repeatedly disowned what he had said in his deposition and insisted that he had refreshed his recollection after he ''was able to concentrate.''

None of these points were what Boies refers to as ''building blocks'' for an appellate record. But Westmoreland, by fighting all these losing—albeit individually insignificant—battles, began to damage his credibility. He started to look more and more like an old soldier who had identified the enemy, and would now do whatever it took to defeat him.

The following morning, Burt announced that Westmoreland would not appear because he had hurt his back. The general did not appear the next day, either, and when he returned to the stand on Thursday, November 29, he seemed to be in pain.

His injury apparently made Boies's job easier, for Westmoreland fared even worse on this day than he had on his previous day of testifying. In fact, by the time he left the stand, he looked again the way he had during his very first hour of cross-examination. The morning testimony centered on a chart that showed enemy troop strength at 207,000 in the third quarter of 1965, 285,000 in the third quarter of 1966, and 242,000 in the third quarter of 1967. Weeks earlier, Walt Rostow, President Johnson's special assistant for national security affairs in 1967, had testified that the 1967 figure—unlike those for 1965 and 1966—excluded the self-defense and secret self-defense forces. This would mean that in briefing the president Westmoreland had demonstrated a decline in enemy troop strength by giving him figures that were not comparable.

At the close of his previous day on the stand, Westmoreland had testified that Rostow had not understood the chart. In fact, Westmoreland stated then, these figures had been arrived at through a ''retrospective analysis,'' in which the self-defense forces were removed for all three years.

But, Boies pointed out, the 1966 figure in the chart corresponded almost exactly with another enemy troop strength estimate from the fall of the same year—one that *included* the self-defense forces. Westmoreland explained: A new, unrelated category, ''administrative services,'' had been added in for all three years. He now asserted that the decline resulting from the deletion of the self-defense and secret self-defense forces had been offset by this new category. Thus, he testified, the fact that the 1966 figure in the chart corresponded almost exactly with the other 1966 estimate was "strictly coincidental."

When Boies pointed out that "administrative services" had been counted in 1965 and 1966 under "combat support"—that they had only undergone a name change—Westmoreland denied it for more than an hour. Boies badgered him until, finally, the general agreed that the categories were indeed the same.

Once again, it was not Boies's victory (in gaining a point of questionable substantive value) that was so marked here, but Westmoreland's defeat. He seemed stubborn, rigid—and wrong.

After gaining this hard-won concession, Boies moved to the subject of enemy infiltration. The documentary charged that Westmoreland's command had blocked reports of higher infiltration in the months before the Tet offensive. Indeed, his command's published reports in the fall of 1967 listed the number of enemy troops infiltrating each month from North Vietnam at 5,000 to 7,000, while Westmoreland, in his interview with Mike Wallace, recalled—six times, emphatically—that there were as many as 20,000 a month. He told Wallace that in view of this "ominous intelligence" he had asked that the 101st Airborne Division, scheduled to arrive in 1968, be deployed early, in 1967.

After the interview, Westmoreland sent Wallace what he has called a "correction letter," containing his command's published estimates of 5,000 to 7,000 for those months, and he has since testified that it was not until late November 1967 that he received highly classified information showing increased troop movements coming south from North Vietnam. Had he received such information earlier, as he told Wallace he had, it would have rendered his optimistic statements on a trip back to Washington in early November—that "the enemy was running out of men" and that he could see "the light at the end of the tunnel"—misleading if not deceptive.

Under Boies's questioning, Westmoreland testified at some length about having requested earlier deployment of the 101st in response to this new, highly classified information. Boies then showed him a passage from the Pentagon Papers stating that he had requested those troops well before November—as he had told Wallace during the CBS interview.

Now Westmoreland contradicted the statement that he had made a few moments earlier. Turning toward the jury, he declared, "I wanted the troops as soon as I could get them, regardless of the intelligence. After all, a bird in the hand is worth two in the bush. I had been promised those troops, and the quicker I got them the better. I mean, the heck with intelligence.''

Westmoreland smiled, but the jurors did not. More and more, his one-liners and speeches seemed to fall flat. By this time, Westmoreland had flatly refuted the testimony of several of his key witnesses. He had also disowned either his Wallace interview or his deposition testimony more than a dozen times, saying that he had since ''concentrated'' or had had his memory ''refreshed.'' On most of these occasions, Westmoreland's new version was free-floating, tethered not to any document but only to his changed memory. While these revisions seemed plausible at first—these events are, as he kept pointing out, 18 years old—they rang ever more hollow as they accumulated.

It was not that Boies ever struck home in one resounding blow, but rather the cumulative effect of Westmoreland's denials and inconsistencies that became so powerful. Having apparently learned his lesson in the early hours of cross-examination, when he had shouted at the general, Boies was now, in a moderate, even understated way, dismantling his witness.

On the general's final day on the stand, however, it was not Boies but Westmoreland's own counsel who provided the opening for the final blow. During his redirect examination, Burt sought to introduce what he said was a document newly discovered in army archives: a memorandum of a weekly intelligence session held at Westmoreland's headquarters in Saigon on May 19, 1967. The memo supported the chronology of events that Westmoreland had offered on the stand.

In order to lay a foundation for it, Burt elicited testimony from Westmoreland that he had seen it before. Under the court's questioning, Westmoreland went on to say that he had probably seen the document ''in draft form'' because it concerned the most important meeting of the week, and he had seen such a memorandum every week.

Boies almost sprang to request voir dire. Westmoreland repeated that he had regularly read memoranda of those weekly meetings ''because it was a very important meeting and any decisions were very important.'' Boies then asked Westmoreland to look at a portion of the cross-examination in which Boies had asked him whether he had received a similar memorandum. Westmoreland had replied, ''Well, a copy of this may have gone over my desk but I rather doubt it. I rather doubt that I noted it. I didn't read documents or memoranda that were unnecessary—were not necessary for the conduct of my business.''

"Did you regularly read the memoranda that were prepared summarizing what had happened at the [weekly intelligence] meetings?" Boies had asked, confirming Westmoreland's answer.

"No, I did not," Westmoreland had replied.

Now, in order to lay the foundation for a document helpful to his case, Westmoreland was completely reversing himself. As Boies attacked this turnabout, the general returned to his refrain: "I just didn't *concentrate* on the questioning," he said. "I didn't reflect on the importance of this and my testimony here is incorrect."

In the end, the fact that this one document lends some credence to Westmoreland's version of the facts is unlikely to tip the scales very much. What will matter more is the impression made by the general in this, his final hour on the stand.

On his direct examination, Westmoreland had been convincing as a man who had served his country and done what he thought was right—having to fight not only the enemy but a press he considered hostile. As he said to Wallace in one of the more revealing moments of his broadcast remarks, "There was a tendency by the President, by Secretary MacNamara, by Secretary Rusk, and by those of us in Vietnam, [including] myself, to accentuate the positive. It wasn't because we wanted to bury the negative, but it was because the negative had been given such emphasis by the media that there was a desire to balance the slate."

That was the battle Westmoreland believed he was fighting 18 years ago, and it is probably the battle that he believes he is fighting in the federal courthouse today. Committed then and now to his version of what was right, Westmoreland looked—by the time he left the stand—like a man willing to lie to prove his truth.

HOW DAN BURT DESERTED THE GENERAL

BY
CONNIE BRUCK

Burt created Westmoreland v. CBS *and rode it to national prominence. Then, when the going got tough, he abandoned the case and negotiated his client's unconditional surrender.*

91

At about 4:30 P.M. on Sunday, February 17, CBS general counsel George Vradenburg met General William Westmoreland's attorney, Dan Burt, in the lobby of Burt's New York hotel, the Westbury, and handed him papers for his client to sign to withdraw his $120 million libel claim against CBS. Westmoreland's entire compensation would consist of a joint statement, which said in part: "CBS respects General Westmoreland's long and faithful service to his country and never intended to assert, and does not believe, that General Westmoreland was unpatriotic or disloyal in performing his duties as he saw them."

No one on Burt's team—neither his four staff attorneys at the Capital Legal Foundation, nor his co-counsel, David Dorsen of D.C.'s Sachs, Greenebaum & Tayler and George Leisure of New York's Donovan Leisure Newton & Irvine—knew that any settlement negotiations were taking place, let alone that final papers were being signed. As Burt took the papers from Vradenburg to bring them upstairs where the general was waiting, he said, according to two sources familiar with the conversation, "I don't trust the son of a bitch. Let me get him to sign them before he changes his mind."

Westmoreland did sign, and several hours later Burt, who declined repeated requests to be interviewed for this article, went alone to the Stanhope Hotel, where his erstwhile adversary, CBS lawyer David Boies of New York's Cravath, Swaine & Moore, was celebrating with his team of associates. According to the Cravath lawyers, they and Burt made champagne toasts to one another: they toasted Burt as a worthy competitor, and he toasted them as having taught him everything he knew. The hotel's small restaurant fairly rocked with good feeling; the CBS lawyers were euphoric at the general's sudden and complete surrender, and Burt must have been relieved at not having to face a jury verdict. He would not go down in history as the lawyer who had lost the Westmoreland case.

For Westmoreland, however, it was not a night of celebration. He and his wife, Katherine, known to her friends as Kitsy, were upset to learn that their other lawyers had not been aware of the settlement. They were besieged with inquiries from the press; Mrs. Westmoreland finally instructed the switchboard at their hotel to hold all their calls, and they went to sleep.

"I feel so bad for Westmoreland," one of his lawyers says. "I keep thinking of this conversation I had with Ellsworth Bunker, shortly before he died. He told me that he could never forget, he'd given his word to those people in South Vietnam—given his word—that we would not withdraw our support. And then we did, and all those people died. Well, I don't mean to be melodramatic," the lawyer continues, "but I feel very bad. I made a commitment to Westmoreland, it was an act of faith—and then for it to end this way. He did not deserve this."

Westmoreland's capitulation only days before this five-month-long trial was to have gone to the jury seemed almost irrational. The four-star general has been faulted for a number of things, but until now being a quitter was not one of them. Friends of his comment that surrender seems out of character for the old soldier; they puzzle over what could have brought his three years' travail to such an abortive and sorry end.

The answer appears to lie not in the character of Westmoreland but in that of his lawyer. Dan Burt created this case, rode high with it in its halcyon days, and then—when it appeared to be heading downhill— engineered its destruction and his own escape. When Burt felt that the time had come to quit, he negotiated with CBS for a statement similar to one the network had offered to make a year earlier, according to CBS's Vradenburg. That earlier version, however, would have been better for Westmoreland: it did not have the key phrase about performing his duties "as he saw them"—an all-purpose caveat that placed the general in a much less favorable light. When CBS made the more favorable offer in February 1984, Burt called it "ridiculous," according to opponent Boies. "Burt said then that there had to be money, there had to be an apology, and there had to be a renouncing of the broadcast," recalls Boies. Westmoreland, when asked recently about the earlier CBS offer that was so similar to the final statement, replies, "I recall nothing like that."

That Burt would have treated this offer so scornfully in February 1984 is altogether consistent with his posture from the start of this case. In the settlement talks that had taken place from time to time since the suit was filed in September 1982, Burt had always asked for some combination of money, an apology, a disavowal of the broadcast, and free airtime without a CBS rebuttal.

Ambitious as these demands were, they seem almost modest when compared with Burt's public pronouncements. "We are about to see the dismantling of a major news network," he promised in an interview with *USA Today* in April 1983, after the court had ordered CBS to turn over to Burt its internal investigation of the making of *A Vietnam Deception: The Uncounted Enemy*. And Burt's threats were not limited to the network. He also fixed his sights on individual players—George Crile, the show's producer; Mike Wallace, its correspondent; Samuel Adams, its consultant; and Howard Stringer, its executive producer—promising publicly, at various times, to savage them on cross-examination.

From the time the suit was filed until the start of trial last October, Burt—all braggadocio and outrage—swaggered across the stage he had created, playing the part of giant-killer. An unknown tax lawyer, he had come from nowhere and used this case to catapult himself to national prominence. He has told the press that he left an extremely successful international tax practice in a small firm he had founded in Marblehead, Massachusetts, because he wanted to do "policy work" at Capital Legal. But according to ex-members of his former firm, Burt was forced out in late 1979 because he was so abrasive and offensive to both partners and clients that, despite his business-getting talents, he became a liability. About six months after he left the firm, he became the president of Capital Legal. He had gotten involved with the conservative public interest group through a former client, Leslie Burgess, then vice president of the Fluor Corporation, and chairman of Capital Legal's board of directors. One former colleague recalls being amused at Burt's sudden political conversion. Burt, he says, had been "very liberal" in his Marblehead days, but the turnabout made sense: Burt had always sought publicity, and Capital Legal might offer high-visibility cases. Besides, as another former Burt colleague puts it, "Dan's only ideology has always been, 'Promote thyself.'"

Coming in the door in the spring of 1982, the *Westmoreland* case must have looked like a bonanza to Burt—sexier than all the rest of his cases put together. As Alan Feld of Boston University Law School, a member of Capital Legal's board of directors, points out, it was "very, very different" from the foundation's other cases, which had to do with promoting a free market and deregulation. Feld declines comment on why or how it was decided to add the anomalous *Westmoreland* case to Capital Legal's otherwise consistent agenda, but he does say that the foundation should perhaps "go back to the other kinds of cases" in the future. James Moody, one of Capital Legal's four staff attorneys, told the press that *Westmoreland* was the foundation's first libel case and probably its last.

By the time Westmoreland came to Burt, he had made the rounds. Clark Clifford of Clifford & Warnke, Edward Bennett Williams of Williams & Connolly, and Stanley Resor of Debevoise & Plimpton had all advised the general not to bring this suit. Only Burt declared it a winner and offered to take it pro bono. And in the pretrial years Burt was able to score one coup after another in the public relations arena. Thanks to CBS's propensity for the self-inflicted wound in its handling of the case from the start, Burt managed to create the impression that he would indeed bring the CBS giant to its knees in court.

Burt liked to tell reporters that he was dedicating himself to this case not as a hired gun or a conservative ideologue, but as a lawyer convinced that his client's cause was just, and willing to take on anybody, no matter how powerful, to prove it. Comments he reportedly made in private during the case's pretrial stage, however, suggest that from the start Burt was motivated less by the client loyalty he trumpeted than by his enthusiasm for a marvelous publicity vehicle for Dan Burt. One *Westmoreland* insider recalls that Burt would refer to his client as "General Asshole," and that when he was told pretrial work was not being done thoroughly enough he replied, on more than one occasion, "Don't worry—he's getting what he paid for."

Burt has often mentioned to his associates and the press the financial sacrifices he made in going to Capital Legal. He is said by a former partner to have made about $400,000 in his last year of private practice; his 1984 salary from Capital Legal was $90,000. But his lifestyle during the Westmoreland case—a case funded not only by the right-wing coffers of Richard Mellon Scaife, the Olin Foundation, and the Smith Richardson Foundation, but also by $10 and $25 checks from retired military personnel and other people of limited means—was one befitting Burt's image of himself as conquering hero. During the trial he occupied a $350-a-day suite at the Westbury (usually discounted to $266 a day for a month-long stay), while the rest of his team stayed at the Harley in $150-a-day rooms discounted to $75 a day. Burt also supplemented his income by being of counsel to the Pittsburgh firm of Thorp, Reed & Armstrong, and it may well be that some of his more extravagant expenditures during the case, such as taking the Concorde to Europe for depositions, were billed to private clients.

In 1984 the board of Capital Legal approved a bonus for Burt, which one source puts at $100,000. According to board chairman Leslie Burgess, he and the other directors considered lending Burt the money, but decided that "for a public interest, nonprofit organization there is always a tinge of duplicity, or shadiness, in giving a loan, interest-free or low-interest." In the end the board settled on a bonus, which "Dan was certainly deserving of," Burgess adds. So, although Burt could probably have made more money in private practice, his life as a pro bono lawyer for Westmoreland was not one of hardship.

And besides, the Westmoreland case, at least in its pretrial phase, offered so many other rewards. Like the Savile Row suits that he liked to tell people he was sporting at trial, this case was tailor-made for Burt. That a man who seems obsessed with his stature and his origins, and who describes himself as "a short, foulmouthed Jew from the streets," had the opportunity to pit himself against the elite, entrenched power of Cravath and CBS was almost too good to be true. There was an old score to settle, too. In his last year at Yale Law School, Burt had been interviewed by Cravath, but had not been offered a job; according to a story he told Boies, that rejection rankled for years. It would be sweet indeed to beat the Cravath lawyers—and also to win their respect.

"When I sued them," he told *TWA Ambassador* magazine just before the start of trial, "they laughed. Nobody expected I could do it. You haven't heard anybody laugh lately, have you? . . . The key to the game is knowing when . . . [to get] the hell outta the line of fire. CBS didn't."

But on Wednesday, February 13, 1985, it was Burt, not CBS, who decided to get out of the line of fire and settle the case. A few hours after Colonel Gains Hawkins, who had been responsible under Westmoreland for the estimate of enemy strength (known as the order of battle), had finished his first day of testimony, Burt called CBS's George Vradenburg and asked to meet the next morning for breakfast. Vradenburg said he already had an appointment on Thursday, so they agreed to meet on Friday morning.

Asked whether he knew at the time that Burt was contacting Vradenburg to talk settlement, Westmoreland says that he does not recall, but that it was possible he and Burt had discussed it in "a fleeting conversation." Westmoreland has told the press that he was shaken by the appearance and testimony of some of his former intelligence officers, particularly that of Colonel Hawkins and General Joseph McChristian. Nevertheless, a source close to the general says that he had no thought of quitting, and that Burt undertook the settlement discussions on his own initiative.

Burt has declined to be interviewed for this article. From interviews with those who know him well, however, it seems clear that the realities of trial—as distinguished from the grandstanding of the discovery period—took a heavy emotional toll. This was his first jury trial. Whatever arrogance had led him to "cut his teeth on this case," as co-counsel George Leisure puts it, seems to have dissipated as he struggled day after day—often futilely—to frame a question or an objection. He was often so inept, so hesitant, that the silence that grew as he struggled to frame a question seemed to embarrass and discomfit even those on the other side benefiting from his paralysis. (Burt's ineptness was not lost upon the jury. One juror, interviewed after the case, says that the jurors often commented among themselves about how "green" Burt was, and speculated about what the trial would have been like if Westmoreland had been represented by Boies and CBS by Burt.)

Less obvious but more damaging to his case was his consistent practice of leading his own witnesses so far beyond the confines of safe testimony that they were ripe for exposure and embarrassment on cross-examination. He did this even with his client. In one such instance, Burt elicited testimony from Westmoreland that he had seen a certain document back in 1967 because he always read such memoranda, although in earlier testimony the general had said he did *not* read them because they were not necessary for the conduct of his affairs. According to Boies, shortly after this testimony, Burt confided that he "had this awful sinking feeling, and was afraid something very bad might happen to him—that he might even lose the case" because this contradiction had damaged Westmoreland's credibility. Burt, however, acknowledged no fault. Instead he blamed his client.

Nervous as Burt felt about Westmoreland—who was in many respects a great witness—it was his confrontation with producer Crile that seems to have shaken him most profoundly. Burt had made it plain from the early days of his lawsuit that Crile, more than any other individual defendant, was the one he planned to dismember on the stand. Burt's success in the pretrial phase of the suit lay in his directing press attention to the procedures of the broadcast, rather than its substance—to what Crile had done in 1981–82, not what General Westmoreland had done in 1966–67. Had he continued this strategy at trial, he would have concentrated the evidence not on truth issues, but on malice issues, where he had more to exploit. Indeed, in his opening, Burt spoke at length about editing practices, charging that CBS deliberately distorted the story, and he repeatedly pointed an accusatory finger at Crile. It was absolutely vital to his case that he damage Crile: he could not win without showing malice, and Crile, as the individual with paramount responsibility for the show, offered him his best chance. Many who know Burt say that besting Crile was vital to him personally, too, because the tall, handsome, and well-connected Crile is everything that Burt seems to chafe at not being.

Since Burt called Crile as a hostile witness, the producer's testimony was in effect a cross-examination—Burt's first. Cross-examination for a novice is hard enough; cross-examination of a witness who has not laid the groundwork by giving direct testimony is harder still. There was heated debate in the Westmoreland team—which included two experienced litigators, David Dorsen and George Leisure—about the wisdom of calling Crile as a hostile witness. "I argued that you are going to lose your momentum by calling Crile," says Leisure, "but Dan was afraid that he wouldn't survive a motion to dismiss at the end of his case, because he would not have made out a prima facie case on malice." Nearly all of Burt's witnesses up to that point had given testimony on the issue of truth only.

Burt kept Crile on the stand for the better part of seven days. While his manner displayed the utter contempt he felt for his witness—he would sneer, make faces, oil his words with sarcasm, put his hands on his hips and roll his eyes toward the ceiling while Crile spoke—his questioning was wholly ineffective. Time after time, Burt was unable to frame questions properly until he got help from Judge Pierre Leval. On editing practices—Crile's weakest ground, where a good trial lawyer would have scored big points—Burt got nowhere. And on the factual basis for the broadcast, Burt would typically build to a denunciatory question so extreme that Judge Leval would give Crile enormous leeway in his response, allowing him to deliver long, self-serving monologues that showed the breadth of his knowledge on *The Uncounted Enemy* and the depth of research that had gone into it.

According to others on the plaintiff's trial team, Burt was disheartened by the drubbing he got from Crile; reportedly he turned to his adversary, Boies, to bolster his spirits. About midway through Crile's examination, Boies recalls, Burt told him that other lawyers on the Westmoreland team were saying that Crile was killing him, and that he should just let Crile go. "I told him, 'I think you're doing great, Dan,' " Boies recalls. " 'I have the same problem with my people sometimes, they just don't understand—and when that happens, I ignore them.' "

By the time Burt released Crile, he apparently knew how badly he had done. Not only had he failed with a key witness for his malice case, but he had expended far too many of the precious 150 hours Leval had allotted each side. He had only about 30 hours left. As though he had just remembered that the clock was running, Burt seemed to overreact. He gave such short shrift to the rest of his malice case that he didn't even call CBS executive producer Howard Stringer, whose derogatory comments about Crile had been taped without his knowledge by *TV Guide* reporter Don Kowet. Burt also rushed through his examination of disgruntled CBS film editor Ira Klein—who had been billed as the star of the malice case—in less than a day.

According to Vradenburg, just before Crile took the stand, Burt had offered to settle if the network would pay $5 million in legal fees and issue a statement saying that CBS now believed Westmoreland had not misled his superiors about enemy strength. By early January, says Vradenburg, Burt had dropped his demand for money and offered to settle for the statement. Both Dorsen and Leisure say they did not know about the December settlement offer. (When the case was over, Burt told *The Washington Post* it had cost about $3 million. Asked about the discrepancy between Burt's December demand and his February claim, Vradenburg says, "Either he was lying then, or he's lying now.")

Burt's beating by Crile caused consternation among his teammates. They began pressuring him to yield the cross-examination of some CBS witnesses to Dorsen. An experienced trial lawyer, Dorsen says he entered the case at the very start with the understanding that he would play a principal role. Then, one Westmoreland insider recalls, "Dan's fantasies got bigger and bigger as the trial approached, until he finally announced he was doing it himself." Leisure—who said the founder of his firm, William Donovan, former head of the OSS, would have wanted the firm to come to Westmoreland's assistance—had come into the case about two months before trial, offering to provide office space, the services of two associates, and his own counsel, for a monthly fee to his firm of $20,000 to $25,000. (By the time the case ended, Burt and his Capital Legal Foundation reportedly owed several hundred thousand dollars to Dorsen, but Leisure says his firm has been paid promptly.)

In the face of mounting pressure from his colleagues, Burt asked jury consultant Jay Schulman, whom he had fired in a dispute at the start of trial, to represent him in a meeting with Dorsen and Leisure. "Dan was experiencing extraordinary trauma as a result of the Crile cross," recalls Schulman. "He was in a state of depression and demoralization." After a two-and-a-half-hour meeting, this committee of three unanimously recommended to Burt that Dorsen cross-examine former CIA official George Allen, Colonel Hawkins, General McChristian, and Mike Wallace. At first Burt relinquished only Allen. Then, through January and February, he gave Hawkins and McChristian to Dorsen. At the end Burt kept for himself Wallace, CBS vice president Roger Colloff, and the summation. When queried by reporters, Burt replied that he had always intended Dorsen to cross-examine the other CBS military witnesses.

This tactic did not save him from humiliation. When Boies called Crile as a witness for CBS, he had the documentary shown on the courtroom's video monitors and walked Crile through it, freezing frames so Crile could document each point—a very effective stratagem. After Boies finished his examination of Crile, he made a brief interim summation. (Leval allowed both sides two hours' worth of mini-summations, to be given whenever the lawyers chose.) With Crile on the witness stand awaiting cross-examination and the broadcast on the monitors, Boies challenged Burt to point to sections mentioning Westmoreland that the plaintiff alleged were false, and to ask Crile why he believed they were true.

Trapped, Burt objected in a sidebar with Judge Leval that Boies was improperly "trying to force" his hand. Leval disagreed, but gave the jurors a mild instruction about Burt's right to choose his own course of action. Burt then cross-examined Crile for about ten minutes, made no references to any part of the broadcast that he was alleging to be false, and retreated.

As the trial progressed, the ebullient, bombastic Burt of pretrial press conferences—the man who would break up CBS—disappeared. One of his teammates recalls Burt's nervous refrain during the later weeks of CBS's case: "How do you think we're doing with the jury? How are we doing?" CBS's case was going well. Both former and active military and CIA officers came forward to testify about their participation or acquiescence in the falsification of enemy troop strength reports in 1967, often using language stronger and more compelling than that in the documentary. In contrast to Westmoreland's witnesses, almost none sustained real damage on cross-examination. Still, as this Westmoreland lawyer points out, any experienced trial lawyer knows that each side tends to look stronger when presenting its case. The game was not over just because CBS was doing well. But Burt, this lawyer posits, lost sight of that.

As the case entered its final days of testimony, Burt learned that—contrary to what both he and Boies favored—Judge Leval was going to instruct the jury to answer specific questions about: defamation; whether the alleged libels were of and concerning Westmoreland; truth; state of mind or malice; and injury. A single verdict would have allowed Burt to claim, if he lost, that the documentary was false, but that the requirements of constitutional malice were almost impossible to satisfy. Now there was no such escape hatch. And worse, from Burt's point of view, Leval had given many indications that he was leaning toward instructing the jurors that, in order to find the broadcast false, they would have to do so by "clear and convincing evidence," rather than by the less demanding standard of "a preponderance of evidence."

On the afternoon of February 13, shortly before Burt called Vradenburg to set up the breakfast meeting, he received more bad news: Ordinarily the defendant offers a summation, followed by the plaintiff; the defendant has no chance for rebuttal. But Boies argued to Leval that he should have an opportunity for rebuttal, reminding the judge that in his opinion Burt had badly misstated the record in his opening statement. In a move that would curtail any impulse of either side to overstate, Leval now offered counsel a series of alternatives. The first was that Burt tell Boies in advance what he was going to say; this, Boies says, Burt quickly rejected. Both of the other options put Boies in a position to rebut, and allowed Burt to respond. And both, therefore, would call upon Burt's powers of extemporaneous speech, which—as his interim summations demonstrated—do not exist. In one of his more memorable interim summations, for example, Burt argued incoherently that there had been "a very bitter dispute" between military intelligence and the CIA, but not a "conspiracy to deceive." He declared that the military and the CIA had the same raw information, then said to the jurors: "Think about it like this. Suppose you are a bank teller and you want to embezzle and so you make out a couple of checks one to D. Duck and one to M. Mouse and then you cash the checks yourself. You are not going to take those checks and go rushing up to the bank manager and say, hey, take a look at this. That just doesn't make sense."

Burt must also have been worried about the gambit Boies had warned in his opening that he would use in his summation. He would point to all the unfulfilled promises Burt had made in his opening statement. "In the course of this trial," Burt had told the jury, "you will hear many people testify that when defendants aired [their] broadcast they either knew the broadcast was false or were recklessly indifferent to its falsity." In his summation, Boies says, he intended to point out that there was only one such witness: film editor Ira Klein, who admitted a personal animus toward Crile. Burt had also promised the jurors they would see "General McChristian's allegedly suppressed report," but it never appeared in the courtroom, Boies points out. Finally, Boies says, he would have reminded the jurors that Burt had told them that Commander James Meecham and former CIA directors Richard Helms and William Colby would all testify on behalf of Westmoreland and that he had told them what these witnesses-to-be would say. But Meecham, Helms, and Colby never showed up.

If Burt had held on to his early enthusiasm for his case, he would have been tempted to step back in as CBS's case seemed to get stronger. For Dorsen's cross-examinations—while not as dramatically disastrous as Burt's first confrontation with Crile—were lackluster. But even the prospect of cross-examining the two CBS witnesses he had reserved for himself, and then presenting the summation, seems to have given him pause. The day after Burt had contacted Vradenburg about settlement, Dorsen recalls, Burt asked him, in an offhand way, whether he might want to do the summation.

Dorsen says he had a much more positive view of the case. Not only was he unaware, that Wednesday afternoon, that Burt had placed a call to Vradenburg, Dorsen says, but he had no idea that settlement was being considered. Of course, he explains, he understood Judge Leval's indications about the verdict and the jury charge on "clear and convincing" evidence—but, he claims, none of this was surprising, particularly after Judge Sofaer's ruling in the Sharon trial. And none of it, he says, was critical. He adds that while he and Leisure discussed these developments with Burt, "it was never in terms of, 'Should we get out?' " Dorsen believed, he now says, that it had been a case with no surprises, that nothing happened to alter dramatically his assessment of Westmoreland's chances. And he says he believed, contrary to how most neutral observers saw it, that although it would be hard to win on malice, there were arguments to be made, and that Westmoreland had a good shot at a *Sharon*-like victory—that is, winning on the question of truth before losing on malice.

On that Wednesday afternoon, Dorsen had just finished part of his cross-examination of Colonel Gains Hawkins, CBS's most powerful witness. Hawkins—bearing an uncanny resemblance to the Jedi master Yoda, of *The Empire Strikes Back*—had given riveting testimony on direct, stating that Westmoreland had imposed a "dishonest" ceiling on reports of enemy strength because higher figures were "politically unacceptable." He was just as effective in his three-hour cross-examination. Early in the cross, Dorsen introduced a rough draft of an article that Hawkins had never completed. It contained comments about another CBS witness, General Joseph McChristian, with which Dorsen clearly intended to damage both Hawkins and McChristian. Hawkins countered that he had meant every word. A little later, when Dorsen asked him to read another passage about McChristian, Hawkins said, "God, this is getting better all the time!'' And at another point, when Dorsen asked him about CBS lawyers having shown him documents in preparation for his taking the stand, Hawkins acknowledged it; then, craning his neck, he peered at Dorsen and asked, ''Is this evil, sir?''

Still, Dorsen was not disheartened, he insists, because he had a five-day recess to prepare for the rest of his Hawkins cross. He claims he had been saving his real ammunition, and was confident that the rest of the cross-examination would be the best and most important of the trial. Dorsen says he planned to focus on Hawkins's deposition testimony that he had been prepared to perjure himself at the Ellsberg trial, and that he had received no direct order from Westmoreland about cutting or imposing a ceiling on enemy strength estimates. Using Hawkins's contemporaneous memorandum book, Dorsen continues, he intended to show that the guerrilla and administrative service categories were not cut when Hawkins said they were. And, Dorsen says, he expected to point out that Hawkins had testified in his deposition that he had remembered little of this period in Vietnam until he started talking to Crile and Sam Adams: ''I started from practically zero and I know a little bit,'' Hawkins testified. Dorsen claims that since the start of litigation, Adams and CBS lawyers made 15 overnight visits to Hawkins's home in West Point, Mississippi, and says he wanted to suggest to the jury that these visits created a memory where there had been none.

Dorsen apparently was convinced then as now that he could do Hawkins real damage—especially since Judge Leval had ordered the CBS lawyers not to talk to Hawkins further before he resumed the stand.

While Hawkins was on the stand on Wednesday, George Leisure was sitting next to Westmoreland at the counsel table, furiously scrawling notes on a legal pad. He was working from an outline that Christopher Hall, an associate at Donovan Leisure, had prepared from the trial transcript for use in Burt's summation.

Leisure outlines his idea for the summation this way: First, take the jurors, step by step, through the 1967 Honolulu conference at which it was decided that the ''irregulars'' category in the order of battle was underestimated, and that studies should be undertaken to form new estimates. Then, develop the series of events that Westmoreland testified about: that McChristian had brought him the cable with the higher estimates; that Westmoreland had said he wanted a further briefing before sending it on; that there had been a couple of briefings, one of them attended by Westmoreland's military superior, Admiral U. S. Grant Sharp. Next, establish that the higher figures were also communicated to the general's civilian superior, Ellsworth Bunker, then U.S. ambassador to Vietnam.

Thousands of pages of trial testimony had focused most compellingly on disagreements about the military capability of the self-defense and secret self-defense forces, estimates which had ultimately been dropped from a special report given to President Lyndon Johnson in the fall of 1967. But, Leisure says, he believed the plaintiff's summation should conclude that this case was not about whether the self-defense and secret self-defense forces should or should not have been included in the order of battle, but about whether Westmoreland withheld information from his superiors.

And Westmoreland's complaint was just that narrow. Only days before the start of trial, Burt had smartly decided not to contest the major assertion of the documentary: that Westmoreland deceived Congress and the American people about enemy troop strength. Rather, he had charged only that CBS libeled Westmoreland by saying he deceived his superiors about the size and nature of the enemy in the year before the January 1968 Tet offensive.

Leisure says he hoped that Burt would listen to his advice. Sometimes Burt seemed to take some odd pleasure in having Leisure—a far more experienced and respected member of the bar—in a subordinate position. (Burt's attitude toward his co-counsel gave rise to one anecdote, possibly apocryphal, that Burt joked about sending Leisure out for coffee.)

It was surely not regard for Burt but loyalty to the case and to the general—with whom he had become "affectionate friends," as Leisure puts it, over the course of this long trial—that kept him at work on this case. He must have known that the Westmorelands felt more kinship with him than they did with Burt, and that they almost certainly trusted his judgment more. One day in court when Burt was questioning a witness, Mrs. Westmoreland was overheard to ask a friend urgently, "Where is George?" Locating Leisure seated against the wall, she settled back in her seat, saying, "I only feel comfortable when George is there."

On Friday morning, February 15—unbeknownst to Leisure, Dorsen, or any other lawyer on Westmoreland's team—Burt met Vradenburg for breakfast at the Westbury. According to Vradenburg, Burt opened the conversation by saying that this would be the last chance to talk settlement before the case went to the jury. Vradenburg's response was a crusher: no money, no apology, no retraction. In fact, he says he told

Burt that CBS would only be willing to issue the kind of statement now that it would make after prevailing with the jury. Vradenburg added, he says, that CBS would be prepared to say something about Westmoreland's patriotism and loyalty. Burt, Vradenburg recalls, countered with a proposal that the CBS statement focus on the May 1967 briefing attended by the general's military superior, Admiral Sharp. A memo describing that briefing in part was discovered in army archives during the trial. Now, according to Vradenburg, Burt asked CBS to issue a statement saying that information about the briefing would have been included in the broadcast if the network had known about it at the time. The two agreed that Burt would write a draft that day and send it to Vradenburg— who then told Boies of the development and kept him informed throughout the weekend.

Vradenburg says he had a brief conversation with Burt Friday evening, after receiving his draft. By Saturday morning, he adds, he had decided it was unacceptable, since it gave too much significance to the May 1967 briefing. Vradenburg then had what he says was a half-hour conversation with Burt at midday on Saturday, before sending back his own draft, which was strikingly similar to the one he had offered a year earlier. He says he dug the earlier statement out of his files and worked from it, adding the phrase about Westmoreland's having performed his duties "as he saw them." Saturday evening, according to Vradenburg, Burt called him with some insignificant word changes—he wanted "issues fully explored at trial" to be "matters explored over two and a half years of discovery and trial," for example—and said he would call the next morning after reviewing the statement with his client. Sunday morning, Vradenburg continues, Burt called to say he had spoken with Westmoreland and that the statement was acceptable, although he asked Vradenburg to remove the words "as he saw them." The two agreed to speak at midafternoon to schedule the signing. In a final, brief conversation, at about 3 P.M., Vradenburg refused to remove the phrase. Burt accepted his decision. The entire negotiating process—from the phone conversations on Friday to the signing at 4:30 on Sunday—took just less than an hour, Vradenburg estimates.

This historic, multimillion-dollar, three-year case was finally disposed of so swiftly and easily—and with virtually no concessions from the defendant—because the lawyer who engineered the settlement did not have to contend with any opposition from his teammates. His client, a man who respects command decisions, heard only Burt's advice. And Burt himself apparently formed his view alone. From interviews with other members of the Westmoreland team, it seems clear that the only input Burt sought was not from his fellow lawyers, but from his jury consultant, Jay Schulman, and Schulman's two assistants—and that his discussion with them occurred only about an hour before Burt put the papers before Westmoreland.

Schulman, who says he flew back from California at his own expense to help his friend Burt prepare for his summation, met Burt at Donovan Leisure at 3:30 Sunday afternoon. Schulman was to videotape Burt doing a mock summation. For about a half hour, Burt, Schulman, and Schulman's assistants, who had been in the courtroom watching CBS present its case, discussed the prospects for a verdict. According to Schulman, Burt asked what they thought of his ability to prevail on the issue of falsity. Schulman's assistants were pessimistic. Basing his views on his assistants' statements and his own assessment of the jurors, Schulman says, he told Burt he thought the odds of prevailing on falsity were 50–50. At about 4 P.M., Schulman recalls, Burt said that he had to leave, but that Schulman should call him about 5:30. Several of Burt's colleagues working in the office were surprised at his sudden departure, since they all knew about the videotaping. According to someone who was present, Burt responded to a query about where he was going, "I'm going to get laid."

In fact, he headed for his appointment with Westmoreland. And it was then, taking the papers from Vradenburg in the lobby of the Westbury, that Burt reportedly remarked, "I don't trust the son of a bitch. Let me get him to sign them before he changes his mind."

It seems that Burt's discussions with the general had been minimal until Sunday afternoon. Westmoreland now says he recalls Burt's mentioning to him on Friday, February 15, that he had proposed to CBS a draft concerning the briefing Admiral Sharp attended. On Saturday, Westmoreland and his wife—a vivacious, perceptive woman who is extremely protective of her husband—traveled to Garrison, New York, to spend the weekend with friends. Westmoreland does not recall speaking with Burt on Saturday. He does recall a conversation Sunday morning, after which he came back to New York, met Burt, and signed the papers at about 4:30. He says he had not committed himself—in his own mind or to Burt—until the moment that he signed. His wife was not with him at the signing.

According to Westmoreland, the fact that it was a joint statement, signed not only by him and Vradenburg but also by defendants Crile and Wallace, was "very, very meaningful" to him. (Defendant Sam Adams, the CBS consultant, could not be found Sunday night, according to Vradenburg.) "It meant to me that the two defendants had accepted the spirit of the document," Westmoreland says, adding that when he signed the statement he thought "it was a subtle way of CBS's admitting that the broadcast was misleading." Westmoreland says he does not recall whether the idea of getting the defendants' signatures was Burt's or his own. It is hard to understand how the general's lawyer did not make plain to him that the statement did not bring CBS even one inch closer to disavowing the broadcast.

Asked about the signatures, Mike Wallace explains that he and Crile were presented with the statement after it had been signed by Westmoreland. "Vradenburg said, 'If you want to sign, fine. If not, it makes no difference,' " Wallace recalls. "George and I looked at each other and I said, 'Well, it's a historical document of a sort, so why don't we sign it?' It had been said over and over again that we didn't have to take back a word of the broadcast," he explains. "I wouldn't call it courtesy, exactly, but it just seemed like an appropriate thing to do."

It is clear that the joint signatures entered the picture only at the very last moment of this hurried episode. According to Vradenburg, Burt did not ask if it could be done until after Westmoreland had signed the papers and Burt had brought them back to the lobby. Vradenburg says he told Burt he would ask Wallace and Crile, but could not promise. Burt agreed.

While Vradenburg took the papers to get the other signatures, Burt joined Capital Legal staff attorney Anthony Murry, Schulman, and Schulman's associates for dinner. He told them about the withdrawal of the suit and read the joint statement from a legal pad.

Without troubling to inform his other associates or his co-counsel, Burt left Schulman and Murry and went to the Stanhope Hotel, where Colonel Hawkins was staying. Boies and his team of lawyers had gathered there for a victory celebration with the witness who had apparently helped them bring the general to his knees. The lawyers toasted each other in high-spirited camaraderie, with Burt finally receiving the approbation from his Cravath adversaries that he had so long sought.

The mood in the Westmoreland camp was not so cheerful. By the evening, there were television news flashes of a possible settlement, and Dorsen and Capital Legal staff attorneys Richard Riese and Patricia Embry were getting calls from the press. Embry reached Schulman, who told her what had happened; she then told Dorsen. Sometime that evening, Dorsen says, the Westmorelands called him. This conversation appears to have been the Westmorelands' first notice that none of their other lawyers—including their trusted friend, Leisure—had been aware of the withdrawal, much less in accord with it.

According to Schulman, Mrs. Westmoreland reached him slightly after 9 P.M. "Kitsy was very, very upset," recalls Schulman. "First of all, because of the process. She and the general had probably made the assumption that all the lawyers knew—I doubt Burt told them one way or the other—and they were shocked to find out otherwise." And, Schulman continues, Mrs. Westmoreland was upset about the decision. "From what she told me, I would say that she had had desultory input into the decision making—and in her judgment, it had not been adequate input." Asked whether Mrs. Westmoreland knew in advance that her husband was going to sign, Schulman says he does not know. Westmoreland, asked about his wife's role in the decision and her reaction to it, says, "She'll have to speak for herself. I'm not going to comment on it." Mrs. Westmoreland also declines comment, saying she's never given an interview— "Age fifty-seven," she remarks dryly, "is late to start"— and "It's Wes's business." What is clear is that Burt's task was easier if she did not know. As he had reportedly remarked to Vradenburg during that final weekend, "Kitsy will be hard to sell."

Schulman says that he told the Westmorelands to refuse all calls for the rest of the night, and to meet him and Burt at the Westbury at 7:30 the next morning. At about midnight Burt, who had just gotten back from the Stanhope, called Schulman. Burt asked Schulman to accompany him to the Harley Hotel, where his Capital Legal team was staying. On the way, Schulman says Burt explained that he had undertaken the settlement alone because "it was his decision to make, it came up on the spot, he had to strike while the iron was hot." Schulman also claims that Burt said he was afraid of leaks to the press. They encountered Dorsen, Riese, and Embry in the lobby of the Harley, but the three lawyers refused to talk to Burt and walked by him.

At about 1 A.M., Burt reportedly called Vradenburg, saying, "Kitsy is livid," and explaining that he was meeting the Westmorelands for breakfast, and had to have one of the signed statements to "show her that it couldn't be undone." Vradenburg, who had all the copies of the signed statements, sent a copy to Burt.

Schulman claims that when he and Burt met the general and his wife at 7:30 A.M., Burt repeatedly asked them both whether they were satisfied, or whether they were having second thoughts. According to Schulman, Burt suggested that if they "couldn't live with it," he and Westmoreland should go to the judge and see about having the withdrawal undone. The general was committed to going forward with it, Schulman asserts, and Mrs. Westmoreland said that although she had been troubled by the decision, she now felt it was the right thing to do.

According to a source on the Westmoreland team, the general also had a conversation with Dorsen that morning in which the feasibility of undoing the agreement was briefly discussed. But Westmoreland didn't need any lawyer to tell him that attempting to take back the statement would have been a debacle, given the fact that the story had already been broadcast and printed across the country.

The decision Westmoreland made on Monday—to go through with the withdrawal—is one to which he has stuck steadfastly. Asked about these Monday-morning sessions, Westmoreland refuses to comment. He makes plain that he will not criticize Burt. "Dan kept me informed," he says. "He made the point, time and time again, that I was the client, and nothing would happen without my approval." Asked about the fact that Burt had not told his co-counsel about the withdrawal until after it was done, Westmoreland says, "I felt Dan had the prerogative to consult with whom he chose. I knew that Dan had talked to a lot of people about this—not about the CBS statement itself, but about all the legal elements, considerations about the jury." Pressed on whether he had believed Dorsen and Leisure were informed and in accord, Westmoreland replies, "Dan was the captain of the ship, and I deal with the captain of the ship."

According to one person inside the Westmoreland camp, however, after the suit was dropped, Mrs. Westmoreland told a Capital Legal staffer that Burt had assured her husband that he had consulted with the other lawyers on the case before withdrawing, and that all were in favor of doing so. (Mrs. Westmoreland, once again, declined to be interviewed.) And, according to another source in that camp, Westmoreland said that, before signing the withdrawal, he asked Burt if he had held a council of war, and that Burt had said he had and everyone had agreed.

Burt, who had masterminded so many public relations triumphs for this case in its pretrial stage, had now created a situation that even he could not save. The timing of the retreat, on the heels of Hawkins's tour de force, could not have been worse; it looked as if Westmoreland and his lawyer had concluded that their case was destroyed. And it quickly became evident that Burt had sprung the withdrawal upon his co-counsel. According to Schulman, Burt was desperate to show a united front at the press conference, and badly wanted Leisure there to give his blessing. But on Monday morning, Leisure resisted first Burt's and then the general's request. He told Westmoreland that he could not come to the conference because, if reporters asked him whether he had known in advance about the settlement, he would feel compelled to answer truthfully and say he had read about it in his morning newspaper.

Westmoreland's performance at the press conference worsened the disaster. It may be that Burt tried, and failed, to control the general. Certainly, if he had any regard for his client, Burt should have tried to dissuade him from declaring, as he did, that the resolution was a "victory," and all he had ever wanted.

The press refused to accept Westmoreland's characterization, and ran headlines such as WESTY RAISES WHITE FLAG (New York's *Daily News*) and THE GENERAL'S RETREAT (*Newsweek*). Paul Conrad captured it all in a syndicated cartoon that shows Westmoreland and Burt, dangling precariously from a helicopter, being airlifted from the roof of the federal courthouse. The caption reads, "Westmoreland declares victory over CBS and pulls out."

Had the general achieved a victory like Sharon's—losing on malice, but winning on truth—it would have been immeasurably better for him than this surrender. Moreover, many of his allies—lawyers, friends, and backers—say they believe that even a finding against him on truth would have been better than this denouement. Reed Irvine of Washington, D.C.'s Accuracy in Media says, "Even if the jury had come in against him on truth, he could have held his head up and said that they didn't understand it, it was too complex." Irvine, who has been feuding with Burt ever since Burt turned down his contributions to the Westmoreland suit rather than comply with his demands for rigorous accounting of how the money would be spent, continues, "This way, it looks like [Westmoreland] had admitted he didn't have a case. I can't imagine that having carried it this far, he would throw in the towel. It's out of character—he's an old soldier, he's a fighter."

Retired Admiral Thomas Moorer, who was chairman of the Joint Chiefs of Staff from 1970 to 1974, and who joined several other high-ranking retired officers in signing fund-raising letters for this suit, says that he and many of Westmoreland's friends in the military agree that it would have been better for him to go "to the bitter end." He adds that knowing the general as they do, they are mystified by his withdrawal. What CBS gave Westmoreland, says Moorer, was "no apology at all. . . . They said he performed his duties 'as he saw them,' " fumes Moorer. "Well, you could have said that about Hitler."

About a week after the case ended, in an interview with *The Washington Post*, Burt offered the only detailed explanation for the withdrawal

that he has given to date. In an article by Eleanor Randolph headlined
FOUR WORDS FELLED LAWSUIT AGAINST CBS, he was reported as saying
that his case was ended by the judge's instruction that the jury must find
the broadcast false "by clear and convincing evidence"—part of the
packets of jury instructions handed to the lawyers on Friday afternoon,
February 15. Burt's explanation defies credulity, for several reasons. He
had called Vradenburg to discuss settlement two days earlier, on Wednesday, and had had the first and only substantive settlement discussion with
him at breakfast on Friday morning. Moreover, contrary to Burt's implication, the judge had not announced a final ruling that Friday; he had
asked for briefs over the weekend. In any case, Boies says the judge
indicated even before the trial started that "clear and convincing evidence" would in all likelihood be the standard on truth, and lawyers on
both sides say that after Sofaer had so ruled in the Sharon case, they
assumed Leval would follow suit.

Immediately prior to trial—during his period of heroic posturing—Burt
had told *TWA Ambassador* magazine, "I made Westmoreland a promise.
When I took his case, I promised to see this to the end, and that he would
have as good a chance of winning as anyone could give him, whatever the
price. I made a promise, and I kept my word."

But in the end, when the going got tough—as any experienced trial
lawyer would have known it would—Burt turned tail and ran. He had
encouraged Westmoreland, plagued for 15 years by the war he had lost,
to try to repair the record for history. Instead, under Burt's aegis, the old
general helped to create a far more damaging record than would otherwise
have existed. And then, at the worst possible moment, Burt negotiated
Westmoreland's unconditional surrender—so that the general seemed to
be ratifying, for all time, everything his accusers had said.

EPILOGUE

The Capital Legal Foundation—which set in motion the bitter dispute
between General Westmoreland and CBS—appears to have lost some of
its former power. Dan Burt has resigned as president to open his own
Washington, D.C., firm, Burt, Maner & Miller. The eight-lawyer firm
primarily does corporate and tax work, but it does handle some media
libel cases. CLF has moved to smaller offices.

There has also been a corporate shuffle at CBS. Van Gordon Sauter,
president and news chief of CBS at the time of the trial, was fired in

September 1986 and was replaced by Howard Stringer, executive producer of *The Uncounted Enemy*. Stringer was made president of the CBS broadcast group in August 1988. George Crile is back as a producer at *60 Minutes*; and Burton Benjamin, who wrote the harshly critical report of the documentary, retired in November 1985 to teach communications at the University of Michigan and write a book about the Westmoreland case: *Fair Play: CBS, General Westmoreland, and How a Television Documentary Went Wrong*. He died in September 1988.

George Allen, one of the former Central Intelligence Agency officers who supported Crile's thesis in a taped interview, now works for the training and education department at the CIA. He shows *The Uncounted Enemy* in his ethics and intelligence presentations to demonstrate, in Crile's words, the "pressure that is placed on intelligence analysts to deliver a report in keeping with the desires, needs, or wishes of their superiors."

Sam Adams, the former CIA agent who approached CBS about the story, died in October 1988. He had been working on a book dealing with the CBS documentary and the Westmoreland trial. Adams had earlier initiated and then quickly dropped a $75 million suit against Renata Adler and her publishers charging that he was libeled in her 1986 book, *Reckless Disregard*, a strong attack on the CBS documentary.

Kevin Baine has continued to represent the *Post* in the areas of libel and invasion of privacy suits, but says that "things have been relatively quiet on the libel front."

Bob Woodward is now editor of investigative news at the *Post*, and Patrick Tyler is chief of the paper's Cairo bureau.

Although he has slowed down a little, General Westmoreland, who continues to live in Charleston, South Carolina, remains a popular speaker at universities, civic clubs, and conventions.

Ariel Sharon
v.
Time

SAY IT AIN'T SO, HENRY

BY

STEVEN BRILL

How sloppy journalism coupled with corporate arrogance made Time *vulnerable in the libel suit brought by Ariel Sharon*

December 17, 1984

Henry Grunwald
Editor in Chief
Time Inc.

Dear Mr. Grunwald:

As the chief editorial officer of Time Inc. and all of its magazines and former managing editor of its flagship, *Time,* you are considered to be the world's preeminent magazine journalist.

So I hope you can appreciate how dismaying this Sharon libel trial has become for those of us in your business who have always looked up to your company as the home of magazines that do what they set out to do as well as or better than any competitor. Yes, the other side's lawyer (Milton Gould of Shea & Gould) has been ineffective and seems to be turning off the jurors; and, yes, the jury does seem to have taken a liking

113

to some of your witnesses, as have our colleagues in the press covering the trial. But the fact that for these reasons you might win is beside the point.

For it seems from the testimony of your own people that *Time* made up its story—that's right, simply made it up—when it reported in a February 1983 cover article that "*Time* has learned" that a secret appendix to a report by an Israeli governmental commission investigating the Phalangist massacre of Palestinian refugees in Lebanon concluded that then-Israeli defense minister Ariel Sharon had visited the Phalangist leaders and "discussed . . . the need" for them to take revenge for the assassination of Phalangist leader Bashir Gemayel.

What's worse—far worse, from the standpoint of your fellow journalists—is that despite the now-compelling evidence that some combination of *Time* reporters, editors, and rewrite people fabricated the story, you recently declared at the New York University law school's prestigious Chet Huntley Memorial Lecture, which you were invited to give in November, that while you "won't say anything about that case" while it's pending, you are certain that *Time* "will be vindicated."

I suppose you define vindication as winning the libel suit against Sharon. True, you might still win it, given the other side's mediocre lawyering and the hurdles a public-figure libel plaintiff faces in suing one of us. But will you and your organization really have been vindicated just because General Sharon can't prove malice or damages? Isn't that a bit like saying Mr. Miranda was vindicated?

Everything that's happened in court as of this writing (December 17, 1984) has already blackened *Time* badly; indeed, your entire defense in court is, in essence: "Even if we got it wrong or made it up, Sharon's such a bad guy that he probably did discuss revenge, even if the investigators who prepared the report and its appendix didn't find it out and put it in there like we said they did." (The Israeli government has kept the appendix secret, though Sharon and an Israeli Knesset member who have seen it both have testified that there's no mention of Sharon's discussing revenge or anything like that in it.)

In fact, your defense argument goes still further. Your lawyers have also been saying, in effect, that "even if Sharon didn't actually discuss revenge with the Gemayels, he still indirectly caused the massacre through various acts or acts of omission."

Is that any way for an organization like *Time* to defend a story that says "*Time* has learned" that such and such is contained in an official report? Will winning that way be vindication?

Besides, you're not likely to win. You haven't even come close to establishing even a reason for believing that Sharon talked about or condoned revenge, let alone that it's in any secret report.

As I write this in mid-December, the rumor is that you're about to settle (with a retraction and an apology and payment of Sharon's legal fees) because the initial weeks of trial have been so rough. Well, it must be the reaction you're hearing from outside (though the press coverage, I think, has been exceedingly mild given the trial record) or perhaps from your board of directors that's making you suddenly consider folding. It can't be the substance of what's happened that's surprising. None of this should surprise you or your lawyers. Nearly two years ago you could have checked the story and seen how bad it was; and as for what's happened at trial, none of that can be a surprise to your lawyers because the pretrial discovery went just as badly. In fact, your own people were so damaging to your case in depositions that Sharon's lawyers have used them as *their* witnesses in the opening weeks of the trial.

Indeed, the pretrial discovery record (you really ought to make your lawyers give you a copy of the whole thing) is enough to make the most absolutist First Amendment invoker (like me) uneasy. I've always been against all libel suits (and still am on pure constitutional grounds), but I've got to tell you this is one I think we deserve to lose. The pretrial and trial record (such as it is so far) reveals an arrogant, bloated bureaucracy in which the reporter of the paragraph that Sharon is suing about is biased to the point of being a near-fanatic, your chief of correspondents isn't much of a chief and has a suspiciously selective memory when he's under oath, your managing editor (the supposed boss of *Time*) doesn't know much of anything about what goes on in his shop, your much-vaunted research department is a sham, and your system for weeding out unreliable reporters is nil.

Overall, the impression created by the depositions of your people and by subpoenaed interoffice communications is of a place where everybody strains to squeeze a "scoop" out of a series of forced assumptions, where stories go through a rat's maze of editing and rewriting that twists their original meaning toward a "scoopier" story, and where nobody ever admits a mistake about anything—which, of course, would explain why you came to trial in the first place.

I don't know how much you know about the reporting process behind the Sharon story, but you ought to be appalled by what happened, as now revealed in the pretrial and initial trial record.

From September 16 to 18, 1982, Christian Phalangist militiamen

115

slaughtered hundreds of civilians at two Palestinian refugee camps in Lebanon. The massacre was apparently done in revenge for the assassination by Palestinian terrorists of Lebanese President-elect Bashir Gemayel, a Christian Phalangist.

Because the massacre took place following the Israeli invasion of Lebanon that past summer and because the Israeli occupation forces had worked in tandem with the Phalangist militia, a special Israeli commission was immediately formed to investigate whether the Israeli Defense Force and its leader, then–Minister of Defense Ariel Sharon, bore any responsibility for the tragedy.

On December 6, 1982, while that commission was still deliberating, a Jerusalem-based *Time* reporter named David Halevy filed a report about a meeting Sharon had had with Gemayel's family just after the assassination and just before the massacre. Halevy's report, telexed to *Time*'s London bureau, said that "according to a highly reliable source who told us about that meeting . . . Sharon . . . gave them the feeling after the Gemayels' questioning, that he understood their need to take revenge for the assassination of Bashir and assured them that the Israeli army would neither hinder them nor try to stop them."

Did you know that that last sentence was rewritten two months later in New York to say that Sharon "discussed with the Gemayels the need for the Phalangists to take revenge," despite the fact that Halevy said in his deposition that he deliberately had used the words "gave them the feeling" precisely because he had been told that Sharon hadn't said anything but had just "used body language"? Yet when Halevy ultimately got the galley proofs of the story back from New York following the rewrite, he made no protest about the strengthening of the language. What kind of a system is that? And, by the way, does it really make sense for there to be a rule, as Halevy describes it in his deposition, that the correspondents aren't "entitled to talk to" the writers and editors in New York who write the stories the correspondents file? How can you do anything but miss a reporter's nuances if your people can't talk back and forth with the guy on the front line? Has your organization grown so large (500 editorial employees and some 100 correspondents) that it is being strangled by this kind of bureaucratic nonsense?

But that's only the beginning of the problem. Halevy's Jerusalem bureau chief, Harry Kelly, has testified in a deposition that Halevy told him soon after he filed that report that his primary source for the story was notes he had seen that were written by an Israeli intelligence agent who, Halevy claims, had been at the Sharon meeting with the Gemayel family.

Yet Halevy refused in his deposition testimony to say whether he ever saw any notes (he said that to answer that question might betray a source), and then conceded in his trial testimony that he had not seen the notes. Instead he cited as his primary source Sharon's own public testimony in October 1982 before the investigative commission, in which Sharon says that "the matter of revenge was discussed among us." In other words, Halevy is now saying that his story wasn't really a scoop. "I think this paragraph is echoing exactly the . . . Commission," Halevy said in his deposition.

Abraham Sofaer, the federal judge in the libel case, pointed out in a scholarly, softly phrased but nonetheless scathing opinion denying your magazine's motions for summary judgment or dismissal (you ought to read his opinion, too) that the Hebrew original of Sharon's testimony more readily means that the matter of revenge was discussed "among Israelis" (not "among us"), meaning that Sharon was merely acknowledging that he and his fellow Israeli officers discussed the possibility that the Phalangists might take revenge. Moreover, as Sofaer pointed out, "if the 'matter of revenge' was discussed by Sharon and the Gemayels and this fact was revealed publicly by one of the participants [Sharon] in mid-October, Halevy's qualification of his report to suggest only a non-verbal communication by Sharon would have had no significance. Furthermore, why would Halevy treat [in that December 6 file report to New York] as newsworthy and describe as potentially 'crucial' the discovery of notes stating little more than the information to which Sharon had already testified, according to Halevy's present reading of Sharon's testimony?"

Thus Judge Sofaer concluded—and I should tell you this is no anti-*Time* judge; if anything he's probably been too nice to your side—that "Halevy's claimed understanding is so questionable in context, and his conduct so inconsistent with his current rationalization, that a jury could find Halevy knew that Sharon's testimony provided no support for his [December 6 file], and moreover that he is not truthful in claiming that it did."

Moreover, if Halevy's source was the public testimony given by Sharon in October, why did he cite in his December 6 memo "a highly reliable source" as the basis for his account? Sofaer ruled that by "ascribing the information in the memo item to 'a highly reliable source,' . . . Halevy implicitly suggested that he had not seen the notes himself. It thus remains possible that Halevy deliberately misled Kelly as to the reliability of his report. Furthermore, whether Halevy told Kelly he had actually

seen the notes may have special significance in this litigation. A jury
could find that Halevy now refuses to confirm having told Kelly he had
seen the notes, because the parties may obtain access to the notes, and
they may not support Halevy's story.''

One source Halevy didn't check with was Ariel Sharon. Why didn't he
call him for comment or confirmation when preparing this December 6
memo? Because, Halevy testified, ''I am not an informer, sir. I don't tell
the ministers of the cabinet about information that I received.'' Is that
Time's policy on getting comment from people?

As you know, nothing much came of that December 6 Halevy memo
until the week of February 7, 1983, when the Israeli investigation commission filed its report. The commission harshly criticized Sharon, saying
he bore ''indirect'' responsibility for the massacre because he should
have known the Phalangists would take revenge.

Yet the report didn't mention anything about Sharon's having talked to
the Gemayels about the need to take revenge. However, there was also a
part of the commission report—Appendix B—that was referred to in the
main text but kept under seal for reasons supposedly having to do with
Israeli national security.

That week, your editors at *Time* decided that the commission report
was worth a major story—it would become the cover story—and Jerusalem bureau chief Harry Kelly began work on the piece with Halevy and
a *Time* stringer. At one point, as Kelly labored over his typewriter, he
called Halevy and asked him what he supposed was in Appendix B.
Halevy, according to Kelly's deposition, said quickly, ''I know one thing
that is in it: my memo item from December''—meaning the information
about Sharon's paying his condolence call on the Gemayel family and his
having given the Gemayels ''the feeling . . . that he understood their
need to take revenge.''

According to his deposition, at this point Halevy was only giving his
hypothesis of what was in Appendix B, based, he testified, on his reading
of the commission report and ''the feeling'' he had when reading it that
''a lot is hidden between the lines, and they make reference and they tell
you where it is hidden, and they say it is in Appendix B. . . . ''

Kelly, too, testified that he'd read the report and noticed references
to Appendix B whenever sensitive subjects, such as the names of intelligence agents, came up. From that, he says, he made ''a logical
deduction'' that the information about the condolence call must be in
Appendix B.

In fact, just the opposite inference can be drawn from the public part of the investigation report. For when the Sharon condolence call is mentioned in the public part of the report there is no footnote to Appendix B the way there is when other subjects are mentioned. As Judge Sofaer put it, "Neither Kelly nor Halevy had seen Appendix B, but Kelly did know that, while the public report referred to many other items as being contained in Appendix B, it at no point referred to Appendix B in connection with the [condolence call] meeting."

Before Kelly sent his report over the wire to New York, Halevy made one additional call to confirm his hypothesis, a call to someone he calls "Source C." After he called Source C, he reappeared in Kelly's office doorway and gave him the "thumbs-up sign," meaning, according to his trial testimony, that he'd confirmed the story about Appendix B.

Mr. Grunwald, I'm afraid that the thumbs-up sign is destined to become a gallows joke around the halls at *Time*. For here's the conversation—according to Halevy's own deposition testimony (some of which has been repeated so far at trial in a more abbreviated form)—that Halevy had with Source C to "confirm" that the information about the condolence call was in Appendix B:

> I put the blunt question and I said, "what the hell is in Appendix B?" The response I got and the kind of response you kind of expect from that level, "hey, hey, this is a secret appendix and I am not going to make any reference to that." I said, "okay. Tell me at least the nature of Appendix B." He said, "it's an index. It's a reference book. The names of the officials appearing there and officers appearing there is a direct reference to their testimony, their minutes, or documents that they provided to the commission."
>
> I said, "okay, is the note taker of Karantina mentioned?" . . . He says yes. "Is the note taker of Bikfaya [the site of the condolence call]?" Yes.
>
> "Is another Mossad agent who presumably was both in the Ashrafiyah meeting mentioned there?" "Yes. This is as far as I can go. Don't ask me more and by the way, they are all mentioned in—there is a reference to them also in the public report."
>
> I went back to the public report. I mean, the report I had in my hands. And correctly so, if you read it very carefully. Intelligence officer A. Intelligence officer that. Intelligence officer this. You get a very clear feeling that we are talking about the same people.
>
> I went into Mr. Kelly's office and raised my thumb to the kind of "Okay, all cleared."

After Halevy went through roughly the same account at trial, Judge Sofaer asked Halevy if Source C had said "anything to you about parts of testimony being there [in Appendix B]."

When Halevy hesitated, Sofaer tried to help him: "So you inferred that," the judge asked. "Yes, I would say so," Halevy replied. A minute later, he continued, "Yes, that is the way I read it. It's my evaluation, my analysis based on my knowledge of forty-three years living in Israel and going through a lot of coverage of governmental official matters."

Whenever I read something like *"Time* has learned," is that what I'm now supposed to think is behind it—the reporter's inference and analysis? Why not say *"Time* reporter David Halevy speculates that Appendix B says . . . "? Why have you been in court defending this journalism? Why has it taken you so long to think about settling a case based on this journalism?

This is why this case isn't anything like the libel suit by General William Westmoreland against CBS being tried in the same courthouse. That case involves debates over editing decisions and editorial fairness— debates that under the First Amendment a jury should never be called on to resolve. Your case involves a fabrication, pure and simple. You said, *"Time* has learned," when *Time* was only guessing.

Sofaer, of course, denied *Time*'s motion for summary judgment—a motion based in part on the absurd claim that Sharon hadn't even presented any possibility of actual malice. (By the way, you ought to have your in-house lawyers explain to your board why that knee-jerk motion was allowed to be made in this case; it simply encouraged Sofaer to focus beforehand on just how bad your journalism had been, allowing him to render a careful, incisive decision that will hurt your appellate chances if you lose at trial.) The judge ruled: "A jury could find that Halevy chose not to ask Source C the ultimate question because he knew or suspected that Source C's answer would undermine his hypothesis. . . . Halevy's actions," the judge continued, "could be read to convey his 'subjective awareness of probable falsity' "—a standard previously enunciated in a federal court decision as establishing actual malice.

With Halevy having "confirmed" his story, Kelly finished his report— that is, his file for the cover story—and telexed it to New York on February 10, 1983.

It said, in part, "Some of that [Appendix B] simply gives the names of agents identified only by single letters in the published report and secret testimony. And some of it, we understand, was published in *Time*'s World Wide Memo, an item by Halevy, Dec. 6 . . . dealing with Sharon's visit to the Gemayel family to pay condolences. Certainly in reading the report, there is a feeling that at least part of the Commission's case against Sharon is between the lines, presumably in the secret portion.''

Now, more than eight weeks after filing that December 6 memo, Halevy attempted to reach Sharon for comment, an effort that would obviously be fruitless given that in the wake of the publication of the commission report everyone in the press was trying to get him to comment. Halevy and Kelly's secretary simply left messages with Sharon's aides that *Time* wanted to arrange an interview; Kelly and Halevy did not do the more forthright thing, and what any good journalist knows they could have done to get their requests for an interview separated from the pack and get a response: tell the Sharon aides exactly what they were about to report and ask for comment.

From that report by Kelly, one of your senior editors at *Time* in New York, William Smith, wrote the following paragraph that appeared in the February 21, 1983, issue—which is the only paragraph Sharon is suing about:

> One section of the report, known as Appendix B, was not published at all, mainly for security reasons. That section contains the names of several intelligence agents referred to elsewhere in the report. *Time* has learned that it also contains further details about Sharon's visit to the Gemayel family on the day after Bashir Gemayel's assassination. Sharon reportedly told the Gemayels that the Israeli army would be moving into West Beirut and that he expected the Christian forces to go into the Palestinian refugee camps. Sharon also reportedly discussed with the Gemayels the need for the Phalangists to take revenge for the assassination of Bashir, but the details of the conversation are not known.

No, there was never any discussion between Smith and Kelly or Halevy, though as part of standard *Time* procedure Kelly and Halevy were telexed a draft of the story before it ran for any suggestions or comments they might have had, and they didn't make any effort to change the paragraph. Nor did they renew any effort to call Sharon.

For his part, Smith testified in his deposition that his only sources of information for this paragraph were Kelly's report, Halevy's earlier December 6 report, and the Kahan Commission Report.

As for your much-heralded fact-checking staff, which I've always heard checks everything that appears in *Time* independently, one of the two fact checkers on this piece testified that in situations where "the reporter files information to which the researcher has no access, he or she must trust what the reporter said. . . ."

Is that really your fact-checking procedure? How can any scoop be checked?

Judge Sofaer had this to say about how you check facts: "No one at *Time*, despite the claim that everyone had read the Commission Report, ever questioned the fact that, in contrast to the Report's discussion of myriad other events, the Report never mentions either Appendix B or any Commission exhibit numbers in connection with the [condolence call] meeting. . . . That seems to be precisely the kind of incongruity which the [*Time*] researcher's guide refers to as cause for checking a story more closely. . . ."

Believe it or not, things went still farther downhill from there. On Sunday afternoon, February 13 (the day the story was being printed and mailed), your PR department at *Time* circulated a press release intended to get the *Time* account of what was in Appendix B publicized as a scoop around the world. Its headline: SHARON SAID TO HAVE URGED LEBANESE TO SEND PHALANGISTS INTO CAMPS. That in turn caused a firestorm of anti-Sharon publicity in Jerusalem, all pegged on the "urged" headline.

A few days later, at a dinner party in Jerusalem, bureau chief Kelly spoke to a member of the Israeli Knesset named Ehud Olmert, who told Kelly, according to Olmert's deposition (which Kelly essentially agreed with in his deposition), that *Time* had made a mistake. Olmert, who is *not* a friend of Sharon's, told Kelly that he, himself, had seen the secret appendix and that it contained none of what *Time* said it contained. Kelly asked Olmert to check again and call him, which Olmert testified he did. When he called Kelly he told him, "There is nothing in this that resembles your story."

Did your bureau chief file *that* report? No, said Kelly, when asked by Sharon's lawyer.

Noted Sofaer: "Despite the weight he had given to Halevy's vague report about the contents of Appendix B, based on an undisclosed source, Kelly says [in his deposition] he did not 'really' consider Olmert's clear representation to be news."

Instead, when Sharon—who had vehemently denied that he'd discussed revenge with the Gemayels and asserted that he'd read the appendix and knew it contained no such report—sued *Time* in Israel a day or two after Olmert's call, a *Time* spokesman said the magazine stood behind its story. Then, when Sharon sued in New York in June, *Time* similarly stood behind the story.

Backing up a reporter is something all editors instinctively do, but in this case you had special reason to question Halevy's veracity, even without Sharon's and Olmert's denials. As I'm sure you know, Halevy, a 43-year-old native Israeli who'd served in the armed forces and had apparently become bitterly disenchanted with the Begin government, had written a story in 1979 that was apparently so totally bogus that *Time* has had to semi-retract it. (I use "semi-retract" because it seems that *Time* never fully retracts or corrects anything; more on that below.)

In a September 1979 issue, Halevy had reported that Prime Minister Begin was in such poor health that he had been secretly examined by three non-Israeli neurologists, who had recommended that he work no more than three hours a day. When Begin's press spokesman wrote to *Time* (following a personal phone call from Begin himself to your then–Jerusalem bureau chief categorically denying all aspects of the story), your *Time* managing editor, Ray Cave, had your chief of correspondents, Richard Duncan, do an investigation.

Duncan wrote back to you and Cave that "I believe our story is wrong. Inescapably, that conclusion then requires a further decision as to whether Halevy was either (a) inexcusably shoddy in his reporting or (b) intentionally misled us, or (c) was the victim of an incredibly well-orchestrated disinformation plot."

Duncan's memo then detailed how then–Jerusalem bureau chief Dean Fischer had investigated Halevy's use of sources for the story. Fischer spoke to all but one source—Source B, whom Fischer, according to Duncan's memo, viewed "only as a tipster and a close friend of Halevy's." Source A, according to the Duncan memo, which you've had to produce to Sharon and the world as part of this case, "denied any knowledge that the meeting had taken place [between the doctors and Begin] and that he was [Halevy's] source." Source C "said the story was 'fantastic' " (meaning he thought it was a fantasy, not a great scoop). Source D "denied any knowledge of the meeting and said that his wife, not he, answered the phone when [Halevy] called."

Moreover, the one doctor identified in the story as having taken part in the Begin examination "denied having any knowledge of the examination," and told Fischer that Halevy had " 'never asked me specifically if I was in attendance.' "

One more detail: in the Duncan memo, Duncan told you that Halevy had told him that "he will be filing what he promises to be dramatic confirmation of the story late Thursday or early Friday.'' That never happened, although five years later at his deposition in the Sharon case Halevy maintained that his story had been accurate.

On October 22, *Time* printed the Begin press spokesman's letter denying the story and then ran the following note:

> *Time* has rechecked all aspects of its story, which was based on what it believed was firsthand knowledge of a meeting between Prime Minister Begin and three consulting neurologists. *Time* was apparently misled as to the meeting and regrets the error. *Time* stands by its report that for a period of weeks following his stroke on July 19 the Prime Minister's work load was significantly reduced.

Before we come back to the question of why Halevy was ever relied on again for anything, let alone relied on for an account that a secret governmental report charged the Israeli defense minister with complicity in a mass murder, I have a few questions about that retraction and *Time*'s general policy of making corrections. Why did you say *Time* was misled? Did you mean misled by your own reporter? If so, who or what is "*Time*" if it's not its own reporters? Where does "*Time*'s" responsibility for inaccuracies start, if anyplace? With its top editors? Its board of directors? Or did you mean that Halevy was misled? Why weren't you more forthcoming?

The chief Time Inc. spokesman, Louis Slovinsky, tells me that *Time*'s policy is to run corrections only by way of printing letters from people with complaints that turn out to be justified. Then, according to Slovinsky, "we may or may not decide to print an editor's note elaborating on the letter."

What if you yourselves discover that something was wrong? Why won't you acknowledge it? Asked those questions, Slovinsky replied, "You sound like a total ass just to ask a question like that. Why should we do that? We don't have to, and we haven't had to for sixty-two years."

Why should you put the burden on someone else to take the role of complainant? Some people don't like to dignify an inaccurate article by having their letters to the editor printed. Why shouldn't they just be able to call you and say you got it wrong and have you print a unilateral correction the way, for example, *The New York Times* does? In this regard, you might take a lead from *Newsweek,* which does print corrections on its own. "It enhances your credibility," says *Newsweek* editor in chief Richard Smith, "to say, 'Look, we blew it.' "

Asked to cite the magazine's last letters/correction, Slovinsky referred first to a playful acknowledgment that a cartoon illustration of a congressman had been mislabeled and then to a letter last October from Senator John Heinz, gently taking *Time* to task for the way it had characterized then-Senator Charles Percy's record. But there was no editor's note appended to Heinz's letter. "The very fact that we printed the letter indicates that we give it some credence," Slovinsky maintained.

Four months after *Time* printed the "retraction" about the Begin health story, Duncan, the chief of correspondents who had written the memo to you about the investigation of this story, placed Halevy on a year's probation and wrote him a letter warning him that he would have to make a more "obvious effort . . . to insure that what you report to *Time* . . . is printable, reliable information. . . ."

Isn't that a bit like telling a bank teller that henceforth he's going to have to let the bank keep all the money? Why wasn't Halevy fired? Isn't a reporter's only value his reliability when it comes to reporting printable, reliable information? Did you keep him because his intelligence community contacts in Israel had given you other apparent scoops that hadn't been challenged?

As Sofaer noted in his pretrial decision denying summary judgment, "[T]he jury might also conclude that the Begin health story reflects a bias on Halevy's part, or a lack of concern with truth, that leads him to publish with actual malice."

Sofaer went on to say, pointedly, that when Duncan was deposed *before Time* had released Duncan's memo concerning the Begin story, "he failed to mention in his account of his criticism of Halevy's work that he actually placed Halevy on probation. In addition," Sofaer noted, "he stated that 'I felt there was a large possibility that Halevy had been set up' . . . despite the fact that his memorandum and decision to put Halevy on probation could suggest that he had rejected that explanation."

Sofaer also noted that "Duncan also mentioned in his deposition that Halevy had read into [what he claimed was] Dr. Fein's [the one named neurologist] cautious denial of the Begin story a confirmation of his story. Taken together with Halevy's apparent failure to ask Dr. Fein directly whether he had been at the examination," Sofaer ruled, "a jury could find that *Time* was aware that Halevy had a tendency to report to his superiors that he had confirmed a story even though the person giving the 'confirmation' had not clearly been questioned about the information for which he was being used as a source. . . .

"Halevy's behavior with Source C [to 'confirm' what was in the appendix]," added Sofaer, "echoes his use of Dr. Fein as a source for his earlier story about Begin's health."

That's pretty strong stuff from an unusually low-key judge, Mr. Grunwald.

Really, Mr. Grunwald, this whole thing is humiliating for *Time*. And there's so much more pouring out of the discovery and trial process that suggests that Henry Luce's 62-year-old miracle of weekly reporting has become bloated and infected with bias and some higher-world sense of itself.

Did you know, for example, that by May of 1984 your man Halevy had taken to comparing Israel to Nazi Germany and that that month he wrote a letter to Duncan asking for a reassignment, in which he wrote of "signs of mysticism, fascism, and radicalism" in Israel? To which your chief of *Time* correspondents wrote back telling him, in part, "Perhaps you could come to the states and rub elbows with all the nice liberal, intelligent, devout jews here and pick up a little much-needed rosy nostalgia for Israel. You know, singing songs together down on the Kibbutz, that sort of thing."

And did you know that in his deposition, Ray Cave, your managing editor at *Time* (the man in overall charge of that magazine), states that he's not informed when a correspondent is found to have inaccurately reported something, that he doesn't know if any correspondents have ever been suspended on his watch, and that he's not quite sure what the fact-checking procedures are? It was as if that stuff didn't matter much to him.

Did you know that Cave, in his deposition, gave this incredibly pretentious and ominous definition of *Time*'s mission: "*Time* publishes and presents for its readers facts plus a point of view"?

QUESTION: Whose point of view is it that the magazine expresses?
CAVE: No person's. . . . The process involves an assessment of the information at hand. The judgment of the editors with respect to that information. The judgment of the managing editor and the judgment of the editor in chief. There are things that *Time* magazine has believed in for decades that are probably at the root of this judgment-making process. The point of view of the magazine is evolutionary, as it should be. It is not only evolutionary, it can change.
QUESTION: Did *Time* magazine, in early 1983, have a point of view as to the issue on Israeli settlements in the West Bank? . . .
CAVE: It is *Time*'s view that . . . a strong Israel is in the best interests of

the United States and the Western world; that the stronger that ally is in the Middle East, the better; that anything that would weaken the State of Israel or endanger it is not in the best interest of the United States or the West. And *Time* tends to evaluate Israeli government policy from that perspective.

QUESTION: Is it fair to say that when *Time*'s point of view became that the invasion was no longer in the best . . . interests of the Israelis . . . *Time*'s view of General Sharon became negative?

CAVE: *Time*'s view of the defense minister's performance as defense minister became negative.

QUESTION: Did the occurrence of the events in the refugee camps in September of 1982 have any impact on *Time*'s point of view about Mr. Sharon at that time?

CAVE: I would say that the view of *Time* about General Sharon—it is important to understand that *Time* does not tend to have views about people. It tends to have views about their actions and the consequences thereof, not about people—would have been that this event in the refugee camps was one of the kinds of consequences that could have arisen out of the invasion. . . .

Earlier, Cave had been asked how the *Time* "point of view" seeps down to the writers and editors and other troops. By means of "verbal consultation with the senior editor of the section handling the story," he replied.

Sure, journalism, especially magazine journalism, can't be fully objective. It needs a point of view. But can that be some amorphous corporate point of view that reporters are supposed to divine and then find facts to fit? Shouldn't it be, in order to insure accuracy, the point of view of the people doing the reporting rather than that of a bunch of editors and corporate people sitting on top of a bureaucracy in New York?

As an example of how that might have affected your story here, Mr. Grunwald, consider what your bureau chief, Kelly, did in considering Halevy's report about the appendix. Kelly testified that one of the ways he and Halevy "deduced" that the condolence call account must be in the secret appendix is that the commission's conclusion about Sharon—that he bore indirect responsibility for the massacre and should, therefore, resign—seemed harsher than the evidence it presented in its public report.

"Such reasoning," said Sofaer, "is based on an unspoken assumption that a jury could find may have affected Halevy and Kelly in all their actions: that Sharon deserved the harsh treatment he received, even though in their view the public Report failed to reflect an adequate case for it. They chose to assume—apparently without even a first thought,'' said Sofaer, ''not that Sharon had been too severely treated relative to others, but that he had been treated appropriately and that somewhere in the secret evidence were minutes of a conversation . . . that would justify the Commission's recommendation.''

Your lawyers recently told the judge that if, through some plan that Sofaer is working on to get limited, confidential access to the appendix and related papers in order to ascertain whether there's any mention of Sharon's discussing revenge, it becomes clear that Sharon did not discuss revenge and that there's no such mention of that discussion in the appendix, ''*Time* will print a correction or retraction of its story, as appropriate.'' That's a pretty lame late attempt to sound reasonable. First, your lawyers, with Sofaer's support, have insisted that they see all these secret papers rather than take the sworn word of an impartial third party (who would be a distinguished Israeli jurist) about whether the papers have material about Sharon's discussing revenge. (By the way, do you, as a journalist, have any doubt today that the stuff is *not* in the appendix?) Second, your lawyers have so expanded the list of secret documents to be looked at—because they want to move the case away from the specifics of what you reported—that there's little chance the Israeli government will agree. And third, it's all irrelevant. You printed that ''*Time* has learned'' what was in the appendix, and it's now clear that *Time*—in the person of Thumbs-Up Halevy, a negligent bureau chief, and a gaggle of eager editors, writers, and press-release drafters in New York—was, at best, speculating.

So what are you waiting for? It's time to settle this thing with an outright apology. Not a ''clarification.'' Not a statement saying you were misled. But an apology saying that when you said you had ''learned'' that an investigative panel of Ariel Sharon's most prestigious fellow countrymen had found, and printed in a secret appendix, that he had discussed the need for revenge, you were lying.

And with that apology should come an admission that even *Time* has people who screw up and perhaps even that this whole mess is a good thing because it will cause *Time*—led by people like you—to reexamine itself.

And then you ought to go about the business of making reforms to prevent further screwups and to fumigate the place so that its arrogance and biases are cleaned out. Like regularly, even eagerly, printing retrac-

tions when you get things wrong. Like reexamining this correspondent/
writer system in which people write things based on reports from reporters
they never talk to. Like revamping the fact-checking system.

Like rethinking who makes it to the top—the best corporate team
players who best convey the *Time* point of view, or the most professional
reporters?

You've got enough lawyers for a constitutional convention working
round the clock on the courtroom defense. But shouldn't you now call off
Tom Barr and his squadrons from Cravath, Swaine & Moore and tell
them you're sorry you gave them an empty if lucrative Christmas season
by having them endlessly brainstorm a defense that shouldn't have been
made? Shouldn't you tell them what they must already know, that this
isn't like their celebrated IBM case, that this time the defendant did do
something wrong, indeed, that their own flailing discovery demands and
defense motions in this case have made them look like the Justice Department lawyers they rightly ridiculed in the IBM fight?

With that in mind, I ought to add that next time you have your people
do a cover story on how America has become overlitigious, be sure they
refer to Cravath's manically broad discovery demands and its absurd
192-page memorandum in support of its motions for dismissal or summary judgment.

Did you know that Cravath subpoenaed stadiums full of documents
from the CIA, the National Security Agency, and the Defense and State
departments, as well as parallel Israeli intelligence agencies, and that, in
quashing these subpoenas against the U.S. agencies, a federal judge in
Washington ruled that they were a "sweeping unfocused request for
documents, in many instances without limitation, [and which] makes
absolutely no effort to demonstrate relevance"? (That sounds like what
Cravath used to say about the Justice Department's IBM subpoenas.)

Responding to Cravath's laughable demand for a dismissal because
many of its discovery requests had been denied, Sofaer described a litigation posture that you ought to be embarrassed about, especially given
your claim in the NYU lecture that *Time* will be vindicated. He noted that
Time "argues that it must be allowed to prove that, irrespective of any
discussions at meetings, General Sharon knew that sending the Phalangists into the camps would result in the massacre . . . and that he authorized or condoned that result." Thus, in his opening statement, we were
treated by Barr (who has seemed in his bullying, discourteous conduct in
depositions to be the litigators' equivalent of what he says Sharon is as a

military and political leader) not to a ringing defense of *Time*'s journalism but to an attack on Sharon as a war criminal who must have done something to cause the massacre and whose reputation was so bad anyway that he can't possibly be awarded damages.

"*Time* seeks to litigate the entire history of the Lebanese civil wars, the Israeli invasion of Lebanon, and the relationship of Israel and the Phalangists," Sofaer continued. "These contentions are far removed from the legitimate issues. They would be important if *Time* had merely stated in the article at issue that it thought that the Commission was incorrect in finding Minister Sharon not 'directly' responsible—an opinion for which *Time* in any event would have been immune from suit. But the jury may find that *Time* said something very different by reporting that the Commission knew, and withheld from the public, details which could reasonably suggest that Minister Sharon condoned or encouraged the massacre as a measure of revenge."

That's the point, isn't it, Mr. Grunwald? You said "*Time* has learned" that the material about Sharon's discussing revenge was in the secret appendix. And it isn't. So how can you have learned it? How can saying you "learned it" be anything other than a lie or reckless disregard for the truth?

Sure, your lawyers are now arguing that if you "thought" it was in the appendix, then it wasn't a deliberate lie or reckless, but I don't buy it and I can't see how the jury will.

Your lawyers are also arguing that, even if it's not in the appendix, if Sharon did discuss revenge at the condolence call or if *Time* believed he did, then the mistake isn't reckless disregard or a deliberate lie. Frankly, I think Sharon's lawyers haven't been vigorous enough in fighting this attempt to broaden the subject matter; and the judge, too, has been too lenient in this regard. (The "news" in your article was that you said *Time* "has learned," not *Time* "thinks," "infers," or "believes." In fact, your people thought it was so newsworthy that *Time* had learned what it learned about the secret appendix that they issued a press release about it.) But I'm not the judge and the jury, and I guess you could win it on this one, though I doubt it.

But either way you shouldn't be making the fight. Because if you do win—if you get away with a clearly reckless, scoop-grabbing, press-release-triggering inaccuracy perpetrated by a reporter who doesn't know, or care about, the difference between a confirmation and a fantasy, when you stood behind your story after the one person you spoke to who read the appendix (Olmert, the Knesset member) told you you were wrong—it will be a terrible loss for all of us who think the First Amendment ought to be more than a license for arrogance.

You must act now, Mr. Grunwald, or this damage will be irreparable. You must act now and do what you'd expect a president or a governor or a corporate president to do in a similar case if you were covering the story: admit the mistake and fire the responsible people. I'm not saying you should give away the store to General Sharon. Fight him on damages if he insists on a draconian payment; it's true he probably doesn't have much of a money claim. And make a constitutional fight that punitive damages shouldn't be allowed in libel cases.

But, please, stop talking about vindication and stop defending what in this instance was your indefensible journalism; you're hurting not only yourself (the jury will probably show you another massacre if you don't call off Barr), but also hurting the rest of us who are constantly defending our profession against charges that journalists are lazy scandalmongers who never admit mistakes.

The theme of your lecture at NYU was that libel actions have become "a serious menace" to a free press. Well, you're right. But even a First Amendment absolutist like me has to admit, in looking at this suit, that this is in large part a problem we've created and that this is one suit we deserve to lose—because of your magazine's arrogance. After all, with your policy on corrections, and your knee-jerk process of standing behind your story, how else was General Sharon supposed to seek redress?

Judge Sofaer, a liberal judge obviously troubled by having to preside over a libel case (so troubled in fact that my sources tell me that he has repeatedly beseeched your lawyers to make some kind of settlement), put it this way in his decision denying you a dismissal or summary judgment:

" . . . *Time* has refused to issue any correction or to print plaintiff's denial. Only through the litigation process has plaintiff been able to uncover and publish the evidence from which *Time* claimed to have learned the contents of the Commission's secret appendix. And only through this avenue has he been able to bring to light the process by which the allegedly offending statement came to be written, including evidence of the possible motivations and truthfulness of its author. That this process has proved enormously expensive, and painfully contentious, is as much the product of *Time*'s all-out litigation strategy as of any plan by plaintiff to intimidate the press. Despite the fact that every single *Time* witness claims to have had no evidence that plaintiff knew in advance that the massacre would occur, *Time* has chosen to pour enormous resources into proving precisely that. *Time* may be entitled to enhance through such tactics the risks plaintiff faces in suing for defamation. But it would be pure fantasy to treat *Time* in this case like some struggling champion of free expression, defending at great risk to itself the right to publish its view of the truth.''

He's right, Mr. Grunwald. For the sake of all of us in the profession you lead, stop fighting the lawyers' fight. Strike a real blow for the free press by admitting your mistake and acting to clean up what caused it.

EPILOGUE

On the eleventh day of deliberations, January 24, 1985, the jury found that the 1983 *Time* article on Ariel Sharon contained a false and defamatory paragraph, but that the magazine had not published the inaccuracies intentionally and was therefore not liable. The jury took the unusual step of issuing a statement criticizing *Time* employees—particularly David Halevy. The employees, the jury said, had "acted negligently and carelessly in reporting and verifying the information which ultimately found its way into the published paragraph of interest in this case."

Both sides claimed victory. Sharon argued that he had achieved his goal, saying, "We managed to prove that *Time* magazine did lie." *Time* managing editor Ray Cave countered, "We are totally confident that the story is substantially true." A statement issued by *Time* attacked Sharon, claiming he brought the suit in an attempt to "recoup his political fortunes."

The Sharon trial prompted some changes at *Time*. Even before the verdict was in, the magazine printed a correction box—the first in its history—admitting the key factual error in its story about the Kahan Commission. "Appendix B does not contain further details about Sharon's visit to the Gemayel family," the passage read. "*Time* regrets the error." According to Edward Adler, a spokesman for Time Warner Inc., the magazine is now more liberal and open-minded, and acknowledges errors of fact. While nothing is labeled a correction, he says *Time* now more frequently prints letters that correct the record, occasionally adding "an editor's answer or acknowledgment of a mistake."

Adler says that the new correction policies were in the works before the Sharon suit, but acknowledges the case gave impetus to the changes.

Less than a week after the trial, the editor-in-chief of Time Inc., Henry Grunwald, sent an internal memo stating, "We must and will continue to make every effort to avoid errors.'' *Time* editors admitted that the fact-checking process broke down in Sharon's case.

Grunwald retired in December 1987, and accepted the post of U.S. ambassador to the Republic of Austria. Although Ray Cave was initially considered by many Time Inc. observers to be Grunwald's heir apparent, he was passed over for the top spot, which went to Jason McManus, *Time*'s managing editor. Cave remained with Time Inc. as editorial director until his resignation in January 1989. He is currently running his own editorial consulting business in New York City.

David Halevy remained with *Time* until December 1987, although he closed out his 19-year tenure at the magazine reporting from Washington, D.C., not Israel. Halevy is writing a book on his experiences as a reconnaisance battalion commander in the Israeli military and co-authoring a book on the P.L.O. Harry Kelly, who worked in Mexico, Chicago, and Washington after leaving Israel, remains on *Time*'s payroll as a consultant and is writing a novel.

Judge Abraham Sofaer has become an important player in the Reagan and Bush administrations, as legal adviser to the Department of State, a position he assumed in June 1985.

Sharon was relieved of his status as defense minister following the Kahan Commission report in 1982. He is currently Minister of Industry and Trade in the Israeli government.

Jeffrey MacDonald
V.
Joseph McGinniss

TRUTH AND BETRAYAL

BY

FRANK JUDGE

Jeffrey MacDonald, the key figure in Fatal Vision, *sued author Joseph McGinniss for fraud—but the real issue was the writer's obligations to his subject.*

The case had all the makings of a best-selling crime novel. In the early morning hours of February 17, 1970, a pregnant woman and her two young daughters were savagely murdered in their army-base home in Fort Bragg, North Carolina. Dr. Jeffrey MacDonald claimed a band of drug-crazed hippies had burst into his home, stabbed him and left him unconscious, then slaughtered his wife and children. But in the summer of 1979 it was the handsome, Princeton-educated physician and former Green Beret captain who was convicted for the brutal killings and sentenced to three consecutive life terms in prison.

Joseph McGinniss, who lived with MacDonald and his defense team during the trial and planned to write a book about the case, visited MacDonald in prison two days after the conviction. "As I left MacDonald there, behind the bars and concrete walls and steel doors of Butner—having just had him tell me that he hoped I was a friend who would stand by him—it was not possible simply to accept the jury's verdict,'' McGinniss recounted in his book *Fatal Vision*. "I had to try to learn more about what kind of man he really was."

This July, 17 years after the murders, MacDonald returned to the courtroom. This time he was pressing a $15 million civil suit against McGinniss. MacDonald claims the writer spent four years as his close friend, confidant, and member of his defense team only to portray him in the best-selling book and NBC miniseries *Fatal Vision* as a "pathological narcissist" who may have killed his family in an amphetamine-induced rage. MacDonald, who steadfastly proclaims his innocence and had expected a favorable book, contends that McGinniss defrauded him and broke an agreement to write a "fair and open-minded" book preserving the "essential integrity" of MacDonald's life story.

The suit sounds like a libel action, but the similarity eluded Los Angeles federal district judge William Rea, who presided over the six-week civil trial. MacDonald's cleverly drafted complaint, which attacked the author's *conduct* during the four years he was writing *Fatal Vision*, defied conventional libel analysis. When Judge Rea chose to ignore the constitutional issues in instructing the jury on MacDonald's fraud and contract claims, he left the author shorn of his First Amendment protections.

MacDonald says that the author's conduct "invited the legal theories" and "that a challenge to McGinniss's fraudulent *conduct*, encompassing four years of lies and deceits, is *no* threat to 'freedom of speech.' " But McGinniss, claiming he was sued for "probing too deep, getting to know the man," calls the suit an attempt to "get back at me because of the content of the book."

From the opening arguments, it became clear that McGinniss's conduct could not be so easily separated from the story he wrote about MacDonald.

MacDonald's lawyer, Gary Bostwick of Santa Monica's six-lawyer Bostwick & Ackerman, put his case simply. "It is a case about a false friend," he told the jury on July 7, the first day of trial. "What you are going to see is evidence of a person who betrayed a friend." In a long series of letters, Bostwick said, the jury would "read the demonstration of friendship, love, support, belief, credibility that Mr. McGinniss communicated to Dr. MacDonald in spite of the fact that [McGinniss] says that he'd already decided [MacDonald] was guilty." The author misled MacDonald, Bostwick argued, and then didn't tell the fair story MacDonald had come to expect.

McGinniss's lawyer, Daniel Kornstein of New York's nine-lawyer

Kornstein, Veisz & Wexler, painted the novel action as a grudge suit brought "by a murderer who did not like the book written about him." Kornstein described how McGinniss had watched MacDonald's criminal trial, reviewed the evidence, and conducted interviews in the process of writing a book Kornstein called "a monument to that thorough investigation." What MacDonald failed to realize, Kornstein explained to the jury, is that "the book *Fatal Vision* was not written *for* him, it was written *about* him."

What was on trial, then, was the fundamental issue of a writer's legal and moral obligations to his subject—an issue neither the judge nor the jury, which deadlocked after four hours of deliberation, would resolve.

McGinniss, 44, author of the best-selling *The Selling of the President,* met MacDonald in June 1979 while the doctor was preparing for his murder trial in North Carolina later that summer. A Fort Bragg military hearing officer had dismissed charges against MacDonald in 1970, but a federal grand jury in Raleigh, North Carolina, had handed down an indictment in January 1975. MacDonald asked if McGinniss, who was writing an article about him for the *Los Angeles Herald-Examiner,* would be interested in traveling to North Carolina and writing a book about the case. McGinniss said yes.

MacDonald agreed in a written contract to give McGinniss "exclusive story rights" in return for a share of his advance, royalties, and other proceeds. Several weeks after the start of the criminal trial, MacDonald signed a broad release that included the following provision: "I agree that I will not make or assert against you, the publisher, or its licensee . . . any claim or demand whatsoever on the ground that anything contained in the book defames me." MacDonald's lawyer, Bernard Segal, a flamboyant criminal attorney who now teaches at Golden Gate law school, scribbled in the qualification, "provided that the essential integrity of my life story is maintained." That ambiguous qualification would form the basis for MacDonald's unusual claim against McGinniss for breach of contract.

Author McGinniss lived with MacDonald and the defense team during trial, even signing an employment agreement to preserve MacDonald's attorney-client privilege, then corresponded with MacDonald for four years while researching and writing the book that became *Fatal Vision.* During that time, MacDonald came to regard the author as a friend and supporter. In June 1983 CBS reporter Mike Wallace, who had received an advance copy of the book, interviewed MacDonald for a *60 Minutes* segment about his case; it was then that MacDonald first confronted McGinniss's startling findings and conclusions. That fall, McGinniss's haunting portrayal of the man who had slaughtered his own family began its climb up the best-seller lists.

Brian O'Neill of Santa Monica's eight-lawyer O'Neill & Lysaght was then handling MacDonald's final criminal appeals. When O'Neill heard his client's complaints about McGinniss, he says he was outraged. McGinniss "suckered [MacDonald] into producing confidential details of his life and the case," O'Neill says. "I knew there had to be a remedy." O'Neill, a partner for eight years at Los Angeles's Manatt, Phelps, Rothenberg & Phillips before starting a solo practice in 1982, says he was too busy to handle a civil action against the author and recommended former Manatt, Phelps associate Gary Bostwick, then 42, who had opened his own office in 1983.

Bostwick recognized immediately that a libel action was "problematical" because his client would have difficulty proving injury to reputation, so he investigated other possible causes of action. "The breach of contract was clear," Bostwick says. And he says he had "no doubt" a claim existed for fraud after reviewing a series of letters McGinniss had written to MacDonald.

In August 1984 Bostwick filed the action against McGinniss in federal court for fraud, breach of contract, breach of covenant of good faith and fair dealing, intentional infliction of emotional distress, and an accounting of proceeds. The following month Bostwick kept MacDonald's potential libel claim alive by filing a libel action against the author and his publishers in Los Angeles County Superior Court. That complaint was never served because the Supreme Court's denial of certiorari last year dashed MacDonald's final hope for a new criminal trial.

FRAUD OR A GRUDGE SUIT?

From the beginning, McGinniss's counsel viewed MacDonald's action as a grudge suit over his portrayal in the book. Attorneys from Los Angeles's O'Melveny & Myers, who represented McGinniss until July 1986, found a sympathetic ear in federal magistrate James McMahon. "It's a bit of a strange fraud case," McMahon observed during a March 1986 discovery conference. "I think it's quite clear the reason it is a strange fraud case is it's a hidden libel case which [MacDonald] contracted out of."

Later McMahon added, "This whole lawsuit smells like a grudge suit" and inquired when O'Melveny would file a summary judgment motion.

But O'Melveny's lawyers faced a serious problem that had nothing to do with the merits of the case. Employers Reinsurance Corporation, the insurer for publisher Putnam Publishing Group, Inc., was refusing to pay author McGinniss's legal bills, claiming the publisher's insurance policy did not cover the suit because it was not framed in terms of libel or invasion of privacy. After paying the first $50,000 of McGinniss's defense costs, Putnam refused to pay any more.

O'Melveny partner Robert Vanderet had hoped MacDonald would lose interest in the case; when he did not, Vanderet advised McGinniss to look elsewhere for counsel. The firm's fees, even discounted, were too steep for McGinniss. Moreover, if O'Melveny sued over McGinniss's policy coverage, the firm faced a potential conflict with Employers Reinsurance, which had frequently approved the firm as libel counsel. "O'Melveny fired me as a client," says McGinniss.

In January 1986 an O'Melveny associate introduced McGinniss to Daniel Kornstein. Kornstein, then 38 and the author of two nonfiction books, said he would handle the insurance case. An action for declaratory judgment would not be prohibitively expensive, Kornstein assured his client. Besides, McGinniss recalls Kornstein explaining, "This is your lottery ticket. You have no choice. You've got six-figure legal fees out there." Delighted by Kornstein's interest in his case, McGinniss says, "There was no question then that he'd handle the [whole] case."

On November 14, 1986, New York federal district judge Robert Sweet ruled that the publisher's insurance policy did cover the author's costs. "The facts [of the fraud and related tort claims] are based upon, and at times indistinguishable from, an allegation of libel," wrote Judge Sweet. "Any alternative interpretation would allow artful and evasive pleading, such as MacDonald's, to render the insurance coverage illusory and deprive insureds of their contractual rights."

Ten days later, with one victory in hand, Kornstein appeared before Judge Rea to argue for summary judgment. Rea, 67, had been on the federal bench for only two years after 16 years on the Los Angeles County Superior Court. Kornstein was confident the judge would see MacDonald's suit as a cleverly concealed libel case. But Judge Rea, who declined through a spokesman to be interviewed for this article, flatly rejected the notion. "I wish Magistrate McMahon had not made the statement that this is a disguised case of violation of First Amendment rights libel case, because I don't construe this as being a libel case,'' he said.

When Kornstein directed the court's attention to Judge Sweet's opinion, Judge Rea snapped, ''It really doesn't matter to the court whether some judge in New York in the district court has found that. . . . That isn't going to govern this court's ruling. I mean, he could be just as wrong as I.''

Retreating to a position he considered secure, Kornstein argued that even if MacDonald's suit was not viewed as a libel action, ''there can't be any question that there are First Amendment implications here.'' Rea, however, wondered aloud whether First Amendment considerations were even relevant. Bostwick, MacDonald's attorney, then volunteered that he, too, believed there were First Amendment issues.

The next day Rea issued a two-line opinion denying McGinniss's motion; he subsequently denied Kornstein's request that the decision be certified for immediate appeal to the Ninth Circuit. MacDonald's case would proceed to trial.

''ESSENTIAL INTEGRITY'' V. TRUTH

On Tuesday, July 7, 1987, Gary Bostwick addressed the jury in an informal, almost folksy, manner and explained that deceit and betrayal were at the heart of his client's suit. This would not be a retrial of MacDonald's criminal case, he promised. ''Now you've all been told by the judge and I'll tell you again that Dr. MacDonald was convicted of the crimes that he was charged with,'' Bostwick said. ''He was convicted of the murders of his wife and two children. That's something that he has to live with and he has continued to deny all this time.''

Kornstein jumped to his feet to object, and Judge Rea patiently reminded Bostwick of his pretrial rulings prohibiting reference to MacDonald's claim of innocence and precluding introduction of evidence from the criminal proceedings without a prior ruling from the court.

''Yes, Your Honor,'' Bostwick acknowledged. ''I will keep that in mind.''

Throughout the trial, however, both attorneys would struggle mightily to admit evidence about the criminal case that might bolster their client's case. McGinniss's questionable obligation to preserve the ''essential integrity'' of MacDonald's story opened the door to such prejudicial evi-

139

dence. "Essential integrity"—and not truth—would apparently form the standard for liability under MacDonald's contract claim.

Bostwick recounted how MacDonald had allowed McGinniss to sit in on defense strategy sessions, mailed him hours of tape-recorded musings about his life, provided intimate personal items, and even turned away other writers at McGinniss's request in the belief the author was a friend.

All the while McGinniss deliberately concealed his belief in MacDonald's guilt to maintain full access to MacDonald and his records, Bostwick argued. In 1980, while staying at MacDonald's condominium, McGinniss discovered notes MacDonald had written describing his use of amphetamines in a diet program at the time of the murders. There in MacDonald's home, Bostwick suggested, McGinniss devised "his own theory of why the crimes had been committed."

McGinniss never confronted MacDonald with his findings or his conclusions, Bostwick said, because he desperately needed MacDonald's help to finish the book. "It had been a long dry spell, and he needed the money," Bostwick said. "He needed this book."

Kornstein countered by reminding the jurors of the nature of the man who had sued for a distortion of the "essential integrity" of his life story. "He was convicted eight summers ago for murdering his 26-year-old pregnant wife, Colette, his 5-year-old daughter, Kristen, and his 2-year-old daughter, Kimberly," Kornstein began. "The evidence will show, and it's a fact in the record, that they were found with multiple stab wounds, dozens of stab wounds. . . ."

Bostwick shouted an objection. Again the judge advised, "I ruled on this and I hope Mr. Kornstein has that in mind."

Nodding, Kornstein continued, steering clear of the inflammatory details of the killings. "They were found with multiple stab wounds and fractures, and they were clubbed. The jury unanimously convicted him." Pausing, he added, "Now he wants two more victims. The victims now are Joe McGinniss and the truth."

Kornstein bristled at Bostwick's accusation of fraud and betrayal. The writer's job is to get close to his subject, he explained, "to understand the subject, to live with him, to see the scene, to be able to recreate it. The subject knows that, the author knows that." McGinniss acted according to the standards of his profession, Kornstein argued. Then, in a voice thick with indignation, he railed, "The only fraud that has been perpetrated here . . . is MacDonald's continuing fraud on McGinniss about the truth of the events way back in 1970 and the continuing fraud on the public."

AN AUTHOR OR A FRIEND?

MacDonald's first witness was Bernard Segal, his lawyer during most of the criminal proceedings. Segal testified that he had encouraged MacDonald to cooperate in the writing of a book to raise funds for his defense. After failing to reach an agreement with author Joseph Wambaugh, they had approached McGinniss. The amiable McGinniss fit in comfortably with the defense team. "After a while we stopped thinking . . . of Joe McGinniss as the author who was there to write a book," said Segal.

Letters from McGinniss to MacDonald would become the most damaging evidence in Bostwick's fraud case. After calling the lanky author as a hostile witness, Bostwick projected onto a large screen a letter McGinniss had sent to MacDonald a few weeks after his conviction in August 1979 and began to read to the jury: "It says, 'Christ, here I sit in Wyoming writing a letter that I'll mail to you in a prison in California when you ought to be in Wyoming too.'

"Did you really believe that he ought to be in Wyoming too?" Bostwick asked.

"Well," McGinniss said, "at that time I think I sort of wished that he was."

MacDonald's lawyer read more of the letter. " 'Jeff, it's all so f——king awful I can't believe it yet. The sight of the jury coming in, of the jury polling, of you standing saying those few words, being led out, and then seeing you in a f——king prison is a hell of a thing. Spend a summer making a friend and then the bastards come along and lock him up. But not for long, Jeffrey, not for long.' "

Bostwick turned from the screen again. "You were trying to tell [MacDonald] that you believed ultimately he would be vindicated, weren't you?" he asked.

"Well, at that time, based on what I was hearing from his counsel, I thought his appeal process had a reasonable chance to succeed on the speedy trial issue," McGinniss explained in a soft, almost academic, manner. "I think I was also telling him, as I felt at that time, that I felt bad for him, I felt a lot of compassion for that man."

Bostwick's assistant slapped a letter written one month after the conviction onto the projector. Bostwick read: " 'Aside from the money and the fact that someday the full story will be told, it seems to me that one very important benefit of the book is that it gives you something constructive to do day by day, something real, something valuable, some-

141

thing essential, a way to channel your anger and reflections, a book about the case, no convict should be without one. Even in jest, it doesn't feel right to type the word "convict" in reference to you.' ''

"Didn't you think it would be real helpful to you if he continued to tell his side of the story?'' Bostwick asked sarcastically.

"Sure," McGinniss replied. "I wanted to get as much of his side of the story as I could, up until the point I realized it wasn't true."

"You couldn't write the book without his help, could you?"

"Oh, I could have written the book," answered McGinniss.

But Bostwick shot back, "You couldn't have written a best-seller, could you?"

"Well, that calls for speculation, Mr. Bostwick."

"Sure does," snapped Bostwick. "I'll withdraw it."

He continued reading: " 'Goddamn, Jeff, one of the worst things about all this is how suddenly and totally all of your friends, self included, have been deprived of your company.' ''

"You were trying to convince him that you were one of his friends so that he would be more likely to cooperate with you in the book?" Bostwick chided.

"There is no question, Mr. Bostwick, that at the time I wrote this letter I continued to feel friendship toward him."

But Bostwick parried, "Even though the evidence had proven that he was guilty?"

McGinniss tried to explain, "It's possible to believe that he's not innocent and still, at least it was at that time, and still think of him as a friend."

"Was it possible to also tell him that that was the case?" Bostwick asked.

"It may have been possible," McGinniss admitted, "but it wasn't my job as a professional writer to tell him what my opinions were."

Bostwick read more from the letter: " 'What the f——k were those people thinking of? How could twelve people not only agree to believe such a horrendous proposition but agree with a man's life at stake that they believed it beyond a reasonable doubt in six and a half hours? The question could keep you awake night after night, no doubt.' ''

Asked Bostwick: "Didn't you try to tell him with those words that you found it hard to believe that the jury had come to the verdict they did?"

"I was surprised it only took them six and a half hours," answered McGinniss, "but my perspective, you'll have to remember, was totally and entirely from one side during that trial. I spent my time only with MacDonald, not with the prosecution.''

"I understand that, Mr. McGinniss," Bostwick interjected, then continued: "What I'm asking you is whether you were trying to get Dr. MacDonald to believe that you believed the jury had been wrong?''

"No," McGinniss replied.

In other letters Bostwick read to the jury, McGinniss expressed a recurring concern other authors might write competing books. The lawyer quoted: " 'At this time to the best of anyone's knowledge, there are no unfriendly MacDonald books on the horizon.' ''

"You were trying to tell him by way of that sentence, weren't you, that your book was a friendly MacDonald book?'' Bostwick probed.

"At that point I was still very much hoping that somehow it could turn out to be,'' said McGinniss.

"Even though you had decided that he was guilty?''

"No," McGinniss answered. "I recognized that the jury had sufficient evidence to convict him. I was going back over everything, the [military hearing], listening to him, doing everything I could to try to find a way not to believe that that man committed those crimes.''

McGinniss asked MacDonald to supply specific and intimate recollections for the book. "I know it's painful, I know it is difficult," wrote McGinniss, in another letter Bostwick read to the jury. "But you've got me involved in this thing, and now I'm deeply involved and I am determined to give it my best and I can get much from the transcripts and much from the other people I talk to, but it is your life, your book in that sense at least, and I need you to take the lid off and climb down in there and accomplish the distasteful task of telling me about your life in minute detail and with as honest an attempt to communicate the emotional content as you can manage. We can't keep putting it off.''

According to the trial testimony, MacDonald sent the author tape recordings rich with personal details. Those edited recordings would later appear in *Fatal Vision* as sections titled "The Voice of Jeffrey MacDonald.'' Yet McGinniss never confronted MacDonald with the facts he found to be inconsistent with the story MacDonald told or with the damning conclusions he published in the final chapters of *Fatal Vision*.

When Bostwick demanded to know why McGinniss had not asked MacDonald about his amphetamine use before writing that he may have killed his family in a drug-induced psychotic rage, McGinniss replied, "By that time I had known him to be a man who had lied under oath repeatedly, so therefore I saw no particular reason to feel that his answer to that question would be something upon which I could reasonably rely.''

Bostwick had set the foundation for his fraud case with the letters. When he called MacDonald to the witness stand, Bostwick clearly hoped to move the jurors with his client's bitter tale of betrayal and distortion in the writing of his life story.

Despite MacDonald's conviction, Bostwick believed the soft-spoken physician would make a good witness. His major concern was MacDonald's discomfort with the truth-seeking process. "He has not been believed on a single issue of his life for the last seventeen years," Bostwick explains. "You want to try to convince any witness to tell the whole truth and not to try to argue his case when testifying. But it's hard to convince a man who feels at every point he has to argue it.''

TEARS OF BETRAYAL

MacDonald, dressed meticulously in a navy blue blazer and gray slacks, recalled that he had liked McGinniss immediately and "felt comfortable with him." When McGinniss first arrived in North Carolina to join the defense team, MacDonald described to the author the story he wanted told. "I told him I wanted the true story told of a false prosecution," MacDonald explained, his soft voice cracking. "I told him that I wanted the truth about my relationship with my wife and children told," he added, choking on a sob. McGinniss, he said, replied that was no problem.

On at least two occasions during the trial, MacDonald recalled, McGinniss told him "my innocence would come out" in the book. Pausing to brush tears from his cheeks, he said the author told him, "I have a book to put it in; you have a book to sell.'' Bostwick then prompted MacDonald to describe the letters and conversations that convinced him he "could count on" McGinniss to write a book that portrayed his innocence.

"Well, I felt the words that he felt the verdict was wrong indicated how he felt. I felt that when he states how could the jury have come to that decision, when he says in the letter that he is saddened by my imprisonment and that he wants me back out of prison, that certainly means to me that that's a friend talking to me and that he believes in my innocence,'' MacDonald replied.

Indeed, MacDonald testified that until the publication of *Fatal Vision,* he regarded McGinniss as one of his four closest friends. When Mac-Donald read the book in September 1983, he said, he felt "sick, like my guts had been ripped out." He testified that he grew depressed at the realization that "I had just spent four years baring my soul to a person who said he was open and honest and was receiving that material with an open eye and ear and hadn't."

With MacDonald's testimony, Bostwick exposed the vulnerability of a subject to an author, a particularly complex human drama in this case. Although the lawyer also attacked the book, particularly McGinniss's conclusions, for failing to maintain the "essential integrity" of MacDonald's story, it was McGinniss's behavior in his relationship with Mac-Donald that many of the jurors would remember in deliberation and condemn.

Kornstein, an experienced trial lawyer, was not about to let MacDonald elicit unwarranted sympathy from the jury. In an incisive and at times devastating cross-examination, McGinniss's lawyer would pick apart MacDonald's complaints about the book. But first Kornstein reminded the jury who was sitting before them on the witness stand.

"Isn't it true that on February seventeenth, 1970, your pregnant wife, Colette, was found dead with a fractured skull, sixteen stab wounds from a knife in her neck and chest, and twenty-one stab wounds from an ice pick in her chest?" Kornstein asked.

"That's true."

"In 1979, weren't you unanimously convicted by a jury for her murder?"

"That's what the jury said, yes."

In similar graphic detail, Kornstein described the killings of MacDonald's two young daughters. Then he forced MacDonald to admit that a jury had convicted him of all three murders and that the convictions have been upheld by all courts, including the U.S. Supreme Court.

After exposing MacDonald's complaints of factual inaccuracies in McGinniss's book as being riddled with holes, Kornstein turned to what he considered the critical issue in the case: who had the right to tell the story in the book. " 'I made myself a promise not to question you on the book,' " Kornstein read from a letter MacDonald had written to McGinniss in August 1982. " 'I've told you, and I mean it, that I have decided to go with you on the book without any controls to protect me, as I could have gotten with a lesser writer, because of my feelings about you as a person.' "

During cross-examination MacDonald described his understanding of the story McGinniss would tell. "The sense that I had was that it was to be Joe's words and my story," MacDonald explained.

"You said that expression a number of times now, Joe's words and your story," Kornstein snapped. "This was a book in which you figured prominently, wasn't it?"

"Yes."

"So it is a book about you and certain events in your life, isn't it?"

"Yes."

"So in a sense it is your story?"

"You mean what eventually came out?"

"It is a story about you?"

"But that's not my story."

McGINNISS'S LIBEL DEFENSE

The case for the defense, beginning with the testimony of authors William Buckley, Jr., and Joseph Wambaugh, showed clearly that MacDonald's claims impinged on McGinniss's constitutional rights. Judge Rea, allowing each lawyer to try his own case even if at times they seemed two different cases, permitted the jury to hear MacDonald's fraud and contract case along with what, in essence, was McGinniss's libel defense. Kornstein would also go on, if only for appeal, to build a case that the book was true or otherwise protected under the First Amendment.

Buckley, author of more than a dozen books and the editor of *National Review,* who was called out of order during the plaintiff's case, pronounced McGinniss "ferociously honest." It is standard journalistic practice, Buckley testified, for writers who are "investigative artists" to woo their subjects into revealing themselves. Writers must avoid confronting a subject with contradictory or incriminating information that might inhibit further disclosures, he said.

"If, for instance, you were writing a book on somebody who was a renowned philanderer," Buckley offered hypothetically, "and he said, 'I mean, you do think my wife is impossible, don't you?'. . . you might say, 'Yeah, I think she's very hard to get along with,' simply for the purpose of *lubricating* the discussion." Added Buckley: "After all, your mission is writing that book."

Author Wambaugh, whom MacDonald first had approached to write the book about his case, took a more dramatic stance. The former Los Angeles police officer and author of *The Onion Field,* a best-selling story

146

of the 1963 murder of a police officer by two sociopaths in an onion field near Bakersfield, California, recalled his only meeting with MacDonald in June 1979.

"I found him to be extremely glib, very charming," Wambaugh testified. But it was MacDonald's detachment that haunted Wambaugh. "He was describing events of, of course, consummate horror in a very detached manner. Not that he wouldn't show emotion. He would show emotion during the course of the conversation, but he would always show emotion when he was discussing the badgering and harassment and hounding that he was suffering at the hands of the government."

Several months later, after MacDonald's conviction, McGinniss visited Wambaugh at his home in San Marino, California. McGinniss was distressed and confused, and as Wambaugh recalled, ruminated aloud that MacDonald was either "a totally innocent man, a good man who was unjustly convicted, or . . . the most evil person I have ever heard of since Hitler."

But Wambaugh offered yet another possibility: "I said, 'There is a third alternative here. You may not be discussing good or evil. Good or evil is irrelevant to the sociopath, and that's the third alternative.' "

"UNTRUTHS"—A TOOL OF THE TRADE

Offering his opinion as an expert on literary custom and practice, Wambaugh testified that a writer should never disclose his views to his subject even if that requires telling an "untruth." He recounted as an example his telling one of the onion field killers, a sociopath, that he believed the killer hadn't shot the policeman. "I did not believe him but I said that I did because I wanted him to continue talking, because my ultimate responsibility was not to that person, my responsibility was to the book."

After gathering enormous amounts of material, Wambaugh explained, the author needs discretion to tell the story. "My job is to make the experiences of life coherent and meaningful and to tell a story that has a beginning and a middle and an end. . . . And I can only do that by having discretion to omit and to edit as I see fit."

Before concluding his testimony on direct examination, Wambaugh recalled his last words to McGinniss at the end of their meeting: "Remember, when you're dealing with a sociopath, do not expect the son of a bitch to fall down on his knees and confess to you."

On cross-examination Bostwick sparred briefly with Wambaugh over the difference between an "untruth" and a lie. The lawyer's casual jabs at the convenience of the distinction were not lost on the jury. In the same vein, Bostwick questioned how Wambaugh could feel responsibility only to the book and not to the people he wrote about.

"Well, because as an author and a literary person, I perceive that the book is a living thing, as you are, as I am—or it will be if I can use all the skill at my command to make it come to life," Wambaugh said. "That book will be much bigger than the subject that I'm talking to, and it will be much bigger than I am if I do my job right and if I have sufficient talent and skill."

"But you don't write books in order to starve," Bostwick said, infusing the talk of art with mundane financial realities.

"I write books in order to tell the truth," Wambaugh retorted. "If they happen to be successful, so much the better."

Kornstein put on several witnesses supporting the substantial truth of McGinniss's account of MacDonald's life in *Fatal Vision,* including the possible explanations he offered for the killings, as if this were indeed a libel action. The strategy was "to demonstrate . . . that [my] assumptions were not unwarranted," McGinniss explains.

Two clinical psychologists testified that, on the basis of MacDonald's tapes, the book, and the testimony of mental health officials at the criminal trial, MacDonald does display characteristics of a criminal personality and "pathological narcissist." MacDonald watched, emotionless.

The next day an army criminal investigator, now employed as a Drug Enforcement Administration chemist—who tested MacDonald's body fluids after the murders and failed to detect any dangerous drugs or narcotics—testified, contrary to MacDonald's contention, that he still could have consumed amphetamines on the night of the murder. The equipment the investigator used could not have detected anything less than a lethal dose of amphetamines, he explained. Another witness confirmed McGinniss's conclusion that consumption of three to five of the diet pills daily could have precipitated a psychotic reaction.

Kornstein then called MacDonald's former father-in-law, Alfred Kassab, who described briefly to a hushed courtroom how he gradually came to disbelieve MacDonald's story about the killings. A drama then developed outside the courtroom when Kassab told reporters that he believed MacDonald had killed his family after his wife caught him sexually molesting their young daughters. "I have reason to believe the

148

children were molested," he said. "I've been looking for a trigger for years."

Kornstein had indicated in pretrial documents that he might call a psychologist to testify about the possibility that MacDonald was sexually abusing his daughters. But Kornstein had decided not to call the witness, and Judge Rea sternly warned the lawyers that such statements could jeopardize the trial. Kornstein declines to comment on this aspect of the case.

On the final day of trial, Kornstein called to the stand a polygrapher hired by Segal, MacDonald's criminal lawyer, soon after the murders. Cleve Baxter, who described himself as one of the best-known polygraphers in the nation, said MacDonald had failed the lie detector test. "The results were very unambiguous," Baxter said. "In my opinion, he was being deceptive" about his role in the murders. Baxter continued, "I told him I could not be of help to him in his defense because he failed the polygraph test. The best thing I did is to keep quiet for seventeen years."

Judge Rea permitted the jurors to hear the evidence only for the purpose of assessing MacDonald's credibility. Earlier in the trial, MacDonald testified that he had failed to mention Baxter's test to the grand jury because he had forgotten about the meeting. MacDonald and Segal also said earlier in the trial testimony the test had been terminated after Baxter asked a series of irrelevant questions about MacDonald's sex life. Although Baxter testified that he could not locate his written record of the test results, he said he remembered them clearly.

When on Thursday, August 13, the attorneys addressed the jurors for the last time, they both spoke of the critical issues the jury had to confront in their deliberations. Threads of First Amendment implications wove through the carefully constructed closing arguments.

For Bostwick, the issue was whether authors have the right to lie. "We need good writers," said Bostwick. "Our liberty depends on them. But we need truthful writers. We do not need people who lie."

For Kornstein, the issue was censorship. "You are being asked to set a precedent," he cried. "A verdict for MacDonald would be a verdict for censorship." If MacDonald prevails, he said, "We'll be going back to the dark ages . . . so that the only light that will remain will be the light from a bonfire of burning books."

Judge Rea then read to the jury instructions on rules of law they should accept in deciding the case. Both lawyers had proposed jury instructions.

Kornstein had included traditional First Amendment libel instructions explaining the constitutional burdens of proof and the defenses available to McGinniss and describing how they should be weighed in deliberation on each claim. But the six-member jury retired that afternoon to begin deliberations with instructions that made no mention of the author's First Amendment interests or defenses.

SEEDS OF JURY DISCONTENT

The judge's failure to define the case until the last day of the amorphous and unwieldy six-week trial and then to rule out any consideration of First Amendment interests provided fertile soil for dissension in an already tense jury room.

After electing Elizabeth Lane, a 64-year-old retired social worker, as foreperson, the jurors began leafing through the instructions, assorted trial exhibits, and the 37-question special verdict form. But one juror, Lucille Dillon, a 59-year-old homemaker, sat apart from the rest of the group reading a newspaper and, she says, thinking about the case. When asked to join the others at the conference table a few feet away, Dillon answered, "I'll stay here."

The peculiar dynamic already unfolding reflected a rift that had been developing over the many weeks of trial. On the first day of trial Dillon had told the jurors she advocates animal rights and offered to bring them literature. She was met by "sly looks and grins," Dillon says. She did, however, bring in animal rights materials and frequently voiced her opinions on the subject.

Alternate juror Jackie Beria, 37, a marketing associate with Pacific Bell who did not participate in the deliberations, says Dillon was a gentle and nice woman, but "very fanatical in her beliefs." Dillon preached to the other jurors not to eat meat, Beria says.

Serious deliberations began the next morning when the jurors attempted to struggle through the verdict form. The first question concerned the first element of MacDonald's contract claim: "Did [MacDonald] perform all of the obligations and conditions imposed on him under the contract?"

McGinniss had presented evidence that MacDonald had breached his contract by suing McGinniss in violation of two broad, signed releases and by cooperating with the author of another book—*I Accuse: The Torturing of an American Hero,* by Melinda Stephens, published in

1987—in violation of his grant of exclusive story rights to McGinniss.

Lane says she was puzzled about whether the jury should consider the releases and competing book in answering this question. The jurors sent a note to the judge requesting clarification on which exhibits to consider and what time frame to apply. He responded that they should consider the underlying contract between the parties. He did not instruct them to consider the releases or supply a time frame, Lane says. The releases were very broad, admits Lane, "but we did not consider them because we were not informed to consider them."

When several jurors criticized McGinniss and his witnesses, Dillon became convinced that they were "looking to get at the author," she says. Dillon says she announced, "I believe the author, I believe the book, and I believe his witnesses. It's a free speech issue." She refused to agree that MacDonald had fulfilled his contractual obligations. Pointing to the releases MacDonald had signed, Dillon says she told them, "An author must have total freedom to write the truth. I didn't see how McGinniss did wrong."

Dillon says she stood up for the author because the others "were not answering the court questions." They would not accept that MacDonald had violated his agreement giving McGinniss exclusive rights to his life story, she says. "To me it was simple." The five jurors did not want to concede the first question to McGinniss, says Dillon, because it would mean MacDonald could not win his contract claim.

The jurors voted 5 to 1 that MacDonald had fulfilled the obligations of his contract up to the date of *Fatal Vision*'s publication. After the vote, says Lane, Dillon "wouldn't deliberate with us," and responded to their questions with "strident combativeness." Dillon claims the other jurors mocked her and McGinniss's witnesses.

After lunch on Friday, only four hours after deliberation began, Lane says the jury sent a note to Judge Rea informing him that "[Dillon] would not deliberate because she had sided with the defendant." A unanimous verdict is required in a civil action unless the attorneys agree otherwise. The judge instructed them to attempt to deliberate. "So we had to go on the best we could," says Lane, but "there was no way we could prevail upon her to change her mind on a single point."

By the following Tuesday, all attempts to deliberate had collapsed. "It was absolutely impossible" to reach a unanimous verdict because of Dillon's obstinate refusal to deliberate, Lane says. Judge Rea, who was attending a judicial conference in Hawaii, conferred with the attorneys by telephone and suggested that Dillon be replaced by one of the alternates. But Kornstein, aware from the jury's note to the judge that Dillon might be the only holdout, flatly rejected the compromise.

Rea decided it was senseless to continue and instructed the jurors to reconvene upon his return. On Friday Judge Rea questioned each juror individually and, after Kornstein again rejected the proposal to replace Dillon, reluctantly declared a mistrial.

Although the jurors agreed on little in their four days in the tense jury room, interviews conducted for this article and those reported in local newspapers after the mistrial suggest that five of the six jurors would have turned in a verdict for MacDonald. But far from awarding the $15 million he sought, they would probably have limited the award to the royalties they believed to be due him under the contract.

"There was an enormous assumption by [Dillon] that we were in sympathy with MacDonald and we were going to give him the earth," Lane says. "It wasn't true." Lane says she believes they would have settled on the $90,000 in royalties that had been placed in escrow for MacDonald. McGinniss says the escrow money would have been distributed to MacDonald "in the normal course" if he had not sued.

Only one juror, Sheila Campbell, 27, who indicated during trial that she had not read a book since high school and that she'd had difficulty finishing *Fatal Vision,* told reporters she would have awarded MacDonald "millions and millions of dollars to set an example for all authors to show they can't tell an untruth" to their subjects. Lane believes, however, that other jurors would have persuaded Campbell not to insist on punitive damages.

The jurors were aware how unsettling the case was to the literary world, but they were trying to consider the evidence within the confines of the judge's instructions and special verdict questions, Lane says. She adds that the jury found the instructions and verdict questions extremely confusing. "I would like to have [said] at the outset that MacDonald got what he asked for and McGinniss did what he said he'd do, but we were asked to go through all the legal points." Lane wonders aloud, "Maybe we got caught up in the thicket of legalities."

The jury felt "a certain amount of sympathy for MacDonald" on his contract claim, Lane notes, because "he was signing his soul away, practically." Nevertheless, she says, he did sign the contract and releases and, as "somebody who should have known better," should be forced to live with the consequences.

Most of the jurors believed McGinniss had deceived MacDonald.

"[MacDonald] had been deceived into thinking the book would have portrayed him as he wanted and it did not," says Lane. McGinniss's conduct offended the jurors. "We're not writers and authors and such behavior is distasteful to us," Lane says. "It's a bit sneaky. Did he have to carry it quite so far?"

Buckley and Wambaugh could testify about the profession's acceptance of this practice "until the cows come home," Lane says, but the fact that "it's expedient and it's done doesn't make it right." At the same time most jurors concluded that what McGinniss did was not illegal, she adds. "I felt MacDonald was manipulating McGinniss and McGinniss was stringing MacDonald along," Lane explains. The jurors did not want to reward either party for dishonesty, she says.

If MacDonald hoped to persuade a new jury of his innocence, he failed. While not a focus of their deliberations, his guilt seems to have been taken for granted by the jury. Even juror Campbell believed in his guilt but felt he had suffered enough, according to Lane. "By now [MacDonald] may have convinced himself he is innocent," Lane notes. "It's possible to lie to yourself so long as you believe it."

Indeed, MacDonald's self-deception was the source of Lane's only real sympathy for him. "It had nothing to do with the legal aspects of the case. If he was guilty and could never admit it [to himself], he could never get any absolution."

The mistrial may be MacDonald's last action against McGinniss. Two weeks before the trial began, Kornstein offered a judgment against his client and $200,000 to MacDonald as provided for under Rule 68 of the Federal Rules of Civil Procedure. "We thought it was a generous settlement offer," Kornstein says. "It also added an element of risk at trial." When ten days elapsed without a response the offer lapsed.

Under the provisions of that rule, if MacDonald were to obtain a verdict for less than $200,000 he would be required to pay all reasonable costs incurred after the offer was made, including the costs of both trials. Kornstein already estimates the costs of the first trial at "tens of thousands of dollars," excluding legal fees. It's a financial risk that Bostwick recognizes and one that his client, who has at least the $90,000 escrow account at stake, cannot ignore—particularly in view of the first jury's reluctance to award MacDonald any punitive damages.

Lawyers for the parties say settlement talks, which occurred sporadically during trial, are continuing. And such a resolution may write the final chapter of this unusual controversy and the book that brought MacDonald and McGinniss together.

"To the extent MacDonald emerges with no new law and no money," McGinniss calls the trial a success. Still he, like many other authors, worries about the impact of this case. "If MacDonald, who may be the world's most unsympathetic plaintiff, can get to trial and even a hung jury," McGinniss wonders, "what's going to happen in other cases?"

EPILOGUE

In October 1987, Joseph McGinniss's lawyer, Daniel Kornstein, moved for summary judgment for his client, arguing that the evidence had failed to prove that McGinnis had damaged Jeffrey MacDonald. But on November 23, Kornstein and MacDonald's lawyer, Gary Bostwick, reached a settlement for $325,000, to be paid by the author's insurance company. McGinniss did not admit liability.

In December 1987, three weeks before the settlement check was due, Mildred Kassab, MacDonald's former mother-in-law, sued MacDonald in Los Angeles superior court seeking to establish a constructive trust for the payment and for the royalties MacDonald earned before the settlement, alleged to be as high as $100,000. Her counsel, Pasadena solo practitioner Douglas Post, argued that under California law MacDonald cannot profit from murder and that the money should instead go to the heirs of the victims, namely Kassab. In January 1989, following a trial, the court ruled that $50,000 be paid to MacDonald, $125,000 to his lawyer, Bostwick, and $75,000 each to Kassab and MacDonald's mother.

McGinniss has finished a new book, *Blind Faith*, about the 1984 murder of the wife of an insurance executive in Toms River, New Jersey, which was published in January 1989.

MacDonald, serving time in Terminal Island Prison in Long Beach, California, continues to make the case for his innocence, publishing a newsletter for his supporters and appearing on network news shows.

WHITE-COLLAR CRIME

Power tends to corrupt. . . .

—LORD ACTON, 1887

U.S.
v.
Ivan Boesky

CAN BOESKY'S SWEETHEART PLEA BARGAIN BE UNDONE?

BY
STEVEN BRILL

How the sentencing judge could have put teeth into Ivan Boesky's deal with the government—and given the admitted insider trader what he deserved.

December 1987

The Honorable Morris E. Lasker
U.S. District Court
Southern District of New York

Dear Judge Lasker:

On December 18, Ivan Boesky is scheduled to appear before you for sentencing. It's now been a year since the fabled arbitrageur's plea bargain with the government was announced. His sentencing has been delayed by the prosecutors twice before, because they claim he's still providing them with vital information related to other cases. So this sentencing date, too, may be postponed.

But whether you're asked to rule two weeks or two years from now, I think you should know that you've been set up to be the final pawn in what may be the most unjust application of justice in the history of plea bargaining.

You've been picked by prosecutors and defendant alike because you're the most lenient judge in the Southern District of New York. You're also one of the smartest, and you ought to be able to see this plea bargain—and this defendant—for what they are.

Boesky will be standing before you having pled guilty to one count of conspiring to file a false 13-D statement with the Securities and Exchange Commission. That's three fewer counts than people like Dennis Levine have had to plead to and even one less than small fry like Ilan Reich had to take.

In return the prosecutors and the SEC have forever waived all rights to come after Boesky for any illegal stock trading he's ever done.

This is the equivalent of Willie Sutton, having been caught robbing 20 banks, pleading to a parking meter violation committed in the course of one of the robberies.

Boesky's agreed-to "crime" is punishable by up to five years in prison. But with the way federal parole guidelines for this type of crime will probably be applied, he'll almost automatically serve just 20 months. That's assuming you impose the maximum sentence, which, as I understand it, you have almost never done.

Based just on the information the government had when it began its plea bargain with Boesky lawyers Harvey Pitt (of Fried, Frank, Harris, Shriver & Jacobson) and Theodore Levine (of Wilmer, Cutler & Pickering), Boesky could have been prosecuted for at least seven felony insider trading counts punishable by up to five years apiece.

There would, of course, have been many more potential counts had the government kept investigating instead of plunging ahead with a plea bargain that, according to lawyers on both sides, took about ten days from the first serious discussion to signatures being affixed on the bottom line.

More absurd than this criminal punishment is what the government did, and didn't do, to Boesky financially. It's been claimed that he paid a $100 million fine representing disgorgement of $50 million in ill-gotten gains and a $50 million penalty. As you'll see below, because of some nifty bargaining by Pitt and Levine, the real cost of that fine is arguably $30.9 million.

And Boesky has admitted to the government that he made far more than that $50 million, anyway, from his illegal trading. Worse, it seems clear that he made far, far more than he admitted to the government—and that he hasn't told the government everything that he could have.

Nor has he told the government about his remaining assets. His lawyers may claim at the sentencing or in a memo to you that he's been wiped out. Don't believe it.

What I'm suggesting is that given the essential, Willie Sutton–like criminality of Boesky's rise to riches, a plea bargain that leaves him basically untouched demands extraordinary judicial intervention. The purpose of this "sentencing memo" is to suggest why you should intervene, and then perhaps how you can do it.

Let's start by analyzing the specifics of what Boesky, himself, has said he's guilty of before we move on to the bigger picture.

I. WHAT BOESKY ADMITTED TO

A. The Levine Deals

Boesky was fingered by Dennis Levine, the Drexel Burnham Lambert managing director whose insider trading arrest in May of 1986 touched off the current scandal. According to an SEC complaint filed in conjunction with a consent decree signed by Boesky on November 13, 1986, Levine told federal prosecutors and the SEC as part of his own plea-bargain-induced cooperation that Boesky had bribed him from February 1985 through February 1986 for inside information relating to seven mergers, acquisitions, and other transactions that moved the stocks of the companies involved.

That would make for a minimum of seven insider trading felony counts, though probably more, since each separate trade in the stocks involved could be a separate count, and Boesky bought the stocks on more than one occasion.

When the SEC exacted its $50 million fine from Boesky, it stated in a "litigation release" and the complaint accompanying the consent decree that the $50 million represented "profits allegedly obtained by his illegal trading."

But on November 24, 1986, *The Wall Street Journal* reported that based on the deal the SEC said that Levine had had with Boesky, the profits seemed to be $203 million, not $50 million.

The *Journal*'s logic worked this way: Boesky had agreed to pay Levine 5 percent of his profits for information Levine supplied on deals Boesky had not already bought into, and 1 percent for information about stocks that Boesky had already bought before Levine provided him with information. Since it was known from the SEC complaint that on three deals—the takeovers of Nabisco Brands, Inc., and Houston Natural Gas Corporation and the restructuring of FMC Corporation—Boesky had bought positions only after Levine gave him information, and since Boesky's purchases in these stocks were listed in the complaint, the *Journal* was able to calculate Boesky's profits from those ''5-percent deals'' at $9,075,000. Therefore, the amount he owed to Levine would be 5 percent of that, or $455,000.

Thus, the *Journal* concluded that if, of the total of $2.4 million that Boesky had owed Levine, just $455,000 represented 5-percent payments due from those three 5-percent deals, the remaining $1,945,000 represented 1-percent payments due from the four other ''1-percent deals''—deals in which Boesky had already had positions prior to getting information from Levine. And if $1,945,000 represents 1 percent of profits, those profits have to be $194,500,000, which added to the $9,075,000 would mean $203 million in profit.

The director of the SEC's enforcement division, Gary Lynch, says that ''the *Journal*'s calculations are just plain stupid'' because they assume that ''all of Ivan's profit in those deals was attributable to Levine, when, in fact, he had bought the stock initially without talking to Levine.

''Ivan agreed to give Levine one percent because it was a round number and a way to avoid arguments over how much credit Levine should get for his information,'' Lynch contends. ''There was no exact way to figure out the value of the information.

''Fifty million seemed like a pretty fair number, based on our talking to Levine and Boesky,'' Lynch explains. ''But it wasn't exact. It couldn't be.''

But as you know, Judge, the only interpretations yet of the relatively new (1984) SEC statute calling for disgorgement make the assumption that *all* profit from trading by a tippee in a stock about which he's been given insider information comes from that insider information. If not, an insider trader could simply avoid the disgorgement penalty by claiming he was going to buy the stock anyway.

As for the argument that Boesky had, indeed, bought the stock before Levine's tips, there's also the argument that he might have sold it, or sold it short, or done something else to hurt his position had he not had Levine's tips. Indeed, the statute even specifies that any ''loss avoided'' is subject to the disgorgement penalty.

In this regard, you ought to be aware that Lynch's position here is completely inconsistent with the position he and the SEC routinely take in dealing with insider traders. As one seasoned securities lawyer puts it, ''The enforcement division always says that all profits are assumed to derive from the information. They usually won't even listen to any attempts to minimize the penalty this way.''

Thus, according to one source, the Boesky side was surprised when the SEC set a profit figure as low as $50 million, though Pitt gamely, and briefly, argued that the number should be lower, probably to make his opponents feel comfortable with the number. Then he and Levine said they'd accept the number if the penalty was equal to one times the amount as compared to the permissible three times the amount. (Under the federal insider trading statute, the penalty part of Boesky's liability could have been as much as three times his profit—or $150 million using the SEC's meek interpretation, or $609 million using the more aggressive interpretation.)

So, in return for a $50 million fine and $50 million in disgorgement of what seems, according to the statute, to have been $203 million in admitted profit, Boesky is forever free from all criminal liability and all SEC action related to any insider trading or any other illegal stock trading that he or any entity he controls or controlled has ever done.

As the SEC's letter of agreement puts it, ''The Commission agrees that, with the exception of the [$50 million fine and $50 million disgorgement] the Commission shall not institute any action . . . against you under the securities laws . . . or any other law, nor will the Commission recommend any action against you to any foreign or United States federal, state, local or self-regulatory agency or body for any conduct occurring prior to the date of this Agreement.''

Similarly, United States Attorney Rudolph Giuliani agreed that in return for Boesky's plea to that one count neither he nor federal prosecutors in Washington or Los Angeles (other conceivable sites of Boesky's stock trading activities) would ever prosecute him for any securities law violations occurring prior to the agreement.

B. The Siegel Deals

As soon as the SEC consent decree and prosecutor plea bargain deals were inked, the government began to see how much it had given up. One of Boesky's first revelations as a cooperating stool pigeon was that from 1982 to 1984 he'd bribed Martin Siegel—Kidder, Peabody's top M&A specialist—$700,000 for information relating to, among other deals, the takeovers of Bendix Corporation, Carnation Company, Natomas, Inc., and Getty Oil Corporation.

In her 1984 profile of Boesky in *The Atlantic, American Lawyer* senior reporter Connie Bruck reported that Boesky made an estimated $50 million profit in the giant Getty Oil deal, a deal that cemented Boesky's reputation as a brilliant, steel-nerved arbitrageur because he had bet so heavily and so relentlessly in the face of the deal's harrowing uncertainties. In fact, as Boesky now told the prosecutors, he'd gotten inside information on the deal from Siegel, who'd been Getty lead shareholder Gordon Getty's closest adviser. ("Making a judgment about Gordon Getty's motives was the main task of an arbitrageur in this deal," Boesky would later write in a book published in 1985.)

Neither the SEC nor Giuliani's office has said yet, assuming they ever will, how many deals other than Bendix, Getty, Natomas, and Carnation Siegel told Boesky about. But according to three sources in positions to know, when the SEC took $9 million in disgorgement from Siegel (his entire net worth minus his two residences) as part of Siegel's settlement, Lynch and others argued that they were exacting what one SEC lawyer recalls Lynch calling "a tiny fraction" of the profit Siegel provided to Boesky with his inside information.

At the time of Siegel's plea, his SEC consent decree said that Boesky made a total of $33.4 million from his Siegel information, including $4.8 million from the Natomas information, $28.3 million from Carnation, and $120,000 on Bendix. But these numbers might be low. For the SEC complaint says that Boesky made just $220,000 on the Getty deal, compared to the report in Bruck's *Atlantic* article that he made $50 million. A former employee of Boesky's says he "can't understand how the SEC could have believed Ivan made a few hundred thousand on Getty. That was one of his biggest scores ever."

Says one source involved with Kidder, Peabody's and Siegel's defense: "We were surprised with the $220,000 number the SEC came up with. But they said that that's what Ivan had told them. So we happily accepted it."

"I think it's because Boesky told us that although he made a large profit on Getty, he told us that he only made $220,000 of it on information Siegel gave him," Lynch says. "And Siegel told us the same thing."

That's an explanation that seems to say more about the SEC's gullibility—remember, Siegel was Getty's closest adviser—than about the profit Boesky really made. Nonetheless, if, as the SEC thinks, Boesky's profit from these four deals was $33.4 million, and you throw in what one knowledgeable lawyer says is "at least another $10 million" for deals as yet unnamed, you get $43.4 million in ill-gotten gains just from the Siegel deals. You get $93.2 million if Boesky made $50 million in the Getty deal. Whatever the numbers, Boesky got to keep it all under his agreement with the government.

The total, then, for Boesky's take in the Levine and Siegel bribe arrangements would seem to be somewhere between $246 million and $296 million.

II. WHAT BOESKY HASN'T ADMITTED TO: A LIFE OF CRIME

Just when Boesky began his bribing of Levine, he published a book called *Merger Mania*, which purported to be a scholarly analysis of the science of risk arbitrage. Its introduction consists of an "analysis" of the Getty deal and how any smart arbitrageur could have applied Boesky's science in that deal to make money. ("Here was a situation that called on all the talents of the arbitrageur and presented the most basic and subtle issues an arbitrageur must face," wrote the man who we now know was bribing Martin Siegel for inside information on that deal.) The book is dedicated to the memory of Boesky's father, who, Boesky wrote, "remains an example of returning to the community the benefits he had received through the exercise of God-given talents."

I mention this desecration of his father's memory to you, Judge, because I think it suggests the nature of the man you are about to sentence. The evidence is now clear—and was, in fact, quite clear even before his plea—that Boesky's entire professional life has been a fraud.

Boesky lawyer Pitt says, gamely, "I believe Ivan had great abilities as an arbitrageur and that one of the really sad things is that he had the acumen to be, and was, at the top of his profession without doing anything illegal."

This is the "Why would he stoop to this with all the money and talent he had?" version of the Boesky story, the corollary of which is that he's now profoundly sorry for what he's done—so much so that while he is waiting for sentencing his limousine drops him off every day at the Jewish Theological Seminary, where he studies the Talmud.

I have to tell you Pitt doesn't even sound as if he believes this version of the Boesky saga. In fact, it seems clear that Boesky did what he did because that's the only way he could get to the top of his "profession" and stay there.

(And if Pitt doesn't believe that, I know from talking to close friends of Stephen Fraidin that Fraidin now does. Fraidin is Pitt's conscientious young partner, who thought of Boesky not only as his major client but as a close friend. An honest, even idealistic lawyer, Fraidin avidly rebutted all the whispers about Boesky over the years and doggedly accompanied him to SEC investigations throughout the 1980s to help Boesky with his indignant denials of impropriety. Fraidin is a spooked shadow of his former self since Boesky copped his plea.)

In hearings held by the Subcommittee on Oversight and Investigations of the House Energy and Commerce Committee four weeks after Boesky's deal with the SEC was announced, William Anderson, the assistant comptroller general of the United States, who headed a Government Accounting Office team that reviewed securities law enforcement activities for the subcommittee in the wake of the Boesky plea bargain, testified that from 1983 through the first 11 months of 1986, "there were forty-seven investigations [initiated by the New York Stock Exchange] of . . . trading anomalies where the name Boesky turned up."

According to someone who worked in a relatively high position for Boesky during those years, 40-odd different trading positions would "just about equal Ivan's big trades over a four-year period."

In other words, to say that the Levine bribes and the Siegel bribes are isolated instances in an otherwise admirable career seems akin to believing that John Gotti is a sometimes-errant plumbing salesman.

What happened to those 47 investigations? According to Anderson, as of the Boesky plea bargain, 24 of these cases were still in "open" status at the stock exchange but had not been moving forward, presumably for lack of evidence. Of the 23 others, 11 were currently under investigation by the SEC, 4 had been "closed" by the SEC after the SEC had "determined that there was no involvement by Mr. Boesky," and in 8 cases "the SEC took no further action."

"We'd call him down and ask him, and he'd refer to research or rumors or some such thing, and we'd have no proof," says one SEC official. "Without a live witness to say he gave Ivan information, we have nothing."

In fact, this SEC official and one lawyer who has worked for Boesky both say that Boesky gave formal testimony before the commission denying any wrongdoing at least five times from 1982 through 1986, including, the SEC official says, testimony on one deal that he later fingered Siegel for providing him information about.

So that's at least one perjury count and maybe more than five, Judge, that the government passed up.

In this regard, Judge, the SEC's incompetence seems incredible. The posture they assumed through the 1980s as Boesky made a spectacle of himself with his incredibly prescient trades (accompanied by a PR apparatus that included his book, his high-profile charitable contributions, and even a press release providing a puffed-up résumé the day his plea bargain was announced) is that they could do nothing but wait for an informant to materialize in the form of another crook who could be flipped to turn against Boesky. And, of course, that didn't happen until someone wrote an anonymous letter that ended up nailing Levine.

What about sending in undercover people? What about wiretaps? Surely there was probable cause. Surely our prosecutors don't sit on their hands this way waiting for a lucky break when an organized crime boss is thriving this blatantly. Why wait and watch while someone corrupts our markets so publicly?

Let's take one example of a deal on which Boesky made out fabulously that could have provided enough probable cause for a real investigation, and about which Boesky has, according to three sources in a position to know, still not admitted anything.

On the afternoon of November 30, 1984, Textron, Inc., announced a bid for Avco Corporation for $47 a share. According to a 13 D he later filed, Boesky purchased 1,875,100 Avco shares on November 29 and 30 at prices as low as $39.75. A coincidence? Deft application of the science of arbitrage?

What about the incredibly prescient positions Boesky took in Lenox, Inc., before its announced takeover by Brown-Forman Distillers Corporation, or in Gulf Oil when Standard Oil of California made its bid?

The only deals where Boesky appears to have lost out big over the years, according to Bruck's article in *The Atlantic,* were deals in which a bribe arrangement with someone operating in the usual constellation of dealmaker insiders wouldn't have helped. Boesky lost big in the Cities Service offer for Gulf, only when the Federal Trade Commission surprisingly scotched the deal. And he lost in T. Boone Pickens's bid for Phillips Petroleum, only when the unconventional Pickens surprised everyone by canceling that deal. (Boesky recovered handsomely on Phillips when Carl Icahn made a bid for the company after Pickens walked away; during the time when Icahn was deciding on his bid, Icahn met with Boesky twice, according to a deposition Icahn subsequently gave.)

The real point here is simple. Here was an arbitrageur whose success dwarfed all of his competitors' gains, so much so that while he was writing a book to cover his tracks, everyone else suspected that he had to have known more than he should have. And now he's admitting that two people, Levine and Siegel, in a total of at least 11 deals (seven involving Levine bribes, four involving Siegel bribes), did, indeed, tip him off. Is there any reason, then, to believe that he *wasn't* tipped off on most or all of the other deals?

Sure, Boesky worked long hours and engaged in prodigious research. But were the work and the research a cover, or a supplement for instances when his inside information wasn't certain or for rare instances when he didn't have any?

Indeed, is there any reason to believe that it was only later in his career, in the 1980s when he'd already made a fortune, that he started bribing people for information, rather than believe that he must have been bribing people earlier on when he especially needed the money?

And then there's the question of a different sort of illegal stock dealing Boesky seems to have been involved in. I have now spoken with three different chief executives who claim that in 1984, 1985, and 1986, Boesky took significant positions in their stock in concert with other arbitrageurs and, in one case, a prominent corporate raider, whereupon Boesky and his cohorts approached the executive and threatened to put the company "in play" as a takeover target unless the executive bought back their positions at a profit.

These stock positions and buy-backs could be kept secret because no one person, including Boesky, had accumulated more than 5 percent of the stock, the 13-D disclosure threshold. But if Boesky and the others were really acting as a group, their failure to file a 13-D disclosing their combined holdings was a crime.

Another executive, Gulf + Western chairman Martin Davis, has been reported in *The Wall Street Journal* as having complained to the SEC about a similar plot in 1985, in which Boesky approached him concerning positions he and others had taken in Gulf + Western stock.

Says one former SEC official: "We knew Boesky and other guys were ganging up and extorting money. We even knew they were ganging up just to put companies into play and create arbitrage action and action for the raiders, but we couldn't prove it. Frankly, I'm surprised that the SEC didn't make Ivan plead to that. It was,'' he concludes, ''one of the key factors in the dismembering of corporate America that's been going on, and the world ought to know.''

I know, Judge, that on sentencing day you can only consider the specific crime to which Boesky has pled, and that all this is only hearsay. But I'll try below to outline how you can deal fairly with all of this.

III. WHY THE $100 MILLION SETTLEMENT ISN'T A $100 MILLION SETTLEMENT

The SEC's Lynch says ''the $100 million settlement is a fantastic settlement for the government.'' It's not fantastic, and it's far from $100 million.

The $100 million was divided into two parts: $50 million in the form of a fine to the government and $50 million in the form of disgorgement to an escrow agent.

Part of the deal negotiated by Boesky lawyers Levine and Pitt was that the $50 million fine would actually be a transfer of what seemed to be $50 million worth of stocks in two companies that Boesky controlled. But eight months after the settlement's announcement, *The Wall Street Journal* reported that the stock in one of the two companies, a London-based closed-end investment trust called Cambrian & General Securities, p.l.c., had declined to the point where the stock package was worth just $37 million.

And as of mid-November 1987, Cambrian & General shares, which represented more than 90 percent of the value of the two-stock portfolio, had declined further in the London market, so that although the shares in the second company, Northview, had increased in value, the total package was really worth about $30,960,305.

Pitt argues that the stock would have been worth more than $50 million if it had been ''disposed of prudently,'' a point the escrow agent, Douglas Rosenthal of Washington's Sutherland, Asbill & Brennan, rejects strenuously.

Indeed, it should have been no surprise that the Cambrian & General stock would decline in value after Boesky's plea bargain. After all, one of Cambrian & General's major holdings was stock in Boesky's arbitrage partnership—which had to liquidate after his plea bargain. Moreover, because Boesky controlled Cambrian & General, it has had to put aside tens of millions in reserves against the lawsuits from plaintiffs likely to attack this Boesky-controlled fund's trades. "The best test of the stock's value," says one neutral source knowledgeable about it, "is the market-place, not Pitt's or the SEC's assessment."

Now let's look at the disgorgement piece. The statute's purpose in providing for an escrow agent to receive those disgorged funds is to ensure that money will be available to plaintiffs who claim they were injured by Boesky's insider trading. In this case, those plaintiffs, as subsequent civil suits have confirmed, include not just people claiming to have lost money by selling stock that Boesky bought with his inside information, but also investors who invested in a giant Boesky arbitrage partnership that had to be disbanded after Boesky's plea was announced.

The plaintiffs who claim to have lost money in trades have difficult suits; there is not yet much settled law on who, if anyone, can have such a claim against an insider trader. But the plaintiffs who invested in the partnership will almost certainly be entitled to recover. And, according to neutral lawyers familiar with these cases, their damages seem likely to be in the range of the $50 million that's now in the fund. That's the best estimate that can be made, given what information is available about the losses the plaintiffs incurred when Boesky closed shop and sold down his portfolio—in part during an SEC-sanctioned selling spree before his an-nounced plea bargain that itself provoked a storm of criticism.

What's so important about the damages apparently being about equal to the disgorgement fund is that these plaintiffs can get that $50 million from the disgorgement fund rather than from Boesky. In fact, the law allows Boesky to make them take it from the fund before they come after him.

This not-much-publicized element of Boesky's bargain, then, is crucial to his financial well-being.

Had Boesky been forced to pay, say, a $100 million fine and nothing into a disgorgement fund, then his partners-turned-plaintiffs would have had to come after him for their damages. Had the mix been a $75 million fine and $25 million in disgorgement, then they'd have had to come after him for $25 million, assuming, again, that their real damages are $50 million.

In other words, if we assume that Boesky was liable to some plaintiffs, presumably the investing partners, for at least $50 million, then his pay-ment of $50 million into the disgorgement fund cost him nothing beyond what he'd have had to pay those litigants anyway.

This, of course, is why, during the negotiations, Boesky's lawyers convinced the SEC people to have the cash portion of the settlement go to the disgorgement fund and the stock portion go toward the fine. If, as Pitt argues, he and his client really believed that the stock was worth more than $50 million if disposed of "prudently," they would have wanted the stock payment to go toward the disgorgement half of the settlement, where Boesky would benefit at least indirectly from that supposed excess in value beyond $50 million.

Disgorgement funds are meant to be used to compensate people who've lost money when thieves steal from them; they're not necessarily meant to pay back people who lost when they invested in the thief's enterprise and the thief gets caught. Thus, Boesky lawyer Pitt, while not wanting to discuss "all the details of the negotiation," acknowledges that "the ability to have the partnership suits be part of what could be taken from the disgorgement fund was an important element of our bargain with the commission."

Yet Lynch, perhaps because he doesn't understand its significance, dismisses the expanded definition of the disgorgement fund as "unimportant," because "this man is probably going to have no money left when all the suits are finished."

Pitt and his co-counsel, Levine of Wilmer, Cutler, also acknowledge that, in Levine's words, "the ratio of penalty to disgorgement is an important point in any negotiation of this kind, because money paid as a penalty cannot be used to pay claimants." In fact, it's more important in the Boesky case than usual because (a) Boesky, more than any other plea-bargaining insider trader, was certain to attract dozens of suits from stock-buying plaintiffs encouraged by aggressive class action lawyers and (b) because of the unique likelihood in his case of more winnable suits from the investing partners.

Both the SEC and Boesky's lawyers also argue that had Boesky not pled he'd have risked no suits and, therefore, that the plea really did cost him that $50 million paid into the disgorgement fund. But that argument assumes, absurdly, that had Boesky not agreed to a plea, the SEC, despite having gotten Levine's testimony about Boesky's bribes to him, would not have brought an action against him. For it's clear that such an enforcement action and accompanying prosecution would have brought on the civil suits, especially those from the investing partners.

Yet Lynch and prosecutor Giuliani also assert that, in Lynch's words, "it's in no way clear that we could have won anything against Boesky had he not made an agreement with us."

Three points about that. First, it seems impossible that with Levine's testimony stacked up against Boesky's incredibly successful stock buying the lawmen couldn't have proven something to a jury. If not, why would the ever-audacious Boesky and his lawyers have folded?

Second, when the SEC sued, and when Giuliani indicted, Richard Wigton and Timothy Tabor of Kidder, Peabody and Robert Freeman of Goldman, Sachs (in the cases featuring the celebrated trading floor arrests last February), they were doing exactly what they're saying they couldn't have done against Boesky—using one person's testimony, Siegel's, along with a paper trail of successful stock trades to make an insider trading case. And in the cases of those three defendants, which the government has since dropped but vowed to bring again, the trades weren't nearly as one-sidedly successful as Boesky's. Moreover, in Boesky's case there was at least one other witness—Levine's partner in crime, Robert Wilkis—who had also turned state's evidence, who knew about the Boesky arrangement, and who was presumably prepared to testify against Boesky.

Third, and most important, there's a big difference between no bargain at all and the bargain that was struck. This was simply a terrible bargain, and it's highly suggestive of the way Pitt and Levine dominated the negotiations for the government people to suggest that the only alternative to this deal was no deal.

Prosecutor Giuliani also defends the Boesky plea bargain as a way to "show all potential defendants the value of coming in early and admitting your crimes before you get caught." Yet Boesky did not strike his deal with the government until three months after Levine made his own plea bargain in June 1986 and, presumably, began talking about Boesky.

In fact, according to two of Boesky's former employees, Boesky first decided to stonewall the government when initially confronted in July or August by subpoenas and queries related to Levine's charges. He reportedly agreed to a deal in September only after his lawyers convinced him his defense was hopeless. He hardly cooperated "before" he got caught.

Asked about that, Giuliani says, "Your sequence of events is not exactly right. . . . Besides, 'coming in early' and 'getting caught' are relative terms. . . . Boesky didn't get arrested or convicted before he cooperated like some people do, and the process took a lot less time with him than it often does."

The fact remains, though, that Boesky has been investigated and questioned about insider trading for years; he only admitted guilt when Levine fingered him and he knew he had no choice.

IV. HOW THE BARGAIN WENT BAD

A. *The Bargaining Mind-set*

To understand how the deal went bad, we first have to understand that at both the SEC and the U.S. attorney's office there is always a bias in favor of doing a deal rather than doing battle in trial. Deals not only bring sure results fast and save resources, they also bring on other deals—new cases that can generate still more deals. It's a bureaucratic keep-the-action-going bias that can sometimes lead to results in which it's hard to believe the people involved are seeing the forest for the trees. (My favorite prosecutorial deal was the revelation that the FBI had supposedly caught Teamsters president Jackie Presser and tried to turn him into an informant in order to investigate labor corruption: How much higher up can a labor corruption investigation go once it nails the president of the largest union in the world?)

So the SEC and prosecutors wanted a deal, badly.

Second, to people in law enforcement, any kind of guilty plea, especially in a white-collar case, is not only a victory for them but a defeat, indeed, a total disgrace, for the defendant. To lawmen, it's the end of someone's life. People whose lives are devoted to enforcing law don't really understand that to an Ivan Boesky there are guilty pleas and there are guilty pleas.

Third, once the defendant does agree to plead, he becomes almost magically transformed in the eyes of most prosecutors. He's seen the errors of his ways. He's now a member of the prosecution team, a redeemed truth-teller who's helping them go after other bad guys. Here's how Boesky's lawyer Pitt says he articulated his client's situation: "I saw him as a man who's made some mistakes, who came in and confessed his wrongdoing, and who made his peace with his government, after which the government extracted a full and complete settlement and got his full cooperation in cleaning up the industry."

Fourth, for the law enforcement people, there's always the specific vision of higher-ups to be nailed that a smart defendant can exploit. And the more momentum and publicity an investigation is gathering, the more enticing and believable that vision becomes.

In all of these respects, the Boesky case was almost destined to become a bad bargain, especially in the hands, as it was, of a weak group of bargainers at the SEC.

B. Doing the Deal

Indeed, it seems that the performance by the SEC, which has pulled the lead oar in the insider trading cases, was worse than the U.S. attorney's. For the problem is not so much that Boesky is only going to go to jail for a year or two or three but that he's going to get to keep a life's work of ill-gotten gains that he accumulated as he became a perverse symbol of sorts of the Roaring Eighties.

Led by Lynch—who had been unable to make much headway in insider trading enforcement, or much of any other enforcement, until someone wrote an anonymous letter that led to Dennis Levine—the enforcement division, it seems, got badly outsmarted by Boesky lawyers Pitt and Levine. (Pitt is a former SEC general counsel, Levine a former associate director of enforcement during the halcyon days of the enforcement division under Stanley Sporkin.)

The first aspect of Pitt and Levine's strategy was to keep things moving fast. From the beginning they tempted the commission and the prosecutors with offers to begin taping Boesky's enormous circle of dealmaking friends and associates as soon as a deal was concluded.

Such was the government's anxiousness to flip Boesky and move on to others that by most accounts the negotiations with Boesky and his lawyers began on approximately September 4, 1986, and concluded with a deal on September 18.

Speed helped Boesky's lawyers because, to put it simply, they were smarter than the other side.

For example, let's go back to Lynch's clearly nonsensical statement about Boesky not having any money left after all the suits against him are litigated. According to four people familiar with the Boesky-SEC negotiations, at no time did the SEC ask for any specific full list of Boesky's assets, nor was one furnished. This despite the fact that one rationale Boesky's lawyers offered for giving the SEC the stock as payment for the $50 million penalty was that their client lacked enough liquid assets to pay the fine in cash.

Whenever someone on the other side argued that the $50 million penalty was too low or that the SEC's setting the profit at just $50 million had been a concession, Levine and Pitt argued blithely that with all the suits to come from this negotiated deal, Boesky would be wiped out anyway. According to two sources, the two Boesky lawyers presented themselves as knowing far more about the prospects of such civil suits than the federal government lawyers could ever know, and they argued that the very idea that Boesky would end up with any money was absurd.

"The question about what his assets really were was deflected [by Boesky's lawyers] whenever it came up," says a lawyer familiar with the negotiations. "They waved it away. They convinced everyone that it just didn't matter because all his assets would be gone."

Levine's pitch today is much the same. "You're kidding yourself if you think he'll be a rich man after all of this," Levine says. "There's really not much question about that." Does Levine know specifically what Boesky's assets are? "I think I have an idea, but, no, that's not something I've gotten into," he says. Does he know what Boesky's wife's assets are, or what's in the trust funds set up by Boesky for his children? "That's just not something we've gotten into," he says.

Levine is now handling Boesky's defense of the civil suits in a spirited way that, of course, contrasts sharply with the notion that Boesky ought to be, or will be, wiped out by his civil liability.

At the SEC Lynch seems almost not to understand the question. "We did have access to all of his tax returns," he notes, "and that gave us a pretty good idea of what he was worth." Even an honest man's tax return reveals little about his assets; and a tax return from Boesky—whose wealth is tangled in partnerships, partnerships of partnerships, corporations, and trusts, and who paid Siegel off in briefcases full of $700,000 in cash and had promised Levine $2.4 million in cash—is bound to be still less edifying.

"We didn't go back and forth like this was a labor negotiation with me presenting one number [for a number of guilty-plea counts or a monetary penalty] and them presenting another," says Pitt. "What I tried to do was fashion a package that I knew would have what they needed, and we pretty much worked from that package."

Indeed, what seems to have happened is that Pitt, with Levine's help, controlled the entire flow of the negotiation. He framed the issues. He framed the solutions.

What Pitt figured the government needed was a civil settlement of unprecedented value, and he offered it: $100 million. But he offered it in a way that helped his client—with a full $50 million going for disgorgement and with investor suits counting in the disgorgement fund, a point that, according to several people who claim to know, was barely acknowledged by the government as even being a deal point.

What Pitt knew the government needed was a sense of whom Boesky might be able to finger—and he offered it: with Kidder, Peabody and Drexel Burnham among the entities enticingly but vaguely named, along with the promise that Boesky would allow his phones to be tapped so that the government could hear him as he dialed everyone he routinely dealt with as soon as the ink was dry on the deal.

It was also apparent to Pitt that the government was frustrated at not having broken into the truly big leagues with its investigation by getting an investment bank and that the SEC would love a way to use Boesky's plea to threaten some top bank into submission. So he offered that, too: by suggesting that Boesky's plea not be to an insider trading count involving Levine—after all, Levine no longer needed scaring—but rather to a scheme, at that point unnamed, involving one of the target investment banks, such as the coveted Drexel Burnham.

As one government official privy to the negotiations but disillusioned by what ultimately happened puts it, "By not naming the crime Ivan was going to plead to [when the deal was announced], by then leaking the fact that Boesky had been wired from the time [Boesky] made the deal to when it was announced"—among some in the press corps Lynch is a widely acknowledged leader—"and by having Rudy [Giuliani] say at a press conference [after the plea] that the Boesky deal illustrated the benefits of turning yourself in early, we were setting up a perfect system of intimidation."

Thus, when the Boesky deal was announced, all that was said was that he had agreed to plead guilty to one felony count related to stock trading. His actual plea was delayed for nearly six months so that he could then tell the government about a stock-parking scheme allegedly involving Drexel Burnham, and, happily for him, so that he could plead in front of the Southern District's most lenient judge—you.

As you well know, Judge, the Boesky plea came at a time when the Southern District's prosecutors, in a practice since eliminated, allowed plea-bargaining defendants six weeks from the time they agree to a plea bargain to enter their pleas in court. This six-week "window," as it was called, gave them the choice of three judges to be their sentencing judge. (Judges preside over plea bargaining for periods of two weeks each during each year.) You were not among the three who could have taken a plea during that six-week period following the November 14 deal. In fact, according to your secretary, the only time in the entire year from November 1986 on that you were the judge taking pleas was in April of 1987, when you took Boesky's plea. In effect, then, Boesky got his choice not just of the apparent best of three judges, but of the best of all the judges in the Southern District.

Moreover, Boesky got to plead to a particular kind of stock trading

174

felony—filing a false 13-D—whose seriousness under parole guidelines is probably lower than would be a plea to insider trading. This might allow him to get out of prison earlier than if he'd pled to insider trading. It also allowed him to help the government still more in its public pressure campaign against Drexel.

In addition, by not pleading to an insider trading count, Boesky was not admitting anything that could hurt him in a civil suit. (His SEC consent decree, like all consent decrees, was neither an admission nor a denial of the insider trading deal with Levine that the SEC complaint outlined.) This doesn't shield Boesky from the civil suits, but it does make it harder for plaintiffs' lawyers to pin charges against him, especially if Boesky, himself, never has to testify in a trial, either because the people he fingers for the government don't get indicted or because they, too, plea bargain and avoid trials at which he would have to testify.

"Let's just call his plea before Lasker [to a 13-D violation] one of those happy situations where both sides were accommodated," explains one lawyer involved in the negotiation.

Finally, there's another question about Boesky's bargain: Has he really told all he knows, as promised? Thus far, his information has nailed Siegel for providing insider tips and Boyd Jefferies, former chairman of Jefferies & Company, Inc., for engaging in a parking scheme. And from all the leaks, it's clear that he has partly implicated Drexel in another alleged parking scheme (the one allegedly involved in his guilty plea to the 13-D violation), though apparently not strongly enough yet for an indictment against Drexel to be brought.

But according to three people in positions to know, Boesky has not provided any more information about insider trading, despite the fact that the circumstantial evidence in trades such as the one involving Textron's Avco deal is overwhelming, and despite the fact that his account of his bribing of Siegel as lasting just until 1984 conveniently eliminates the possibility that he got help from Siegel on several major trading coups he scored in 1985 and 1986 (such as GAF's bid for Union Carbide), even though Siegel was a key player in those deals.

Could Boesky be holding back about more deals with Siegel, or, more important, about other deals with other bankers or lawyers—either because he's been paid off to keep quiet, or because he's trying to avoid more civil suits that would come from more insider trading revelations? Could he be holding back because he knows that potential defendants such as Drexel have hired hordes of private investigators to gather dirt on his notorious personal life and on the rumors, thus far unsubstantiated, that through friends such as Houshang Wekili, a mysterious Iranian who has long been his closest confidant, he's hiding still more wealth? (Wekili could not be reached for comment.)

One reason I raise this possibility, Judge, is because I'm told by two people who should know (those directly involved won't comment) that Boesky's debriefing by the SEC was sloppy.

Again, because Pitt and/or Levine seemed to control the flow of the discussions, there was never a thorough review of all the trades Ivan Boesky had ever done, with specific questions asked about how and why he had done what he'd done and who, if anyone, had helped him. Dominated by superior lawyers, the SEC people and the federal prosecutors simply lost sight of the fact that they had the Willie Sutton of stock traders in front of them. They debriefed him more on the basis of his limited agenda than on the broader picture of his entire career.

It wasn't that Pitt or Levine counseled Boesky not to be candid, even forthcoming; it's just that they made it so that for the most part he controlled the conversation.

As I'll suggest below, you can change that.

V. BOESKY'S CURRENT ASSETS

The man standing in front of you for sentencing will be worth, counting his wife's and children's assets, over $300 million. And because much of it is not under his legal control, it won't be susceptible to recovery in the civil suits pending against him, assuming those suits will absorb the $50 million disgorgement fund.

A real estate agent reports that Boesky's holdings in the Bedford area of northern Westchester are worth $15 million to $20 million. But much of that, as well as his 52-percent share of the stock in the company that recently sold the Beverly Hills Hotel for $140 million, is reportedly in his wife's name. Soon after his plea bargain was announced, Boesky and his wife filed for divorce. That would allow those assets to be shielded from the civil suits. The divorce is seen even by Boesky's remaining friends as suspiciously convenient.

Beyond that there are the trusts for each of Boesky's four children. There are 13 trusts in all, nine of which feature Ivan Boesky as the trustee. One lawyer who claims to be familiar with the family's finances says the trusts are worth a total of $65 million.

The same lawyer says Boesky himself has assets worth approximately $195 million from the 1986 liquidation of his key arbitrage trading vehicle, plus some $35 million in bank accounts and other assets in Europe.

VI. WHAT YOU CAN DO ON SENTENCING DAY

Yes, Boesky has already pled guilty, and you've accepted the plea. You can't change that, and you can't order the government to bring new charges. You're a judge, not a prosecutor. But here's a choice of what you can do:

A. *Delay Sentencing Pending a Report from the Government and from a Special Master*

While you can't change the plea, you don't have to pronounce a sentence when the government asks you to. Instead, when the prosecutors finally bring Boesky before you, you can put a hold on the sentence pending more information.

For starters, you can question the bargain in the context of questioning the government's sentencing memo and the defense's predictable brief for leniency. You can say that you're withholding the sentence pending a full, new investigation by the government of every major Boesky arbitrage trade, as well as a full report of all his assets in the United States and abroad. Tell the prosecutors you want them to get all the facts so that the full dimensions and meaning of this deal can be known and acknowledged by everyone before you close the books on it.

At the same time, you can appoint a special master with a law enforcement background to render a report, or even ask for a special grand jury to investigate and render such a report. In either case the subject matter would be an exploration of Boesky's activities and conduct as the backdrop for a review of alternatives to the government's using as its only investigative strategy the passive one of waiting for someone to get named by an informant, who, like Boesky, they can then flip in order to catch someone else. In this way, you can, and should, raise the question of whether this method and rationale—which always makes sense case by case—doesn't often get carried too far, too unthinkingly, as it has been here, in a way that contradicts the very idea of deterrence by sending the message that a white-collar criminal who gets caught can always reduce his punishment to a triviality by turning the searchlight on someone else.

B. "Sell" Boesky a Light Sentence

Under the law, the most you can fine Boesky is $250,000. And, again, the most time you can give him is five years. You should certainly do that. Yet even that sentence will probably become about 20 months if the parole board applies its guidelines in a way (which you can be sure Boesky's battery of lawyers will press on them) that minimizes the money amount seemingly involved in the crime to which Boesky pled.

But you might be able to influence the way the parole board will apply its guidelines by stating explicitly from the bench that you see Boesky's parking scheme, to which he pled guilty in the 13-D violation, as a conspiracy. Under the parole guidelines that would mean that his five-year sentence will only be reduced to 40 months, or three years and four months.

With the possibility of three years and four months as leverage, you could then tell Boesky that if he makes "restitution" to a public fund— say, for the homeless—of all but, say, a million dollars of his and his family's wealth you will sentence him only to one year, meaning he'd be out in about eight months.

You should allow him to keep a million dollars or so because you have to allow some credit for his wife's inheritance. But you needn't allow too much, since that money seems to have been mixed in with his funds and parlayed in his insider trades. (As for how you can get Boesky to break open the trusts established for his children, what you would probably have to do is get him and the government to agree to void the part of his deal that protected the trusts, then have the government seize the funds as an additional penalty.)

Of course, you can't force this money deal on Boesky because that would be a fine exceeding the limits of the statute. Instead, you'd have to get him and his lawyers to agree to it, and perhaps even initiate it, because he wants to avoid 40 months in prison.

Beyond that there's also the problem of piercing the veil, assuming it is a veil, of his divorce to get at more of his wife's assets.

But if there's any way you can do all or some of this, you should. Stripping Boesky of all but a tiny fraction of his wealth and endowing $200 million or $300 million to a charity would do much to redeem his prosecution and his plea bargain.

C. Urge the Manhattan District Attorney to Investigate Boesky's Crimes

As an alternative, you could try to exact more of a criminal penalty from Boesky by looking a few blocks north to the Manhattan district attorney's office.

By custom, a federal plea bargain precludes local prosecutors from going after people for crimes that are similar to or related to those subject to the plea bargain. But all that the double jeopardy law actually precludes is prosecution for the same crime that has actually been pled to in the plea bargain. Thus, Manhattan District Attorney Robert Morgenthau could only be prevented from prosecuting Boesky for filing a phony 13-D, and that's not a violation of state law anyway.

Morgenthau is said by a top official in his office to be contemplating investigating Boesky for crimes such as commercial bribery. (That's what Boesky did with Levine.) He might also look at whether Boesky committed perjury in Manhattan during any of those old SEC investigations.

But for now, Morgenthau is being held up because the federal law enforcement people are keeping all the witnesses from him, claiming that a local case would interfere with their cases.

You should consider giving the D.A. a road map and encouragement and helping to clear the way for his investigation to proceed by ruling that, if asked, the federal prosecutors cannot withhold witnesses from Morgenthau beyond a specific deadline.

Perhaps at the same time, you could encourage Morgenthau to offer Boesky the $300 million–plus plea bargain outlined above; he might buy it, given that the state prisons are so much worse than federal facilities.

No matter what you do, Judge, you should speak out. You especially should speak out, because as one of the most respected judges in New York and as the man widely regarded as the most lenient, your voice against this one-sided plea bargain will carry special weight.

Until Ivan Boesky found arbitrage, he was a failure, a frustrated grade-C lawyer and stock trader unable to pay the rent without his wealthy father-in-law's help. Only his life of insider trading gave him great wealth.

So, if you let this plea bargain go through unchallenged, Boesky will have parlayed a life of crime into vast riches for himself and his heirs in return for a year or two in a low-security federal prison. He'll have netted $300 million for 20 to 40 months in prison—$7.5 million to $15 million per prison month. That will have been his upside gain and his downside risk. The man who has been the symbol of the garish corruption of the get-rich-quick Roaring Eighties will now embody a classic Roaring Eighties bargain—a bit of prison for hundreds of millions in cash.

It's a bargain that stands the idea of deterrence and retribution on its head. It's not a bargain that any prosecutor—or any judge—should want to make.

EPILOGUE

On December 18, 1987, U.S. District Judge Morris Lasker sentenced Ivan Boesky to three years in prison. Two months later, the Wall Street speculator John Mulheren was arrested on charges of threatening to kill Boesky and other witnesses against Mulheren in a government securities investigation.

At Lasker's suggestion, Boesky was assigned to the minimum-security federal prison in Lompoc, California, where he began serving his term on March 24, 1988. With time off for good behavior in prison, as well as prison furloughs, Boesky was scheduled to be released in March 1990 after serving two years.

On September 7, 1988, the Securities and Exchange Commission filed a long-awaited civil complaint against the Wall Street investment firm Drexel Burnham Lambert Inc., charging the company with insider trading, stock manipulation, fraud, and other securities law violations. The complaint also named Drexel senior vice-president Michael Milken, who heads the junk bond department, two other Drexel employees, and two Drexel clients. Of the 18 deals cited in the complaint, 16 are alleged to have hinged on Boesky. "Boesky is a central figure in the [alleged] scheme," says Thomas Newkirk, chief litigation counsel at the SEC.

Three months later, in December 1988, Drexel pleaded guilty to six counts of mail and securities fraud. As part of the deal with the government, Drexel agreed to pay $650 million in fines and to fire Milken, who was waiting trial at publication time.

Dennis Levine served 14 months of his two-year sentence in federal prison in Lewisburg, Pennsylvania, and was released in July 1988. At publication time, Martin Siegel had not yet been sentenced.

U.S.
v.
Beech-Nut

BRENDAN SULLIVAN BOMBS IN BROOKLYN

BY
TIM O'BRIEN

Jurors in the Beech-Nut apple-juice case found the company's former president guilty—and its renowned lawyer overbearing.

"You know who that is?" asks an excited Frank Livorsi as he steps into the jury room. "That's Ollie North's lawyer!"

The jury room adjacent to federal district judge Thomas Platt's courtroom in Brooklyn is abuzz. "Big time!" jokes one juror. Another shakes her head and says, smiling, "Oh, my goodness."

Juror Livorsi, 28, a New York City subway motorman, has just recognized Brendan Sullivan, Jr., of Washington, D.C.'s Williams & Connolly, whose combative "I am not a potted plant" defense of retired Marine Lieutenant Colonel Oliver North in the Iran-contra hearings had put him on national television.

It is November 16, 1987, day one of the fake-apple-juice fraud trial of the two top executives of Beech-Nut Nutrition Corporation. The trim, bespectacled Sullivan, 42, protégé of Edward Bennett Williams, is sitting coolly at the defense table, surrounded by a formidable Williams & Connolly team. Next to Sullivan sits partner Barry Simon, his colleague in the ongoing North case.

Sullivan and Simon have, in tandem, gained a reputation for torpedoing prosecution cases. In a 1987 tax evasion case against the president of Omni International Corporation, they won a dismissal by convincing the judge that federal agents had back-dated documents. And in defending executives of GTE Corporation on allegations of illegally obtaining classified Pentagon documents, the pair convinced another judge to admit classified documents, thus forcing the government to drop the charges. One Williams & Connolly associate told *The New York Times* in 1987, "First [Sullivan and Simon] go over the ground with a fine-tooth comb. Then they scorch it."

But now, after months of voluminous motion practice, they are trying a case that has reached a jury, and they face trouble.

Sullivan and Simon are in Brooklyn representing former Beech-Nut president and chief executive officer Niels Hoyvald, 54. Co-defendant John Lavery, 56, former vice president for operations, is represented by Steven Kimelman, a former assistant U.S. attorney who headed the fraud squad in the Eastern District of New York, where the Beech-Nut case is being tried. Kimelman now has his own two-lawyer firm in New York.

Hoyvald and Lavery face 450 counts of conspiracy, mail fraud, and violations of the Food, Drug and Cosmetic Act. They are accused of selling, from late 1981 through March 1983, millions of jars labeled "100 percent pure apple juice—no sugar added" that contained little or no apple and were nearly 100 percent sugar. The consumers of the fake apple juice, as the prosecution will often remind the 18 jurors and alternates, were babies.

"A classic case of big corporate greed," is the way prosecutor Thomas Roche characterizes Beech-Nut's apple-juice maneuver, which he attributes to a corporate decision to save money by buying phony apple concentrate at 20 to 25 percent less than the real thing.

The government team is solid: career prosecutor Roche, 44, who as executive assistant ranks third in the Brooklyn office of U.S. Attorney Andrew Maloney; John Fleder, 41, director of the Justice Department's Office of Consumer Litigation; and Kenneth Jost, 38, a veteran federal trial attorney in Fleder's office.

Roche, who also heads the financial crime section in Maloney's office, has prosecuted several major multi-defendant drug and white-collar cases. Fleder has supervised big cases against the Reader's Digest Association, Inc., Eli Lilly and Company, and Smith Kline Beckman Corporation.

But it is Sullivan who gets the jurors' attention. Juror Salvatore De-Blasi of Queens, a retired claims officer with the New York State workers' compensation board, recalls being impressed by Sullivan's association with North. "Ollie North is more of a hero than a villain to me," says DeBlasi, an ardent conservative who calls former President Richard Nixon "a saint."

Yet by trial's end last February, any goodwill that may have flowed from Sullivan's relationship to North was spent. Asked about Sullivan today, DeBlasi sneers, "He used every trick in the book. . . . From his opening, his thing was, how can I deceive the jury?"

In interviews with ten of the eighteen jurors and alternates, Sullivan received some praise for his courtroom skills—skills employed in a tough case that would have challenged any lawyer. But the words most often used by the jurors to describe the combative litigator, and to a lesser extent his sidekick Simon—neither of whom agreed to comment for publication—are enough to indict hard-nosed tactics in front of a jury and to make Ollie North a little wary when and if his case comes to trial: "Tricky." "Nasty." "Sneaky." "Too polished." "An artist." "An actor."

Those jurors who were the harshest critics of the Williams & Connolly scorched-earth tactics became the strongest advocates of the government position during deliberations—deliberations that ended with guilty verdicts and jail sentences for Sullivan's client and his co-defendant. One Williams & Connolly lawyer says it is the first time since 1973 that a Sullivan client has drawn a jail sentence.

Sullivan's and Simon's zeal also rankled Judge Platt, who sparred with them daily and who ruled against them on most points. "Maybe I better get a tape and play my rulings over and over until you understand them," the judge snapped at Simon during one sidebar conference. At another point, trying to stifle Sullivan's insistence on arguing a point long since decided in favor of the government, Platt snarled, "Do you think I am a congressional committee?"

In fairness to the Beech-Nut defense team, Platt is viewed as pro-government by litigators on both sides. Nevertheless, the judge was consistently harsher toward Sullivan and Simon than toward Lavery's attorney, Kimelman.

The Sullivan-Platt skirmishes were usually outside the presence of the jury, but not always. After Sullivan insisted on referring to a former Beech-Nut outside counsel as an expert because he specialized in Food and Drug Administration matters, Platt took to correcting Sullivan before the jury, saying, "so-called expert." Platt once admonished a key Sullivan witness for trying to "sneak" in testimony on direct examination that had been ruled inadmissible. Several jurors say they were left with a feeling that Hoyvald's lawyers were trying to dupe them by breaking the rules.

Perhaps a potted plant would have been better.

WHERE ARE THE APPLES?

Andrew Rosenzweig was crawling around in a Dumpster in the Woodside section of Queens, New York, on a hot June night in 1982. Flashlight in hand, the private investigator was searching through mounds of paper looking for vouchers, anything that had the word *apple* on it. He had been staking out Food Complex Company, an apple concentrate manufacturing plant, for days, but he had yet to see any apples going into the place.

Rosenzweig was in the employ of Processed Apples Institute, Inc., a trade association whose members make products from apples, including the concentrates that become apple juice when mixed with water. PAI suspected widespread adulteration in the apple-juice industry.

One day late in June Rosenzweig followed a tanker truck as it pulled out of the yard. Hours later it rolled into Beech-Nut's plant in Canajoharie, New York, near Albany. The following day, June 25, 1982, Rosenzweig walked into the plant and confronted operations chief Lavery with the information that there was a problem with a Beech-Nut supplier.

"Universal is the one," Lavery blurted out. Universal Juice Company was then buying concentrate from Food Complex and reselling it, via a broker, to Beech-Nut. "There have been reasons that we've had to question their product," Lavery said.

Rosenzweig then told Lavery he had documentary proof that the concentrate was bogus. He asked Lavery for samples and urged Beech-Nut to join PAI in a suit against Universal and Food Complex.

What he didn't tell Lavery was that he was wearing a hidden body mike and taping the conversation, which was played for the jury this winter.

That was the beginning of the end of Beech-Nut's fake-juice caper.

As the PAI filed suit—which Beech-Nut declined to join—the FDA and New York State inspectors began asking questions of their own. The government charged that Universal and Food Complex were part of a bogus concentrate network that was grossing millions of dollars annually, with Beech-Nut by far its biggest customer. (The companies are now out of business, and their owners have either pled guilty or are awaiting trial.) And, thanks to a voluminous paper trail and information from more than a dozen Beech-Nut insiders, the government charged Beech-Nut and its two top corporate officers with fraud.

A "SMOKING GUN"

From the start, the case was a tough one for the defense. Documents produced in discovery made it clear that for three and a half years before Rosenzweig made his appearance in Lavery's Canajoharie office, the vice president had been receiving warnings about the concentrate—memos from his research and development director, Jerome LiCari, as well as reports of lab tests that labeled Universal's concentrate as nothing more than cane sugar, corn syrup, and assorted acids.

Those lab results had led LiCari to dispatch company scientists to check out the blending facilities at Food Complex's Queens plant as early as 1978. All they were allowed to see was a warehouse full of drums marked "Israel." (Food Complex claimed to be importing apples from Israel.) The visit heightened suspicions in Beech-Nut's research department, yet Lavery continued to buy from Universal.

Lavery's counsel, Kimelman, argued that his client could not have dropped Universal without absolute proof that would hold up in court that the product was adulterated. According to LiCari and other witnesses from Beech-Nut called by both sides, there was no foolproof method to distinguish between real and fake juice concentrate. Universal's product did look, smell, and taste like real apple juice.

But in an August 5, 1981, memo sent to Lavery that prosecutor Roche dubbed the "smoking gun," then–research director LiCari warned of the "tremendous amount of circumstantial evidence that suggests" that Universal's concentrate was fake. "It does paint a grave case against the current supplier," LiCari wrote. Lavery refused to meet with LiCari to discuss these findings and continued to buy the cheap Universal concentrate.

Kimelman and Sullivan both argued that Beech-Nut was victimized by Universal. They presented a theory of separate conspiracies, saying that Universal was conspiring to defraud Beech-Nut and therefore Beech-Nut and the suppliers could not have been engaged in a single conspiracy as charged in the indictment. Had the jury agreed with that position, Kimelman explains, it would have had to acquit Hoyvald and Lavery on the conspiracy count.

The jurors, however, say they spent little time agonizing over conspiracy theory. Several say they simply believed government witness Raymond Wells, the Food Complex owner, who testified that Beech-Nut understood full well it was paying 25 percent under market price for concentrate because it was getting sugar and malic acid.

"[Hoyvald and Lavery] knew why they were getting it cheap. Business is business," says juror Livorsi.

FAKING OUT THE FDA

For Sullivan and his client, Hoyvald, the June 25, 1982, date was crucial. Hoyvald had joined Beech-Nut in 1980, a year after its purchase by the Switzerland-based food giant Nestlé S.A., and had become president in April 1981. Unlike Lavery, Hoyvald could—and did—claim that until Rosenzweig's visit he knew nothing about the concentrate problem, even though products with apple concentrate constituted 30 percent of sales.

Unfortunately for Sullivan, the prosecution had assembled a formidable case that for nine months after June 25, 1982, Hoyvald knowingly continued to sell what one government witness called a "chemical cocktail." Documents and trial testimony from more than a dozen Beech-Nut employees established that, as inspectors from the FDA and the New York State Department of Agriculture and Markets began to test samples and interview company officials, Hoyvald and Lavery ordered employees and attorneys to delay, stall, and obfuscate—in prosecutor Roche's words, to "fake out the FDA." Meanwhile they hid the bogus juice, dumped it on overseas markets, destroyed it before inspectors could seize it, and sold it wherever they could before they finally agreed to a limited FDA recall.

Three incidents, spelled out in testimony and memos, were particularly convincing to the jury. The first was dubbed "the midnight move" by prosecutors Roche, Fleder, and Jost; juror DeBlasi recalls it as "the Warner Brothers movie without Humphrey Bogart." On August 11, 1982, after a state inspector visited the Canajoharie plant and said he would return to seize one lot of apple juice for testing, Hoyvald ordered Beech-Nut's transport firm to send nine trucks to the plant in the dead of night. Some 26,000 cases of juice were hauled away and stashed in a Secaucus, New Jersey, warehouse.

Four days later, Hoyvald okayed a "special offer" to Beech-Nut's Puerto Rican distributor, telling the distributor the company was "closing down stocks held at our public warehouse in New Jersey." Two weeks later a second telex offered the distributor in San Juan 16,000 cases of juice from the Secaucus warehouse, promising a big discount and extended credit terms to "move the merchandise fairly rapidly." Undaunted by the distributor's refusal, Hoyvald shipped the phony juice anyway; some of it wound up in the San Juan city dump. (Roche charged at trial that company officials feared the cases could be seized by FDA inspectors in Puerto Rico.)

Says juror Anne DiStefano, a dental assistant from Long Island, of the Puerto Rican deal: "That convicted both of them. The deal they were willing to give [the distributor] was outrageous. It was the straw that broke the camel's back."

Finally, in mid-September 1982, as inspectors were closing in to seize juice for a recall, Beech-Nut hurriedly shipped to the Dominican Republic another 20,000 to 25,000 cases of apple juice. The juice was in Beech-Nut's San Jose, California, plant and had just been red-flagged by the FDA as phony. When no ship could be booked immediately in California, Hoyvald and Lavery ordered the cases trucked to Galveston, Texas, where a ship was available.

"The Dominican Republic deal was a dead giveaway . . . pure fraud. . . . I know what the shipping costs involved must have been," says juror DeBlasi, explaining that his first job was as a civilian analyst in the army's transportation corps.

ADVICE OF COUNSEL: THE LAWYERS MADE ME DO IT

To counter the government's case Sullivan devised an advice-of-counsel defense that attempted to shift responsibility from Hoyvald to two Washington, D.C., law firms that Beech-Nut had consulted. The essence of this defense: the lawyers made me do it.

In a case characterized by bad judgment on the Beech-Nut side, beginning with the company's decision to play hardball with the FDA, the advice-of-counsel defense may have been the worst mistake of all.

"A lot of crap," was one juror's assessment of the advice-of-counsel ploy. Another juror, Robin Marcus, a 32-year-old telecommunications analyst from Brooklyn who was excused for personal reasons about three weeks before deliberations, is equally vehement if less blunt: "If a lawyer gives that kind of advice, they should be disbarred," says Marcus. "It's illegal advice. If it's a legitimate defense, then the lawyers should be here on trial."

Sullivan's advice-of-counsel strategy began to unravel on January 20, when he was about to call the man he had identified in his opening statement as the central figure in Hoyvald's defense.

"When people ask what is proper and lawful, they can rely upon a lawyer to tell them what is proper and lawful and reasonable," Sullivan said in his opening. "That's what Mr. Hoyvald did. The minute he learned about the June twenty-fifth incident [he called] in the lawyers. Virtually immediately. He reached out to a lawyer in the law firm in Washington, D.C., headed by Thomas Ward . . . a man who had represented the giant mother company, Nestlé. A man whose advice was respected, a man who a layman could rely upon when trying to understand the tangled webs of rules and regulations."

As Ward, senior partner in six-lawyer Ward, Lazarus & Grow, waited to take the stand, prosecutor Roche told Judge Platt in a sidebar conference that he intended to cross-examine Ward, on credibility grounds, on his "bad conduct . . . as an attorney," particularly his role in the ongoing fraud case involving London-based Arthur Guinness & Sons, PLC, the biggest securities probe in British history.

Sullivan and Simon argued vehemently that such questions should be off-limits because Ward has not been convicted. "If his honesty is up for grabs, he is entitled to be cross-examined," said the judge.

Roche handed Platt a file on Ward, which the judge began referring to as the "list of horrors." On the list was not only Ward's central role in the Guinness insider trading scandal, but also his involvement in the fight against the 1981 boycott of Nestlé products triggered by the World Health Organization's denunciation of Nestlé's promotion of infant formula in the Third World.

As counsel to Nestlé, Ward had allegedly disseminated a study supporting Nestlé without revealing that the Ethics and Public Policy Center, which produced the study, had been given a $25,000 grant by Nestlé. The connection became public when Ernest Lefever, the head of the center, became President Reagan's nominee for assistant secretary of state for human rights and humanitarian affairs. During his confirmation hearing, Lefever conceded that his center had accepted the money from Nestlé, although he insisted that the center's support of Nestlé's position was unrelated to the grant.

But it was Ward's alleged involvement in the Guinness case that was Sullivan's biggest problem. In fact, the same day as the sidebar, Justice Department lawyers in Washington, D.C., acting on a request from the British Crown Prosecution Service via the State Department, were winning permission from a federal judge to begin gathering evidence in the Guinness case. Court papers subsequently filed by Justice list Ward's alleged role in the insider trading scheme as one subject of the probe.

Ward, 49, is a key suspect in the Guinness scandal, which stems from the successful $4 billion takeover in 1986 of Scottish whiskey maker Distillers Company by Guinness. Ward, who was a Guinness director, officer, and company counsel, is the subject of a British arrest warrant charging him with theft, false accounting, and related securities violations. He is accused, along with others—including former Guinness chairman Ernest Saunders, who as an officer of Nestlé in 1980 hired Hoyvald for his Beech-Nut job—of manipulating the price of Guinness stock to help the company outbid a rival suitor in the bitter battle to take over Distillers. (Ward did not return phone calls.)

At the Beech-Nut trial, Simon, citing recent case law, seemed to convince Judge Platt to bar the government from cross-examining Ward on the Guinness case. Platt ruled that because Ward had declared that he would invoke his Fifth Amendment privilege, questioning him about Guinness would only serve to prejudice the defendants. Later, however, the judge suggested he might allow cross-examination of Ward if the government was willing to risk a reversal on appeal. "The judge was unclear, and so calling Ward was a risk," says one defense lawyer.

Sullivan, apparently mindful of Ward's credibility problems, did not call him.

"PEE-WEE HERMAN"

Without Ward, Sullivan had to rely on attorney Sheldon Klein to make his case about the legal advice provided to Hoyvald in 1982. Klein, 32, who is now of counsel to Ward, Lazarus, described himself as "the junior associate" of the firm in 1982.

Dubbed "Pee-wee Herman" in the government camp because of his slicked-back hair and youthful appearance, Klein proved to be a disaster for the defense. Even his looks counted against him. In interviews after the trial, several jurors mentioned his youth and rejected the notion that, at the age of 25, he had advised Beech-Nut on a major crisis.

On direct examination, Klein impressed the jury as being too eager to help Hoyvald and Lavery. Once, after Klein described Hoyvald as having been upset by an FDA action, Judge Platt ordered him not to "characterize [Hoyvald's] state of mind." Undeterred, Klein responded, "May I characterize his tone of voice?"

During Klein's direct examination, Sullivan tried unsuccessfully to have admitted into evidence three thick bound volumes containing Ward, Lazarus's entire Beech-Nut file from 1982 and 1983. Sullivan and Simon had come to court with copies of the volumes for each juror, as well as 50 charts detailing Ward, Lazarus memos, time sheets, and telexes. Over strenuous objections from the Williams & Connolly team, Platt ruled that both the books and the charts were hearsay and therefore not admissible.

Sullivan then guided Klein through the file as the witness sat on the stand with a book in his lap.

The objective seemed to be to overwhelm the jury with the sheer volume of paper generated between client and lawyer, including dozens of time sheets that Sullivan asked Klein to read. But, again, it backfired.

"How much coaxing did he get, with that book? . . . Lawyers are very shrewd. They can manipulate. They had time to put together that book," says juror Napoleon Cockern, a Long Island engineer. (Cockern began deliberations but became ill and was excused, leaving 11 to reach a verdict.)

On cross-examination prosecutor Fleder devastated Klein and the advice-of-counsel defense. Fleder made the most of a December 17, 1982, report from Ward to Hoyvald in which Ward says, "We had two main objectives . . . to minimize Beech-Nut's potential economic loss . . . conservatively estimated at $3.5 million, and to minimize any damage to the company's reputation." The way to do this, Ward advised, was "by delaying, for as long as possible, any market withdrawal of products produced from . . . Universal Juice concentrate." Ward bragged in the letter that Beech-Nut had been successful in preventing the FDA from recalling mixed fruit juices even though those juices "constituted the bulk of the products produced with Universal concentrate. . . . One of our main goals became to prevent the FDA . . . from focusing on those products, and we were in fact successful in limiting the controversy strictly to apple juice."

Juror Marcus says the Ward report convinced her that Hoyvald "was calling the lawyers to see how much he could get away with."

Fleder also confronted Klein with Hoyvald's November 1982 management report to his Nestlé superiors, in which the Beech-Nut president boasted of his success in blocking the FDA. "If the recall had been effectuated in early June, over 700,000 cases . . . could have been affected," Hoyvald wrote. "We received much assistance from Mr. Tom Ward's law office . . . as well as Food and Drug attorneys [Washington, D.C.'s Kleinfeld, Kaplan and Becker] in delaying recall of the suspected apple juice codes."

"[Hoyvald] just didn't want to take those losses," concludes juror Portia Crafton, a home health aide from Brooklyn.

Klein's credibility—and the advice-of-counsel defense—was perhaps most undercut by his testimony regarding the September 1982 shipment to the Dominican Republic. Klein had wired Lavery, saying, "We understand that approximately 25,000 cases of apple juice manufactured from concentrate purchased from Universal . . . is currently in San Jose. It is strongly recommended that such product, and all other Universal products in Beech-Nut's possession anywhere in the U.S., be destroyed before a meeting with [FDA compliance officials] takes place."

Not only were the cases not destroyed, they were exported. Klein and Hoyvald both testified at trial that Hoyvald, after receiving the advice to destroy, called Klein and asked if it would be lawful to ship the product to the Dominican Republic, and that Klein reversed himself and said such an export would be legal.

The government noted, however, that no advice approving the exportation of the phony juice was put in writing, unlike the advice to destroy the product.

Most jurors simply dismissed Klein as a mouthpiece for Beech-Nut or, in the words of jurors DeBlasi and Livorsi, "a wise guy." Fumes Livorsi: "He was such a son of a bitch I wanted to punch him."

The testimony of the second lawyer Sullivan called to prove his advice-of-counsel theory was even more damaging to the defense.

According to testimony at trial, Ward had enlisted Kleinfeld, Kaplan, a nine-lawyer firm that specializes in FDA regulatory work, as the agency was closing in on Beech-Nut in August 1982. Sullivan told the jury that name partner Vincent Kleinfeld, 81, had advised Hoyvald to ship the fake juice but was now too old and ill to be called.

That left Kleinfeld, Kaplan partner Richard Morey, 50. Morey testified under cross-examination that he would not have recommended the selling of the juice in 1982 had he been told that Beech-Nut knew its juice was adulterated. Morey further testified that he would not have made the same representations to the FDA in 1982 had he seen the memos that documented Beech-Nut employees' long-standing suspicions about the concentrate.

"That blew them out of the water," says juror DiStefano, the Long Island dental assistant, who says the advice-of-counsel defense died with Morey's stark admission that he had not been told the facts by his clients in 1982.

"That hung them," says juror Livorsi. "When Morey said he wouldn't give them the same advice because he hadn't got all the test results [on adulteration], I said, 'Why wouldn't you tell your lawyer the truth?' "

The Beech-Nut episode has left a bitter taste with Morey. Being called as a witness by Sullivan "certainly wasn't pleasant," Morey says. "A client has every right to rely on their lawyers' advice, but if the facts [the lawyers] receive are wrong, it will affect that advice. . . . The advice is only as good as the information on which it was based."

"GET OFF MY BACK"

Whatever the wisdom of advice-of-counsel as a concept—Sullivan, after all, was at a serious disadvantage in the face of the physical evidence—it is clear that the Williams & Connolly scorched-earth style alienated both jurors and judge.

Simon, who argued the legal points for Sullivan and is identified by lawyers on both sides as Sullivan's henchman, particularly vexed Platt. The judge, a Yale Law graduate, would sometimes chide Simon, a graduate of Harvard Law, saying, "That's Cambridge law school." But more often Platt was angered by Simon's refusal to accept negative rulings. In one sidebar Platt exploded at Simon, "Get off my back, will you?"

"Simon, he was smart, but childish," Armenian-born juror and Brooklyn dance teacher Newart Babaian says, "always trying to argue with [the] judge . . . trying to get stuff in against [the] rules." Sullivan, she adds, "was [a] tricky man."

Platt once threatened Sullivan with a Rule 11 sanction for frivolous litigation for repeatedly trying to introduce Ward, Lazarus's Beech-Nut files, which the judge had already dismissed as "irrelevant . . . telephone books." Sullivan also flirted with a contempt charge when he ignored Platt's instructions not to read inadmissible notes to the jury. Peeved at the Williams & Connolly pair for slapping a midtrial subpoena on prosecutor Fleder, Platt said he felt like jailing them for the stunt. The subpoena, for documents that Fleder had already said did not exist, was quashed.

One attorney familiar with Sullivan's and Simon's struggles with the judge says, somewhat bitterly, "I think Platt wanted a conviction and did everything he could to get it. He undercut the . . . advice-of-counsel defense because I think he believed that Hoyvald could have been acquitted with it."

But repeatedly the defense was hurt by its own witnesses, or during cross-examination of prosecution witnesses. One case in point was the cross-examination of ex–research chief LiCari by Lavery's lawyer, Kimelman. LiCari, the lone Beech-Nut officer called by the government who was not an unindicted co-conspirator and did not receive immunity, was the prosecution's star witness. He testified that he left Beech-Nut in January 1982 because he couldn't sleep at night knowing what was going on. He said he made the decision after two conversations with Hoyvald in which the president refused to take action against the bogus juice.

Hoyvald denied under oath that LiCari ever discussed the problem with him. But Hoyvald did not make a favorable impression on the jury. "Hoyvald was haughty," says juror Babaian of both the former Beech-Nut CEO's 1982 actions and his demeanor in court. LiCari, on the other hand, seemed to fit Roche's description of him as "the conscience of the company."

During the cross, Kimelman took LiCari through all of his annual employment evaluations, pointing out the shortcomings that Lavery had noted. One was Lavery's 1981 criticism that LiCari's decision making was "at times colored by naïveté and impractical ideals."

On redirect examination, prosecutor Fleder asked LiCari, "Were you naïve in June of 1981?"

LiCari's response was devastating to the defense. "I guess I was," he replied. "I thought that apple juice should be made from apples."

In fairness to the defense counsel, they were facing a strong government litigation team armed with a strong case. Every time the trial threatened to get mired in technical language or legal fine points, prosecutors Roche, Fleder, or Jost would swing it back to basics, usually reminding the jury that the ultimate victims of the fraud were babies.

But in the end, most of the Sullivan-Simon arguments failed, and many of their strategies backfired. Hoyvald and Lavery were both convicted. The predominantly blue-collar jury found Lavery guilty on all counts but was hung on several charges against Hoyvald—conspiracy, mail fraud, and FDA violations relating to the juice shipments before June 25, 1982.

But the advice-of-counsel strategy failed to protect Hoyvald from conviction on the remaining counts. In June Judge Platt sentenced the two defendants to a year in jail and fined each $100,000. They remain free pending appeal.

BABIES CAN'T TALK

In retrospect, the obvious question is why Hoyvald and Lavery went to trial against such tough odds.

On the eve of trial the Beech-Nut company took the more cautious route. It pled guilty and agreed to a $2 million fine, the largest in FDA history. As the jury was being selected, Beech-Nut's new president, Richard Theuer, was issuing a mea culpa press release admitting the company had violated "a sacred trust" by selling fake apple juice to the mothers of America and the world.

Lawyers on both sides confirm that in the months before trial there were plea negotiations, in which U.S. Attorney Andrew Maloney played an active role. Asked to comment on the trial, Maloney quotes a comedian's quip: "It was the perfect crime, because the victims were babies, who can't talk."

Beech-Nut finally decided to plead after a package deal proposed by the defense—in which the company would plead to the most serious charges, Hoyvald and Lavery would plead to two misdemeanors, and the government would recommend no jail—failed to materialize. The government was unwilling to reduce the charges from felony counts to misdemeanors or to recommend that there be no jail sentence. On those terms, "Hoyvald just wouldn't go for it. He wouldn't plead guilty," says one lawyer familiar with the defense position.

"It was understood," this lawyer continues, "that Judge Platt would in all likelihood not jail [Hoyvald and Lavery] if they pleaded because that's the way he is. He's pro-government but lenient, especially if you cooperate. The bottom line is to keep your client out of jail. That they are going to jail is a shame."

One government lawyer agrees. "Absolutely, had they pleaded there would have been no jail," he says. He adds that Lavery appeared to follow the lead of his former boss, Hoyvald, in turning down a plea bargain. According to this attorney, Lavery dropped New York solo practitioner Thomas Fitzpatrick and retained Kimelman after Fitzpatrick recommended that Lavery accept a plea. (Both Fitzpatrick and Kimelman decline comment on this matter.)

One defense attorney familiar with the bargaining explains that Sullivan "lost a client to jail fifteen years ago on a plea that carried no guarantee of no incarceration," and from that point on his "philosophy is not to plead without a government recommendation of no jail." This attorney says Sullivan tells his clients, "At least you have had the full benefit of the adversarial system of justice."

At the sentencing hearing in June Judge Platt seemed to agree with the assessment that going to trial was yet another in a series of faulty judgments in the Beech-Nut case. After hearing a tearful Hoyvald beg for mercy and Sullivan argue for a noncustodial sentence, Platt said: "I must say that when you hear all of the facts in the case, as of course I did over the three and a half, four months we were all here, you get an awful lot more detail than perhaps you would get if the case was just presented to you on a set of papers. . . . And the detail involved . . . was, as far as the economic fraud . . . pretty extraordinary and pretty bad. I don't really think any judge would do other than what I'm going to do. . . . I think the fraud was too extensive, too long, and too involved for it to go completely unpunished."

Sullivan and Simon are now preparing for the North Iran-contra trial. They have already had the kind of run-ins with Judge Gerhard Gesell that they had with Judge Platt. In late July Gesell angrily called the pair examples of "a breed of lawyer that assumes that the minute they come into the courtroom, the judge is against them."

Perhaps in some quiet moment the Williams & Connolly duo will contemplate the counsel Platt gave Sullivan at the conclusion of one of the many skirmishes at the Beech-Nut trial.

During a break in the testimony, Sullivan surreptitiously erased a diagram a government witness had written on a blackboard. He did it instinctively, Sullivan told Platt sheepishly, because the nuns in his fourth-grade class "mandated clean boards." Then he crowed, "When I got to be a trial lawyer, if it was not marked in evidence I always erased it."

Platt, who had suggested photographing the blackboard to preserve the diagram as evidence, was not amused.

The judge's advice: "Restrain yourself."

EPILOGUE

In March 1989 a dividend panel of the U.S. Court of Appeals for the Second Circuit reversed Niels Hoyvald's and John Lavery's convictions on the FDA-related counts, citing technical venue grounds. The panel agreed with Brendan Sullivan and Barry Simon, partners at Williams & Connolly, that the pair should have been tried in Albany, N.Y., near the company's Canajoharie plant.

The court, however, affirmed Lavery's convictions on the conspiracy and mail fraud charges.

Hoyvald was retried in the summer of 1989, in upstate New York, but the trial ended in September when the jurors said they were hopelessly deadlocked after voting 9 to 3 for a conviction.

On October 30, 1989, the U.S. Supreme Court rejected review of Lavery's 18-count mail fraud and conspiracy convictions. At publication time Lavery was close to beginning his one-year prison term.

On November 13, 1989, on the eve of his third trial, Hoyvald finally admitted he knowingly sold sugar-water to consumers labeled "100 percent pure apple juice." Under a plea agreement worked out between Sullivan and prosecutor Thomas Roche, Hoyvald pleaded guilty to ten felony counts of violating the Food, Drug and Cosmetics Act. The former president received no jail time, but was sentenced to five years probation, a $100,000 fine, and six consecutive months of full-time community service. Both Beech-Nut and Hoyvald were barred from doing business with the federal government, with Beech-Nut's suspension lasting until 1991 and Hoyvald's until 2001. When Judge Platt took Hoyvald's plea, he made it plain he was unhappy with the deal that in effect undid Hoyvald's original 1988 jail sentence. Platt said he believed the Second Circuit had erred, and called the overturning of the convictions "a miscarriage of justice."

The last two defendants who had not pleaded guilty before the initial trial did so in September 1988. Nina Williamson, who worked for the juice concentrate supplier Raymond Wells, and Danny Shaeffer, who ran a parent firm that connected several suppliers of the bogus concentrate, pleaded guilty to selling a misbranded product, but were not sentenced to jail. All told, six individuals and two companies either pleaded guilty or were convicted, with total fines reaching about $2.4 million. Beech-Nut also settled a class action by purchasers of the phony apple juice for $7.5 million. The company is still trying to recover from the case, which has cost it an estimated $25 million in fines, judgments, legal fees, and lost business.

Prosecutors Roche, John Fleder, and Kenneth Jost, in addition to being nominated for the Justice Department's annual John Marshall Award, also received a citation in August 1988 from then-Attorney General Edwin Meese for the Beech-Nut prosecution.

Thomas Ward of Ward, Lazarus & Grow, Beech-Nut's lawyer whom Sullivan decided not to call at trial, was handcuffed and arrested in his Washington, D.C., office on Oct. 5, 1989, by FBI agents who were acting at the request of Britain's Crown Prosecution Service. The former Guinness director is facing charges in Britain of stealing $8.3 million from the Guinness till. At press time extradition proceedings were under way in the U.S.

Jerome LiCari, the former Beech-Nut research chief who was the government's star witness, is director of clinical development for Sandoz Nutrition Corporation in Minneapolis, where he went after resigning from Beech-Nut in January 1988.

CRIMINAL JUSTICE

Lawmakers ought not to be lawbreakers.

—GEOFFREY CHAUCER, c.1386

U.S.
v.
John DeLorean

ENTRAPPED?

BY

STEVEN BRILL

The unsettling questions raised by the Abscam and DeLorean cases

"The DeLorean case is the dream entrapment case," says San Francisco litigator and criminal defense specialist John Keker, referring to the recent undercover drug bust that snared the auto impresario. "The law on entrapment isn't all that clear," he adds, "but the case you make to a jury for entrapment is clear. You tell them, 'Okay, he's shown on the video-tapes doing all that stuff. But what was the process that led to his ending up there in front of the camera? How do you feel about what they did to get him to say and do all that in front of the camera?' "

The DeLorean cocaine caper is one of three videotaped scam extravaganzas orchestrated by the FBI and federal prosecutors that have dominated the headlines of the last two years, and each has made the crime fighters look good and a bunch of white-collar big shots look awfully bad. The other two are the FBI video-sting of alleged trade-secret thieves from Japan's Hitachi, Ltd., and of course, the Abscam prosecutions that netted several local officials in Pennsylvania and New Jersey and seven members of Congress, including Harrison Williams, then the senior senator from New Jersey.

Talks with an FBI agent involved in the DeLorean case and an examination of defense and prosecution papers filed following the indictments of the Hitachi executives last June suggest, as we shall see below, that the answer to Keker's question—what was done to get the defendants to the point of the sting—might be unsettling to those who believe that prosecutors should care as much about justice and the integrity of the system as they do about filling jail cells.

Yet it's the first of the three stings, Abscam—which has already been adjudicated to the appeal stage in most instances—that should be considered now as a clear warning about the prosecutorial abuses these kinds of cases allow. Recent testimony during Senate and House investigations of Abscam, a strongly worded bipartisan report just released by the House Judiciary Committee's subcommittee on civil and constitutional rights, and memos found in the prosecutors' files (some produced during the trials but given scant press attention and some just recently made public as a result of the congressional investigations) provide clear, convincing proof that Abscam was as much a scandal for the prosecutors as for the defendants. There is now strong evidence that the prosecutors in charge of Abscam—Philip Heymann, Irvin Nathan, and Thomas Puccio—ruined the life of at least one innocent defendant (former New Jersey Casino Control Commission vice chairman Kenneth MacDonald), unfairly convicted several other utterly unsympathetic but not appropriately prosecutable public officials (such as Senator Williams), and then stained the reputations of those professional prosecutors who had the guts to say, in internal memos of dissent, that the simple integrity of the system was more important than a sexy indictment or conviction.

To try to write about Abscam is to understand the true power of television. What follows may seem long and tedious, and it may not hold every reader's attention. Indeed, how can any number of pages of print compete with the overwhelming visual image of Abscam: clever lawmen capturing crooked politicians in the act, all brought to you on a grainy film from some seedy hotel room?

The place to start is with the case of Kenneth MacDonald, the New Jersey businessman and state casino commission vice chairman who was indicted for taking a $100,000 bribe to help the fictitious Arabs of Abscam get a casino license.

Like every other case, MacDonald's began with Melvin Weinberg, the government's chief undercover informant in the sting. Following a mail-fraud conviction in 1977, Weinberg agreed, in return for a sentence of probation, to work for the FBI. He was to set up an operation similar to the fraud scam he'd been running prior to his conviction, only now he'd be working for the FBI.

Weinberg established himself as a business agent for Abdul Enterprises on Long Island, a company ostensibly owned by a group of fabulously wealthy Arabs looking for American business opportunities, honest or otherwise.

Weinberg and the FBI's goal was to catch crooks looking to sell stolen art or securities. Through 1978 they had no success, but toward the end of that year another opportunity presented itself: word of Abdul's limitless funds and yen for a good deal had spread to southern New Jersey, and Camden Mayor and State Senator Angelo Errichetti soon arrived on the scene. According to FBI tape transcripts and files released at subsequent Abscam trials, Errichetti told Weinberg, and then the FBI undercover agents posing as Abdul's top executives, that he could help them get an Atlantic City casino license ahead of other license applicants because he had all kinds of political influence at the casino commission.

In March 1980, a month after the Abscam caper was leaked to the press, Philip Heymann, head of the Justice Department's Criminal Division, would testify before the House subcommittee on civil and constitutional rights that "we seek to take every possible precaution against involvement of the innocent," noting that "such precautions involve a careful evaluation of anything we are told by intermediaries. . . ."

Heymann, who has since returned to a law professorship at Harvard and who now declines all comment on Abscam, can't have been thinking of the real world of the investigation he ran, for the record of the Mac-Donald case suggests no such precautions. On January 9, 1979, there was a taped discussion in which Errichetti bragged to FBI agent John Mc-Carthy (posing as an Abdul executive) that he controlled three of the five casino commissioners because these three had been his nominees. He referred to them as "Roth," a "black man," and "Collozzi." Had Heymann made sure that his agents conducted "a careful evaluation" of Errichetti's information, they'd have found that Errichetti nominated no one to the commission, that the commission's only black member was a woman, and that none of the commissioners was named Roth or Collozzi.

The discussions with Errichetti continued nonetheless. By February, Errichetti—who at all times during Abscam was a scammed politician, always believing that he was dealing with Arabs and their agents, not the FBI—had come up with the name of a real commissioner: MacDonald. But this was only after he'd gotten some help from FBI informant Weinberg.

On February 12, Errichetti, Weinberg, and an FBI undercover agent discussed Errichetti's planned meeting with McCarthy, the supposed Abdul kingpin. "The main thing you ought to speak to him [McCarthy] about is MacDonald," Weinberg said, according to a tape of the meeting. "The big thing is you give him those assurances on . . . MacDonald." The agent then asked whether MacDonald would meet McCarthy; obviously, he was thinking of a taped bribe meeting. Errichetti replied that MacDonald probably wouldn't talk to McCarthy and that the best he could do would be to arrange a social dinner.

A dinner meeting between Errichetti, McCarthy, and MacDonald took place on March 5, 1979, at a New Jersey hotel. It was videotaped. Nothing happened. MacDonald, apparently at the behest of Errichetti, the mayor of a major New Jersey city, was there simply to tell Errichetti's friend what the normal, legitimate procedure was for applying for a casino license.

(Bear in mind that this all took place at the inception of Abscam's foray into the scamming of politicians. The fact that the FBI, with undercover informant Weinberg leading the way, kept going in this direction even after there were no signs of wrongdoing by MacDonald—who enjoyed an impeccable reputation—should already indicate a desire by the agents *and the prosecutors in charge of them* to generate headline cases rather than to catch people engaged in criminal activity.)

On March 8, during another videotaped meeting, the increasingly frustrated Weinberg (who, as we shall see later, was being paid on a per-indicted-politician basis) suggested a meeting at which McCarthy would give a bribe to MacDonald or give it to Errichetti, who in turn would give it to MacDonald. Errichetti got extremely upset. "Oh, no way, no way," he said, according to the tape. In fact, Errichetti then conceded what everyone else who ever knew MacDonald prior to his Abscam indictment always believed—that he was totally honest. "MacDonald ain't doing it for money, ya know. . . ," Errichetti said. "No, believe it when I tell you MacDonald isn't getting a fucking quarter. I may buy him a cigar, a three-dollar cigar, that's it. But there ain't no fucking way I'm gonna offer, give him the money."

Weinberg, of course, wasn't pleased. But he wasn't completely discouraged, either. "Well, we'll work on that," he said. "We'll hold that in abeyance."

Weinberg and the FBI continued to work on it. By the end of March Weinberg had convinced Errichetti, according to other taped meetings, that the Abdul people would be sure that a bribe to Errichetti was worthwhile only if they knew that MacDonald had gotten some money, too. Finally, a compromise was worked out: there would be a meeting on March 31 between McCarthy, Errichetti, and MacDonald, at which time McCarthy would give Errichetti a briefcase with $100,000 and Errichetti would in some way acknowledge that the money was for both him and MacDonald.

Just prior to that March 31 meeting, Weinberg met with Errichetti. According to FBI regulations, that meeting—between an undercover agent and a public official—should have been recorded. At a minimum, the FBI agent in charge of Weinberg should have filled out an FBI Form 302 immediately afterward, recording exactly what had happened. But no record of any kind was made of the meeting. All the evidence gathered since suggests why: at that meeting Weinberg and Errichetti, both aware that MacDonald would not take the money, agreed to dupe the Abdul people (at least, Errichetti *thought* they were Abdul people) and keep all the money for themselves. In short, Weinberg scammed the scammers while framing MacDonald. Here's how.

At the March 31 meeting, the $100,000 was passed in a briefcase from McCarthy to Errichetti. When McCarthy then turned to MacDonald and said that a portion of it was for him, MacDonald insisted, "I had nothing to do with that." In fact, he angrily left the meeting. Errichetti caught up with him and suggested that they stop at a Holiday Inn, where he had arranged to meet Weinberg and an agent posing as an Abdul executive. Weinberg and the agent apologized profusely to MacDonald for McCarthy's conduct.

Enter Errichetti's nephew and chauffeur, Joseph DiLorenzo. The briefcase with the $100,000 was passed from Errichetti to DiLorenzo, who put it in the trunk of Errichetti's car. DiLorenzo later testified (at the Abscam trial of Philadelphia Congressman Ozzie Myers) that the money was never given to MacDonald or opened in his view. In fact, DiLorenzo stated that he drove Errichetti back to Long Island the next day, April 1, 1979, and that Errichetti had the briefcase with him. They drove to a rest stop on the Long Island Expressway, where Errichetti met with Mel Weinberg, according to DiLorenzo.

Weinberg never recorded or reported that meeting with Errichetti, either. In fact, he denied it took place, although DiLorenzo was able to describe Weinberg's wife's Lincoln Continental in detail—a car he would never have seen before or after that alleged meeting.

To impeach DiLorenzo's testimony and thus defend Weinberg's credibility, the government introduced a tape of a telephone conversation between Weinberg on Long Island and Errichetti in New Jersey at 2:30 P.M. on April 1, 1979—the exact time Weinberg was supposed to be meeting with Errichetti in Long Island.

Curiously, the time given for the conversation—2:30—was supplied on the tape because Weinberg stated it in a preamble to the conversation. No other tape in all of Abscam contains such a preamble.

More curiously, when prosecutors in New Jersey were later considering the MacDonald case, they examined Weinberg's telephone records more closely than the prosecutors who introduced the tape and its preamble at the Myers trial had. The New Jersey prosecutors found no record of a 2:30 long-distance call between New Jersey and Long Island. What they did find was a call between Weinberg and Errichetti at 4:54 P.M.

Later, when he learned he was under investigation, MacDonald hired recognized polygraph experts to test him. He was found to be truthful as to his claim of innocence, according to his lawyer, Justin Walder of Newark's Walder, Sondak, Berkeley & Brogan. MacDonald then offered, through Walder, to have the FBI test him. The offer was declined, Walder says.

In 1982, Errichetti, who had by then been convicted on other Abscam counts, testified before a Senate select committee investigating Abscam that he had used MacDonald—that MacDonald had never agreed to do anything and had never recovered any money. He also told the senators that he split the money with Weinberg.

Walder offers as further proof of his client's innocence the fact that other Abscam projects subsequent to MacDonald's alleged bribe taking had involved casino applications, and yet the Abdul people had never followed up with MacDonald—their alleged bribe recipient—to ask him for help.

Moreover, during a grand jury proceeding in the MacDonald case on June 4, 1981, McCarthy, the FBI agent who had made the bribe, testified that there was no evidence that MacDonald ever received any money.

Yet MacDonald was indicted on June 18, 1981, for conspiring to accept the $100,000 and for accepting it.

How come?

JUSTIFYING THE INDICTMENT

One reason for MacDonald's indictment may be that although he was one of the last to be indicted, his case was the one that initially raised Abscam from a common stolen-property fraud operation to a political-corruption scam. If the first case bore no fruit, the legitimacy of the rest might become more questionable. That, in fact, is exactly how Gerald McDowell, then deputy chief of the Justice Department's Organized Crime and Racketeering Section, argued in pressing for the indictment in a January 23, 1981, memo to higher-ups in the criminal division. The memo was recently uncovered by Ralph Soda, a Gannett News Service reporter who, along with Nat Hentoff of *The Village Voice,* has done the best retrospective reporting on Abscam thus far.

In his memo McDowell conceded that there were problems with the MacDonald case, but he advocated the indictment because, as he put it, the case was "the heart and soul of the [Abscam] investigation. A decision by the department not to prosecute . . . would cast doubt on all that has been accomplished thus far."

McDowell's memo also suggested an inventive strategy for dealing with the April 1 meeting on Long Island between Errichetti and Weinberg (the one in which the two may have split the money meant for MacDonald) and for handling the April 1 telephone tape and its apparently phony 2:30 preamble (which, by the time of McDowell's memo, even the FBI, having scientifically tested it, thought was a fabrication). "By ending the conspiracy [charge] on March 31, [1979]," McDowell wrote, "we lose use of the April 1 tape, evidence that . . . must at this time be viewed as suspect."

MacDonald was never tried. He died of cancer ten months after his indictment.

As head of the Justice Department's organized crime strike force for New York's Eastern District, Thomas Puccio ran most of the Abscam prosecutions out of his Brooklyn headquarters and personally tried five of the seven cases against members of Congress. For Puccio, a witty, likable man, Abscam was the capstone of a spectacular career as a prosecutor that saw him able to leave the government last May at age 38 and step into a partnership at Park Avenue's Booth, Lipton & Lipton. Asked about the MacDonald case over lunch recently, Puccio says, "At the very least, the guy [MacDonald] allowed Errichetti to use his [MacDonald's] office for private gain." When it is pointed out that that's a far cry from what the indictment charged and that for it to have been a crime, MacDonald would have to have known Errichetti's criminal intention, Puccio seems exasperated by the way this reporter fails to understand the basic nature of Abscam the way most other journalists have. "Look, the guy was crooked," he exclaims. "Why else would he have had anything to do with Errichetti?'' Soda, the Gannett reporter who found the McDowell memo, ''is just a wacko,'' Puccio adds, and the memo (pressing for MacDonald's indictment on seemingly nonlegal grounds) is ''insignificant bullshit.''

Actually, Puccio would not have had the MacDonald case but for the fact that the New Jersey federal prosecutors refused to indict him. When they balked, the Justice Department, apparently motivated by concerns such as those expressed by McDowell (whose memo was written at exactly the time the New Jersey officials decided not to indict), transferred the case to a Brooklyn grand jury and to Puccio, under whose aegis the Abscam operatives had been working in the first place. Asked about that, Puccio says, ''You know, you hear all this pious bullshit from the New Jersey guys about how it sometimes takes courage not to prosecute. That's garbage. It takes courage *to* prosecute. Because if you do, and *you* don't win—if the guy gets off—look how bad you look. I won the other cases and I'd have won this one if the guy hadn't died. The New Jersey guys were weak, lax. I'd like to think it's just weakness. Who knows? Maybe it was something else.''

On that note of character assassination, we turn to New Jersey.

THE ''LAX'' PROSECUTORS FROM NEW JERSEY

When Mayor Errichetti and informant Weinberg first made contact in early 1979 and Abscam started to focus on New Jersey public officials, Robert Del Tufo was the U.S. attorney in that state. A 1958 law review editor and graduate of Yale Law School, he had served as a law clerk to the chief justice of the New Jersey Supreme Court, as a county prosecutor, as a member of the state board of bar examiners, and as director of the state division of criminal justice.

It is true that Del Tufo was appointed U.S. attorney in 1977 by a Democratic president and that the Democratic senator—then the later-to-be indicted Harrison Williams—traditionally passes on such appointments. But it is also true and well known to Puccio and other government lawyers (and recently confirmed to me by former attorney general Benjamin Civiletti, who was then chief of the Justice Department's Criminal Division) that Williams had appointed a screening panel to choose five possible U.S. attorney nominees and that while Del Tufo was on the list, he was not Williams's choice. Williams lobbied instead for a state senator, but Civiletti, aware of Del Tufo's impeccable reputation, urged the White House to choose him.

In February 1979 Del Tufo got a call from Puccio in Brooklyn. Puccio told Del Tufo that Errichetti and MacDonald had been drawn into an undercover sting—Abscam—that he had been running on Long Island, adding that Del Tufo and his office should be aware of what was going on. (U.S. attorneys are higher in rank than strike-force chiefs such as Puccio but are not above them in the chain of command; a strike-force chief technically operates outside the purview of the U.S. attorney's office, reporting directly to the Justice Department.)

Del Tufo met with Puccio on February 28. He brought with him Robert Stewart, head of the Justice Department's Newark organized crime strike force. Among law enforcement people and reporters who cover organized crime, Stewart is something of a legend. He never talks to the press. He just makes cases—so many and so well, in fact, that when I was writing a book about the Teamsters I was told by sources associated with mobsters Tony Provenzano and Russell Bufalino about repeated discussions in which a mob "hit" on Stewart was considered. (The idea was repeatedly rejected because Stewart was so liked and admired by other prosecutors that the mobsters figured the feds would leave no stone unturned to catch his killer.)

As Abscam progressed, Heymann, the head of the Criminal Division in Washington, requested that Del Tufo, Stewart, and their people become more involved.

According to Del Tufo, at an April 4, 1979, meeting with Puccio, he and Stewart were told that MacDonald had accepted a bribe on March 31. In recent testimony before the House subcommittee on constitutional and civil rights, Del Tufo recalled that Puccio "advised us that at a taped luncheon meeting [after the $100,000 had changed hands], MacDonald had made incriminating, corrupt statements." Of course, Del Tufo would later learn that this was untrue. (Puccio now says he doesn't remember saying that; in subsequent memos and testimony, Stewart remembered the meeting the way Del Tufo had.)

Soon after the April 4 meeting with Puccio, Del Tufo assigned Executive Assistant U.S. Attorney Edward Plaza and Assistant U.S. Attorney Robert Weir to work with Puccio's people. After visiting the Brooklyn strike-force offices several times in April to review evidence, Plaza and Weir, who are both experienced prosecutors, reported several problems to Del Tufo. The required FBI 302 reports for various conversations and events involving informant Weinberg's contacts with the politician-targets of Abscam were missing or had not been completed in the first place, they said. Various recordings and videotapes were missing or mysteriously contained only fragments of conversation. As Del Tufo recently testified before the House subcommittee, "Those and other circumstances suggested that Weinberg was being selective, thereby raising the possibility of duplicity on his part and calling for tighter controls over him and his activities."

Yet, in a recent interview, Del Tufo recalls that "at the time, I thought Plaza and Weir were being a bit too difficult. I told them to work with Puccio's people. These seemed like good cases."

Plaza and Weir got no place with Puccio. Justice Department guidelines call for the "careful monitoring" of any informant "whose reliability and credibility may be open to question." But when Plaza and Weir urged Puccio and his assistants to keep better track of Weinberg's activities and conversations, they were told that Weinberg had to be left alone to be effective. At one point, according to Plaza, when he told Puccio that Weinberg had accepted a microwave oven from a target of the investigation, Puccio replied, "Mel is Mel. You have to accept that sort of thing from him."

"We were trying to tell Bob [Del Tufo] that these cases were going to be lost because the guys in Brooklyn were sloppy," says Plaza. "At first, we thought that that was all there was to it. Just sloppiness." At Plaza and Weir's urging, Del Tufo spoke to Puccio about the problems his assistants were encountering. "The remedial management controls necessary to proper evaluation of the investigation and to proper supervision of Weinberg were, however, not established, although the situation was called repeatedly to Mr. Puccio's attention," Del Tufo testified before the House subcommittee on November 23. "Moreover, Messrs. Plaza and Weir were soon denied by Mr. Puccio any meaningful access to information. When Mr. Plaza and Mr. Weir described to me their fruitless trips to Brooklyn, I would contact Mr. Puccio. Typically, he would either deny the existence of a problem or assure me that any difficulties would be promptly remedied."

"Puccio's assurances were like the guy who says the check is in the mail," recalls William Robertson, who was Del Tufo's first assistant and later succeeded him. "He was very nice, but nothing happened. He was jerking us off."

At one meeting between Del Tufo and Puccio, according to both men, Puccio told Del Tufo that he didn't believe in "overmanaging" cases. "I was trying to give Bob some friendly advice," Puccio explained during our interview. "You shouldn't push the FBI people around too much. They resent it."

THE COACHING TAPE

Undercover scam artist Weinberg also resented it, especially when Plaza and Weir happened upon evidence of his misconduct. During one August 1979 visit to Brooklyn, Plaza and Weir were invited by Puccio's secretary to make themselves at home in an office containing much of the Abscam evidence. "In a bottom drawer," Plaza recalls, "we happened on a [transcript of a] tape that seemed to be discarded. It was what turned out to be the coaching tape."

This was a tape of Weinberg and Errichetti with Senator Williams. The three had met in June 1979 just before Williams was to see the fictitious sheik who ran Abdul Enterprises. The Abscammers' plan was for Williams to get the sheik to give a multimillion-dollar loan to a fledgling mining company that Williams owned a piece of in return for Williams's promise to get government contracts for the company.

Weinberg was obviously worried that Williams would not perform corruptly. So, as the tape reveals, he told him, "You tell him [the sheik] in no uncertain terms, 'Without me there is no deal. I'm the man who's gonna open the door. I'm the man who's gonna do this to use my influence.'. . .

"And that's it," Weinberg assured Williams. "It goes no further; it's all talk, all bullshit."

Williams asked what the sheik knew about the mining company's properties. "Don't even mention it," Weinberg counseled the senator. "Let me tell you, he's interested in you. . . . You gotta just play and blow your horn."

Weinberg then told Williams how low an interest rate the mining company would have to pay on the loan and that there was more money available for other projects. "That's why you gotta sell him like mad. . . . If we wanna buy something else, we have carte blanche. . . . He came here at an expense of anywhere from fifty to a hundred thousand dollars," Weinberg added with characteristic flair. "He has a whole entourage down here . . . for twenty minutes with you. All right? So you gotta take the position, you're the boss. . . . You're on stage for twenty minutes."

Having thus been coached that his pitch was "all talk" and that "it

211

goes no further,'' Williams indeed went "on stage"—in front of the secret FBI video cameras—for 20 minutes. He bragged shamelessly about how high up he was in the Senate and about all the influential people he knew. But he never promised to do anything but try to sell the mining company's products on their merits.

This embarrassing performance in front of the sheik became the key videotape in the Williams trial. Indeed, in Puccio's summation in the Williams trial, he said of the postcoaching tape, "This tape, ladies and gentlemen, stands at the heart of the government's case."

According to Plaza, "I doubt that the coaching tape would have seen the light of day if I hadn't discovered it in the bottom of that drawer." Puccio denies that, saying, "Of course we'd have turned it over [to the defense]." The coaching tape was, indeed, turned over; we will see below why it wasn't enough to get Williams acquitted. But there's no denying that Plaza's discovery of the tape and his reaction to it exacerbated tensions between the Brooklyn and New Jersey prosecutors.

Plaza would later testify, in an account substantiated by two New Jersey FBI agents who were there, that on August 9, 1979, he and Weir met with Weinberg and two Brooklyn FBI agents at the home of an Atlantic City FBI agent. At that meeting Plaza vehemently scolded Weinberg, telling him that he had to stop coaching targets such as Senator Williams. Weinberg replied, according to Plaza's testimony as confirmed by the two FBI agents, that "if we don't do that, then we won't have any cases."

After that meeting Weinberg and the Brooklyn FBI agents broke off almost all contact with Plaza, Weir, Stewart, and everyone else from New Jersey. At a rare and tense session about two months later on Long Island, FBI special agent John Goode told Plaza, according to Plaza, that "Weinberg had been insulted by my criticism of him and didn't want to work with me and that my criticism of Weinberg had jeopardized the entire investigation." Goode's account in later trial testimony is, in essence, that Plaza had been too harsh and not tactful enough in dealing with Weinberg. Puccio puts it this way: "At that meeting Mel [Weinberg] started not to trust the New Jersey guys. I mean he figured, they've been in New Jersey all this time with all these crooks and hadn't prosecuted anyone, so who knows if they're straight. I mean I trust Del Tufo and Plaza and Weir, but I think Mel and the [FBI] agents didn't, and I could sympathize with them." (In fact, the New Jersey strike-force office has had an exemplary record prosecuting corrupt public officials and organized crime operatives for more than a decade.)

THE INFORMANT TAKES CHARGE

By September, Abscam was moving merrily along almost totally unencumbered by the New Jersey prosecutors' involvement. This was despite the fact that in mid-July Justice Department Criminal Division head Heymann and his deputy Irvin Nathan (who has now returned to a partnership at Washington's Arnold & Porter) had told both Puccio and Del Tufo that *all* jurisdiction over Abscam was to be transferred to New Jersey. Heymann and Nathan had acted after receiving memos from Del Tufo expressing concern that the way the case was being run jeopardized Abscam's potential for getting convictions, and the switch in jurisdiction made sense since the targets were now New Jersey organized crime figures and politicians who might be drawn into the Atlantic City casino scam.

"Puccio and his people simply ignored Phil and Irv," says Del Tufo.

"You see, my agents didn't trust Del Tufo," says Puccio. "And I sided with them.

"What this was," Puccio continues, "was a plain old turf fight. I won. I won because I was no ordinary adversary. I was the most respected prosecutor in the country and Del Tufo was just a lawyer from New Jersey. He took on the wrong guy."

Heymann declines all comment on Abscam. Nathan, during a series of long telephone interviews, acknowledged what the written record of several Justice Department memoranda indicates: that, in his words, "transfer of jurisdiction from Puccio to New Jersey was never carried out as effectively as I had hoped."

Unbeknownst to the New Jersey prosecutors, who supposedly now had jurisdiction over Abscam, the Brooklyn lawmen had shifted the scam in August 1979 to what they called "the asylum scenario," in which they attempted to get congressmen to take bribes in return for helping the fictitious sheik emigrate to the United States. This was a spontaneous idea of Mel Weinberg's, which he had blurted out to Errichetti one day. It would prove to be the linchpin of most Abscam indictments.

Beginning in September, Stewart, the New Jersey strike-force head, started sending a series of memos sounding the alarm about Abscam to Justice Department officials. A September 12 memo to David Margolis, the chief of the Organized Crime and Racketeering Section, detailed Puccio's obvious evasion of Heymann's jurisdictional decision. A five-page memo dated October 31 went further, noting that "it is the Informant [Weinberg] who is dictating the course of this investigation." A

January 8, 1980, memo from Stewart to Margolis's deputy chief, Gerald McDowell, declared that "the informant persists in formulating the criminal scheme rather than simply allowing the suspects to do this."

Stewart went on in that memo to present a succinct analysis of the legal issues associated with Abscam:

> It appears to me that the substantive problem with respect to this investigation is that it is being conducted in the manner of a conventional "sting" operation—that is, the predominant modality is to videotape anyone willing to meet with the Undercover Operatives in order to determine what, if anything, they have to say which might be incriminating. The problem with this approach is the fundamental difference between the subject matter of a conventional "sting" operation and that of the present operation. In the former, the subject matter under discussion (such as a stolen television set in the hands of a junkie thief) is contraband per se and any discussion about it is ipso facto incriminating.
>
> The suspect's mere presence in an ostensible "fencing" location with an item which is being offered for sale at a fraction of its face value provides more than an adequate basis for further investigative action—namely, recording the suspect's conversations about the contraband item. In the present investigation, the circumstances are fundamentally different because there is nothing inherently illegal about either the nature of the meeting place or the general topic of conversation. Indeed, absent specific facts to the contrary, there is an initial presumption of legality because of the positions which the suspects occupy and because of the ostensibly legitimate nature of the things under discussion— whether those things be the operation of a business, economic development in a particular area, or the protection of the human rights and indeed the very life of a foreign national who is touted as nothing more than a legitimate entrepreneur. [This refers to the asylum scenario.] Hence, the decision for further investigative action cannot be controlled by the criteria which govern such decisions in a conventional "sting" operation, but must depend instead upon the demonstrable existence of special facts which infect the particular transaction with illegality.

To illustrate his point, Stewart then accused Puccio of having lied about the original reason to investigate Senator Williams. He charged that Puccio had assured him in March and in May that the reason to investigate Williams was that Williams then had a hidden interest in the mining company, with the *hidden* nature of the interest being the appropriate cause for suspicion. Yet, Stewart charged in this memo, when the New

Jersey prosecutors finally got to see some previously "missing" tapes in October, they discovered that the only reference to Williams's "hidden interest" was a prediction by one of his business associates that Williams might have a hidden piece of the company in the future.

A month prior to that January 8 memo, on December 17, 1979, Del Tufo and his staff had written a memo about the Williams case. They concluded that Weinberg's coaching and other government overreaching had ruined any chance for a conviction. Puccio, Nathan, and others involved in the later decision to indict Williams now say they disagreed with the Del Tufo analysis. Yet on November 27, 1979, FBI section chief W. D. Gow wrote a memo to then–assistant FBI director Francis "Bud" Mullen, Jr., reporting on a November 19 meeting attended by various FBI people *and* by Puccio and his field people. The memo—which was not available to defense lawyers at Williams's trial—substantiates Del Tufo's position. Gow states:

> Relative to the matter concerning U.S. Senator Harrison Williams of New Jersey, the following was decided:
>
> 1. It will be necessary to recontact U.S. Senator Williams in an attempt to obtain an overt action on his part regarding his sponsoring of some type of legislation; i.e., tax cover for titanium mine, environmental standards for titanium mine and/or import quotas for titanium mine.
> 2. It was also suggested that attempts should be made to elicit from U.S. Senator Williams whether or not he wanted his shares hidden, through discussions concerning reporting of personal taxes and official acts that he promised to provide.
>
> *If the above information is obtained,* prosecutors at the meeting felt that they could prove that Senator Williams was in violation of title 18, section 201 of the U.S. Code and conspiracy to defraud the Government. [Emphasis added.]

In short, the FBI and Puccio, like Del Tufo, didn't believe they had a case against Williams yet—and this was now eleven months since his name had come up and at least five months since Weinberg had started meeting with Williams.

It was for this reason that yet another videotaped meeting with Williams was planned for January 15, 1980, at the Plaza Hotel in New York. There, the asylum scenario would be tried on Williams: he would be offered a bribe in exchange for sponsoring an immigration bill for the sheik. To Puccio, the meeting was so important that he personally monitored the session from the next room; he had not shown up for any other Abscam meetings. Puccio and FBI agent Goode set up a phone line so that if things didn't go well and needed adjusting, they could communicate with their sheik.

The meeting had been arranged by Weinberg, who had told one of Williams's associates that the sheik had a "little favor" to ask of Williams. Thus, unlike many of the other congressmen snared in the asylum scenario, Williams was given no hint in advance that he would be offered a bribe at this meeting.

By most standards, the meeting would seem to have been a flop. After the sheik mentioned what his "little favor" was, Williams stressed that he could help only if the sheik could meet the legitimate criteria for special immigration legislation. The sheik then said, "I would like to give you, er, you know some money for—for permanent residence." But Williams interrupted. "No," he said. "No, no, no . . . when I work in that area, that kind of activity, it is purely a public . . ."

The conversation was then abruptly interrupted by a call from FBI agent Goode, who was in the next room with Puccio. It seems that they wanted to stop the taping of Williams's innocent statements. Goode, according to his later testimony, said he instructed the agent to get the senator to be more specific about what he intended to do to help with the immigration bill.

When Williams persisted in matter-of-factly stressing the importance of the merits involved in such legislation, the sheik received another phone call: Goode, according to subsequent testimony, told him to get Williams to tie his immigration help to the loan for the mining company. Williams indeed allowed himself to be diverted to a discussion of the loan and then, when asked again about the immigration bill, said, "I will do all that is necessary to get that to the proper decision."

This promise, along with Williams's earlier promise (in the postcoaching tape) to help convince all those public officials he had bragged about knowing that the government needed the mining company's products, was the basis of his indictment and conviction.

It didn't matter that it was Weinberg who had first brought up the subject of government contracts—not Williams or his business partners, who were interested only in getting private customers for the company. Nor did it matter that Williams had been coached and prodded for eight months and still had not done anything overtly criminal. What he had done, at most, after all the prodding, was tell a sheik who was about to lend tens of millions of dollars to a business Williams was involved in that he'd sponsor an immigration bill *if it was legitimate to do so*.

How, then, did Williams get convicted? For starters, his lawyer, George Koelzer of New York's Evans, Koelzer, Marriott, Osborne & Kreizman, was ineffective and disorganized. More important, Williams's performance on the witness stand was like his performance on many of the tapes: he came across as a stupid, pompous, arrogant, shady politician. In fact, Williams seems to have been so arrogant and stupid that he was oblivious to the trouble he was in. Thus, he reportedly refused Edward Bennett Williams's offer to represent him because he wanted to spare the expense. He also tried to impress the jurors by telling them that Weinberg's coaching hadn't had all that much effect, even though he had desecrated the office of senator with his bragging to the sheik about all of his influence. And he blithely defended his many business interests and those of his wife, as if being a senator were part-time work. In short, when it came time for the jurors to apply criminal defense lawyer Keker's test (as he explained it above with regard to the DeLorean case) of how they felt about what the government had done to get Williams to say what he'd said in front of the camera, their sympathy for him was nil.

But Williams was not indicted by Del Tufo and his people in New Jersey. They refused, despite the pressure that mounted on them after February 2, 1980, the day the Abscam investigation was leaked to the press and its covert phase was ended.

"Once Abscam went public and there was all this controversy about it," says Del Tufo, "Heymann and Nathan were under all kinds of pressure. And they looked to the one guy who could pull them out of the fire—justify it all with indictments and convictions—and that was Tom Puccio."

By February, Puccio's turf grabbing had succeeded to the point that New Jersey had been left with jurisdiction only over the MacDonald case and that of another New Jersey politician who was never indicted. Del Tufo assigned Plaza and Weir to pull the MacDonald evidence together. (It was then that they learned from Errichetti's driver that Errichetti and Weinberg had probably kept for themselves the money that was meant for MacDonald.)

By June, Plaza and Weir's problems with Weinberg were mounting. They had found that he'd received gifts that he had not reported, such as the microwave oven, from targets of the investigation and that several million dollars' worth of forged certificates of deposit that Weinberg had allegedly recovered for the government—for which he had received bonuses from the government—had actually been manufactured and forged by Weinberg himself. Plaza and Weir met with Puccio and complained that all of this would undermine Weinberg's credibility. According to Plaza, Puccio said that he saw "no problem" with the certificates of deposit because they were not involved in any case and said he would see that the microwave was removed from Weinberg's home. (Asked about that, Puccio says, "You think I'd tell those clowns to remove evidence? I'd have to be crazy.")

That session between Plaza, Weir, and Puccio was followed by a confrontation with FBI agent Goode on June 18, in which Goode refused to let Plaza or Weir interview Weinberg without Goode's being present— an obvious problem since Goode and Weinberg were likely to be co-witnesses to the same event during the trials. In late June, Del Tufo relented. Realizing that there was no way that Plaza and Weir could get along with any of the Abscam field agents, he asked Nathan to send two new lawyers from Washington to complete work on the MacDonald case. Nathan agreed, but only after first telling Del Tufo that MacDonald ought to be indicted quickly and that it was up to the defense to raise the kinds of due process or evidentiary problems that were bothering Del Tufo. (Nathan confirms making that statement.)

In August 1980, Del Tufo resigned. He says his decision to go into private practice in order to support three college-age children had been made long before the Abscam problems.

Del Tufo's successor was his top assistant, William Robertson. A career prosecutor, Robertson was named, as is statutorily mandated, by the district judges in New Jersey to fill Del Tufo's vacancy pending a presidentially appointed replacement.

The two prosecutors sent up from Washington, Reid Weingarten and Eric Holder, quickly began to see what Weir and Plaza had seen about the Abscam irregularities and Weinberg's credibility problem. In fact, according to Robertson's recent testimony before the House subcommittee, it was Weingarten and Holder who discovered the discrepancy in telephone records that put the lie to Weinberg's 2:30 P.M. preamble, which had allowed him to deny meeting with Errichetti for their apparent split-up of MacDonald's "bribe." The telephone records, incidentally, had been requested from the Brooklyn people by Plaza and Weir over a year before Weingarten and Holder arrived, according to Robertson's testimony.

THE PERJURY MEMO

In early December 1980, Weingarten and Holder, according to Robertson's testimony, told Robertson that they were under great pressure from Heymann, Nathan, and McDowell in D.C. to indict MacDonald by December 18.

Robertson says it had been his intention "to bring in Weinberg and the FBI people to the grand jury, but as usual, there was resistance. I was told Mel didn't trust us. So, I thought I could avoid a fight on this—I didn't want to fight—simply by having all the testimony by these guys in the Abscam trials that had already been held pulled together so that maybe we could simply read that testimony to the grand jury."

Robertson assigned Plaza and Weir to pull together all the prior testimony of the FBI agents and of Weinberg and prepare a memo of their findings.

The memo was explosive. It suggested that Weinberg and the government had committed perjury in some of the other trials. For example, Weinberg had denied under oath that he had ever been admonished by anyone concerning his coaching conversation with Williams or his failure to record all conversations. No one from the government had made any effort to correct the record. Similarly, during the trial of two local Philadelphia politicians, the government had submitted to U.S. district judge John Fullam an incorrect schedule of payments made to Weinberg, a schedule different from the one submitted to the court in Brooklyn in the trial of Congressman Ozzie Myers. Worse, Weinberg had testified before Judge Fullam that with the exception of a $5,000 bonus he had received for work done in Florida, he had received no special rewards or bounty payments from the FBI. Yet Plaza and Weir had seen an FBI memorandum justifying payment of a $15,000 bonus to Weinberg for his "skillfully establishing a major federal violation against a major political figure." (The figure involved was MacDonald; the use of the phrase "establishing a violation against" may be the most honest, if unwittingly so, description to come out of Abscam.)

Plaza and Weir further pointed out in their memo that in the Myers trial, in which the government's new schedule of payments included the $15,000 bonus for the MacDonald case, the defense had pressed Weinberg about why he had received it. He had refused to be specific. Finally, after conferring with the government prosecutors, Judge George Pratt had declared to the defense at a sidebar conference that Weinberg's government-informant file showed that the payment had been made "in connection with a matter in which he [Weinberg] was nearly killed,'' hardly a precise description of the MacDonald investigation.

Plaza and Weir also noted in their memo that they had been told by FBI agent Goode and by Nathan that Weinberg's payment schedule was ''based upon the number and status of indicted officials but was not conditioned upon their convictions.''

After reading the memo Robertson ordered it sent to himself and to Criminal Division chief Heymann (as well as to then–District of Columbia U.S. Attorney Charles Ruff, who was prosecuting another Abscam case).

Between December 17, 1980, and January 7, 1981, the New Jersey people heard nothing from Washington about the Plaza-Weir memo. On January 7, Robertson was notified by McDowell, the deputy chief of the Organized Crime and Racketeering Section, that the matters raised by the Plaza-Weir memo had been sent to all defense counsel and judges in current Abscam cases and that Judge Pratt in Brooklyn, who was then trying the cases of several Abscam defendants, wanted Plaza and Weir to appear to testify the next day.

What Robertson was not told, and what Plaza and Weir didn't know until they got to court, was that what was being submitted to the courts and defense lawyers was not their memo but a memo by Heymann's deputy, Irvin Nathan, that purported to summarize the Plaza-Weir memo and then rebut it.

Nathan's memo started by maligning Plaza and Weir for having ''complained bitterly in the early summer of 1979'' about not having played enough of a role in Abscam and for having done ''very little, if any, work'' on the MacDonald case. The memo also notes that ''Weinberg, in particular, was suspicious of the motivations of the New Jersey prosecutors''—as if he is a credible character reference—and then goes on to rebut selected portions of the memo in a way that is wildly at odds with facts on record.

Asked about the memo, Nathan says, ''I stand by every fact in it,'' though his superior, Heymann, conceded some factual errors in later testimony, including the assertions that Plaza and Weir had been lax in working on the MacDonald case and that either of them had even met Nathan in the summer of 1979, let alone complained to him then about jurisdiction in the Abscam cases.

Nathan further defends his memo by writing that Judge Pratt, in his decision on due process defense claims of several Abscam defendants, "totally substantiated my memo." This is not exactly true: Pratt, whose rulings were obviously pro-government throughout Abscam, simply accepted and parroted back as fact everything in Nathan's memo, including the overall claim that the New Jersey people were simply resentful that their turf had been invaded. He conducted no independent fact-finding.

TARRING THE NEW JERSEY LAWMEN

After the Nathan memo, disciplinary charges were brought against Plaza, Weir, and Robertson for their supposedly having improperly helped the defense by Plaza's having produced the December 17 memo and other memos in Judge Pratt's court—after the judge had requested them, and after Plaza had protested unsuccessfully that the judge first review them *in camera*. The three were also charged with improper conduct because Plaza and Weir had written a letter to all Abscam judges rebutting the Nathan memo. Plaza, Weir, and Robertson were later cleared when the charges were referred to the Justice Department's Office of Professional Responsibility. But other than acknowledging that they had been cleared, Associate Attorney General Rudolph Giuliani has refused to release the report. (Puccio acknowledges that "Rudy [Giuliani] and I are good friends; we go way back.")

The recently released House subcommittee report notes that while the committee, too, was denied access to the report, it was orally briefed on it by Office of Professional Responsibility lawyers, who said they had found Nathan's memo to be "a twisted analysis . . . libelous, and slanderous" and Robertson's, Weir's, and Plaza's actions to be thoroughly justified.

Nonetheless, when Plaza and Weir understandably became defense witnesses, they were viciously cross-examined by Puccio, who used several obviously bad-faith questions. For example, Plaza was asked about the fact that George Koelzer, Williams's hapless defense counsel, had attended the New Jersey U.S. attorney's office Christmas party. (Plaza pointed out that because Koelzer was once an assistant in that office, his invitation was traditional.)

Del Tufo was also called as a witness, and with him Puccio went right for the jugular, repeatedly asking about Del Tufo's "political" connections to Williams and others involved in Abscam and even asking if Del Tufo thought it was proper for him to be working on the case. For

221

example, Puccio asked this kind of have-you-stopped-beating-your-wife question: "Did it bother you in any way that Senator Williams was . . . one of the subjects of the Abscam investigation and that in some way he was responsible in your appointment for U.S. attorney?"

In an interview, Nathan picks up on that theme, saying, "I always thought it unseemly of Del Tufo to be involved at all. He should have recused himself. You ought to look into that." Of course, Nathan, as Del Tufo's boss, could always have removed Del Tufo himself; instead, in July 1979, he placed him in charge of Abscam, perhaps because he knew that Del Tufo had been appointed in spite of Williams's preference for another U.S. attorney.

Actually, that kind of attack on Del Tufo began soon after someone had leaked the existence of the Abscam investigation to *The New York Times* and NBC in February 1980. Two days after Abscam went public, the *Times* ran a story quoting "law enforcement officials" as saying that Del Tufo had recommended "against any prosecution of . . . Williams." The *Times* story went on to report the falsehood that Del Tufo had been appointed "on the strength of a recommendation by Senator Williams." At about the same time, I received a call from a news producer at NBC asking if, based on my prior reporting about Teamsters in New Jersey, I knew anything about Del Tufo. The NBC person explained that he'd heard from Brooklyn strike-force sources that Del Tufo was crooked.

Weir and Stewart (the New Jersey strike-force chief) are still in their jobs; actually, Weir now works for Stewart and just tried a big New Jersey racetrack scandal case. But Plaza, Robertson, and Del Tufo, the three most outspoken Abscam critics inside the Justice Department, are now in private practice.

From the small office in Jersey City that he shares with his brother and another lawyer, Plaza says, "The whole thing hurt me terribly. Here and even in the local papers at home [in Asbury Park] I became known as the lax prosecutor." Robertson, a partner at the 60-lawyer Newark firm of Hannoch, Weisman, Stern, Besser, Berkowitz & Kinney, says, "We were all tarred by this, especially Plaza and Bob [Del Tufo], all because we wrote internal memos. Isn't that what you're supposed to do?"

Del Tufo is prospering at Newark's 45-lawyer Stryker, Tams & Dill, but friends say it's what might have been that has been lost for him: he had once hoped to seek high state office, and his work as U.S. attorney on environmental cases (in which he opposed local businessmen as powerful in their spheres as Williams was in his), on corruption cases, and in a nationally headlined Russian spy case had given him a sterling reputation. Had he acquiesced in Abscam and gotten some share of the credit with Puccio, he'd have been quite a comer. "I guess I've been forestalled from anything in politics by this," Del Tufo concedes, in the only trace of bitterness that comes during long interviews which otherwise are full of warnings-against-interest. For example, Del Tufo cautions that a reporter should "not be too harsh on Irv [Nathan] or Tom [Puccio]; they were under a lot of pressure and they're not bad people. It's just that Irv was inexperienced and Tom didn't quite have the sensitivity a good prosecutor should have."

Puccio, like Nathan, cites Pratt's opinion upholding the Abscam cases and also notes that James Neal, the Tennessee lawyer of Watergate fame who was chief counsel to the Senate select committee's investigation of Abscam, "tells me that their final report [not yet public as of this writing] will say that the New Jersey guys' complaints were bullshit." Neal says that he considers the objections of Del Tufo, Robertson, Plaza, and Weir to be "totally justified," and he directed me to statements in the Senate committee's interim report which substantiate the New Jersey lawyers' charges about Weinberg's misconduct, the apparent sharing of the MacDonald bribe by Weinberg and Errichetti, and related New Jersey claims. "I think the way Puccio ran things was distasteful," Neal adds. "I think he's a good prosecutor. But he was so overbearing in this thing that the Department of Justice couldn't control him. And he was definitely unfair to the New Jersey people."

On the other side of Capitol Hill, the bipartisan report of the House subcommittee on civil and constitutional rights, released in mid-December, should go a long way toward restoring the reputation of the New Jersey prosecutor. Puccio calls the subcommittee "biased" and "a real low-life operation," and says its chairman, Congressman Don Edwards of California, is "a fool." The subcommittee report backs the New Jersey version of Abscam events: it is sharply critical of Puccio's attacks on the New Jersey prosecutors' motives and integrity, and it endorses Del Tufo's call, made during his testimony before the subcommittee, for a special prosecutor to investigate Weinberg's misconduct and the possibility that Weinberg may have committed perjury during the Abscam trials, a crime to which the government agents may have improperly acquiesced.

Yet the press and public may take the two committees' reports with a grain of salt; after all, they may be seen as a group of congressmen attacking law enforcement people who were clever enough to nail their congressional colleagues.

CREATING CRIMES IN ORDER TO SOLVE THEM

It was when outsiders Weingarten and Holder, together with Robertson, continued to refuse to indict MacDonald in the spring of 1981 that the Criminal Division in Washington shifted that case to Brooklyn's jurisdiction and to a grand jury there. MacDonald was then promptly indicted, though the case was never tried because he died ten months later.

There were, of course, stronger Abscam cases than *MacDonald* or *Williams*. For example, it is hard to argue with the conviction of the thug Camden mayor, Errichetti, who immortalized himself on tape with the pronouncement that in politics, "money talks and bullshit walks."

Yet there are other cases that fall in between MacDonald's and Errichetti's. For example, Congressman Frank Thompson was snared after first rebuffing the idea of a bribe and then being invited back—on the premise of the Arabs' interest in making investments in his congressional district—to be offered it again. In Thompson's case, as in many others, the target was a public official with a long-held reputation for honesty. Like MacDonald, Thompson was targeted only after a crooked, unreliable middleman told the FBI, with no substantiation, that he knew Thompson, which he didn't, and could deliver him for bribe taking.

Thus, Stewart's basic point in the memo quoted above bears repeating: Abscam did not infiltrate ongoing criminal activity. Rather, it created that activity and then set up a sort of integrity test for various public officials aimed at seeing if they would be willing to participate.

Thus far, two district judges have thrown out Abscam convictions, although one was reinstated by a Third Circuit Court of Appeals ruling in the case of two Philadelphia politicians. The only other court of appeals decision was in the less problematic case of a low-level immigration official snared for bribe taking; the Second Circuit upheld the conviction. A Second Circuit decision on Williams is expected shortly.

The case law on entrapment is ambiguous, though it seems to center on two questions: (1) Was the defendant predisposed to commit the crime; and (2) was the government's conduct so outrageous so as to warrant a dismissal of the case? In the most recent Supreme Court case (*Hampton* v. *United States;* 425 U.S. 484; 1976) all the justices seemed to think that the defendant drug dealer, who was given drugs by a government informant to sell to an undercover agent, was predisposed. But three justices thought that the government's action in setting up the crime was so outrageous as to merit a dismissal, while three thought that government overreaching or misconduct should *never* result in a dismissal. The pivotal other third, with Justice Powell writing the concurrence, upheld the conviction because, while the government's conduct was a valid issue, it had not been so egregious in this case that it warranted a dismissal.

At least some of the Abscam cases seem to present clear instances of government overreaching in the person of Weinberg. But if the court, in cases such as Williams's or Thompson's, takes a milder view of this governmental conduct, as Judge Pratt and the Third Circuit have in cases less defense-sympathetic than Williams's or MacDonald's, then the first test—predisposition to commit a crime—becomes meaningless. For it can be argued that *by definition* the trap set by Abscam measures some-one's predisposition to commit *a* crime—i.e., if he succumbs, he must have been disposed to succumb. It would seem that for the court's test of whether this is permissible to be meaningful, it would have to come back, as it apparently did in the case of the drug dealer's drug-dealing convic-tion, to the question of whether the defendant was predisposed to commit *the crime in question*.

Thus, we approach New Jersey strike-force chief Stewart's notion of the government's having to be involved in intercepting some *ongoing* criminal activity; and surely no one would argue that MacDonald, or Williams, or Thompson, was conducting as an ongoing activity a bribes-for-official-conduct operation.

President Reagan has often argued that one reason that government cannot afford to be "soft" on crime by taking account of poverty or other supposed root causes in trying to fight crime or punish criminals is that he believes that "man is inherently evil." If he's right, then we are all predisposed to commit some crime, and any Abscam-type test will ulti-mately catch anyone if the inducement is high enough.

Take the example of the most typical street-crime sting: an undercover policeman posing as a derelict lies in the street waiting to catch a man who is said to be cruising the neighborhood slashing derelicts with a knife. This is clearly proper police work aimed at ongoing criminal ac-tivity. But what if the derelict lies down in the street with his wallet hanging out of his pocket and a $100 bill sticking out of his wallet? What if the wallet is simply placed three feet away from the derelict and the $100 bill is on top of the wallet? Many people will be seduced by that integrity test. Are they practicing criminals? Is catching them the proper function of police work?

Puccio argues that "we knew a lot of people in Congress were cor-rupt," which seems to make a case for "ongoing criminal activity." Yet he readily concedes that Williams and Thompson, for example, were thought to be honest and that he has nothing particular in mind when he refers to his prior knowledge of congressional corruption, which, of course, is consistent with the fact that Abscam in no way began as a congressional probe.

DeLOREAN AND HITACHI

The John DeLorean case illustrates similar problems. What is known so far from government filings is that DeLorean, desperate to save his car company, was put in touch with a drug dealer by a conman-turned-informant named Hoffman. The drug dealer and Hoffman told DeLorean that he could make $60 million by financing a major cocaine deal. Government agent Hoffman then put DeLorean in touch with an FBI agent posing as a banker, who lent DeLorean the money to finance the deal. In short, DeLorean, about whom there is no evidence of prior involvement in drug dealing, was provided by the government with the money to finance a drug deal and provided with a drug dealer with whom to do business. Here is a crime clearly created by the government: how else could the money-strapped, inexperienced (in drug dealing) John De-Lorean, any more readily than you or I, become a drug dealer about to make $60 million?

What we don't know in the DeLorean case is whether informant Hoffman first suggested the drug deal to DeLorean or vice versa, and that is certain to be the key fact issue at trial. But an FBI agent familiar with the case recently told me that "Hoffman told the agent he was working with that DeLorean was a neighbor of his [in San Diego] and was eager for ways to make money. He [DeLorean] knew Hoffman was a shady guy. Hoffman told us that DeLorean suggested drugs, but that was only after we told Hoffman to go back and see if DeLorean might be interested [in a drug deal]. So who knows?"

The point is that for the FBI agents and their undercover agent, De-Lorean was a big catch, just as Williams and MacDonald were big catches for Weinberg and Puccio, both of whom stood to gain financially from their big indictments—Weinberg via FBI bonuses and Puccio with the notoriety that helps a prosecutor later establish a private practice. In that situation, dare we allow a verdict to turn on the assurance of a criminal-turned-informant that the crime was first suggested by the defendant? That's why all those incomplete and missing tapes and reports of Weinberg's are so important, and why the Williams coaching tape (other

Abscam defendants claim they, too, were coached) is so important. And that's why the concerns raised by Del Tufo, Stewart, Plaza, Weir, and Robertson should have been hotly heeded, not ignored and denigrated.

In the case of the Hitachi executives charged with buying IBM trade secrets, an equally strong though different incentive seemed to be at work encouraging the FBI informants to create crimes: they were IBM employees who, the defense has already contended, were simply using the FBI to wipe out a competitor. In fact, the key undercover person in this case is an IBM security operative named Callahan who posed as a *lawyer* advising the Hitachi people in procuring the alleged trade secrets. We don't yet know how far Callahan advised his "clients" to go in committing their alleged crimes, but why should we be faced with that question? Why pose someone as a lawyer, especially given the Japanese tendency to defer to lawyers as prophylactic advisers on legality, if the goal is to bring absolutely legitimate cases rather than to bag some high-powered suspects?

Undercover sting operations are, of course, necessary. Crimes like bribery or drug dealing or even trade-secret stealing don't occur out in the open or produce victims who can identify perpetrators in a police lineup. But when the police go underground and lie about who they are and what they're doing, special protections and special vigilance are necessary. And these protections should arguably be not only operational but structural, going beyond the simple pleas of Del Tufo and his men for better monitoring of how far the undercover people pushed their targets. The vigilance should start with restrictions on the nature of the operation itself.

At a minimum, an undercover operation should be directed at an ongoing criminal activity in which the police believe the target is participating, such as a drug sting of a reputed drug dealer. Or the scam might be directed at unknown targets if they are targets who, because of the nature of the sting, will soon materialize on their own—such as purveyors of stolen goods snared in a feigned fencing operation, trade-secret thieves caught by undercover agents trying to buy IBM trade secrets, or congressmen caught in a scam that simply spreads the word that there's a sheik in town eager to bribe legislators for votes on AWACs. Even then, the undercover operatives must be careful not to overdo it: the operation must make the criminal activity absolutely unambiguous in nature and subject to the targets' clearly intentional and active participation.

Another reason to limit stings to ongoing criminal activity has to do with simple law enforcement priorities. Frustrated as they may be by their inability to curb the kinds of violent crimes that infuriate all taxpayers, police may like the idea of looking clever by catching big-name crooks on television with these kinds of video-stings. But does creating a crime in order to test a man's honesty do anything to curb crime? Did giving John DeLorean the means to become a drug dealer and then catching him at it do anything to curb drug dealing?

Following DeLorean's arrest there have been all kinds of leaks concerning his allegedly dishonest stock deals and other financial manipulations. If the government had reasonable cause to suspect him of that kind of wrongdoing, why couldn't it set up that kind of sting to catch him—thereby intervening in ongoing criminal activity?

It seems probable that the Second Circuit or even the Supreme Court will veto government overreaching such as that which occurred in the Williams case with Weinberg's coaching followed by his continued attempts over eight months to get the senator to incriminate himself still more. But it seems that a broader rule is necessary, lest the police get the idea that an appealing substitute for solving real crime is creating already solved ones with a star cast on camera.

This broader protection would be based on a citizen's basic constitutional right to be left alone and not have his privacy invaded by police and their criminals-turned-informants laying integrity-test traps. Put differently, it would be based on the constitutional principle that in the United States the function of police is to catch criminals, not test people for possible criminal tendencies.

"I'm not big on guidelines for undercover operations," says Puccio. "The best safeguard," he explains, "is the honesty of the target. An honest man will not succumb. If MacDonald had been thoroughly honest, he'd have not been there." Doesn't that ignore the probability of the police working so hard and in such bad faith at getting an innocent man that they find the right inducement and the right set of circumstances? "The honesty of the individual is still the best safeguard," Puccio maintains.

What about this case: The Justice Department becomes concerned that leaks of grand jury proceedings are compromising investigations and the integrity of the process. It decides to send a reporter out to solicit leaks. The reporter, who has a solid reputation for writing about organized crime that easily wins him friends among prosecutors, invites a high-profile former prosecutor to lunch. The prosecutor, now in private practice in New York, seems eager to please the reporter, who now runs a publication about lawyers, and eager to talk about the challenges of his new practice. The reporter commends the lawyer on his fabulous career, drawing an appreciative smile.

Having thus made friends, the reporter asks for help on an article he's writing. Could the prosecutor tell him about the proceedings of a grand jury that he ran in his most well-known case? The former prosecutor readily offers the information (about whether and how some supposed witnesses had testified and how the grand jurors had reacted to the proceedings). It's not a major transgression, but arguably, in the hands of an able, eager prosecutor, enough to be a violation of Rule 6E of the Federal Rules of Criminal Procedure which constitutes criminal contempt of court.

Thomas Puccio has been successfully stung, though only in print.

INSIDE THE DeLOREAN JURY ROOM

BY

STEVEN BRILL

The jurors share their notes with Brill on the trial proceedings, their perceptions of key witnesses, and their recollections of their seven-day deliberation.

"I had all these people—friends, relatives, even strangers—come up to me and say, 'We knew you'd find the son of a bitch innocent. He's too rich to get caught,' " recalls Linda Wolfe, 27, who served on the jury in the drug conspiracy trial of John DeLorean. "It was *so* frustrating." Wolfe had been the staunchest holdout for a conviction. And she does not like the idea that her service on this now celebrated jury brands her as some kind of softie or social reformer.

Nor does John Holladay, a 64-year-old self-described conservative who served 30 years in the army and retired as a colonel. Like nine of the other eleven jurors, he voted for President Reagan last month.

Holladay's was an early not-guilty vote, as was that of W. Vern Lahr, 57, the jury foreman—who spent ten years as a California highway patrolman. For Lahr, the press coverage following the acquittal, which stressed the jury's supposed reliance on entrapment as a defense, has been as unnerving as the ribbing he has taken from friends for letting DeLorean off. Like many of the others, including Holladay, Lahr never needed to worry about entrapment. The government simply hadn't met what Lahr calls its "hellacious burden of proof."

Harry "Hal" Graves, 49, did believe DeLorean guilty of a drug conspiracy, but yielded when some of the others pushed the entrapment issue. His basic strategy for dealing with friends who kid him about the verdict, he says, is "to get them to wipe the word *innocent* from their minds. John DeLorean is not innocent. We just couldn't find him guilty and do our jobs the way we were sworn to," he explains.

This is not the story of what John DeLorean did, or what the government did to snare him, or what either side's lawyers did. Rather, it is a story, perhaps even a celebration, of twelve people doing their jobs as they were sworn to.

Eleven of the twelve jurors (and three of four alternates) were interviewed for this article, most more than once. There was also one three-hour group interview involving eight jurors and alternates. Theirs is a story filled with ironies and things that are not supposed to happen. For example the youngest, seemingly most liberal juror—Wolfe—became the holdout for a verdict of guilty, while the oldest, seemingly most conservative member of the panel—Holladay—became a pivotal voice for acquittal. But above all, it was the story of the system working—and of all the tensions that arise when the popular expectation that bad people should be punished brushes against the safeguards necessary to assure that the state does not overstep.

"WHY ELSE WOULD THEY HAVE ARRESTED HIM?"

"Sure I thought he was guilty," says Jo Ann Kerns, 39, who works as an assistant manager in sportswear at the Broadway department store in Montclair, California. "Why else would they have arrested him?"

Like many of the other jurors, Kerns had not only heard and read about DeLorean's arrest on October 19, 1982, but also saw the videotape that porn publisher Larry Flynt had procured and given to CBS to broadcast a year later. The tape, which Kerns recalls seeing one night while preparing dinner, showed DeLorean in a hotel near the Los Angeles airport with two undercover agents, reaching for plastic bags of cocaine and exclaiming that they were as "good as gold," then toasting to the group's success, whereupon he was arrested.

Howard Weitzman, DeLorean's chief defense lawyer, says a poll he had done before the trial *and before the airing of the Flynt-procured tape* showed that 92 percent of the people in the far-flung area of the federal court's Central District of California had heard about the DeLorean case and that 70 percent believed him guilty. All the jurors and alternates interviewed told me they knew about the case before the trial. With two claimed exceptions, all said they assumed the automaker guilty.

"SOME DEFENSE LAWYER HAD ALWAYS REJECTED ME"

"I had always wanted to be on a jury," says Vern Lahr, who later became the foreman. "But I had reconciled myself to the fact that because of my background in law enforcement and the job I have in the insurance industry I never would be." Lahr, in addition to having been a highway patrolman, has been an insurance claims adjuster and is now a claims superintendent for State Farm Mutual Automobile Insurance Company. "So, I reassured everyone at work when I got called for jury duty that there was no chance I would get on a panel," he says. "Several times before, I had been called but had never had the chance to serve; some [defense] lawyer had always rejected me."

Called for federal jury duty in January, Lahr, like those who would be his co-jurors, waited around for several weeks. On Friday, March 2, they were told that, if they were willing to volunteer to be considered to serve on a panel that might involve a very long case, they would be free to go if they were not chosen for that case. They were also told that if they were chosen—the odds of which were fairly slim because many would be disqualified for one reason or another—the trial might last as long as two months, but that court would be in session from just 8:30 to 1:30 (with two 15-minute breaks) from Tuesday to Friday. Later, when the trial started, Lahr, like Kerns and others, would go to his regular job every day at about 2:30 and work past normal closing time. Despite this schedule and the fact that some jurors lived as many as 80 (and in two cases more than 100) miles away from the courthouse, not one juror or alternate missed a day or even arrived late during what would become a four-month trial.

Clarence Berman, 56, also wanted to be on the jury, and for him the prospect of a long case was especially appealing. "I had just retired," he says, "and the idea of steady work at the courthouse seemed okay. It was like a new civil service job.

"But," adds Berman, "that Sunday night I was reading the paper in bed and saw a small article about the DeLorean case about to begin. I figured, 'Shit, I can't get on that panel; I know too much.' I had seen and read so much about it, and I figured the guy was guilty. Also, my job had been in law enforcement"—as a county environmental inspector—"and I knew that would disqualify me."

"Because, like Vern, I'm an insurance adjuster, I was sure I'd never get on," says Hal Graves. "So when they told the group of us to raise our hands and be sworn in, Vern and I looked at each other in disbelief."

"The jury selection process was probably the most important thing for us about the trial," says Donald Ré, Weitzman's co–defense counsel and his partner in the small Los Angeles firm of Weitzman & Ré. "The key," Ré adds, "was the judge."

In the conventional jury selection process in the federal courts, the judges question the prospective jurors. Judge Robert Takasugi, a 54-year-old Gerald Ford appointee and former general practitioner and municipal court judge, did the voir dire differently in the DeLorean case.

Keenly sensitive (perhaps oversensitive) to the problems associated with pretrial publicity, Takasugi, whom all the jurors praise to the point of near-worship, had issued an order in 1983 enjoining the airing of the Flynt tapes. It was quickly overturned as unconstitutional by the Ninth Circuit. Now, Takasugi decided to have all prospective jurors fill out a questionnaire detailing their backgrounds, what they knew about the case, whether they knew any of the dozens of people involved in the case, what they had read and seen generally in the news media, what their political leanings and religious beliefs were, whether they had used certain kinds of drugs, and what their attitudes were about various aspects of law enforcement. Takasugi allowed lawyers on both sides to study the completed questionnaires and then to question the potential jurors about their answers.

On Monday, March 5, 143 potential jurors filled out the questionnaire, which the prosecutors and defense lawyers had helped to draft. It was 42 pages long and had 99 questions. On Tuesday, March 13, the lawyers' questioning and their process of moving to eliminate jurors they didn't want began. It would last for seven weeks.

"The prosecutors were uneasy about the process, because they'd never done state cases, where [lawyers doing the questioning] is standard," asserts Ré, referring to James Walsh, Jr., and Robert Perry, two highly regarded veteran assistant United States attorneys who respectively were the number-one and -two men on the prosecution team. (Walsh declined to be interviewed for this article; Perry says that he had done voir dire himself in one prior trial. Judge Takasugi also declined to discuss the case.)

"Walsh and Perry," claims Ré, "never understood what we were after in the process. They always figured we were so worried about the tapes that we'd want to put on a few jurors who are the typical types to be sympathetic to defendants—liberals, people who themselves have used drugs—who'd hang the jury. They thought we thought the case against us was so bad that we want to hang, which we often do. But here what we really wanted were people who were thoughtful enough to see this complex case and understand that the tapes didn't show a conspiracy, or to understand the unusual entrapment issues in this case."

"Of course, Vern Lahr's police background threw up a red flag," says Weitzman. So did Colonel Holladay's military background. "But we figured from the kinds of answers he and Holladay gave to our questions that they were thoughtful enough to think this case through."

"Jo Ann Kerns expressed a bias, no doubt about it," Ré recalls, "but at that point we were losing too many intelligent jurors because they said they thought he was guilty. So we decided based on her answers that she'd be open-minded enough to take a chance on her."

"You use that opportunity of questioning jurors to begin your case," notes Weitzman. "You set it up, by saying things like, 'You're going to see lots of tapes; are you prepared to believe that they may not mean what they seem to mean or that the government may have orchestrated them?' "

"It dawned on me," says juror Berman, "that there might be a different story from what I'd seen on TV when Weitzman asked me a question about the tapes and if I was prepared to consider that they might not be what they seem to be. From then on, I was skeptical." Berman adds that prosecutor Perry's warning that the chief witness in the case—informant James Hoffman—was a convicted drug dealer and perjurer also shook his original presumptions. Several of the other jurors say their assumption of guilt was eroded at least somewhat by the voir dire.

The prosecution's questioning may even have contributed to that: it seems to have raised the expectations of the jurors to levels that were never met. For example, Berman recalls that "Perry asked me what I thought of government sting operations. I said they were okay if they stop crimes, but that I didn't like Abscam because it seemed like that hadn't focused on criminals and had set up the crime. So he said, 'Would something like Abscam be okay as long as the defendant thought up the crime first?' And I said, 'Sure.' Well, because I was ultimately seated on the jury, I figured my answer was the acceptable one for Perry and that Perry was prepared to prove to me that DeLorean thought of drugs first. But they never showed that he thought of it first.''

"We, too, were looking for intelligent people, and got them," says Perry. "They were intelligent, but not smart enough to see the truth." (Beyond commenting generally on the case and the jury selection process, Perry would not discuss specific trial strategy or the merits of the case against DeLorean.)

"All in all," says Ré, "all sixteen jurors and alternates were among the twenty-five people we had decided from the questionnaires and voir dire would be best for us."

In addition to Kerns, Berman, Holladay, Graves, and Lahr, the jurors were:

- Ruthe Sutton, 61, an administrative aide in the Los Angeles County school system.
- Jackie Caldwell, 33, a sometime housewife and sometime bill collector for an auto repossession company.
- Linda Wolfe, 27, a sometime teacher, actress, and singer.
- Carl Hoover, 36, a tax administrator for the Fluor Corporation.
- Fred Gelbart, 34, a research scientist with California Institute of Technology. (Gelbart, who is said by prosecutor Perry to be working on a book about his jury service, is the only juror who declined to be interviewed. Positions attributed to him in this article are taken from the accounts of his fellow jurors.)
- Evelyn Dowell, a sometime housewife who has worked on divorce arbitration workshops and has a master's degree in chemistry. (Dowell consented to only two brief interviews and refused to be quoted directly.)
- Nancy Andersen, 35, a registered nurse. Incredibly, Andersen was allowed to serve despite the fact that she'd recently been on a jury in another case in which Weitzman had been the defense counsel. That jury, including Andersen, of course, had convicted Weitzman's client on several counts. After the DeLorean trial was over Andersen would ask Weitzman why he had allowed her to serve. "He told me," she recalls, "that he remembered that after that first trial I had seen him on the courthouse steps and told him that the evidence offered by the undercover agents was convincing and that he figured I was intelligent

enough to see that the evidence in this case from the undercover people was a contrast, that it was not convincing.'' Prosecutor Perry says, ''We heard she'd served on a jury in front of Weitzman, but not that she'd had a conversation with him. No one told us that.''

Altogether there were six men and six women, seven college graduates, eleven self-described political moderates or conservatives, four people with some prior involvement in some aspect of law enforcement (including bill collector Caldwell), and five who worked, or had worked, for some governmental body.

THE TRIAL

''This case is a story of a man with a dream . . . and how he turned that dream into a nightmare composed of failure, drugs, and disgrace,'' prosecutor Walsh charged in his opening.

Walsh—who had been in charge of the DeLorean investigation from the start—outlined his case as follows: In June of 1982, DeLorean, desperately in need of cash to save his Northern Ireland–based car company, had asked James Hoffman, a drug dealer whom DeLorean had met when the two had been neighbors in 1980 in Southern California, if Hoffman still had ''his [drug] connections in the Orient.'' When Hoffman said yes, DeLorean told him that he had $2 million he wanted to invest in a heroin deal. Later, according to Walsh, a cocaine smuggling operation had been substituted for the heroin deal, and still later DeLorean had been allowed to put up stock as collateral when he couldn't come up with the $2 million.

What DeLorean hadn't known, Walsh said, was that Hoffman had been caught in 1981 and forced to become an undercover agent, that the other men to whom Hoffman had led DeLorean—a supposed organized crime drug czar and a supposedly crooked banker—were Drug Enforcement Administration (DEA) and FBI agents respectively, and that many of their meetings with DeLorean were videotaped. The videotapes, Walsh promised the jurors, would provide a ''candid camera'' show in which ''John DeLorean is caught in the act of being himself.''

''This case is a sick case; it is a tragedy and a travesty of justice, and the evidence will show you that,'' Weitzman countered, whereupon he ripped into informant Hoffman and the coming tape show that Hoffman and federal agents had ''orchestrated.''

The jurors recall that they were generally unmoved by the openings, though they thought then, as they would later, that both sides' lawyers were effective.

"HE COULDN'T BE THAT STUPID"

Linda Wolfe says she thought to herself when FBI agent Benedict Tisa—who had posed in the DeLorean sting as a crooked banker—first took the stand, "Wow, he's impressive. So good-looking. So well tailored." Her enthusiasm did not last long. "Soon," she says, "I got upset about him. God, his answers were so evasive. It was so obvious he was trying to say just the right thing to cover his ass."

"I was so angry," says Jo Ann Kerns. "A guy who pays as much attention as he does to the crease in his pants when he sits down could not have been that unprepared and stupid. . . . It had to have been deliberate. This guy took up three weeks on three days' worth of testimony. He just wouldn't answer, especially on cross-examination."

"Ask him what time it was," says Hal Graves, "and he'd start to tell you how to make a watch." But the problems with Tisa's testimony were a matter of substance as well as form.

Walsh, an intense veteran prosecutor, used Tisa to present the basics of the case Walsh had put together, including all the tapes. Says Berman, the retired environmental enforcement officer, "By the end of Tisa's direct examination I knew that if this was the government's case I could not in good conscience find guilt beyond a reasonable doubt." Berman says he recorded in his notebook—some jurors would reportedly fill in as many as seven steno pads during the four-month trial, and Cal Tech scientist Gelbart would index his seven books—that "Tisa was interpreting things in ways that just weren't necessarily justified. He kept repeating 'DeLorean's drug deal' or something to that effect to refer to every event, as if he'd been programmed to, when it wasn't clear that any of those events necessarily had anything to do with a drug deal."

For example, the first videotape showed DeLorean with Tisa at a San Francisco savings and loan that had allowed Tisa to pose there as a crooked banker. Berman and the other jurors saw DeLorean, having been directed to Tisa by informant Hoffman, start to discuss an investment in the DeLorean car company. Tisa told DeLorean that, yes, he had an investor, but that it was someone who'd "been very successful in bringing in cocaine" and now needed some way to invest the illicit profits.

DeLorean clearly offered to launder the money through his company by creating a back record of consulting payments to the drug dealer.

What did all that have to do with DeLorean, himself, doing a drug deal? Because, Tisa explained, DeLorean later acknowledged that he was investing $2 million for a drug deal involving this drug dealer and Hoffman, the informant. Yet it wasn't clear from the tape that DeLorean was talking about investing in the drug deal, per se, and, more important, DeLorean had never come up with the $2 million. "He was never charged with laundering money," notes Berman, "and he never invested the two million."

Indeed, another tape had DeLorean telling Hoffman that he could not come up with the $2 million. Tisa testified that the day after that conversation he had called DeLorean and suggested that he could put up collateral instead of cash, which, the prosecution contended, is what DeLorean did—in the form of stock in a DeLorean car company shell corporation that, by all later accounts, was worthless.

"When I heard that they had called DeLorean back after he said he wasn't putting in the money, that was it for me," says Nancy Andersen, the registered nurse. "As far as I am concerned because they called him instead of him calling them no one can say beyond a reasonable doubt that he ever intended to do a drug deal."

Yet Graves, Wolfe, housewife/bill collector Jackie Caldwell, and accountant Carl Hoover say that at this point, if not throughout the trial, they thought DeLorean was clearly involved in culpable activity. Graves adds that he felt the government "was just following up" by calling DeLorean back. "There's no reason DeLorean had to take the offer [of putting up collateral instead of cash]," he explains, making a point seconded by many of the others, especially Wolfe.

Weitzman would later suggest that DeLorean had seemed to accede to Tisa's offer to put up collateral only because he was afraid of Tisa and the others and of backing out on their deal. After all, Tisa, supposedly a mob-connected banker, had told DeLorean in one of the taped conversations that DeLorean's not coming up with the $2 million had put Tisa and his confederates "in a bad spot." But none of the jurors, except nurse Andersen (who seems to have accepted almost everything Weitzman argued), would buy that part of the defense, though Colonel Holladay recalls being upset that "Tisa sounded angry when DeLorean said he wasn't investing in the drug deal. What business does an FBI agent have being angry when someone won't invest in drugs?" It was a point that Weitzman would make almost word for word in his summation.

Weitzman's cross-examination of Tisa—which lasted 12 days but "could have lasted two if the man had answered the questions," says Kerns—intensified the skepticism now shared by many of the jurors.

Weitzman hammered away at the FBI agent on why he had called DeLorean back to suggest he put up collateral. "So, as I understand it, if Mr. DeLorean had not come up with the promissory note, he would have been out of the deal, correct?" Weitzman asked. "Yes," said Tisa, in a rare one-word answer.

"And whose plan was it, sir, to come up with that alternative?" Weitzman continued. "I guess it was ours, the government's," Tisa answered.

In all, if the jurors' own accounts are accurate, the testimony of the government's lead witness produced three seemingly unshakable not-guilty votes—those of Andersen, Berman, and Kerns—and more strong not-guilty leaners, such as Ruthe Sutton and Evelyn Dowell.

Linda Wolfe was the strongest guilty proponent at this point, just as she would be throughout. "I really felt kind of sorry for Walsh and Perry watching Tisa testify," she said. "It seemed to me they didn't want him to be so evasive. . . . It was even brought up at the trial that Perry yelled at him for not answering the questions."

Indeed, at several points at the beginning of a new day or after a recess Weitzman would sarcastically ask Tisa if "there is anything you would like to change, amend, modify, delete, correct," whereupon Tisa would pathetically say that, yes, there were some changes to make. "I had a whole shtick about asking him if he wanted to change anything," says Weitzman, calling this "part of my flair for humor."

One day, after Tisa had duly made some corrections, Weitzman said, "You only changed your testimony after Mr. Perry yelled at you during the recess. . . . Isn't that true?"

Tisa replied, "If you're asking me if I'm changing my story because Mr. Perry talked to me, no. I sat and reflected on what I had said and what I had done, and I realized that I had mistakenly said some things that were not correct."

Unlike Wolfe, other jurors seized on the daily corrections by Tisa (and later by others) as still more evidence of the government's efforts to fabricate a case. "The prosecutors had to tell him what to say every day," says Kerns. "That's part of why it took three weeks. The whole thing made me angry. From Tisa on, I didn't see that they had a case."

Even Wolfe says that the Tisa testimony made her skeptical enough that "I began to rethink some of the assumptions I had coming in." Thus, it was sometime during Tisa's cross-examination, Wolfe recalls, that she and Berman and ''one or two other'' jurors had a conversation that signaled the new sensitivity to the presumption of innocence that they were developing. Says Wolfe, ''We were sitting around [in the jury room] during one of the sidebar conferences [between the judge and the lawyers] and someone was reading about a highly publicized child molestation case out here. And one of the jurors remarked, 'I could never be fair to a defendant who did something like that.' Well, Clarence and I found ourselves at the same time saying, 'Wait a minute, that person didn't *do* anything; it's only an accusation.' ''

Other than moments like that, the jurors report that they had not the slightest inkling about what each of them was thinking about this case; they each say that they so scrupulously observed the judge's warning not to discuss the case until deliberations that they had no idea when the trial closed whether anyone agreed with their view of the case or how the verdict would come out.

Some, however, ventured some guesses to themselves or spouses. Graves recalls, based on some discussion that he had with Lahr about recent developments in insurance laws (they are both insurance adjusters), ''I assumed he was very inflexible and very conservative.'' Other jurors say that Linda Wolfe's youth, effusive speaking manner, political views (she's a liberal), and what one calls her ''liberated life-style'' made them assume she was pro-defense. Similarly, former cop Vern Lahr's strong protestation when Jackie Caldwell announced one morning that she'd gotten a speeding ticket (two other jurors got tickets during the trial), and accused all police of going out of their way to ticket people driving new cars, led many to believe Lahr felt that lawmen could do no wrong.

Such differences in outlook, though, were always expressed kiddingly; for something else was going on among the jurors and alternates. It was a phenomenon that all would bring up in later interviews, but that they had trouble explaining. Perhaps it was the desert-island-like unifying effect of having to sit through the testimony of someone like Tisa. Maybe it was the boot-camp aura created by the seven-week selection process. Or perhaps it was Judge Takasugi's solicitousness in explaining what was going on, in asking after their comfort, and in joking with them, all of which made them feel so special as a group.

Whatever it was, the meticulous Cal Tech researcher with the Ph.D. (Gelbart); the quiet schoolroom painter (alternate Al Walker, one of two blacks on the panel); the tough, opinionated former cop (Lahr); the ebullient young sometime actress and teacher (Wolfe); the easygoing insurance adjuster (Graves); the outgoing, vivacious nurse (Andersen); the stern-looking school board administrative aide (Sutton, the second black); and the others were becoming like an extended family. They joked and gossiped with each other about politics, religion, their love lives, their jobs, and anything else except the case. Many of them would later say that they had come to like the group so much and, indeed, were to become in many instances so touched by the sense of friendship and shared mission they developed, that the thought of having a party-pooping debate over a verdict sometime later scared them.

TESTIMONY FROM A "CREEP"

Ruthe Sutton remembers that when James Timothy Hoffman, a jowly 43-year-old 225-pounder in a government-purchased brown polyester suit, took the stand as the prime witness against John DeLorean, "he never looked anyone in the eye. He was just not believable from the minute he spoke."

"I believed nothing Hoffman said," recalls Jo Ann Kerns. "And I kept thinking to myself, 'If Hoffman can do this to DeLorean, he can do this to any of us.' " Kerns's point should not be mistaken for a broader argument about entrapment or sting operations: "I'm all in favor of going after people if the government knows or has reason to believe that they are dealing in narcotics. Then anything goes. Any tricks that the government can come up with. But here it was just Hoffman's word. And then we never saw DeLorean on the tapes actually participate in the conspiracy."

Prosecutor Walsh took Hoffman through the story of how he had befriended DeLorean because his son and DeLorean's had played together when the two were neighbors near San Diego in 1980. Hoffman explained that it was the sons' friendship, not an intention to try to snare DeLorean in a drug deal, that had led Hoffman to call DeLorean two years later (on June 29, 1982)—by which time Hoffman, coincidentally, had become a government informant. "This guy's father of the year," Holladay recalls thinking to himself. "He's using his own son to make up a story to get money as an informant."

But the reaction was not unanimous. Hoffman's testimony had occasioned the playing of more tapes, the most notable being one in which DeLorean is clearly listening and nodding agreement as Hoffman outlines

240

a drug wholesaling operation, and another in which Hoffman and De-
Lorean are in a room while DeLorean calls a real drug smuggler named
Morgan Hetrick and urges him to get on with a smuggling trip to Colombia. Hoffman and the government agents were also stinging Hetrick,
and had decided to put DeLorean in touch with him; ultimately Hetrick,
having flown in a large cocaine shipment from Colombia, would be
arrested the day before DeLorean, and he'd plead guilty to the same
conspiracy that DeLorean was charged in. Some jurors, particularly
Wolfe and Graves, were impressed by these tapes; they indeed show
that DeLorean at that point was ready and willing to take money generated from a cocaine deal. But it was the government agents, not De-
Lorean, who had promised to give Hetrick the money to buy the
Colombian drugs, and it was impossible from the tapes to understand
what arrangement DeLorean and Hetrick—the supposed co-
conspirators—had had.

More important, it was never clear how DeLorean had come to be
involved. Had Hoffman lured him, or had he really approached Hoffman
only after Hoffman had called to ask about getting their sons together to
play? This was the focus of Weitzman's cross-examination, and it brought
many more jurors on their way over to Holladay's and Sutton's view of
Hoffman and the case.

If Hoffman had first met DeLorean and chatted with him during a brief
period in 1980 when DeLorean and his family were out at their California
home (they lived mainly in New York and New Jersey) for an Easter
vacation, why had Hoffman told the grand jury just after DeLorean's
arrest that he had gotten to know the auto magnate over a nine-month
period in 1980, Weitzman asked. Could it be that when federal investigators checked further they realized that DeLorean, busy with his auto
company, hadn't been out to California during those nine months?
Hoffman said he had simply been mistaken when he'd testified earlier.

Hoffman now said his discussion with DeLorean about drugs had come
on June 30, after he had called DeLorean the day before (DeLorean
wasn't in and had returned the call the next day) to inquire about their two
sons' getting together during some upcoming holiday. If that's true,
Weitzman continued, why had Hoffman told the grand jury that De-
Lorean had called him first on June 29? Could it be that when government
agents later checked toll records they could find no record of DeLorean
calling Hoffman on June 29, but could find a record of Hoffman calling
DeLorean? Hoffman said he had simply been mistaken. And why, asked
Weitzman, after two years, would Hoffman's son, who is four years older

than Zachary DeLorean anyway, suddenly express an interest in playing with the ten-year-old DeLorean boy? Hoffman didn't know.

Why hadn't all of Hoffman's conversations with DeLorean been taped, once DeLorean had made his supposed drug deal overture? Because the equipment hadn't been available or had been faulty, Hoffman said.

If DeLorean had really asked on June 30 whether Hoffman still had his "connections in the Orient" necessary to do a drug deal, and Hoffman had said yes, why had DeLorean, desperate as he was, waited until July 11 to come to California to meet with Hoffman? And why, asked Weitzman repeatedly, hadn't that meeting been taped? Hoffman said he didn't know why DeLorean had waited and that the meeting hadn't been taped because the federal agents didn't think it was important enough to arrange for a taping on a Sunday.

"I still figured I was pretty sure DeLorean had been in a conspiracy with Hetrick after Hoffman testified," says Hal Graves, "but I knew one thing for sure: Hoffman is a pitiful, psychopathic liar—the kind that believes what he's saying but can't tell the truth. I can tell people like that. My own father used to tell stories and they'd change over the years, yet he'd still believe them. That's how this guy was."

Every juror, except Wolfe, uses words and phrases like "completely unbelievable" (Jackie Caldwell's description) in assessing Hoffman, while Wolfe says "he was probably lying a lot." For some, like Andersen, Sutton, Kerns, Dowell, Lahr, and Holladay—jurors who would never see the full elements of conspiracy—this was not as important as it was for the others, like Graves, Caldwell, Gelbart, and Hoover. Later, their view of the case—that DeLorean had indeed conspired in some way with Hetrick but that Hoffman couldn't be counted on to be telling the truth about his initial contact with DeLorean—would be the fulcrum of the jurors' entrapment decision.

"LIKE A BUNCH OF TEN-YEAR-OLDS PLAYING MAKE-BELIEVE"

DEA agent John Valestra had posed as the kingpin organized crime drug dealer in the sting. Perry and Walsh put him on the stand to detail the government's relationship with Hoffman and to redescribe the nature of the drug deal into which DeLorean was supposed to have entered.

But Valestra seemed at a loss to pin down what the drug deal was. Why would DeLorean share in the profits if he was putting up no cash and, by everyone's admission, playing no role in either getting the drugs or selling them once they were smuggled in? Valestra contended that DeLorean's role was that of an investor because Tisa, the FBI agent posing as the banker, had relied on DeLorean's stock as collateral in order to give Hetrick the money to buy the drugs. "Drug deals are a rocky road," Valestra said, explaining the various changes in the arrangement—from when DeLorean and Hoffman were supposedly discussing a heroin deal, to when DeLorean was supposedly putting up $2 million for a cocaine deal, to this collateral/cocaine deal. No, DeLorean and Hetrick hadn't necessarily had a meeting of the minds about what DeLorean's share of the profits would be, he conceded. But that wasn't necessary to find a conspiracy, he asserted.

To Lahr, it now seemed as if the only possible conspiracy had to involve the government agent Tisa and the informant Hoffman with DeLorean, since it seemed that if any deal had been struck it involved Tisa's and Hoffman's promise to DeLorean that he would share in their profits. But the jurors had already been told by the defense team that a conspiracy with government agents or informants was not an illegal conspiracy under the law. And that deal seemed ludicrous anyway since DeLorean would be putting up worthless stock to get $40 million for a cocaine deal without doing anything to procure or sell the cocaine.

"I thought after hearing Valestra," says Berman, "that if DeLorean was guilty of anything it was taking money from drug dealers either for nothing or for some kind of laundering scheme. But I guess he really thought he was getting something for nothing, or scamming them. The whole plan was childish. He puts in no money; he doesn't do anything; and he gets forty or fifty million dollars." (Incredibly, the numbers changed, too, from $40 million to $50 million, during Hoffman's, Tisa's, and Valestra's discussions of the deal.)

"Why doesn't someone offer me that plan?" continues Berman. "It just doesn't happen in the real world. If you could make forty million bucks in a couple of weeks or months without putting up a penny or doing anything, why would you be interested in making cars? . . . If a guy like me walked in and said, I've got two million and want to do a drug deal, and then said I don't have the two million, they'd throw me out. The collateral he put up [in a shell corporation that had no assets] was obviously worthless; a child with a pencil could have figured that out. This whole thing was like a bunch of ten-year-olds having a club and playing make-believe."

The government called three other witnesses, all federal agents who tried to fill in other aspects of the case. The prosecution rested on July 11. Its case had taken three months.

"We were certain we'd won," says prosecutor Perry. "We thought Hoffman had been our best witness, by far. Weitzman was obnoxious and theatrical, but he never touched Hoffman. Hoffman was unshaken through the whole thing."

A FAST DEFENSE

Weitzman's and Ré's case was over a little more than three weeks, or 12 trial days, later. Weitzman says he was "pretty sure that the government witnesses were so bad that we had it won, or hung." He was dead right, although at this point, it would have been impossible to tell from the news coverage of the trial, which seemed to indicate a strong government case. (For example, after Weitzman's 14-day-long cross-examination of Hoffman, the *Los Angeles Times* reported that the informant's testimony had been "unshaken.")

In addition to two relatively insignificant federal agents and DeLorean's secretary (who disputed one of Hoffman's key claims about the timing and circumstance of his initial call to DeLorean, and had a logbook to prove it), Weitzman and Ré called William Waters, a local DEA supervisor who had testified for the government. Their purpose was to prove that the government had rushed its final Los Angeles hotel scene (the one with the cocaine bags) and its arrest of DeLorean so that this crowning element of the sting would take place before the scheduled collapse of DeLorean's company. (The defense's contention was that the government investigators knew that DeLorean would not be desperate for money—via either a drug deal or an investment, depending on whom you believe—once the DeLorean Motor Company went under for good.)

Although Weitzman had requested before the trial all government documents relating to the timing of the arrest, and hadn't gotten any, he had also initiated a Freedom of Information Act request; and now, just as Waters was about to testify, the request had produced something: a cable from the L.A. DEA office to Washington DEA officials citing news reports of the imminent demise of the car company and asking permission to arrest DeLorean before his company went under. Weitzman ripped into Waters and the government for not having yielded the document originally; prosecutor Walsh responded, as he had following similar discoveries of prior requests for documents during the trial, that it had been overlooked.

By now the prosecutors had long since lost most of the jurors, though, according to Perry, they didn't know it. But this constant disclosure of previously requested documents and what seemed to the jurors to be the government's lame excuses about why they hadn't been produced before, intensified in at least four jurors their determination to vote not guilty. As Kerns puts it, ''The government's conduct made me feel less uncomfortable about freeing a guy like DeLorean.''

Using the cable, Weitzman got Waters to concede that the case had been rushed at the end and that the Los Angeles FBI agents had argued with their New York counterparts over who would get the chance to arrest DeLorean. Accordingly, he also got Waters (and a prior witness, FBI agent Jerry West) to admit that DeLorean's presence in the Los Angeles hotel room, let alone the presence of the cocaine in the room, had nothing really to do with the charges against DeLorean, since he was not charged with having imported or sold the contraband and since the conspiracy that he was charged with had taken place prior to that scene. The two agents conceded that the scene was staged basically as a clincher in proving DeLorean's knowledge of the illicit nature of the undercover agents' business—an admission that Weitzman characterized as a concession that this scene had been orchestrated purely for its dramatic effect on the jury.

Then Weitzman struck more pay dirt. He noticed that the cable Waters had written referred to ''demands being made by the informant'' and asked Waters what that meant, whereupon Waters revealed that, just before the first videotaping of DeLorean, Hoffman had demanded ''as a bounty'' 10 percent of any drugs that would be seized from Hetrick. Reminding Waters that the government had allowed Hoffman to tell the jurors that, in addition to the living expenses he had received from the government, he had helped with the DeLorean investigation only because he ''enjoyed the feeling of doing something that was worthwhile,'' Weitzman demanded to know why Waters hadn't disclosed the demand before. Because he had rejected Hoffman's demand immediately and therefore had considered the ''matter put to rest,'' Waters answered.

Out of the jury's earshot, Judge Takasugi, who had given not a hint of what he thought of either side's case, now called the Waters admission about Hoffman a ''smoking gun'' in terms of the informant's credibility. Weitzman cites it as the high point of the case—the time ''when I really thought for sure we had it won.''

The jurors were not nearly so moved, perhaps because they didn't need to be. Most call Waters, who if nothing else answered succinctly, the strongest of the government's witnesses, because, as Graves puts it, "he was straightforward; he admitted mistakes." And everyone was already so down on Hoffman that, in Ruthe Sutton's words, "we didn't really need Waters."

Weitzman's final witness was Gerald Scotti, a former DEA agent who had worked on the DeLorean case. Scotti had been forced to resign from DEA after it was discovered that he had given minor information about the status of a suspect to a defense lawyer. He had finished law school and was awaiting the bar results while co-hosting a sports radio show.

Scotti, 36, testified that on the morning of June 29—the day before Hoffman first reached DeLorean by phone (supposedly to arrange their sons' social visit) and a few hours before he first tried to call the auto magnate—Hoffman had boasted to Scotti (who was with Hoffman for a court appearance on another case) that he was going to "get John De-Lorean for you guys. . . . The [financial] problems he's got, I can get him to do anything I want." Scotti explained that at that time Hoffman was nearing the end of his work on the cases for which DEA had agreed to pay his living expenses in return for his undercover work.

Scotti then asserted that the case soon became a major priority for his fellow DEA agents, for the FBI, and for prosecutor Walsh, who had taken charge of the investigation. And, claimed Scotti, after one seemingly successful videotaping of DeLorean with Hoffman and Valestra (posing as the drug kingpin), the agents and Walsh had celebrated with more than $300 worth of wine. At one point in the post-taping festivities, Scotti declared, Walsh had raised his glass and said, "Gentlemen, I can see this on the cover of *Time* magazine."

Scotti faced three days of harsh cross-examination from Perry, which concentrated on the troubles he was having in his personal life during the DeLorean investigation. (Perry implied that Scotti's personal problems clouded his judgment and distracted him from what was going on in the case.) At one point, when Perry was questioning Scotti on the state of his failed marriage, based on what Scotti had confided at the time to his partner, Valestra, the witness broke into tears and a recess was called.

Perry also lashed out at Scotti about the reasons for his forced resignation, implying that it had embittered him about the DEA and his colleagues. Scotti replied that he respected his supervisor, Waters, his partner, Valestra, and Walsh. "I think we all cared," he said. "But I think we were being blind in what we were doing. It just seemed that we were on a steamroller and we lost sight of where we were. The case was so important that a lot of us who would have used better judgment on other occasions used bad judgment."

"The *Time* magazine thing didn't convince me of anything new," recalls Kerns. "It just helped pull it all together for me. Now I could understand the whole thing."

Five other jurors recall being persuaded by Scotti's testimony, particularly the *Time* magazine story, but, like Kerns, they say that it was icing on the cake.

For Ruthe Sutton, the most decisive moment in Scotti's testimony was Perry's bitter cross-examination. "I was offended by the personal questions they asked. It showed me they would go to any lengths in this case," she recalls.

"I listened to Scotti, and though I believed some of it, I felt so bad for Walsh and Perry," recalls Wolfe. "I could feel them wince when he said those things. I'm sure Walsh gave that toast, but he never expected anyone to talk about it. . . . And it didn't change my view of DeLorean."

"Scotti wasn't totally believable," says Graves, "but the judge told us after the case was over that if the defense hadn't put him on he would not have given us the entrapment instruction. So he turned out to be very important." Although Judge Takasugi declined to be interviewed for this article, other jurors share Graves's recollection about the judge's comment; and it is possible that without someone like Scotti laying a defense foundation, the entrapment instruction might not have been given.

After Scotti, the defense rested, which left some jurors wondering about a missing witness: prosecutor Walsh. "I couldn't figure out why Walsh didn't testify," says Lahr, a quandary shared by at least Berman and Graves. ("If the guy's gonna wear two hats, as investigator and prosecutor, he ought to have to testify when questions about his investigation come up," reasons Graves.) None of the three knew that during many of the long sidebar conferences that sent them out of the courtroom Weitzman and Ré had pressed for Walsh to testify but Takasugi had rebuffed them.

The government declined to recall any witnesses—including Valestra—to deny Scotti's assertions (which Weitzman made a point of reminding the jury of in his summation). "We could have rebutted Scotti with two or three people, including Valestra. But we were sure we had the case won," claims Perry (who also says that Walsh "has denied" the *Time* magazine toast).

Now only the summations were left. DeLorean himself was never called to the stand, an omission that the jurors say did not surprise them.

The jurors unanimously view the summations as having further helped DeLorean. They were either "disgusted" (Andersen's and Kerns's word) or "offended" (pro-government juror Graves's word) when Walsh *for a fourth time* played the videotape of the final arrest scene in the hotel, with DeLorean calling the cocaine good as gold. ("Didn't they think we got the point the first time?" asks Graves. "I had all these doodles in my notebook where they kept replaying those stupid tapes over and over and over.")

Yet some jurors recorded in their notebooks several of Walsh's and Perry's better points (the two prosecutors and two defense counsel each made a closing statement), including the fact that DeLorean had been taped making phone calls to Hetrick urging him to get on with the drug deal, and that the government would have been derelict had it not investigated DeLorean's professed interest (as relayed by Hoffman, of course) in investing $2 million in narcotics.

Many more jurors were impressed by Weitzman's ploy in beginning his summation by reading several pages of his opening, and then declaring, "How far off was I?" And they filled their notebooks with quotes from Weitzman and Ré. Among the most popular points transcribed or nearly transcribed were:

- the defense's calling the ever-changing account of what DeLorean's drug deal really was a game of "pin the tail on the donkey";
- the reminder that agent Tisa said he meant to sound angry when DeLorean said he didn't have the money for the drug deal;
- the reminder "that the instruction says that reasonable doubt is the state of mind which would leave a reasonable person hesitant to act," followed by the plea that "when you talk about James Hoffman, ask yourself, if Mr. Hoffman came to you and gave you information which you wanted to rely on or needed to rely on to buy a house, to make a loan . . . to buy a car, would you rely on Mr. Hoffman without hesitation?"

Following the summations, Judge Takasugi carefully read a list of 68 instructions. Most involved the usual matters of proof beyond a reasonable doubt, circumstantial evidence, the definition of conspiracy, and the like. Number 56 involved entrapment. At about 10:30 in the morning on Wednesday, August 8, the jury went out.

The alternates were then dismissed, but not before they exchanged addresses and phone numbers with their newfound friends on the panel. "The bailiff told me that it was absolutely amazing that I hadn't been moved up to the jury," says Jeanette Schniedwind, a retired civil servant, who was alternate number one. "For five full months those twelve people drove from all over and never missed a day or were late or got sick. He said he had never seen that happen, even on juries where the trial lasts a week or two. This was an extraordinary group of people."

USING ROBERT'S RULES

"It was such a relief to be able to go back into the room and talk about it after all those weeks," recalls Linda Wolfe. "We soon discovered that we all thought Tisa was an ass and things like that. It was great."

"I remember a few of us laughed hysterically when one of us made some remark about Tisa," recalls Andersen. " 'You mean, you thought that, too?' I said to someone."

Indeed, for all the jurors the beginning of deliberations was a tremendous release. Finally, all the chitchat about politics—the jury was 10 to 2 for President Reagan—and the jokes over accountant Hoover's silly puns, and the women's fascination with the network TV artists' courtroom portraits could be dropped in favor of the subject they all wanted to discuss. Finally, this group of friends—real friends—could talk about the issue that had brought them together.

Yet they also knew that real agreement was not imminent. It was going to take hard work, especially if the job was to be done without anyone's feelings being hurt.

The first order of business was selecting a foreman. Vern Lahr, the former highway patrolman, was the first to mention it, and he stood at the blackboard asking for nominations as the others sat in the armchairs around the conference table. Lahr himself was nominated, as were Carl Hoover, Colonel Holladay, and Evelyn Dowell, a housewife with a master's degree in chemistry, who seemed to most jurors to be among the most intelligent in the group. Dowell got one vote, Holladay a few, and Hoover and Lahr the rest, with Lahr emerging the victor.

"Vern was there and seemed to take charge of the vote, so we voted for him," recalls Andersen, the nurse.

After that the jurors worked on other housekeeping matters, such as deciding to eat in—"that was our first unanimous vote," says Hoover—

and to work the same 8:30-to-1:30 shift that they'd endured through the trial.

At Dowell's, Hoover's, and Gelbart's suggestion, Lahr then led a discussion on procedure. "Evelyn, Fred, and I picked up on the same thing," says Hoover, the accountant. "This was a wonderful group, and the group meant a lot to all of us. We had become such good friends and didn't want the argument to get personal. We just didn't want people arguing with each other." Dowell was especially solicitous in stressing that everyone's point of view was worth something and ought to be heard, a point she would make so often that it became annoying pabulum to some.

Foreman Lahr, picking up on the point, noted that above all their job was to come to a unanimous decision, and he recalls saying, "That's not going to happen if people get personally so identified with defending a point of view that they're backed into a corner." Everyone agreed that coming to a decision was vital, if it could be done without pressuring anyone. Someone remarked that the defense and prosecution lawyers—all four of whom everyone seemed to admire, though a vote for best performance probably would have gone to Weitzman—had worked too long and hard for the group not to come in with a verdict. Judge Takasugi, if no one else, deserved a verdict, a second juror added.

Lahr says that as onetime president of a local insurance adjusters' association and a former leader of his Masonic lodge he had become familiar with Robert's Rules of Order, and he and Hoover suggested some form of that parliamentary procedure as a way of avoiding over-personalization of the debate. "We figured that if people addressed the chair instead of each other, it would help," he recalls.

Thus, for at least the first few days—"until we became relaxed enough and were working well enough so that Vern allowed us gradually to break out of it," says Kerns—the DeLorean jury operated under a form of Robert's Rules, with people making motions or arguments to the chair (Lahr), and Lahr writing down people's names on a pad as they raised their hands, in order to set the sequence in which they would speak.

"Vern cheated a bit," jokes Graves. "I saw him sneak his name to the top of the list when he couldn't hold himself back from talking any longer.

"The important thing we did after electing Vern," adds Graves, "was to demand a set of jury instructions for all of us. We'd only gotten one copy and the bailiff told us that that was all we could get. So I said, Fine, we're not deliberating. They gave us each a copy."

The jurors then spent some time reading their notes, after which they took turns reading the eight-count indictment and instructions aloud, going over their sense of definitions.*

"We did everything calmly and methodically," recalls Hoover. "When you read about a case in the press or see it on television, you don't see the indictment, the judge's instructions, and the evidence all put together. We were going to put it all together."

"Reading the indictment against the instructions was very important for me," says Lahr. "It's what formed the basis of my decision that there was no conspiracy that was proven beyond a reasonable doubt. The press," he adds, echoing Hoover, "has made a lot of this verdict—that we were sitting in judgment on the government or trying to make some point. As far as I'm concerned all that we were doing is reading the indictment against the instructions and the evidence."

At 1:30 they went home.

A VETO OF A VOTE, THEN A "TENTATIVE" VOTE

Lahr began the session on Thursday, August 9, by suggesting that, to avoid wasting time in the event that they all already agreed on the verdict, they should take a preliminary vote on count one, which was the basic conspiracy count. Holladay agreed eagerly, but Gelbart, who would prove to be the most deliberative, or some say fastidious, of the decision makers, objected. He argued that they had spent five months on the trial and owed everyone involved more time to consider things methodically. When Hoover, Dowell, and Graves agreed, Lahr and Holladay backed off.

There was then some debate as to the procedure for considering the various counts, with Gelbart arguing for a day-by-day review of the trial, and Hoover, followed by most of the others, pushing for a count-by-count analysis and references back to the trial only when needed. Hoover's plan, as he terms it, carried.

But first Holladay got up, walked to the blackboard, and drew what he called his "big picture."

"I told them that I like to look at the big picture," he says, "not get paralyzed by analysis of details."

* It should be noted that in my interviews with the 11 jurors (all except Gelbart) not all of them always agreed on the exact sequence of events during the seven days of deliberation. In instances such as this one, where there was some disagreement, the consensus recollection is stated. No sequence is described where there was no consensus.

Holladay's picture was a straight line that he called "the line of doubt." He then marked various points on the line as denoting degrees of doubt, putting reasonable doubt about a fourth of the way along. Next, he marked where he was, which was far past simple reasonable doubt. Calling Hoffman "a shabby creep" and citing the book *Nineteen Eighty-Four*—which Weitzman had also cited in a reference that Holladay had doodled several times in his notebook—the retired colonel argued that no one could honestly deny being anyplace but where he was on the doubt line.

"John [Holladay] wanted to look at the big picture," recalls Jackie Caldwell, "but I for one wanted to do it step by step, and so did most of the others." Indeed, they did, and so began a deliberative process that would put most law students to shame, in which they carefully read, usually out loud, the count in the indictment, the relevant instructions, the tape transcripts, and then from their own voluminous notebooks.

They began with count one.

Toward the end of the second day, after not more than two hours of general discussion about this conspiracy count (in which Caldwell did the most talking, as she would most days, and Ruthe Sutton the least, but in which everyone participated as Lahr kept his list of raised hands), Lahr again suggested a preliminary vote. "I wanted to see where people stood," he says. He did not, he recalls, expect a unanimous vote, since it was clear that Caldwell, Graves, Wolfe, and probably some others believed that DeLorean had participated in the conspiracy, while many others, led by Berman, Andersen, Kerns, and Lahr himself, did not.

Dowell suggested that this first vote be "nonbinding," and Lahr agreed. He then listed all the names on the blackboard, put "not guilty" next to his own (which surprised many people, particularly Hoover and Graves), and asked which of the other jurors had a not-guilty vote. Andersen, Sutton, Kerns, Holladay, Dowell, and Berman raised their hands.

When Lahr asked for the guilties, only Wolfe and Caldwell responded, leaving Gelbart, Graves, and Hoover. These three said they were abstaining. The tally: seven not guilty, two guilty, and three abstentions.

Now the real debate began. Berman insisted that there hadn't been a conspiracy, a point seconded by Lahr. When Jackie Caldwell said the conspiracy was there because Hetrick had been DeLorean's partner in the deal, Hoover referred to his notes, he recalls, and found "that Hetrick was a separate wholesaler whom the undercover people were buying from; yet DeLorean hadn't made any deal with Hetrick to buy.

"Jackie's point was one of the things that eventually pushed me over to not guilty," says Hoover.

Hoover's use of his notes typified the proceedings; the jurors dove into their steno pads to find support for an argument, unless they quoted from the tape transcripts spread out on the large conference table. The group's reliance on notes is the reason no one needed to call for trial transcripts during the deliberations.

On the way out that afternoon, they were accosted in the courthouse parking garage by dozens of reporters and cameramen, who took their pictures and tried to write down the license plate numbers of the cars they entered so that they might obtain their names and addresses. (To avoid juror harassment, Judge Takasugi had kept the jurors' names secret.)

"They were like cockroaches in that parking garage," Wolfe recalls. "Tell me what thrill a cameraman gets out of taking our pictures getting into our cars," adds Andersen.

DEADLOCK?

As the debate over the conspiracy continued, "it began to look like a hung jury," recalls Graves, whose abstention had really had to do with his view that a vote shouldn't be taken so early. "I knew I wasn't going to be convinced that he hadn't been involved in a conspiracy," he says, "and I knew people like Clarence [Berman] and Nancy [Andersen] and Jo Ann [Kerns] were not going to be convinced that he had."

The group argued back and forth, with Lahr usually unable now to keep everyone addressing the chair. The argument was heated, often blunt, and sometimes even testy; yet by all accounts there was never any bitterness and hardly a raised voice. There was some personal bickering and even some one-on-one animosity. Linda Wolfe and Evelyn Dowell, for example, did not get on well, nor did Lahr and Berman.

But generally, people disagreed in words, not in tone, and usually took the trouble to address each other by first name (as in, "Nancy, I hear what you're saying and respect it, but I really don't see it"). Of the group, according to most of those interviewed, Holladay, Graves, and Andersen were the most plainspoken and took the least trouble to avoid offending the others; but even they were unusually affable and deferential. And Berman was the most outspoken about refusing to consider a guilty vote.

At one point, Caldwell recalls, "I said, Let's try to find some conspiracy we can agree he is guilty of." But Berman, Andersen, and Kerns would have none of that. Berman asked why Hetrick, DeLorean's supposed co-conspirator, hadn't testified or been tried (he had pled guilty), and the pro-guilty people, pointing accurately to one of Judge Takasugi's instructions about how other defendants' cases were not to be considered, said that was irrelevant.

The man working for Hetrick in transporting the drugs had also been named in the conspiracy (like Hetrick, he'd pled guilty and didn't testify); but he had not been mentioned in the trial as being involved with De-Lorean. For that reason, one of the not-guilty contingent (some remember it was Dowell, but she declined comment on what she thought or what was said in the jury room) argued that this showed the government's case hadn't been proved. But the pro-guilty people convincingly pointed out, again referring to the instructions, that DeLorean only had to be found to have acted with one of his co-conspirators (each of whom, in turn, could have acted with the other one).

Reading from the transcripts, with Jackie Caldwell helping her, Linda Wolfe argued passionately, from a more moralistic standpoint, that De-Lorean sitting in a room talking about drugs and drug flights to Colombia, even discussing with Hetrick how much gasoline the flight took, was a guilty man who ought to be punished. Berman and Lahr insisted that this was only talk, indeed arguably only the talk of a man trying to be polite while two drug dealers who are going to invest money in his company discuss their trade. It was a point that Ruthe Sutton, who spoke hardly at all, seconded vehemently but with a whisper, recalls Berman, who sat next to Sutton.

"I know I can be in a room and turn off a conversation and just nod or be polite and say something but not really be involved," Sutton recalls. "And I gave DeLorean the benefit of the doubt and assumed he could do the same thing."

Holladay, reading count one aloud again, argued more simply that, as he recalls it, "John DeLorean is no lily-white Baptist from Biloxi, Mississippi. He is not a good man. But they haven't proven a conspiracy between John DeLorean and William Hetrick beyond a reasonable doubt."

The group went home for the weekend deadlocked.

"I lay awake Friday night sorting out the evidence, but I still couldn't find the conspiracy," Lahr recalls.

"It was a terrible weekend, so stressful," Wolfe remembers. "I told my boyfriend that I didn't know what we were going to do. But I didn't want to see this jerk get off free."

A BREAKTHROUGH

Almost immediately, John Holladay proposed an approach that had been mentioned at the end of the day Friday and that he had thought over during his two-hour drive into court that morning from his home near Palm Springs. Since it was clear that the group was getting nowhere deciding whether DeLorean had engaged in a conspiracy, the retired colonel argued, why not move on to consideration of the entrapment defense? "I pointed out," he says, "that if we agreed that, even if DeLorean had committed the conspiracy, he had been entrapped into doing so, then it wouldn't matter what we thought about the conspiracy."

Lahr seized on the idea, and soon the others did, too. "It moved very quickly then," recalls Hoover. "We read through the entrapment instructions and began the discussion."

Judge Takasugi's instruction number 56 had outlined three conditions for entrapment:

1. The idea for committing the acts had to have come from the "creative activity" of the government agents or informant;

2. DeLorean had to have been induced by the government into committing the acts; and

3. DeLorean had to have not been "ready and willing" to commit the acts before the government agent or informant induced him to become involved.

For the defense to use entrapment it had to meet all three conditions.

It soon became clear that only Jackie Caldwell and Linda Wolfe were now hesitant about a not-guilty vote. The others—Graves, Hoover, and Gelbart—readily saw entrapment when they went through those three conditions. The second phone call, in which Tisa offered to let DeLorean use collateral after DeLorean had said he didn't have the money; the Scotti testimony; DeLorean's references throughout the tapes to an investment in his company; and, of course, the unlikeliness of Hoffman's having only called DeLorean to set up a meeting of their sons, were just too much. As Hoover puts it, "I thought Hoffman was as pitiful and as much of a liar as anyone. . . . I remember driving in Monday and thinking how terrible Hoffman was, and then seeing the entrapment alternative."

When Caldwell argued that the defense had to prove entrapment beyond a reasonable doubt, Holladay quickly countered that the last line of the judge's instructions said exactly the opposite—that once DeLorean's lawyers lodged the defense, the government had to prove beyond a reasonable doubt that DeLorean had *not* been entrapped. No one, said Berman, could know beyond a reasonable doubt that Hoffman's account of his contacts with DeLorean was true. Caldwell quickly came over to the not-guilty side. "She said, 'Okay, I give up. I want to find him guilty, but I guess I can't,' " recalls Graves.

Only Linda Wolfe was left.

"I just don't believe people are ever victims," she says. "People make their own fates. He could have chosen not to be involved. He could have chosen not to have those conversations. . . . He should have called the police when he saw what Tisa was up to. It's just the way I feel, and I just couldn't face letting him off."

As the others tried to persuade Wolfe, she stuck to her point about people never being victims. They recessed Monday still deadlocked.

A VERDICT

The debate picked up immediately, focusing on Linda's "no one's a victim" contention. One of the group walked her through the three conditions for entrapment. Yes, she saw that the idea of committing the crime—the Colombian drug deal—had come from the creative activity of the government. Yes, she saw that the government had induced DeLorean through the promise of the investment in his company, or the profits that were to come from the drug deal that they were setting up, whichever it was. But no, she refused to believe he had not been predisposed, because only a criminal would sit and listen to people like that talk about things like that.

The debate dragged on; by now it was getting repetitive. People were frustrated with Wolfe, as she was frustrated about the notion of letting a man like DeLorean off.

Then Jo Ann Kerns spoke up. "Linda," she began, "you have to stop judging this man by the moral standards you apply to yourself. Just because you wouldn't sit in that room doesn't mean we convict him."

It was the most emotionally charged moment of the deliberations. "You can't judge him like that. And you can't punish him if the government hasn't proven its case as it is supposed to," Kerns concluded. Andersen, then some of the others, chimed in, seconding Kerns's point.

"I had been thinking about it all night," Wolfe recalls, "and what Jo Ann said was part of what I had been thinking. I began to see that I was taking it on myself to punish him because the government hadn't made its case. Well, it wasn't my fault the government screwed up. I saw that now. It just wasn't my fault, and I wouldn't be doing anything wrong by voting not guilty."

Soon a vote was taken on the first count. It was 12 to 0 not guilty. In all, four, maybe five, jurors had been won over by the entrapment defense, while the others simply hadn't found the conspiracy.

"No, there was no real euphoria," recalls Nancy Andersen. "We just moved on."

Five counts dependent on the first one were now moot. Still to be voted on were two counts related to traveling in interstate commerce with intent to sell drugs.

A DELAY

"I viewed the travel counts as kind of nothing add-ons," recalls Hoover, "and so did most of the others. But not Linda and Jackie. They were still hanging on."

Again, Caldwell folded before too long. But Wolfe seemed to focus on the act of traveling to do a drug deal—and meeting with real or masquerading drug dealers on these trips—as even less susceptible to "victimization" (that is, less susceptible to entrapment) than the conspiracy.

No one made DeLorean travel and meet with those people, Wolfe argued. The debate dragged on through the day, with Lahr joining Kerns and Andersen in insisting that Wolfe not hold DeLorean to her standard but only the court's. Hoover recalls asking Wolfe how the government's act, via Hoffman and Tisa, of calling DeLorean in New York and telling him to hop on a plane for California and pick up his money (which was how he got to the hotel room for the final scene in the sting) could be anything *but* entrapment.

At lunch the group was forced to leave the courthouse, although they had voted the first day to eat in. The marshal told them that for some reason the building needed to be cleared and they had to eat out. (Later they heard over the radio that a telephoned bomb scare was the reason they'd had to leave.) They were piled into a marshal's van whose windows hardly opened and whose air conditioner didn't work. It was excruciatingly hot.

When they got back from lunch, "everyone was tired," Holladay recalls, "but we still treated Linda with respect."

"We kept telling her that as much as we wanted a verdict, we were not

257

going to pressure her,'' Graves remembers. ''They were real nice about it,'' Wolfe recalls. ''They were trying to help me through it.''

THE END

As the other jurors tell it, Linda Wolfe arrived seemingly ready, or resigned, to go along with them. As she puts it, ''I finally faced up to the idea that it was entrapment and that just because I might not be entrapped doesn't mean he wasn't.'' After voting not guilty on the three counts, the jurors notified the bailiff at about 11 that they had a verdict, then ate a last lunch while they waited for the court to reconvene. According to Andersen, the group talked about the public controversy their verdict was likely to engender and promised each other not to reveal what individual jurors had said in the deliberations. Some jurors later broke that vow in talking to this reporter, but only after others had, in the view of those who broke the vow, misstated in postverdict interviews the group's reasons for acquitting DeLorean.

''We the guilty,'' the court clerk began before correcting herself and reading the jury's verdicts, whereupon, says Lahr, ''Weitzman and Ré and DeLorean and his wife went up to the clouds.'' Walsh and Perry ''seemed thunderstruck. . . . I think [the prosecutors] really thought they had a case,'' adds Lahr in an assessment heartily endorsed by prosecutor Perry. ''And I could empathize with them. They had a terrible burden, and just didn't meet it.''

Following the verdict, Judge Takasugi asked the jurors to join him back in the jury room, where he thanked them and they thanked him. He then asked if they had any questions. Graves asked why Walsh hadn't been called to testify. The judge chuckled, said it was an excellent question, then told him that he had denied several of Weitzman's motions that Walsh be called to the stand.

Weitzman and Ré and their associate Mona Soo Hoo then came in to shake hands with the jurors. Weitzman asked if DeLorean and his wife could meet with the jurors. Lahr, who says the prospect made him uncomfortable, nonetheless agreed, although many, especially Linda Wolfe, did not like the idea and today view it as a DeLorean PR ploy in which they were the pawns.

According to DeLorean, ''After the verdict, the jury asked to see us. It was extremely emotional. They were crying, and telling me how they felt for me. It was incredible the feeling these people had for me.''

Weitzman, too, told me—and told the press at the time—that the jury had asked to see the defense lawyers and the defendant, a point that became a key aspect of postverdict press stories recounting the jurors' strong feelings of happiness and relief for DeLorean. All of the jurors deny it and resent it. "Weitzman asked us if he and John and Cristina [DeLorean] could see us," says Graves. "And then we read where we asked to see them. It really made us angry."

The jurors also were angered by reports, quoting Weitzman again, that the meeting with DeLorean had been extremely emotional. "It was all straightforward and objective," says Wolfe. "He thanked us and told us that it had all been as his defense said it was"—"which none of us believed," interjects Graves. DeLorean also tried to explain to the jurors that what they had seen on camera—him talking about drugs—was the picture of a desperate man who had been making trips back and forth to Europe trying to save his company and who had lost his judgment for a while. "John, they know all that," his wife, Cristina, interjected. "Let's get out of here."

At one point, Weitzman told the jurors that "they were sending a message" that the government could not get away with law enforcement tactics such as those used in this case. Gelbart—who had been noncommittal through most of the trial and certainly had never talked about sending messages—chimed in, "That's right, we're sending a message."

"Where he got that idea, I'll never know," says Ruthe Sutton. "We weren't sending any messages. We were just being fair with the evidence that we had and the case that we had."

"After Fred agreed about sending a message, which I never understood," says Graves, "Carl [Hoover, the accountant] said something about how this could happen to you or me or your children if it could happen to DeLorean. Well, that's bullshit, too. I hope I've instilled in my children better conduct than that. . . . I don't think the government entrapped anyone. They didn't do anything wrong, other than get a little excited and go a little too far by believing Hoffman and by pushing the case too fast when they saw DeLorean's company was about to go under. DeLorean would have broken a law in a way they could have proven if they'd given him the time."

Other jurors similarly resent Gelbart's and Hoover's declaration of a larger purpose and what they see as the two men's eagerness, as one of them puts it, "to use this to become media heroes." (Hoover says he meant only that he hoped that this verdict would cause the government to "go a little more carefully" in setting up stings. Gelbart is the one juror who declined to be interviewed.)

The good feeling shared by everyone in the privacy of the jury room seems to have been shattered a bit when they were thrown into the spotlight following their verdict. Seven jurors went out of their way to tell me in interviews that they had meant to do nothing more than render a verdict on this case. And most were bothered or even infuriated by the news reports that night declaring that they had intended to "send a message" about stings and entrapment and the like.

For most, the ordeal was not over when they left the courtroom. When they got home that afternoon they found reporters flocking for interviews. "My husband had let them in and was serving drinks and hors d'oeuvres," recalls Andersen.

"They were swarming all over my parents' house, because that's where my car is registered," says Wolfe, referring to the reporters' trick of tracing license plates.

The next morning, two jurors appeared on the *Today* show and three on *Good Morning America*, with Vern Lahr being the worst guest because he refused to say that the jury meant to say anything other than that the government had not proved this particular case beyond a reasonable doubt. The other four allowed themselves to be pushed into generalizing a bit, but not much.

Today, the jurors—many of whom were united for the group interview occasioned by this article, during which they exchanged news like relatives at Thanksgiving and speculated that the DeLoreans had separated in order to split, and thereby protect, their assets from bankruptcy proceedings and lawsuits—still seemed peeved at the notion, advanced particularly by Gelbart and Hoover, that they were trying to do anything other than read the indictment, read the instructions, review the evidence in their notebooks and in the transcripts, and render a decision on guilt beyond a reasonable doubt. For them that was a far higher calling and a much more challenging one; and, in their eyes, to assume that they meant to do anything else, such as "make a statement" about entrapment, denigrates what they did do.

"We never talked in that room about sending messages. We talked about the facts and the law," says Holladay. Yet some are more willing than others to generalize and draw lessons from what they decided: Andersen, the most pro-DeLorean juror, has even spoken at law forums along with defense lawyer Weitzman, and Hoover and Dowell say they are thinking of turning their journals of the trial and the deliberations into books. According to prosecutor Perry, Gelbart, too, is "hard at work on a book." (Having already come to the age of the lawyer as celebrity, could we now be approaching the era of the juror as celebrity?)

Others remain more uncomfortable about their role, or at least the public perception of it. "I feel terrible about letting him off," says Wolfe, "but I just tell people it's not my fault the government didn't prove guilt beyond a reasonable doubt."

Meanwhile, DeLorean has taken to rubbing salt in these jurors' wounds by running ads that ask for money to pay his defense fees. The ads cite the government's horrible prosecution of him, paint him as a thoroughly innocent victim, and claim to be sponsored by a group whose name—the American Civil and Economic Liberties Association—seems concocted to sound like the ACLU.

Recently, some jurors got a chance to provide some feedback on the experience—to a Justice Department task force convened to investigate the government's conduct of the case.

Several jurors report that in late October they were called by William Hendricks, a lawyer with the Justice Department's public integrity section in Washington, who asked them to meet with him and a committee he chairs that is investigating the DeLorean case and the trial. Those who met with Hendricks say the sessions (involving one juror at a time) took two or three hours and that Hendricks and his cohorts (three or four other Justice Department lawyers) asked them to talk about how they reacted to each witness and to the prosecuting attorneys.

According to Lahr and one other juror, Hendricks also mentioned that Judge Takasugi was to be interviewed and his group would be investigating the way documents needed by the defense seemed not to have been produced when initially asked for and Walsh's role as investigation leader and then lead trial counsel.

Stephen Trott, assistant attorney general in charge of the Justice Department's criminal division, says that the task force investigation, which includes "people from DEA, the FBI, and Justice," is a "routine management review." Would it be possible that having government lawyers question jurors might even inadvertently intimidate them or future juries once the existence of that investigation is known? "Absolutely not," says Trott. "This is being done with the full cooperation of the judge, and all the jurors are being told it is purely for the purpose of improving our operations"—an account confirmed by the jurors. It should be noted that prosecutor Perry has also called jurors, and invited a few to his office to explain why he and Walsh lost the case. Wolfe says that one of Perry's questions—which were always asked very politely—was, "Do you know you're going to set this guy [DeLorean] up as some sort of a hero?" Perry says he "might have said something like that, because it's true."

Of course, what the Justice Department lawyers will hear that their agents made terrible witnesses; that informant Hoffman couldn't meet the reasonable doubt burden if he were testifying about the weather; that many in the jury simply couldn't find the conspiracy because, they felt, in Lahr's words, that "the facts in the indictment weren't established yet—they should have let the case go on longer or tried to indict him for money laundering"; and that for some the entrapment issue was real, especially given the second call after DeLorean said he had no money to invest.

But there are other points that should not be forgotten when the story of the DeLorean case and its jury is considered.

For starters, there's something alluringly deceptive about a 12–0 verdict, for it implies more unanimity than really exists. The jurors here only agreed on the verdict, not on the reasons for it, not on the entrapment issues, and not on anything of policy import about the government's conduct. (Remember, Graves thought the government's second call to DeLorean asking him just to put up collateral was an appropriate follow-up, and Andersen thought it was an outrage.)

Second, the generally accepted speculation that pretrial publicity spoils things for the defendant gets no support here. Indeed, the facts of this jury's conduct and approach compared to the general assumption (even in the press's own arguments defending pretrial publicity) that pretrial publicity endangers the fairness of a trial, but that it's still worth it for First Amendment reasons, make that general assumption seem debatable, at best.

This brings to mind another point about the press and juries. Nearly everyone on this jury said he or she came out of it thinking much less of the media. Kerns's comment is typical: "Before the trial, I believed everything I saw in the media; now I believe maybe thirty percent." Why? "Because," Kerns explained, "before the trial I believed De-Lorean was guilty. The media never told me the facts of the case, and I now assume, when I see or hear a story about something else, I'm not getting the facts."

But wasn't what Kerns and the jurors experienced simply the tension between legal definitions of guilt and popular standards of good and of evil worthy of punishment? After all, didn't the press accurately report the accusations and denials and then accurately write about or show John DeLorean in a room talking drugs and holding drugs? And isn't this gap between perceived good and evil versus legally culpable criminal activity the reason that the jurors now find themselves kidded and even upbraided by friends, relatives, and acquaintances for refusing to punish DeLorean? In short, isn't it not so much that the media are inaccurate, but that the media convey general and popular perceptions of good and bad, not legally binding ones?

It would be impossible to come away from an examination of this trial and its jury without renewed appreciation for the role of the judge. Takasugi's good humor, scrupulous fairness, and attention to the jurors gave them the appreciation for the process and the inspiration to make it work that impelled them to meet a very high public calling. He raised the level of the proceedings to the highest plane, and his jurors met him there.

One of Takasugi's last instructions said, "Remember also that the question before you can never be: Will the government win or lose the case? The government always wins when justice is done, regardless of whether the verdict be guilty or not guilty." In that sense, the Justice Department investigators should find that the government won.

"We weren't trying to make policy or send messages, but there is a message here," says Colonel John Holladay. "It's that our citizens will not let our government go too far. We just looked at the evidence, and I for one saw that the government had gone too far in this case. It was like the book *Nineteen Eighty-Four*. They set one trap after another for DeLorean and then tried to prove a case when they still didn't have the evidence. In this country, the government can go only so far and then its citizens will draw them back into line.

"And that's what we did—*in this case only*," he says. "We were not making any kind of statement about what the government does generally. We were simply telling the government that it went too far on this one. You see, we just did our job as jurors, which is one hell of a responsibility."

EPILOGUE

Since his acquittal on cocaine charges in 1985, John DeLorean has been involved more than twenty lawsuits, according to his lawyer Mayer Morganroth, of Detroit. In 1986 he was acquitted of criminal charges alleging that he defrauded the limited partners of the DeLorean Motor Company of $17 million and that he conspired to evade income taxes. The trustees of DeLorean's bankrupt company brought a civil action to keep him from transferring his Palmer Valley Ranch house in California to his lawyer, Howard Weitzman, for payment of attorneys' fees.

In May 1987 Weitzman negotiated what he calls a "global settlement" that requires DeLorean to pay $9.36 million to his creditors over time. In September 1987 the court allowed DeLorean to transfer his house to Weitzman and in May 1988 it was sold for $1.1 million.

Also in 1987 an English court awarded $54 million to the British partners of DeLorean's bankrupt car company in Northern Ireland who had sued him for fraud, deceit, and breach of fiduciary duty, claiming that DeLorean stole millions from the company, DeLorean Motor Cars Ltd., before it closed in 1982. In December 1989 a federal appeals court in Cincinnati upheld the award, but it was vacated by the British High Court.

In November 1987 residents in DeLorean's New York apartment building sued to evict him, claiming he violated his lease by using his apartment as collateral for the $9.36 million he owes his creditors. The case was later dismissed, and DeLorean still lives in the building.

In April 1988 DeLorean brought a $200 million suit under the Racketeer-Influenced and Corrupt Organizations Act against the accounting firm Price Waterhouse & Company and several executives of the British accounting firm Cork Gully (the British affiliate of Coopers & Lybrand). Price Waterhouse & Company was the court-appointed accountant for the creditors' committee in DeLorean's company's bankruptcy proceedings and Cork Gully executives were on the creditors' committee. Also named as defendants are the creditors' committee lawyers Honigman Miller Schwartz & Cohn of Detroit, two of its partners, Sheldon Toll and Robert Weiss, and the chairman of the creditors' committee, Malcolm Schade, of counsel to New York's Mudge Rose Guthrie Alexander & Ferdon. DeLorean charges that the defendants humiliated and embarrassed him when they conspired to have his assets frozen and instituted conversion charges against him during his company's bankruptcy. In addition to the RICO charge, DeLorean has sued for malicious prosecution and intentional infliction of emotional distress. The suit is pending in federal court in the Eastern District of Michigan.

In January 1989 Howard Weitzman, who is now managing partner at the Los Angeles firm of Wyman, Bautzer, Kuchel & Silbert, sued De-

Lorean for $680,000 in unpaid attorneys' fees. The suit is pending in Los Angeles state court.

Weitzman's former partner Donald Re has his own office in Los Angeles. Robert Perry left the U.S. Attorney's office in February 1985 and is now a partner at Douglas Dalton in Los Angeles. Joseph Papelian, who had been with the U.S. Attorney's Office prosecuting DeLorean in Detroit, joined the legal staff of General Motors Corporation in June 1987.

DeLorean is currently the chairman of the Utah-based Logan Manufacturing Co., which makes snow-grooming equipment. According to his lawyer, he plans to be involved in the manufacture of another car soon and has had numerous movie offers. He was divorced from his wife, Christina, in April 1985.

The study of the DeLorean case by William Hendricks was never made public. Hendricks has used the report's findings in speeches he makes to law enforcement students and officials. He says the report addressed the problems of working with informants and cited the need for greater verification of statements given by informants and for better accounting of their expenses. Hendricks was chief of the fraud section of the Justice Department's criminal division until August 1989.

There were no books published about the DeLorean trial by jurors Hoover, Dowell, or Gelbart.

State of Alaska v. John Peel

A BURNT-OUT CASE

BY
PETER CARBONARA

After eight people were killed aboard the Investor, *Alaska prosecutors spent six years and $3 million pursuing an accused murderer. They lost—twice.*

It was an unlikely time and place for a beach party—late April in Alaska.

Still, even if the shore was a little rugged and the water forbiddingly cold, most of the 20 or so invited guests were happy to spend the afternoon of April 26 at Sandy Beach in Douglas on the state's southern coast, eating hot dogs, unwinding, and shooting the breeze.

The gathering looked like a reunion of far-flung relations: At first everyone was a bit stiff. Gradually, though, the self-consciousness faded and eventually the women were embracing, the men swapping stories. The prevailing mood was one of relief.

No one felt it more than the guest of honor, John Peel, a slight 28-year-old whose open face and ice-water-blue eyes make him look much younger.

Three days earlier a jury across the Gastineau Channel in Juneau had found him not guilty of eight counts of first-degree murder and one count of first-degree arson. Now Peel, his wife and five-year-old son, and the members of his defense team were spending a quiet afternoon at the beach with the jurors and alternates who had seen things their way.

It began just after Labor Day 1982, when the charred corpses of five adults and one child were found on the burning wreck of a fishing boat about a mile off the Alaska coast. In 1984, after two years of investigation, police pointed to Peel, a boatyard worker and fisherman from Bellingham, Washington, as the man who had shot the crew of the *Investor* before torching their boat. *State of Alaska* v. *John Peel* became the longest and most expensive criminal case in Alaska history, taking six years, two trials, and more than $3 million.

It was also a fiasco, an entirely circumstantial case that degenerated into a personal vendetta between attorneys. Hamstrung by a botched police investigation, the prosecution, headed by Anchorage, Alaska, Assistant District Attorney Mary Anne Henry, asked two juries to convict without being able to provide a motive, a weapon, or any physical evidence linking Peel to the crime. Worse, the state was baited into a series of personal confrontations by Peel's bombastic trial counsel, Anchorage solo practitioner Phillip Weidner.

Distracted by Weidner's tactics—and anxious to vindicate the state's massive investment of time and money—the prosecution overplayed a weak hand. After the first trial ended in a hung jury leaning toward acquittal in 1986, the state elected to go after Peel again, despite the absence of any new evidence. Two years later, the second jury laughed Henry's case out of court without having heard a single defense witness.

Arleen Ryan, 45, then a librarian, was the forewoman of the jury in the second trial. "I waited to hear something and it never came," she says softly. "They didn't convince me that they had anything." Another member of the second jury, Geraldine Alps, 52, a Juneau housewife, agrees: "I still can't figure out why the state thought they had any kind of case."

After the verdict, when Weidner invited the jurors to the picnic he had organized at Sandy Beach, most had misgivings about accepting. All of them showed up, however, mainly to look John Peel in the eye and satisfy themselves that they had done the right thing. None say they had any significant doubts about the verdict. Later Barbara Costello, 30, an alternate, presented Peel with a husky born the day of the verdict. She named the dog Justice.

"He was an appropriate puppy," she says.

Prosecutor Henry concedes she never thought it would be easy: "It was a very difficult case to prove." She says the state had the goods on John

Peel but wasn't allowed to use them. Months after the verdict, the assistant D.A. is still fighting the case. She's trying to get information suppressed at trial made public. Henry will not discuss the evidence while the matter is pending, but sources close to the defense say the key piece of evidence in question is a segment of a taped police interview with the defendant. The prosecution has called it a confession; the defense calls it 11 minutes of unintelligible muttering.

"Given the amount of time and money," the assistant D.A. adds, "the people have a right to know." Wiping the self-righteous smirk off Weidner's face after six long and humiliating years would just be gravy.

THE KILLINGS

Several years ago the state of Alaska started paying people an annual stipend to stay. The stipend came from a tax on the oil companies that were enjoying the use of the state's new pipeline and was designed to encourage those who had come north to work on the thing to stick around once it was finished. When the bottom fell out of the oil market about five years ago, though, the state reverted to its usual condition: a vast chunk of frozen real estate, rich in natural beauty and not much else. Some of the discouraged started selling their rights to the government checks and used the money to go home. A bumper sticker on a car in Juneau, the state capital, reads, "God, please give us another boom—we promise not to piss this one away!" Now the people coming to Alaska are not oil-field workers and engineers; they are the same kinds who have always come: frontiersman-types, tourists, and fishermen.

Fishing is near the top of Alaska's list of reasons for being—and the *sole* reason for places like Craig, Alaska, a tiny town on the northwestern edge of Prince of Wales Island, one of the largest of the hundreds of islands off the state's southern coast.

Labor Day marks the close of the fishing season, and around then normally quiet Craig is filled with young men and women looking for a few laughs before heading home. In September 1982 the town was filled with the usual assortment of itinerant fishermen whooping it up one last time before packing it in for the winter. One of them was John Peel, then 22. Another was Mark Coulthurst, also of Washington, who turned 28 that Labor Day. Peel and Coulthurst knew each other—Peel had once dated one of Coulthurst's sisters—and had spent previous summers together on fishing boats in Alaska. In 1982 Peel was working on a boat called the *Libby 8*, skippered by another friend from Washington, Larry Demmert, Jr. The *Libby 8*, like a lot of boats in Craig, was a beat-up black hulk owned by the Columbia-Ward cannery.

Coulthurst's boat was in another class altogether. Brand-new and gleaming white, the 58-foot *Investor* was a Rolls-Royce among battered Buicks. Stripped, she had run Coulthurst about $750,000, but with all the gear he added she was worth an estimated $1.5 million. On board the *Investor* late that summer with Coulthurst were his wife Irene, 28, and their two children, Kimberly, 5, and John, 4, and four crewmen, Dean Moon, 19, Michael Stewart, 19, Christopher Heyman, 18, and Jerome Keown, 19.

On Sunday, September 5, Craig was typically noisy for the end of the season. That evening Coulthurst and his crew arrived at Craig's North Cove dock, planning to spend a few days in town before making one last salmon run. Early the next morning, other fishermen who weren't still asleep or hung over saw the *Investor* heading out from the dock. Late the following afternoon, a column of smoke filled the sky near Craig. When rescuers got out to the scene, they found the *Investor* furiously ablaze; she was made of wood and fiberglass and burned hot and long.

During a lull in the fire, Alaska state troopers boarded the boat and found the incinerated corpses of six people. All of them had been shot. The bodies of crewman Dean Moon and four-year-old John Coulthurst were not recovered. Investigators speculate the boy's body was consumed in the fire, which was immediately labeled arson. Moon was listed as missing. As for the *Investor* herself, the boat was almost a total loss, burned practically to the waterline.

As troopers examined the wreck, they found almost no useful evidence. They also made a number of mistakes that would come back to haunt the prosecution. The first was allowing local fishermen to cut a hole in the *Investor*'s hull to release water used to put out the fire. As the tide rose and fell, ashes and debris—and possibly evidence—were swept out of the wreck and into the sea. The second major foul-up had to do with the boat in which the killer was believed to have made his escape. While the *Investor* burned, several people had seen a man pilot the boat's skiff back to Craig. There he abandoned the small boat and disappeared. The skiff was soon discovered but never examined for fingerprints. It had been blocking access to other boats and police reasoned that by the time they got to it, practically every fisherman in Craig had put his hands on it.

Police searched for the skiff operator in vain for two years. Most of their efforts were devoted to finding the missing crewman, Dean Moon.

"[The troopers] were thinking Dean Moon was still alive," says lead prosecutor Henry, "and if he was, he had some explaining to do." After a year went by, however, Moon was declared dead. No arrests were made until two years after the killings.

On September 10, 1984, John Peel did what he always did; he woke up at his home in Bellingham, Washington, got out of bed, and drove to work. When he pulled into the parking lot of the Chris-Craft boatyard he was greeted by about a dozen police officers. A week later, he was arraigned in a Whatcom County, Washington, courtroom for the *Investor* murders.

The main evidence against Peel was a series of eyewitness descriptions of the skiff operator. The police also had a putative motive: Peel and Coulthurst had had a falling-out the summer before the killings. Peel had worked for the murdered man aboard another boat, the *Kit*, and had been fired. The state's scenario was this: At a birthday party for Coulthurst aboard the *Investor*, the two men had gotten into a brawl. Using a gun from the *Libby 8*, Peel shot the skipper in anger and then, realizing that there were seven witnesses, killed the rest of the crew. He took the boat out into deep water and attempted to scuttle it, escaping on the skiff. The next day, when he saw the *Investor* was still afloat, he returned with gasoline.

There were problems with this version, however. The largest was that there was no physical evidence linking Peel to the crime and no witnesses who could put him at the scene. Patrick Gullufsen, a former Juneau district attorney who was lured out of private practice to assist the prosecution with the case, concedes it looked like a hard sell from the outset. "I won't say the evidence is compelling," Gullufsen says, between dips of snuff. "I didn't think the case was in the bag by any means."

"The decision we made to arrest [Peel]," Henry says, "was the right one."

HOW A MASS MURDERER ACTS

For three months last winter, juror Russell MacDowell, a 51-year-old Juneau high school teacher, sat in a courtroom looking at John Peel. "How does a mass murderer act?" MacDowell still wonders. "How does anyone know? How do you know when you're talking to one?"

If there is anybody in the case who *doesn't* look like a Central Casting mass murderer, it's John Peel. Peel is the kind of generically good-looking young man who should be modeling permanent-press slacks in a J. C. Penney catalog. Perhaps his most distinctive expression is a wounded one; like a little boy falsely accused of breaking a neighbor's window, Peel doesn't look angry exactly, merely hurt. "They just have your life dangling on string," he says of the police and D.A. "They have too much power and not enough checks." Married with one child, Peel has lived most of his life in his hometown, 90 miles north of Seattle. He had no police record until he was picked up on a DWI charge just prior to his 1984 arrest. He is not a choirboy, but neither does he seem a likely candidate to kill eight people.

His attorney seems made to order for the part. A tall, rangy man with a chest-length black beard, Phillip Weidner, 42, is an unreconstructed student radical. When he smiles, which is occasionally, his face lights up like a pinball machine; when he is morally exercised, which is most of the time, he looks like John the Baptist just in from the desert, or as an opponent once described him, "a cross between Rasputin and Charles Manson."

Weidner says he was convinced absolutely of Peel's innocence from the start. Peel remembers that he and his parents were impressed with the attorney, especially after talking to William Bryson, a former partner, and others who had worked with him. One of them told him, Peel recalls, that "Phil would be like a dog with a bone."

After he was retained, Weidner pursued a strategy of hectoring assistant D.A.s, police officers, judges—anyone who represented authority. It seemed to come naturally. Between Massachusetts Institute of Technology and Harvard Law, Weidner is proud to recall, he spent a few days getting teargassed by the Chicago police during the riots outside the 1968 Democratic convention. In 1972 he found his way to Alaska, where his father had sat out World War II in an army base designed for enlisted men with incorrigible attitude problems. The weather and scenery did nothing for the elder Weidner's outlook. It doesn't seem to have mellowed his son much either.

After a stint as a public defender, Weidner went into private practice. He represented mostly drug defendants and became known for two things: papering courtrooms with every conceivable kind of motion and attacking prosecutors head-on.

One D.A. he skirmished with was Mary Anne Henry. Like Weidner, Henry is a product of Harvard Law. Her interest was strictly prosecution; back in Cambridge, she had briefly tried defense work and hated it. There were plenty of criminal cases to be tried up north, and she moved to

Anchorage in 1976 and found work with the D.A.'s office. After five years as an assistant in the Anchorage district attorney's office, she graduated to the top prosecutorial slot in Ketchikan, Alaska, a district that includes Craig.

As she discusses *Peel,* Henry's voice is soft and deliberate, the persona she projects extremely earnest. Like the defendant, she can't seem to believe how the people on the other side behaved. "[The defense] tried to reduce this case, in my view, to personal attacks on the state's attorneys," Henry says. The main targets were Henry and her chief assistant on the case, Ketchikan Deputy District Attorney Robert Blasco, a strident man whose tone of whiny exasperation endeared him to neither the defense nor the two juries. (Blasco, now in private practice in Juneau, declined to be interviewed for this article.)

"[Weidner] tried me and Bob Blasco rather than John Peel," Henry says, "and I think it was improper and I think it was false, but that's the way he runs his practice."

Before *Peel,* Henry had faced Weidner once before at trial, in a vehicular homicide case that ended in a mistrial. Henry recalls the defense attorney had been up to his usual tricks, generating a barrage of motions and accusations.

That experience, says Henry, came to mind quickly when she learned Weidner had been retained by John Peel. "I figured it was coming," she says, forcing the weakest of smiles, "and it was."

"THEY HATED OUR GUTS"

Weidner took the *Investor* case knowing the Peels had little money with which to pay him. Because Peel was indigent, Weidner was assigned Brant McGee, director of Alaska's Office of Public Advocacy, as second chair on the first trial.

McGee, 38, a prematurely gray Vietnam vet, comes across as casual yet serious, like a particularly hip high school guidance counselor. In court, he played Mr. Reasonable to Weidner's wrathful avenger, a difference in style that reflected their disagreements over tactics. "I would just grit my teeth over some of the things he'd try," McGee says, "but goddamn if he didn't win."

One thing the two had no trouble agreeing on was how the prosecution felt about them. "They hated our guts," McGee says. "There was a

272

feeling of deep personal hostility.'' During pretrial hearings, the two sides baited each other—the defense making splashy accusations of ineptitude and misconduct, the state responding with charges that Weidner was playing to the press.

The tone of the trial itself was just as belligerent, with even the smallest points blossoming into debates that required the judge, Thomas Schulz, 52, presiding judge of Alaska Superior Court, to send the jury out for extended periods while he entertained heated argument. Schulz reportedly interrupted one of these shouting matches to say, ''It appears the attorneys would be more than happy to try each other rather than try the facts.''

While Weidner's contentiousness irritated Schulz, the state's relations with the judge were no more tranquil. Henry was given to angry outbursts and shouted objections. ''I would get irritated and jump up and yell,'' Henry admits, ''and [Schulz] didn't like it.'' The proceedings were punctuated by contempt citations and motions for sanctions.

In August 1986, after nearly 150 witnesses and close to six months of trial, the case was sent to the jury. Six days later, forewoman Heidi Ekstrand, then managing editor of the *Ketchikan Daily News,* sent a note to Schulz saying the jury was deadlocked. After a brief conference with Ekstrand and attorneys for both sides, Schulz declared a mistrial, putting both the jurors and attorneys under gag not to discuss the jury tallies publicly.

''It was kind of a sick, frustrating feeling,'' Ekstrand recalls. In the absence of any physical evidence linking Peel to the murders, the case—and the jury's inability to agree—rested on eyewitnesses, chief among them Larry Demmert, the skipper of the boat Peel had been working on in the summer of 1982. Demmert, a longtime friend of Peel's, told investigators he had seen someone he believed to be Peel aboard the *Investor* the night of the murders. His testimony, however, was problematic. Demmert had waited until after Peel's arrest to tell what he knew. At trial, he backed off from key parts of his story, saying his memory had been clouded by heavy use of Valium, an admission that hurt his credibility with the jury. ''Demmert,'' says juror Bernie Besherse, a merchant seaman, with disgust, ''has been involved with drugs half his life.''

The jury split 8 to 4 not to convict on seven of the eight murders, 9 to 3 on the murder of the missing crewman, Dean Moon, and 7 to 5 on the single arson count. Not all of the jurors could explain their votes logically. The question of whether Peel had killed the crew of the *Investor* was far from resolved.

MISTRIAL AND RETRIAL

Shortly after the mistrial Mary Anne Henry publicly announced her intention to retry Peel. The final decision rested with then–Attorney General Harold Brown.

Not everyone in Alaska law enforcement had been a fan of the state's handling of the case. The chief of the Ketchikan police department complained that his cases were going neglected while Henry was on television speaking into banks of microphones on the courthouse steps. Brown, however, supported the prosecutors. "I was satisfied that the evidence pointed to Mr. Peel," Brown says. "I was convinced that Mr. Peel is guilty."

Brown says questions about the time and expense involved in a new trial were secondary to the urgency of getting a verdict one way or the other. "It was the most notorious case in southeastern [Alaska] history," he says. "A jury should decide." Brown's inquiry into the matter consisted of discussions with defense counsel and prosecutors as well as several hours spent with jury forewoman Heidi Ekstrand.

Just for insurance, he dispatched Herbert Soll, then the director of criminal prosecution in the state, to Washington to spend the better part of a day with Larry Demmert. "The case turned on his credibility, which had been attacked by the defense," Soll says. "I came up with the opinion that he was a trustworthy person.

"If the investigation had been done properly," Soll concludes, "we would have won the case."

Soll and Brown both say they heard little in the way of opposition to retrying the case from anyone but Weidner, who fired off a 30-page "position paper" explaining with his usual understatement that the state's case was totally unwinnable. Brown met with Weidner and the prosecutors separately but was never tempted to hear them out together. Assistant Attorney General Dean Guaneli, who had become involved in the case for the prosecution, says, "The animosity that existed between the attorneys was such that it wasn't conducive to such a meeting." Brown says Weidner's complaints and accusations cut little ice with him.

In the meantime, the state was working to rid itself of Judge Schulz. The judge had made no friends on either side, but the state was particularly wounded by his evidentiary rulings. One of the most important was his decision not to admit an 11-minute portion of a taped police interview with John Peel made in March 1984. Peel had been recorded talking to himself when he thought he had been left alone. The state maintained the tape contained a muttered confession. The defense argued that it was unintelligible and had been made in violation of Peel's right to privacy. Schulz agreed and was upheld by the Alaska Supreme Court.

After the mistrial, a romance had developed between Weidner and Camille Oechsli, who had recently left her job as a clerk to the judge. Schulz declined to recuse himself over Weidner's relationship with Oechsli but was removed from the case by another Superior Court judge. As presiding judge, Schulz appointed his own successor in the matter, Walter Carpeneti, 42. The case was transferred to his court in Juneau.

The buildup for the second trial in January 1988 was just as intense as the first. A large Juneau federal courtroom was commandeered to accommodate spectators. Most days, the attorneys gave them the show they had come to see.

On the day of his opening argument, Weidner appeared in his usual costume, his somewhat scraggly beard and cowboy boots offset slightly by his three-piece suit. He was accompanied by his jury expert, Josef Princiotta. With his beard, rose-tinted eyeglasses, and hands covered with rings, Princiotta—a man who claims to be able to pick juries entirely on the basis of panelists' physical characteristics—would go entirely unnoticed among the senior members of the Grateful Dead's road crew.

That day, Princiotta brought with him eight wooden easels. On each was a portion of a time line that began with the date of the *Investor* murders and ended with the future. As Weidner made his remarks to the jury, he marked out the events on the time line. When he got to the last item—JANUARY 1988. WHERE DO WE GO FROM HERE?—he wrote the words *Not Guilty*.

"RESULT—DREAMS"

In the middle of the time line were a number of items concerning the prosecution's most important witness, Larry Demmert. One of them read, STATE LIES TO AND THREATENS LARRY DEMMERT / RESULT—DREAMS. Two others read, DEMMERT GIVES TESTIMONY WHICH REQUIRES PERJURY IMMUNITY and LARRY DEMMERT, SCARED AND INFLUENCED BY HYPNOTIC

DRUGS AND THE THREAT OF JAIL, FLIP-FLOPS ON HIS STORY, CLAIMS TO *SUDDENLY* REMEMBER PEEL.

Demmert was the linchpin of the state's case. "Demmert was the only one," prosecutor Gullufsen says, "who could put John Peel there." He was also the prosecution's biggest liability.

Back in September 1984 when Demmert was called to testify before the first grand jury, the state had no witnesses who claimed to have seen Peel around the *Investor* near the time of the murders. When Demmert arrived in Ketchikan, prosecutors expected only that he would reiterate that Peel had worked for him and that they had been in Craig at the time of the murders. Instead Demmert swaggered into Henry's office, apparently intoxicated or drugged, and toting a loaded pistol, muttering that he was a "star witness." The D.A. sent him back to his hotel. Two days later he appeared before the grand jury with a new and substantially improved story.

Demmert testified that he had been asleep on the *Libby 8* on the night of the killings and had been awakened by shots and screams. Deputy D.A. Blasco asked, "How were you feeling then, Larry?"

"Real scared. I mean, there was evil—evil presence in the air so thick you could breathe it," the witness replied.

Three times, Demmert said, he had seen the killer from his bunk on the *Libby 8*—once crossing over the boats tied up next to the *Investor,* another time in the wheelhouse of the *Investor,* and a final time standing on the dock holding what looked like a rifle. The man was John Peel.

Blasco pressed him to explain to the grand jury why he had withheld what he knew. "Because I was in a state of shock," Demmert said. "I had known the person, he was a crew member of mine, and . . . I didn't want it to be true, or whatever, I guess."

Demmert's testimony was a major windfall for the state, but it came with a price tag. Before testifying at trial, he wanted immunity for perjury related to his grand jury testimony. After being granted immunity, Demmert told a less electrifying story to the second grand jury. Now he wasn't sure if he had been awakened the night of the murders by a scream or merely a nightmare. He maintained that he had seen Peel on the dock but was less confident about the other sightings. Asked if he was sure he had seen *someone* aboard the *Investor,* he said, "I may have—well, that's an area I'm having trouble with, whether it was a dream or not . . . and it's something I can't really be sure of."

The reason for the confusion and his need for immunity, Demmert explained, was his dependence on Valium during his first grand jury appearance. The drug impaired his memory and made him more inclined to tell prosecutors what he thought they wanted to hear, he said. While the story he told was true, he said, he had filled in a few key details: he was afraid that *he* would be accused of the murders if his testimony was not convincing.

Henry says Demmert was never a suspect in the case. "Some witnesses are more afraid than they have to be," she says, "and Larry was just one of those witnesses." Still, the state knew Demmert could hurt them as much as he could help. During the first trial he had testified on direct for a day and a half. In the second trial, Blasco questioned him for about 45 minutes, avoiding anything that might give Weidner grounds to bring up drugs or the first grand jury.

Despite their caution, Demmert gave the defense almost as much to work with as he gave the state. Weidner kept him on the stand for three days, hammering on Demmert's Valium use and whether the witness considered himself a drug addict. "The A word," as Weidner laughingly refers to it, had been ruled taboo by the judge, and Weidner's use of it produced a steady stream of angry objections from the prosecution table.

Demmert's erratic behavior was a cue for Weidner's theme song: the police and the D.A. had behaved in a manner befitting the KGB. First they had bungled the investigation of the case, now they were exploiting vulnerable witnesses. Demmert had been presented to the grand jury loaded on Valium and thoroughly intimidated by the D.A.

Henry denies those allegations categorically. "I don't think we should stoop to that kind of thing," she says. "It's kind of a shock. He's accusing me of giving drugs to a witness. He's accusing Bob Blasco of suborning perjury." Special prosecutor Pat Gullufsen admits Demmert was a highly problematic witness but calls Weidner's charges garbage. "If you know Mary Anne Henry and you know Bob Blasco and how they operate," Gullufsen says, "you know it's bull———."

Like Judge Schulz in the first trial, Judge Carpeneti grew increasingly annoyed at having to send the jury out every few minutes to hear argument. Demmert's first day on cross, for instance, was almost a complete loss. "This is a debacle," the judge said. Juror Russell MacDowell says the breaks gave him and a few other jurors plenty of time to work out a number of large and intricate jigsaw puzzles in the jury room. During a particularly tedious bench conference one juror slipped the bailiff a note that read, "I wonder what would happen if they came back from the bench and we were all gone? Let's open the door and find out." The note produced a laugh from the bailiff, but not from Deputy D.A. Blasco, who demanded the note be turned over to the court.

"OH NOOOO, MR. BOB!"

By the time Demmert left the stand, the tone of the case had reached a new low. The lightning rod for much of the tension was Blasco, whose indignant manner proved very unpopular with the jury.

Weidner was not shy about provoking the prosecutors, particularly Blasco, into endless objections, which came to be met by audible groans from the jury. One alternate took to whispering, "Oh noooo, Mr. Bob!" when Blasco rose to speak, in emulation of the hapless clay puppet on *Saturday Night Live*.

At the close of his redirect exam of Demmert, Blasco repeated a question he had asked the witness before the grand jury: "Are you still having trouble accepting that you saw your crew member on the *Investor* that morning?"

Weidner objected on the grounds that since Demmert had backed off about being able to identify Peel positively, the question misstated the record. Blasco sneered, "Defense counsel certainly doesn't want this answer out." With the jury again sent outside, Weidner demanded a mistrial for "intentional prosecutorial misconduct" and launched a bitter attack on Blasco. "The gentleman seems to be having some trouble following those rules, but—and I use the word 'gentleman' advisedly— . . . the fact is, Your Honor, that he made a calculated decision to prejudice Mr. Peel." Weidner went on to tick off a quick list of other alleged prosecution atrocities. "They know that they got hurt bad with Mr. Demmert. They know their big-gun witnesses haven't made it, and they're goading us into a mistrial. . . . This is not some situation where they haven't had a chance. . . . Now they've had another chance, and they got beat."

Carpeneti, civil almost to a fault, sat through Weidner's lecture and many more like it. After hearing both sides out, he cautioned Blasco, but declined to characterize the prosecutor's remark as misconduct.

"This case was just litigated to the *n*th degree," the judge says today. "It was a case of the technique overwhelming the substance." He adds, however, "The lawyers were good. Even if you have a lot of paperwork from people who are bright, you have to take it seriously. An inept attorney could be dealt with more easily."

While both sides seemed to do about equally well with the judge, the jury made a clear choice almost from the beginning of the trial. Blasco lost the jury for good in February when the state called Brian Polinkus, a friend of Peel's and a member of the crew of the *Libby 8*. Early in the case Polinkus and Dawn Holmstrom, also a friend of Peel's and a witness, claimed they had been pushed by police and the D.A. into making stronger statements than they could back up. Polinkus had told the grand jury that before any bodies were discovered, Peel said he thought the crew of the *Investor* had been shot. Polinkus subsequently backed off, saying that he wasn't sure when Peel had made his remarks.

Blasco tried to head off any possible cross of Polinkus's claims of intimidation. As he was preparing to complete his direct, Blasco asked Carpeneti to rule that he had not asked the witness about the grand jury and the subject was therefore beyond the scope of cross. When Carpeneti declined to do so, Blasco brought it up himself, asking Polinkus if he had any complaints about his treatment.

Polinkus responded that Blasco had threatened him. "I was in your office," the witness said. "You were quite upset. Foul language was used. I think it was because my answers weren't the way I was expected to answer them. . . . You said if I wasn't straight with you and I didn't cut the bull——, you would send me into the grand jury room alone and you would let them rip me apart. That was exactly what you said." Polinkus then added a new charge to his catalog of complaints, saying that Blasco had suggested specific answers to him.

Blasco's efforts to discredit Polinkus—including the suggestion that he smelled of alcohol on the stand—worked against the state. "Blasco said, 'I didn't harass those witnesses. I didn't harass Brian Polinkus,' " says alternate Barbara Costello. "And we sat there and saw him do it right in court."

Another witness who backfired was Charles Samuelson, who had cropped up only after jury selection in the second trial was complete. Samuelson claimed that during a fishing trip in the summer of 1983 Peel had confessed to having killed the crew of the *Investor*. Clouding Samuelson's testimony was the fact that he had not agreed to tell his story at trial until he was granted immunity on an unrelated pending assault charge in Palmer, Alaska. Late in the trial the state called his mother, who corroborated his account of why he had waited to tell the police what he knew: he had been advised by his father not to get involved. After a few minutes of fairly gentle interrogation, Weidner asked her about her son's deal with the state.

"And isn't it true that he was very interested in getting those charges dismissed up there in Palmer—getting out of trouble?" Weidner asked.

"Well, I think—no comment," replied the witness. Laughter was heard from the jury box.

"Pardon me?"

"No comment."

"No further questions," Weidner said. "Thank you, ma'am."

The court asked if the state had any questions on redirect. There were none. Two weeks later, John Peel got a phone call from his attorney. Peel says he held the receiver with trembling hands. Weidner told his client that he did not intend to call any witnesses. "Okay," said John Peel.

A QUICK AND ANGRY VOTE

On April 19, 45 days and 50 witnesses after the case began, the state presented closing arguments. Henry began with a description of the case that was not exactly charged with certainty: "One shot fired from a gun held by the defendant, John Peel, started what has been called the *Investor* tragedy. The state can't tell you why the first shot was fired, but after that first shot, he kept on shooting, whether out of panic or fear or whatever reason, because everyone on the *Investor* knew John Peel and could identify him."

When his turn came, Weidner waxed up a high sheen on the tone of righteous indignation he had been developing throughout the whole case: "We didn't put a case on; there was no reason to. The fact is, there simply is no evidence in this case and there certainly is not evidence to demonstrate beyond a reasonable doubt."

The prosecution's fits of temper, Weidner told the jury, were just proof that the state's case was conducted in bad faith. "You saw who got irate and angry when we tried to pursue reality," he said. The attorney was proud to admit who had pushed their buttons: "mean old Mr. Weidner."

The jury was charged on the afternoon of Wednesday, April 20. On Thursday they took a preliminary vote. There were nine not-guilty ballots and three marked "not sure." The undecided jurors said they just wanted to go through all the evidence methodically. On Saturday afternoon, the jurors voted again. At about five o'clock, they returned to the courtroom. For a few moments, John Peel sat impassively, then broke down in tears as Carpeneti announced that the jury had found him not guilty on all counts.

The jury's response to the state's case was hostile. They didn't like the way the investigation had been conducted, they didn't like the witnesses the state presented, and they didn't like the way Henry and Blasco handled themselves in the courtroom. "There were comments that the state had kids in there practicing," juror Geraldine Alps recalls.

"Disgust in the jury room was very high every day," says alternate Barbara Costello. "Mary Anne Henry lost it because she couldn't keep her composure when Weidner was egging her on," Costello adds. "It was fun watching him do it. He did a very good job of doing it."

Some jurors were angry that their time had been wasted. "I kept thinking that maybe one of these days we might get something real," Vicki McMillan, 35, a state employee, says with a sigh.

Forewoman Ryan, like many of the jurors, says she was surprised at the thinness of the state's case. "I assumed," she says, "that they would have their act together." Ronald Hilbert, 41, a state records handler, is more vehement. "A travesty of justice happened against Mr. Peel," he says, "and the right thing happened. He was let go."

Henry seemed at times to be motivated by a personal grievance against the defense, jurors say. "She let her emotions get the best of her," alternate Phillip Smith recalls. "Sometimes it seemed like Phillip Weidner was on trial and not John Peel."

"I did not prosecute John Peel," Henry says, "because I had a personal vendetta against Phil Weidner." Rather, she says, it was her strong belief in Peel's guilt that led her to pursue the case at great personal expense for six years. Between the first and second trials Henry put in for a transfer from Ketchikan back to Anchorage, where she had begun her career in Alaska. The reasons, she says, were partly personal, partly connected to the Peel case.

"I asked for a demotion," she says, "so I wouldn't have to think about anything but the Peel trial." Asked if she derailed her career with that move, she pauses a moment. "I suppose I did, in a way."

Henry is obviously weary of the Peel case and the aggravation it has caused her, but she has taken a "you can't win 'em all" attitude and has refused to assign blame for the loss of the case. "You can't say it was anybody's fault. It happened," she says.

"I was disappointed," Henry says. "I was disappointed but not surprised." She's not finished, either. Not long after the trial ended, Henry asked Carpeneti to make evidence suppressed at trial public. As of early October Carpeneti had yet to rule on her request and Henry will not discuss the evidence while the matter is pending, except to say that there are a number of pieces of evidence at issue. Given the amount of time, money, and publicity the case received, Henry says her obligation is to the public. "I think they have a right to know the whole story," she says.

John Coulthurst, 55, the father of the murdered *Investor* skipper, says he supports Henry's continued efforts. "We were very pleased with the prosecution," he says, and approves of Henry's attempt "to show that her office didn't do a bad job." Coulthurst is convinced Peel murdered his son out of jealousy and that the errors of the state police prevented the D.A. from proving that in court. Coulthurst says, "We feel that John Peel is definitely guilty and there's no two ways about it."

Sources close to the defense say the most important item currently being held *in camera* is the portion of Peel's March 1984 taped interview with police, which was the subject of a pitched evidentiary battle in the first trial that the state lost. Peel says the tape contains only a few minutes of him mumbling, "Oh, God," to himself after police first accused him of the *Investor* murders.

Weidner has opposed the move to release the evidence, but maintains there is nothing in the suppressed material to incriminate Peel. "It's exculpatory, as far as I'm concerned," he says.

Meanwhile, in August Weidner was sanctioned $150 for remarks made at the first trial and $250 for his use of the word *addict* in questioning Larry Demmert at the second trial. Carpeneti also declined his motion for attorneys' fees. Weidner says he knew such a motion in a criminal case was probably quixotic but pursued it to make a point. "I just want them to face what they've done," he says. Weidner says he and Peel are considering a civil suit against the state but have decided to hold off for a few months until the dust from the second trial settles. He and Peel have been approached with book and film offers but haven't seen any to their liking so far.

Peel has returned to Washington and says he is trying to start life over again someplace where he won't be recognized. While some lingering parts of his case are being dragged out in the Alaska courts, the whole thing is over as far as he's concerned. He can't be tried again. He says he still can't believe how the police and the D.A. behaved. "I thought they were supposed to be professional," Peel says sarcastically. Instead he encountered a district attorney he derides as "wacko."

As for Henry's continuing efforts against him, Peel laughs and shakes his head.

"I think," he says with a broad, boyish grin, "that's fine."

EPILOGUE

Judge Walter Carpeneti ruled in favor of the motion by the Anchorage assistant district attorney, Mary Anne Henry, to make public evidence suppressed at trial. John Peel's attorney Phillip Weidner, however, asked the Alaska Court of Appeals for a stay of the order. A decision is pending. Weidner maintains that there is nothing damaging to his client in the material held *in camera*.

Weidner says that his success in a number of personal injury suits has helped him recover from the financial losses he sustained defending Peel. "I'm beginning to see daylight," he says. In December 1989 the attorney returned from a trip to Costa Rica where he says he's considering investing in a hotel.

Meanwhile, John Peel and his wife Kathy have moved to a small town near Bellingham, Washington. November 1989 saw the arrival of their second child, a girl.

BUSINESS
BEHAVIOR

It must be remembered that all trade is and must be in a sense selfish.

—LORD CHIEF JUSTICE JOHN DUKE COLERIDGE, 1888

Pennzoil
v.
Texaco

GETTY GAMES

BY

STEVEN BRILL

How a mix of bad lawyering, bad tactics, and bad faith character-
ized the legal work done in the giant Getty-Texaco deal

On the morning of Friday, November 11, 1983, the board of directors of
the Getty Oil Company met in Houston to ratify a truce recently signed
by its chairman and by Gordon Getty, a son of the company's late founder
and the trustee for a trust that controlled 40 percent of the company's
stock. After a few preliminary matters were discussed, Getty was asked
to leave the room while the board formally voted on the agreement that
would, it seemed, ensure a 12-month cease-fire between management and
the Getty heir by pledging each not to do anything that might upset the
current balance of power.

But as Getty was ushered out through one door, the oil company's
lawyers—Barton Winokur of Philadelphia's Dechert Price & Rhoads and
Herbert Galant of New York's Fried, Frank, Harris, Shriver &
Jacobson—were shown in through another. Whereupon they explained to
the board that, despite what the truce agreement said, the company could,
and should, join a lawsuit the following Tuesday aimed at stripping

Gordon Getty of his control over the trust. That discussion finished, the board voted to ratify the truce. Gordon Getty was then called back into the room and told that the 12-month agreement had been adopted. He went home to San Francisco a happy man—until Tuesday.

Two weeks later, Winokur of Dechert Price and Galant of Fried, Frank rendered a 15-page "opinion" to company management that nitpicked its way through the truce agreement with a can't-see-the-forest-for-the-trees approach that would do a first-year law student proud. The agreement had not been violated by the litigation, Winokur and Galant opined. But by then a humiliated, angry Gordon Getty had reacted to the suit against him with a series of moves designed to overthrow the management and that ultimately delivered his father's company to Texaco in the biggest merger in history.

That Winokur and Galant were almost certainly wrong legally is not as important as how wrong they were tactically to go into court against Gordon Getty, whatever the justification. Nor could any of their forced legal reasoning transcend the bad-faith nature of their tactics.

That mix of bad lawyering, bad tactics, and bad faith characterizes much of the legal work done in this biggest deal ever. Whether it was a senior partner at Baker & Botts not getting his team in place to close Pennzoil's deal with Getty on time, or a famed New York lawyer, Arthur Liman, attacking the integrity of some of his most highly regarded colleagues, or Getty's general counsel—in the presence of his Dechert Price lawyer—destroying key documents in the suit filed when Getty switched to Texaco, this was not a story of grace under pressure.

GORDON GETTY "WANTED IN"

It began as a three-sided battle. On one side there was Sidney Petersen, 53, Getty's urbane chairman and chief executive, who joined the company in the 1950s and worked his way up through a series of finance-related jobs. Under Petersen the company had not done well finding new oil; and either as a result of such problems in its core business, or as a cause of them, Petersen has been diversifying Getty into areas such as cable TV and insurance.

Then there was Gordon Getty, the 50-year-old son of the company founder, J. Paul Getty, whom reporters like to describe as a semiprofessional opera buff fond of setting Emily Dickinson poems to music. Which is true. But, as we'll see, it's also true that Gordon Getty is not a total flake. He was right that the oil company that bears his name was not doing well, and its stock was depressed, and that something could be done about it.

As the sole trustee of the Sarah C. Getty Trust that his father established as his main legacy, Gordon Getty controlled 40.2 percent of the company stock, a position that recently caused *Forbes* magazine, apparently overestimating Getty's own share of the trust by a factor of three, to name him number one in its annual list of the 400 richest Americans. Nonetheless, his share of the trust is large enough to have netted him $28 million in Getty stock dividends last year.

From the time his father died in 1976 until 1982, Getty never used his position as trustee for the 40.2 percent of the shares to influence the company. Instead he deferred to C. Lansing Hays, Jr., his father's longtime friend and legal adviser and a co-trustee of the family trust.

According to advisers who know Gordon Getty well, Hays, who ran the 11-lawyer New York firm of Hays & Landsman, acted as his surrogate father. As such, Hays was the bridge between the heirs and company management, including Petersen. Hays, like Getty, had a seat on the board, and Getty almost always cast his vote with his mentor.

In 1980 Hays merged his firm with the New York office of Dechert Price, a 109-year-old, 200-lawyer Philadelphia powerhouse. Dechert Price, which had done some work for Getty in the past, now became the company's lead counsel. Within a few months of the merger, Hays, who by then was 64, had handed off much of the Getty work to Barton Winokur, then a 40-year-old partner regarded as a rising star. Winokur, strong-willed, outgoing, and articulate, quickly cemented a relationship with Petersen. But it was Hays, and Hays alone, who retained Gordon Getty's confidence.

In May of 1982 Hays died. Almost immediately, Getty began to reassess his relationship to the company as well as his own career, and, according to lawyers and bankers who are close to him, he soon began to believe that the family's company was not being run well and that it might be time for him to try his hand at it.

Getty had worked intermittently at minor positions in the company, never achieving much to make his father proud before dropping out of the business altogether in the mid-1970s to pursue interests in anthropology and music. Now, recalls one of his close advisers, "with Hays dead and with Petersen acting like he disdained him, and with Winokur having no relationship with him because he was a Petersen man, Getty felt left out and like he wanted in."

Which brings us to the important third party and erstwhile referee, Harold Williams. In 1981 Williams—a former Norton Simon chairman and chairman of the SEC—became chairman of the board of the Malibu, California–based J. Paul Getty Museum, the fabulously endowed lesser half of the Getty legacy. A man of Williams's background was not nearly as out of place running a museum as it might seem: in addition to housing one of the world's most valuable private art collections, the museum owned 11.8 percent of the Getty Oil Company's stock.

Thus, in a fight between the company and Gordon Getty, Williams became the pivot. If he sided with Getty, who controlled 40.2 percent, they would form a block of 52 percent; if he sided with the company's management, which likes to think of itself as being responsible for the individuals and institutions that collectively own the remaining 48 percent of the stock (it is listed on the New York Stock Exchange), then they would command a majority capable of beating Gordon Getty back.

For this reason, Williams's 11.8-percent block had a premium value to either side, or for that matter to any other would-be purchaser of Getty— but only if he maintained that balance of power by making sure neither side built up a majority any other way.

GORDON GETTY REBUFFED

By early 1983, without Hays as a buffer, Gordon Getty maintained that the company's stock price—about $50—was much too low and that changes were needed at the Los Angeles headquarters. He presented the chairman of his father's company with numerous proposals, including an equity restructuring that would see the company buy back enough shares so that the stock price would rise and, not incidentally, so that the shares owned by the trust Gordon Getty controlled would go from 40.2 percent to a majority. Other Getty proposals called for a retreat from Petersen's diversification strategy in favor of renewed efforts to build oil reserves.

Gordon Getty's lawyer in these discussions was Moses Lasky, the then-75-year-old former Brobeck, Phleger & Harrison partner who had left that large San Francisco firm in 1979 to start what is now the 14-lawyer office of Lasky, Haas, Cohler & Munter.

Through the winter, spring, and summer, Petersen rejected almost everything Getty suggested. The only ground he gave was to head off Getty's announced intention to hire investment banker Goldman, Sachs &

Company to explore alternatives for Getty Oil by having the company hire Goldman instead.

In July, Goldman, Sachs presented its findings, and among many recommendations, it, too, spoke favorably of a stock repurchase plan as a way of boosting the company's market value and stock price. Tensions grew as Petersen and his board refused to act on the plan. Finally, Petersen countered with a proposal that the stock repurchase go forward but that while Gordon Getty's stock percentage would go to 51 percent, he would be limited to 40 percent of the shareholder votes. Getty bitterly rejected the idea.

According to a variety of subsequently filed court papers, by now Williams was concerned that the museum's 11.8 percent premium position was in danger; worse still to him was the prospect of being a minority shareholder in a company that was controlled by Gordon Getty. In the late summer of 1983, Williams retained Martin Lipton, the takeover specialist from New York's Wachtell, Lipton, Rosen & Katz.

Few lawyers have played as key a role in any mega-transaction as Lipton would in this one. Lipton is one of Williams's oldest and closest friends, and although Williams is a tough businessman, Lipton had little trouble acting unilaterally in his name. (Indeed, when the final deal price for Getty was set, it was Lipton, negotiating with Texaco chairman John McKinley in the lobby of New York's Pierre Hotel, who set it.) Lipton is also a man of exceptionally strong will with an ego to match, and he quickly converted the pivotal role enjoyed by his client into an equally central role for himself—which, it should be added, was made all the more easy by the fact that until Texaco jumped in at the eleventh hour, using a team from Skadden, Arps, Slate, Meagher & Flom, he was the only seasoned mergers and acquisitions lawyer in the whole affair.

"LAYING DOWN THE GAUNTLET"

In late September, according to Winokur, the Dechert Price partner working for Petersen, "the company heard that Gordon planned to team up with the museum to take control; so we decided we had to do something."

Petersen called a special board meeting for Sunday, October 2, in Philadelphia, with notice delivered by telegram to Getty's San Francisco home on that Saturday afternoon. (The other members of the board were called by telephone, according to Getty and two of the members.) But Getty was in London for a museum meeting.

With Getty not present, the board authorized the issuance of an additional nine million shares to an employee stock ownership program. These new shares, if issued, would have diluted the combination of Gordon Getty's and the museum's shares to less than 50 percent.

At the same meeting the board also discussed doing something about Gordon Getty's status as the sole trustee of the Getty family trust (the entity that owned the 40.2 percent of the company's shares). According to a board member who was there and to subsequent accounts contained in court papers, Petersen and Winokur said that Winokur had been in contact with other Getty heirs, especially J. Paul Getty, Jr., a 51-year-old recluse living in England (it is one of his sons who was kidnapped in 1973 and had his ear severed), and was encouraging the heirs to file suit seeking the appointment of a second trustee on the ground that Getty's interference with the company was not in the best interests of the trust. Winokur and company officials, Winokur told the board, had helped Getty, Jr., hire a Los Angeles lawyer, Seth Hufstedler of Hufstedler, Miller, Carlson & Beardsley, to represent one of Getty, Jr.'s sons, 15-year-old Tara Gabriel Galaxy Gramaphone Getty, in such a suit. It was likely, he noted, that the company would want to intervene in that suit or, in fact, bring the suit unilaterally if a plaintiff such as this Getty grandchild could not be found.

After a brief discussion, the board authorized the company to encourage the suit, to bring it itself, or to intervene when the suit was filed.

Having received their authorization to issue the nine million shares and to get involved in the suit against Gordon Getty, Petersen and Winokur flew to London. With them was Herbert Galant, a 55-year-old corporate partner at Fried, Frank whom Winokur has retained as special counsel. "We wanted to make a last-ditch effort at a deal with Gordon," Galant explains. "We knew that actually issuing the shares would be laying down the gauntlet. It would dilute Gordon and the museum, but it would so advertise all the strife that a new buyer could come in, buy shares on the open market, and team up with Gordon or Gordon and the museum and take control. So we went over to make a deal."

But Gordon Getty and his lawyers had other ideas for a deal—with the museum. On the morning of Monday, October 3, Lipton and Williams met in London with Gordon Getty and two of his lawyers from Lasky's firm, Charles Cohler and Thomas Woodhouse. But no deal was agreed to, nor was the company contingent able to get Getty to agree to anything when they met with his people later that evening.

Now it was Lipton's turn to try something. The next day, October 4, he met with Petersen, Winokur, Galant, and Geoffrey Boisi, the head of the mergers and acquisitions department at Goldman, Sachs, which was still on retainer to the company. According to Winokur and Lipton, the company people told Lipton that because they had feared that Getty would try a linkup between himself and the museum, they had authorized an action, which they refused to specify (it was the stock issuance plan), that, as Lipton recalls them describing it, "would frustrate the trust [Getty] from exercising control over the company if it tried to act in concert with the museum."

LIPTON'S SHUTTLE DIPLOMACY

As a way out of all the threats and counterthreats, the ever-resourceful Lipton proposed a three-party "standstill" agreement, under which the company, the museum, and Gordon Getty would cease all hostilities for 18 months and forgo any plans for altering their various stock interests. To mollify Getty, Lipton proposed allowing him to add Lasky or someone else of his choosing to the board. In addition, Williams would be added to the board as the museum's representative. During that time, Lipton told Petersen, Winokur, Galant, and Boisi, tempers would cool and the company could put together a constructive business plan.

The company people told Lipton they thought such a plan might be a good idea.

Later that afternoon, Lipton pitched the standstill agreement to Gordon Getty and his lawyers. At first Getty balked, but then he agreed to think about it.

That night Lipton, working with an associate who had flown over with him, drafted the proposed tripartite agreement. (Although the associate, 27-year-old Patricia Vlahakis, was just two years out of Columbia Law School, she would play a key role in the three months of fighting ahead.) The next day Lipton submitted copies of the handwritten draft to lawyers for the company and Gordon Getty, and flew home.

Two weeks later, the group reconvened in San Francisco at Moses Lasky's office. Lipton flew out to the meeting with Martin Siegel, Gordon Getty's investment banker from Kidder, Peabody & Company. During the fight, Lipton accepted Siegel's suggestion that Getty be allowed to add four members to the board instead of one, and that the four be independent-minded businessmen who would steer the board on a more even course. One of the four they discussed was Laurence Tisch, the founder and chairman of the Loews Corporation, who is a client and close friend of Lipton's; Tisch would end up playing the key statesman's role in the fight in the weeks ahead.

In San Francisco, Getty and his lawyers were in one room and Petersen, Winokur, and Galant were in another, with Lipton—by now "thinking of himself as some kind of goddamn Henry Kissinger," says one lawyer who developed an intense dislike for him—shuttling between the two.

By this time Winokur and Galant had turned Lipton and Vlahakis's two yellow pages into a 16-page, single-spaced contract, which, says one adviser who was there, was "hammered away at by Winokur, who lectured Moses Lasky like Lasky was some kind of kid."

"Gordon just wouldn't deal with it," says Galant. "He said he'd only sign Lipton's draft." Getty also insisted that the agreement last only 12 months instead of the 18 Lipton had proposed.

Before he even signed that, one of his lawyers from Lasky's firm objected to the fact that the draft didn't seem to give Gordon Getty an explicit out if Petersen's board didn't ratify Petersen's agreement. "I don't care," said Getty, overruling his lawyers. "Sid Petersen is a man of his word, and if he says he'll get his board to go along, then I know he will."

"It was Lipton who got Gordon to sign this," says one of the people who were there. "Gordon was scared. He knew what he was giving up, and he literally turned green when he signed it; but he did it on Lipton's say-so."

Lipton then took Getty's signed copy and, says Winokur, "presented it to us as a take-it-or-leave-it fait accompli. So we signed that version."

"YOU SNOOKERED ME"

It was three weeks later, at the November 11 meeting, that the Getty board formally ratified the truce with Gordon Getty—and decided that the standstill agreement did not prevent them from intervening in a suit to dislodge Getty as the sole trustee for the family trust (after Getty was asked to leave the room on the pretext that the board wanted to discuss the agreement without him present).

On the night of November 15, Boisi of Goldman, Sachs was at a dinner with Siegel of Kidder, Peabody, and with Lipton, and he took them aside to tell them about the intervention. Siegel called Gordon Getty later that night and asked if he hadn't been at the November 11 board meeting at which the intervention had been discussed. Of course he had, said Getty. Had he listened to everything carefully? Of course he had, he replied. Had he left at any point to go to the bathroom? No, he replied. But they had asked him to leave at one point, he said.

Siegel then explained what had happened when he'd left the room. "I was shocked, hurt, and embarrassed," Getty recalls. "However," he adds, "I also knew it was a dumb thing for them to do, because it proved that neither the museum nor I could deal with the company."

Petersen says that the chief strategist in encouraging the suit and then intervening in it was Winokur, but adds, "I thoroughly support what he did. I knew Gordon . . . would be pretty upset, but we took that into account when we decided to file the suit, or rather have it filed, and then intervene," he recalls. "What we didn't figure on was how Lipton would react."

"I felt utterly betrayed personally," says Lipton. "I'd never dream Fried, Frank would do something like this. Here I had stuck my neck out. I had begged Gordon to sign this, and look what they did. . . . A standstill agreement means peace, not two people suing each other."

The next day Lipton called Galant.

Galant and Winokur got on the phone. "We expected," says Galant, "that Marty would be calling to find out what we knew about Gordon's reaction and to tell us that the museum would continue to work with us"—an expectation that Lipton says was "ridiculous," and that he quickly dashed.

"You snookered me," Lipton angrily told them, according to both Galant and Lipton. "No, if we snookered anyone, Marty, it was Gordon, not you," Lipton says Galant replied—a version that Galant says is almost true. "I said, 'If anyone should feel snookered, it's Gordon,' not that we snookered him," Galant asserts.

WORRYING ABOUT THE LETTER, NOT THE SPIRIT, OF THE LAW

Within two days Lipton had dashed off an opinion letter to Williams telling him that the company's involvement in the suit violated both the letter and the spirit of the standstill agreement and urging that Williams call for a full board meeting (Williams was now a board member as a result of the agreement) to air the issue and seek a reversal of the company's action. Williams forwarded the letter to Petersen, along with his demand for such a meeting. Similarly, Laurence Tisch—the chairman of the Loews Corporation, whom Lipton had convinced Getty to name as one of the four new board members allotted him under the tripartite agreement—called Petersen demanding the same thing. Petersen refused to call the meeting, asserting that the holiday season precluded the board's being able to convene. Instead, on December 1, Winokur and Galant rendered their opinion that the company's intervention in the suit had not violated the standstill agreement.

Galant and Winokur maintain, in Galant's words, that the filing of the motion to intervene was "thoroughly and completely permissible under the agreement," whereupon they offer, in the opinion letter and in a series of interviews, this interpretation of the agreement:

• Point number one of the ten-point agreement had called for the company to rescind "any action or authorization for issuance of securities or other change of control type transaction that was heretofore taken." Lipton had maintained in his letter that this should have included the board's action at that Sunday, October 2, board meeting (the one Getty had been in London for and had apparently not received sufficient notice of) to authorize the motion to intervene in the suit. Galant and Winokur argue that since the suit hadn't yet been filed, there was no "action" that could be rescinded on the date the tripartite agreement was ratified.

• Also, because the suit to add a trustee to the trust was not intended to change the trust's equity position in the company but only Gordon Getty's status as sole trustee, it was not a "change of control type transaction," even conceding, which they do not, that any suit was a "transaction."

• Point number two required that all directors "be advised in advance of all matters to be brought to the board." But, according to Winokur and Galant, this provision was not violated by the board's not telling Gordon Getty in advance of its discussion of the lawsuit at the November 11 meeting, or by the exclusion of mention of the discussion of the suit from the minutes of the October 2 meeting that were presented at the November 11 meeting, because "the board as a board" did not act on the intervention at the November 11 meeting. The discussion of the intervention by members of the board after Getty had been asked to leave, they argue, was not a board discussion because Getty was not there and because no formal vote for authorization to intervene in the suit against him was taken.

"We think what we did was entirely within the bounds of the agreement," Winokur concludes. "And we can understand why Gordon Getty might not agree, but not Marty Lipton. He had every reason to go along with us. His reaction was utterly irrational."

Therein lies the failure of the company's strategy. During our first interviews, Winokur and Galant maintained that the only reason they made the motion to intervene was to be up-front about their activities—in Winokur's words, "to put on the record in the court that we had played a role in encouraging the suit." It is a reason, according to Galant, "that Lipton completely acknowledged and agreed with; he said he understood that that was our reason."

But Lipton calls that account of their conversation completely untrue. And when pressed later on why they couldn't simply issue a press release acknowledging their complicity in the suit while smoothing things over by telling Getty that they had acted in this manner before the agreement but would not now support the suit, Petersen and his two lawyers offered a different, and more crass, explanation for the intervention: What they really expected to happen, Winokur, Galant, and Petersen said, was that they'd intervene and Getty would then say that the standstill had been violated and proclaim himself free of it. But then they would sue to uphold the standstill—that is, they intended to enforce the standstill on Getty while they took part in the suit to get him removed as sole trustee. And they expected that Lipton and the museum would side with them. "We would never have agreed to the standstill if it specifically precluded our intervening in the suit," says Petersen. In fact, Winokur points out that he had told Lipton about the possible intervention in London, a point that Lipton concedes. "Marty Lipton is being totally disingenuous. We were signaling him all along about the suit," says Winokur.

"We figured Marty knew about it and that that was why he worded the standstill as vaguely as he did," adds Galant. "We were going to use the year we had with the standstill to go into court to get the additional trustee appointed."

To Lipton that strategy is absurd because, though he says that Winokur had "mentioned the possibility of them intervening in a trust suit before the standstill was agreed to, I never dreamed they would do it after a standstill was signed. That's why I didn't mention it in the agreement. I never dreamed they would do it with an agreement signed."

Gordon Getty's lawyer, Charles Cohler, was similarly trusting or naïve. After the trustee suit was brought, Cohler filed an affidavit describing conversations he had had with Winokur in which the possibility of the suit was discussed. (His purpose in the affidavit was to have the suit dismissed as a sham because the company, rather than named plaintiff Tara Gramaphone Getty, was really behind it.) But he, too, never asked Lipton to make a prohibition against the company intervening in, or financing, the suit part of the agreement.

"You know," says Galant, "people like Lipton keep talking about how we violated the spirit of this thing. Well, we're all lawyers, and we should be concerned with the letter of the law, not the spirit."

"IF MARTY HAD ONLY ASKED US"

Instead of siding with the company, Lipton did just the opposite. As the company had always feared might happen, he threw in with Gordon Getty. On December 5, Williams and Getty signed a consent to action by majority shareholders. Using the convenient Delaware corporate law that allows a majority of shareholders to change the company's bylaws, the two parties revised the bylaws so that a vote by 14 of 16 directors was necessary to do any of the things prohibited under the tripartite agreement, such as issuing new stock, recommending the sale of stock, or, as was stated explicitly this time, initiating any action or proceeding relating to control of, or voting power over, more than 5 percent of the stock. Also, the motion to intervene in the trustee litigation was ordered withdrawn.

Winokur and Galant maintain that Lipton's action, as Winokur explains, "put his own client's position in jeopardy because it allowed Gordon to be free of the standstill provisions while the company was now tied to it." Thus, anyone could come along, he asserts, and buy up 10 percent of the stock and combine with Gordon Getty.

Indeed, although Lipton had gotten some protection when he had the museum sign the majority consent with Gordon Getty by also getting Getty to sign an agreement that neither party could sell its shares without the other having the opportunity to sell at the same price, it is true that the blowup of the standstill "put the company into play" (the phrase investment bankers and M&A lawyers use for making a company a likely takeover target) by advertising more resoundingly than ever the standoff between these majority shareholders and management, and by freeing Getty again to make a deal with someone else. The difference is that

Lipton argues that it was the company's warlike intervention in the trustee suit that caused the trouble, whereas Winokur, Galant, Petersen, and others on the company side, including investment banker Boisi, assert that what they call Lipton's "irrational" reaction was the problem.

But the company people do offer one explanation for Lipton's reaction other than irrationality: Williams's ambition. They speculate that Williams wanted to combine with Gordon Getty to take over the company, and that Getty's anger at the company's intervention in the trustee suit provided the perfect pretext for the museum to run to his side at a time when he was feeling most under assault and most in need of help. "The only way I can figure out Lipton's reaction," says Petersen, "is that I suspect his client [Williams] saw the lawsuit as a way to combine with Gordon against us. . . . I'm not saying Williams wants my job. Hell, he's not willing to work that hard. But he probably did want to be the power behind the throne."

Williams was unavailable for comment. But Lipton and two Getty board members who know Williams well dismiss that speculation as, in Lipton's words, "sheer nonsense." Rather, Lipton argues, "we were presented with a board that had snuck this guy out one door and brought the lawyers in the other. They hadn't even told us about authorizing the suit at the last meeting. Who could tell what they'd do next? Besides, how did we know what Gordon was going to do on his own if we didn't get together with him? The man was off the wall he was so mad."

"Marty Lipton is a liar," replies Getty Oil counsel Winokur. "He just won't tell the truth. Instead, he blames us for doing something that was thoroughly rational and would have worked if not for his willingness to put the museum's stock in jeopardy."

"Wars start," says Galant, "because people don't know what the other side is going to do; they don't communicate. If Marty had only asked us, we'd have told him that all we intended to do was pursue the [trustee] suit and that we intended to stand by the standstill. The only reason I can offer for why he didn't ask us was that he saw this as an opportunity for Harold [Williams]."

"There's an old Chinese proverb," says one adviser on the Getty deal. "You don't piss off forty percent of your shareholders. That's what these guys did, and in the process they pissed off another twelve percent [the museum's] by betraying Lipton."

Thus, by the first week in December the standstill agreement had come apart and the consent had been signed pitting Gordon Getty and the museum against the management. The company was, indeed, in play, and investment bankers Felix Rohatyn and James Glanville of Lazard Frères, representing Houston-based Pennzoil, had a plan for taking advantage of that.

PENNZOIL MAKES AN OFFER

On December 28 Pennzoil made a $1.6 billion tender offer for 20 percent of Getty's stock at $100 per share. Lipton and Williams were now worried. Though Getty stock was then selling at about $80, they considered the $100 price much too low. Yet, if that deal went through, Pennzoil could then offer to buy Gordon Getty's shares at the same price and the best the museum would be able to do would be to sell its shares for the same $100. Nor, of course, were Petersen and his people happy with the offer; they also thought it too low, plus it spelled the end of their reign as managers of an independent company.

By Saturday, December 31, Lipton had convinced the company, as well as Getty and his investment banker, Siegel, to agree to an alternative plan: The company would do its own tender offer for the 20 percent of the shares, but for $110. Gordon Getty would then hold a majority interest in the company (because 20 percent of the shares would have been taken out of circulation by the self-tender), but he would agree to refrain from exercising control for 90 days while a sale at a higher price, or some other solution, was sought. Lipton celebrated New Year's Eve thinking he had found at least a temporary end to the hostilities.

The next evening Siegel showed up at a New Year's Day party Lipton was giving and took Lipton and Tisch aside to give them some startling news. Gordon Getty was balking at signing the self-tender agreement because he didn't trust Petersen anymore. And because Siegel thought the worst thing was to have no plan to repel the $100 Pennzoil offer, he had structured a new one: Pennzoil chairman J. Hugh Liedtke and Glanville of Lazard had met with Siegel and Gordon Getty earlier that day and struck a deal in which, for $110 a share, Pennzoil and Getty would do a leveraged buyout of all the public shares and the museum's shares. The result would be a new Getty oil company of which Gordon Getty would own four-sevenths and Pennzoil would own three-sevenths. Getty would be president and chairman of the company and Liedtke the chief operating officer. If at the end of a year they were not in agreement on how the company ought to proceed, they would then divide up the assets of the company into two new companies, with Getty owning and running one and Pennzoil the other.

A meeting of the Getty board was convened at 6 P.M. the next day at the Hotel Inter-Continental in New York. (The meeting had been planned a few days before to consider the now-discarded $110 self-tender for 20 percent of the shares.)

Lipton and Williams wanted to take the latest Pennzoil deal at $110. "The Museum is a seller at $110," Lipton wrote in notes he prepared for Williams in advance of the board meeting. But other members of the board objected that the price was too low. Throughout the meeting, in fact, it would be Tisch—Lipton's friend and Gordon Getty's designated board member—who went against both Lipton and Getty in challenging the Pennzoil deal as not being good enough for Getty's public shareholders; if any unselfish statesman emerges from this story, it is he.

The lead lawyers for Pennzoil were Arthur Liman, a senior partner at New York's Paul, Weiss, Rifkind, Wharton & Garrison, and Moulton Goodrum, Jr., a senior partner at Houston's Baker & Botts. Liman officially represented Lazard Frères, Pennzoil's investment banker, while Goodrum represented Pennzoil, his longtime client. The key contact between the board and Pennzoil as the meeting wore on was between Liman and Lipton and Siegel. At several points either Lipton or Siegel left the meeting to ask Liman, who was posted outside, if the offer couldn't be sweetened, but to no avail. The meeting lasted until 2:30 A.M., when the board, after a great deal of heated argument, formally rejected the deal.

The board reconvened about 12 hours later. Soon thereafter, Liman appeared and told Lipton that he had gotten instructions to offer a complicated formula involving an extended payout from proceeds of a planned sale of a Getty insurance subsidiary. This add-on, called a "stub," was considered to be worth $1.50 per share in current dollars. The board discussed it extensively but rejected it.

It should be noted that all the while Lipton and Williams had declined Pennzoil's entreaties that they simply sign another majority consent with Gordon Getty, remove the current board, and put their own members in to approve the sale. Lipton says he felt that it would have been unfair for the museum to so impose its will on the board; it also would have been awkward for him, since he had recruited Tisch and the other board members brought in by Getty under the original tripartite agreement and they were now among those opposing the sale as being too low.

By about 6:30 P.M., however, Liman had come back to tell Lipton that if he could get the board to agree on a stub that was worth $2.50 per share, Lazard could get Pennzoil to go for it. Lipton informed the board, and Williams made a motion to accept the offer. His motion carried with a 14-to-1 vote. Lipton and Siegel of Kidder, Peabody went out to tell Liman, who phoned the Pennzoil people and got their okay. At 6:55 Siegel informed the Getty board of the Pennzoil decision and the meeting adjourned. According to a later deposition, congratulatory handshakes were exchanged all around, and Gordon Getty went home to his suite at the Pierre Hotel and cracked open a bottle of champagne.

"NO ONE REALLY KNEW WHAT THE DEAL WAS"

But had the board approved the whole deal or just the price? By now they had been meeting for 12 of the last 24 hours, and with everyone exhausted, no one wanted to go into the details of the transaction. Would it be a merger or a tender offer? How would the stub really be structured? Who would buy the museum's shares, and when? (Lipton wanted an immediate buyout of the museum's stock to avoid the risk of the deal falling through, but other board members, including Tisch, opposed such preferential treatment). With a total of 17 lawyers and bankers in the room, plus the 15 directors, there was all kinds of cross talk on these and other issues.

Nonetheless, everyone departed, leaving the lawyers to work out the details. As Williams would later put it in a deposition, ". . . the best thing to do at that point was to let those tired and angry directors go home and leave it to the lawyers to work out the structure of the transaction." It was decided, according to several people who were present, that the board would meet again the following day in the early afternoon to consider and ratify a definitive agreement, and that to do that the lawyers would have to have drafts by about 10 A.M. the next day.

That never happened, and why it never happened remains, as of this writing, the subject of a bitter lawsuit.

Following the board meeting, lawyers for all sides convened at the Paul, Weiss offices on Park Avenue. According to several who were there, the scene was total chaos. As one associate recalls, "No one really knew what the deal was or what they were supposed to do." What followed was about five hours of heated discussions, even shouting matches. For example, Vlahakis, Lipton's associate who was there representing the museum, argued with Winokur about whether the company should be buying out the museum's shares immediately. (Finally, they agreed that some kind of escrow arrangement might be acceptable, though it seems that Winokur never actually signed off on that.) Similarly, what the provisions of the stub were to be confused almost everybody. Worse, there was no agreement on whether Pennzoil or the current shareholders would get Getty Oil's first-quarter dividends—which amounted to $30 million.

But beyond these substantive points, there was general confusion about what form the deal was to take. At about midnight all the lawyers except those from Paul, Weiss and Baker & Botts left. "Everyone agreed that . . . the Pennzoil lawyers would draft a proposed definitive merger agreement for receipt by the other parties the next morning, January fourth," Vlahakis later stated in an affidavit.

BAKER & BOTTS: A LEAN AND LATE TEAM

The Wachtell, Lipton and Fried, Frank people point the finger for the subsequent delay at Paul, Weiss and Baker & Botts, arguing that whenever a hostile or semi-hostile deal is being negotiated, there is not a minute to spare, and that the acquirer's lawyers should have documents from the very beginning that can be constantly revised in the word-processing machine as the negotiation goes on. Such a draft would have at least given everyone something to focus on.

Seymour Hertz, the lead Paul, Weiss corporate partner on the scene that night, counters that "Baker & Botts made it very clear that they were doing the drafting." Moulton Goodrum of Baker & Botts says that "we don't draft documents before we reach a deal," and he adds that "the idea that we were slow is just something the Wachtell, Lipton people are telling you because they want the world to think they're the only people who can operate in this area."

Yet not only did Goodrum not have papers prepared in advance, he also did not have much of a team on hand once a deal was in the works. Working through the night on the drafting were just Goodrum, a tax partner, and a corporate associate.

Goodrum maintains that "we were not shorthanded." But in an interview in mid-January Joseph Cialone, another Baker & Botts partner, told me that he was called by Goodrum in the middle of the night on the night the drafting was being done and told to get on the first plane to New York to assist the three Baker & Botts lawyers. "I got there around noon and began the difficult parts of the drafting,'' Cialone said. ''There was still a lot to be done, and I do much more of this kind of drafting than Moulton does.''

When asked to comment in mid-January on Cialone's account, Goodrum said, ''Joe is in error; he could not have told you that. He was brought here just to finish a few details.''

Another lawyer at Baker & Botts says that Cialone was reprimanded by Goodrum and managing partner E. William Barnett for what he had told me, and was told that his comments had put the firm in danger of a malpractice suit. Cialone did not return subsequent phone calls. Managing partner Barnett says, ''We didn't call Joe [Cialone] on the carpet. We simply asked him why he gave out inaccurate information, and we decided to coordinate our responses to the press more carefully by having Moulton or me talk with you.''

Whatever the reason, drafts were not sent from the Paul, Weiss offices to the other parties until after 6 P.M. the next day, Wednesday, January 4. (Actually, Paul, Weiss has no record of the package's ever going out, according to partner Seymour Hertz.) And, according to records in the Wachtell, Lipton mailroom, they were not received until 8:25 P.M.— some ten hours after the 10 A.M. target time.

In fact, after 7 P.M. eastern standard time on Wednesday, the delivery of the drafts became temporarily irrelevant, for at 4 P.M. that day in California a state judge signed a temporary restraining order sought by one of the Getty trust's other beneficiaries enjoining Gordon Getty from closing the Pennzoil deal for at least 24 hours, which meant that the deal could not go forward until at least 7 P.M. the next day.

A ''CRAZY'' PRESS RELEASE

But the lawyers had gotten one thing done Tuesday night. They had drafted a press release announcing the basic terms of the Pennzoil deal.

However, the release also said that the agreement was ''subject to execution of a definitive merger agreement.'' Such in-progress press announcements are usually issued only in situations involving friendly deals; to issue one in this situation, where everyone knows that the holders of various blocks of stock are at odds, simply invites new bidders. Thus, it is the consensus among every experienced mergers and acquisitions lawyer I interviewed that Pennzoil should have insisted on no release pending the completion of the deal (Getty could simply have requested a halt to its stock trading without explaining it) or have made sure that the signing of a completed deal would follow the release by an hour or two at most. "When we saw that press release come over the wire saying there was no agreement," says one investment banker, "we knew the company was up for sale to anyone who could top $112.50 [the $110 cash price plus the $2.50 stub]. It was crazy."

"Pat Vlahakis was the one who insisted on the press release," says Pennzoil counsel Goodrum of Baker & Botts, referring to Lipton's twenty-seven-year-old associate. "Maybe she was tricking us, because we believe a deal is a deal and she doesn't." Vlahakis denies insisting on the press release; it was Pennzoil's and Getty's idea, she says. She and other lawyers involved for the museum, for Gordon Getty, and for Getty Oil note that it was an idea that made sense if the papers were to follow shortly. She only insisted that Goodrum read it before it went out, Vlahakis asserts, adding that the company lawyers prepared it with the expectation that they'd have papers with which to execute the deal within hours of the 9 A.M. release.

ENTER TEXACO

It was now the morning of Wednesday, January 4, and Bruce Wasserstein, who with Joseph Perella runs the hard-driving M&A department at First Boston Corporation, was one of those who read the press release as an invitation to join the bidding. According to subsequently filed court papers, he quickly phoned Boisi of Goldman, Sachs (the company's investment banker) to ask how much time he had to hunt up a new buyer. When Boisi told him there were no papers drafted yet, Wasserstein had all the encouragement he needed. Soon he was on the phone to Texaco.

By the next morning, Wasserstein—who understood that Lipton and the museum would be the fulcrum in any deal—was on the phone to Lipton, telling him that a better offer from Texaco was in the works. Lipton told him that the papers had finally been delivered to him the previous night and that in reviewing them earlier that morning he had found all kinds of problems. (For example, the museum's demand to have its stock purchased immediately upon signing the deal, as opposed to awaiting the lengthier and hurdle-filled completion of a tender offer, had still not been resolved.)

Later that afternoon, the judge in California continued the restraining order prohibiting Gordon Getty from selling the trust's stock.

By seven that night, Wasserstein and Perella, along with Texaco chairman John McKinley and lawyers from Skadden, Arps, Slate, Meagher & Flom, were in Lipton's office offering him $122.50 per share if he could get Gordon Getty to go along. (Williams was celebrating his fifty-sixth birthday with his children, and he delegated all bargaining to Lipton.) Obviously, the company would have to follow the museum and Gordon Getty, since it had agreed on $112.50. Besides, it was the company's investment banker, Boisi, who had been instrumental in encouraging Wasserstein to bring Texaco in; in fact, subsequently filed court papers indicate that Boisi had spent a good part of Wednesday and Thursday phoning around for higher offers than Pennzoil's.

Lipton told McKinley that he wanted $125 a share. (The difference for Texaco was $200 million.) McKinley said that might be possible, but only if he could get Gordon Getty to go along that night so that the deal could be consummated quickly before others might jump in.

The group then left for the Pierre Hotel, where Gordon Getty keeps a suite, but not before Lipton had called Loews chairman Tisch and asked him to join them at the Pierre and help convince Getty to become a seller at $125 rather than a buyer (with Pennzoil) at $112.50—and, thereby, give up his dream of running the company. Lipton and Tisch went up to talk to Getty, who was with Siegel, his investment banker, and Thomas Woodhouse, one of his lawyers. They spent about two hours before Lipton came down to the hotel lobby and told McKinley that there could be a deal for $125. McKinley pushed for $122.50, but capitulated on the condition, again, that Getty agree to the deal now.

There was the problem, though, of the California state judge's restraining order: How could Getty agree now and not violate it? Lipton took McKinley up to Getty's suite and on the way got an idea. Getty would sign a letter to McKinley saying he would sign a deal with Texaco but for the restraining order and intended to do so as soon as it was lifted. Woodhouse took down Lipton's dictation. They then waited for about an hour while Woodhouse searched for his senior partner, Lasky, who was in some San Francisco restaurant. At 1 A.M. Getty signed.

By 6 A.M. Lipton had signed a definitive agreement for the museum, and by 9 A.M. California time the company had held a telephone board meeting to ratify the new deal. The papers had been prepared within five hours by Skadden, Arps, whose lawyers, led by takeover specialist Morris Kramer, had already prepared drafts (and the word-processing disks to match) by the time they had first come to talk about a deal.

THE JILTED PARTNER'S SUITE

When the Texaco merger was announced Friday morning, January 6, Liedtke of Pennzoil immediately announced that he would sue to enforce his deal, which included an option clause that would have allowed Pennzoil to buy seven million shares of Getty stock at $110 immediately upon signing. (Liedtke, Liman, and everyone else on the Pennzoil side heard about the deal through the press announcement; no one on the other side had called them.)

Later that day, Getty Oil, seeking to ensure that Delaware, as opposed to a possibly friendlier forum for Pennzoil, would be the site of the litigation, sued in Delaware court seeking a declaratory judgment that no binding agreement between Pennzoil and Getty Oil had been made. On January 10, Pennzoil filed its suit in Delaware naming Getty Oil, Gordon Getty and his trust, and the museum as defendants for breaking the deal. They sought an injunction against the Texaco deal going forward (which couldn't happen anyway until the Federal Trade Commission completed its antitrust investigation of the merger) and specific performance of the option clause and the entire sale. Two weeks later, at a January 27 hearing, Pennzoil, represented by John Jeffers of Baker & Botts, amended its request for relief to include a more limited, and realistic, performance demand—that it simply be able to buy the three-sevenths of the company it had contracted for but at the higher price offered by Texaco. (By then the price had been raised from $125 to $128 in order to mollify a group of heirs who had sued to block the $125 deal; Gordon Getty had brought the stock a long way from the $50 it had been trading at just 12 months before.)

On February 7, Delaware State Chancellor Grover Brown ruled against the Pennzoil motion for a preliminary injunction and denied the immediate relief Pennzoil demanded. However, he also declared that, in his view, a contract between Pennzoil and Getty Oil, Gordon Getty, and the museum had existed and been broken. As of this writing, on that basis, a renewed suit by Pennzoil seeking damages is imminent.

The outcome of such a suit is uncertain (though I'll bet it results in Texaco, which indemnified the company, the trust, and the museum when it made its deal, paying a hefty settlement).

The museum's defense seems strongest. Although the museum signed a memorandum of agreement with Pennzoil on January 2, Lipton had Williams handwrite in next to his signature that the museum would not be bound in any way if the plan was not approved at Getty's January 2 board meeting, which it wasn't. It was rejected then, and an amended offer was approved the next day. Then again, it was Williams, the museum's president, who had made the motion at the board meeting to accept the amended Pennzoil deal.

Another point in the museum's favor in the Pennzoil suit is that it seems undisputed that the museum, Getty Oil, and Pennzoil had never come to terms on the immediate purchase of the museum's stock. (The museum had insisted on an immediate purchase, but no draft prepared by Pennzoil had included that provision.)

As for the company—which never signed any agreement with Pennzoil—it also seems clear that the board had spent most of its time in the marathon meeting debating price, and that it, indeed, had not resolved the other structural but important details of the deal and was awaiting a draft agreement to do so.

In this sense, the case against Gordon Getty, who had negotiated the three-sevenths/four-sevenths deal with Pennzoil and who had signed a letter of agreement similar to the one Williams signed but without his footnote, seems strongest.

PLAYING HARDBALL

But whatever the merits of the case against Gordon Getty and the company, there can be no doubt that reneging on the deal in favor of Texaco was harder hardball than many people like to play or think others should play. It is no surprise, then, that the briefs and accompanying affidavits offer a variety of embarrassing revelations. Among them:

• Gordon Getty might now take the position that he had made no deal with Pennzoil, but as late as January 5, Cohler, his lawyer who was attempting to get the TRO in California lifted, told the court that "there is presently a transaction agreed upon among [the defendants] and Pennzoil Company." Worse, on January 5 Cohler also filed an affidavit in the same court declaring that on January 3, "After the board of directors had considered other alternatives, the executed agreement in principle among Pennzoil, the Museum and the Trustee was approved by the Getty Oil board of directors." However, a day later, on January 6, following the announcement by Texaco concerning its acquisition of Getty, Cohler filed what he called a "corrected" affidavit in which he added to the above sentence the words, "as to certain terms but which was changed to a new proposal by Getty Oil to the Museum, the Trustee and Pennzoil as to other terms.''

• At the marathon January 2–3 board meetings, Getty corporate general counsel and secretary Ralph Copley took voluminous handwritten notes. He dictated them into a transcriber on January 4 and 5. They were then typed and circulated to Getty executives and to Dechert Price lawyers at the firm's New York branch office for what Copley said in a deposition were their ''comments.'' The tapes were erased on January 6 or 7, according to Copley's deposition. And he threw the original notes themselves into the garbage on January 9, after Getty chairman Petersen had had a chance to comment and make some corrections on the already-edited typewritten version. Present when Copley threw away the originals was Richard Seltzer, a Dechert Price partner. He declines comment on what the plaintiffs now call the ''destruction of evidence,'' but his partner Winokur says that the notes were destroyed before the lawsuit was filed and, therefore, do not constitute destruction of evidence. Winokur's only half right: the notes were destroyed the morning before the Pennzoil suit was filed against Getty but four days *after* Getty filed its preemptive suit against Pennzoil seeking a declaratory judgment. Winokur also points out that ''if we were going to doctor anything, we could do a better job; some of those typewritten notes [which indicate that the board heard investment banker Siegel report that Pennzoil had agreed to the final offer] hurt our case.'' He's right about that, and it's probably a good bet that Copley's action and Seltzer's acquiescence in it were just plain stupid. But who knows? Might there have been references to discussions and decisions on the nonprice aspects of the deal that the defendants now say were still left to be resolved?

• There seems to be evidence that once the prospect of Texaco's coming in was clear on the morning of Thursday, January 5, Dechert Price and Fried, Frank were less than candid with their opposite numbers from Paul, Weiss and Baker & Botts in explaining why they were taking so much time reviewing the drafts. ''We could tell there was some kind of stall going on,'' recalls Cialone of Baker & Botts. ''The Fried, Frank people kept telling us every hour that they'd be back to us in an hour.'' It actually didn't matter because Gordon Getty was still enjoined from acting that day, but no one knew how long he'd be enjoined, and the Pennzoil people by then were pressing to get everything ironed out so that the papers would be ready the minute he was free to sign them.

• On the other side, Baker & Botts, as co-counsel to Pennzoil in the suit, is in an awkward position. To explain the delay in getting the papers drafted, they have to admit either that they were unnecessarily slow in doing the work or that the work took time because there were still complicated issues to resolve. So far, they're trying to have it both ways by simply ignoring the issue of the delay, which has to hurt their case.

Liman, whose firm is handling the suit for Pennzoil along with Baker & Botts and Wilmington's Potter Anderson and Corroon, has been telling friends that it has more of a chance than most think, and he is quick to point to the circumstances surrounding the suit as evidence of the low standard of honor to be expected from takeover lawyers. For two successful lawyers who are contemporaries and travel in so much the same circles, he and Lipton have always been conspicuously unfriendly, and Liman, a man to whom sanctimony comes easily anyway, seems to take pleasure in deriding Lipton and his fellow dealmakers for their conduct in Getty: "This used to be a profession where deals were done on a handshake," says Liman. "But I guess not with certain firms when there's billions of dollars at stake." ("Write that I laughed when you told me what Arthur said," Lipton says.) But one investment banker responds to Liman's attack this way: "If that's what Arthur Liman thinks about billion-dollar deals, that it's all in a handshake, then all I can say is, 'Welcome to the world of big deals, Arthur—where it's never over till it's over.' "

BLOOD FEUD

BY
STEPHEN J. ADLER

Houston's top lawyers clash bitterly and nobody's bored but the jury.

It's August 8, at the end of a long day of testimony in a dingy courtroom in Houston state court, and plaintiff's lawyer Joseph Jamail leaps to his feet to address the judge. With the jury out of the room, Jamail points to opposing counsel Richard Miller, who is seated in the spectators' area near the jury box instead of at the counsel's table. He accuses Miller of whispering to jurors and currying favor with them during the trial. "I think if they get real close to him, they will learn to hate him," Jamail snarls, adding, "I think it's demeaning, and if that's what he thinks he has got to do, the court ought to be aware of it." Miller responds in disgust, "I don't believe I ever saw a lawyer so goosey." After the issue is resolved and Miller is allowed to sit where he wants as long as he doesn't talk to jurors, he mutters to a New York lawyer, "They don't pull that kind of chickenshit stuff in New York."

It is one in a series of nasty exchanges between opposing counsel—and particularly between Jamail and Miller—that have marked Pennzoil's marathon $14 billion suit against Texaco for allegedly busting up a planned merger between Pennzoil and Getty Oil in January 1984 so that Texaco could buy Getty. The lawyers have even gone to the absurd length of filing disciplinary complaints against each other with the Texas bar, and the judge has threatened them with sanctions for making abusive remarks to one another.

It's no wonder tempers are running high. The suit pits some of Houston's best and most flamboyant lawyers against each other in a high-stakes case that could produce an important precedent in the case law that governs mergers and acquisitions and contract law in general. More to the point, the rancor of one of the most bitter takeover fights ever seems to have passed like a baton to the trial lawyers.

Pennzoil's lead counsel is Jamail, 59, a longtime friend of Pennzoil chairman J. Hugh Liedtke and a master at getting huge jury verdicts in personal-injury cases. It is an article of faith among Houston lawyers that in good years Jamail pulls in $10 million in fees. (Jamail declines comment on his earnings.) Although not primarily a corporate litigator, he has proved adept at reducing this complex corporate dispute to a simple morality play.

Working closely with Jamail are six lawyers from Houston's Baker & Botts, Pennzoil's regular outside counsel, led by partners John Jeffers, 43, and G. Irvin Terrell, 39. Baker & Botts represented Pennzoil in the botched Getty negotiations and seems to have a huge stake in vindicating itself with a victory at trial.

For its part, mammoth Texaco has chosen a feisty 13-lawyer Houston firm: Miller Keeton Bristow & Brown. Miller, 59, who is leading the defense, was formerly head of the litigation department at opposing counsel Baker & Botts and is one of the most feared litigators in the city. His close ties to the other side have increased the bitterness of the trial: at Baker & Botts, Miller was considered a litigation guru; he occasionally did work for Pennzoil and tried cases for other clients with the assistance of the two much younger Baker & Botts litigators who are Pennzoil's counsel in this trial. He even defended Jamail in a defamation suit three years ago. (Miller got the case dismissed.)

Yet despite the strong matchups and the important issues at stake, the trial—which began July 9 and is still in progress at this writing—has at times been a disappointing and even embarrassing spectacle. It features a judge who probably shouldn't be hearing the case, a jury that certainly can't understand it, a law firm that appears to have a conflict of interest, and lawyers who sometimes seem more intent on taking cheap shots at each other than in bringing the case to life for the jury. Indeed, by burdening the jury with infinitely too much detail, Pennzoil's lawyers seem to be risking defeat in what otherwise might be a strong jury case. It's as if they're trying so hard to be thorough that they're unable to perceive how boring their presentation has become.

For Houston lawyers, the case is an irresistible daytime soap opera that many sneak off to watch while they're at the courthouse. But much of the warfare among the attorneys takes place beyond the hearing of the jurors, who have to be wondering why all those spectators are *voluntarily* sitting through the proceedings.

GETTY GAMES REVISITED

The trial focuses on events in the pivotal first week of January 1984—a week in which Pennzoil chairman Liedtke fell abruptly from triumph to humiliation. On January 3, after a marathon two-day meeting, the board of Getty Oil Company had agreed to a deal in which Pennzoil and Gordon Getty would pay $112.50 a share to take the company private. Gordon Getty, who as trustee for the Sarah C. Getty Trust controlled 40 percent of the company's stock, would own four-sevenths of the newly constituted company and would be its president; Pennzoil would become owner of three-sevenths, with Liedtke serving as Getty's new CEO. The J. Paul Getty Museum, which owned almost 12 percent of the shares before the deal, had agreed to sell its shares to Getty Oil immediately as part of the overall transaction.

Late on January 3 lawyers for the parties were dispatched to write a press release announcing an agreement in principle and then to draft the necessary merger documents. Baker & Botts corporate partner Moulton Goodrum, Jr., representing Pennzoil, accepted chief responsibility for drafting the merger papers.

After the board meeting, however, Getty investment banker Geoffrey Boisi of Goldman, Sachs & Company called Texaco officials and assured them that no binding deal had been reached and that Getty might still be amenable to a higher offer. Texaco quickly put together a proposal to purchase Getty Oil for $125 a share (the price was later increased to $128). On January 6, while lawyers for Pennzoil were still trying to pull together documents to complete their deal, Texaco and Getty announced that they had reached terms. The Pennzoil deal was dead.

Throughout the Christmas-week negotiations with Getty Oil and its major shareholders, Liedtke had expressed fear that New York lawyers and investment bankers would try to take advantage of him, according to his deposition testimony and that of his advisers. Now he was furious that they had. He shot off a telex to Getty Oil: ''[I]f you fail to keep your agreement, we intend to commence actions for damages . . . against Getty Oil Company, your individual board members, the Getty Trust, the Getty Museum, and all others who have participated in or induced the breach of your agreement with us.''

Texaco and Getty refused to back off. Liedtke ordered his lawyers to sue the Getty interests for backing out of the agreement in principle and to sue Texaco for tortiously interfering with the Pennzoil-Getty deal.

LIEDTKE TAPS BAKER & BOTTS—AGAIN

Liedtke immediately asked Baker & Botts to handle the litigation. In one sense it was a routine choice, because Baker & Botts had especially close

313

ties to Pennzoil. The company typically brought the firm some $4 million in business a year, according to a source at the firm. Also, Pennzoil's then–general counsel Perry Barber, Jr., and its then-president Blaine Kerr had been partners at Baker & Botts. Kerr, a prodigious rainmaker, had brought in the Pennzoil business in the 1960s. In addition, Baker & Botts lawyers knew everything there was to know about the Getty deal, having handled the negotiations.

On the other hand, the choice of Baker & Botts was fraught with risk because of potential conflicts of interest. And the job of dealing with the conflicts fell to a brand-new manager, William Barnett, who had just been elected to take the helm at Baker & Botts. Although he resolved the conflict problems in a way that permitted his firm to serve as trial counsel against Texaco, the resolution proved costly to the firm.

The initial conflict issue arose because Texaco, which has substantial business operations in the Houston area, used Baker & Botts as one of its chief local counsel and provided the firm with close to $1 million a year in billings. In 1983, for example, Texaco had paid Baker & Botts some $920,000, according to Texaco in-house lawyer Robert Fuller. This included $486,000 in billings for personal-injury and property-damage defense work, according to Fuller. Barnett declines comment on the figures.

Because a firm is prohibited from representing an adversary of a current client without the client's permission (even in an unrelated matter), Baker & Botts had to get Texaco's permission to proceed. With the rule in mind, Barnett called Texaco general counsel William Weitzel, Jr., the week of January 9 and asked for a conflict waiver.

Weitzel promised to talk it over with the Texaco brass and report back. On January 16, Weitzel called with Texaco's decision: Baker & Botts would be permitted to bring the case against Texaco. But, according to Barnett's testimony in a later pretrial hearing, Weitzel explained "that he could not tell me, ever, that that would not jar the relationship we had had a long time with Texaco or it necessarily would be a healthy thing for the law firm or our relationship with them. . . ."

Weitzel's warnings about jarring the relationship turned out to be understatements. As Pennzoil prepared its case—seeking astronomical compensatory damages and suing for punitive damages on the grounds that Texaco officials had behaved unethically in stealing Getty away from Pennzoil—Weitzel and others at Texaco became more and more disturbed about doing business with Baker & Botts. "It was all the circumstances [that disturbed Texaco]," says Weitzel. "It was not only the fact that they were adversaries, but the way they were handling it, and the direction in which the case was wandering.''

Meanwhile, in late January, Texaco retained Miller Keeton as trial counsel. The firm was a collection of top Houston litigators who had tired of big firm practice and banded together just five months earlier, in September 1983. At first, Miller says, he had balked at taking the case because of his former ties to Baker & Botts and to Pennzoil. ''This might be a case that turned out to be unpleasant,'' Miller remembers thinking. ''Perry Barber [then general counsel of Pennzoil, now a partner at Baker & Botts] is a friend of mine, and Baker & Botts is likely to be very intense about this case because people are saying they f——ed up the deal.''

Nonetheless, the prospect of getting such an important case for his fledgling firm—and, he says, some pressure from his partners, who were anxious to try it—overcame his hesitation. Miller Keeton became trial counsel. The firm put 6 of its 13 lawyers on the case.

According to Miller, the firm's involvement rankled partners at Baker & Botts, where Miller had been such a superstar, and litigator John Jeffers called Miller to complain. ''He said he didn't want to make this phone call but he was asked to call me and say that in their view, I and my firm were disqualified because I had done work for Pennzoil and [Daryl] Bristow [a Baker & Botts partner], who had just joined us, had done Pennzoil work,'' Miller recalls. Asked specifically about that conversation, Jeffers declines comment, as does Barnett.

Miller says he first made sure that Bristow hadn't worked on the Pennzoil-Getty deal while at Baker & Botts. (Bristow hadn't, although his wife, Elaine Bristow, had. She has since left Baker & Botts.) Miller then discussed the issue with Pennzoil's then–general counsel Barber. At first, he says, Barber said he had no objection if Miller represented Texaco. But later Barber called back, Miller says, and told him: ''I want you to know that if you get involved in this case your friends at Pennzoil are going to be plenty pissed off.'' Nonetheless, Miller says, he decided that the firm didn't have a conflict and would represent Texaco. ''I didn't owe the guys at Baker & Botts anything because what little work I did do for Pennzoil had nothing to do with this case,'' Miller says. (Barber didn't return phone calls.)

It wasn't long before Miller crossed swords with his former partners. On March 28, 1984, Miller and partner Richard Keeton, formerly a top litigation partner at Vinson & Elkins, went to visit Baker & Botts managing partner Barnett to bring some costly news from Texaco. Miller told

Barnett that Texaco officials had decided that their relationship with Baker & Botts had indeed become strained beyond repair—and Texaco was pulling all of its business from the firm. Miller instructed Barnett, his former partner, to arrange for the transfer of various pieces of litigation and other matters to other law firms.

In addition, Miller informed Barnett that Texaco was no longer willing to let Baker & Botts represent Pennzoil in the Texaco suit. The Texaco conflict-of-interest waiver, Miller explained, had applied only to Pennzoil's earlier (and unsuccessful) suit in Delaware to enjoin the deal. Now that Pennzoil had moved its case to Houston and had accused Texaco of bad faith and even fraud, Texaco officials no longer believed that the waiver was valid.

Having taken all its business away from Baker & Botts, Texaco couldn't move to disqualify Baker & Botts for simultaneously representing one current client against another. Instead, Miller told Barnett, Texaco intended to challenge Baker & Botts's role as trial counsel for Pennzoil because several of its lawyers were likely to be called as witnesses at the trial. The lawyer-witness rule provides that a firm may be disqualified if any of its lawyers ought to be called as witnesses at trial or if it becomes apparent that the testimony of a lawyer will be prejudicial to his client.

At least four Baker & Botts lawyers, led by corporate partner Goodrum, had participated in aspects of the dealmaking and had been deposed by Texaco during discovery. There were mutterings among lawyers involved in the dealmaking for some of the Getty interests that Goodrum had understaffed the Getty deal and had been slow in preparing the final merger documents. Even within Baker & Botts, there were grumblings about how the deal was handled, according to a former associate who was there at the time. "There are a lot of people at the firm who think the firm screwed up," says the former associate.

If Goodrum had been quicker in drafting the final papers, some lawyers argued, Texaco might not have had time to make its competing bid and negotiate the terms that it announced January 6. It's Pennzoil's position— as explained by its lawyers in deposition testimony—that the delays were primarily the result of stalling tactics by lawyers for the Getty interests, who repeatedly put off meeting with the Pennzoil lawyers so Getty could cut a better deal with Texaco.

Miller suggested that some Baker & Botts lawyers might have to be called as witnesses to explain the delays in drafting the definitive merger documents. In addition, they might be in a position to discuss the intentions of the parties as to whether the agreement in principle was meant to be binding.

It was a hardball tactic by Texaco, given that the lawyer-witness rule generally is intended to protect the client of the lawyer-witness, in this case Pennzoil, rather than the opponent. And Pennzoil hadn't objected to keeping Baker & Botts as trial counsel, nor had Baker & Botts shown any sign of taking the lawyer-witness question seriously.

After Miller raised the question in March, Barnett looked into the problem further. After discussing it with litigators Jeffers and Terrell, he said, he concluded that Baker & Botts lawyers "were not important to the case, would not be called, and were not adverse to the Pennzoil position in any event." Nonetheless, Miller placed in the record at the next deposition that Texaco reserved the right to move to disqualify Baker & Botts sometime before trial.

ALMS FOR THE JUDGE

Jamail was brought into the case as lead counsel for Pennzoil in late January, before Texaco threatened to have Baker & Botts disqualified. Jamail and Liedtke had been friends for the past 20 years and had often vacationed together with their families along the Gulf Coast beaches. At various times, Jamail had represented members of Liedtke's family, although this was the first time he had been brought in on company business. But Jamail's grand entrance brought about a bizarre plot twist that continues to cast a shadow over the case. On March 7, 1984—just two days after Texaco had filed its answer to the Pennzoil complaint—Jamail gave the trial judge in the case, Anthony J. P. Farris, a $10,000 campaign contribution. The contribution was the largest Farris had received. (Farris received a total of $101,000 in campaign contributions in 1984).

By the time Miller learned of the gift in August 1984, Farris had already ruled against Texaco on several motions involving the discovery schedule. Miller says he and his partners had known nothing about the facts of the Pennzoil case when they became Texaco counsel and were rushed ill-prepared into discovery. As a result, he says, "I'd have to say we did a half-assed job." When he discovered the Jamail contribution, he linked it to the judge's adverse rulings in the discovery dispute. Miller filed a motion to disqualify the judge that raised what appeared to be reasonable questions about whether the contribution might cause an ap-

317

pearance of bias in the judge. However, his motion promised more than it could deliver—and boomeranged on him and his client.

Miller alleged that client Pennzoil must have been behind the Jamail gift, even though—as it turned out—he could produce no evidence to prove it. "The sheer size of the gift, far beyond the resources of one lawyer to give to one judge when many judicial candidates are seeking election and reelection, suggests that Jamail's client Pennzoil is involved," Miller declared in his motion.

Miller also charged that Pennzoil had dismissed its initial case against Texaco in Delaware and moved the case to Houston so it could take advantage of Jamail's hometown connections. According to Miller's motion, the change of forum gave Pennzoil the chance "to employ a lawyer who was known by Pennzoil to have contributed heavily to judicial races."

Although the $10,000 gift was properly reported to the county clerk, neither the judge nor Jamail informed Texaco that the gift had been made. In a risky move, Miller went beyond the allegation that Judge Farris might appear to have a conflict and attacked Farris directly. "His acceptance of such a massive contribution from a lawyer who is known by him to be the lawyer for a litigant in an important case just filed in his court—and at the very commencement of that case—is highly questionable, but his failure to disclose the gift to the other litigant and its counsel is a clear breach of his legal, ethical, and moral responsibilities as a judicial officer," Miller alleged. It was strong language to use about a judge who, if Miller lost the motion, would be trying the case.

Pennzoil responded with a torrent of righteous indignation, escalating the tone of personal attack and assuring that the trial itself would become a grudge match. After attacking Miller for lashing out at the judge and slandering the good names of opposing counsel, Pennzoil's written reply, signed by Baker & Botts's Jeffers, asked: "Why would he do this? Perhaps it is as a precautionary alibi for the ultimate outcome; the evidence of Texaco's liability in this case will be difficult even for him to explain to a jury and the potential damages are of an order of magnitude he has not previously faced and cannot face now."

Pennzoil denied that it had anything to do with Jamail's contribution and cited the state constitutional provision that a judge can only be disqualified for having a monetary interest in the outcome of the trial, being related to either of the parties, or having previously served as counsel in the case. Campaign contributions by attorneys are customary in Texas and don't provide any basis for disqualification, Pennzoil argued.

The October 25, 1984, argument on the motion before retired state judge E. E. Jordan proved nastier than the written exchange. Jamail came out storming at having been maligned by Miller. Jamail first insulted Miller by insisting that Miller be sworn before he testified, a requirement generally waived for lawyers because they are officers of the court. Judge Jordan refused to let Miller be sworn but otherwise kept a low profile while Jamail and Miller exchanged blows.

Jamail quickly got Miller to concede that he had no evidence—only intuition based on "what I know about this case and what I know about Mr. Liedtke and his past"—that Pennzoil was behind the contribution. And Jamail, after calling one of Miller's remarks "cowardly," characterized the motion as "a long whine and a pout by Mr. Miller who has not been able to run over Judge Farris."

Somehow Jamail managed to turn the argument into a rout: "It's a disgrace for an officer of the court to come and, with suspicion and surmise, smear the judicial system," he declared. "I have contributed money, Your Honor, to almost every judge. . . . To say that I have never given a contribution [to] a sitting district judge [of] ten thousand dollars before is a lie. I have. And he knows it. [Miller actually had said that lawyers never give as much as $10,000 to judges in county races.] But to stand here and deliberately perpetuate falsehoods on this court is unbecoming, undistinguished, and not respectable, and it's an attack on the judicial system." (Miller responded that Jamail's contribution had been described as a "princely sum" in a letter by Farris to another backer, which Miller read into the record, and that such a big gift suggested that "something is rotten in Denmark." According to Miller, "It's like Sherlock Holmes says to Mr. Watson, 'Watson, I don't believe in coincidences.' ")

It took some fancy footwork to make a virtue of giving a contribution to a sitting judge in a $14 billion case, but when he sat down, Jamail seemed to have succeeded. And he had lots of help from a sympathetic judge. Judge Jordan sat quietly through much of the argument, but prefaced his ruling with an anecdote that suggested how futile Miller's bid had been. "I did have one contested election," the retired judge reminisced. "And I told [the lawyers], 'I don't even know who contributes or how much. Give it to my campaign manager.' I've got the records at home. To this day I haven't looked at them because I didn't want anybody to be able to do to me what has been done to this judge today."

Turning back to the Texaco-Pennzoil case, Jordan said it would "tear up the whole judicial system in this state" if lawyers filed motions to disqualify the judge anytime they thought there might be some impropriety. "Because," he said, "then the judge is placed in the unenviable position of having to say, yes I'm a crook, or fight it, which the judge in this case is doing. . . . He can't recuse at this point. I wouldn't. No other judge would." It came as no surprise that Jordan rejected the motion.

Winning wasn't enough for Jamail, however. At the end of the proceeding, he ordered a certified transcript so, he said, "I may forward it to the Grievance Committee for the Grievance's consideration of Mr. Miller's conduct." Jamail now declines to comment on whether he filed a complaint against Miller, although he and Miller confirm that someone filed a disciplinary complaint against Miller in connection with the motion to disqualify Judge Farris. According to a source in a position to know, one of Pennzoil's lawyers, but not Jamail personally, filed against Miller. In turn, Miller filed a counterclaim alleging that his accuser had filed a frivolous disciplinary complaint, and both complaints were dismissed summarily without a hearing.

The dispute over the Jamail contribution was a pivotal event in the Pennzoil-Texaco suit. But like so many of the battles that make this case intriguing to lawyers, the fight over Jamail's gift—and Miller's response to it—was not going to be replayed before the jury. For those jurors who were now to be selected, it would be a boring trial involving the maddeningly complex details of a corporate transaction. The passion of the players and their lawyers would remain hidden.

CHOOSING A JURY, TEXAS-STYLE

Restored to the bench by Judge Jordan, Farris ruled against Texaco's motion to disqualify Baker & Botts on July 5, 1985. With tempers high on both sides, it was finally time to go to trial.

Jamail had played a minor role in discovery, and during the motion to disqualify Baker & Botts, he had emphasized that he wasn't familiar enough with all aspects of the case to handle it himself. But starting on July 10, he demonstrated his value as a trial lawyer by taking the lead role in jury selection. Although Jamail's campaign contribution had been covered in the press several months earlier, it seemed unlikely the potential jurors would remember the story.

From the start of the voir dire, it was clear that Jamail's strategy was to harangue the potential jurors—and swing them to his side—under the guise of asking questions to help him eliminate jurors he didn't want. Observers call the three-day event one of the most extraordinary jury selections they have seen. Said one, "I was amazed at the latitude the judge gave [the lawyers] to talk about evidence and documents that weren't in evidence yet. It was the broadest voir dire I had ever seen in Texas."

Jamail started by laying out Pennzoil's basic theme: The Pennzoil-Getty deal had been sealed with handshakes and evidenced by an earlier memorandum of agreement (even though the final merger documents were never completed), and the jury's job was to affirm that a handshake still means something. "The question ultimately that you are going to have to decide, those of you [who] get chosen to serve on this jury, is what a promise is worth, what your word is worth, what a handshake is worth, what a contract is worth," Jamail began. He personalized the case by repeatedly calling Liedtke "my friend" and reminding the jury that promises are binding "the way I grew up and the way I am sure most of you did."

The us-versus-them theme intensified as Jamail identified what he called "a conspiracy between Texaco and a group of New York investment bankers and New York lawyers." In contrast, Jamail pointed out, "I have my own small law firm. I was born here. I was raised here. I went to school here and I live here." With nothing less cosmic at stake than the value of a man's word in the oil patch, Jamail told the jurors that the suit is "the most important case ever brought in the history of America. There isn't any question about that."

Then Jamail embarked on a clever line of questioning to enlist the jurors to his cause. After telling the jurors that Getty issued a press release on January 4 announcing the agreement in principle, Jamail asked: "Is there any one of you who would not accept that as evidence in considering the issues at the end of this case . . . as to whether or not the Getty interests thought they had a binding agreement? If there's anyone who could not accept that as evidence in this case, *powerful* evidence, I need to have a show of . . . hands and we can discuss it."

When no hands were raised, Jamail said with satisfaction, "I take it each of you would do that."

Jamail then explained that Texaco had indemnified the Getty interests against any liability arising from making the deal with Texaco and breaking the deal with Pennzoil. Again Jamail asked the potential jurors, "Is there any member of this panel who could not and would not accept that indemnity . . . as evidence of the fact that Texaco had knowledge of the Getty and Pennzoil agreement and binding contract? . . . I see no hands. I didn't expect any.''

Jamail developed a rhythm, describing evidence in a manner most favorable to Pennzoil and then challenging the jurors to join with him in accepting it. By the time Jamail was done—three days after he began— the jury probably could have been counted on to vote for Liedtke for president. Miller acknowledged this when he began questioning jurors on behalf of Texaco on July 15. He did his best to counter Jamail with an appealing folksiness of his own. But it became apparent as he proceeded that Texaco's case—although probably supported by existing case law— is a tougher one to sell to a jury.

Miller started out by deflating Jamail's claims about the importance of the case. ''I tried a case two months ago where a father was trying to get his children back. I consider that case considerably more important than I consider this case,'' Miller said. ''This is a suit over money. . . . The idea that money turns this into the most important case that's ever been filed I think tells you something about the company that's bringing this case.''

Miller went on to emphasize that Getty Oil investment banker Boisi invited Texaco to bid, that ''we didn't crash this party.'' Then he launched into Texaco's main defense: The agreement in principle did not constitute a binding contract because the parties contemplated that a final document would have to be signed before anyone was bound. The Getty board didn't approve a final deal, Miller said, but rather ''the evidence will show that what they voted on was price. That is to say, they voted upon a price at which negotiations would commence.''

Miller also sounded the theme that the deal was so complicated, involving so many parties in such complex arrangements, that anyone would be a fool to be bound by an agreement in principle until all the essential elements had been worked out. And to show they hadn't been worked out, he went through a litany of questions that were still unresolved between Pennzoil and Getty at the time Texaco and Getty made their counter-deal. For example, the parties had never determined whether Getty Oil shareholders would be entitled to some $30 million in first-quarter dividends when they were bought out. Nor had they resolved whether a potential $2 billion tax penalty would require the deal to be restructured so that the Getty Museum sold its shares directly to Pennzoil, instead of to Getty Oil, as the agreement in principle had contemplated.

The U.S. Court of Appeals for the Second Circuit seemed to back

322

Texaco's legal position in its recent opinion in *Reprosystem, B.V.* v. *SCM Corporation,* in which the court found that the magnitude and complexity of a deal were factors in determining whether the parties intended to be bound by an agreement in principle. In extremely complicated deals, wrote Judge George Pratt, there is "a practical business need to record all the parties' commitments in definitive documents."

Miller tried hard to prepare the jury for what appeared to be a stretch of logic: "Just as the oil patch has certain expressions, just as the legal profession has legal expressions, [in] the financial community that's made up of New York City . . . the word[s] agreement in principle [are] always recognized as a statement that you do not have a contract."

Will the jury buy it? Or will they prefer the notion that a handshake still means something and a man's word is his bond, even in the alien world of finance? It may depend a lot on the background of the 12 jurors and four alternates who were selected in this five-day process. The 16 (they were not told which are alternates and which are jurors) include a ward clerk at a hospital, a mailman, an unemployed woman who takes temporary secretarial jobs, a housekeeper at the University of Houston, another professional housekeeper, a housewife, four clerical workers, a salesman, a man who works in the heating business, a woman who works in the county's insurance office, a man who does "communications" work for the city, an accountant, and a registered nurse. Texaco lawyers say they believe the nurse, who has been taking notes, will be selected foreperson. Both Miller and Jamail say they are happy with the jury. Miller says he was looking for hardworking, intelligent jurors who will study the case closely and take copious notes (at least three jurors are writing in their notepads). Jamail says he wanted individuals who have the common sense to recognize that a deal is a deal.

For the jury, the case is a challenge both to their intellects and their endurance. They are being asked to evaluate financial analyses of the cost of discovering oil (which will be crucial if damages are assessed), to follow the structure of the Getty-Pennzoil buyout, to figure out whether all of the "essential" elements had been covered in the agreement in principle, and to understand terminology such as tender offer, definitive merger agreement, leveraged buyout, stock option, stub payment, no-shop, top-up, golden parachute, and indemnification.

At the outset, it looked more like a Jamail jury—not highly educated, unfamiliar with corporate transactions, and possibly more comfortable with hometown company Pennzoil and its hometown executives. But Miller is hoping that Jamail's harping on Pennzoil's Houston roots will backfire. "They say, 'We're going to pick twelve boobs who will vote for us because we're local.' If I was on a jury, I'd resent that," Miller said in an interview early in the trial.

PENNZOIL'S DOWNHILL COURSE

For Pennzoil, jury selection may have been the high point of its case. Once Pennzoil started presenting witnesses, the pace slowed—and Pennzoil's previously clear and easy-to-understand case began to get muddled and increasingly dull.

Baker & Botts's Jeffers doggedly steered the first witness, retired Pennzoil president Blaine Kerr, through almost seven days of redundant testimony, including a torturously complete recitation of all the events at the time of the takeover attempt. Kerr's main contribution in almost 2,000 pages of testimony (including cross-examination) was to make clear that Pennzoil officials didn't believe that an agreement in principle was an invitation for others to bid, as Texaco had claimed.

In all, it was a soporific performance that dulled the sense of excitement Jamail had created. "Kerr was the opening witness and should have been among the strongest. Pennzoil ought to have been well ahead on points when they got through with Kerr, and I think they were only slightly ahead," says a Houston lawyer who has been observing the trial.

On one of Jamail's main themes—the broken handshake—Miller scored strongly on cross-examination. First, Miller quoted Jamail's opening remarks: " 'They made a deal and they evidenced the promises by signing it with a handshake.' " Then Miller asked Kerr, "Now, you never shook hands with anybody [at] the Getty Oil Company, did you?" Kerr responded lamely that he had only shaken hands with Pennzoil's partner in the deal, Gordon Getty. Kerr also conceded that Liedtke hadn't shaken hands with all the parties to the contract.

After Kerr stepped down, the Pennzoil case got worse. Pennzoil put on videotaped depositions of two Texaco officials to provide evidence that Texaco knew that an agreement had been reached between Pennzoil and Getty, yet brazenly induced the parties to breach it anyway. The Texaco witnesses couldn't be brought to testify live, Jeffers says, because they were outside the subpoena power of the state court. (Their depositions had been taken in New York, where discovery orders from the Texas court could be enforced by a New York court.) Miller Keeton partner Michael Peterson counters that Texaco would have been happy to produce their officials as witnesses if Pennzoil had asked. Jeffers dismisses the idea: "It would have been foolish to ask that question," he says.

The result was a week of television in a darkened room, with four screens flickering and everyone's attention flagging. And the testimony wasn't even very compelling: the Texaco officials, president Alfred De-Crane, Jr., and senior assistant treasurer Patrick Lynch, never admitted to wrongdoing and didn't do much to advance Pennzoil's case. Asked about the wisdom of putting on videotaped witnesses, Jeffers responds: "The jurors are paying attention as best as they can, and it's better than the alternative, which is reading the depositions." Jamail, however, who thrives on live courtroom confrontation, seemed uncomfortable with the videotapes. "I never have been a fan of that. I just never have," he says. However, he adds, "I think in this case they've been more helpful than I've seen before."

One Houston lawyer who was observing the trial had a different viewpoint. "I think they're killing the jury with videotapes. . . . When they play the videotapes, I leave."

The videotapes had another negative impact on Pennzoil. Its lawyers didn't want to play their four videotapes—which lasted roughly two weeks in all—one after the other, for fear of putting the entire courthouse to sleep. Thus, they had to bring in live witnesses periodically to break up the tedium. So rather than continue building its liability case, Pennzoil presented damage witnesses—generally a dry breed of number crunchers—in these interludes between videos. The interruptions didn't liven up the case much and they brought an air of disorganization to Pennzoil's presentation. One lawyer wearily watching the case offered a suggestion: "You need to show some *Roadrunner* cartoons between witnesses in this trial."

The problem of the videos was most apparent when Martin Siegel's deposition was shown five weeks into the trial. Siegel, an M&A specialist at Kidder, Peabody & Company who represented Gordon Getty in the deal, can be charismatic in person but turned out to be a boring TV personality. By 4:15 on August 20, the jury had been fidgeting furiously for much of two days. For perhaps the tenth time, they had heard a narrative of the events of the last week in December 1983 and the first week in January 1984. The main purpose of putting Siegel on, according to Jeffers, was to introduce an affidavit Siegel prepared on January 4 in connection with a California court proceeding. The affidavit stated that the Pennzoil-Getty deal had been completed as of that date.

It was a good, although relatively minor, point for Pennzoil, in that it

325

showed that at least one of the key players appeared to believe that a binding contract existed prior to Texaco's bid. Yet surrounded by so much extraneous video testimony, the point got lost. Jeffers responds that some background had to be let in to lay the groundwork for the affidavit and that a good deal of the Siegel video was shown at the direction of Texaco, which wanted the jury to hear other sections to weaken or rebut Pennzoil's strongest material.

Nonetheless, on the whole the video was a bust. One juror, a 42-year-old clerical worker seated in the back row, appeared to be snoozing by day's end, his mouth wide open. The others seemed increasingly bored and annoyed, their summer ruined by repetitious testimony concerning the intricate and financially complex details of the Pennzoil-Getty-Texaco fight.

Meanwhile, the judge was setting a pattern for his handling of the trial. It quickly became apparent that Farris, a former U.S. attorney, wasn't always familiar with the players in the New York takeover arena. At one point in the proceedings, the judge interrupted to ask: "[D]id you say that the First Boston company is a New York firm?" When told it was, he added, "If the name is First Boston, it should be in Massachusetts. Why didn't they call it the First Staten Island Company or something?"

Farris also had a habit of frequently scolding the bailiff for some perceived infraction and ordering the few spectators, basically an orderly bunch, to be quite. He spent a lot of time during breaks talking about the sketches of the trial that a courtroom artist had been drawing. During one break, he asked all the attorneys to sign their names to the sketch that was being done for him.

In mid-trial, the Houston Bar Association released the results of its ratings of state judges—and Farris finished a bleak 15th out of 19 state civil district judges in Houston. Roughly 40 percent of the lawyers who responded to the bar poll gave him a grade of "poor" for courtesy and attentiveness to attorneys and witnesses. And slightly more than a quarter of the respondents graded him "poor" for impartiality.

Nonetheless, as the trial progressed, Farris seemed to gain a better understanding of the case and to be more facile at settling evidentiary disputes among the lawyers. He bore the extra burden of having to appear strictly impartial as Jamail, his contributor, and Miller, who had tried to oust him, each sought favorable rulings. Although Farris frequently overruled Miller's objections, Miller said in an interview that he thought Farris was doing a good job of putting the disqualification motion out of his mind.

Ultimately, Farris's role will become crucial. In Texas jury trials, jurors are typically asked a series of questions, called special issues, and return only answers to those questions—not a single verdict. According to some of the lawyers involved, the case may well come down to how Judge Farris decides to word those questions and thus define the issues in the case. Given the complexity of the case, this would be a challenge even for a Delaware chancery judge who has tried numerous M&A-related cases. It remains to be seen whether Farris will be up to the challenge.

LIMAN TAKES THE STAND

There were bright spots in Pennzoil's eight-week presentation of the evidence—and one ironic high point was the testimony of Arthur Liman, who had represented Pennzoil in the deal but came from the same group of big-firm New York lawyers that Pennzoil had been criticizing for conspiring against it.

During the motion to disqualify Baker & Botts, Pennzoil wanted to emphasize that it didn't believe lawyers were good witnesses and therefore it was prepared not to call any Baker & Botts lawyers to testify in this trial. Lawyers were just agents of the corporate executives, who did the real negotiating, Pennzoil lawyers claimed. In one exchange during the disqualification argument, Pennzoil lawyer W. James Kronzer (a Houston trial lawyer and tort law specialist who is helping with the case) asked his colleague Jamail whether he intended to call lawyers as witnesses. Said Kronzer, "Mr. Jamail, you have to have the finest circumstances possible to call a lawyer under the best cases, don't you?" And Jamail responded: "Let me tell you, big man, that is flirting with disaster."

Yet Pennzoil's second witness—and possibly its best—was Liman, a partner at New York's Paul, Weiss, Rifkind, Wharton & Garrison who negotiated the Pennzoil-Getty deal on behalf of Pennzoil investment bankers Lazard Frères & Company. Trial lawyer Liman proved to be an excellent witness, turning toward the jury to answer each question posed by counsel, and frequently ignoring the lawyers to make his points with jurors. He seemed at ease, bantering with the judge and with spectators during breaks, and commenting teasingly about the slow pace of lawyering in Texas. Several times he made the jury laugh with little self-deprecating jokes about New Yorkers and about lawyers.

Liman explained to the jury that the Getty Oil board had approved all essential terms of the agreement with Pennzoil on January 3 and that the board and the dealmakers understood at that point that they had a binding contract and only needed to wrap up a few nonessential details. He described the moments after the Getty board meeting as follows:

> Within a few minutes, Marty Lipton [the museum's lawyer] and Marty Siegel [Gordon Getty's investment banker from Kidder, Peabody] came out [of the board meeting], the door opened and they said, "Congratulations, Arthur. You got a deal. . . ." I said, "I'd like to ask for permission to go into the board meeting and to shake hands with all of the directors because they've been at it for so many hours and I'd like to just shake hands with all of them." . . . I went around the room and I introduced myself and I shook hands with everyone I could. I said, "Congratulations." They said, "Congratulations to you."

Finally, somebody from Pennzoil—even if not a Pennzoil executive—had testified that he had actually shaken hands with Getty Oil executives.

Liman was even sharper during Texaco's cross-examination, when he counterpunched effectively against Miller Keeton partner W. Robert Brown. Brown, who was hoarse from a cold, generally spoke in a dull drone—although when he reached a point when he thought he had cornered Liman, he raised his voice and seemed excited. In one exchange, Brown questioned Liman about his views of Martin Lipton of Wachtell, Lipton, Rosen & Katz. The point of the question was to get Liman to speak well of Lipton's integrity and thereby weaken Pennzoil's claim that New York lawyers, including Lipton, had conspired to unlawfully break up the deal with Pennzoil.

Instead, Liman turned the tables and explained how Lipton's actions in the takeover fight demonstrated that Lipton knew he was breaching a contract and was doing so only because Texaco had agreed to indemnify the J. Paul Getty Museum. And Liman noted approvingly that Lipton had expressly refused to provide the usual warranty that the museum knew of no prior claims against the stock it was selling. (The museum's sale contract states in parentheses that the museum "makes no representation with respect to . . . the Pennzoil Agreement.")

Liman's handling of the question left the jury with the impression that Lipton was personally honorable and that Texaco—the only defendant in this case—was well aware that it had induced a breach in the Pennzoil contract and was now refusing to acknowledge it and pay up.

Liman's testimony should have been a prelude to Pennzoil's sewing up the case. Instead, Pennzoil again let the momentum flag by moving into video depositions. Pennzoil's lawyers appeared a bit concerned that the trial was dragging, but seemed insufficiently sensitive to the effect of the drawn-out testimony on the jury. "You can't help but be concerned about [the amount of testimony]," Jeffers noted in an interview during a lunch break on August 20. "But we had to put on all the testimony we felt we needed to make our case, and you have to include a lot of background to get that testimony in. . . . No question it's a hard decision-making process to get all your proof in without losing the jury."

Pennzoil finished strongly by putting Pennzoil chairman Liedtke on the stand and letting its best trial lawyer, Jamail, handle the direct examination. It remains to be seen, however, whether they did so much damage by making the jury wade through eight weeks of testimony that Liedtke's performance will be lost on them.

Liedtke was on the stand to make two basic points: first, that in his experience as an oilman, a deal is a deal, and second, to express sufficient indignation that the jury would be more likely to assess large damages. He made both points well. In his second day of testimony, the harmonizing between Liedtke and Jamail reached its highest pitch:

Q. "Would a company like Pennzoil have any interest or incentive to enter into an agreement such as it entered into with the Getty interest as it was approved by the board of directors on all its essential terms if the only meaning of such agreement was that the other parties could use it as the starting point to go shop it and trade it?"

A. "Of course not. At some point, the trading stopped. And when you have a deal, when you've agreed to something, which we had done, we had met the requirement. We'd done what they asked us to do. The shopping stopped. You have a deal. That's the end of it."

However, Miller was prepared with a spate of objections, making this the best head-to-head competition between Jamail and Miller since the motion to disqualify the judge. Repeatedly Miller objected to Jamail's questions on the grounds that they were eliciting legal conclusions from Liedtke—rather than his understanding as a businessman—about the nature of the Pennzoil-Getty contract. But generally Judge Farris overruled his objections, and Liedtke got the chance to state his opinion again and again that, among oilmen at least, an agreement in principle is binding.

At one point during an argument over evidence (as usual, outside the hearing of the jury, which was missing all the excitement), the exchanges between Miller and Jamail became so heated that Farris warned them about contempt. Jamail had been trying to get Liedtke to attack Texaco for treating Getty employees poorly after the takeover. The issue wasn't directly relevant to the case, but it was a good way of painting Texaco black, and Miller had arguably opened the door to such a discussion by mentioning earlier that Texaco was a good employer. Miller strenuously objected, and the jury was quickly dismissed so that the attorneys could take their gloves off and fight it out. Jamail told the judge that he wanted Texaco to produce "the evidence that they have in their possession that they extracted . . . $250 million from these [Getty] employees' benefit and pension fund and whatever document that's in and wherever it's concealed in Texaco's instruments." Miller responded angrily, "Do I have to put up with these cheap shots like 'concealed' and 'extracted'?"

Judge Farris admonished, "If they're made before the jury, I will then use this [contempt] form that is waiting to be used." After another such exchange a few minutes later, he added, "Please do not make denigrating remarks about each other. And I've decided to include nonjury denigrating remarks. . . . Remember, after the column that has time of day that the remark was made, the next column is amount of fine. And the one after that is jail time." The jury was then ushered back in, and questioning resumed.

At this writing, Miller was just beginning to cross-examine Liedtke. Then Texaco will get its chance to put on witnesses. Miller says Texaco will take three to four weeks to make its case and will call as many as ten witnesses, including top Texaco executives, and probably including museum counsel Lipton. There's also the possibility, he says, that Texaco will call Baker & Botts tax partner William Griffith to testify about a potentially significant tax problem that came to light after the agreement in principle was reached. His testimony, if adverse to Pennzoil, will raise questions about Judge Farris's decision to permit Baker & Botts to stay in the case.

In his deposition, Griffith stated that he learned on January 4, 1984—in the crucial period after the agreement in principle between Pennzoil and Getty but before Texaco announced its deal—that there might be a serious tax problem if the Pennzoil-Getty deal went forward as originally planned. Under skillful questioning from Miller in the deposition, he agreed that the problem, if not resolved, was potentially deal-breaking because of the risk of a $2 billion tax penalty. "Were the penalties small or large?" he was asked. He answered, "If there were a prohibited transaction, the consequences were too horrible to contemplate." Miller coaxed on: "Just make you want to cut your throat? Is that right?'' And Griffith replied, ''If they had gone into it when I was present [and] I was supposed to know it and didn't, yes, I'd cut my throat.''

This appeared to be a crucial admission because Pennzoil had claimed that all essential elements of the deal had been agreed to when the agreement in principle was reached. If the structure of the deal had to be changed to eliminate the tax problem, Texaco maintains, that suggests that the deal wasn't yet complete in its essential terms—and thus wasn't yet binding. If the deal wasn't binding, Texaco was within its rights to make its own offer to Getty. Pennzoil claims that the tax problem was a technicality that the parties were well on their way to solving when Texaco broke up the party. Thus, the company claims, Griffith's testimony would be irrelevant. But Miller may be able to make good use of it at trial.

$14 BILLION GAMBLE

Who will win? Pennzoil's broken-handshake theme retains its elemental appeal. But the company's lawyers have been only sporadically effective in presenting the case.

With so much passion evident in their behind-the-scenes battles with Texaco's lawyers, it seems that Pennzoil's lawyers could have channeled some of that passion into convincing the jury that Pennzoil had suffered a terrible injustice. Instead, they sucked much of the life out of the case with tedious recitations of the details of the takeover attempt and with two weeks of dreadful videotapes. With the exception of never-a-dull-moment Jamail, Pennzoil lawyers have committed the sin of boring the jury, and it's unclear whether the jury will forgive.

Texaco now has the opportunity to please the jury by keeping the evidence short and to the point and staying away from videotapes as much as possible. ''It's going to be a lot more focused and directed, and most of our witnesses will be live,'' says Miller Keeton partner Peterson.

But Texaco is relying on what Jamail calls ''loopholes'' and ''excuses'' to justify breaking up a corporate marriage and running off with the bride. And that defense may come in for some pounding when Jamail launches into his closing argument.

Case law (in particular the Reprosystem case) seems to favor Texaco's position that in big, complicated deals, it's generally necessary to consolidate the various agreements into a single final document before the deal becomes binding. But a big wild card is how Judge Farris—hardly an M&A expert—will construe the law in instructing the jury. So as Texaco begins its defense, the $14 billion case still seems very much up for grabs. Says a prominent Houston lawyer who is avidly following the trial, "Anytime you're dealing with a jury in state court, it's a throw of the dice."

EPILOGUE

In March 1988 the two oil giants finally ended their battle. Texaco paid Pennzoil $3 billion to settle the litigation, but only after several more rounds in the courts.

On December 10, 1985, Judge Casseb entered a judgment for the full amount of the verdict—plus $600 million in interest—for a total award of $11.1 billion. Although Texas law required Texaco to put up a bond equal to the amount of the judgment while it appealed, the oil company was given a reprieve a week later by U.S. District Judge Charles Brieant; Jr., of White Plains, New York, who granted Texaco a temporary order barring Pennzoil from enforcing the Texas court order.

On January 9, 1986, Judge Brieant resumed proceedings to hear arguments over Texaco's request for an injunction against Pennzoil. Meanwhile, in Houston, Texaco asked for a new trial and sought the removal of Judge Casseb from the case. (The Texas Supreme Court later refused to order a hearing on Casseb's removal.) The next day, Brieant granted an injunction against Pennzoil and ruled that Texaco need put up only $1 billion for bond while it carried out its appeal in Texas courts. Pennzoil quickly appealed.

On February 5 Texaco posted the $1 billion security bond; 15 days later a federal appeals court in New York upheld Judge Brieant's ruling.

Pennzoil asked the U.S. Supreme Court on May 2, 1986, to review the appeals court decision. After oral arguments in January 1987, in which Texaco was represented by David Boies, a partner at New York's Cravath, Swaine & Moore, and Pennzoil by Harvard's Laurence Tribe, the court ruled unanimously on April 6 that Judge Brieant should not have excused Texaco from posting the full $10 billion appeal bond. The Supreme Court decision did not address the legality of the state court's award of damages against Texaco or the constitutionality of the state's appeal bond law, but concentrated solely on jurisdictional issues. In the majority opinion written by Justice Lewis Powell, Jr., and joined by four other justices, the court stated that the lower federal court should have abstained rather than engaging in an "unprecedented intrusion into the Texas judicial system."

Six days after the Supreme Court decision, Texaco filed for bankruptcy. On June 15, 1987, Texaco, represented by Boies, appealed its case to the Texas Supreme Court. Later that month Texaco got help from an unexpected ally—the Securities and Exchange Commission—which filed an amicus brief with the Texas Supreme Court, urging it to accept Texaco's appeal of the jury verdict. On November 2, the Texas Supreme Court upheld the appeals court decision without issuing an opinion, leaving Texaco with only the U.S. Supreme Court to overturn the award.

On March 23, 1988, federal bankruptcy judge Howard Schwartzberg of the Southern District of New York approved Texaco's $5.6 billion plan of reorganization, permitting it to emerge from Chapter 11 proceedings. The $3 billion Pennzoil settlement was central to the plan. Texaco also consented to sell $5 billion of assets to pay its creditors.

Johnson v. Johnson

THE $8 MILLION ASSOCIATE

BY

ELLEN JOAN POLLACK

*Shearman & Sterling associate Nina Zagat fights for her cut of the
Johnson estate.*

It was about 3 P.M. on April 14, 1983, when Shearman & Sterling
associates Jack Gunther, Jr., and James Hoch arrived at the home of
multimillionaire J. Seward Johnson in Fort Pierce, Florida. They had
come to witness the signing of his will. Gunther, a 20th-year associate
who had known Johnson for 12 years, chatted with him about the balmy
Florida weather. They then joined fellow associate Nina Zagat in the
dining area of the Johnson home for the signing ceremony. Unlike the 33
other wills and codicils Seward had signed in the preceding 17 years, this
was truly to be his last will and testament. He died five weeks later.

In his April 14 will, Seward left the bulk of his $400–500 million estate
to his young wife, Barbara, a former chambermaid known as Basia. He
also designated Nina Zagat as co-executor with Basia, presenting the
43-year-old associate with the prospect of great wealth—about $8 million
in executor fees plus millions more in trustee fees.

But Seward's legacy also included what has become a bitter fight in
Manhattan surrogate's court over the events of that warm April afternoon
and the contents of the 48-page document. Seward's six children from his
two previous marriages insist that their father was too ill with cancer to
know what he was doing when he scribbled his name and the date—their
lawyer says Seward wrote "Aprul 14"—on the will. The children main-

334

tained that their father would not have wanted to exclude from his will Harbor Branch Foundation, Inc., the world-renowned oceanographic institute he had co-founded in 1971. Before April 14, Seward's will had stipulated that Basia was to receive income from an approximately $75 million Qualified Terminable Interest Property Trust, known as a Q-Tip trust, until her death, at which time the trust would go to Harbor Branch. But the April 14 document gave Basia wide discretion as to the disposition of that trust.

The children claim their 49-year-old stepmother, Basia, exerted undue influence on their ailing father. Shearman & Sterling associate Zagat, they say, was her accomplice—"the means by which Barbara rewrote Seward's will," in the words of their lawyer Edward Reilly of New York's Milbank, Tweed, Hadley & McCloy. Reilly steadfastly maintains that Zagat treated Basia—not Seward—as her primary client. In one memorandum filed with the court, Reilly accuses Zagat of a "woeful failure to provide Mr. Johnson with independent and disinterested legal advice."

"I know that my father wouldn't separate me from the other children," says Seward Johnson, Jr., the only one of the siblings to receive a bequest in the April 14 will—$1 million and some property on Cape Cod. "And [my father] never would have cut out Harbor Branch." The challenge to the will "started out only as principle," he says, although he acknowledges that money is also a factor. The children could receive part of their father's estate if the suit is settled or if the jury overturns the April 14 will.

There are no poverty-stricken widows and orphans in this crowd. No matter what the outcome, Basia will be more than comfortable in her $20 million 140-acre estate, and her six stepchildren—who had not been named as their father's beneficiaries for about 20 years, apart from a handful of token bequests—will continue to live on the trusts he provided in the 1930s and 1940s. The poorest of the siblings must make do with assets of about $23 million. Even Harbor Branch, the charitable foundation, has about $67 million in assets.

It is Zagat who has the most at stake. Her $8 million in fees may seem piddling next to the riches of her co-executor, Basia. But if Zagat is removed as executor, as the children demand, she will revert to the life of a permanent associate—toiling away in the individual clients department at Shearman & Sterling, where she earns $115,000 after 19 years at the firm. If she gets the money she will be allowed to keep it all. A Shearman & Sterling partner confirms that, had she made partner, she would have had to share it.

335

Standing between Zagat and that $8 million is the trial in surrogate's court that began last winter and will probably last until Memorial Day. At issue is how she represented the Johnsons—and which spouse she really represented.

On February 27, an array of high-priced New York legal talent settles in at the counsel table in the appropriately sumptuous, mahogany-paneled courtroom of Surrogate Marie Lambert. Representing Basia and Zagat as executors are partners Donald Christ and Robert Osgood of New York's Sullivan & Cromwell. In the children's corner are Milbank's Reilly and his partner Charles Berry. Jack Kaufmann and associate Robert Hirth of Dewey, Ballantine, Bushby, Palmer & Wood are acting for Harbor Branch, which has chosen to take a second-seat role to its champions, the Johnson children.

Zagat takes a front-row seat with Basia and Shearman & Sterling partner Arnold Bauman, a former federal judge whose role today is something akin to a legal chaperone. After the judge's opening remarks to the jury, Zagat's lawyer Christ describes the life of the Johnsons as "virtually a dream. It was a dream that they could afford because of the tremendous wealth that Mr. Johnson had."

What will emerge from the nine days of direct testimony and cross-examination that Zagat is to begin later in the day is that, in the early 1970s, when she was assigned to handle work for Seward and Basia by Thomas Ford, then-head of Shearman & Sterling's individual clients department, she, too, was swept into that dream. She visited the Johnsons at their villa in Italy, at their mansion just outside of Princeton, New Jersey, and at their home in Florida overlooking the Atlantic. She accompanied Basia to Paris. When Seward journeyed to Poland to pick up a spanking new yacht, the *Mazurka*, she went along. Zagat and her husband vacationed on Children's Bay Cay, her client's private island in the Bahamas. She flew to Florida to attend Basia's birthday party. When a horse owned by Seward's daughter Diana raced at Royal Ascot in Great Britain, Zagat was there to cheer it on.

Eventually Zagat had much more contact with the couple than Ford, the Shearman & Sterling partner who was obstensibly in charge of the account. She handled most of the work of Harbor Branch, for which Shearman & Sterling was general counsel. She helped draft more than a dozen wills and codicils for Seward and often supervised at least two other associates working on his account. She oversaw the couple's checking accounts. She paid millions of dollars' worth of bills for art and antiques. She even took care of the couple's Shearman & Sterling bills, which were sent to her at the firm.

In the middle of the afternoon, Zagat commences her performance as star witness. As with game show contestants, her challenge and the reward are equally clear: to win her $8 million, she has to lay out the long history of Seward's estate planning and convince the jury that there was a logical pattern of wills from 1971 to 1983.

But Zagat barely has time to tell the jury that she went to Yale Law School and to describe her duties at the firm and the events of April 14, before she is pulled off the stand. In chambers, Judge Lambert rules that the April 14 will cannot be admitted until the attesting witnesses, associates Hoch and Gunther, testify. And so Zagat goes back to her front-row seat and watches for two days as Gunther and Hoch tell the jury that Seward was of sound mind and memory when he signed the April 14 will.

On the afternoon of March 3, Zagat again takes the stand. In response to Christ's queries about the first will Shearman & Sterling drafted for Seward in 1973, she explains, amid objections from Reilly, "Mr. Johnson wanted to be absolutely sure that Mrs. Johnson got the maximum amount that he could leave her under the federal tax laws."

Zagat's testimony the next day seems almost rehearsed, as she recounts the execution of the February 1976 will, when Johnson first penned in her name as one of his executors. "Can you recall anything else that he said?" asks Christ. "Yes, she replies, "Mr. Johnson said, 'Nina, what about you? Would you be willing to be one of my executors and trustees? I would really like that,' and I said, 'Yes,' that I would be happy to. And Mr. Johnson said, 'Well, I hope this will be helpful to you.' "

Christ deftly leads Zagat through the sticky issue of commissions. Two days earlier, Reilly had severely rattled associate Gunther on that very subject. After establishing that Gunther had helped draft a May 1981 codicil removing a cap on executor and administrative fees, Reilly showered him with a series of clearly unexpected questions about why he thought it was Seward's wish to increase the fees substantially by stipulating that New York statutory rates be applied.

"Then how do you know you were doing it at his instructions?" Reilly demanded, when Gunther reluctantly testified that he had had no direct conversation with Seward about fees and hadn't heard Zagat tell her client what the fees would be. "Because Mrs. Zagat told me he had instructed her," Gunther replied. "And you believed Mrs. Zagat?" returned Reilly. "Absolutely," said Gunther.

"Did you feel it would be in the best interests of your client, or in the best interests of Nina Zagat, to remove that limitation?" Reilly asked.

After an exchange between the lawyers and the court, Gunther responded, "It was in the best interests of my client because that's what he wanted to do."

When Reilly's questioning revealed that Seward signed the codicil just hours before he was to leave for Princeton's medical center to have a cancerous tumor removed, the whole incident looked fishy.

And so when it is Zagat's turn to explain the commissions, she testifies that she and Seward had discussed revamping the commission clauses in 1979, two years before he signed the codicil. "I went over the provision that was in the will at that time and I explained that essentially that provision had been taken from an arrangement that Mr. Johnson had originally with Mr. [Robert] Myers, his former lawyer, and that we had always had some concern as to how that would work," she says, explaining that Myers had lumped legal and executor fees together.

Based on the value of Seward's estate at that time—$200 million—and the probable cost of legal and accounting work, Zagat continues, the four then-executors would earn $375,000 each. Under the New York statute, she and the three other executors would be entitled to almost $2.5 million each. (Later there would be just two executors—Zagat and Basia Johnson—and the value of the estate would have increased to yield Zagat the $8 million she is now fighting for. Seward, Jr., was also named executor, but he refused to accept the appointment in order to challenge the will.)

Zagat's history of the removal of the cap helps to counteract the impression that the change was slipped under Seward's nose just before he went into the hospital for major surgery. And yet it is more than likely that Reilly's inquiry to Gunther about whether removing the fee cap was in the client's interests or Zagat's will stick in the minds of the jurors longer than Zagat's tedious and uncorroborated rendition of her conversation with her client.

Zagat is not an appealing witness. She is nervous, overly cautious, and uncomfortable with the microphone. Christ asks for painstaking detail. One juror, dubbed "the sleeper" by a courtroom observer, holds her head in her hand as Christ leads Zagat through 12 long years of representation. Seward, Jr., sitting with his grim-faced siblings in view of the jury and only a few feet from Basia, often sits forward in his seat, sometimes slowly shaking his head in disgust.

Even Judge Lambert is impatient. "Let me tell you something," she complains in chambers near the end of the day on March 6, Zagat's fourth full day on the stand. "All day it has been very slow. The words come out of Mrs. Zagat's mouth as if she didn't go past elementary school. She . . . speaks . . . at . . . this . . . rate. And then there are pauses, and there are pauses between the questions, and it really has gotten to the point at which it begins to give an appearance of stretching this out."

Basia and Zagat's lawyer Christ, a trust and estates partner, exhibits a dry charm that must be exceedingly appealing to his wealthy clients. He can unleash a series of pointed questions, but he is too subtle. His Adolfo-clad wife, who often sits behind him with Basia, further softens his image.

For the courtroom audience of family members and press, Reilly provides the dramatic relief. Reilly, a litigator, attacks. He never quite lets loose; his repertoire does not include emotional displays for the jury's benefit and his attitude to the judge is a touch ingratiating. But he emerges from his corner throwing punctuated, carefully calculated jabs. His lines of inquiry always have a payoff, and he doesn't hesitate to rough a witness up if it will create the right effect. Even his objections are dramatic. Until Christ complained, Reilly would stand a second or so before making his objection known, shifting the attention of the courtroom to him and away from Christ's witness.

By the time Reilly starts his cross-examination of Zagat on March 7, everyone is expecting them to clash. During the four-day grilling it is almost as though she, and not Christ, is Reilly's opponent. He questions her with a crusader's fervor. He glares at her from the podium. She does all she can to evade his questions and deflect his accusations, then finally lashes out.

Reilly opens his cross-examination by firing an unexpected shot, as if to put his witness and the courtroom on warning. "Mrs. Zagat," he says, "as I look around, perhaps I can ask one question of you before dealing with your testimony. Could you tell us who the man is who is seated next to Barbara Johnson? Will you identify him for us?" Reilly is referring to Jack Raymond of Jack Raymond & Company, Inc., the public relations firm retained by Basia.

Christ objects. "This is a sideshow," he tells the judge at the bench. "It is prejudicial."

"I don't call it a sideshow if they are disseminating things to the press," Reilly retorts. "He's been here every day. I think the jury is entitled to know it. I think he has been paid a lot of money by Barbara Johnson and Nina Zagat."

Although Judge Lambert admits she doesn't know whether Raymond's role is relevant, she sustains the objection. Nevertheless, Reilly leaves the jury wondering, and at the luncheon break two jurors are overheard guessing correctly that Raymond is Basia's press representative. The arrival on the scene about two weeks later of John Scanlon of Daniel J. Edelman, Inc., the children's press representative, will receive no such herald.

The first topic Reilly raises with Zagat is what has been dubbed the May 3 trust. On direct, Zagat testified that on March 10, 1983, the day Seward signed the first of his three 1983 wills, he had inquired whether his will could be challenged. That seems to have set off an alarm at Shearman & Sterling. Twelve days later, without conferring with Seward, Zagat returned to Fort Pierce and had him sign another will, identical to the March 10 document except for a clause explaining that he was leaving nothing to his children because of his substantial gifts to them during his lifetime.

Then in late April, she testified on direct, Seward, Jr., told her that two of his sisters might contest the will. On May 3, she again flew to Fort Pierce, this time with a trust agreement in hand. She presented Seward with documents transferring about $9.5 million in bonds to a trust for Basia. Seward, largely bedridden and in the final throes of his battle with cancer, had less than three weeks to live.

"You have always referred to your bond portfolio as your anchor to windward," Zagat said she told her ailing client, using one of his favorite nautical terms. "And the time may come when Basia will need an anchor to windward, and I thought that you might want to consider putting those bonds into a trust, so that if there are any delays in the probate of your will, there will be funds available to Basia immediately upon your death." Zagat had named herself as the trustee.

Under Christ's questioning, Zagat had told the jury of long, detailed conversations she'd had with Seward about his financial affairs. But her descriptions of his responses as he signed the trust papers on May 3 had been extremely brief—not surprising, considering his condition.

Now, on cross, as Basia looks on with her usual slight smile, Reilly hammers away at Zagat for not having conferred with Seward before arriving at his bedside in Florida with completed trust documents. "During that period of time, did you pick up the telephone and call Mr. Johnson?'' he asks.

"No, I did not," Zagat answers.

"You didn't call him and say, 'Mr. Johnson, I think it would be a good idea to transfer nine or ten million dollars' worth of your bonds into a trust?' '' he continues.

"No," she says.

"You were prepared to prepare the trust agreement and go all the way to Florida to have it executed by him and then just have him say, 'No, I'm not interested'?'' Reilly inquires several questions later.

"Without question," Zagat replies.

"Isn't it a fact that he was simply not able to hold a telephone up to his ear and speak into it at that time?'' Reilly demands.

"Not to my knowledge," she replies.

Reilly also presses Zagat on the morality of naming herself as the sole trustee of the May 3 trust. The exchange makes it seem that she is twisting the truth:

ZAGAT: Mr. Johnson had nominated me as a trustee.

REILLY: You mean when you presented this document to Mr. Johnson, the identity of the trustee was simply blank, and he wrote in your name?

ZAGAT: No.

REILLY: Your name had already been typed in?

ZAGAT: Yes.

REILLY: By Nina Zagat?

ZAGAT: No.

REILLY: You didn't actually do the typing?

ZAGAT: That's correct.

REILLY: But you were the one who designated yourself?

ZAGAT: It was a decision made at the office, not by me alone.

REILLY: By Shearman & Sterling?

ZAGAT: Yes. I had discussed it with many people in the office, and the conclusion was that it was appropriate.

Zagat then testifies that she received approximately $22,000 in trustee commissions in May 1985 and admits that she had never discussed the potential amount of the fees with Seward.

Finally Reilly underlines his point by asking Zagat how long she's been a lawyer.

"Since 1967," she replies.

"In those nineteen years," he continues, "have you ever prepared a trust instrument for any client other than Mr. Johnson involving the transfer of securities to a trust without discussing the matter first with the client?"

Zagat's response—"I don't recall"—is unconvincing.

Zagat is fuming. When Reilly asks her to check her time records to see if she had ever created trusts under similar circumstances for other clients, she snaps, "No, I could not do that."

Reilly is also frustrated. A few questions later, he complains, "I believe I am entitled to an answer of just one word, consisting of three letters. The first one is 'y,' " he says, turning to Zagat. "And you know what the other two are."

Finally, at 11 A.M., Judge Lambert calls a break. When Zagat returns to the stand 20 minutes later, Reilly turns to her corporate housekeeping for Seward's closely held or wholly owned corporations. He asks her to identify the minutes of a meeting of the one shareholder, Seward, and the directors of REI Company, which owned the couple's antiques. The minutes were signed by Zagat. Referring to the document, he asks, "Was a meeting of the shareholder held at Fort Pierce, Florida, at 9:30 A.M. on May 3, 1983?" Zagat answers, "No."

Christ objects on grounds of relevance, but the judge admits the document to evidence: "[Zagat] says that she prepared the document, and now she says that there was no meeting held on May 3 at 9:30 A.M. [Reilly] has a right to offer this document over her signature to contradict her."

Reilly then presents Zagat with the minutes of meetings for companies holding Seward's paintings, antiques, and an island in the Bahamas, and for the Barbara Piasecka Johnson Foundation—meetings all held at ten- to twenty-five-minute intervals on May 3, according to the documents. In all, Reilly questions her about the time and date of nine meetings. In each case, she acknowledges that the time was incorrect on the minutes she signed.

"You signed them anyway?" Reilly asks.

"I can't answer it yes or no when you include in your question 'anyway,' " she answers fruitlessly. Reilly never lets her testify about why the documents contain the errors.

Reilly then moves on to another document signed on May 3—the revocation of Seward and Basia's prenuptial agreement. Under the terms of that agreement, signed in 1971, Seward was required to leave Basia

$10 million, which he did in his 1971 will. Seward's youngest daughter, Jennifer, testified at her deposition that Basia once told her she had left Seward and refused to come back until the prenuptial agreement was ripped up and its author, Robert Myers, of Washington, D.C.'s Williams, Myers and Quiggle, was fired. (According to two sources close to the case, Myers always refused to represent Seward's wives and kept a tight cap on the estate fees.) Myers did almost no estate work for Seward after 1972 and was wholly replaced by Shearman & Sterling in 1973.

Under Reilly's questioning, Zagat testifies that she prepared the revocation at Shearman & Sterling partner Ford's suggestion, "since we had been advised that the agreement had been revoked many years ago and since we had no evidence in our files."

Reilly sets out to show that the revocation was designed to protect Basia's interests in the event of a will contest, implying that Basia and her lawyer were nervous that the April 14 will would not survive. "Did Mr. Ford tell you that he was concerned that there would be a will contest and that in the event of intestacy Mrs. Johnson would receive only the amount specified in the prenuptial agreement?" Reilly asks Zagat.

"No," she replies.

After a battery of questions about her efforts to find the original agreement and what she claims was its earlier revocation, Reilly asks if "this instrument of revocation would become relevant only in the event Mr. Johnson were intestate?"

Her reply—"I don't know"—occasions a sarcastic response from Reilly: "And you have been a lawyer for how many years?"

Reilly's concluding question in his campaign to unveil the revocation as a desperate move to save Basia's fortune in the event of a will contest exacts a defiant but nonsensical answer. "Can you tell me any way in which this instrument of revocation would be of any interest to anyone if this will is admitted to probate?" Reilly asks.

"Yes," Zagat answers.

"In what way?"

"It tidied up Mr. Johnson's files and his affairs."

The tussle over the revocation takes half an hour. Some of Reilly's questions about Zagat's search for the original prenuptial agreement and its revocation seem unnecessary, but they have worn Zagat down. For her, it is not the ideal time to have to field questions about what is known as the April 14 letter.

Handwritten and signed by Basia on April 14, immediately after her husband had executed his will, the one-page letter has become a major point of contention in the will contest. (It was also central in a New Jersey case in which Basia tried—unsuccessfully—to wrest control of Harbor Branch from Seward, Jr.)

The letter, written on Basia's personal stationery, opens, "Dearest Seward," and refers to the provision in the new will that allows Basia to decide which of Seward's descendants and charitable organizations will receive the Q-Tip trust after she dies. "I hereby agree," the letter continues, "not to exercise said limited testamentary power of appointment in my will so that the property subject to it will go to Harbor Branch Foundation, Inc., at the time of my death."

On direct, Zagat testified that Seward said, "Basia, you don't have to do that," when he was told about the letter. According to Zagat, Basia replied, "Seward, I want to," and asked the three associates, "Can I sign it, 'Love, Basia'?"

Seward, Zagat, and associate Jack Gunther also affixed their signatures to the letter—Seward to acknowledge it and Gunther and Zagat as witnesses. But Zagat insisted in her direct testimony that she had told the group "that we are not telling anybody that this letter has any legal effect."

The children and Harbor Branch believe that the letter is binding and enforceable. In November 1984, when a Milbank paralegal found the letter among thousands of documents produced in discovery, the children were furious that it had not been brought to Harbor Branch's attention when the will was probated. The failure of Basia and Zagat to disclose immediately the letter's existence—their "most egregious dereliction," in the words of a Milbank memorandum of law—is at the heart of the argument that the two women should be removed as executors.

When Reilly questions Zagat about the letter, she testifies that she and Gunther helped Basia write it. Reilly then launches into an inquisition about its enforceability.

REILLY: What reason did you have for not saying that this had any legal effect?
ZAGAT: Because I didn't believe it did.
REILLY: And why didn't you believe that it did?
ZAGAT: Because that was my belief.
REILLY: And I am asking you why was that your belief?
ZAGAT: Because this was a letter written by Mrs. Johnson to her husband expressing her intention not to exercise the power and expressing an enormous amount of love to him and to Harbor Branch Foundation.

REILLY: You are saying this is an expression of an enormous amount of love?

ZAGAT: That is correct.

REILLY: Is that what I heard you just say?

ZAGAT: That is correct.

REILLY: When she refers in fairly technical language to provisions of the will and then says, "I hereby agree not to exercise a limited testamentary power of appointment," you consider this an expression of love?

ZAGAT: It certainly was. I was there.

REILLY: Signed by her and acknowledged by him?

ZAGAT: That's right.

REILLY: And witnessed by two lawyers in your firm and you are calling this a love note?

ZAGAT: I didn't say it was a love note.

Reilly continues his attack until Zagat is fairly bursting with frustration. "You can't look at this piece of paper without understanding the whole background," she finally blurts out. "And it seems to me as though that is all terribly, terribly important. Her belief in the future, her knowing that her husband would be at peace if he had more confidence than he was able to have on his own in the future of Harbor Branch Foundation."

Reilly tangles once more with the resistant Zagat when he tries to make the point that as general counsel to Harbor Branch, Shearman & Sterling had an obligation to alert it to the existence of the letter. He tries to get her to say that her firm counseled Harbor Branch until two months after Seward's death, but she claims she is not sure when the representation ended. "You are not aware of a letter advising you and your firm of your replacement as general counsel to Harbor Branch?" Reilly inquires.

"I am aware of that letter. I am also aware of other things," she retorts, perhaps referring to the fact that Reilly's own firm was tapped for the general counsel role. (Dewey, Ballantine was brought in as trial counsel because it became clear that conflicts might develop in representing the children and the foundation.) Reilly's comeback—"Undoubtedly you are, Mrs. Zagat. I hope we all are"—prompts an objection from Christ. Judge Lambert moves in to separate Zagat and Reilly.

"Didn't you feel any obligation, as the lawyer with the firm that was general counsel to Harbor Branch, to bring to Harbor Branch's attention the existence of this letter?" Reilly asks.

"Not at all," Zagat replies.

*   *   *

As the first day of Zagat's cross-examination draws to a close, Reilly turns to the document that cements Basia's control of Seward's fortune—the April 14 will. His goal, it seems clear, is to convince the jury that, in the months preceding Seward's death, Zagat's main concern was to protect Basia's interests.

Zagat had testified on direct that on April 11, shortly after she'd returned to New York from a vacation on the Johnsons' Children's Bay Cay retreat, she received a call from Basia. As a result of the phone call, which she was unable to describe because of an objection by Reilly on hearsay grounds, she reexamined the March 22 will. She then redrafted it with the help of Ford, associates Hoch and Gunther, and Henry Ziegler, who had recently succeeded Ford as the head of Shearman & Sterling's individual clients department. The major change was the restructuring of the Q-Tip trust. Zagat flew to Florida on April 13, she testified on direct, and spent part of the following morning reviewing the will's provisions with Seward in his bedroom.

Reilly focuses on Zagat's instructions to rewrite the will. Did she have any "direct communication" with Seward between the previous will signing on March 23 and the bedroom conference on April 14? No, says Zagat, "other than the telephone call from Mrs. Johnson."

"I am not talking about your telephone call with Mrs. Johnson," Reilly tells her. "I am talking about whether you had any conversation with Mr. Johnson."

"I did not," Zagat concedes.

"You didn't bother during that period of time to call him up and say, 'Mr. Johnson, before I go to the not inconsiderable expense of bringing two lawyers down to Florida, I would like to know whether you would be interested in signing this document.' You didn't call him up and ask him that, did you?" Reilly demands, several questions later.

"Of course not," Zagat says.

Reilly continues angrily in this vein. It is a tense exchange punctuated by quibbles from Zagat and infused with Reilly's obvious disdain. When Reilly spits out, "It is a fact, isn't it, that [Seward] did sign [the will] as presented to him without making a single change in this so-called draft?" Zagat retorts that she has "trouble with the word 'presented.' "

"You don't know what is meant by the word 'present'?" he shoots back incredulously. "That's right, I don't," she replies.

When he asks, "Didn't you consider it appropriate to call him and get his thoughts on his will, whether he wanted these changes made?" Zagat inexplicably begins to giggle. After an exchange involving Christ, Reilly, the witness, and the judge, Zagat replies, "I didn't consider it."

Nearly 15 minutes later, Reilly has made his point: Zagat took her instructions from Basia and did not consult with Seward until she arrived at his sickbed with the will, complete with ribbons and seal.

After a 12-day reprieve—during which three doctors who treated Seward in Fort Pierce testify that their patient was mentally sound and Reilly quoted nurses' notes describing Seward's confused state on April 14—Zagat returns to the stand on March 19. Reilly spends much of the morning asking her to sift through letters she had written to Citibank, transferring millions of dollars from Seward's $24 million line of credit to his various checking accounts and to Basia's personal account. Basia has not been called to the stand, and Reilly is trying to document the fortune she spent on arts and antiques. It is tedious work, and Zagat refuses to make connections between the transfers and the art purchases.

Following a morning break, Reilly gets Zagat to testify about the power of attorney that allowed her to make transfers from Seward's line of credit. On the same day that he signed the May 3 trust and the revocation of the prenuptial agreement, she asked Seward to sign another power of attorney and to increase his line of credit to $25 million, she explains to Reilly and the jury.

When Reilly asks why the new power of attorney was necessary, she says Citibank had lost its copy. The earlier power of attorney excluded the power to sell Seward's $350 million in Johnson & Johnson stock, the Milbank attorney points out. The new version contains no such qualification. "Why didn't the May 3, 1983, power have a similar exclusion?" he asks.

"I don't know," Zagat replies.

"When Mr. Johnson executed the second power on May 3, didn't he ask any question about why this power did not exclude the ability to sell his Johnson & Johnson stock?" Reilly inquires.

"I don't believe I had a copy of the prior one with me," she responds, prompting a protest from Reilly and a plea from the judge to listen to and answer the question. "Otherwise, we will be here until Christmas," says the judge. "And we will have to take a month's vacation this summer because I can't let the jury sit until Christmas."

Reilly asks Zagat why she didn't have a copy of the first power of attorney in her files. "I was unable to find it at the time that I prepared the second one," she says, adding that both she and Citibank have since found their copies.

Zagat denies Reilly's insinuation that her client was too ill to focus on the contents of the document she placed before him. She finally blurts out, "It was always understood that the stock would not be sold and that I certainly wouldn't sell it."

"If it was understood," counters Reilly, "then why did you have to have the provision in 1982 that denied you the right to sell it?"

"Mr. Johnson was concerned about what the bank might do, not what I would do," Zagat responds.

Zagat's evasiveness reaches a peak when Reilly asks about Seward's shaky signature on the power of attorney. Did anyone at Citibank question Seward's signature or his competence? he asks. Her response—that she can recall no questions about the signature and no worries about his competence—seems to surprise Reilly. He presses her to recall. "I remember a conversation with somebody from Citibank, but I don't remember it being about the signature," she finally says.

"I'm not asking you about conversations," says Reilly impatiently. "I'm asking you about any question being raised concerning this signature. Didn't someone at Citibank raise a question as to whether there was something wrong with Mr. Johnson?"

"I believe people at Citibank knew that Mr. Johnson was sick," she says.

"Do you know anyone at Citibank named Joyce Hirsch?" he asks.

"Yes."

"Does that refresh your recollection as to whether anyone at Citibank raised a question concerning Mr. Johnson and his signature on this document?"

"I remember Joyce Hirsch calling me and talking to me about Mr. Johnson's health."

"Did she talk to you about Mr. Johnson's signature?"

"I don't recall that specifically. I remember her saying that she knew that Mr. Johnson wasn't well and that she could see that there was some change in his signature and was there anything that Citibank could do to be of help."

A soft collective gasp is heard in the courtroom as Zagat contradicts herself. She looks utterly defensive and unreliable.

By late afternoon, Zagat's credibility has been severely damaged. Reilly asks about a final $3,760,000 she transferred to Basia's account only three days before Seward's death. He inquires if she thinks it likely that he would have understood the transaction on that date? "I was acting in accordance with instructions . . . that Mr. Johnson had given to me on May 3, and he knew just what he was doing," she says loudly and deliberately—but with no supporting paper trail.

According to the testimony Reilly painfully extracts from Zagat, Seward's checking account was then overdrawn by $180,000. She couldn't transfer money from his line of credit because she had already emptied the remaining $3,760,000 into Basia's account. So on the day Seward died, Zagat transferred $180,000 to his checking account from Basia's account. On the 706 estate tax form she later filed with the IRS, Zagat recorded the transaction as a loan from Basia to her dying husband.

"Mrs. Zagat, doesn't it seem to you inconsistent to view transfers of some $5,270,000 by Mr. Johnson to Mrs. Johnson as gifts and the transfer of $180,000 from Mrs. Johnson to Mr. Johnson as a loan?" Reilly finally asks, toward the end of the day.

"No," is Zagat's answer.

On March 20, Reilly spends a good part of the day finishing his questions about Basia's art purchases. He presents Zagat with lists of art-related assets valued at close to $57 million and bills for more than $1 million from art dealers around the world. The bills, sent to the Johnsons in care of Zagat at Shearman & Sterling, were paid by Zagat from Seward's checking accounts. Most of the bills were initialed not by Seward, but by Basia. Zagat's suggestion that there is no set procedure for handling such bills serves only to make her record-keeping look slipshod.

Reilly then launches a line of questioning about why, as of the next-to-last will, she was replaced as an attesting witness by Hoch, who didn't know Seward. As Reilly asks why Hoch was chosen, Christ interrupts, asking the judge to stop Reilly from yelling at his witness. But Zagat, too, is raising her voice. "Mr. Christ, now who is yelling?" the judge interjects, none too softly.

Zagat tells Reilly that under New York law she was not precluded from acting as a witness, but that it had been decided "that it would be probably best to have someone else."

"Why would it be better? If there was no reason under New York law, why would it be better that someone else do that?" Reilly demands.

Zagat pauses, then snaps: "Because there are people like you who will turn anything around."

Reilly looks stunned. "Your Honor," he says after a few seconds, "I was going to ask initially that the answer be stricken, but I think it is better to leave it in the record."

In the courtroom, there is jubilation in the executors' camp. Basia giggles in the corridor with Zagat and Shearman & Sterling partner Bauman. Zagat, they seem to believe, has finally scored a point against Reilly.

It took a few days for observers to understand the success of Reilly's cross-examination. All along, the children have been considered the underdogs. But both the substance and style of Zagat's testimony so far—she is expected to be called back for further cross-examination and redirect—have strengthened the children's argument. After Reilly's attacks on her credibility, motives, and legal work, the jury has to be wondering whether Zagat's judgment hasn't been clouded by too much fun, too much travel, and too close a relationship with her good friend Basia Johnson.

After Zagat left the stand, Harbor Branch trustee Marilyn Link testified that Seward had started losing his memory as early as 1980. Combined with Reilly's trouncing of Zagat, Link's testimony put the children's position in a new, stronger light. As Reilly prepared to begin his own case, it looked as if he had caught up. For the first time, it seemed, Basia stopped smiling. And for the first time, too, there were smiles in the children's corner.

SULLIVAN & CROMWELL STUMBLES

BY

ELLEN JOAN POLLOCK

The Wall Street firm gets its white shoes scuffed in the J. Seward Johnson estate battle.

Izabella Poterewicz looked slight and waiflike as she entered Manhattan surrogate's court on March 27. Flanked by lawyers from Milbank, Tweed, Hadley & McCloy and clutching a large folder, she had come to testify at the bitter will contest over the $500 million estate of J. Seward Johnson. Seward's six children, represented by Milbank, Tweed, are challenging the will offered for probate by his widow, Barbara (known as Basia), its primary beneficiary, and her co-executor Nina Zagat, a 20th-year associate at Shearman & Sterling who will collect about $8 million in executor fees if the will is allowed to stand. The courtroom was nearly full: word had been passed that Milbank, Tweed's Edward Reilly would begin his case with a surprise witness.

Poterewicz came to the United States from Poland in 1981. Her English, while adequate, is not yet fluent. She now works at a discount department store in New York, but in 1982 and 1983 she cleaned house for Basia Johnson, herself a Polish émigré and onetime maid.

Before the jury filed in, lawyers from Sullivan & Cromwell and 50-odd observers watched as Reilly showed Poterewicz how to speak into the microphone. It seemed hard to believe that Poterewicz could be the nemesis of Sullivan & Cromwell, counsel to Basia and Zagat. But in a very real sense she was. By the time she completed her two days of testimony, Sullivan & Cromwell was well on its way to losing two wars.

The first was being fought in chambers—before an increasingly hostile judge—over the admission of evidence. The second and more significant was unfolding before the jury. Poterewicz was only the first in a long string of witnesses hungry to prove Basia's undue influence over the elderly and ailing Seward. And her testimony proved so invincible—and the contents of that folder she tightly clutched so damaging—that Sullivan & Cromwell stumbled badly. For the duration of the children's case, the firm was able to summon up only the feeblest of defenses. By the time Reilly finished presenting his witnesses on May 8, Basia's floundering legal team had resorted to a tactic destined for failure: they filed a motion for a mistrial, a strategy that only further infuriated the judge.

Poterewicz was a made-to-order witness. She was so eager to testify that she had appeared at the courthouse about a week before she took the stand, offering her services to one of Seward's children.

In charmingly halting English, Poterewicz regaled the jury with tales of Basia's outrageous and uncontrollable temper—the juicy gossip they had been waiting for. And although other witnesses would impart more fantastic stories, it was the way Sullivan & Cromwell's Robert Osgood lost his cool during Poterewicz's testimony that made a bad situation worse.

In the first two hours of her testimony, Osgood objected more than 100 times. He continually argued with Surrogate Marie Lambert over her decision to admit certain out-of-court statements into evidence. His com-

351

bativeness contrasted sharply with Poterewicz's almost vulnerable demeanor on the stand.

Osgood had picked a disarming witness to attack. When Reilly asked Poterewicz on direct how she got her job at Jasna Polana, the Johnsons' New Jersey estate, she replied: "I wrote to Johnson & Johnson Company." She had gotten the address, she said, from a bottle of baby oil.

Osgood objected as Poterewicz painted a grim picture of life as Basia's servant—making $130 a week, with few weekends and no holidays off. She told the jury how Seward's condition deteriorated after he moved to Fort Pierce, Florida, just months before he signed his last will and died. "In Florida, usually when he had some vegetables, he had puree every time. . . . He was much slower than in Princeton, and many times he needs help from somebodies, like Mrs. Johnson was helping him to cut his meat, or take something from—when the dinner was serving, take something from a platter on his plate."

Spoken loudly, Osgood's abrasive objections took on a panicked edge when Reilly led Poterewicz through her testimony about Basia's yelling at Seward. Surrogate Lambert, worried that Reilly's questions were too complex, constantly interjected her own questions to aid the witness and allowed Reilly to lead at some points.

"Many times I heard her yelling on Mr. Johnson, but I didn't listen what she was yelling about, so many times I didn't know why," Poterewicz testified. "But sometimes . . ."

"I object and move to strike. Unresponsive, particularly the last part," said Osgood frantically. Lambert struck part of the answer but allowed Poterewicz to testify about the tone of the conversations.

"How frequently did you observe Mrs. Johnson yelling at Mr. Johnson?" Reilly continued.

Osgood: "Objection to form."

Lambert: "Overruled."

Poterewicz: "Many times."

Reilly: "Did it occur every day?"

Osgood: "Objection."

The judge again interrupted to ask what Poterewicz meant by "many times."

"Maybe I should tell this way," Poterewicz explained. "She was yelling almost every day, but not every day on Mr. Johnson exactly."

Osgood: "Objection. Your Honor, may I state the grounds of my objection?"

352

Lambert: "She said she was yelling every day, but not always at Mr. Johnson."

Osgood objected again on hearsay and competence grounds but was overruled. His objections reached a crescendo when Reilly asked what words Basia used when she yelled at Seward. "Many times I heard she called him names," Poterewicz replied, after Lambert had overruled one more Osgood objection.

"What names?" asked Reilly.

Responding to yet another objection Lambert struck the word *names*. "Do we have a time period?" Osgood futilely demanded. "It's the same time period," said the judge. "She said she cannot specifically give you the dates."

Finally the names slipped out: " 'Stupid Englishman,' 'idiot,' and even I heard 'You son of a bitch,' " Poterewicz testified.

During the next six weeks, other witnesses would tell the court of similar and worse insults hurled at Seward by his wife. But this was the jury's first exposure to the couple's life, as portrayed by Reilly's witnesses. By prolonging the testimony with his objections, Osgood only exacerbated its effect.

Shortly before lunch Poterewicz revealed the contents of the folder lying on her lap. It was a tape recording of Basia screaming at her in Seward's presence. Sullivan & Cromwell's lawyers had never heard the tape; indeed until that day they did not know of its existence. Lambert dismissed the jury for lunch and heard arguments on its admissibility.

When the jury and spectators filed in after lunch, it was apparent that Sullivan & Cromwell had lost: a huge tape recorder—purchased several days before by Milbank, Tweed—sat in front of the witness stand.

In its mistrial motion almost a month later, Sullivan & Cromwell would insist that the playing of tapes "served no purpose but to appeal to the emotions of the jury. Their introduction brought these proceedings to a new low and turned the courtroom into a circus."

But in the thirty minutes of rapid-fire argument and questioning that preceded the playing of Poterewicz's tape, Osgood only added to the carnival atmosphere. Perhaps he misjudged the mood in the courtroom as he conducted voir dire about the tape before the jury. His near-hysterical probing backfired and further heightened the tension and sense of anticipation.

Some of Osgood's questions seemed to insinuate a Watergate-like tampering with tapes. "Have there been times between January 16 and

March 24 when you have been outside of your house and without the tape in your pocket?'' Osgood asked.

"May I inquire as to what years counsel is referring to?'' Reilly demanded.

"Any time between January 17, 1983, and March 24, 1986,'' answered Osgood.

"I have my tape recorder with me but not all the time in my pocket,'' Poterewicz replied incredulously.

Poterewicz told Osgood that she had made a copy of the tape two days before in the offices of Milbank, Tweed. "Did you ever leave the room when the copy was made in the office?'' he asked. She said she had not.

Finally, the judge allowed speeches from both sides. Osgood almost shouted: "I object. [The tape] is hearsay. It is incompetent evidence. It is designed to influence the jury and it is not probative on the question of undue influence.''

Answered Reilly: "We want each member of the jury to realize the manner in which Mrs. Johnson terrorized.'' That prompted another outburst from Osgood.

Reilly continued. "This was a daily or several times a day occurrence, and I think the jury is entitled to know the atmosphere, the ambiance in which Mr. Johnson survived during that period,'' he said. Osgood began to argue again. He worried that playing the tape in the echo-chamber-like courtroom, on a large machine, would unfairly amplify Basia's voice. To allay his fears, Lambert promised to take the jury to a smaller room to listen to the original tape on Poterewicz's tiny recorder, but only after the copy was played.

Finally the tape was played. And for the courtroom spectators, salivating for a dose of melodrama, it was worth the wait. It featured six minutes of Basia's almost nonstop shrieking in Polish. When it was over, there was silence.

"We will now take a five-minute recess and find a smaller room,'' the surrogate finally piped up. "I think it is unnecessary,'' Osgood told her.

He should have left it at that. Instead, he offered to take the jury to the scene of the conversation—a large bathroom at the Johnsons' estate in New Jersey—to hear the tape again. Observers were shocked that Osgood would allow the jurors to view the sumptuous Jasna Polana. The offer was quickly snapped up by the judge, Reilly, and Robert Hirth of Dewey, Ballantine, Bushby, Palmer & Wood, counsel to the Harbor Branch Foundation, Inc., which is also contesting the will. (Seward had co-founded Harbor Branch, an oceanographic foundation, and donated considerable funds to it. The foundation, which was named in some previous wills, had been cut out of his last one.)

A recess was taken, and the court took on a party atmosphere. Poterewicz's translator, mobbed by the press in the corridor, said Basia had used words like "dumb broad" and "whore" to describe Poterewicz. (Basia later denied this.) A Sullivan & Cromwell associate blew up when he discovered what was going on. "Is this proper?" he demanded. "This whole thing is a f—— outrage. Reilly probably told her to get out here and talk to the press."

Five days later, while a bus waited to take the jury to the Johnsons' luxurious $20 million home near Princeton, Sullivan & Cromwell partner Donald Christ tried to defuse the bomb Osgood had created. The visit to Jasna Polana was finally scotched—amid frantic backsliding. Basia, Christ said, was unwilling to have the press in her home, even though the television stations were willing to limit the number of reporters on the premises.

"It's reasonably plain to me that Mr. Christ and Mrs. Johnson and others may have had second thoughts about the matter, and they have chosen to use this as a scheme to reverse their original position," said Milbank, Tweed's Reilly. "I think it's untenable."

Osgood's suggestion that the tape be played in a bathroom at Jasna Polana was the last he would utter before the jury. After about two and a half years on the case, he was relegated to a back office role. Christ, a trust and estates partner, was left without the backup of a litigation partner. He would sorely need it in the weeks ahead.

THE HEARSAY TURNABOUT

Although Poterewicz and other witnesses were allowed to testify about how Basia spoke to Seward and the Jasna Polana household staff, Lambert had barred what Christ and Osgood thought was similar testimony during their case. Lambert had refused, for example, to allow Zagat to testify about some conversations she had had with Seward, Basia, and Seward, Jr.

Lambert reversed her position on hearsay during the testimony of Marilyn Link, a witness put on the stand by Harbor Branch just before Reilly launched his case with Poterewicz. Dewey, Ballantine's Hirth asked Link, a Harbor Branch trustee, to tell the jury what Basia had said about Seward's onetime lawyer Robert Myers, of Washington, D.C.'s Williams, Myers and Quiggle.

The question launched a behind-the-scenes argument that would change the course of the trial. Lambert sustained Christ's objection to the testimony on hearsay grounds, but she called the lawyers to the bench at Hirth's request.

Hirth explained that Link was about to testify that Basia had called Myers a "stumbling block" and an obstacle to getting money Seward wanted her to have. "It is not being offered for the truth," he told the surrogate. "It is being offered to show her state of mind . . . [and to shed light] on the undue influence charge in this case."

Reilly called the judge's attention to a memorandum that Milbank, Tweed had filed a week before on the admissibility of evidence it had yet to present. The memorandum cited episodes where Basia allegedly had called Seward "stupid," "crazy," and "gaga," had claimed she had left Seward until he ripped up their prenuptial agreement, and had threatened to hit her husband with a cane. "Evidence of this type is relevant because considered as a whole it shows, among other things, Mrs. Johnson's tyrannical disposition and her near-total control over Mr. Johnson," Milbank, Tweed wrote in the memo. "The full picture will become clear, however, only if objectants are permitted to place in evidence each of the tiles that is a part of the mosaic."

The argument at the bench moved to chambers, and Lambert said she would reverse herself on some of the previously excluded testimony. "I was in error, and my error has now come to my attention, and I am not going to have a record that has error in it when we are still in the middle of trial and we can cure that error, especially since Ms. Zagat has not finished with her testimony," Lambert explained.

Reilly, Hirth, and Lambert's law clerk, Harvey Corn, agreed that relatively few rulings would be affected by the change. But Christ insisted that doubling back on direct was prejudicial to his case. Osgood, who had remained silent, antagonized the judge by asking for an adjournment. "We should have an opportunity to review the direct case and the trial transcript, the various rulings that the court made and kept evidence out on hearsay grounds, and see whether in our judgment it is curable or whether we must move for a mistrial," he said.

"Stop having pipe dreams. Nobody is going to get any mistrials in this case. So stop with your pipe dreams," Lambert retorted. "I am not going to compound an error if I have made an error."

Lambert was angry, but Osgood pushed even harder for adjournment—

until she lost her temper. "Tell you what I'll do," she said. "I'll give it to you overnight. You can read it. Put ten people in your office each reading four hundred pages of testimony. Put twenty people. I'll give you to tomorrow morning to come up with all the areas."

"There are four thousand pages of transcript," Osgood complained. Lambert pointed out that Sullivan & Cromwell and Shearman & Sterling could marshal hundreds of troops to plow through the transcript.

Finally Reilly reentered the fray, pointing out that the errors were confined to 700 or 800 pages of testimony. "The whole thing is just sort of a blown-up, exaggerated attempt to create an image of prejudice which I think is very unfair," he said. "We have had interruptions that I could easily lay at the feet of other counsel and claim that, well, I was prejudiced." Lambert reminded Sullivan & Cromwell that it had forced an interruption of Reilly's cross-examination of Zagat when it was learned S&C had failed to turn over many of her time cards.

Tempers began to cool. Lambert gave Sullivan & Cromwell four days to go over the transcript, promising that she would allow the firm to put their questions in context.

Osgood and Christ refused to let the issue die. Osgood even suggested that to correct the problem they might need to present their case again. The next day Sullivan & Cromwell filed a memorandum that was filled with vitriol: "The court has already acknowledged error with regard to rulings it has made against the proponents; those errors are serious, and it may well be that they cannot be cured."

At this point, Harbor Branch was only one day into its case. The children hadn't even started theirs. But Sullivan & Cromwell was laying the groundwork for an appeal.

Zagat's return to the stand for continued cross-examination and re-direct was delayed until after the completion of the children's case, largely because Milbank, Tweed had to sort through Zagat's recently produced time cards. Sullivan & Cromwell had plenty of time to identify 62 rulings they wanted reversed, but they won only six.

LOST OPPORTUNITIES

In early April, with Osgood gone, Christ had to shoulder the burden of Basia and Zagat's case. Although Christ had always been the Sullivan & Cromwell partner in charge of the trial, his expertise is in trusts and estates. He had relied on Osgood for litigation support.

Christ seemed incapable of effective cross-examination. The points he did score seemed insignificant next to Reilly's. Reilly had brutally examined Zagat and Jack Gunther, Jr., another Shearman & Sterling associate who had worked on the Johnson account. When the trial began last winter, few expected the children to put on such a strong case, but at times Christ's vapid technique made it seem as though there was no contest at all.

As his firm had promised in its memorandum on the admissibility of evidence, Reilly's undue influence case consisted of a "mosaic." He placed each piece against the background of two points he'd scored earlier in the case. One was his devastating cross-examination of Zagat, which showed her favoring Basia's interests over those of Seward. The other was the playing of the tape, which was a tangible—and certainly audible—reminder of the fury that Basia was capable of mustering.

A parade of 33 witnesses made brief appearances on the stand to testify about the Johnsons' marriage. Basia was portrayed as an unusually manipulative shrew, Seward as an increasingly doddering, passive, sick old man.

Sullivan & Cromwell had good reason to want to limit the testimony. The jurors were not likely to soon forget what was dubbed the "papaya juice episode," a dispute between Basia and a nurse over some juice Seward wanted. It resulted in a colorful tirade by Basia. Nor would they soon forget "the orange juice episode"—Seward thought a nurse giving him orange juice was choking him. The testimony was offered by Reilly to show Seward's confused and dependent state during the months in which he signed his last wills, which gave increasing financial control to Basia.

While Christ's direct case had been dominated by upper-crust lawyers and cool doctors, the cast of characters directed by Reilly was far more appealing. The private nurses who cared for Seward during his last illness were just plain folk. Seward's children and in-laws were alternately witty and entertaining, and nervous and sympathetic. Former Jasna Polana servants mangled their English but nonetheless conveyed that Basia manipulated the lives of her husband and everyone else around her. Former security guards testified about Seward's isolation and fears.

One of the family members who testified is Martin Richards, a Broadway theater and movie producer who is married to Seward's daughter Mary Lea. Basia, he said, "was very much a disciplinarian and acted like a very stern mother, and my father-in-law spoke like a baby, in baby talk." He told of Basia's hysterical yelling and her bragging that "she spent more money than Queen Elizabeth does in a year.'' Richards also recounted a story about a stormy family lunch at Children's Bay Cay, Seward's private island in the Bahamas.

On cross-examination the next day, Christ tested Richards's memory on the minute details of that occasion. Indeed, the witness was uncertain when questioned about how long Seward's daughter Elaine Wold and her husband, Keith, had stayed on the island during that 1980 visit. It was too small a point. As Christ moved on, he set a trap for himself that obscured any small weakness he had revealed.

"What was the argument about? Do you recall?" Christ asked.

"Yes," Richards answered.

"What was it?"

"Some poor soul, a steward that had worked on one of my father-in-law's boats, was taking over as a cook and butler for the day, and he put a plate down in the wrong position. That's what I believe started it. And a lot of screaming went on, and a lot of throwing around things, and a lot of name-calling to him, and then following him around, and, as I described it yesterday, just screaming louder and louder and louder and louder. And then my father-in-law was screamed at. And it continued for quite a while."

"What do you recall Mr. Johnson saying on that occasion?"

"He first said, 'Basia, please,' for which he was screamed at and insulted," Richards testified. He added, "Seward turned to us when she was not . . . in that dining area, and said, 'Don't anyone say anything, because if you say anything it's going to go on forever,' or 'an hour,' or 'longer,' or whatever the word was."

Christ simply allowed Richards to repeat his direct testimony without trying to shake him off the story. This was typical of the way he conducted his cross-examinations.

During the examination of Seward's daughter Elaine, Christ pushed too hard, asking a potentially explosive question. "Was there ever a time, prior to your father's death, when you did not get along well with [Basia]?" he asked.

"I was uncomfortable," Elaine replied.

"Always?"

"At times," she answered nervously.

"Not always?"

"No," she said.

"Did there come a time when you became uncomfortable?" Christ asked.

"Yes."

"When was that?" he continued.

"The dates that there was any discord between my father and Basia, any yelling, I became uncomfortable."

"How many times did that happen?" he asked. Quickly thinking the better of it he said, "I withdraw the question," before Elaine could answer.

Christ seemed determined to pick away at the fringes of Reilly's case rather than attack its substance. "Basia said she threatened to leave my father unless he were to tear up the prenuptial agreement," Elaine told the jury on direct. "She appeared very proud of the fact that she had such power over my father to cause him to tear up this agreement." On cross-examination, Christ hammered away at her because she confused certain dates.

Christ sometimes chose his battles badly. Anthony Maffatone, a body-guard for the Richardses, testified that at Jasna Polana he saw Basia slap Seward with the back of her hand. Christ made an unsuccessful attempt to cast doubt on the witness's motives for offering the testimony by asking Maffatone, a Vietnam War veteran with 19 decorations, to tell the jury about the bodyguard fees he receives from the Richardses. He also allowed Maffatone to repeat the incident—in excruciating detail.

Several minutes later, Christ asked Maffatone whether it was true that he didn't like Basia. "No, I don't," he said simply. "And isn't it also a fact that you consider the Richardses to be your friends?" Answered Maffatone: "Absolutely."

Reilly took Christ's cue for his three-question redirect, and Maffatone's answers could have been part of Reilly's summation. "Mr. Maffatone, is there any particular reason why you do not like Barbara Johnson?"

"Yes, there is," he replied.

"Will you tell us what it is?"

"I feel that she enjoys berating people. My mother and father were working-class people, and when I witnessed the way she treated her employees and everyone that she felt was beneath her, it brought out an anger in me that—I put myself in empathy with the people that she would scream and yell at and berate and hold their jobs in the palm of her hand, and it was like if they didn't become subservient to her they would lose their jobs. And it disgusted me."

"Did that include also the way she treated Mr. Johnson?" Reilly inquired.

Christ objected strenuously. "Overruled," said Lambert. "You opened the door by asking the question."

Continued Maffatone: "When I see a man humiliated by anyone in front of guests or friends, it repulses me, and I kept wanting him to react or to do something, to defend himself. And it just—it turned me off like a switch. I just wanted to be away from her and the whole thing."

Christ also bungled some chances to damage Reilly's case. For example, he could have chipped away harder at the testimony of Judith Abramovitz, but he didn't. Abramovitz, who nursed Seward at Jasna Polana in 1982 and 1983, had two lurid stories to tell. The first took place in the mansion's library, when a security man told Seward that a crockpot Seward had ordered had arrived.

Basia, according to Abramovitz, was furious. "She picked [Seward's] cane up and stood up, not completely straight, but somewhat towered over him and did attempt to come down on him with the cane but never connected, and she was screaming the entire while. Some of the things she said were, he was 'senile,' '[a] stupid old man.' "

Story number two was more comical. The issue: papaya juice. Seward had indigestion, and Abramovitz recommended the juice. Basia overruled the nurse, because she thought the two-day-old juice was stale. That night Seward asked for papaya juice, and Abramovitz handed it over. The next day Basia found out. "The screaming started: louder and more furious than I had ever heard, and I never thought it was possible that she could get louder, but she did," testified Abramovitz. "If anybody has ever done any work in institutions, psychiatric, they would know what I was talking about. She raved like a lunatic."

It was powerful, ghastly testimony. On cross-examination, Christ made an important score; he got Abramovitz to testify that Basia's mother had died the day of the papaya juice incident. Yet he didn't try to discredit some of her most damaging testimony. On direct Abramovitz said she had spent three months working in a mental institution, but Christ never questioned her expertise to characterize Basia's behavior as that of a "lunatic." And his effort to show that Basia had not hit her husband with the cane was halfhearted.

"But she didn't swing at him, did she?" he asked.

"Yes, she swung it. Shall I demonstrate?" Abramovitz retorted. That Basia could have easily hit Seward if she really wanted to—but chose not to—was never exploited by Christ.

Throughout his case Reilly tried to drive home to the jury that Seward was uncomfortable in the palatial home Basia insisted they build. Christ blew a chance to undercut that claim when Abramovitz was on the stand. Seward "had preferred to be home than in the hospital, is that right?" he asked her.

"Oh, absolutely. He loved his home," she told him. Instead of dwelling on the point, Christ quickly moved on.

Near the end of Abramovitz's testimony, Christ asked whether she thought Seward was a "gentleman." It was an inquiry he made to many of Reilly's witnesses. The point was never clear.

Christ rarely seemed to know when to stop. This was most apparent during his cross-examination of Roger Cook, a Harbor Branch executive. Cook was a terrible witness but was put on the stand by the foundation to tell the jury about Harbor Branch's submarine work. Dewey, Ballantine partner Jack Kaufmann had Cook answer just a few questions about Seward's declining state in the final years of his life and turned the witness over to Christ.

Christ quickly—and conclusively—established that Cook could tell the jury everything about submersibles but had little memory for anything else. Nevertheless he kept Cook on the stand for hours. He hammered away needlessly, even after Cook told the jury that a head injury had affected his memory. Lambert kept the jury late until Christ completed his examination. By the time court adjourned for the evening, the resentment was obvious.

Finally, on April 23, Sullivan & Cromwell sent in another lawyer to assist the flagging Christ. Partner Philip Graham, Jr., had joined Basia's entourage in mid-April, observing the proceedings from the spectators' gallery. It wasn't long until he was cross-examining his first witness, nurse Mary Banks.

Banks testified about Seward's episodes of confusion in the period just before he signed his last will on April 14, 1983. His disorientation had been well documented by Banks and other nurses in their notes, which became some of Reilly's most powerful evidence. By skillfully questioning her accuracy, Graham came close to neutralizing Banks as a witness. Graham asked Banks about an entry in her notes: "Asked for drink then refused." She testified that Seward had asked for a glass of water and then, when it came, denied he had requested it.

"And yet that is not what you wrote down, is it?" Graham asked.

"No, you're right. I didn't write the whole conversation down," she said.

"In fact, you left out the part you thought was significant, is that right?"

"Evidently," she answered.

Graham went on to do competent cross-examinations of another nurse, Bonnie Weisser, and Reilly's expert witnesses. Courtroom observers agreed that Christ could never have matched his partner's work and that Graham had arrived too late.

A THREE-RING CIRCUS

The progression of the Johnson will contest regularly provided headlines, but the events of April 16 seemed to top them all. That day, 15 workers from Jasna Polana descended on the courtroom in a protest, screaming "liar," "communist," and "spy" as one of Reilly's Polish witnesses left the stand. Lambert had the jury removed and sentenced the apparent ringleader—Basia's estate manager—to 15 days in jail. (The sentence was later reduced to time served, one night; five of the workers had fines levied against them.)

That night Reilly's shaken witness received a menacing phone call from one of the courtroom intruders. "As Your Honor knows from applications we have made in this court during the past year, we have experienced considerable difficulties in getting witnesses to appear in this jurisdiction from Florida and elsewhere," Reilly told the judge, out of the presence of the jury, when he reported the harassing phone call. "It has been in no small measure because of efforts made by proponents [of the will] and at least one of their counsel, Mr. Osgood, to intimidate witnesses who otherwise would freely appear and testify."

Milbank, Tweed had previously alleged that Osgood had improperly approached, and even paid, former employees of the Johnson family and Harbor Branch. In mid-1985 Milbank, Tweed had sought to make Osgood's pretrial work an issue in the case. Reilly had moved for permission to depose Osgood. Lambert refused.

Now Reilly said, "We have argued in connection with earlier attempts at intimidation that the fact of the intimidation should be admissible before this jury as evidence of an admission by conduct, admission of the weakness of the proponents' own case." He asked for an injunction to prevent Basia, Zagat, and their representatives from approaching his witnesses.

"I am personally offended by the suggestion that an injunction should be somehow levied against Sullivan & Cromwell, Mrs. Johnson, Mrs.

Zagat, [and] the other attorneys involved in this proceeding,'' Christ countered.

On March 4, Reilly had filed an affidavit describing Sullivan & Cromwell's allegedly improper dealings with seven potential witnesses. It was kept under lock and key in Lambert's chambers. The surrogate eventually allowed Reilly to read from the deposition of Harbor Branch employee John Peach, who had helped look after the dying Seward during the period the last will was signed.

Peach had testified in the deposition that after Seward's death, Sullivan & Cromwell paid him about $25,000 to help prepare the case. He submitted other bills for about $135,000 to Zagat, who paid them from Basia's accounts. He described his visits to Seward's nurses on behalf of Sullivan & Cromwell and revealed that Basia had paid $23,000 in medical bills for one potential witness. Nurse Weisser testified briefly that when Osgood paid her a visit, he offered to help get her employment at Johnson & Johnson.

But this testimony was severely diluted because Lambert made Reilly include selections chosen by Sullivan & Cromwell in his readings from the deposition. "Seward, I love you, I love you,'' Peach recalled Basia saying as Seward died on May 23, 1983. Basia sniffled into her hand as Reilly and a paralegal read that portion to the jury.

In the end, the deposition was deadly boring. The jury laughed when it was mentioned. It became a courtroom joke.

A PROBLEM WITH BIAS?

By late April many of those watching the trial unwind had come to two conclusions: It seemed obvious that Sullivan & Cromwell was losing its case. But it was equally clear that Lambert favored Reilly and the children over Christ, Basia, and Zagat. Throughout the proceedings, the Sullivan & Cromwell lawyers suffered at the hands of the judge—so much so that her behavior became the central issue of the firm's April 22 motion for a mistrial.

To say that the surrogate has a short fuse is to understate the obvious. She constantly expressed her exasperation and impatience with Christ's long-winded and aimless cross-examinations. Lambert almost always had good reason to believe that Christ was wasting the jury's time. But her disdain for his performance and even his case was so obviously telegraphed to the courtroom that she unwittingly provided grist for the mistrial motion. One spectator opined: "The judge is Mr. Reilly's co-pilot."

Sometimes her disapproval took the form of grimaces or quick, sharp outbursts. When Christ posed a question she felt was inappropriate she would flash Reilly a look, as if to invite him to object. Other times Lambert would simply lose control. Her temper was especially virulent during Christ's seemingly endless cross-examination of Robert Myers, Zagat's predecessor as Seward's lawyer. Myers tried her patience with his long, lawyerly answers, but she reserved the brunt of her frustration for Christ.

At one point, Christ led Myers through the impact of a complicated IRS revenue ruling that was an issue in Seward's estate planning in 1973 "And this all has to do with a will in 1973, am I correct?" interjected Lambert, as if to underscore its irrelevance to the will offered for probate.

Myers: "You're correct."

Lambert: "It had nothing to do with an April 14, 1983, will, does it?"

Myers: "No."

Lambert: "Okay."

Christ followed up with yet another question related to the 1973 wills. Charles Berry, Reilly's partner, objected.

"Overruled," said Lambert. "I will let him ask anything he wants. Let's see how many weeks we can go on with this."

Almost an hour later Christ pushed Myers to pinpoint a 1973 meeting that the witness had already said occurred on or about May 9. "Was it May 9? Was it May 10? Was it May 12? Was it May 13 or May 14 of 1973?" asked Lambert, her voice filled with sarcasm. "It's very crucial to find out if it was any one of those dates. Would you tell us please? We will do them one at a time. Did you meet with them on May 9?"

Myers: "I don't know, Your Honor."

Lambert: "Did you meet with them on May 10?"

Myers: "I don't know, Your Honor."

Lambert: "Did you meet with them on May 11?"

Myers: "I don't know, Your Honor."

Lambert: "Did you meet with them on May 12?"

Myers: "I don't know, Your Honor."

Lambert: "Did you meet with them on May 13?"

Myers: "I don't know, Your Honor."

Lambert: "Let's go. Go ahead, Mr. Christ. Keep asking."

Not surprisingly, this exchange made it into the papers filed by Sullivan & Cromwell to support its mistrial motion. "It has become apparent that the proceedings have become so infected with irreparable error prejudicial to the proponents that any verdict rendered in favor of the objectants will not be sustainable on appeal," the firm suggested.

The documents accused Lambert of hostility toward Sullivan & Cromwell's witnesses. "The one held in least regard by the court is proponent Nina Zagat," Sullivan & Cromwell argued. Indeed, throughout Zagat's testimony, Lambert's in-chambers talk seemed sprinkled with disapproval for the way Zagat had conducted her representation of the Johnsons. The motion quoted the most outrageous of Lambert's in-chambers comments, made after Zagat had snapped at Reilly during his pounding cross-examination. "Let me tell you something," Lambert told the lawyers. "If I had been [Reilly], I would have said, 'At least I'm not a crook and a thief.' "

The motion also attacked the judge for treating Sullivan & Cromwell lawyers unfairly and harshly. "In stark contrast," the memorandum continued, "the court allowed Mr. Reilly to lead Mrs. Poterewicz blatantly with such questions as . . . 'Were his hands steady?' " The firm argued that the judge's rulings—especially the shift on hearsay—were irreparable.

Milbank, Tweed's reply brief argued that Lambert did not treat Sullivan & Cromwell unfairly. It called many of S&C's objections "frivolous" and criticized the firm's "sorry record of concealment, evasion, and deception. . . . Proponents have put the record under a microscope and labored hard to find even the slightest imperfection. That their labors have produced such a grab-bag of worthless nitpicks is a compliment to the court and its sound, practical management of this complicated case."

Harbor Branch's reply detailed Lambert's promise, after she reversed herself on the hearsay issue, to allow Sullivan & Cromwell to requestion Zagat in context and explain the problem to the jury. "Virtually all of the testimony proponents claim was improperly excluded remains inadmissible," the brief reiterated.

For a while after the mistrial motion was filed, Lambert toned down her management of the trial. She seemed to respond more favorably to Graham's thoughtful cross-examinations. She looked solemn, interrupted counsel less often, and carefully worded her rulings. On May 2 she denied the motion from the bench.

Six days later, Sullivan & Cromwell launched its rebuttal case. For the second time, the firm went back to the bull pen for relief. The new addition to counsel table this time was Marvin Schwartz, a senior litigator. He immediately incited Lambert's fury by ignoring her instructions and asking leading questions. But Schwartz seemed not to care. He confidently plowed ahead, determined to shore up the faltering Christ and undo Reilly's devastating damage.

EPILOGUE

On May 30, 1986, after a week and a half of negotiations, Basia Johnson agreed to a settlement with the Johnson children and the Harbor Branch Foundation. According to the terms of the settlement, the children received approximately $140 million and Harbor Branch $20 million; Basia took home the remaining $350 million.

As counsel to the executors, Shearman & Sterling led Basia's team at the beginning of the settlement talks. But in the last three days of negotiations Frederick Lacey, a partner at LeBoeuf, Lamb, Leiby & MacRae who had been brought in by Basia one month before to assist in her representation, took control of the talks and hammered out the settlement with the Johnson children.

That settlement put an end to the family squabbling, but did not halt the financial wranglings spawned by *Johnson* v. *Johnson*. Soon after the 17-week trial ended, Basia—who by this time had dropped Shearman & Sterling as her personal counsel in favor of Lacey—continued her fight for control of the Seward Johnson fortune. This time she took on trial counsel Sullivan & Cromwell, refusing to pay the full $10 million in legal fees billed by the firm. After months of fighting—during which Basia balked at paying the $5.5 million Sullivan & Cromwell insisted was still owed—the two sides worked out an agreement by which Basia would only pay $2.3 million more.

During the trial, Milbank, Tweed, Hadley & McCloy partner Edward Reilly, who represented the children, charged in a memorandum that Sullivan & Cromwell had engaged in improper dealings with seven prospective witnesses. Reilly maintained that his opponents had "embarked on a scheme to corrupt or silence" witnesses, charging among other things that improper payments were made to a former Harbor Branch employee who helped recruit witnesses for the defense and to a former nurse of Seward Johnson's whose deposition—favorable to Basia's case—contradicted her medical notes. A disciplinary panel of the New York State Supreme Court is now investigating Reilly's allegations.

Nina Zagat, still at Shearman & Sterling as a trusts and estates associate, never cashed in on her full share of the Johnson fortune. She too discovered that Basia Johnson was a tough client: During settlement negotiations, LeBoeuf's Lacey whittled the executor's fees to be paid Zagat from the $8 million stipulated in Johnson's will to the less princely sum of $1.8 million. And for Zagat, the outcome of the trial carried a second blow. When the Johnson trusts were collapsed as a part of the settlement, it meant she lost an estimated $900,000 a year in trustee fees.

In January 1988, Shearman & Sterling filed a petition with Manhattan Surrogate Marie Lambert seeking $3.75 million in fees and almost $300,000 in disbursements it claims the estate owes the firm for its work as counsel to the executors. Negotiations were begun, but in April 1988, Basia filed a malpractice action in Florida against Zagat and Shearman & Sterling, alleging that they mishandled the execution of the will and opened the way for the will contest. The suit seeks the return of more than $115 million the estate paid out in the settlement, unspecified punitive damages, and the voiding of attorneys' fees and commissions already paid and still owed.

Zagat, in turn, has asked Lambert to compel the estate to pay $500,000 of the $1.8 million in executor's commissions, as well as her attorney's fees in the malpractice action.

In August 1988 Shearman & Sterling was granted a preliminary injunction barring Basia Johnson from proceeding with her malpractice suit in Florida rather than in New York. On December 27, the Appellate Division, 1st Department, affirmed the injunction.

A hearing on the issues of a permanent injunction, Shearman & Sterling's fee petition, and Zagat's commission and fee request was scheduled before Surrogate Lambert for April 1989. However, on March 10, Johnson filed a motion for Lambert's recusal from matters concerning the malpractice suit, claiming the judge had displayed bias against the heiress. Lambert denied the motion.

On April 18 Surrogate Lambert began hearing arguments on whether she should permanently enjoin Johnson from proceeding in Florida. However, Johnson's case suffered a devastating blow when it was revealed that during the hearing in New York, without her counsel's knowledge, Johnson had settled an unrelated case in Connecticut which involved payment of $150,000 to a potential witness against Johnson in return for his agreeing not to testify against her in New York.

Three weeks later, after a month on the stand, Johnson finally agreed to settle the case in New York. On May 17 Surrogate Lambert mediated the 11-hour negotiating session in which it was agreed that Zagat would receive the $1.8 million in commissions, plus about $400,000 in interest, and Shearman & Sterling would receive about $3 million of the $4 million in fees and disbursements it was seeking as counsel to the estate.

It appeared that the case was finally over; however, on August 28, four months after Surrogate Lambert issued a decree effective July 17 approving the settlement, J. Seward Johnson's children moved to have it thrown out. The six Johnson children said they should have been given notice of the decree which, they claim, makes unsupported findings of fact regarding their father's mental capacity. The motion sought to resettle Lambert's decree and remove findings of fact, but did not request any additional relief. In early December 1989 Lambert denied the motion.

Basia Johnson is now involved in a widely publicized effort to aid the Solidarity movement in Poland.

Richard Lord
V.
Martin Sorrell

IN THE WAR FOR DICK LORD'S AD AGENCY,
TOUGH WASN'T SMART

BY

STEVEN BRILL

*Martin Sorrell hired Philip Reiss to defend his investment in the
Lord, Geller ad agency. Reiss's scorched-earth tactics hurt the
agency they were designed to save.*

Martin Sorrell's fight with Richard Lord over the future of the glitzy ad
agency Lord started and Sorrell now owns would seem to deserve better
than a grubby lower Manhattan courtroom meant for landlord-tenant disputes and small-time civil claims.

What an unlikely place for such an uptown clash of egos (flashy copywriter Lord's against British accountant-cum-mogul Sorrell's); of social
values (the touchy-feely agency creative types against people who get
chills reading balance sheets); and of legal principles (a purchaser determined to protect his assets versus a man who refuses to be pigeonholed
as one of those assets despite the fact that he did, indeed, sell his personal
services company).

What an inadequate setting for a case involving the people who brought us those classy ads from IBM, Hennessy cognac, Tiffany, *The New Yorker,* and *The Wall Street Journal,* let alone a case that might be pivotal in deciding the nature of ownership in what is fast becoming a national economy built on personal services businesses.

Just as unlikely is the man who will have to render at least the initial jurisprudence that will decide it: Judge Herman Cahn, a former civil litigator at a three-lawyer Manhattan firm, who spent six years hearing plea bargains and felony cases as an acting New York State Supreme Court justice in the criminal division and was switched to the civil division only seven months ago.

Yet the judge and his courtroom aren't nearly as much out of their league as Martin Sorrell's lawyers have been.

Sorrell's lead lawyer is Philip Reiss, a senior partner at 32-lawyer Davis & Gilbert in New York. For Reiss, Sorrell's much-publicized war with Lord is a perfectly timed opportunity. Davis & Gilbert is well known for its specialty in ad agency work, but as the agency business has become the province of giant conglomerates, his firm has, as one lawyer there puts it, "felt under some pressure to prove to our clients that they shouldn't go to big firms just because they're so much bigger now."

"In this case, we're a small firm going against Skadden, Arps [Slate, Meagher & Flom] and Shearman & Sterling," says Reiss, whose firm had a fifth of its lawyers working the Lord-Sorrell fight by mid-April. "And the ad trade press has been calling it David against Goliath. That's given us a big lift here. . . . We're showing we can go toe to toe against the big firms."

The case hasn't, however, given Reiss's client much of a lift.

Skadden is representing Lord and his compatriots who fled their old agency—Lord, Geller, Federico, Einstein, Inc., which is now owned by Sorrell—to start anew; Shearman & Sterling is representing the large agency, Young & Rubicam, that has staked Lord's new venture.

The two big firms have out-lawyered Reiss's people not only in court but, more important, before the case ever got to court.

Goliath has beaten David. Badly.

And it's mattered. This clash over who owns "people assets" and over what's fair and what's foul in the age of takeovers and management buyouts is a case where the lawyering, good and bad, has really counted. The whole saga could be the stuff of a commercial about the value of good lawyering and the dangers of not-so-good lawyering.

In Dick Lord's ad world, a commercial like that would be organized around storyboards, each illustrating a scene. Like this:

STORYBOARD #1:
THE CASE OF THE BADLY DRAFTED
CONTRACT CLAUSES

It's 1974 and Dick Lord's little agency, then called Lord, Geller, Federico, Peterson, Inc., is seven years old. Lord and his colleagues, all refugees from larger agencies where they were hot copywriters and art directors, have been making headway creating a boutique that specializes in what Lord calls "ads based on considered purchases—purchases people have to think about, not impulse buying. Ads that people have to think about. . . . No one goes out and buys our stuff skipping down the aisle of a supermarket."

They're doing quirky, creative ads and running a fun, informal shop (where, for example, the Christmas party is held in January "to give everyone a lift then, and because we could afford to rent a better place in the off-season," Lord explains). But Lord is frustrated because he hates running a small business that "lives from day to day," as he puts it, and more important, because "the big clients are still afraid to use such a small agency. . . . We made a pitch to Seagram," he remembers, "and we almost had it won until [Seagram chairman] Edgar Bronfman piped up at the end that he wanted a big, established agency. . . . It was driving me crazy."

So Lord talks to some friends at the big agencies, and before too long he's got a deal: giant J. Walter Thompson will buy Lord, Geller for "about $360,000 split between a whole bunch of us," Lord recalls.

"But they agree that we'll be totally autonomous, that we can run our own show," Lord explains. "The difference is that if we pitch an IBM account and we win the competition, and the IBM ad people go back to the CEO and he asks who we are, they can tell him we're part of J. Walter and have their backing and their staying power."

"In our view we weren't buying much except a stake in some very creative guys who might build a good small agency," recalls Hugh Connell, who was general counsel of J. Walter in 1967. "If Dick Lord tells you that the key ingredient of the deal was that they would be autonomous, except for a few corporate decisions, he's telling you the truth," adds Connell, who retired in 1986. "He was totally focused on that, much more so than on the money. He really didn't care much about the money; what he cared about was having his own freedom while being able to get the support of a larger agency.''

At the time, Lord, Geller has only about $5 million in billings—that is, its clients place about $5 million in advertising, from which Lord, Geller receives about 15 percent in commissions, or $750,000 in revenue. Profits in 1974 "were negligible," Lord recalls, "maybe $100,000 because we only took $18,000 each in salaries."

In addition to the purchase agreement, Lord and his partners and J. Walter sign a management agreement and employment agreements. The management agreement, Connell recalls, "was meant to give them all the autonomy they wanted consistent with our responsibilities to our shareholders."

Thus, the agreement calls for Lord and his partners to be the only members of a new Lord, Geller board of directors and "to have the right to conduct the business on an autonomous basis."

There are five exceptions to this autonomy: major capital expenditures, the selection of outside auditors, the compensation of Lord and his partners (which is set anyway by the employment contracts), the setting of profit-sharing contributions for employees, and, most important, "the acceptance or resignation of any account assignments."

That last exception, regarding accounts, would become a key point of contention after Sorrell bought J. Walter (and in turn Lord, Geller) in a hostile takeover. The clause is there because J. Walter fears that if it has, say, a giant car account and Lord, Geller goes after another car company, J. Walter's car account will be offended by the conflict and fire J. Walter. These kinds of client conflicts would, in the 1980s, become the central controversy of the ad business, as agencies merged and conglomerated, and it was just that issue that would force the ultimate split between Sorrell and Lord.

It is hard to imagine a provision less up to the task of dealing with those issues than the one fashioned in this deal.

(Connell says he supervised Stephen Salorio, then assistant general counsel, and Stephen Lang of New York's Breed, Abbott & Morgan, then J. Walter's outside counsel, in the drafting. Salorio declines comment. Lang says the entire agreement was handled in-house.)

The agreement's statement about autonomy is in an opening "Whereas" clause. But the agreement's provision for the five exceptions to the autonomy is in a paragraph (labeled Section 2) that follows a paragraph (labeled Section 1) that begins, "Except as hereinafter provided, for a period of five years from the Effective Date [J. Walter] shall, as sole stockholder of the Company," let Lord and his partners be Lord, Geller's sole directors.

That second paragraph then states, "During the period provided by Section 1 . . . the Managers [Lord and his partners] shall . . . exercise all the powers . . . of a board of directors . . . provided, however, that they shall . . . comply with the wishes of [J. Walter] with respect to" the five exceptions, including accepting and resigning accounts.

How could they be as generally autonomous as an introductory "Whereas" provision would suggest if their unilateral powers as board members only lasted for five years? On the other hand, couldn't it be assumed that the five limits on their board powers, including the limitation on accepting accounts, only lasted for the five years while their general autonomy (again, as stated in the "Whereas" provision) would last forever?

"I don't remember," says Connell, "but I'd imagine we meant for everything—the autonomy, subject to the limitation on client assignments—to last forever. . . . I guess, in light of today's climate of disputes, it was rather ambiguously drafted."

Lord's lawyer at the time, R. Todd Lang of Weil, Gotshal & Manges, says he has no recollection of the specifics of the deal.

Worse still is the no-compete clause in the employment agreements signed by Lord and his partners. It provides that "except in the event of the breach . . . of the Management Agreement"—assuming one could figure out what constituted a breach—"for a period of one year . . . he shall not, directly or indirectly, solicit or accept any of the advertising business being handled by the Company at the time his employment with the Company terminates.

"For the purposes of this provision," the all-important clause continues, "Employee shall be conclusively deemed to have indirectly solicited or accepted any business acquired by any advertising agency during his employment by . . . such agency . . . if, in connection with the solicitation or acceptance of such business by such agency, Employee has contact with or arranges for a meeting with any representative of a client or former client of the Company or if Employee has any contact or attends any meetings with any representative of such a client after the acquisition of the account by such agency."

It hardly takes great lawyers to figure out what this provision does *not* do:

a. It in no way prohibits Lord from hiring away any Lord, Geller employees.

b. Because the phrase "Employee shall be conclusively deemed to have indirectly solicited or accepted any business" doesn't say "conclusively but not exclusively," it arguably makes what follows—the individual involved personally contacting or meeting with clients—the only definition of what constitutes Lord's soliciting or accepting business; and it seems, therefore, not to bind Lord from being at an agency, even a new one that he starts, that solicits or accepts such business. Indeed, the clause clearly envisions that Lord and his partners might go to such an agency.

Why didn't Connell or anyone else add a "but not exclusively" modifier?

"It's not like it was a great bone of contention with Lord," Connell remembers. "It's probably just that we didn't see it as that important."

Connell adds that "as I recall, we fashioned the noncompete clause after what the Duane Jones case said we could do."

Duane Jones Company, Inc. v. *Burke et al.*, a 1954 case involving renegades from an ad agency run by a man named Duane Jones, would, indeed, become a focal point of the 1988 Sorrell-Lord litigation. But the idea that anyone fashioned this clause after the law made in that case is almost inconceivable.

In the Jones case, a large group of Jones's employees confronted him one day and told him that they'd already lined up most of the agency's clients and employees and were prepared to relocate the entirety of his agency across the street without him unless he sold the business to them immediately at their offering price. The New York court of appeals upheld an award to Jones, ruling that the employees' solicitation of clients and employees before having left Jones's employ constituted a breach of their duty to him as employees.

That case, then, had to do with an employee's common law obligations; it had nothing to do with what a purchaser, such as J. Walter, could require from Lord and his partners in return for purchasing the goodwill and other assets of their agency. Although no-compete clauses are generally looked at skeptically by judges, the ones that do survive typically are those that are linked to a purchase of a business. After all, J. Walter was buying little more than Lord's reputation, clients, and the employee team he had built; it had a right to protect those assets.

The clause he was asked to sign, however, said nothing about goodwill and, therefore, wasn't nearly as encompassing or binding as it could have been in keeping him from competing for clients or employees.

Likewise, the Duane Jones case had had to do with the pre-solicitation of clients and employees; it said nothing about employees, let alone owners who are selling their goodwill to a buyer, soliciting clients and employees *after* they leave.

Then there was the question of how long the Lord no-compete clause lasted, which brings us to the second storyboard.

STORYBOARD #2:
"ALL IS WELL," DESPITE AN IN-PERPETUITY NO-COMPETE CLAUSE AND A LAPSED CONTRACT

The Lord no-compete clause provides that it runs for "a period of one year from the termination for any reason of his employment with the Company, whether during, at the end of, or after the [five-year] term of employment."

But can a clause in a contract run beyond the term of the contract—i.e., "after the term of employment" envisioned by the contract? Maybe, but not necessarily, as Lord's lawyers will later argue.

What would have clarified the clause would have been a provision adding that "the employee's continued acceptance of employment beyond the term of the contract in the absence of a new contract shall constitute his continued acceptance of the no-competition provisions of this contract." In short, another lapse in draftsmanship.

More important, though, was the J. Walter lapse in not signing Lord and his people up for new contracts when these expired in 1979, five years after the original purchase. That would have clarified whether the autonomy limitations and the no-compete provisions had lapsed.

But in 1979 no one, including the J. Walter legal department, is focusing on any of this.

"I guess it just slipped everybody's mind," recalls Connell. "Everyone was happy. The agency was successful, and everyone was getting along."

"We weren't important to J. Walter," Lord recalls. "They were so big; we were a pimple to them. They didn't care, and they weren't managed well enough to remember it, anyway. . . . We set our own compensation and bonuses, and all was well. We were never pigs about it, and they never cared. And *we* certainly didn't think we needed contracts," he adds, tellingly, "because it was our shop."

By 1983 J. Walter would approve a "phantom stock" plan for Lord and his partners, which, in effect, gave them an equitylike stake in Lord, Geller. They'd each have "phantom stock" valued at a multiple of earnings that they could cash in, with vesting in the stock beginning with the 1983 fiscal year and reaching full value in 1989, after the calculation of earnings for 1988.

By 1983 Lord, Geller would also capture the IBM business. That and other new business would turn Lord, Geller into a fabulously successful shop. By 1987 it would have about $220 million in billings (more than half from IBM) and, according to documents later made part of the court record, some $5–6 million in profit. Still, the only documents binding Lord and his people to J. Walter were the contracts signed in 1974.

STORYBOARD #3:
RESTLESS AND RESENTFUL AT LORD, GELLER

By 1987 all is not well with the Lord, Geller–J. Walter relationship. Lord and key partner Arthur Einstein aren't getting along with J. Walter's chairman, G. Donald Johnston, an imperious CEO who is fighting his own internal turf wars.

Worse, Lord, Einstein, and the others at Lord, Geller are reading almost every week about a friend of theirs in the business who has made a killing selling his agency to a larger one in what has become a near-frenzy of multimillion-dollar agency consolidations. Lord, Einstein, and the others had sold their business for peanuts, and, says one Lord, Geller principal, "We were more than a little resentful that Johnston owned us for nothing."

In early 1987, Lord approaches Johnston and asks if he'd be receptive to Lord and his partners doing a leveraged buy-back of their agency. Johnston says he'll consider it.

The lead buyer in many of the other bonanza agency deals had been London-based Saatchi & Company. And one of the key law firms on the other side of the Saatchi deals was Davis & Gilbert, a 67-year-old boutique known for its advertising specialty.

The Saatchi brothers were impressed enough with Davis & Gilbert to give the firm some real estate contracts to handle after its clients were bought out. But the real opportunity for Davis & Gilbert came when former Saatchi group financial officer Martin Sorrell formed his own holding company (called WPP Group PLC) and used Reiss, a 55-year-old senior partner, for some purchases of small advertising-related businesses in the U.S.

Now Sorrell, 42, is on the prowl to do his own deal for a giant American ad agency. Only this one is to be a hostile takeover, of J. Walter. Though the lead oar in what becomes a hard-fought but success-ful battle is pulled by M&A specialists from Fried, Frank, Harris, Shriver & Jacobson, Reiss and his people will play an important role.

"Phil [Reiss] resented that Fried, Frank ran the deal and was charging so much more, with its premiums and everything, than he was," asserts one source close to Sorrell. "You could tell he was anxious to please Martin and get an in with him."

Reiss denies any jealousy but acknowledges that he was "anxious" to get the J. Walter business once the deal was consummated.

"Phil was very much involved in the deal," says Sorrell. "And it was quite natural that, given his specialty, he act for me once the deal was done."

STORYBOARD #4:
UNSUBTLE ADVICE ABOUT "OWNERSHIP"

"You do have to remember that they sold that agency, that we bought that agency, and that we own it," says Sorrell, introducing his side of the argument. It's a line of reasoning that almost everyone who has dealt with Sorrell quickly attributes to him.

"Martin's a financial man who takes ownership of his assets quite seriously," says one of his closest advisers.

"Martin's hung up on ownership," echoes Lord. "He kept telling us he owns us."

So in this storyboard Martin Sorrell is determined to own what he's bought—and Reiss is cheering him on.

M&A specialists have developed a kind of subspecialty helping clients make the transition after a takeover; and among the first matters they consider is what they can do to lock in key employees. Whether it is because Fried, Frank isn't around now to do that for Sorrell, or because Reiss and Sorrell are preoccupied with troubles at their larger entity, the J. Walter agency itself, or because of Sorrell's unsubtle appreciation of the difficulties of "owning" a personal service business and Reiss's unwillingness to sensitize him, no early effort is made to deal with the restless "assets" at Lord, Geller.

"The first time I met [Sorrell]," Lord recalls, "was in the summer of '87 just after he took over. We sat down for a drink in the bar at the Mayfair Regent [in New York]. I asked for a Perrier, and he told me to get an Evian because it's more expensive and, therefore, I'll like it more. That's how he thinks. . . . I mentioned to him," Lord continues, "that I had been talking about a management buyout, and he just brushed me off. He said he didn't sell good assets." (Sorrell confirms the basics of the conversation, though he says, "It was Vittel water.")

Reiss says that although Sorrell took over J. Walter (and, therefore, Lord, Geller) in July 1987, "we probably didn't really focus on Lord, Geller until the fall." After all, Reiss explains, Sorrell had paid $560 million for J. Walter, and Lord, Geller's "portion of the value was maybe five or ten percent of the total."

Nor do Reiss or any of his or Sorrell's people look at the old Lord, Geller management or employment agreements until the fall.

Thus, when Lord approaches Sorrell again later that summer with a more serious discussion about doing a buy-back, Sorrell recalls rejecting the idea out of hand.

"We just rebuffed them every time they asked," says Reiss. "Which was our right."

Another Sorrell adviser recalls that in the fall, despite the fact that the no-compete clauses were so narrow and now so dated, "Reiss gave us a kind of casual report on what the contracts covering the Lord, Geller people said, and he assured us that they couldn't walk with our business. So we rebuffed their LBO offers and tried to negotiate decent employment contracts with them, but from a position of strength."

"Sure, I told them they couldn't steal the business, and when this case is done, I'll be right," Reiss says.

STORYBOARD #5:
A TACTLESS CONTRACT DRAFT

In the fall of 1987, the Lord, Geller group demands that if a buyout isn't in the cards, they'd like to see a Sorrell proposal for a new working arrangement. They focus their demands on five points, including a premium on their phantom stock equivalent to the premium Sorrell paid for the J. Walter stock, a new incentive plan, and renewed assurances of autonomy for Lord, Geller. In response, Reiss drafts (and sends over the signature of the chief financial officer of J. Walter) proposed new contracts for Lord and his partners. No premium for the phantom stock is offered, and, incredibly, the contracts include no provisions for autonomy but do have a sweeping two-year no-compete clause.

STORYBOARD #6:
LORD GETS GOOD COUNSEL

Jerome Traum of the literary law boutique of Janklow & Traum knows when to refer business that's out of his specialty. So when his friend Dick Lord talks to him in September about getting a lawyer to help him consider some sort of leveraged buyout, Traum doesn't hesitate to recommend Skadden, Arps.

On November 17, 1987, Lord, Einstein, and Lord, Geller vice chairman Edward Yaconetti meet at Skadden, Arps with corporate partner Michael Goldberg and litigation partner Thomas Schwarz.

Schwarz is apparently well versed in the Duane Jones case.

"We discussed all of our options," recalls Lord. "A buyout, a buyout with another agency, a partial buyout with Martin keeping a minority share, even quitting. And from the very beginning they stressed to us that we couldn't talk to any clients, that we couldn't give anyone, any third party, any information about the agency, and that we couldn't even talk to our employees about what we were thinking about."

Other participants at the meeting recall that Schwarz said that while the provisions of the no-compete clause probably should not, and would not, be enforceable because of its lack of a deadline and because it was now 15 years old, the participants ought to assume and plan as if the clause, limited as it was, might be enforceable.

Finally, the Skadden lawyers advise their clients to write what one participant terms "a nice, unthreatening, but strong letter for the record," rejecting Sorrell's proposal.

The letter concludes, "We've also decided, based on the contracts we received, that the baggage outweighs the benefits. Therefore, we've decided to go ahead and run our business without employment agreements."

STORYBOARD #7:
REISS FAILS TO FIRE BACK

Rather than worry about that letter, Reiss and Sorrell assume, in Reiss's words, "that it's just all part of a negotiation over their contracts." Thus

Reiss doesn't write back reminding Lord and his people that they're bound by the surviving no-compete provision of the 1979 contract.

Schwarz of Skadden will later argue that "in a letter dated November 19, 1987, defendants put plaintiffs on notice that they were no longer working under any employment contract."

Thus, Reiss's litigators will later find themselves arguing for an injunction reading broad no-compete provisions into the old contract much like the ones spelled out in this new proposal—and rejected, in writing, by Lord and his partners.

STORYBOARD #8:
WAR OVER AUTONOMY

It's mid-December 1987, and Lord, by his own account, gets a call from the J. Walter manager in Milan, who asks if Lord can be in Milan by Saturday to begin pitching the Alfa Romeo Europe account.

"Burt Manning [J. Walter's new chairman] had told me about us going for Alfa a few weeks before, and I had told him it sounded good, that that's our kind of account. But now I wanted to know more," recalls Lord. "It seemed serious, so I wanted details.

"So I ask the guy what it's all about, and he says we'll need to have ten offices in Europe. I ask how much it's worth, and the answer he gives me makes the billings seem like it won't come close to the expense. So I tell him that, and he says I needn't worry because it'll be staffed with J. Walter people who'd worked on Ford. And I asked who would run it, and he said not to worry about that either, because he would.

"Now, I'm getting the picture. You see, J. Walter [which has Ford's U.S. business] had had Ford's Europe business but had been fired. But in Europe you can't lay off people the way you can here; you have to pay them. So what Martin is going to do is take the people who screwed up the Ford account so badly that they got fired and call them Lord, Geller people and have them get the Alfa work. So I tell the guy to forget it, that they can't use our name or me."

Then, in early January, Lord reads an article in *Ad Week* reporting that Sorrell has announced that a new European entity, Conquest Europe, affiliated with Lord, Geller, was pitching the Alfa account. "I went nuts."

Sorrell says that "Lord first agreed and then reneged on going after Alfa."

"If you really own something when you own something, then Martin can use that name," says Reiss. "It's a f——ing fact of life, whether these guys like it or not."

They don't like it. Nor would they like being ordered in February not to pursue the business for General Motors' new $100 million Saturn account after they have already made the first competitive cuts and become one of five finalist agencies. Under the old regime they'd been allowed to pursue other car companies, but Sorrell, fearing a backlash from Ford, whose domestic business is worth $300 million in billings to J. Walter, again exercises his owner's prerogative.

Also in January, according to Lord, Sorrell refuses to release money for Lord, Geller to give its employees their traditional bonuses. When the funds are finally released, money is withheld so that Lord and key executives can't draw their own bonuses until they agree to sign new contracts. (Sorrell asserts that only the bonuses for the executives were an issue.)

STORYBOARD #9:
FINDING A PARTNER

Through February Lord and his people still harbor hopes of being able to do an LBO. (In December Lord had asked Sorrell to consider the proposal once again and even mentioned a price range—$30–40 million. Sorrell told him the right price was $90 million, but that he wouldn't sell it for that price either.)

All along, Lord and his people have known they can't finance a deal on their own; thus, Lord had approached friends at larger agencies for possible backing. By late November the Lord group has settled on Young & Rubicam, a giant agency, as a likely backer and minority partner. Lord is friendly with Y&R CEO Alex Kroll, and Kroll sees the potential deal as a ripe opportunity.

But Kroll's executive vice president and general counsel, R. John Cooper, is cautious.

First, according to Lord and Schwarz, Cooper gets an opinion from Skadden that there is nothing in any contracts between Lord and the others and J. Walter that precludes them from starting a new agency. (Schwarz finds great comfort in the old no-compete clause drafted by Connell and his people.)

Second, Cooper continually warns Lord and his people not to provide any confidential information about Lord, Geller to anyone at Y&R.

"He drummed that into us," says one of the key Lord, Geller people. "It was like a broken record."

STORYBOARD #10:
QUITTING TIME

By March Lord and his people are ready to quit.

"I'm sixty-two and the last thing I wanted to do was quit and start over," says Lord. "Yes, I was even willing to pay someone else [albeit with the agency's own profits] the forty million dollars in value I had built up. I just wanted to run my own show again. . . . If you don't have autonomy, if you can't take on accounts because potential clients know there will be a conflict with the agency that owns you . . . they won't even come to you. And that means I can't feed [what by now were] three hundred twenty employees.

"What Martin should have done," Lord adds, "is give me and my top twenty people a great new incentive plan, a great reward from our old phantom stock plan, and our autonomy; then he could have kept us. He just didn't realize that he didn't own us, just the name Lord, Geller. . . . The difference between the Saatchis and Martin is that when the Saatchis buy an agency they spread all kinds of money around to the managers to keep them and give them all kinds of attention. . . . Martin's problem is that he's been laboring in the financial kitchens presiding over these financial stews he cooks up—all his complicated deals and financings. He didn't understand that he had to come out of the kitchen and deal with people."

In early March Lord and his top five managers (or partners as he calls them)—Einstein, Yaconetti, Lewis Eichenholtz, Kevin O'Neill, and Conrad Freeman (Norman Geller and Gene Federico were ostensibly retired)—trigger their phantom stock payouts in anticipation of quitting and starting their own shop, with Y&R as a 49-percent equity investor. (They can only request the phantom payouts while still employees.) Their strategy, explains Lord, "is to use that as a signal to Martin that we were going to walk so that maybe we could make a deal of some kind."

Indeed, while Schwarz continues to iron out their deal with Y&R, Eichenholtz, the group's financial manager, continues a dialogue with Reiss in the hope that things can be worked out.

"Reiss's attitude all along, which he kept expressing, was that we were employees, not owners," says Eichenholtz. "I said that if this is going to work the concept of partnership has to be understood. He just didn't want to hear that. . . . I remember earlier on," says Eichenholtz, "when I'd told him the same thing, and he'd said, 'This is crazy. You guys are employees working for an employer!' I'm convinced that he reinforced that view with Martin. There was no getting through to him."

At Y&R, Cooper and CEO Kroll are sensitive to Lord's autonomy needs, and they and Skadden's Goldberg come up with a plan that will ensure that Lord can deal with Y&R on key questions such as account assignments without a war. If Y&R wants to block Lord from taking on an account it can do so, but its act of blocking an account in the face of Lord's continued desire to accept it will trigger a deadlock that will allow Lord to seek financing from a new partner—a situation presenting difficulties for both Lord and Y&R, and, explains Cooper, "assuring that we deal with each other as partners in good faith, not as owner-employees, which is just how we mean to deal with each other." Later, that arrangement will head off claims by Sorrell's lawyers that Lord's complaints about autonomy were a sham, as evidenced, they will assert wrongly, by the fact that he won't have autonomy at Y&R either.

On Thursday, March 17, the group, in concert with Cooper at Y&R and the Skadden lawyers, decide that Friday will be departure day.

There is a clause in the Lord, Geller employee manual requiring all employees to give two weeks' notice, but Schwarz decides that his clients will have to violate it because were they to stay for two weeks after giving notice (assuming Sorrell would have them stay) they might have contacts with employees or clients that could constitute, or could be claimed to constitute, pre-departure solicitation.

"I decided that that would be too messy," Schwarz explains. "Besides, it's not at all clear in New York that an employee manual constitutes a contractual obligation."

"I wanted to have a meeting and tell all the people Wednesday or Thursday what we were doing and why," says Lord. "These employees were like my family. But the lawyers wouldn't let me do anything except tell my secretary on Thursday that I might be leaving—and that's only because I fought with them on that," he recalls.

Indeed, these are not sophisticated business clients, easy to control, and on Thursday three of the group break their silence enough to tell another secretary or a close colleague that they may be leaving. Beyond that, though, no one knows; the lawyers' instructions are followed to a T.

In fact, they are arguably followed too literally. The Skadden lawyers told their clients to take no papers with them, so the six even leave behind personal papers, such as household utility bills.

They were also told to keep doing Lord, Geller work right up to the end; accordingly, on the morning of March 18, the Friday the six quit, Einstein comes in early to finish work on three *New Yorker* ads, while O'Neill works up to the minute the six walk out at 10:30 A.M. coordinating the filming of some IBM commercials that have to be finished before a threatened actors' strike.

"These guys must have been tightly controlled by their lawyers," says one Lord, Geller client who intends to switch to the new agency, called Lord Einstein O'Neill and Partners. "I called Friday morning looking for Arthur [Einstein] and was told that he'd quit," this client recalls. "I told his secretary that she must be kidding, that I'd talked to him the night before about my ads. She wouldn't even tell me where to reach him."

Also at Schwarz's instruction, the six leave behind a memo for all Lord, Geller employees, urging them to "do everything possible to keep the machine ticking smoothly and continue to give LGFE clients the service and advertising they have come to expect."

STORYBOARD #11:
REISS'S OVERREACTION

To Reiss and Sorrell, the good-bye memo is a cynical charade. "These guys were pissing on the place on their way out, trying to wreck it," says Reiss. "It's what they'd wanted to do all along because they just didn't like Martin and they were bitter about all their friends who'd made five, ten, a hundred million dollars selling out when they'd made nothing. . . . You can bet I was pissed off when I found out."

Reiss got the news of the departures, he says, when copies of the resignation letters were hand-delivered to him at about 10 A.M. "I thought it was a joke. I mean, we were still negotiating with these guys," he recalls.

"I called Martin [who had come to New York to negotiate with Lord] and then, yes, I sat down with my litigators to figure out how we could sue."

Great damage has already been done either by the unwise legal advice Sorrell has received—that his "assets" are secure, that these people can't or won't walk—or by Sorrell's own intransigence, or by some combination of the two. But now that damage is about to be compounded by Reiss's scorched-earth litigation.

Rather than work quietly to stem the losses at the agency while preparing a damage suit against Lord once damages, if any, were ascertained, Reiss and his people "went right to work that weekend" preparing a complaint, he says.

Thus, what would have been a one-day story in the trade press (and in the media business sections of *The New York Times* and *The Wall Street Journal*) becomes an ongoing saga based on an immediately launched court fight—centered on Reiss's claim, as spelled out in his complaint filed the following Tuesday, March 22, that the defendants' actions would "cripple" Lord, Geller.

The complaint—which seeks damages from both the six defectors and Y&R equivalent to the value of Lord, Geller and an injunction prohibiting them from taking any Lord, Geller business or employees—assures that Lord, Geller clients and employees will presume the worst about their agency.

The case is assigned to Herman Cahn. Because of vacancies on the higher trial court, Cahn is sitting as an acting supreme court justice and he's just recently been assigned to handle civil cases. Cahn seems intelligent and hardworking. But he'll have trouble dealing with this high-powered, complicated civil suit.

Davis & Gilbert files a separate motion the next day (Wednesday, March 23), seeking a preliminary injunction to keep the new Lord Einstein from soliciting or accepting any Lord, Geller clients or employees or using the Lord name. Again the agency's threatened destruction is stressed, accompanied, as could have been expected, by new press stories of the agency's destruction.

Reiss will later assert that the injunction effort was necessary because several key Lord, Geller employees had defected to Lord Einstein on Monday. But those employees would later file affidavits swearing that they were not solicited by Lord and his émigrés but were so put off by Sorrell, who met with them over the weekend, and so eager to keep working with Lord and the others, that they decided to quit on their own.

Reiss's lead litigator is Patricia Hatry, 51. Hatry has a good reputation, especially in trademark, unfair advertising, and similar types of cases that are her firm's standard fare. But the papers she files in this case are disorganized, almost desperate in tone, perhaps because she and others at the firm have so little to go on in moving so fast—or perhaps because they're just not used to moving so fast.

All that Sorrell's lawyers are accomplishing, at best, is putting Lord and his people on the defensive, while torching their own shop by undermining whatever confidence any clients may continue to have in Lord, Geller.

"We had pep rallies on Tuesday and Wednesday with Sorrell, and he assured us that the agency was in fine shape," recalls one man who quit later that week. "But then we'd read in the papers that he was in court declaring that Lord had destroyed his agency. You can imagine the effect this had on us, and on our clients."

By March 23 IBM's ad people demand that Sorrell detail for them how he intends to staff their work; when a good enough answer is not forthcoming they switch some projects to Lord Einstein, which by now is housed temporarily in some extra Y&R space.

On March 28 Hatry files a memorandum in support of her preliminary injunction motion. It begins with a nice rhetorical flourish that must have pleased Sorrell: "The individual defendants sold their advertising agency in 1974. In 1987, they decided they wanted it back; when the owner refused to sell, they proceeded to steal it."

It is nicely put, but as one lawyer who knows Judge Cahn puts it, "This is a guy who sees real people steal real things; he's probably not thrilled with rhetoric like that."

The rest of Hatry's memorandum is disjointed, presenting a pet point of Reiss's—that Lord and his key managers had breached fiduciary responsibility by so damaging Lord, Geller—along with half a dozen others. But in essence the memo makes no point other than that the Lord group's exodus had ruined the Lord, Geller agency.

However, Hatry is helped by one set of documents the Lord group has left behind. In Ed Yaconetti's office private detectives hired by Davis & Gilbert to canvass the émigrés' offices find several memos, most importantly one that is described at the top as notes of the November 17 meeting with the "legals"—Schwarz and Goldberg of Skadden. (The detectives, from the usually sophisticated Kroll Associates Inc., also make fools of themselves by reporting such "discoveries" as the fact that Lord's and Einstein's personal desks had few client files, the baseless implication being that they had taken them, and that Yaconetti had been seen leaving his office with a duffel bag—which, he later explained in a lighthearted affidavit, contained his jockstrap and other gym equipment.)

But the Yaconetti memo is good stuff, at least on the surface. It outlines a series of options supposedly discussed at the November Skadden meeting, including a "slowdown" at the agency in order to cause a "confrontation" with Sorrell and a "hardball walk to the door" if Sorrell refuses a leveraged buyout.

(The same memo seems to indicate that Schwarz had opined to the group that in the event they quit, Sorrell was unlikely to sue, not only because he wouldn't win, but also because of the "potential disruption and negative impact a court fight of this type could have on client relationships." Schwarz apparently overestimated Sorrell's wisdom, or that of his counsel. Hatry, ironically, misuses this notation in her memorandum as evidence that the Lord group planned to disrupt client relationships.)

Another of Yaconetti's notes lists "clients we would probably want to take or hope to take with us," which Hatry presents as evidence of a conspiracy to solicit clients before departing.

STORYBOARD #12:
SCHWARZ HOLDS HIS FIRE

It would seem that the first question raised by Yaconetti's memo is why it isn't privileged as a lawyer-client communication. After all, notes of a discussion with one's lawyer about one's options would seem to be protected.

Schwarz first learns of the Yaconetti memo when he gets a call from a reporter who has been furnished a copy of Hatry's memorandum with accompanying exhibits (of which a printout of the memo was one) by Davis & Gilbert. Schwarz toys at first with the idea of asking the judge to exclude it. But he decides that because there is mixed case law on the issue (some courts have ruled that lawyer-client documents left where others can find them are not protected) and because the judge and the press already have it, asking for a separate hearing on the question of its admissibility would only magnify its importance. In short, Schwarz doesn't do what Reiss and Hatry have persisted in doing— litigate with a flourish without regard to his client's real, long-term best interests.

(That, of course, begs the question of whether it might have been more appropriate for Reiss and Hatry first to contact Schwarz and ask him if he was inclined to contest the admissibility of the questionable document before releasing it to the judge, let alone to the press. Reiss says, "We knew there was no question about the document being protected because the guy had left it in his office.'')

STORYBOARD #13:
Y&R CHOOSES THE RIGHT COUNSEL

Reiss and Hatry have named Young & Rubicam as co-conspirator co-defendants in the suit (and, inexplicably, as co-defendants in the injunction motion, even though they really aren't seeking to enjoin Y&R from anything and, thus, are giving the defendants two lawyers instead of one at any hearing). Indeed, if there is a culpable conspiracy Y&R is, indeed, a likely defendant. After all, Y&R provided financing to the new agency, is a major big-agency competitor of J. Walter, and is now housing the new Lord Einstein in its own offices.

For just those reasons Y&R general counsel Cooper decides that he wants Y&R's counsel to be one that will not get the firm into the public eye, and, therefore, into any fallout from this litigation, any more than it has to. So, while he wants a big-firm lawyer to look after his interests in dealing with Skadden, he doesn't want someone who would push himself and Y&R into the limelight as, say, a swashbuckling litigator from Cravath, Swaine & Moore might do. (Cooper, a Cravath alumnus, has frequently used that firm, as well as Rosenman & Colin.)

Thus, Cooper chooses Stephen Oxman, a friend at Shearman & Sterling, whom Cooper knows to be highly skilled but not at all overbearing.

It's a wise choice; Oxman and his associates do an excellent job backing up Schwarz, but Y&R stays out of most of the press stories about the litigation.

STORYBOARD #14:
DAVIS & GILBERT OUTCLASSED IN COURT

It is March 28 in Acting Justice Cahn's dingy courtroom in the civil court building. Patricia Hatry is trying to get her injunction.

''I represent the once-proud advertising agency of Lord, Geller,'' she begins. ''This agency until March 18 enjoyed one of the finest reputations of any advertising agency in the city or in the country. . . . That was, until March 18. . . . Ten days ago . . . six men walked out . . . like thieves in the night.''

Thus Hatry negates her own client's continuing attempt to assure the world and the Lord, Geller staff that Lord, Geller is still functioning.

But she achieves little else. Her presentation, such as it is, is halting, disorganized, formless. The judge cuts her off quickly, giving the floor to Schwarz.

His brief has strongly argued that the employment agreement's no-compete clause was not valid because it had long since expired and/or been negated by Sorrell's usurpation of Lord, Geller's autonomy with the Alfa Romeo and Saturn disputes. But Schwarz senses, unlike Hatry, that the judge wants, or can only cope with, a brief, simple argument; he'll save the no-compete clause for an appeal, if necessary. So he argues the invalidity of the no-compete clause only briefly, then quickly jumps to his key points:

- That the Yaconetti memorandum is only a series of ''ruminations.''
- That there is no evidence anyone at Lord, Geller had slowed down anything prior to the walkout, and that the only direct evidence—a series of affidavits Schwarz had submitted from the defecting six and from others describing their work up until the minute of the walkout—proved just the opposite.
- That unlike the situation in the Duane Jones case there is no evidence of any pre-solicitation of employees (again, his brief had included convincing affidavits) or clients.
- That despite the fact that he doesn't believe the no-compete clause in the 1974 contract to be valid, his clients were nonetheless abiding by it and not soliciting or meeting with any Lord, Geller clients.
- That no doctrine of employee fiduciary responsibility prohibits employees or directors from soliciting employees or clients after they have left their company.
- And most of all, that Sorrell's side, which had already put a price tag on its damages, would not suffer irreparable harm—the crucial test for granting an injunction before the evidence has been heard at a trial—because damages could be awarded were Sorrell to win. Schwarz's clients, on the other hand, would suffer irreparable harm if they were enjoined from accepting business, hiring employees, using the Lord Einstein name, or otherwise going about their start-up.

As for Y&R, Oxman argues briefly that Y&R had acted properly, had instructed the Lord group to act properly, and wasn't really involved in any activity that Hatry sought to enjoin anyway.

STORYBOARD #15:
REISS CLAIMS VICTORY

On April 5 Cahn hands down a decision on the preliminary injunction motion that is hardly a masterwork but seems clearly to side with Schwarz and his clients. He begins with an overbroad, even bizarre, interpretation of the Jones case—declaring that "the common law implies a duty of loyalty between an employer and employee which prohibits employees from conspiring to set up a competing business while they are still working for their employer." (Of course, a group of employees can plan to set out on their own as long as they don't solicit clients while still on the job.) But he goes on to accept most of Schwarz's argument, if for reasons he leaves unclear.

The new Lord Einstein agency is enjoined, he rules, but only from soliciting employees of the old Lord, Geller. Moreover, Lord and Einstein individually—the two men of the six who had signed those 1974 contracts—are enjoined from personally soliciting or accepting any business from Lord, Geller clients; but such soliciting or accepting is defined, along the lines of the old contract, as meaning only that they can't personally meet with those clients.

Thus, to take one example, *The New Yorker* and its president, Steven Florio, who has announced his switch to Lord Einstein, can meet there with Kevin O'Neill, the creative director for the account, but Florio can't converse directly with Lord or Einstein.

Because Schwarz had instructed his clients to abide by the 1974 agreement as if it were valid, and since the Lord people were not soliciting employees anyway but were accepting them as they departed Lord, Geller, the judge's decision has no negative impact on the agency's operations.

Nonetheless, Reiss declares it a victory, and the press, giving at least some credence to his spin on things—and the spin offered up by PR men from Kekst & Company, whom Sorrell has hired despite the fact that his WPP Group owns a rival PR firm, Hill and Knowlton—reports the ruling as a mixed result and, in some cases, even one that is favorable to Sorrell.

Yet, when it comes time for each of the two sides to draft an order for the judge to sign enforcing the injunction, Davis & Gilbert submits a draft—along with a new memorandum of law—rearguing the motion and asking that the entire agency be enjoined from accepting the business of former clients or hiring former employees. (Schwarz, for his part, submits a draft order that is simply consistent with the ruling that Reiss and the men from Kekst had told the press was their "victory.")

STORYBOARD #16:
SORRELL'S COUNSEL OUTCLASSED AGAIN, BUT GAIN A SMALL VICTORY—FOR NOW

A week later, on April 14, Hatry, Schwarz, and Oxman are back in court, and Hatry is arguing not only for her draft order but for a new injunction that will do what she had wanted the first injunction to do—stop Lord Einstein from hiring any Lord, Geller employee or doing work for any Lord, Geller client.

This time she seems even more unsure of herself than in the first appearance. Her voice cracking and barely audible in a courtroom that is an acoustical abomination, she wanders from point to point as the judge interrupts to try to help her.

"An injunction that says an individual cannot accept an account is meaningless," she says, referring to last week's "victory."

Perhaps now mindful of the PR damage her prior litigating has done her client, Hatry declares that Lord, Geller is still able to service the IBM account, then asserts in the next breath that the agency has been stripped of its IBM copywriter, art director, and others working the account.

But, at least in the judge's mind, Hatry has something extra going for her this time. Discovery since the first hearing has revealed documents at Lord Einstein and Y&R in which the Lord group seems to speculate further about which clients it plans to get, and, worse in the judge's eyes, which key Lord, Geller employees it hopes to hire. The list of those employees, Hatry argues in her memo and, with the judge's urging, in her oral presentation, is remarkably similar to a list of those employees whom the Lord group has, in fact, now hired—which suggests that they planned to lure them away and did, in fact, lure them away.

Schwarz argues, though, that those discovered documents simply indicate who the Lord group hoped might join them and, most important, that they present no proof at all that there was any solicitation of those employees, let alone any pre-solicitation. (He doesn't mention, as Lord later explains, that it was their lawyers' warnings that headed off whatever pre-solicitation Lord and the five others might have been inclined to attempt.) Schwarz adds that he has just submitted affidavits from all employees hired by Lord Einstein specifically rebutting any suggestion of solicitation. He also reiterates his irreparable harm argument.

But the judge seems impressed by Hatry's documents. "Something in his stomach told him something was wrong," Reiss would explain gleefully the next morning. "This is a judge with a good stomach."

Thus, despite the lack of any hard evidence of solicitation, after hearing more argument in chambers Cahn announces from the bench that he's withholding a decision on Hatry's new motion pending testimony from the hired employees and perhaps from some clients. He also says that pending that hearing and his decision, which together will take at least two weeks (Schwarz wanted the hearing to begin the next morning, but Hatry prevailed on the judge to wait a week), he is expanding the injunction to forbid Lord Einstein from hiring any more Lord, Geller employees, whether they solicit them or not. Moreover, he says that at least until the hearing he won't allow the Lord Einstein agency—not simply Lord and Einstein personally, as he had decided before—to take on any Lord, Geller business that it has not already taken on.

Finally, Hatry and Reiss have won something, though by now the press has grown tired of the fight and the headlines are relatively tame.

But what they've won, I'll bet, is short-lived and hardly worth all that they lost before.

Amid buoyant pronouncements the next morning about how the "judge's stomach" has "given us real relief," Reiss is unable to claim any direct evidence Hatry will be able to present at the following week's hearing of the Lord group soliciting clients or employees, let alone soliciting them before their departures. Schwarz, on the other hand, promises 43 witnesses (the number of hired employees) who will all say they were not solicited, and "as many clients as the judge wants me to bring in" to say that they, too, were not solicited.

Schwarz also says he intends to ask the judge to expand the hearing to include the question of irreparable harm, and in that regard he may have a new ace up his sleeve. At press time he and Oxman were talking about having Y&R indemnify the Lord Einstein agency, plus the Lord group as individuals, against all damages—which would give Sorrell a way to recover the full value of his Lord, Geller agency were he to win at a trial and prove those damages.

That indemnity would come on cue from Judge Cahn, who at the April 14 hearing asked Schwarz pointedly if he was asserting that there was no possibility of irreparable (that is nonrecoverable) damage to Sorrell because Y&R had indemnified the new agency and was certainly big enough and rich enough to cover any damage claim. Cahn misunderstood Schwarz to be saying that, but at the time no such indemnity existed. "However, it sounds like a good idea and something the judge will like," noted one lawyer after the hearing.

STORYBOARD #17:
RIDING THE VICTORY TO NOWHERE

"I suppose," says Reiss, the morning after the second hearing, "that if Y&R offers the indemnity, we'll lose our irreparable harm argument." And, he concedes, "We have a ways to go filling in the gap between the memos [in which the Lord group speculated about whom they would like to hire] and finding pre-solicitation. But," he asserts, "if we can't find hard evidence of soliciting and lose the injunction we'll still have a real damages case based on this theory of mine of fiduciary responsibility.

"It may take until it gets to the court of appeals," Reiss continues, "but I'm convinced that in this age of management buyouts some judge is going to come along and say that there comes a time—especially when the owner says, 'No, I won't sell to you managers'—when the directors and managers have a fiduciary responsibility to abandon the idea and run the business or to quit—but not to plan a new business while they're running the old one.

"You know," Reiss concludes, "there are some fascinating issues here. America is becoming a service economy, based on personal service businesses. And some judge is going to have to decide what assets really are in a personal service business. It's a case of the rights of the owners against the rights of people who are the assets the owners own."

It's a thoughtful argument, about an engaging, important issue. But it's a case Reiss and his client could have brought without the destructive hoopla of their injunction motions, their press releases, and their PR men, all of which operated to exacerbate the damage caused by the Lord Einstein walkout.

Managements plotting to buy the company out from their owners, let alone plotting a competing company as an alternative, do, indeed, have inherent conflicts. A manager who has already sold his company seems an especially unsympathetic balancer of those conflicts. And owners who buy personal service businesses arguably have a right to own what they've bought.

Then again, what of Lord's argument that simply because he is seeking the independence he once enjoyed, and because his personal talents and those of the people loyal to him are so unique, he cannot be restricted from exploiting those talents by his "owner" as if he were a patent or a steel mill? As he put it in one affidavit. "Plaintiffs are . . . seeking to prevent me and other individuals named as defendants from earning a living in the business in which some of us have been engaged for in excess of thirty years."

In short, it could have been an interesting case—one that Lord Einstein and Y&R, cognizant of the possible appeal of these issues to some jurisprudentially minded judge at an appellate level, might have been willing to settle. Confronted with these issues in a clearly reasoned, focused argument by skilled counsel, they might well have been willing to give Sorrell (who seems to be experiencing some of the same talent-drain problems at his far larger J. Walter purchase) a portion of the money he lost when he didn't sell to Lord and his group.

At press time Judge Cahn's hearing with the employee and client witnesses had just started (and Lord Einstein, which had just won a lucrative account from Saab, had filed a counterclaim against Sorrell for interfering with the new agency, for spreading "false and defamatory" information about the new agency to the press and to prospective clients, and for not paying Lord and his partners their 1987 bonuses and phantom stock entitlements). Cahn was at least a week away from rendering his decision on Hatry's motion for the expanded injunction.

But for now all that Sorrell has—courtesy, at least in part, of lawyers who counseled him aggressively but unwisely in the face of opposing lawyers who did just about everything right—is a wounded ad agency, wounded worse by litigation that put his lawyers front and center in the trade press while magnifying his agency's troubles. And he faces opponents who aren't nearly as likely to settle the main complaint, much less drop their new countersuit, because they'll be so buoyed when, I'm willing to bet, either the judge or an appeals court gives them their injunction victory.

Moreover, assuming Sorrell goes ahead with the damages case (and he might not for fear of still more publicity, once he's discouraged by what's so likely to be the loss of the injunction motions), his best claim—Reiss's fiduciary conflict idea, which is a long shot, anyway—will likely be blurred by all the other claims Hatry threw in front of the same judge in her frenzied injunction papers.

Whether he gets it from Judge Cahn or, if Cahn is still too befuddled, from an appeals court, Richard Lord will have his freedom because his lawyers didn't miss a trick. And Sorrell will have killed off his classy ad agency because his lawyers, from the day he took over his "assets," were tough when they should have been wise.

EPILOGUE

Hearings on the injunction were held intermittently from April until mid-July 1988. Once the hearings ended, the agencies expected that Judge Herman Cahn would rule promptly, since there was a temporary order in place barring Lord Einstein O'Neill and Partners from accepting Lord, Geller clients or employees. But no ruling came until the fall.

In October 1988, Lord Einstein advised Judge Cahn that it had no plans to do business with existing Lord, Geller clients pending a decision on Lord, Geller's motion for a preliminary injunction. Accordingly, the two agencies agreed that the temporary restraining order would be lifted. Judge Cahn finally vacated the order on October 18, 1988.

IBM passed over both disputing agencies to split its approximately $100 million account between two other New York City advertising firms. The decision stripped Lord, Geller of about two-thirds of its $180 million billings and raised the possibility that it would be disbanded and merged into one of Sorrell's companies, such as J. Walter Thompson or Ogilvy & Mather. In September 1988 Lord, Geller laid off more than ninety people, close to a third of its staff.

Lord Einstein had been one of five finalists for the IBM business and while it lost out on that account, it has achieved billings of $94 million, with a staff of 92.

Cipollone
v.
Liggett Group, Inc.,
et al.

THEY DIDN'T REALLY BLAME THE CIGARETTE MAKERS

BY

AMY SINGER

The Cipollone *jurors handed the tobacco industry its first defeat in a product liability case. But the verdict may mean less than it seems to mean.*

One juror was crying. It was June 13, and the jury in *Cipollone* v. *Liggett Group, Inc., et al.* had just announced its verdict. But this woman regretted the decision. She would have preferred announcing that the jury was hung. The others, however, had finally persuaded her to vote with them.

"I was told no way were they letting me out," she says. "I was told I blew the whole case because I didn't want to give any money. . . . They made me think maybe I was wrong. Pressure can be very bad. . . . I gave in. But now I'm sorry."

Banner headlines the next morning proclaimed the first victory against a tobacco company in a product liability suit. Even if it was against her

397

will, this juror and her five colleagues had found that by advertising cigarettes with such phrases as "Play Safe" and "Just What the Doctor Ordered," Liggett had made express warranties to consumers—pledges that cigarettes were not harmful—and had breached those warranties. They also found that Liggett had failed to warn consumers of the potential hazards of smoking. The panel awarded $400,000 in damages to plaintiff Antonio Cipollone—but no damages to the estate of his wife, Rose Cipollone, who smoked for more than 40 years and died of lung cancer in 1984, 14 months after filing the suit.

While the verdict was generally perceived outside the jury room as a brilliant victory for plaintiff's counsel Marc Edell of Short Hills, New Jersey's Budd Larner Gross Picillo Rosenbaum Greenberg & Sade, inside the jury room it was another story. Certainly, if upheld, the verdict may prove to be a devastating blow to the tobacco industry. But it could have been much worse. In fact, the decision should give the tobacco companies some comfort. For a majority of the jury thought that Rose Cipollone didn't deserve one penny from the cigarette makers. They viewed her as an independent woman who made her own informed decision about smoking and who was responsible for her own death. They agreed to award damages only after two of the six jurors refused to give in unless a compromise—granting her husband some small amount—was reached.

The jurors had four basic claims to consider against Liggett and its co-defendants, Philip Morris Incorporated and Loews Corporation, the parent company of Lorillard, Inc.: fraudulent misrepresentation and/or concealment; conspiracy; failure to warn; and breach of express warranty. Since Cipollone had not smoked Philip Morris or Lorillard cigarettes until after 1966—the year warnings went on cigarette packages—the failure to warn and breach of express warranty claims against those two companies were dismissed in a directed verdict. Liggett, facing all four claims, had the most at risk.

The jurors rejected all claims of fraud, conspiracy, and concealment, thus completely exonerating Philip Morris and Lorillard. They found that Liggett had breached its express warranties and that the company should have warned consumers prior to 1966 about the health risks of smoking. But they also decided that Cipollone was 80 percent at fault.

A certain feeling of gloom and confusion had passed over many of the 11 jurors in federal district judge H. Lee Sarokin's ornate Newark, New

Jersey, courtroom on June 7 as the clerk handed each of them copies of the 72-page charge and the 20 interrogatories they would have to answer. Six jurors would be chosen, by lottery, to deliberate after the charge was read. Throughout the trial each of the four men and seven women (a fifth man was excused midway) appeared to listen attentively—some even took copious notes—to testimony that covered everything from the location of Cipollone's tumors to the internal documents of the three companies. The issues had always seemed complex, but now as the judge was about to instruct the jurors, the true difficulty of their task became apparent. "I was shocked," says one woman who was selected to deliberate. "I wanted to raise my hand and say, 'I resign.' "

"I didn't know it was going to be like different charges," says Ralph Eliseo, another of the six jurors chosen. "I thought it was just going to be, did she smoke cigarettes because she wanted to or because she was forced to? Was it her fault or was it the tobacco companies' fault? Period. I didn't know it was going to be fraud and conspiracy. When I think of conspiracy I think of overthrowing governments. Conspiracy? It's like everyone's running around in secret and the secretaries don't know what the executives are doing."

To some extent that was the idea that plaintiff's counsel Edell wanted to impart. But for most of the three men and three women who deliberated, his portrayal of an "evil-minded conspiracy" just didn't wash. Four of the six jurors felt the company documents that Edell had emphasized amounted to nothing. Strongly convinced that Rose Cipollone was to blame for her death, these four went into the jury room ready to vote not guilty on every count. "I thought we were gonna be in there five minutes," says Eliseo. Indeed, the first vote went 4 to 2 in favor of the defendants on all counts.

What the four defense-minded jurors encountered were two jurors who, "if they had their whole say, would have found [the tobacco companies] guilty of anything and everything," says one of the majority. One of the dissenters, says this juror, was especially adamant. His attitude was, "Let's be the first jury to hang them," she recalls. For the next five days the six jurors battled it out. Ultimately there was a compromise, but the four stood firm on the one thing they felt most strongly about: Rose Cipollone knew what she was doing when she chose to smoke.

Edell had focused his case on the tobacco companies' responsibility, but he knew that Rose Cipollone's awareness of the hazards of smoking was a hurdle he had to get over. He asked the jurors to try to put themselves back in 1941 and forget everything they know today about smoking and cancer. For many that task was just too hard. "We're in 1988 and you're supposed to blot out in your mind everything that happened in the fifties, sixties, and seventies," says one juror. "How can you make believe you don't know what happened after that?"

The two jurors who felt strongly for the plaintiff declined to comment for this story. (In fact they were so secretive about the deliberations that right after announcing the verdict, they shredded the materials the group had used.) But the comments of four jurors and five alternates make one thing quite clear: the defense strategy of focusing on the plaintiff's awareness of the risks of smoking—a tactic that was successful in previous tobacco cases and that was again found to be successful during jury research in preparation for *Cipollone*—worked once more.

The four-and-a-half-month trial was a pull-out-all-the-stops affair with impressive lawyering on both sides. Chief among those representing the defendants were Donald Cohn, Francis Decker, Jr., and James Kearney of New York's Webster & Sheffield, for Liggett; Peter Bleakley and Thomas Silfen of D.C.'s Arnold & Porter, for Philip Morris; and Robert Northrip, Steven Parrish, and Patrick Sirridge of Kansas City, Missouri's Shook, Hardy & Bacon, for Philip Morris and Lorillard. Representing the plaintiffs were Edell, his associate Cynthia Walters, and Alan Darnell, a partner at Woodbridge, New Jersey's Wilentz, Goldman & Spitzer.

The three defendants opened their case on April 7 with Fred Carstensen, an economics professor from the University of Connecticut, whose testimony was intended to prove that by the late 1940s, the public was aware of claims that cigarettes could cause cancer. He gave a slide show on the history of tobacco usage and testified about the abundance of information available to the public on the hazards of smoking. In a striking display of blowups, he showed excerpts of some 700 articles that appeared in the three newspapers he searched; each juror also received a binder that contained more than 300 articles that Mrs. Cipollone might have read. (Edell tried to establish that Carstensen was not qualified to discuss the "information environment" since he had never done a study of smoking and health. Several jurors, nonetheless, say they enjoyed his presentation.)

Following Carstensen was Claude Martin, a professor at the University of Michigan School of Business Administration, who testified that advertising and public relations have very little effect on a consumer's decision to smoke. Tobacco companies spend billions of dollars advertising, he said, because they are afraid not to. They also want to convince smokers to switch brands.

The most interesting thing about Martin's testimony was a question from Judge Sarokin. During a break in the professor's cross-examination, while Edell was preparing a document to show the jury, Sarokin asked, "If a cigarette manufacturer put out an ad showing an attractive young woman in a tennis outfit in a nice setting or put an ad showing a funeral for that woman and said, 'Smoking kills,' you mean that second ad would not have an impact upon the information environment?"

When Martin equivocated, Sarokin rephrased the question twice. Arnold & Porter's Peter Bleakley, representing Philip Morris, finally objected and approached the bench. "A jury is inevitably going to come to the conclusion that Your Honor has very strongly held views on this subject and I think it is extremely prejudicial and I must object," Bleakley argued.

In fact, several jurors seem to have shared the defense counsel's annoyance with Sarokin. "I thought that was terrible of the judge. I felt that [question] was something the attorneys should have argued, not the judge," says one juror. "Who would ever put out an advertisement of someone in a coffin? That was stupid. . . . It didn't sway how the jurors felt, that's for sure."

Nevertheless, most of them were quite fond of Sarokin, though some feel he sometimes went a little easy on Edell and associate Cynthia Walters. Walters was in charge of the plaintiff's medical witnesses, and several jurors were flabbergasted at some of the things they thought she got away with during cross-examination. The plaintiff and defense differed on the type of cancer Cipollone had, and Walters asked some witnesses if they agreed with certain medical authorities. "The witness would say no," recalls one juror. But this juror and several others noticed Walters wrote something else on an oversized pad of paper. "No one objected," this juror says. "I couldn't understand it."

Actually, the defense lawyers had objected, though the substance of their objections was heard at sidebar. For her part, Walters says, "I wasn't writing anything different from what the authorities said."

"[Walters] got away with a lot," agrees another juror. "She sat there at the table and made faces all the time. I don't think she was very professional." Replies Walters: "I probably didn't even know I was doing that."

Walters did get some high marks. "I admired how she could compete with all the doctors," says alternate juror Zlata Janegova, a 43-year-old high school math and physics teacher who grew up in Czechoslovakia. "I was wondering if she had a doctor degree."

The first medical witness for the defense was Dr. Sheldon Sommers, one of six pathologists who had diagnosed Rose Cipollone's cancer and a former scientific director of the industry-sponsored Council for Tobacco Research. Three pathologists—who examined the tumor after Sommers—had diagnosed it as a small cell carcinoma. Sommers and two others, however, called it an atypical carcinoid—a rarer cancer less clearly linked to cigarette smoking than small cell.

The defense succeeded—at the very least—in raising considerable doubt about the kind of cancer Cipollone had and whether smoking had caused it. Only one juror was convinced that Cipollone had small cell cancer and that it had been caused by smoking. The other five weren't certain but thought she probably had atypical, or possibly both. "If these men who graduated first in their class can't figure it out, how can you expect twelve people who never heard of carcinoma to figure it out?" says juror Eliseo.

The defense closed its case on May 18 with a short reading from Rose Cipollone's deposition, chosen in part to emphasize the idea that Cipollone smoked because she enjoyed it despite her fear of cancer. Budd Larner associate Walters objected to portions of the selection on the basis that the jury had already heard several references to the pleasure Cipollone got from smoking. Sarokin limited the portions that Liggett counsel James Kearney could read but did allow him some leeway. The passages Kearney chose showed Cipollone to be stubborn and implied that the difficulty of quitting frightened her.

Kearney read the questions and a Shook, Hardy secretary, playing the part of Rose Cipollone, read the answers:

You said earlier, and I don't want to repeat this, but just by way of background, that you enjoyed smoking cigarettes. Correct?
Yes.
That they gave you pleasure?
Yes.
You liked to smoke when you had a cup of coffee?
Yes.
You liked to smoke after meals?
Yes.

You liked to smoke at card games?
You have to slow down. I can't talk as fast as you. I'm sorry. I can't.
You liked to smoke at card games?
Yes.
You liked to smoke at bingo games?
Yes.
You liked to smoke when you were sitting talking to your sister?
Yes.
You liked to smoke while you were watching wrestling matches?
Yes.
So there were a lot of situations where you enjoyed smoking. Correct?
When I smoked.

Kearney skipped ahead:

But anyway, you smoked while doing various activities in your daily life.
    Isn't that true?
And I smoked when I didn't do activities. I have sat and I smoked, too.
    I read and I smoked.
You enjoyed reading?
Yes, very much.
You were an avid reader, I think you told us?
Yes, I still am.
This was a pleasure that we can fairly say you didn't want to give up.
    Isn't that true?
I wouldn't say I wouldn't want to give it up. I said it was very hard for
    me to give it up.
I remember you said in 1965 when you were talking to your doctor who
    was treating you, I think you were hospitalized around that time, that
    you probably held out on him as to the number of cigarettes you
    smoked. Do you remember telling us that?
Yes.
You didn't want the doctor to hassle you about your smoking at that time,
    did you?
Correct.
You didn't want the doctor to tell you to give up your pleasure, did you?
Correct.
You weren't going to tell him that cigarettes were safe, were you?
Why would I tell him that?

Skipping again:

You wanted to avoid the whole discussion with your doctor about ciga-
  rettes?
Probably.
That is because you wanted to continue smoking and you didn't want
  anybody to interfere with your pleasure of smoking, did you?
No.
What I said is true? When you said no, it was a little ambiguous. What
  I said is true, isn't it? You didn't want anybody to interfere with your
  pleasure of cigarettes, even that doctor. Isn't that true?
I will put it another way. I didn't want to give up cigarettes because it was
  hard to give up cigarettes. Let us put it that way.
It might have been hard. We can also put it that you wanted—
I was weak.
And maybe you wanted to continue your pleasure. That was part of it,
  wasn't it?
Okay. If you say so.
I say so. Does that make it true?
If you say so. Fine.
When you say that, you will understand that we can't know later whether
  you are agreeing with the fact or just agreeing with me so I
  will stop asking questions. You know that, don't you? Don't you know
  that?
Know what? I don't know what you are trying to say.
I am probably not being clear.
Maybe you are not. I am sorry.

The defense selection made a distinct impression. "It changed the
whole picture," says alternate Gloria Gooden, a 43-year-old nurse's aide.
"The lady knew what she was doing. She was an intelligent woman. . . .
She was a well-read woman. She was strong. . . . She did it because she
wanted to do it."

For rebuttal, Edell recalled his first witness, Dr. Jeffrey Harris, an
M.D. and Ph.D. who teaches economics and health at Massachusetts
Institute of Technology and Harvard Medical School. Harris's initial
six-day testimony had focused on what the scientific community knew
about the possible ill effects of cigarette smoking as early as the 1930s.
In his original appearance he had testified that if he had been advising

Liggett in 1955, he would have recommended that the company tell consumers about the potential hazards of smoking.

Harris returned in part to testify about the significance of some 30,000 internal Philip Morris and Lorillard documents that he had reviewed since his first appearance. One of these documents referred to a "gentleman's agreement" among the tobacco companies to refrain from doing in-house biological research. It seemed to buttress Edell's theory that the industry had conspired to do nonproductive research and to withhold information from the public, but not all the jurors thought so. "All the major companies stick together in cahoots," says Eliseo. "I think it was just a phrase."

Though several jurors thought Harris was smart, some were discouraged when they heard he was coming back to testify. "Remember your impression of your first blind date?" asks one. "I thought he was gonna drone on for another week, but he only droned on for another day."

On cross, Harris deflected much of the defense hostility and stood his ground. But this bothered one juror. "They kind of pinned him down where he should have said something favorable to the defendants, and he just wouldn't admit he was wrong," she says. "That had a distinct impression on me. I wanted to hear the facts. If he found something bad I wanted him to admit it. Of course, you expected it. Mr. Edell was paying him."

Following a prearranged schedule, Webster & Sheffield partner Donald Cohn, representing Liggett, closed first, starting on Wednesday, June 1. Before a standing-room crowd, Cohn gave a low-key, three-and-a-half-hour summation in which he continually repeated his theme of Rose Cipollone's personal choice: "She was intelligent. She was strong-minded. She was well-read. She had a mind of her own. She was used to making decisions for herself and her family. This is a woman who was in control of her life. She wanted to do what she wanted to do. She wanted to smoke. She smoked."

Cohn also argued that Liggett didn't have to warn consumers about the hazards of smoking because the hazards were already well known. Besides, he said, it would have made no difference to Rose Cipollone. She continued to smoke once they did put a warning on. And, if she continued to smoke because she was addicted, "what good would a warning have done?"

Cohn, who would often turn to the jury box with a smirk during cross-examinations and who spent many hours at trial doodling on a legal pad, nonetheless appealed to several jurors. "I felt in the beginning a little leery," says one. "But when he got on his feet he did all right."

Says another: "I didn't like his smile at first. But I came to love him."

One alternate, however, never got past her distrust of Cohn. "He's like a con to me," she says. "That smile—and then he'll cut your throat."

Cohn's summation was followed the next day by Shook, Hardy's Robert Northrip—speaking for Lorillard—whose succinct and well-organized closing focused mostly on Cipollone's cancer and whether it had been caused by smoking. Northrip argued that no claims could succeed if the jury believed she had had the atypical carcinoid not statistically associated with smoking.

Northrip also tried to cast doubt on the significance of the company documents. "Over one hundred thousand documents were produced," he said. "You have seen less than one percent. I don't suggest you should have seen more. We have been here long enough. But when you consider the documents, you should put them in the context and recognize that these are samples of the writings of literally hundreds, perhaps thousands, of people over forty years from several organizations."

On behalf of Philip Morris, Peter Bleakley of Washington's Arnold & Porter argued that people start smoking because of peer pressure, not advertising, and denied that the industry had misrepresented the risks of smoking. Industry assertions that smoking is not a proven cause of cancer are merely opinions, Bleakley argued. And an opinion cannot be the basis for fraud. "There is no such thing as a false opinion," he said. "We guard very jealously the right of people and institutions and corporations to state their opinions in this country."

The defense had argued that statistical associations between smoking and cancer do not prove smoking causes cancer. Bleakley—employing a sort of have-your-cake-and-eat-it-too defense—managed to turn to his advantage the association between quitting smoking and reducing the risk of cancer. "If you accept that it is relevant that there is a statistical association between cigarette smoking and cancer, then you have to accept the evidence on the record of this case that Mrs. Cipollone could have reduced that risk, probably to the level of a nonsmoker, after fifteen years, but in any event very, very substantially by quitting."

Concluding, Bleakley repeated more firmly a notion Cohn and Northrip had already mentioned: "You are not the conscience of the community in this lawsuit. You are the judges of the facts in this lawsuit, and you apply the facts to the law that will be given to you by the Court, and your job is to decide whether Mr. Cipollone gets money. That is what this case is all about."

Most of the jurors who deliberated were convinced that the case *was* about money. But one alternate was not. "I really don't think it's a case of money. I really don't," says Evelyn Perkins, a 42-year-old telephone operator, who admits she was shocked by the verdict. "I really thought they would have given more money than they did. . . . I think the lady really had the feeling the companies had done something wrong. . . . I think she was courageous. . . . That takes a lot of guts to go up against a big company like that."

Edell was scheduled to close the following morning—Friday—but when he met with his associate Walters on Thursday night to go over the medical portion of the closing, he says, he realized that the material was not organized as he wanted it. Edell notified the defendants' counsel and the judge that he needed a postponement, but that did nothing to ease the tension when they convened the next morning.

"Logic took over from ego," he explained to the incredulous group gathered in Sarokin's chambers. Several defense lawyers had enjoyed trying to second-guess Edell and occasionally made bets about what he would do in court. But they hadn't wagered on this move, and they were furious. The closing schedule had been settled the week before, and the three defense teams had abided by it. "I was up till three-thirty Wednesday night preparing for my closing, and I didn't feel like I was ready," argued Bleakley. "You never feel like you are ready. That is part of the life of being a trial lawyer."

But Edell was insistent. He told Sarokin he was prepared to go to jail rather than sum up. "I cannot close this morning, and that is the bottom line," he said, adding, "It is like a pack of wolves that are smelling blood, and I can see the eyes glaring down at me in the middle of the wolf pack with my foot up in the air."

Sarokin ruled that to compensate for the possible prejudice to the defendants of Edell's getting a weekend to prepare, each defendant could have a half hour of rebuttal. But Edell asserted that *he* should then get a half hour of surrebuttal. Over angry defense objections, Sarokin granted his request.

Edell certainly seemed to make good use of the weekend. In a strong and smooth closing he blasted the motives of tobacco manufacturers. "What you have seen in this case is an evil-minded conspiracy intended for one purpose and one purpose only—profits on their part, deceit of the public on the other."

He tried to unravel the defense strategies. "If everybody knew all the way back here, in the 1930s, 1940s, if everybody knew [about the hazards of smoking], why weren't they doing research if everybody knew? On one hand they said there is not enough research. Not enough scientific research to warrant doing research, but, on the other hand, they say everybody knew. Do you want to know the truth of the matter? That is nothing more than a fabricated legal defense.''

The defense, Edell said, deflected attention from the big picture and focused it on Rose Cipollone. "They put Rose Cipollone on trial," he said. "She did something wrong. They argued to you freedom of choice. . . . If you don't know what your options are or risks are, it is not free and informed choice.

"Well, the defendants had a choice, too. Theirs was an informed choice because they knew what the facts were, and they chose a carefully orchestrated strategy designed by public relations counsel, designed by lawyers. . . . It boggles the mind.''

The rebuttals that followed were unremarkable, but in Edell's surre-buttal, he confidently took on the defendants' assertions, batting each of them off with clean, sharp blows.

Some jurors just couldn't stir up the outrage that Edell tried to impart. Others, however, were impressed with him. "I think he did a very good job," says alternate Perkins, who favored the plaintiff. "Most of the time when he made a statement or an accusation against something he had a piece of paper to back it up.''

"I thought Mr. Edell was an excellent lawyer," says a juror on the final panel. "I think the tobacco companies should hire him. He really left no stone unturned.'' She nevertheless was unconvinced by most of his arguments.

The next day, when Sarokin read his charge, neither side was completely satisfied with the wording. Edell was upset that there weren't more examples of the defendants' allegedly deceitful conduct in the charge. He had also wanted Sarokin to instruct the jurors that when apportioning fault they could not consider what Rose Cipollone knew about the hazards of smoking after 1966.

For his part, Liggett counsel James Kearney found the failure-to-warn charge confusing. "It permitted the jury to find a manufacturer liable for failing to warn about what everybody already knows," Kearney says. "The charge was heinous, virtually unwinnable.''

Another defense complaint concerned whether Rose Cipollone had relied on the defendants' actions, and whether her reliance was one cause of her lung cancer and death. Unlike the failure-to-warn, fraud, and conspiracy charges, the express warranty charge against Liggett related only to industry action, not to Rose Cipollone's behavior. "On all of the claims except express warranty," says Shook, Hardy partner Elwood Thomas, who represented Lorillard and Philip Morris, "we had some sort of requirement that she had to rely on the information she got. That was extremely important to us because that was obviously one of our major defenses."

It would prove to be important in the jury room as well. The express warranty claim gave the two pro-plaintiff jurors their best argument for awarding *something*. Had the charge instructed that the plaintiff had to prove Rose Cipollone relied on the express warranties, the jury quite possibly would have let Liggett off on that claim, too.

The group returned to the jury room after the charge on Tuesday afternoon feeling tense. "We kind of looked at each other and said, let's just calm down and relax," recalls one. "The charge was overwhelming," says another. "That was uppermost in my mind. I felt it was quite complex, the legal terms. We were told we're just to accept his instructions. I was sort of anxious to read it again."

They would read it over and over again—aloud and to themselves—before they were through. Seventy-two pages long, the charge led the jurors through a labyrinth of instructions. The jurors even listed each claim and the elements needed to prove it on large sheets of paper that they taped up on the wall.

A bit of fate and a 22-page questionnaire had brought together these six people to decide where to place the blame for Rose Cipollone's death. They had been among 233 prospective jurors who, in January, had filled out a 108-question form as part of an eight-day selection process. The six jurors were:

James Dwyer, a 64-year-old loan adviser for Bergen County, New Jersey. Dwyer smoked over two packs of cigarettes a day for nearly 23 years. He quit in about 1962. Why? "Uncertain," he wrote on his questionnaire. "Just decided to give it up. Odors, wife, dirty ashtrays." Quitting was "somewhat difficult," he said.

Ralph Eliseo, a 35-year-old smoker who works in financial marketing. Eliseo has smoked two packs a day for 16 years and, he wrote on his questionnaire, has found quitting "extremely difficult." The only smoker on the jury, Eliseo bet another juror that he could easily quit for a couple of days. He succeeded in cutting down but not quitting.

Marie Mickens, a 57-year-old nonsmoker who packs bowls and lids in a plastics factory. She was voted forewoman.

Evelyn Miller, a 64-year-old housewife who smoked a pack a day for 22 years. Quitting, she wrote on her questionnaire, was "relatively easy." What influenced her to quit? "Bad press," she answered.

Ralph Pochank, a 52-year-old nonsmoker who works as an engineer for a utilities company.

Barbara Reilly, a 52-year-old nonsmoker who does research in a food laboratory.

That first afternoon, before tackling the 20 interrogatories, they took a vote to see what kind of cancer they thought Rose Cipollone had. The vote was 5 to 1 in favor of atypical carcinoid—the type not usually linked to smoking—with only former smoker Dwyer convinced she had small cell. "If we all thought it was atypical and we all thought it wasn't caused by smoking, we could have stopped right there," says one juror. (Had the defendants' counsel been in the jury room, they surely would have been pleased, since they had proposed that a similar question should be first on the verdict form.)

But since the jurors couldn't stop right there, they went through the interrogatories and took a tentative vote. It was then that their battle lines were delineated. Siding with the defense were Mickens, Miller, Reilly, and Eliseo—the three women and the only smoker. Voting for the plaintiff were Dwyer and Pochank—the loan officer and the engineer.

They spent much of the second day, Wednesday, reading aloud the charge, one claim at a time. Housewife Miller did much of the reading. As they went over each claim, everyone tried to get a word in. "There was screaming and yelling for two days," says smoker Eliseo. The deliberations continued at an emotionally charged level until one juror pointed out that they could hear the deputy's radio through an open window. Concerned that the lawyers might be listening, the jurors toned down their arguments.

They skipped from one claim to another, but the focus kept returning—just as the defense hoped it would—to Rose Cipollone. Not only did most of the jurors feel that she knew what she was doing but they also regarded her as stubborn and domineering. She was so difficult, they say, she had even sent her husband—a sympathetic figure—out late at night to fetch her cigarettes. When he came back with the wrong brand she insisted he go again. The defense emphasis on Rose Cipollone's strength and independence had made a deep impression. "He was madly in love with her and she drove him into the ground," says one juror. "I'm surprised he didn't die first."

A counterpoint to all the talk about Rose Cipollone's pigheadedness was the assertion by loan officer Dwyer that, as plaintiff's counsel Edell had argued, she was a young girl led astray by the tobacco companies. But he and engineer Pochank were alone in believing that the tobacco industry had deceived smokers. To the others the companies' actions just seemed like business as usual, the kind of thing you'd expect from any major industry. Indeed, early on the majority of the jurors rejected the fraud and conspiracy claims without much difficulty, although Pochank and Dwyer kept trying to go back to them.

Several times the jurors read an industry response to a study showing that mice developed tumors when cigarette tars were painted on their backs. The response, called "A Frank Statement to Smokers," asserted that smoking had not been proven to cause cancer, and that the industry would do all it could to find the answers. "The four of us saw nothing wrong with that," says one pro-defense juror. "Mr. Dwyer and Mr. Pochank didn't like it." But the four wouldn't budge from their positions.

While the jurors could not agree on whether Rose Cipollone had been addicted to smoking, they all believed that she was in large part responsible for her own death. Thus, one of the easiest questions was interrogatory number 12: the percentage of responsibility attributable to her. Under New Jersey comparative fault law, a finding that Rose Cipollone was more than 50 percent responsible precluded her estate from collecting damages on the failure-to-warn claim. All the jurors agreed that she was more than 50 percent at fault. (Two thought she had 100 percent responsibility.) They batted around figures with Pochank and Dwyer but 80 percent was the lowest the four pro-defense jurors would agree to. "We wanted people to know that we strongly felt she was wrong," says one of the four.

The jurors had more than 20 binders of documents and other exhibits in the jury room. (The plaintiff's exhibits alone totaled more than 15,000 pages.) But even with all this, smoker Eliseo and some of the others were frustrated because they thought that important documents may not have been admitted into evidence. Perhaps they were struck by defense attorney Northrip's closing suggestion that they had seen less than 1 percent of the documents produced. "I didn't see why we couldn't go through everything," Eliseo says. "How can you make a decision without having all the facts? If Mr. Edell really had stuff that proved fraud and conspiracy, why couldn't we read it? If I read absolutely all that stuff maybe I'd have a different opinion."

Eliseo felt strongly that when faced with the knowledge of possible dangers in 1954 Liggett had acted responsibly and done research—and

411

that it was *good* research. "The way I feel is that when the tobacco industry found something worth looking into, they spent money and looked into it," he says.

He was especially convinced by one Liggett document—notes from a 1954 internal conference—that he came across while flipping through the binders. The passages he fixed on were the same ones that Webster & Sheffield partner Donald Cohn had emphasized in his closing. One paragraph dealing with the mouse-skin studies stated that: "Obviously, you cannot get the answer with mice. But by using mice you can satisfy people. Otherwise, it would be necessary to wait at least thirty years and watch the death rate change."

The paragraph intrigued Eliseo and prompted him to send a note—without first telling the other jurors—requesting the Surgeon General's 1984 report to see if it had any information or findings about the death rate. "I was looking for actual people facts to back up mouse facts," Eliseo says. "I wanted to see if the mouse tests were indeed accurate." The report, however, had not been admitted into evidence.

Ultimately, Eliseo and the other three defense-minded jurors conceded that Liggett should have made more of its research findings public and warned consumers of the risks smoking posed. "I felt pretty strong that they could have and should have warned," says one. "They had the information."

But the other three did not believe Liggett was seriously at fault. "We didn't feel we found them guilty of much when we found them guilty of [failure to warn]," says one. "I think we all thought they were trying to find what the problem was. We felt that back then there wasn't a lot of research going on. It was just a different time period then."

These three pro-defense jurors also say they found it easier to compromise on the failure-to-warn claim since they had already agreed Cipollone was more than 50 percent responsible for her death and so could not collect damages on that claim.

The answer to question number 8—"was that failure to warn prior to 1966 a proximate cause of all or some of Mrs. Cipollone's smoking?"— proved more elusive. She didn't stop smoking when a warning went on the package in 1966, the four argued. And, says one juror, "We felt like even if they had a warning on a pack in 1940 it would have made no difference to her." Still, the four were persuaded to answer yes to this question. One says, "We felt they should have acknowledged [the risk] just by saying, 'Yes, we tested it and found there's carcinogens in there and we're going to work to improve it and cut it down.' "

Having answered yes to question 8, the jurors next had to decide whether Cipollone's smoking was a proximate cause of her lung cancer and death. The mouse-skin studies were not convincing to everyone, since all the mice did not develop tumors. "If a person is susceptible to cancer they'll get it. She had it in her bloodline," says Eliseo. But since the proximate cause charge required only that Cipollone's smoking be "probably a substantial contributing factor in bringing about Mrs. Cipollone's illness and death," the jurors voted yes on the question. They still had not all drawn a definite conclusion. "I don't think we really were sure it was a proximate cause of her cancer," says one. "That was an iffy thing."

Perhaps the most difficult claim for the jury to tackle was that of express warranty—the contention that Liggett's advertisements had misrepresented the risks of smoking. Pro-defense jurors Mickens, Eliseo, and Reilly believed that the ads weren't *very* misleading. And, like defense expert Professor Claude Martin, Eliseo argued that no one takes advertisements seriously; he didn't start smoking because of an advertisement, he asserted. But one juror says that pro-plaintiff juror Dwyer felt that Cipollone had been duped. He kept bringing up the "Play Safe" and "Just What the Doctor Ordered" ads, she recalls. For her, the only really disturbing ad was one that said, "The Mask Is Off in Cigarette Advertising." The ad proclaims that Chesterfield is the first to name all its ingredients: "1. Best Tobaccos, 2. Natural Sugars, 3. Costly Glycerol . . . NOTHING ELSE!"

Three of the defense-minded jurors were reluctant to find that Liggett breached express warranties because they did not want to award any money. And, they interpreted the charge and the interrogatory form to mean that if they found Liggett liable for breach of warranty, they *had* to award money. "I think the way [the form] was worded, the question said if you answered yes to a particular question you were asked what damages did Mrs. Cipollone sustain, what damages did Mr. Cipollone sustain," says one juror. "There were dollar signs next to [the damage question], and it certainly indicated there was some figure [called for]."

Throughout the discussions, forewoman Mickens, smoker Eliseo, and lab technician Reilly had stated very clearly that they would not give any money to Mr. *or* Mrs. Cipollone, even if it meant a hung jury. In fact, after three days of deliberating, Mickens suggested sending the judge a note saying that they could not reach a verdict.

But engineer Pochank was vehement that they try to work it out. "We have enough intelligence to come to some kind of agreement," one juror recalls he said. "We can't go down and say we're a hung jury. There's an answer here and we've got to find the answer."

By Friday, the fourth day of deliberations, there was general agreement that they would award damages if they found the ads had breached an express warranty. They decided to think over the weekend about how much money was appropriate. Loan adviser Dwyer—pro-plaintiff from the start—suggested a figure in the millions. One juror recalls it was $5 million, but "right away we were, no way were we anywhere near five million or even one million," she says. "The rest of us didn't want to give a figure." Still, most of them went home thinking they would agree on something Monday morning and be done early.

But the end turned out not to be so close. On Monday, the four pro-defense jurors came in and said they'd changed their minds. "She did it to herself. How can we award money?" said one of them. "Everybody was like, 'Oh, I don't believe this,' " recalls another who had changed her mind. They thought they would never reach a verdict.

One juror thinks this frustration made Dwyer and Pochank soften. Having reached a standstill, they seemed more willing to come down in their money demands. By the afternoon awarding a token amount to Mr. Cipollone only seemed an acceptable compromise.

So again they tossed around numbers. One person suggested $500,000, but Eliseo—who still preferred to give nothing—argued that a damage award would make insurance rates go up. Another juror disagreed, and joked that the price of cigarettes would go up. Finally they reached a consensus. Mr. Cipollone would receive $400,000 from Liggett for breach of express warranty and, as the jurors had decided earlier, Liggett would be found liable for failure to warn—but would pay no damages on that claim. Punitive damages were something the four refused to consider.

By the time the jurors notified the judge that they had reached a verdict, most of them still did not feel any outrage toward the tobacco companies. But they did have a sense—if only a fleeting one—that it was important to tell Liggett and other tobacco companies that it was not acceptable to mislead the public. "They should have had some kind of little acknowledgment that there were things in cigarettes that could be harmful to some people," says one juror. "Not that it *was* harmful, but it *could* be harmful. . . . We thought it was a small amount to the tobacco company and not too small to Mr. Cipollone, and it would more or less get across a message."

"That man should get something," says another juror. "He certainly was a good husband and stuck by her. But he should have never gone out for those cigarettes."

* * *

Liggett has moved to set aside the verdict, arguing that Sarokin was wrong not to instruct the jury that to find a breach of express warranty they had to find that Rose Cipollone relied on the warranty. Edell has requested prejudgment interest of $223,237.39 on the damages, asked for an amendment of the judgment under the New Jersey consumer fraud statute (which would treble the medical costs of $124,500 and require Liggett to pay attorneys' fees), and moved for a partial new trial on the issue of damages for Rose Cipollone. "Although we have no way of determining the motive for the omission of damages," Edell's brief says, "a reasonable conclusion would be that the jury improperly applied the doctrine of comparative fault (which it found as to the failure-to-warn claim) to the breach of warranty claim. . . . There can be no justification for the non sequitur of no damages."

But for four of the jurors, damages for Rose Cipollone were never a possibility, and they resent the implication that they didn't understand that they *could* award damages to her. "We know we could have given to her. We knew that. We didn't feel that we wanted to give [to] her. And most of us felt very strongly about that," says one. "Why have a jury rack their brains? This was terrible to go through. . . . I hope [Edell] doesn't succeed in that [motion]."

Another juror was shocked and offended that Edell would ask for a new trial. "I felt that we had rendered a verdict," she says. "It's like going to a doctor. Do you keep going to one until you find one that gives you the right answer?" This juror was hesitant to discuss the case in great detail because she feared it would help Edell in his next trial. "I'm just not going to give any ammunition," she says. "I can just see Mr. Edell coming out with a whole new approach." Still another juror feels Sarokin should just have decided the damages himself.

Two of the jurors say their friends were shocked that they awarded any money at all. One—who is satisfied with the decision—sent those friends a copy of a *Bergen Record* editorial that praised the verdict. Another juror says she is too embarrassed even to talk to her friends about the verdict.

That juror also feels angry that Sarokin—who other jurors say thanked them in chambers after the verdict—didn't express any gratitude in the courtroom. "He really never thanked us," the juror says. "I guess the trial didn't go the way he wanted and that was it."

The juror who cried after the verdict was handed down, sorry about the outcome, still questions her decision and wonders if she was too weak.

She is not alone. "I don't know if I'm right or wrong on my decision," says smoker Eliseo. "If I had another five months to go through all the evidence I might have come up with different opinions. . . . I look back at the whole thing as one of the low points in my life. Why do I have to have the responsibility of deciding if a person was responsible for smoking, was responsible for their own death? If Rosie knew she was smoking a bad product why didn't she stop? I didn't think it was fair that she put this burden on me."

CIPOLLONE V. LIGGETT GROUP, INC., 83-2864
JURY INTERROGATORIES

1. Has plaintiff proven all of the elements necessary to establish fraudulent misrepresentation or concealment by defendant Liggett, prior to 1966, of material facts concerning significant health risks associated with cigarette smoking?
Yes _____ No _____

2. Has plaintiff proven all of the elements necessary to establish fraudulent misrepresentation by defendant Philip Morris, prior to 1966, of material facts concerning significant health risks associated with cigarette smoking?
Yes _____ No _____

3. Has plaintiff proven all of the elements necessary to establish fraudulent misrepresentation by defendant Lorillard, prior to 1966, of material facts concerning significant health risks associated with cigarette smoking?
Yes _____ No _____

4. Was there a conspiracy prior to 1966 to fraudulently misrepresent and/or conceal material facts concerning significant health risks associated with cigarette smoking?
Yes _____ No _____

5. If you answered "yes" to question 4, were any of the defendants members of that conspiracy?
Liggett Group,
   Inc.   Yes _____ No _____
Philip Morris
   Incorporated Yes _____ No _____
Lorillard, Inc. Yes _____ No _____

6. If you answered "yes" to question 5, has plaintiff proven all of the elements necessary to establish fraudulent misrepresentation or concealment, prior to 1966, by any member of the conspiracy?
Yes _____ No _____

7. Should Liggett, prior to 1966, have warned consumers regarding health risks of smoking?
Yes _____ No _____

8. If you answered "yes" to question 7, was that failure to warn prior to 1966 a proximate cause of all or some of Mrs. Cipollone's smoking?
Yes _____ No _____

9. If you answered "yes" to question 8, was such smoking a proximate cause of Mrs. Cipollone's lung cancer and death?
Yes _____ No _____

10. If you answered "yes" to question 9, did Mrs. Cipollone voluntarily and unreasonably encounter a known danger by smoking cigarettes?
Yes _____ No _____

11. If you answered "yes" to question 10, was this conduct by Mrs. Cipollone a proximate cause of her lung cancer and death?
Yes _____ No _____

12. If you answered "yes" to question 11, what is the percentage of responsibility for Mrs. Cipollone's injuries attributable to each of the following parties:
Mrs. Cipollone   _____ %
Liggett Group,
   Inc.   _____ %

[*NOTE: The sum of these percentages must equal 100 percent.*]

13. Did Liggett make express warranties to consumers regarding the health aspects of its cigarettes?
Yes _____ No _____

14. If you answered "yes" to question 13, did any Liggett products used by Mrs. Cipollone breach that warranty?
Yes _____ No _____

15. If you answered "yes" to question 14, was Mrs. Cipollone's use of these products a proximate cause of her lung cancer and death?
Yes _____ No _____

16. If you answered "yes" to any of the following questions: 1, 2, 3, 6, 9, or 15, what damages did Mrs. Cipollone sustain?
$ _____

17. If you answered "yes" to any of the following questions: 1, 2, 3, 6, 9, or 15, what damages did Mr. Cipollone sustain?
$ _____

18. If you answered "yes" to any of the following questions: 1, 2, 3, 6, or 9, is plaintiff entitled to punitive damages against one or more of the defendants?
Yes _____ No _____

19. If you answered "yes" to question 18, to what amount is plaintiff entitled?
$ _____

20. If you awarded a sum under question 19, what amount of this total is attributable to each of the following parties?
Liggett Group, inc. $ _____
Philip Morris Incorporated $ _____
Lorillard, Inc. $ _____
[*NOTE: These amounts should add up to the total awarded under question 19.*]

EPILOGUE

On August 24, 1988, U.S. District Judge Lee Sarokin denied the motions by plaintiff's counsel Marc Edell for a partial new trial on the issue of damages for Rose Cipollone, for trebling of damages under the New Jersey consumer fraud statute, and for prejudgment interest. At the same time, Judge Sarokin denied Liggett Group, Inc.'s motions for a judgment notwithstanding the verdict and for a new trial. Liggett and Edell both appealed.

Approximately 100 cases similar to Rose Cipollone's are pending in several states against one or more of the tobacco companies involved in *Cipollone*. Edell is representing the plaintiffs in six of these. He has brought no new suits of this type since the *Cipollone* verdict and notes that the case has not started an avalanche of new litigation.

On January 5, 1990, the Court of Appeals for the Third Circuit overturned the verdict and ordered a new trial, ruling that it had not been proved that Mrs. Cipollone either saw or believed Liggett's advertising.

U.S. v. International Brotherhood of Teamsters and SEC v. Drexel Burnham Lambert, Inc.

WHEN THE GOVERNMENT GOES JUDGE SHOPPING

STEVEN BRILL

How government lawyers manipulated the system to steer suits against the Teamsters and Drexel to sympathetic judges—and why that should worry everyone.

The two most important civil suits pending in the United States are the Securities and Exchange Commission case against Drexel Burnham Lambert, Inc., Michael Milken, and related defendants, and the Justice Department's case against the International Brotherhood of Teamsters. In one, the government is suing the nation's most aggressive investment bank and its leader for basic, sweeping violations of the securities laws. In the other, the government is trying to get the largest union in the free world declared a racketeering organization so that the court will appoint an honest trustee to take it over.

If ever there were two cases where we should want the system to shine—to be a model of justice dispensed fairly, credibly, effectively—these are the cases. If ever there were two cases where we want the government to behave as if it isn't just another litigant but is the one litigant that is supposed to care more about a fair trial and about justice than it does about winning, these are the cases.

Which is why it is so embarrassing, so destructive that these cases have started out in kangaroo court, each overseen by a judge who is anything but evenhanded, and each steered to that judge by cynical government lawyers who have forgotten the higher values they're sworn to uphold.

STEERING THE TEAMSTERS TO EDELSTEIN

On the merits, you can't get me to say a word in favor of the Teamster defendants; I wrote a book about the union ten years ago detailing not just its *involvement* in organized crime but that it *is* organized crime incarnate.

In 1982 the Justice Department had brought this type of civil RICO suit in New Jersey to remove the Teamsters' corrupt local leadership and replace it with a court-appointed trustee until honest, democratically elected leadership could be assured. That kind of suit is what RICO was meant for: federal assaults on racketeering organizations that attack the organization itself. Now, in the winter and spring of 1988, the Justice Department was preparing a monster version of this local suit: a RICO fight to take over the union's Washington, D.C.–based national leadership. On June 28, the long-awaited national suit, which could have been filed anywhere in the country, was filed in the Southern District of New York by U.S. Attorney Rudolph Giuliani.

In the Southern District, as in all federal court districts with more than one or two judges, cases are assigned randomly. When a case is filed at the courthouse in Manhattan's Foley Square, a judge's name is picked, bingo-style, out of a bowl that spins on a wheel. But there's one exception to the wheel: If a case is related to another case, the plaintiff's lawyer can fill in a box on the complaint form citing the related case. If he does, his case is automatically routed to the judge handling the supposedly related case. The judge can then accept it, or he can reject it if he deems it unrelated.

When Assistant U.S. Attorney Randy Mastro, the 32-year-old former Cravath, Swaine & Moore associate and superstar in Giuliani's office who is running the Teamsters case, filled out the complaint form, he filled

419

in the related case box, citing a RICO suit brought earlier in the year against two small local units of the Teamsters operating in Queens.

The local union case is being handled by Judge David Edelstein.

A 37-YEAR EMBARRASSMENT TO THE BENCH

I'll give a free subscription to anyone who's ever litigated a case with Edelstein who on a one-to-ten scale rates him anything higher than a .5 (and who's willing to be hooked up to a lie detector as he renders his rating). Edelstein, who at 78 is a senior judge, was appointed in 1951 by President Truman. For 37 years he has been an embarrassment to the federal bench.

I interviewed 30 lawyers of all different stripes who have practiced before Edelstein. None had a good word to say about him. The words "stupid" or "dumb" were used 27 times, "bully" or "arrogant" 24 times, "incompetent" 27 times, "lazy" 20 times. And 26 of the 30 lawyers offered "pro-government" to describe Edelstein, including 6 such assessments from the 7 present or former federal prosecutors interviewed.

Edelstein is widely remembered as the judge who turned the government's antitrust case against IBM into our civil law version of Vietnam, allowing it to run 13 years, including two years in which depositions were read out loud into the trial record by lawyers playacting in Edelstein's courtroom.

Edelstein did everything short of bring in a hanging rope to help the government win its unwinnable case. He harassed IBM's lawyers from Cravath, Swaine & Moore with name-calling and knee-jerk denials of objections and motions, ruling for the government in 74 of 79 contested motions while upholding 60 percent of the government's objections versus 3 percent of Cravath's. He allowed the government to amend its complaint whenever the mood struck and to take discovery and question witnesses endlessly.

But Edelstein's damage spreads far beyond the IBM case, which ended when the government—over Edelstein's objection!—dismissed it in 1982. Print out a WESTLAW search of run-of-the-mill cases he's handled and you get a roll call of lawyers who say it was the worst experience they've ever had in front of a judge. Except that lawyers for the government (five chosen at random) who had cases before Edelstein after the mid-seventies (a period when he seems to have gone from being simply incompetent, slow, and bullying to being incompetent, slow, bullying, and pro-government) admit that they had an easy, if humiliating, time with him.

Because the Teamsters case involves requests for equitable relief, including the appointment of a special trustee, it will all be decided by Edelstein, not a jury.

THE "RELATED CASE" MANEUVER

The local court rule about related cases under which Assistant U.S. Attorney Mastro got this landmark suit in front of Edelstein seems clear. "Cases are related," the rule states, "if they present common questions of law and fact, or arise from the same source or substantially similar transactions, happenings, events, or relationships, or if for any other reason they would entail substantial duplication of labor if assigned to different judges."

The small civil case Edelstein already had, upon which Mastro now piggybacked the civil case against the national union, had been brought against John Long and John Mahoney, Jr., who are officers of two local units of the Teamsters union in Queens. Long and Mahoney had allegedly misappropriated local pension-fund investments.

The national union consists of 742 locals, hundreds of which are far more corrupt—and far more the real grist of the national suit—than the two Queens locals. The two locals aren't charged in the small suit with overall, systemic corruption, only with pension-fund corruption. Nor is the government seeking a trustee to take over the locals.

Indeed, the complaint in the national suit is 113 pages long and contains all of two sentences referring to the local Queens suit. It is impossible, therefore, to imagine any of the overlap in witnesses, fact issues, legal issues, or anything else that the rule was designed to accommodate.

When a lawyer moves on the complaint form to have his case deemed related to another one so that it goes to the same judge, he is required to attach a brief statement explaining its relatedness. Thus, Mastro wrote: "In both this case and in *U.S.* v. *Long* [the local case] . . . the United States has brought suit under the civil remedies provisions of RICO . . . to remedy corruption within the International Brotherhood of Teamsters. This case deals with alleged corruption at the International level [the Teamsters call the national union an "international" one because it has units in Canada], while *U.S.* v. *Long* deals with corruption at the local

421

level which the International Union leadership has failed to redress.''

True, the allegations against Long and Mahoney are among the dozens of examples of corruption alleged in the national case that the national leaders have allegedly tolerated, but that hardly makes the cases related in the way the rule requires. (And, as we'll see below, there's evidence that the Long and Mahoney allegations were added to the national complaint only to get the national case related to the Long and Mahoney case once Edelstein got the Long and Mahoney case.)

More important, Long and Mahoney are also under criminal indictment, and Mastro and his office have agreed to stay the civil case against them—and all discovery related to it—pending the outcome of that criminal case. In fact, the government has now taken the inconsistent position that because of the Long and Mahoney criminal case, the national union's lawyers cannot now take discovery of witnesses related to the minuscule Long and Mahoney portions (two sentences of a 113-page complaint) of the national civil case. Thus, the very reason for the related-cases rule, to speed the process and to avoid duplication, has been negated by the government.

The complaint form also states that the plaintiff can fill in the box designating a related case "ONLY if you intend to move for consolidation." (The capital letters are the form's, not mine.) Consolidation means that the cases would be tried together.

According to chief Southern District judge Charles Brieant, Jr., that admonition about consolidation was added in 1981 because "we began to think too many people were being a bit loose about what a related case was.''

Asked if he intends to move to consolidate the cases, Mastro declines comment. But he hasn't moved to do so, and it's clear that he won't and shouldn't, for several reasons. First, the two cases have so little to do with each other that consolidation would be a farce (as would consolidation of discovery, which Brieant asserts is another option under the admonition). Second, at least one of the two Queens locals is generally viewed by law enforcement officials as not endemically corrupt in the way the national suit seeks to portray the national union; so having that local be part of the national case would undercut the national case. Third, neither of these two locals is under the rigid control of the national union leadership the way so many larger, more corrupt locals are; so including those two locals, and those two alone, as part of the national case would similarly undercut the national case.

Asked how a litigant could fill in the box and then not move to consolidate, Brieant explains that the internal rules of the court on the assignment of judges are "for the benefit of the judges only. We can do it any way we want to." He adds, "If I want to give one of my cases to another judge because I want to go to the beach, that's fine. . . . No one has the right to any judge or to any system of choosing judges . . . and these rules don't give anyone any rights."

As for how a judge should deal with a litigant who ignores the admonition about moving to consolidate, Brieant says that the instruction is "only a guideline, because it's entirely for Judge Edelstein to decide whether he should take that case.

"When the controversy dies down that has arisen lately [because of the Teamsters and Drexel cases] about this rule," adds Brieant, "we'll probably look at changing the form. It's really not meant to be as rigid as it seems. The part about consolidation was put there just to slow down this trend to consolidate. . . . The important thing is that it's the judges' decision to make about who handles what cases."

A LONG WAY AROUND THE "WHEEL"

The government's maneuvering to get the case to Edelstein seems to have started well before Mastro filled out the form claiming the cases were related. Originally, Edelstein didn't have the Long and Mahoney civil case. When that case was filed on May 11, 1988, it was assigned, via the wheel, to Judge Richard Daronco. What's interesting about that is that two other civil cases brought by the government were already pending against one of the two Queens locals and two of its officers, including one of the defendants in this May 11 case (Mahoney). The other two cases had to do with the same pension-fund corruption allegations made in the Long and Mahoney case that went to Daronco via the wheel.

Those two earlier cases were in Judge Louis Stanton's court. Giuliani's office apparently doesn't fancy Stanton, because no move was made to have this new Long and Mahoney case sent to his court as a "related" case, which it clearly was.

On May 21 Judge Daronco was murdered at his home by the father of a disappointed litigant in an unrelated case. The Long and Mahoney case was then transferred to Judge Vincent Broderick.

Meantime, a criminal RICO indictment against Long had been filed on December 14, 1987. Edelstein had drawn this case off the wheel. On April 27, 1988, a new indictment was brought in the Long criminal case, superseding the first one and adding Mahoney as a defendant. Because it was an addendum to the first indictment, the new indictment stayed with Edelstein.

But in May of 1988, Mastro—who was not the lawyer in Giuliani's office handling the Long and Mahoney civil or criminal cases but was handling the national Teamsters case—called Long and Mahoney's lawyers and asked if they would agree to have their *civil* case transferred to Edelstein, who had the Long and Mahoney criminal case. There is no provision in the rules for civil cases to be transferred to "related" criminal cases, because a criminal case, obviously, is supposed to be tried independently of all other cases and kept untainted by any extraneous evidence. But according to an affidavit subsequently filed by Mahoney's lawyer, Jo Ann Harris, Mastro made a good practical argument for moving that civil case to Edelstein; he promised that the civil case would remain dormant while the criminal case went forward and that, according to Harris's affidavit, "if Mahoney [was] acquitted in the criminal action the Government would . . . drop the civil action. . . ."

Faced with nothing to lose—she already had the bad luck of having Edelstein in the criminal case, and if she won that she'd be rid of the civil case—Harris and her co-counsel agreed.

Now Edelstein had the Long and Mahoney civil case.

A month later, Mastro filed the national Teamsters case, called it related to the Long and Mahoney case, and got it into Edelstein's court.

In August the Teamsters' newly retained lawyer, Jed Rakoff of Wall Street's Mudge Rose Guthrie Alexander & Ferdon, figured out what had happened. In an angry motion—which he had to make before Edelstein— he demanded that the government be enjoined from prosecuting the case before Edelstein and that the case be sent back to the wheel for reassignment. Rakoff accused the U.S. attorney's office (where he was once chief of the frauds unit) of "sharp practices and constitutional infringements" in its "attempt to steer the . . . case to this Court by a manipulation of the local Rules. . . .

"[A]ny overlap between this case and the *Long* case," Rakoff contended, "is so demonstrably *de minimus* as to render incredible any claim that the Government sought to promote any meaningful or substantial savings of time by the Court, as contemplated by Rule 15. Rather, the logical and compelling inference which arises from these facts is that the Government's acts, at least beginning with its successful effort to transfer *U.S.* v. *Long* to this Court, were undertaken not to aid the Court in the proper application of its Rules, but instead to give the Government the improper and unconstitutional advantage of affecting the selection of the tribunal for this case.''

Rakoff also asserted that ''any doubt as to the almost total lack of relationship of *Long* to this action has now been resolved by the fact'' that the government had now opposed any discovery of Long or Mahoney in the national case, despite ''the expedited discovery schedule'' in the national case. The government ''could only defend such a position,'' he charged, ''on the basis of an admission that allegations relating to Long and Mahoney are insubstantial in the context of'' the national case.

Mastro replied that he'd only been following the rules, as he was obligated to. He argued that the cases were, indeed, related and contended that he'd promised Harris, Mahoney's lawyer, only that the civil case would stay dormant pending the criminal case and that if she won the criminal case he would ''discuss'' what should happen to the civil case. Most important, he declared in an indignant reply brief that it is the judge, not the litigants, who decides if the cases are related. That is true, but it skirts the reality that a senior judge like Edelstein looking for a high-profile, important case will grab it if offered, and that, according to his own chief judge, he can grab it once offered no matter how minimally related it is.

Teamsters counsel Rakoff had cited the fact that Mastro personally had called Harris to get the Long and Mahoney case moved to Edelstein, even though he wasn't working on that case. as evidence of Mastro's carefully planned effort to ''steer'' the case. Mastro replied that as deputy chief of the Southern District's civil division he had supervisory responsibility over the Long and Mahoney case, too, even if he wasn't working on it. Asked in an interview how many times he had ever made similar calls—related to a case he wasn't working on himself rather than have the assistant running the case do it—he declined comment.

On October 13, Edelstein, to no one's surprise, denied Rakoff's motion, ruling that the judge alone has the right to accept or reject related cases.

According to two government lawyers who say they saw an earlier draft of the national case complaint that was written several weeks prior to Mastro's move to get the Long and Mahoney case moved to Edelstein, the earlier draft had nothing about Long or Mahoney. Those two sentences about Long and Mahoney, which Rakoff had argued appeared in the complaint ''as a grain of sand appears on a beach,'' and had ''all the earmarks of being added simply for the purposes of manipulating the local rules,'' didn't appear in that earlier draft at all, according to those sources, but were, indeed, added to a draft that was written after Mastro got the Long case moved to Edelstein.

Mastro declined comment when asked about the contents of earlier drafts of the complaint.

Mastro, Giuliani, and others in Giuliani's office take the position, as one puts it, that "it was our duty to call the relatedness to the attention of the court." They even say it with a straight face, although they didn't see that duty when it came to relating the Long and Mahoney case to the clearly related cases being handled by Judge Stanton, and although around the office, steering the case to Edelstein was seen, according to two sources in the office, as a coup nearly worthy of celebration.

The Teamsters' lawyers aren't free of hypocrisy either. Rakoff's papers take pains to point out that he's not suggesting that the union wouldn't get a fair trial from Edelstein, perish the thought. Indeed, because such motions to get a judge off a case have to be made to the judge himself, reality always has to be avoided. Which, of course, allowed Edelstein, in his ruling denying Rakoff's motion to take the case away from him, to note that the Teamsters' due process rights weren't violated because "the Union has not pointed to any prejudice as a result of the case being heard by this court. In fact, the Union has stated in open court and in its moving papers that it has no question of the court's impartiality. . . ."

So all three players are engaged in an elaborate charade, one that anyone who cares about our system should be embarrassed about, and one that will produce anything but evenhanded, credible justice in this landmark case. Indeed, the Teamsters' only hope now is that Edelstein will be more incompetent than biased—it's always a close contest with him—and that the case will get mired in years of discovery and pending motions.

DREXEL GOES TO KANGAROO COURT

As almost every newspaper-reading American knows (courtesy of a two-year cascade of leaks), Drexel Burnham Lambert, Inc., and its junk-bond king, Michael Milken, have been under investigation by the SEC and by Giuliani's office from the moment pseudo-arbitrageur Ivan Boesky got caught in the Dennis Levine insider trading scandal and turned informant.

During the first week in September, members of the multimillion-dollar legal team representing Drexel and Milken were told, they say, by the SEC that formal charges were finally coming. According to two lawyers on the Drexel side, because they were mindful of what the government had just done in the Teamsters case they feared that when the SEC did file its case, the commission would claim that it was related to cases being handled by Judge Milton Pollack, and that, therefore, Pollack would get the case.

The cases Pollack was already handling (via the wheel and then the federal courts' multidistrict consolidation procedure) were those that had been filed against Ivan Boesky and other defendants by assorted plaintiffs claiming to have been injured by Boesky's insider trading. The two main categories of plaintiffs were class action plaintiffs who had bought or sold stock in the companies Boesky had traded on, and investors in an arbitrage fund Boesky had organized that had lost millions when Boesky had been forced to liquidate after he was caught.

Drexel was a tangential co-defendant in these class action cases against Boesky, because Levine and another confessed insider trader, Martin Siegel, had been employed at Drexel during part of the time they and Boesky had done their dirty work. Drexel is a co-defendant in the suits by Boesky's investors because it was the underwriter in the Boesky fund offering. Thus, the allegations the SEC was preparing against Drexel, though broad and damning, had nothing to do with Drexel's status as a defendant in the shareholder suits and were only tangentially related to the arbitrage fund suits. Nonetheless the Drexel lawyers feared that the SEC would call its case a related case in order to get it in front of Pollack.

THE PROSECUTORS' FAVORITE JUDGE

Milton Pollack, 82, a former plaintiffs securities lawyer appointed to the bench by President Johnson in 1967, is smart, indeed brilliant. He is anything but lazy. Although tough on lawyers in court, he is usually respectful. Off the bench he's a candid, direct, witty man. His clerks and former clerks revere him.

And when it comes to running a courtroom, he is everything that Edelstein isn't and everything a judge should be. Under Milton Pollack lawyers attempting discovery abuses or anything else that avoids the merits are stripped bare; Pollack is the model of how the system *can* work when a judge wants it to work.

But around the Southern District it is an open secret that Pollack has two bedrock problems. First, he's so sure of how smart and how "right" he is that he chooses sides early. He then gives no quarter to the other side, pushing the case to his chosen result.

Second, when the government is the litigant, and especially when the government is the accuser in criminal cases, Pollack almost always chooses the government side. Once he does, evenhandedness all but vanishes, so much so that he has a long-whispered-about habit of calling assistant U.S. attorneys who have cases pending before him and discussing the case with them ex parte, even advising them on how to handle the case.

"When you have Judge Pollack," says one experienced litigator, echoing what seems to be a unanimous sentiment, "you have a scale of justice with a fist on one side."

From Drexel's perspective Pollack's general attitude was only part of the problem. Almost as bad was the fact that Michael Milken's lead lawyer is Arthur Liman of Paul, Weiss, Rifkind, Wharton & Garrison. Liman has a platinum reputation, but a first-year law student would be a better bet for Milken in front of Milton Pollack.

In the early 1970s Liman had earned Pollack's enmity while arguing the celebrated Chris-Craft Industries, Inc., securities case against Bangor Punta Corporation. Pollack, according to third-party accounts, had early on decided that Bangor Punta should win the case (as did the Supreme Court, ultimately). But Liman, a man not known for his humility, was far from a willing victim. He fought Pollack at every turn. Pollack is known as a judge who holds grudges, and he is especially known in Southern District circles as a judge who has held a bitter grudge against Arthur Liman.

CHECKING THE BOX

The Drexel defense team suspected that the case was going to be filed on the afternoon of September 7, just after the 4 P.M. close of the stock markets. Having failed to get a copy of the complaint directly from the SEC, Michael Armstrong of Lord Day & Lord, Barrett Smith, who represents Milken's brother Lowell, and Martin Flumenbaum, a partner-protégé of Liman's, went to the clerk's office at the federal courthouse in Manhattan to try to get the complaint as it was filed. They also were hoping they could head off having the case filed with Pollack by raising with the clerk at the filing window the issue of whether the SEC could file it as a related case unless they really did intend to consolidate it with the Boesky cases.

When Armstrong, according to his subsequent affidavit, arrived at about 3:45, he saw several SEC lawyers, led by enforcement division chief Thomas Newkirk, and an SEC paralegal waiting in the room where the line forms to file cases. According to his affidavit, Armstrong—a gregarious litigator who knew the SEC lawyers because he'd dealt with them during the long Drexel investigation—chatted with them "amiably" before they stepped up to the filing window at 4 P.M.

Meantime Flumenbaum, according to his subsequent affidavit, went to find a supervising clerk who, he thought, might be willing to question the SEC lawyers about whether they really intended to consolidate this case with the other Pollack cases, as the form required, before he would let them check the box claiming related-case status.

At 4 P.M., the SEC paralegal stepped to the window. Armstrong, according to his affidavit, asked the clerk to wait before accepting the filing because the clerk's supervisor was expected momentarily and might have a question for him and the SEC lawyers. Newkirk, according to Armstrong's affidavit, got between Armstrong and the paralegal and urged the paralegal and clerk to continue on with the filing.

But Flumenbaum had no luck with the supervising clerk. For when he approached the clerk, he was told, he says, that a clerk from Pollack's chambers had already arrived, had spoken with the supervising clerk, and was waiting at the window to receive the filing and bring it to Pollack.

The Pollack clerk having already talked the supervisor out of worrying about any argument concerning consolidation, the supervisor refused to interfere with the filing and Pollack's clerk happily took the case off to the judge's chambers.

No one at the SEC will comment about it, but it seems clear that the enforcement division's move to get the case to Pollack was coordinated in some way with the judge. His clerk, after all, had known to post himself in the clerk's office to wait for the case. More important, just before 4 P.M. Pollack had appeared in the federal court press room and told at least two reporters, according to the two, that they should, as one recalls the conversation, "wait around this afternoon, because something interesting is going to happen."

The next evening, at the Second Circuit Judicial Conference, a conclave in Hershey, Pennsylvania, of all the circuit's district and appellate judges plus a few hundred prominent litigators, the landing of the Drexel case in Pollack's court was the subject of hot gossip. Pollack seemed ebullient that evening, telling this reporter that "of course" he was going to keep the SEC case. And he was positively beaming the next morning when his picture was on the front page of the business section of *The New York Times* in an article on the case that called him a "tough" judge.

"Here's Milken," remarked one judge at the conference, "who's like Svengali in the financial world, who controls everything and hires the best lawyers in the world, but he ends up in front of Milton Pollack and he can't do a damn thing about it."

THE $30 MILLION CONFLICT

By the day after the *Times* story, though, it seemed that there could be something done about it. According to subsequent affidavits, on September 9 Drexel CEO Fred Joseph returned a call from W. Mitt Romney, managing general partner of an investment group called Bain Venture Capital in Boston. Bain is a client for whom Drexel had agreed to provide junk-bond financing for Bain's buyout of a Houston-based retailer called Palais Royal, Inc. Romney reminded Joseph of the pending Palais Royal deal, then dropped what the Drexel side asserts was a bombshell. He'd just read about Milton Pollack being the judge in the SEC case and thought Joseph should know that Palais Royal's chairman and major shareholder, through an inheritance from her first husband, was Moselle Pollack—the wife of Milton Pollack.

Mrs. Pollack, who under the law of judicial conflicts is considered to be the same person as her husband, stood to gain some $30 million if the deal went through, Bain's Romney reported.

Joseph called his two lead lawyers, Thomas Curnin of Cahill Gordon & Reindel (Drexel's longtime outside counsel) and white-collar crime specialist Peter Fleming, Jr., of Curtis, Mallet-Prevost, Colt & Mosle, both of New York. The next afternoon, Saturday, September 10, Fleming and Curnin called Pollack at home, briefed him quickly on the apparent conflict, and scheduled a meeting in his chambers for Tuesday, September 13 (the first business day after the Jewish holiday that Monday).

On Sunday, September 11, Fleming and Curnin also called Gary Lynch of the SEC's enforcement division and briefed him.

At the September 13 meeting, which was held in secret, Pollack angrily refused even to consider recusing himself, calling the Drexel conflict claim a "cockamamy story." If the Drexel lawyers filed a recusal motion, Pollack said, "I intend to exercise whatever rights I have to sanction anybody.'' He then ordered the record of the meeting sealed. (He later unsealed it.)

The Drexel lawyers wanted the conflict question resolved quickly. They had seen in the SEC's filing of its case a way to turn adversity to opportunity—provided they could get Pollack out of the way.

Even a believer in the general merits of the government's assertions of egregious wrongdoing by Milken and Drexel (and I am a believer) would agree that it had been stupid for the SEC to bring its case before Giuliani brought his expected criminal indictment. So stupid, in fact, that the only possible explanation is that the SEC's Lynch is so consumed by his rivalry with Giuliani that he wanted to beat Giuliani to the headlines by going first. (Indeed, since criminal charges are inherently so much more sensational and full of photo opportunities—people get arrested, booked, arraigned—had Lynch's case come at the same time or after Giuliani's it might have received little notice.)

By bringing his case first, and, as it now turns out, significantly before the criminal case, Lynch had given the defendants an apparent right to get discovery of the government's witnesses, including Boesky. In a criminal case they'd have no such right.

But getting that discovery depended on getting a judge other than Pollack, for Pollack was likely to buy the government's catch-22 plea that, yes, ''we'' (the government as represented by the SEC) brought the civil case and want it to go forward (or we wouldn't have brought it), but no, ''we'' (the government as represented by the U.S. attorney's office) can't allow discovery because it will jeopardize our pending criminal investigation.

Another Southern District judge, John Sprizzo (who is no bleeding heart), had recently refused to allow the government to whipsaw a defendant by accusing him in an SEC civil case but then saying he couldn't go forward with the discovery to clear his name because of a pending criminal case. Sprizzo had ruled that the government was the government and that if the government didn't want the SEC case to go forward it shouldn't have filed it.

(The Drexel lawyers were also counting on using the same logic once the criminal indictments came; they planned to argue that the civil case, and discovery for it, should not be held in abeyance, a notion that Pollack was sure to reject.)

Three days after the September 13 conference in chambers, at which he had refused to consider recusal, Pollack ordered on his own motion that all discovery in the SEC case be stayed pending a hearing on September

22. On September 20 the Drexel defense lawyers filed a formal motion for Pollack's recusal.

Pollack refused to hear that motion at his September 22 hearing, promising that he would hear it on October 11. He instead confined the hearing (which he laced with some barbs at Liman and the others) to discovery issues, all of which he decided, to the extent he decided them, against the Drexel lawyers. Five days later, he issued another order, this one delaying all depositions at least until after November. Just as bad from the standpoint of the defendants, he ordered that all discovery in the SEC case be consolidated with discovery in the Boesky cases, which is absurd. The multiparty, multilayered cases have little overlap with the Drexel cases. Consolidating their discovery will result in dozens of plaintiffs' lawyers and lawyers from Boesky's old arbitrage fund and their defense counterparts having to be present at depositions related to the SEC case and vice versa.

Pollack also gave the SEC until November 10 to produce documents requested by the Drexel defendants.

In short, Drexel's lawyers were going to lose the advantage Lynch had given them for the impending criminal case. Worse, they could see that even after the criminal case was filed Pollack would do the government's bidding in the civil case—which he, not a jury, would decide, and in which he might decide discovery issues in a way that could hurt Drexel's criminal case.

Indeed, according to three of the Drexel lawyers, who say they see Giuliani's office as more cautious than Lynch's unsophisticated headline-hunting crew, they still entertained the thought at this point in late September that they might strike some kind of plea bargain with Giuliani, only to be left with Pollack and his court as the main arena, and with Pollack able to impose all kinds of nightmarish penalties.

GOING FOR MANDAMUS

On September 30, three days after Pollack's discovery order, the Drexel lawyers took the drastic action of filing a writ of mandamus, asking the Second Circuit Court of Appeals to remove Pollack from the case or at least to order him to stop issuing discovery orders until he had ruled on the recusal motion.

The mandamus and the recusal motion that was attached to it outlined the case under the federal law that governs judicial conflicts. Section

455(a) of the law states that a judge must remove himself whenever his "impartiality might reasonably be questioned."

"How could Judge Pollack ever make a ruling in favor of Drexel or the other defendants without that decision being questioned—and without creating public suspicion, no matter how unfounded, that he was influenced by the multimillion-dollar payment to his wife," the brief argued—as if that was what was worrying Liman and his cohorts.

"And the converse is equally true," it continued. "How could Judge Pollack ever rule against Drexel without raising suspicions that he was bending over backwards to avoid favoring Drexel?" (In Pollack's case, of course, there would be no such suspicions, because everyone would see it as Pollack just being the same old Pollack.)

"With 22 active and 13 senior judges in the Southern District of New York," the brief concluded, "it simply makes no sense to allow this new litigation to be handled by a judge about whom there will be even the slightest question concerning an appearance of impartiality."

THE SEC'S SMEAR REPLY

The SEC's reply brief, written by enforcement division litigation chief Newkirk, 46, and his deputy Barry Goldsmith, 38, seems less the product of lawyers working for the republic than the work of hunters consumed with getting and keeping their prey.

Even a paralegal was enlisted by Newkirk and Goldsmith in the lies and innuendo. "From literally the moment this case was instituted," the brief began, "the Drexel defendants have brazenly tried . . . to prevent Judge Pollack [to whom their motion was addressed] from hearing this case. . . .

"These tactics," the brief declared, included an attempt by Armstrong "to physically stop [SEC paralegal] Barbara Bailin . . . from filing the complaint. . . . While towering over Ms. Bailin, and not identifying himself . . . Mr. Armstrong objected to her filing the complaint," the brief asserted, citing an appendixed affidavit from Bailin.

In fact, Armstrong hadn't had to identify himself because he'd been talking—"amiably," he claims—to the lawyers with whom Bailin was standing for ten or fifteen minutes before she went to file the papers. And he says he hadn't at all physically interfered with her or been impolite to her in any way.

Not only is that what Armstrong claims in a sworn affidavit, which, it should be noted, is far more direct and clear than paralegal Bailin's, which uses such words as "towering over" only to have them translated into "physically stop" in the Newkirk-Goldberg brief. It is also what the clerk who was in the filing room that afternoon told me. File clerk Dennis Pomarico, who says he remembers the incident "very clearly," recalls that Armstrong was, indeed, chatting "in a quiet, friendly way" with the SEC lawyers, that he was "always very polite" to Bailin and "never blocked her or anything like that," and that he spoke "politely to me at all times. He never raised his voice." Pomarico also says that, as Armstrong asserts in his affidavit, it was Newkirk of the SEC who introduced the only physical confrontation by "forcing himself in front of Armstrong to speak to me. Mr. Newkirk got very excited."

Yes, this seems like trivial stuff. But it isn't all that trivial for government lawyers to misrepresent the facts to a court this way—much less make what has now become a much publicized accusation against another lawyer of physical intimidation or, as much of the press has played it, of a lawyer being so desperate to help his obviously guilty client that he tried physically to stop a suit from being filed.

This accusation is followed in the brief by the more substantive one that the Drexel defendants are estopped from bringing the motion to recuse because the Boesky cases in which Drexel (though not Milken and others of the SEC defendants) is a defendant have been pending for 18 months, while the transaction between Palais Royal and Bain has been pending since early 1988. Drexel, therefore, must have known about the conflict for a long time, the argument goes.

In other words, the Drexel defendants—and their lawyers—are lying to the court about first having known about the conflict on September 9.

"It strains credulity to believe that Drexel, either itself or through its counsel, was unaware of Moselle Pollack's relationship to Judge Pollack until two days after this case was filed," the SEC asserted.

We need to examine carefully what Newkirk, Goldsmith, and the SEC are saying here and how they are saying it.

Here is how they establish this supposed prior knowledge (and, therefore, the lawyers' perjury), taken directly from their brief's "statement of facts" arguing the estoppel point:

1. According to an appendixed affidavit by an investment banker from Shearson Lehman Hutton Inc., which was representing Palais Royal in the buyout deal, one of the Shearson people told someone from Bain during the summer of 1988 that one of the selling shareholders

was married to Judge Pollack. *Nowhere does the SEC say that anyone from Bain told anyone from Drexel or Cahill about one of the shareholders being married to Judge Pollack.*

2. The same Shearson banker's affidavit declares that he gave a copy of a list of shareholders to a Cahill associate sometime in July or early August of 1988. *The affidavit does not say that anyone pointed out to anyone at Cahill that the Moselle Pollack listed there was related to Judge Pollack.*

3. "Bain, no later than summer of 1988, told its legal counsel, who were negotiating with Drexel and with Cahill Gordon & Reindel, of the relationship of Judge Pollack to Moselle Pollack." *Nowhere does it say that the counsel for Bain actually told anyone at Drexel about the relationship, nor does it name the lawyer. In fact, Bain's lawyer, Karl Lutz of Chicago's Kirkland & Ellis, says that he was contacted "several times" by the SEC and asked if he had told anyone at Drexel about the relationship. According to Lutz, whose firm, it should be noted, has also represented Drexel in the past, "I told them I was sure I hadn't mentioned it to anyone at Cahill." Needless to say, the SEC did not ask him for an affidavit. What clearer evidence could there be of the SEC lawyers' effort to mislead the court than the sentence quoted above combined with the fact that the SEC had spoken with Lutz?*

   "I don't think we actually said that Drexel or Cahill learned this from Bain," says Newkirk. "I think the implication was that here you have a transaction where Bain and Bain's lawyer knew, and they're negotiating with Cahill. And that is relevant as to whether Cahill knew. It may be that the Bain lawyer [Lutz] just didn't recall telling Drexel."

4. "While meeting with potential lenders—including Drexel—Bernard Fuchs, the president and chief executive officer of Palais Royal, generally told them about the history of Palais Royal and identified Moselle Pollack by name as the widow of the founder . . . and as a selling shareholder. In addition, on a number of occasions, Mr. Fuchs pointed out to potential lenders and financiers in these meetings that Moselle Pollack is married to Judge Pollack of New York." *This subterfuge is more obvious, though no less excusable: Nowhere does it say that Fuchs actually told Drexel about the Judge Pollack relationship, nor does the affidavit backing this statement—from the Shearson banker, not from Fuchs—say that Fuchs told anyone from Drexel. (Fuchs, who works for Mrs. Pollack, declined comment when I asked, through his secretary, whether he recalled ever telling anyone at Drexel about Moselle Pollack's relationship to Milton Pollack.)*

435

THE BIGGER SMEAR

Beyond the obvious lack of proof, one is left wondering why the Drexel defendants and defense counsel would do what Newkirk and Goldsmith try so hard here to accuse them of doing. If Liman, Fleming, Armstrong, Flumenbaum, and the others were so concerned with the SEC case getting to Pollack that they tried to get the court clerk not to send it to him, and if they knew about the conflict beforehand and could have raised it in the context of the Boesky cases that Pollack was handling, why would they have waited until *after* the SEC case was filed to raise the conflict?

"That's easy," says one of the SEC lawyers. "We think they purposely planned the conflict, and if they were going to do that, they couldn't raise it immediately after they got into the Palais deal because then it would have seemed too obvious."

Indeed, not content to accuse Drexel and their defense lawyers of lying about when they knew of the conflict, the SEC goes on, in a footnote that has now received wide publicity, to suggest this bigger fraud. "The facts of this case," says the footnote, "suggest that the defendants not only delayed filing their motion, but may have purposely created the alleged conflict."

Asked what evidence they have of the fabrication of the conflict, the SEC's Goldsmith and Newkirk would only say that the papers they filed speak for themselves. One enforcement division lawyer, insisting on anonymity, offered this new standard of evidence: "With these people you just never believe in coincidences."

Yet all the affidavits filed in the recusal battle, even those submitted with the SEC's brief, make it clear that Shearson solicited Bain to buy Palais Royal and that Bain then solicited Drexel and, again, that Drexel, as far as any of the evidence shows, knew nothing about Judge Pollack's involvement until September 9.

WHAT CONFLICT?

The rest of the SEC's argument was that there was, in fact, no conflict for which Judge Pollack needed to recuse himself.

As you read the following description of that argument, imagine that the SEC is in front of a nonpartisan judge, not one like Pollack, and that a defendant investment bank is arguing *to keep* the judge in the case despite the fact that his wife is about to get $30 million in a deal financed by the defendant. Would the SEC argue the same way?

Drexel, wrote Newkirk, Goldsmith, and their team, is far removed from a relationship with Mrs. Pollack in this deal because it is simply helping the buyer raise money to give to Mrs. Pollack, not giving her the money itself. Drexel's involvement in the Palais Royal transaction, the SEC argued, "is no different than that of a mortgage broker in the sale of a house to a buyer who is obligated to obtain mortgage financing." In fact, the SEC added in a triumphant footnote, Drexel's relationship to the Pollacks is no different from that of a dealer in government bonds who helps the government raise money from the bonds so that the proceeds from those bonds can, among other things, be used to pay judges' salaries.

All of that turns on the curious notion, coming as it does from the SEC, that Drexel is some kind of fungible entity, not the leading and most aggressive and most successful junk-bond financier in the world, which is basically how Drexel is described in the SEC's own complaint. Any old bank could have and would have done this deal, the SEC argued.

To back that up, the SEC submitted affidavits from the Palais Royal Shearson banker (who, of course, is working for Judge Pollack's wife) saying that Drexel was not crucial to the deal, and, later, one from former Lehman chief Louis Glucksman (a renowned trader, not LBO financier) saying that the deal was financeable by other bankers.

Drexel has, indeed, faced competition of late in junk-bond financing. And it may be that some other bank would do the deal. Bain counsel Lutz, however, says, "Drexel is the only bank that would . . . do this deal. We know that. Hell, when Romney [of Bain] called Joseph with the news about Pollack, he was terrified it would kill the deal." (Lutz says the SEC asked him about Drexel's indispensability, too.)

But the important point is that Drexel was the bank that Bain had settled on as offering, if not the only deal, then surely the best deal—and presumably the deal most likely to give Mrs. Pollack her $30 million. (The SEC countered by saying that Drexel hadn't yet signed an irrevocable contract to finance the deal but instead had agreed only to make its "best efforts" to do so, again a curious argument coming from the SEC, which surely is aware that "best efforts" commitments are the standard fare for investment banks in deals like this one.)

A Bain executive working on the deal later submitted his own affidavit saying that Drexel was "indispensable to the deal." This was echoed in an affidavit from a banker from Citicorp Venture Capital, Ltd., saying that his firm, which is also involved in the buyout, regarded it as a high-risk deal that only a few banking firms would agree to finance, and that of these firms Drexel was the leader in expertise and market share. (The Citicorp banker also said that an SEC official had contacted him six days before submitting the SEC brief charging Drexel with creating the conflict and asked if he thought it was possible, based on what he knew about the deal, that Drexel had "set up" the conflict. He had told the SEC that this was "highly improbable," he declared.)

In short, the only other two parties to the buyers' side of the deal—Bain and Citicorp—both said unequivocally that Drexel was indispensable.

But, again, all of that is beside the point. The judicial conflict statute deals with two possibilities. The first is that the outcome of the litigation could in some way affect a judge's financial interest. Drexel argued that this could apply here because, in essence, some ruling that Pollack might make, even at the early stages of the litigation, could weaken Drexel's ability to do deals and raise money in the junk-bond marketplace, thereby hurting its effort to raise the Palais junk bonds. That argument, speculative as it is, isn't indisputable, but I think it holds.

The second possibility under the statute is that the public will *perceive* that a judge might not have been impartial because of some relationship he has with one of the litigants. That one does seem indisputable.

Suppose, for example, that no one had raised the conflict and the Pollacks' connection had never been made public. Suppose also that Pollack had, for whatever reason, decided the case for Drexel. And then suppose that six months later *The Wall Street Journal* learned of the Palais Royal transaction and the Pollacks' $30 million take from it. Is there any question that there might then be some public doubt about the disinterestedness of the judge's decision?

After the Drexel defendants filed their recusal motion and writ of mandamus, Yale Law professor and routinely quoted ethics specialist Geoffrey Hazard, Jr., told *The Wall Street Journal* that he didn't "see anything to indicate there's any case for disqualification here." Mrs. Pollack's financial interest was unlikely to be affected by the outcome of the case, he explained.

What about the other leg of the conflict statute, the appearance problem, I asked Hazard a few days later. "Drexel is not giving her the money, and I think sophisticated people will understand that the odds are high that another bank would do the deal," he replied.

I posed my six-months-later newspaper hypothetical to Hazard. "How the press might misconstrue the facts isn't the issue," he replied. "The real question of perception isn't really about the man in the street's perception," he added. "It's about what world-wise, sophisticated people would think, what the power structure would think, not people recruited from a jury."

In the only case it has decided on the judicial conflict statute, the U.S. Supreme Court ruled in June 1988 that a judge who served as an unpaid trustee to a university indirectly involved in a case before him had to remove himself, because "if it would appear to a reasonable person" that the judge might be partial, "then an appearance of partiality is created even though no partiality exists."

Although I think Hazard believes what he's saying, it's also worth noting (as the *Journal* didn't, because Hazard didn't tell its reporter, he says) that Hazard is on retainer to Wall Street's Fried, Frank, Harris, Shriver & Jacobson in that firm's defense of itself in the Boesky-related cases. (Fried, Frank is a defendant because one of its partners, Stephen Fraidin, who was Boesky's lead lawyer for years, is alleged to have helped lure investors into Boesky's fund.) Fried, Frank is said by three sources familiar with its defense to welcome Judge Pollack's role in their case because the firm believes he is sympathetic to its arguments that Fraidin and the firm cannot be held culpable under the securities laws.

Hazard seemed to back off his position a bit after the Drexel defense team submitted a reply to the SEC brief, which stressed the public perception problem and chastised the SEC because it "of all parties should not be heard elevating the form of a transaction over its economic substance." The brief also included a strong "expert" affidavit from Hazard's alter ego on the legal ethics guru circuit—New York University law professor Stephen Gillers—supporting the Drexel position. Hazard told me that the Drexel reply, which he had read, "may have some merit." But, he added, "What's bothersome about this is that it's all devoid of reality, because they're not worried about Pollack favoring Drexel; they want him off the case because they're afraid he'll be against them. So it's all a lot of baloney."

In other words, Hazard's best argument—a sound, commonsense one, but one which, because of the charade required in court that all judges are equally fair, must be unspoken in court—is based on Pollack's known bias: Pollack's bias precludes him from favoring Drexel, or being seen to favor Drexel, even if his wife is getting $30 million indirectly from Drexel. The public, or even Hazard's "power structure," will never suspect that Pollack favored Drexel because of the $30 million because he, in fact, never *will* favor Drexel. And if he sides with the SEC, the "power structure," at least, will know that he did it because he always sides with the government, not because he's bending over backward, as the Drexel lawyers' brief had hypothesized. In short, only if Pollack were a fair judge would Drexel have a claim for getting him off the case.

On October 7, the court of appeals, as expected, turned down the Drexel mandamus petition, saying that because Pollack was scheduled to hear the motion for recusal on October 11 it was unnecessary to preempt him. "We expected that," said one Drexel lawyer, "but we wanted to file the mandamus anyway so that if the court of appeals said that they would wait for Pollack to rule on October 11, they would be preventing Pollack from exercising a pocket veto by refusing to decide. This way, he'd have to decide it on the eleventh, and then we could appeal."

POLLACK GOES AFTER LIMAN

But on October 10, Pollack dropped a thunderbolt. Although it was a court holiday (Columbus Day), that afternoon he had his clerk call Liman and Flumenbaum from Paul, Weiss and tell them to have someone pick up a "show cause" order pertaining to them.

What the Paul, Weiss messenger brought back from the court was a sloppily typed (as if Pollack and a clerk had worked on it alone during the weekend and that holiday Monday) two-page paper with 20 pages of attachments.

"Upon the attached exhibits," the order began, "from which a fiduciary relationship appears to exist between respondents [Liman and Flumenbaum] and Palais Royal and its stockholders, and it appearing that respondents may have participated herein on the pending motions for recusal of the court adversely to Palais Royal and its stockholders . . . let said respondents show cause [the next day] at 11:00 [three hours before the recusal hearing] why an investigation and hearing should not be held to determine whether respondents are proceeding herein in breach of fiduciary duties and obligations and with professionally conflicting interests in the pending matter seeking disqualification of the Court . . . and why respondents should not be required to identify and withdraw the papers on said disqualification motion which they drafted . . . and why plaintiffs and any other parties should not have such other and further relief as may be just and proper."

How could Liman and Flumenbaum have a "fiduciary relationship" with Palais Royal and its shareholders?

Pollack's 20 pages of exhibits were copies of letters from a Paul, Weiss tax partner, Alfred Youngwood, from April 1987 through November 1987 rendering tax advice to George Asch, who is the husband of Mrs. Pollack's daughter from her prior marriage and a shareholder in Palais Royal. There was also one letter acknowledging some tax work done for Palais Royal. Another of Pollack's exhibits indicated that Paul, Weiss's charges for 1987 had totaled $13,000, which had been billed to Palais Royal.

According to an affidavit subsequently filed by Youngwood, he had been a boyhood friend of Asch's and had occasionally provided him tax advice related to his interest in Palais Royal. Also, Youngwood and a Paul, Weiss associate had spent seven hours during the summer of 1988 doing research and advising Asch about the New York residency laws with regard to what Asch had told Youngwood might be the sale of Palais Royal. But, said Youngwood's affidavit, he had never been told anything about the proposed sale—not its terms, not who the buyer was, and not which banker was providing financing.

Youngwood also swore in his affidavit, as would Liman and Flumenbaum, that neither Liman nor Flumenbaum had ever known of Youngwood's work for Asch or Asch's connection to Palais Royal until after Paul, Weiss and the other Drexel lawyers had filed the Pollack recusal motion.

True, it can be argued that any partner's knowledge about a client is imputed to all partners at a firm. But for Pollack to argue that Paul, Weiss's divulging of the conflict would adversely affect Palais Royal and its shareholders is to concede that Drexel is key to the Palais Royal deal. (For what he's saying is that the revealing of the Drexel conflict might somehow cause Drexel to get out of the Palais Royal deal, which would hurt the shareholders in exactly the way that the SEC claims they wouldn't be hurt if Drexel bowed out and another banker was sought to replace Drexel. Surely, Pollack couldn't mean only that the shareholders were hurt by the Drexel lawyers' simple act of revealing the pending deal with Bain to Pollack in the recusal motion; for they had revealed that—under seal—only to Pollack and the SEC, which is supposed to be good at keeping secrets about pending financial transactions.)

Moreover, for Pollack, who declined repeated requests for an interview concerning Palais Royal and the Drexel case, to argue that Liman and Flumenbaum had a fiduciary duty to the Palais Royal shareholders—who

441

include his wife and, therefore under the law, him—is to argue that Pollack must immediately recuse himself from this case or any other case involving Paul, Weiss, and that he should have done so long before the recusal motion was filed, assuming his wife or son-in-law told him earlier.

In short, Pollack's "show cause" order was a rare lapse. Pollack may be biased but he is not known to vent his biases in such an illogical, poorly fashioned manner. "He hates Arthur [Liman] so much that he must have just lost his cool when Liman and the others tried to recuse him and he saw that they had him," ventures one lawyer indirectly involved in the case.

THE EX PARTE JUDGE ATTACKS
EX PARTE LAWYERS

When the 11 A.M. hearing came, Pollack mounted the bench for about three minutes, seemed to forget the part of his order seeking to throw Paul, Weiss off the recusal motion, and told the gathered lawyers (who included those from the "related" Boesky cases) only that he imputed knowledge to Flumenbaum and Liman of the "conflicting representation" in 1987 and was, therefore, referring "the conduct of the parties in this case for disciplinary resolution . . . to the chief judge. . . . And I will hear no more about this motion."

The 2 P.M. hearing started out quietly. Fleming began an almost obsequious Drexel presentation by stressing that the issue, of course, wasn't His Honor's actual impartiality but the possible misperceptions of it. SEC enforcement division assistant litigation chief Barry Goldsmith repeated the government's arguments about Drexel's role not being important to the Palais Royal transaction, and urged that ethics expert Gillers's affidavit supporting Drexel's conflict claim be stricken from the record. Pollack granted the motion before Goldsmith had finished making it, dismissing Gillers as "a former clerk of one of the parties." (Gillers had been a Paul, Weiss associate, which he revealed in his affidavit.)

Goldsmith also repeated his proofless contention that Drexel and Cahill Gordon knew about the Palais Royal conflict "months ago."

The private plaintiffs counsel, delighted to have Pollack on their case, piled on. In fact George Reycraft of Wall Street's Cadwalader, Wickersham & Taft, which represents the plaintiffs from the Boesky arbitrage fund, made the SEC's footnote about Drexel "creating" the conflict his keynote.

The alleged conflict was Drexel's own "creation," Reycraft charged. (Asked later what evidence he had, Reycraft told me that what he really meant was that because Drexel could still walk from the Palais deal, it was responsible for the continuation of the conflict—as if Drexel's walking from the deal now and thereby endangering or changing the terms of the $30 million payout for Mrs. Pollack's stock would eliminate rather than exacerbate a conflict.) Reycraft also urged an investigation of what Cahill Gordon and Paul, Weiss had "known about this matter." He contended that because a Cahill associate had seen Mrs. Pollack's name on a shareholder list during the summer, the firm is "chargeable with this knowledge" of the Palais Royal deal and Mrs. Pollack's role in it.

That, of course, ignores the question of whether the associate is charged with the knowledge that the Moselle Pollack he saw on the list was Milton Pollack's wife—which he said in a sworn affidavit he did not know. But Pollack, who seemed to enjoy Reycraft's presentation, interrupted, saying Cahill is charged with the knowledge of who Moselle Pollack is for 17 years because partner Thomas Curnin, the litigator representing Drexel, had known his wife that long. In other words, everyone in a law firm is charged not just with knowing about client matters, which is what the relevant conflict law is, but with knowing anything any of its members knows, including the name of a judge's wife.

When Curnin spoke, Pollack attacked him for having claimed that "Cahill Gordon did not know that Moselle Pollack was married to Judge Pollack," as if that were the issue. Curnin replied with "a declaration pursuant" to the federal perjury statute that his firm hadn't learned of the real conflict—that Pollack's wife was a shareholder in a Drexel-financed buyout—until September 9.

Through most of the hearing Pollack seemed to control his anger. Finally, though, he lost his cool, and when he did he chose a curious point of attack.

It came near the end of the hearing, as Peter Fleming began a rebuttal. Pollack interrupted, attacking Fleming because Fleming and Curnin had called Pollack on that Saturday afternoon, September 10, without first informing their adversaries at the SEC that they were going to make the call and giving them an opportunity to participate. (Fleming and Curnin had called Lynch the following morning, and no substantive discussion of the matter was held until the hearing in Pollack's chambers, with all parties attending, on September 13.)

That ex parte call, Pollack said, getting visibly angry for the first time, according to observers who were at the hearing, was "totally irresponsible and improper . . . and that is a rule of ethics that you cannot just fob off. And I resent it very much." He kept at it for several minutes.

Fleming and Curnin say they thought they were obliged to inform the judge immediately, and briefly, of the facts of the conflict and then schedule a hearing, but that, yes, they should have involved the SEC in the first call. Of course if Pollack had really thought that the call was improper, he could have told Fleming and Curnin to hang up until they got the SEC lawyers on the phone for a conference call.

But beyond that obvious point, it must be said that ex parte contact is an odd, even pathological, issue for Pollack to have waxed so indignant about. Pollack's own ex parte calls to litigants who have cases pending before him are legendary in the Southern District. Ex parte contact has long been the much-whispered-about way in which Pollack acts out, and even gets results from, his well-known biases. Indeed, the more one tries to find out about Pollack and ex parte contact, the more one finds a 20-year-old pattern of startling impropriety.

I spoke with 23 lawyers who acknowledged personally getting ex parte phone calls from Pollack while having cases before him. The earliest reported call was in 1969. All 23, who include six present or former bureau heads or higher in the U.S. attorney's office, said they had won their cases. All but four said the calls related to the substance of their cases. Seven said that Pollack had even suggested arguments they might make or questions they might ask a witness.

Two of the government lawyers recalled that during their tenure the calls from the judge had gotten so frequent at one point that Robert Morvillo, who was the head of the criminal division from 1971 through 1973, had instructed his people that all Pollack calls be routed to him so that he could fend them off because he thought the ex parte contacts so improper. (Morvillo declined comment.)

Two other former government lawyers said that their boss in the prosecutor's office, then–U.S. Attorney John Martin, had been so bothered by the calls that he had called Pollack to request that he stop making them. (Martin declined comment.)

Two of Pollack's former clerks confirmed the stories about ex parte contact; three others declined comment. Pollack, through his secretary, declined comment when asked if he had ever made ex parte calls to litigants which involved substantive discussion about the cases before him. (He also declined comment on all other issues related to this article.)

Others recalled Pollack's having forced ex parte contact on them even without having initiated the contact himself. One lawyer who was the beneficiary of this variety of ex parte discussion (in a private party case about three years ago) recalls that he "became kind of addicted" to the discussions, "even though I knew it was wrong.

"I called one afternoon to ask his clerk about a scheduling matter, purely a scheduling matter," he says. "But the clerk put me on hold and then the judge picked up the phone and started talking about the case and what I ought to do. . . . I called a week later and the same thing happened. So I started developing excuses to call the clerk. . . . I feel kind of dirty about it, but I did it."

Whether Rudy Giuliani's troops feel dirty about it is not known, but they do seem to benefit from the calls. Several former assistants in the office during Giuliani's five-year tenure recalled getting calls from Pollack; others said that John Carroll, who is running the Boesky and Drexel criminal cases, has been getting calls from Pollack concerning discovery motions pending in the Drexel SEC and private party civil cases, in which Carroll has interjected himself as a party (seeking to hold off certain discovery). Carroll says he is "not comfortable commenting about any discussions I may or may not have had with Judge Pollack."

Giuliani, through spokesman Dennison Young, was asked whether he or, to his knowledge, any of his assistants had ever received ex parte calls from Judge Pollack concerning substantive case matters. After checking, Young reported that Giuliani declined comment.

A CHARADE THAT NO ONE SHOULD
BE PROUD OF

Although Pollack had promised the Drexel lawyers "the prompt decision you request" at the October 11 hearing, Pollack didn't decide the case then and hadn't decided it by week's end. Finally, on October 17 he ruled, as expected, not to recuse himself.

Calling the Drexel lawyers' conflict claim "ludicrous" and "bizarre," and declaring that there is "an utter and admitted lack of any privity between Mrs. Pollack and Drexel," Pollack declared, "This court can confidently respond, unhesitatingly," that there will not be "even the slightest doubt . . . of the judge's impartiality.

"The antics of counsel," Pollack added, "are an affront to the civility which must attend the conduct of litigation. The case is as clearly related to the earlier 13 cases before the court as the interest of my wife and her family is unrelated to the merits of this litigation.''

As of this writing the Drexel lawyers' appeal to the Second Circuit—in the form of a renewed mandamus petition—is pending, as is Pollack's ostensible disciplinary action against Liman and Flumenbaum (referred to Chief Judge Brieant) for their purported violation of their duty to Palais Royal and its shareholders, including Mrs. Pollack. The Drexel lawyers' new mandamus petition, which restates the first one but also cites Pollack's bizarre ''show cause'' order and disciplinary charges against Liman and Flumenbaum as evidence that the judge, himself, has become a litigant in the case, seems to have at least made a good initial impression on the Second Circuit. The day after it was filed, the appeals court, on its own, issued an order stopping Pollack from making any more discovery rulings until it renders its decision.

But even if the Second Circuit throws Pollack off the case, the system will have been disgraced by the charade played out in this case, as in the Teamsters case, in which government lawyers have smeared other lawyers, misstated the facts, taken legal positions (on judicial conflicts) that seem certain to come back to haunt the government in other cases, and otherwise fallen all over themselves to hang on to a judge who promises to provide anything but the justice these lawyers are being paid to seek.

Even those sympathetic to the SEC's cause in the Drexel case should muffle their cheers over what's gone on so far. Getting the case in front of Pollack may prove to be too much of a good thing. For, as a *Wall Street Journal* column incisively pointed out in mid-October, the brouhaha over Pollack has diverted public attention from the meticulous, far-reaching accusations made in the SEC's 184-page complaint, and, in fact, may result in Drexel being cast as the victim of a hanging judge rather than a wrongdoer brought to justice.

Likewise, in the landmark Teamsters case, some bright young Giuliani protégé, with a wink and a nod, found a way to manipulate the system. Randy Mastro probably went home that night feeling pretty clever. But over the long term the case that he so skillfully put together will be undermined, even if he wins, by Judge Edelstein's involvement in it.

The problem, then, is twofold.

First, the judges themselves. Southern District chief Brieant is an excellent jurist who cares mightily about the system. His concern that litigants shouldn't think they have a right to any particular judge is well-founded, based as it is on the notion that for judges to be independent they have to be insulated from personal attack. But Brieant's ''all judges are the same'' posture ignores a reality that judges, like any insulated bureaucracy that wants (and in this case needs) to stay insulated, don't like to face: some among them are unfit and should be thrown off the bench, because they are anything but fair, and because some litigants will seek them out for that reason.

Nothing I have written about Edelstein or Pollack will surprise a single judge who knows either man. Yet to my knowledge no judge has spoken out or done anything else about these ongoing threats to justice. Whether as a group, through their supervising judges, or through their appellate judges, federal judges ought to establish aggressive peer review panels that, like some of their state court counterparts, will solicit complaints and send regular questionnaires to lawyers asking them about judges. And if the panels can't unseat judges who turn up rotten in these reviews, they can at least pressure them to improve, or limit the cases they get, or, in extreme cases, embarrass them into improving by making the most negative reports public. (Pollack's ex parte activities, for example, would have probably stopped if they'd been publicly exposed.)

There's also one simple rule that judges or the Congress can promulgate so that the farce of a Pollack or an Edelstein hearing his own recusal motions is eliminated. Recusal motions should be heard by a different judge, perhaps even by a different judicial district.

But there will always be bad judges. And that brings us to the second problem: government lawyers who, among other acts of overreaching, are willing to manipulate unjust judges in the cause of winning.

The majority of government lawyers are, understandably, young, eager, and self-righteous. But that means they need to be led by people who can teach them that justice, not winning, is their real cause, and that even a just result isn't justice if it is achieved indecently, unfairly, or outside the law.

The people in charge of these lawyers have to make them see these higher values. To take another example of the same kind of winning-is-everything conduct, the leaks about the Drexel investigation—which are felonies and which, according to reporter-sources, come from an SEC that has used the leaks to pressure targets and to garner headlines—should not be winked at, but should be investigated by those in charge with Giuliani-like relentlessness. (Yes, making cases will be hard because reporters can, appropriately, invoke shield laws protecting the confidentiality of their sources; but Giuliani could at least put his people and the SEC people in front of a grand jury to see who will deny what under oath, or who will seek immunity.)

Similarly, because government lawyers are supposed to care about doing justice, they should work to rid the court of clearly unjust judges, not do anything they can to take advantage of them, as if they were some kind of house advantage.

Giuliani and the SEC's Gary Lynch should never have allowed the hypocritical, deceitful, and downright improper efforts to get Edelstein and Pollack enlisted in their cases. As officers of the court and lawyers for the Republic, they should not have forgotten that winning isn't everything.

EPILOGUE

On March 14, 1989, the national RICO Teamsters suit was settled. In the consent decree filed with Judge Edelstein, several individual International Teamsters officers agreed to leave their posts, and the union accepted court-appointed officers to supervise union administration, investigations, and elections. The Teamsters also agreed to a mandate for the first-ever secret-ballot election of officers by all the union's members.

In December 1988 John Long and John Mahoney, Jr., were convicted of criminal RICO offenses in federal court in Manhattan. Discovery in the civil cases against Long and Mahoney, which was never consolidated with the national RICO case, resumed as of March 14, 1989. At publication time, the cases were still being litigated before Judge Edelstein.

The Second Circuit denied Arthur Liman and Martin Flumenbaum's renewed mandamus petition to remove Judge Pollack from the Drexel case. According to Flumenbaum, as of publication time the ostensible disciplinary action against him and Liman had not gone forward.

In December 1988 Drexel pleaded guilty to six counts of mail and securities fraud before Judge Pollack. As part of the deal with the government, Drexel agreed to pay $650 million in fines and cooperate with the government in its ongoing investigation of individual Drexel employees.

HUMAN RIGHTS

The law is for the protection of the weak more than the strong.

—CHIEF JUSTICE WILLIAM ERLE, 1850

U.S.
v.
the Arizona Sanctuary Workers

LAW OR JUSTICE

BY

MITCHELL PACELLE

Jurors in the Arizona sanctuary trial say their verdict followed the law. But, they ask, was justice done?

Moments after a Tucson jury came to a decision in the criminal trial of 11 church workers who were charged with smuggling Salvadorans and Guatemalans into the United States, juror Dennis Davis looked out the window of the federal courthouse. Scores of people were rushing toward the entrance. Among them he saw "the defendants and their lawyers walking arm in arm, just smiling," Davis recalls. "They were so sure the decision would be not guilty." Another juror, Ethel Smathers, remembers, "We looked out the window and said, 'My God! What have we done?' "

What Smathers, Davis, and their ten fellow jurors did last May 1 was convict six out of eleven church workers of conspiring to violate federal immigration laws. Various defendants were also convicted of lesser charges of helping aliens sneak across the border, driving them up into Arizona, and sheltering them in churches and homes.

All of the defendants were part of the sanctuary movement—a loosely knit coalition of some 300 churches and synagogues, 20 cities, and two states—New York and New Mexico—that are offering haven to Central Americans believed to be fleeing political oppression. Some saw the convictions as a verdict on the sanctuary movement itself.

The decision was not reached lightly. As the 12 jurors waited one long hour in the jury room for the defendants and their lawyers to assemble, "the emotion started to climb," says juror Arthur Mathieson, a 47-year-old building inspector.

"We were all just kind of cold and clammy," recalls juror Lynn Cobb, 39. "I was just terrified to go in there and face the defendants. . . . I had an awful feeling that I was going to sit and cry through the whole thing."

Then, as the bailiff finally read the verdict to a stone-silent courtroom, "You could see all of [the defendants'] faces dropping," says Smathers. One defense lawyer lowered his head to the table. Another started to cry.

Their clients seemed stunned. Among them were the Reverend Ramón Quiñones, 50, a Roman Catholic priest who counseled fearful Central Americans who showed up at his Nogales, Mexico, church; Maria Socorro Aguilar, a 60-year-old Mexican widow who brought food and clothing to Central Americans in Mexican border jails and helped some cross into the U.S.; the Reverend John Fife III, the outspoken 45-year-old pastor of Tucson's Southside Presbyterian Church (U.S.A.), which posts a huge sign declaring itself a sanctuary to fleeing Central Americans; and Sister Darlene Nicgorski, who had fled her Guatemalan ministry when her pastor was murdered in 1981 and who has occasionally housed aliens in her Phoenix apartment.

After the verdict, the jurors were whisked out the back door of the courthouse. Their six months of public service were over—but not their questions about it. Cobb, who works in a Tucson bookstore, says she still second-guesses herself about voting to convict on conspiracy. "I waver back and forth on this since the trial," she said in a recent interview with *The American Lawyer.* "Some days I feel we had to do it. Other days I'm real upset."

For another juror, the verdict has become quite literally haunting. When reporters phoned Anna Browning, the 25-year-old who came close to hanging the jury, she was getting sick to her stomach. Browning now declines to be interviewed, saying it makes her sick to think about the case. Browning's mother, who lives with her, blames the trial for her daughter's continuing migraine headaches and nausea.

Recent interviews with nine of the twelve jurors reveal something even more disturbing. Four of the jurors who voted to convict—Dennis Davis, Susan Hagerty, David McCrea, and Ethel Smathers—stated flatly that, although they followed the law as instructed by the judge, *justice* was not done. Two others questioned the laws on which their votes for conviction were based. "We felt that these people probably shouldn't have been prosecuted," says Smathers.

Defense lawyers say that the government's handling of the case—using wiretaps and unsavory informers to infiltrate church meetings and secretly tape the defendants—was morally and legally wrong. They hoped to instill in the jury such a sense of outrage at the government's investigation that jurors would simply throw the charges out the window. And many jurors did enter the jury room torn between following their consciences or the letter of the law. But, say several jurors, forewoman Catherine Sheaffer, backed by several vocal supporters, exhorted the jury to disregard their emotions and stay focused on the indictment and the judge's instructions.

It was not easy to dismiss moral judgments, especially with such defendants. "I found it real tough to be in a position of finding the guilt or innocence of people engaged in what I consider lifesaving activities," reflects Davis, who left town on a rail pass after the verdict to "clear my head . . . to get some peace and quiet."

Davis adds that his jury experience ultimately left him "feel[ing] like a piece of a jigsaw puzzle. When we got sworn in and agreed to go by the rules of the court, I started to feel that I was sworn into a game without knowing what the rules were."

For the jurors, the trial that would end in paradox began in mystery. When they filed into the courtroom to hear opening arguments on November 15, 1985, they knew little of the nearly two weeks of legal wrangling that had just ended; of the political tensions of the trial, indicated by—among other things—the blood smeared on the courtroom wall by a protestor; or of the severe evidentiary restrictions imposed by the judge. Defense lawyers say that, judging from voir dire, none of the jurors had more than a vague notion of what the sanctuary movement was.

The movement had been making headlines in Arizona and other Southwestern states since January 14, 1985, when the Arizona U.S. attorney handed down indictments against 16 sanctuary workers in Tucson, Phoenix, and the border towns of Nogales, Arizona, and Nogales, Mexico.

453

There were dozens of counts, the most serious being criminal conspiracy. Five defendants were later dropped from the indictment, leaving 11 church workers to stand trial that fall.

The arrests grew out of Operation Sojourner, an investigation by the Immigration and Naturalization Service of church groups and individuals that were openly assisting aliens from Central America. The nine-month investigation relied heavily on government informants who infiltrated several church groups and secretly recorded 91 tapes of sanctuary planning sessions and church meetings.

With illegal immigration a red-hot political issue in southern Arizona, the prosecutor, Special Assistant U.S. Attorney Donald Reno, Jr., and the 13 defense lawyers spent three weeks considering some 80 potential jurors to empanel 12, plus three alternates. Trial judge Earl Carroll, a Carter appointee, conducted the questioning.

The defense lawyers functioned as a team but had no clear-cut leader. It was a varied group that included lawyers from New York and California as well as Arizona. James Brosnahan, a partner at San Francisco's Morrison & Foerster, handled the case *pro bono,* and Ellen Yaroshefsky flew in from New York's Center for Constitutional Rights. The eight Arizona attorneys included Tucson's A. Bates Butler III, a former U.S. attorney in Arizona and now a partner at Butler & Stein; Robert Hirsh of Tucson's Hirsch, Sherrick & Murphy; and Michael Piccarreta of Tucson's Davis, Siegel & Gugino.

Prosecutor Reno, 43, had joined the Phoenix U.S. attorney's office three months before the investigation began as a special assistant charged with prosecuting interstate alien smuggling conspiracies. After working in his father's practice in Champaign, Illinois, for eight years, Reno had taken an eight-year detour from law as a developer of restaurants, fast-food outlets, and nightclubs. Nine months after he joined the prosecutor's office, he was devoting nearly all of his time to the sanctuary case.

The lawyers eventually wound up with a jury that neither side says it was comfortable with. The group of twelve who eventually delivered the verdict included nine women, seven jurors under the age of 35, four college graduates, three Evangelical Christians, and three Catholics.

Prosecutor Reno must have felt that the defense used its 12 preempts deftly, for he came out of voir dire feeling that the defense lawyers had "sanitized the jury," leaving him "starting behind the starting line," he says.

Yet the defense lawyers felt similarly handicapped. They were most worried about one juror, 47-year-old Catherine Sheaffer. Concerned about the year she spent in law school and her Evangelical Christianity, they debated vigorously about whether to preempt her, deciding eventually to preempt others they considered more objectionable. When they later learned that she was selected forewoman, many felt they'd made a mistake.

HAMSTRUNG FROM THE START?

In some respects, the most important part of the trial took place before it even started. Defense lawyers assert that a series of lengthy and hotly contested pretrial motions and pleadings left them hog-tied before they got a chance at the jury. Prosecutor Reno filed a pretrial motion in limine that anticipated critical defense arguments and argued to prohibit lines of questioning on matters that were—he argued—irrelevant and prejudicial.

Tucson's Robert Hirsh, who represented the Reverend John Fife, explains that the intended defenses were based on both the U.S. Refugee Act of 1980 and international law. The act defines a refugee as an alien who has "a well-founded fear of persecution" if sent back to his native country. International law, argues defense lawyer Bates Butler, does not require aliens to apply to the INS to qualify as refugees. Testimony on conditions in Central America would have been introduced to bolster the defendants' claim that they believed the Central Americans—none of whom had applied to the INS at the border for refugee status—were refugees.

Hirsh had planned to tell the jurors that given the church workers' belief that the Salvadorans and Guatemalans were refugees, the defendants had no intent to break any laws and certainly were not conspiring to do so. Defense lawyers also had planned to tell the jurors, says Hirsh, that the defendants were required by their religion to give food, shelter, and clothing to refugees, no questions asked.

In response to Reno's motion—and in spite of defense pleadings—Judge Carroll ruled that all such testimony had to do with intentions and was therefore irrelevant and inadmissible. The jurors were to hear none of it, he ruled, torpedoing what the defense team considered its most potent defenses.

"That was a real tough blow to us," says Butler. The defense quickly retrenched, launching what would be a spirited and skillful battle. Despite the judge's numerous restrictions, they were able to move jurors by slipping in evidence about torture, killings, and other forms of terror in Central America.

A DEFIANT DEFENSE

In his opening statement, prosecutor Reno said he would present a "routine alien smuggling case" to the jury. Nonetheless, his first witness was highly controversial. Jesus Cruz had agreed to work for the government in exchange for immunity on separate charges of smuggling aliens. Cruz, who would become the prosecution's star witness—albeit a tarnished one—was a key operative in "Operation Sojourner." For 23 days, Cruz testified in Spanish about what he witnessed after being accepted by the defendants as a co-worker.

The defense lawyers began a blistering cross-examination of Cruz, impeaching him several times. Juror David McCrea recalls that the defense "proved time and time again that [Cruz] was lying." Jurors Ethel Smathers, 44, a cafeteria department head, and Janice Estes, 33, who lives on an army base with her husband, were left wondering whether to believe anything Cruz had said. "I believe at least ninety-six percent of his testimony was worthless," remarks Smathers.

Cruz's testimony disturbed other jurors less. "The whole jury saw him for what he was," says Cobb, "a sleazy character. But that didn't change that he saw these things." Computer programmer Lori Dorazio recalls, "I trusted what he said. I thought of myself trying to remember a conversation that happened a year ago." Says Sandra Johnson, the 37-year-old nurse who later argued strongly for convictions: "I just thought he was someone doing his job. . . . Cruz, I felt, really did care for [the aliens]." That view was shared by Dorazio.

Jurors did not hear from a Central American alien until January 15, two months after the trial started. Prosecutor Reno called to the stand Alejandro Rodriguez, a 45-year-old Salvadoran labor organizer who had fled overland with his family in a grueling journey from El Salvador to Arizona in 1984. Rodriguez, a hostile prosecution witness, testified that Mexican lay worker Aguilar was "the only person that offered me a roof over my head when I was most in need."

Even the jurors who later pushed for convictions were deeply moved by the testimony of Rodriguez and the aliens who followed. After hearing from Rodriguez, says Dorazio, "I just went home and cried all night." A later witness from El Salvador, Silver Palacios, 20, was scheduled to be deported after the trial. Juror Ethel Smathers remembers, "At first we thought he was stoned. But when you looked closer, you could tell he was just terrified." (With the jury out, defense attorney Butler revealed that Palacios had lost three brothers and an uncle in the violence in his homeland.)

In their cross-examinations, defense lawyers immediately began to push against the evidentiary boundaries drawn by Judge Carroll. In order to refute Reno's charges that the defendants induced Rodriguez to cross the border, defense lawyers pressed the witness to explain why he brought his family north. Carroll allowed the defense team to use such terms as "political persecution" and "concern" for one's safety but warned against any graphic discussion of violence. (The jury was sent out before Rodriguez chronicled his kidnapping, imprisonment, and torture by Salvadoran armed forces.)

When cross-examining the Salvadorans and Guatemalans, defense lawyers engaged in a delicate dance around the rulings, using euphemisms such as "fled involuntarily" to clue jurors in on just what the judge had declared off limits, or occasionally, just blurting out impermissible questions. For the jurors, it was a confusing and disturbing new phase during which a broader story began to emerge.

"The attorney would stand up and say, 'Without going into detail, tell us how your brother died,' " recalls Cobb. "Or, 'How do you live being on a death list?' Reno got up [to object] in three seconds. Meanwhile, we already heard it."

As the defense stepped up its tactics, they came in conflict with the judge, whom they believed had shown bias against them from voir dire on. Indeed, the animosity between Carroll and the defense lawyers grew so severe that later in the trial, defense lawyer William Walker would accuse the judge (out of the jury's hearing) of making "a last-gasp effort . . . to muzzle us and to engage in grasping a victory for the prosecutor. . . . The judge has exhibited, again and again, bias against us."

Jurors didn't share the defense's view about Carroll. "I thought he was very patient," remarks Cobb.

DISORDER IN THE COURT

As defense lawyers repeatedly breached the boundaries of admissible evidence, the judge time and again ordered the jury out of the courtroom. At one point, Reno asked Guatemalan farm worker organizer Joel Morelos about a certain conversation he'd heard between sanctuary workers. Morelos blurted out that he probably hadn't heard the whole exchange because he had lost hearing in one ear after being tortured. He was later asked by defense lawyer Michael Altman to show his scars. "Boy, they got us out of the courtroom fast!" says Smathers.

The jury was marched out so often, says Dorazio, that "we would joke, 'Here we go, we're getting our exercise.' " Says Davis: "Sometimes it felt like they could hardly get the door closed before there was going to be a donnybrook. The electricity was there."

On his return to the courtroom, Davis, for one, would scrutinize the faces of the judge and defense lawyers. "I'd catch an idea as to which side had won," he recalls. Reno, Davis adds, remained impassive throughout.

Some jurors say they found their patience for courtroom disorder wearing thin. What with lawyers jumping up repeatedly to object, spectators breaking into laughter, and the judge threatening to clear the courtroom, says Smathers: "At times you'd get the idea that it was like a three-ring circus."

"Some of the [defense] lawyers would make cracks back and forth that made Judge Carroll mad. I thought that was kind of childish," Smathers complains. Several jurors cite comments made by defense lawyer William Walker of Tucson's Stompoly & Even that angered Carroll. Walker dismisses the remarks as jokes. Sandra Johnson recalls, "There were times that I thought the defense lawyers conducted themselves less than professionally. . . . I was getting really irritated." She and other jurors claim, however, that their reactions to defense lawyers had nothing to do with their deliberations.

Defense lawyers Bates Butler and James Brosnahan both deny any improper comments were made by the defense team. Walker adds, however, that "the chemistry was very wrong between us and the jury. We thought this jury would like it if we played the fighting lawyers. We were wrong."

Butler agrees, adding: "If there was a negative response [by jurors], I suspect it was because the judge conditioned them. . . . If he would have said jump, they would have said, 'How high?' "

Although Judge Carroll barred discussion of the Refugee Act of 1980, he did allow it to be mentioned. Cruz, for example, testified that defendants had declared at sanctuary meetings that they thought their actions were legal under the act. This left some jurors perplexed about the restrictions imposed by the court. "It sounded like one set of valid laws being pitted against another set of valid laws," says Davis. "I would have liked to hear why [the Refugee Act of 1980] does not apply. It bothered me that I didn't hear more about it."

"There were so many things that they wouldn't let us know," complains Smathers, who was sympathetic to the defense in deliberations. "I thought we were supposed to hear the whole story."

According to defense lawyer Michael Piccarreta, the defense team "wanted to paint a picture of what evidence was off the record. . . . We wanted them to realize they were being told half of a story."

Despite the restrictions, all of the jurors interviewed reported that they indeed had gotten a good idea as to why the aliens were fleeing their homelands and why the defendants were helping them. "I think that I had a pretty good understanding of what was going on and filled in the blanks for myself," says Johnson, who nevertheless was a pro-prosecution juror. "We got a fairly decent picture of at least some of the war zone conditions," adds Davis. Jurors later would differ over whether to disregard such information.

A STUNNING CLOSE

The prosecution rested on Friday, March 7. On Friday, March 14, the 11 defense lawyers rose one by one and informed the court that they were resting their cases. None had called a single witness.

"I didn't even understand what that meant," Cobb admits. "The judge said, 'This surprises me. We'll have to talk about this,' and we were whisked out of the room." Says Johnson: "Some of us said that we wanted an instant replay of that, because something important had happened and we just missed it."

Defense lawyers told reporters at the time that the government simply hadn't proven its case. "When you're ahead twenty-seven to nothing, why bother playing the fourth quarter?" Piccarreta remarked to reporters.

Hirsh now admits to another consideration: "We couldn't put our clients on, because the fact is, [they] did do these things that the government accused [them] of." The problem, Hirsh argues, is that the defendants were not allowed to testify as to their intent. Defense lawyer Butler adds, "If we had put the defendants on, they would have been convicted on more counts"—counts the prosecution could not prove without a crack at the defendants.

The abrupt defense move filled several jurors with dread. "It took me until the next day to get it into perspective that we weren't going to hear anything else and what we had was what we were going to work with,'' says Johnson. Davis remarks: "It felt like a great weight coming down on us.''

The 12 jurors had two full weeks to mull it over, due to yet another protracted struggle among defense lawyers, the judge, and the prosecutor, this time over jury instructions. "We slugged it out over every instruction,'' explains Reno. Defense lawyers complain that the final instructions were slanted toward the prosecution.

In his closing statements, Reno stressed the jury's obligation to follow the law—not moral, religious, or humanitarian factors. "The final consensus of what the law is comes from Congress. It doesn't come from Southside Church,'' declared Reno, referring to defendant Fife's church. Reno concluded by telling the jurors, "Have the courage and come out, look these people in the eye as I have done, and tell them that there is no higher law than that passed by Congress.''

In their closings, defense lawyers harped on the credibility of Cruz and picked away at Reno's case, trying to convince jurors that the government simply hadn't met its burden of proof. "What we did was all that was left,'' says defense lawyer Ellen Yaroshefsky. "We gave them a road map to get out—to acquit.''

Reno attacked Hirsh, arguing that the defense was doing far more than just reminding the jury about burden of proof. With the jury once again sent out, the prosecutor charged that Hirsh was arguing for jury nullification, an argument Judge Carroll had warned defense lawyers he would not tolerate.

Jury nullification refers to a jury's refusal to apply the law when it decides that to follow the letter of the law would produce an unjust verdict. In federal courts (and all but two state courts), defense lawyers are prohibited from telling jurors to depart from the law to render justice. "It's almost a joke in law,'' says former U.S. attorney Butler. "They're supposed to be able to do it, but you can't tell them they can.''

Hirsh now admits that the defense was hoping to suggest the concept to jurors. But, he adds, the defense tried to show the jurors that they could acquit without ignoring the facts. "The message that we tried to get across,'' says Hirsh, "was that it's within your power to simply reject the testimony [of Cruz and government investigator Nixon] to get a result. It's a game. . . . You find the facts in accordance with what you believe is just.''

"In [closing] arguments," recalls Brosnahan, "we came at every possible angle on the discretion and common sense and power of the jury." In his closing statement Brosnahan told the jury. "[A]ll of us realize that when defendants go on trial in a criminal case, there is only one group of people that can decide it. . . . It is the character of Americans to try and be fair. It needs no words heaped upon it by a lawyer."

THE DELIBERATIONS

On Thursday, April 17, the 12 jurors took their seats at the large rectangular table in the jury room. Although the jury would ultimately convict, it was not because jurors started out carrying the government flag. In fact they stumbled on the very roadblocks that the defense had laid: distrust of the government witnesses and plain sympathy for the defendants.

Catherine Sheaffer—the juror who some defense lawyers had insisted should be stricken—was chosen forewoman. Sheaffer, the onetime law student, would tell fellow juror Smathers that "her loyalties lay with the letter of the law," Smathers recalls.

The first two days were spent in nearly fruitless debate. Sheaffer, computer programmer Lori Dorazio, and nurse Sandra Johnson had detailed notes, while others, like Susan Hagerty and final holdout Anna Browning, had little to offer the group.

The first big decision came over which charge to address first. Defense lawyers had hoped that jurors would take on the conspiracy count, which would tie them up and perhaps lead to a defense verdict. "If they acquitted on conspiracy, they would have been less inclined to go count by count," suggests defense lawyer Piccarreta.

But the jury decided to put aside the conspiracy charge, a rambling 27-page description detailing all of the defendants' actions and involvement, and to address the simple overt acts first. The jurors started with counts two and three, which charged Mexican lay worker Aguilar and Quiñones, a priest, with helping several aliens to sneak across the border. Aside from beginning discussion on counts two and three, the jury didn't accomplish much during the first two days. Cobb remembers going home that Friday afternoon upset by the jury's lack of progress. "I fumed about it all weekend," she recalls.

Three jurors—Dorazio, Johnson, and Arthur Mathieson—were troubled that first weekend by something else: the very thing that defense lawyers *hoped* would trouble them. "My first impulse was, you want to find them not guilty of anything. You like these people," says Dorazio. "You think, 'Should we follow the instructions, or should we follow our emotions?'

"I thought about it a lot," Dorazio continues. "I came to the conclusion that if every jury went in and decided that they didn't like the laws and didn't go with them, it wouldn't be a very good system. I kind of decided in my mind that we had to follow the instructions.

"I talked to Art [Mathieson] a couple of days later, and he had gone through the same thing," recalls Dorazio. "He said, 'You know, I was worrying about it all night, and I finally decided that these people did break the law.' " Says building inspector Mathieson: "I realized that we had to stop anguishing for these people and get on with our work."

Johnson also came to that conclusion over the weekend. She explains, "When I came back that Tuesday, I was ready to look at [the charges]."

Thus, those with detailed notes were the first to come to terms with the sympathy factor, dealing a blow to defense hopes for jury nullification. In the first few days of debate, jurors also talked over their main problem with the state's case: informant Cruz. While Dorazio and Johnson said they believed Cruz, Smathers says that she, Estes, Hagerty, McCrea, and Jackie Schoonover, the high school dropout, didn't want to give any credence to Cruz. "We all agreed that if he lied once he'd lie again," Smathers recalls. Davis says the group decided that no conviction should ride solely on Cruz's testimony—it had to be corroborated by another government agent or an alien. The jury followed that test throughout the deliberations.

During these preliminary talks it became clear that computer programmer Dorazio and nurse Johnson, both college-educated, articulate, and not afraid to speak their minds, were becoming leaders in the debate. Both would later become vocal leaders for convictions when deliberations bogged down in the final stretch over the difficult conspiracy count.

That second week, with leaders like Johnson and Dorazio no longer anguishing over whether to apply the law, the jury methodically worked through most of the 29 overt acts, such as transporting and harboring aliens. Dorazio—the 26-year-old who throughout the trial recorded nearly verbatim all of the questions and answers—typically kicked off the discussion by reading aloud from her notes.

Nonbinding votes kept the deliberations rolling. Forewoman Sheaffer,

Johnson, Dorazio, Estes, and McCrea were the most vocal, while other jurors, especially Hagerty, said practically nothing. McCrea, the 26-year-old electronics worker who had drawn pictures through most of the trial—and dozed off more than once after working night shifts—was surprisingly vocal in the deliberations and amazed others with his recall of the facts. In most cases, the jury came to a preliminary consensus, which Dorazio duly recorded.

Sheaffer, who consented only to brief interviews, told a reporter after the trial that she rose at dawn during deliberations and read her Bible to prepare for the day. She says now that it was "very, very difficult" to keep her instincts and her beliefs as an Evangelical Christian out of the deliberations but adds, "I wouldn't have any peace in myself if I bent the rules."

"I think she was so conscientious and wanted to make sure that her religious convictions wouldn't interfere," notes Cobb of Sheaffer, "that she followed those jury instructions to the letter."

Other jurors were still struggling with their sympathy for the defendants. "It really was a strain for me to face the fact that there really was enough evidence to convict them . . . that what appeared to be charitable works were against U.S. laws," Dennis Davis explains.

Estes, an Evangelical Christian with a husband in the army, frequently put it more bluntly. "So we're going to hang these people for helping other people," Smathers remembers Estes saying more than once.

Forewoman Sheaffer took it upon herself to steer jurors who were still struggling. Frequently, says Johnson, Sheaffer would begin the morning by urging others "not to disallow evidence on strictly an emotional basis"—a statement that would have made defense lawyers cringe.

"She was just doing her job," comments Smathers. "But I didn't see the need to say it every morning." Sheaffer says that all she did was direct the jurors back to the instructions, and only when the need came up.

Jurors who still couldn't set aside their strong sympathy for the defendants often found themselves in the minority. In most cases, the holdouts—Lynn Cobb, Anna Browning, and Janice Estes—were swayed by the majority.

By the end of the sixth day of deliberations, as the second weekend approached, the jurors had reached a preliminary consensus on all but a few of the overt actions. The jury eventually found the defendants guilty of 12 of the 29 overt actions they were charged with. Consensus on the 17 acquittals came easily. "Most of the acquittals were just cut and dry," says Dorazio.

A CONSPIRACY DEADLOCK

Sanctuary sympathizers awaited with greatest interest the jury's decision on whether the defendants' actions constituted a criminal enterprise. Mathieson notes that the decision on the conspiracy charge, which carried the possibility of a five-year prison term, was tantamount to passing verdict on "what the whole sanctuary movement is about."

At the opening of debate on the conspiracy count, "I was sure nobody thought they were guilty [of conspiracy]," says bookseller Cobb. "I had a feeling that everyone was leaning toward [not guilty]." But when Cobb suggested taking a preliminary vote before any discussion, Sheaffer was "very fast to move. She said absolutely not," Cobb recalls.

Cobb may have been right about which way the others were leaning. Judge Carroll had instructed them, "If you find that the conspiracy charged did not exist then you must return a not guilty verdict, even though you may find that some other conspiracy existed." Dorazio explains, "We wanted so bad to find them not guilty of that, we grabbed that and started to look for another conspiracy." Several alternative conspiracies were proposed and rejected—including whether the defendants had conspired "to help people in general, that their intent was not to break any laws," Dorazio says.

Early on, McCrea was the only juror who favored convictions, according to Davis. "Until we started digging, we thought there was not enough evidence," says Smathers.

Sidestepping a debate on the justice of a conspiracy conviction, jurors decided to discuss one defendant at a time. In short order they determined that defendants Anthony Clark, a priest; Nena MacDonald, a Tucson lay worker; and James Corbett, a founder of the sanctuary movement, were not guilty of conspiracy. Verdicts on eight more remained to be decided.

"A lot of us knew that we were going to have to find [some of] them guilty," claims Dorazio. "But we were trying not to do it at the time." Then the group discussed a secretly taped meeting at which some of the defendants talked about bringing a refugee from Mexico to Seattle. The tape convinced most of the jurors that four of the defendants, all Americans, were laying plans to break the law.

Davis says he was swung when he saw that the defendants' activity "started to involve a kind of division of labor, where no person was doing anything big." Davis reasoned that the consistent cooperation among defendants constituted an agreement to carry out the unlawful activity. But some jurors—namely Browning, Cobb, and Estes—continued to resist conspiracy convictions. Preliminary votes were coming out 9-to-3 for conviction.

On Tuesday, Johnson stepped to the blackboard to sketch what she saw as the conspiracy. Her drawing was much like the charts Reno used in his closing—it depicted a trail from El Salvador to Nogales, Mexico, to Nogales, Arizona, to Tucson's Southside Church to Phoenix to points beyond. "I worked different [aliens] through the chain," explains Johnson, "and brought in defendants and where they participated and how they related back to one another. . . . There was always a thread that tied them all together."

Defense lawyer Butler complains that the jurors, in their efforts to make sense of the evidence, were simply not assessing reasonable doubt. Johnson counters that reasonable doubt was discussed and adds, "It wasn't a decision we arrived at lightly."

As the majority attempted to convince the holdouts, Johnson and Dorazio stood out as the leaders. "They were the brightest and the firmest in what they felt," says Cobb. But by late Tuesday afternoon, "We started showing some very emotionally tired people," says Johnson.

A TRAUMATIC CONCLUSION

Wednesday, the second-to-last day of deliberations, Cobb, Estes, and Browning had yet to be convinced there was a conspiracy. Says Cobb: "I didn't think they planned to break the law." David McCrea tried to sway her. Cobb recalls, "I said to David, 'I'm not stupid. I voted with you on these other counts. But I don't think that there was a plan.' "

Estes and Cobb were the first to hint at a reluctance to convict despite the evidence. Sandra Johnson recalls that for Cobb and Estes "there was no real argument. They just wanted to say, 'I'm feeling real bad about this. But I can't look through the evidence and deny what you say.' "

Eventually, however, both Estes and Cobb changed their votes. "I'm not a go-along-with-the-crowd kind of person," says Cobb. "But I saw what they were saying" about the cooperative effort of the defendants.

Only Anna Browning, the part-time student and housekeeper, was left for the others to convince. But, comments Johnson, "It was a whole different ball game trying to talk to Anna." According to one juror, Browning is "really inarticulate" and "just didn't understand" the nature of the charges. "It just went right past her." Browning declined comment on the deliberations.

Davis says that on the second-to-last day of deliberations, he, Mathieson, Dorazio, and McCrea took turns trying to sway Browning. Davis recalls that Browning raised a wall against their arguments: "She said, 'I don't believe any of this. I don't believe there's a conspiracy. I've heard the arguments. I don't buy it.' "

Says Davis: "We were speaking from evidence and logic, but she was coming straight from the heart. . . . There was a lot of emotional pressure, although we were trying to keep it off of her."

The pressure eventually erupted that afternoon, when Johnson lashed out at Browning for doing crossword puzzles during the deliberations. "She'd sit there and work those word puzzles," recalls Smathers. "Sandy [Johnson] blew her cool." Browning put the book away, but she was clearly nettled.

With Browning incensed, the jury was stuck. "My getting angry [at Browning] was not conducive to good group functioning," Johnson confesses. The jurors decided to turn to unfinished business. Two American lay workers were found not guilty. But were the two Mexicans—Quiñones and lay worker Aguilar—part of the conspiracy?

McCrea was the only juror who thought so. He recalls telling the others, "I can't see why [you don't include them]. They knew what was going on. They didn't just take people across the border and say, 'Here's your cross. So long.' . . . If I say no to them, I'll have to say no to everyone." After discussing it further, the others agreed that there was sufficient evidence to tie the two Mexicans to the four Americans.

Johnson came in on the last day of deliberations, Thursday, May 1, and apologized to Browning—who was wavering at the time on conspiracy convictions. But before discussion even started, Cobb asked to address the group. Cobb, who despite her vote to convict the day before had yet to feel comfortable with conspiracy convictions, poured out her troubled feelings about the decision.

Cobb, who prepared notes the evening before, recalls saying, "First of all, these jury instructions were written by the judge, and we all know the defense lawyers are having problems with the judge. He's the one who wrote these jury instructions. This isn't the law." Cobb admits to having seen a headline during the trial about defense lawyers charging the judge with bias.

Sheaffer, Cobb recalls, snapped back at her, "We know nothing of the kind. You have no right to be telling us that." Sheaffer went on to argue that the 11 defense lawyers simply wouldn't have allowed faulty instructions. "I believed her," says Cobb. "The lawyers did meet with the judge." (The defense lawyers, in fact, had argued with Carroll over the instructions and did feel the instructions were biased.)

Cobb touched on another point that defense lawyers—despite restrictions—had suggested to the jury. Cobb says she told the others, "Even if we're not allowed to use the Refugee Act of 1980 or international law in this case, [the defendants] were following it." Cobb had heard trial testimony that the defendants knew about the law and were attempting to abide by it, but neither Cobb nor her fellow jurors knew what the law was. "Cathy [Sheaffer] just said, 'That's not part of what we're looking at,' " Cobb says.

Finally, in an impassioned plea, Cobb declared that she just didn't want to find the church workers guilty of conspiracy. "I just felt that enough was enough," she recalls telling the others. "I said, 'You know jurors can do whatever they want.' . . . I said it firmly with tears in my eyes." Recalls Davis: "It was a very tempting thought to many of us . . . [but] the instructions said we couldn't decide arbitrarily."

Although she had no idea she was doing so, Cobb was articulating the concept of jury nullification. Cobb explains that she has "always known" that jurors can do what they want—"I suppose just from reading about past cases." Cobb did not know that lawyers are not allowed to tell jurors about the concept, although it seemed to her that defense lawyers "came awfully close."

As Dorazio remembers it, "[Cobb] said, 'We're all human and we all have human emotions. We can act human in this. We don't have to follow the law.' " Dorazio says that Davis responded, "No. We do have to follow the law." Forewoman Sheaffer seconded Davis. Cobb had failed to turn the jury around.

After a break in deliberations, recalls Davis, Anna Browning simply announced, "I'm sorry I have to do this to you, but I'm going to have to hang the jury."

But Johnson, for one, was not about to give up. Says Johnson: "I said to her, 'I am unwilling to turn in that kind of a verdict to Judge Carroll after a commitment of the courts for so long, and our commitment here, without a lot of discussion."

Juror Jackie Schoonover—the high school dropout who had contributed little during deliberations—told Browning and the others that she once had been on a hung jury. The judge had sent the jury back to deliberate when they first emerged. "Everyone felt for sure that would happen to us," says Dorazio.

Deliberations became tense and emotional. Johnson remembers Browning tearfully telling the others, " 'These are good people, and you can't find good people guilty.' All we wanted her to do was listen—that there was more to it than that and none of us were denying that these were good people."

According to Browning's mother, Julia Browning, her daughter's conviction was so firm on that final day that she was on the verge of taking a rather unusual step: "She was getting ready to write a letter to the judge [telling him] 'I'm never going to change my mind.' "

Frustrated by their efforts to turn Browning around, the jury once again turned to other business. After lunch, and after taking final votes on other counts, the jury once more voted on each of the four questions the instructions directed them to answer to convict on conspiracy. To everyone's shock, Browning voted with the others on all four.

The startled jurors asked why. "Because all of *you* say it," McCrea recalls Browning saying. Jurors urged her not to follow them without believing herself that there was a conspiracy, says McCrea. Dorazio recalls Browning declaring, "You just better be sure that the way you're interpreting [the law] is right."

Jurors are still hard put to explain the reversal. Davis speculates, "Something inside of her just collapsed." Says Browning's mother: "She said she got mad and gave in. . . . She was convinced she was going to get in trouble." None of her fellow jurors claim to have a clue as to what trouble Browning was concerned about. Her mother is not sure, and Browning herself would not comment.

What Julia Browning is sure of is that the verdict devastated her 25-year-old daughter. "For the first five nights [after the verdict] it was just like having a five-year-old back. She was crying and just wanted to be close to me. . . . She said, 'If I'd have known I wouldn't get in trouble, we'd still be down there today.' "

Later, when a reporter asked Browning whether she knew that the jurors could have based their decision on their consciences, even if it was in conflict with the law, she said she hadn't known. She added, "It doesn't seem right that nobody could tell us that."

In July, Judge Carroll sentenced the six convicted sanctuary workers to terms of probation requiring them to comply with all immigration laws. The sentences came as a great relief to jurors. "I didn't want to see any of these people go to jail," says Johnson, who had argued for convictions. Many defendants have since declared that they would continue to support the sanctuary movement.

Even today, defense lawyers remain a bit mystified over why they didn't win the case. "We defense lawyers were filled with such righteousness in this that we never believed that the jury would do anything but acquit," says Hirsh. "I told all the members of the press we were going to acquit. I came out with egg on the face."

After juror Dennis Davis got back from his postverdict vacation, he paid an impromptu visit to Hirsh in the lawyer's office. The lawyer says he told Davis that if the jury had felt that guilty verdicts were not just, they could have simply said, "I don't believe Cruz. I don't believe [government investigator] Nixon. I have a reasonable doubt. I'm not going to convict." Davis, says Hirsh, "looked at me kind of mystified."

Other early conviction proponents, such as Dorazio, offer only a qualified endorsement of the verdict. "We didn't agree with what we had to do, but a lot of it was cut and dry," explains Dorazio. "It didn't mean we thought it was right that the law was that way."

Lynn Cobb, for one, still has misgivings about the jury's adherence to the judge's instructions during deliberations. "I just think we went overboard by following them too closely," she reflects.

Says Davis: "We probably had a lot more power and a lot more latitude than we ever imagined. I think Lynn was right on that one. . . . We just didn't have it within us to do that." He adds, "It might have gone differently if we discussed whether justice was met."

EPILOGUE

Lawyers for the Sanctuary defendants argued before the Ninth Circuit Court of Appeals in December 1988 and the convictions were affirmed on March 30, 1989. Coordinating the appeal was Karen Snell, formerly of San Francisco's Riordan & Rosenthal. Snell, who left the firm in March 1989 to join the federal public defender's office in San Francisco, worked on the Sanctuary trial with James Brosnahan while she was an associate at Morrison & Foerster. Joining the original defense team for the appeal were Dennis Riordan, name partner at Riordan & Rosenthal, and Michael Tigar, a professor at the University of Texas Law School, who argued the case before the Court of Appeals.

In briefs to the appellate court, and in the December 1, 1989, petition to the Supreme Court for writ of certiorari, the defense argued that Judge

Carroll erred in his jury instructions on the meaning of criminal intent and in the definitions of the criminal actions at issue. The appellants also questioned the constitutionality of infiltrating churches and the impact on religious freedom. The judge, according to the appellants, also unfairly barred testimony on political conditions in El Salvador and Guatemala. Donald Reno, Jr., who is now an assistant U.S. attorney with the Immigration and Naturalization Service in Seattle, says the judge's definitions of the crimes "precisely followed precedent," that the question of intent had no bearing on whether laws were violated, and that "the court admitted a large amount of testimony from the aliens regarding political conditions in those countries." He handled the government's case throughout the appeal.

Penny Deleray, administrator of the San Francisco–based National Sanctuary Defense Fund, says the number of congregations in the movement has grown from 280 to more than 500 since the trial. Although fewer groups are sheltering refugees, she says, they are instead aiding Salvadorans and Guatemalans not eligible for amnesty under the 1986 Immigration Reform and Control Act and lobbying for congressional support of a bill that would grant extended voluntary departure status to Salvadorans.

Two sanctuary cases decided since May 1986 have turned out favorably for the defendants. Defense lawyer Michael Altman, now of Boston's Silvergate, Gertner, Fine & Good, won a dismissal in June 1988 for a Maine resident charged by the INS with illegally transporting a Guatemalan from Maine to Canada. In August 1988 an Albuquerque federal jury acquitted a priest and a journalist of criminal conspiracy and immigration law charges. The Reverend Glen Remer-Thamert, with reporter Demetria Martinez in tow, had smuggled two Salvadoran women to New Mexico in 1986.

The Reverend John Fife III, the Presbyterian minister who helped found the movement, has resumed his pastoral duties with the Southside Presbyterian Church (U.S.A.) in Tucson, and has expanded the church for refugees.

Darlene Nicgorski left the Sisters of St. Francis in December 1986, and worked as an employment counselor at Roxbury Community College in Roxbury, Massachusetts. She is now involved with the issue of the Catholic religion and the role of women in a male-dominated church. In January 1987 she was named one of *Ms.* magazine's "Women of the Year." The Reverend Ramon Quinones is ministering to homeless people and refugees in Nogales, Mexico.

Beulah Mae Donald v. the United Klans of America

SLAYING THE DRAGON

BY

FRANK JUDGE

How Morris Dees and the Southern Poverty Law Center vanquished the United Klans

On the spring morning in 1981 when a black teenager was found brutally beaten and hanged from a camphor tree in Mobile, Alabama, a group of Klansmen sat on the front porch of the house across the street admiring the spectacle. As local television news cameramen filmed the scene, Bennie Hays, an elderly Ku Klux Klan official, eyed the body of 19-year-old Michael Donald and muttered that the lynching would play well on the news. "It's gonna look good for the Klan," he said.

But Bennie Hays's perverse delight would later come back to haunt him.

The trail of evidence in the grisly murder would lead to the conviction of two Klansmen of Mobile's Klavern 900, one of them Hays's own son, and ultimately to a civil suit that devastated what was once the most powerful Klan group in the nation. In February 1987, an all-white federal

471

jury in Mobile awarded Beulah Mae Donald, the victim's 67-year-old mother, a $7 million judgment against the United Klans of America, the nation's oldest and largest Klan organization.

The verdict was a staggering setback to the Klan. For the first time a jury had found an entire Klan organization responsible for the violent acts committed by its individual members. Other Klan groups, fearful of similar liability, are now openly discouraging acts of violence by their members. The $7 million judgment also dealt a potentially lethal blow to the financially strapped United Klans. In May the still-grieving mother of Michael Donald took possession of the United Klans' only major asset: its two-story national headquarters in Tuscaloosa, Alabama.

The Donald case would have ended in 1983 with the convictions of his two killers if not for a tenacious Alabama civil rights lawyer and his team of experienced investigators. Morris Dees, Jr., 50, executive director of the Southern Poverty Law Center and a veteran of courtroom battles with the Klan, saw in the killing unmistakable signs of a larger conspiracy— one that might embrace not only other members of the local Klan unit but also Imperial Wizard Robert Shelton's United Klans of America.

After filing suit on behalf of Donald's family and the NAACP, Dees and his team of investigators labored to break through the shroud of secrecy that surrounds the "Invisible Empire." Success at trial, they knew, depended on their ability to unmask the hooded society, exposing the killing as not simply the vicious act of two rogue Klansmen but the brutal expression of the violence at the Klan's core. So they tracked down former Klansmen, including several hidden within the federal witness protection program, gathering startling details of the Klan's inner workings and its lurid history of violence. Dees then persuaded these Klan outcasts to come out of hiding, to violate secrecy oaths punishable by death, and to testify against the United Klans. When the Donald case went to trial, Imperial Wizard Shelton would be shocked to discover that the most damaging evidence against his United Klans came from those it had least feared: its own members.

At one time it seemed Michael Donald's killers would never be found. On the day Donald's body was discovered, Mobile County District Attorney Christopher Galanos announced that race did not appear to have been a motive in the killing. When black community leaders objected, calling the killing a lynching, local white politicians charged them with fanning the flames of racism. Within days, police arrested three young white men described by authorities as "junkie types fired up on drugs" for the murder. But two months later a state grand jury refused to indict the men after one witness withdrew her statement and another was discredited. (The latter was subsequently convicted of perjury and as an habitual offender—this was his fifth felony conviction—was sentenced to life in prison.) With no new leads, the state investigation soon sputtered and stalled. An FBI investigation into possible civil rights violations also came up empty.

Donald's killers eluded detection by police and the FBI for more than two years. Interest in the case waned. But Thomas Figures, 42, a black assistant U.S. attorney then in charge of the Mobile office's civil rights matters, pressed for another, more thorough FBI probe. "I was disenchanted with the first investigation," he says. The FBI had merely tracked the district attorney's investigation, according to Figures, who is now in private practice with Mobile's four-lawyer Figures, Ludgood and Figures. "I pleaded personally for a second investigation," Figures says. Veteran civil rights investigator James Bodman of the Mobile FBI office was assigned to the case. Although he declines to comment on the investigation, Bodman unearthed enough new leads for Barry Kowalski and Albert Glenn, trial attorneys in the Justice Department's civil rights division, to proceed with the case.

Kowalski, 43, now deputy chief of the Justice Department's criminal section, had joined the department in January 1980 following a stint teaching at Antioch Law School. Finding the killers of Michael Donald would pose the biggest challenge of his young government career. The Klansmen of unit 900 told investigators repeatedly that they were at an all-night poker party at the home of Klansman Henry Hays on the night of the murder. "Everybody was sticking to their story that they didn't know anything," Kowalski says.

The attorneys tried a critical final gambit, going to a grand jury in May 1983 to "break the roadblock," Kowalski recalls. "We brought to the grand jury all the people at the party that night and other people who might know anything."

The Klansmen and other witnesses were paraded before the grand jury day after day, asked time and again to describe their activities on the night of the murder. Each time the federal prosecutors obtained a little more information and a better sense of what occurred that night. "It was a process of catching witnesses up in a little lie," explains Kowalski, then playing on their fear of a perjury conviction. The attorneys also wanted to engender "a distrust among these people that someone's talking," he says.

After more than a month of intense grand jury scrutiny, James "Tiger"

Knowles cracked under the pressure. He confessed to the lynching and implicated fellow Klansman Henry Hays. "We were pretty close to having enough evidence to convict [Hays]," recalls Kowalski. "He didn't know how much we did know, but he thought we had enough to get him."

On June 16, 1983, Knowles, a rough-and-tumble 19-year-old who Kowalski said "cried like a baby" when he confessed, pleaded guilty to federal civil rights charges and was sentenced to life in prison. "He was grateful to get life," Kowalski says, because Knowles was convinced the "state would electrocute him." Henry Hays, 28, arrested later that day, would be convicted of capital murder and sentenced to death.

During the murder trial of Hays in December 1983, Knowles described how the two randomly abducted and killed Donald. Several Klansmen from Mobile unit 900 had gathered at Henry Hays's house on the evening of Friday, March 20, 1981, to await the 10 P.M. television news for details of the verdict in a local criminal case. Josephus Anderson, a black man accused of killing a white Birmingham policeman, was being retried at the Mobile county courthouse. The first trial had ended with a jury of 11 blacks and one white deadlocked.

Knowles calmly testified that on the drive to the Hays house he was "tying a hangman's noose for the purpose of hanging somebody." Soon after they arrived, a report came over the news that the jury had again failed to arrive at a verdict. Henry Hays and Knowles bolted outside and drove to a predominantly black neighborhood "looking for someone to hang," Knowles told the jury. The two men saw an elderly black man but decided against him because he was too far from the car and was using a public telephone. Later they came upon Donald. "He seemed like a good victim and no one was around," said Knowles.

"PLEASE DON'T KILL ME"

Michael Donald, a technical student who worked part-time in the *Mobile Press Register* mailroom, was on his way to a corner gas station to buy a pack of cigarettes. Hays pulled his car alongside Donald, and Knowles motioned him over to the car. "I asked him if he knew where a nightclub was and he started to direct me," Knowles testified. "I asked him to come closer and he leaned over and I pulled the gun out. I told him to be quiet and he would not be hurt." After forcing Donald into the car, they drove to a remote area across Mobile Bay. Donald kept saying, " 'I can't believe this is happening. I'll do anything you want, beat me, just don't kill me.' He kept saying, 'Please don't kill me,' " recalled Knowles.

When the three got out of the car, "Donald acted like he was a crazed madman," Knowles said. "I had the gun in my hand and he jumped me." The three struggled over the gun; it went off once but no one was hit. Later they struggled over Hays's knife. Donald managed to get free and grabbed a tree limb on the ground, but it was knocked from his hand. "Hays got the noose and both of us managed to get it around [Donald's] neck," Knowles testified. "Hays started pulling the rope and I started hitting [Donald] with the limb." Finally Donald collapsed.

They dragged Donald to the car and lifted him into the trunk. "He was laying on his back and Hays had the utility knife," Knowles told the jury "I asked [Hays] if he thought he was dead. He said, 'I don't know but I'm gonna make sure' and he cut his throat three times." After brushing their tracks away, the two drove back to Henry Hays's house. Later Knowles and Hays hung Donald's body from a tree across the street from Hays's house. From the porch, Knowles said, "you could see the body if you strained real hard. Ted Kysar pinched me and said, 'Good job, Tiger.' "

Later that night Klansmen Kysar and Frank Cox burned a cross on the grounds of the county courthouse. It was a deliberate act of defiance. Knowles would tell the jury that Donald was killed "to show the strength of the Klan in Alabama."

Morris Dees watched the state's criminal case with keen interest. After Hays's conviction, Mobile Acting District Attorney Thomas Harrison told the press, "I'm not sure this was a Klan case. It was a deliberate, intentional homicide that happened to be perpetuated [sic] by members in the Klan." But Dees suspected otherwise.

For nearly a decade, Dees and the Southern Poverty Law Center have kept a watchful eye on Klan groups across the country, bringing dozens of civil rights actions against Klansmen. Dees formed the nonprofit organization in 1971 with Joseph Levin, Jr., a law partner and fellow graduate of the University of Alabama Law School. After making a fortune in the direct-mail business in the 1960s, Dees had turned his attention to the political and civil rights arenas. The same year he founded the Law Center, Dees raised more than $24 million for then-Senator George McGovern's campaign for president. In return, McGovern gave him a list of 700,000 liberal contributors to the campaign. Direct-mail marketing campaigns have formed the financial backbone for the Law Center ever since.

The Law Center's suits against the Klan have resulted in indictments of Klan leaders who planned an attack on a peaceful black demonstration in Decatur, Alabama; injunctions against Klan harassment of Vietnamese fishermen in Galveston, Texas; and court orders shutting down Klan paramilitary operations in Texas. In July 1983, Klansmen struck back, burning the Law Center's offices. (Three Klansmen were convicted of arson and sentenced to up to 15 years in prison.) More recently, Louis Beam, Jr., a former Vietnam helicopter gunner and member of the radical right-wing Aryan Nations, threatened to kill Dees. Still Dees has remained the Klan's most vigilant and successful adversary.

Born the son of an overseer for a plantation in the cotton country outside Montgomery, Dees understands the Klan's appeal to some men. "They've been losers in life in many ways," he explains. "They find roles of leadership in the Klan to give them some status in their family and community." While Klan groups are frequently led by fanatics and racists, Dees says, "The average rank-and-file members are not that zealous; they're good folks. They're just people who have a bias against blacks, but they're not basically bad human beings. They'd have been good labor union members if the labor union had got there first."

Although the Klan's role in the Donald killing seldom surfaced during the criminal proceedings, Dees recognized signs of a larger conspiracy. In June 1984, he and Beulah Mae Donald's personal attorney, Michael Figures, 39, a state senator and brother of the former assistant U.S. attorney, filed a civil rights action on behalf of Donald's family and the NAACP for "all black citizens of Alabama" against the United Klans of America, the local unit, and several of its members. "I could tell from just the evidence that I saw [at Hays's trial] and what little investigation we were doing that there were a lot of other people involved," Dees recalls.

Searching for leads, Dees and his team retraced the investigations conducted by state and federal authorities. Staffers from the Mobile district attorney's office had questioned the members of Klan unit 900 soon after the murder but turned up nothing. Dees noted that investigators had interviewed a young Klansman named Johnny Matthew Jones but, suspecting him of being mentally retarded, cut the interview short. Several months later, Jones sold his trailer home, leaving Mobile and the Klan.

Dees, however, was more persistent. Joseph Roy, an investigator for the Law Center's Klanwatch Project and a former detective in the robbery and homicide division of the Montgomery police department, tracked Jones to Houston. Dees spoke several times with Jones by telephone and learned that Jones was not retarded but epileptic. Jones spoke slowly; he grew inarticulate under pressure. But when Dees asked calmly about the Klan, Jones recalled quite clearly his experiences in the Mobile unit, including a meeting held two days before Donald was killed.

CRACKING THE KLAN'S WALL OF SECRECY

Dees wanted to meet with Jones but the former Klansman was "stand-offish," recalls Dees. "He didn't want to get involved. He was afraid of the Klan." Yet Dees pressed him, cajoling and arguing with him to tell the truth. At last, Jones agreed to a meeting.

Dees brought a court reporter to Jones's apartment. The questions began simply: name, former residence, and age. Dees continued:

"Do you know your Social Security number?"

"Yes," Jones answered. "It is 2—" He then fidgeted nervously in his chair. He glanced uneasily at the hands of the court reporter.

"Do you have it in your billfold?" Dees asked reassuringly.

"Yes, I have it in my billfold," Jones said.

"Why don't you get it so we can get that down," Dees offered in a soothing drawl, easing the tension.

Then slowly and with some obvious physical difficulty, Jones began to recount his life in Theodore, Alabama, living with his father in a trailer camp, working odd jobs, then his adoption by the Klan. Neighbors Frank Cox and his wife befriended him and suggested he join. They assured him that "it was a good thing to join, and I wouldn't be getting into anything that was wrong or anything like that," Jones told Dees. So in 1980, at age 19, Jones swore an oath of allegiance to the Klan and joined unit 900. The unit met weekly in Bennie Hays's barn. "Then after the meeting was over we would go in [Bennie Hays's] house and sit inside there and watch TV," Jones explained.

As Jones tired, his answers came more slowly and the words began to slur together. Worried that Jones might be unable to complete his statement, Dees quickly turned to the meeting that preceded the killing. Jones remembered the group had discussed the retrial of Josephus Anderson. Bennie Hays, a United Klans Titan who controlled Klan activity in southern Alabama, rose to his feet and ordered his son Henry to "get this down: If a black man could kill a white man, a white man should be able to get away with killing a black man." The other Klansmen chortled in agreement. Jones remembered that Henry Hays added, "A nigger ought to be hung by the neck until dead to put them in their place."

When the meeting ended, Tiger Knowles asked to borrow Jones's .22-caliber pistol. Jones also learned that Knowles and Hays had borrowed some nylon rope. Several days later Knowles returned the pistol. "It had sand in the barrel, one shell missing," Jones told Dees.

Dees had his first major break in the case—evidence of a broader conspiracy carried out under the direction of a United Klans of America corporate officer. And it had come from a former Klansman, an eyewitness.

Tanned and lean, Dees in his madras sport shirt and blue jeans looks more the part of the cotton farmer he once wanted to be than a shrewd and relentless civil rights lawyer. But that down-home style has played a part in his uncanny knack for unearthing this kind of evidence and his success in battling the Klan. "I'm from the South and I kinda think I can talk a little bit their language," he explains in the gentle cadence of the Deep South, one word spilling into the next. "And I treat Klansmen like human beings. I don't act like a civil rights lawyer and jump down on 'em and look down on 'em or criticize 'em for what they've done. I just take 'em the way I find 'em."

Jones's statement implicated eight Klansmen who had attended the unit 900 meeting. Several weeks later, Dees would add three more of them as defendants to the suit.

But "the second aspect of the case was much more difficult—that was to prove that these people were acting as agents of the United Klans and therefore the United Klans should be held responsible," Dees says. "Nothing's unusual about agency theory; it's as common as dirt," he says. "You have to show the person was acting in the line and scope of his authority and carrying out the purposes of the corporation. [But] what's the line or scope of authority for the United Klans?"

Dees was aware that Bennie Hays and Knowles were the two highest officers of the United Klans in southern Alabama, but he knew little more about the secretive organization's corporate structure and operation. The United Klans of America was formed in 1961 when 500 Klan leaders met near Indian Springs, Georgia, to organize a unified national Invisible Empire that could halt the civil rights movement in the South. Robert Shelton, a young charismatic Klan leader, emerged as the commander or Imperial Wizard of the new Klan organization, a post he has held ever since. Operating under a shroud of secrecy enforced by threat of death, the United Klans has successfully resisted government efforts to investigate the organization over the years. Shelton even served nine months in federal prison in 1969 for contempt of Congress after he refused to produce corporate records to a House committee investigating Klan activity in the South.

HELP FROM UNEXPECTED SOURCES

But in what Dees calls a "stroke of luck," he was able to obtain all the important corporate records of the United Klans: documents that had never circulated publicly. Dees and the attorney representing the United Klans in the case, John Mays, 39, a criminal lawyer from Decatur, Alabama, who is regular counsel for the United Klans, were in court arguing a pretrial motion in the case. After the hearing, Dees spotted Bennie Hays and his wife sitting at the back of the courtroom. "I went over and sat down and talked to him," Dees recalls. "I said, 'Mr. Hays, I'm sorry about your son being on death row.' I was just being nice to the guy. His life was falling apart." After his son's conviction, Hays and his wife were indicted for insurance fraud in connection with a claim filed after their home was destroyed by fire in July 1983. State investigators suspected they had burned the house to raise $50,000 for their son's criminal defense.

Several days later, after this brief conversation, Dees received a letter from Bennie Hays. "You talked very nice to me and my wife," Hays wrote, "much different than I expected after being told what I had about you." He had information Dees might find helpful, Hays wrote. "As I explained the other day I am broke and cannot afford an attorney. I will be glad to work out any deal with you and get my life straighten [sic] out. . . . So here is my start with you to straighten out my life." He enclosed with the letter the official Klavern 900 charter issued by the United Klans in 1973 and signed by Shelton. "I hope it will help you in doing the work that needs to be done, since I found out what kind of people I was working with," Hays added.

Although Dees knew intuitively that Klavern 900 was a chartered unit of the United Klans, he had had no way to prove it. Now he could make that link.

"I picked up on [Hays's offer] real quick," says Dees. He and William Stanton, director of the Law Center's Klanwatch Project, drove to Bennie Hays's house. "We set with Mr. and Mrs. Hays and tried to talk to him about cooperating and telling us more about what happened," says Dees. But Hays dwelled on his gripe with the United Klans' lawyer, Mays, telling them Mays came to the house after his son's indictment, stood in his front yard, and said, "We're not going to help you," according to Dees. (Mays, at the request of his client, declined to be interviewed for this article.)

Bennie Hays, while bitter about his treatment by the Klan, remained "cagey," recalls Dees. "But he showed me all the files he had on the Klan and he had a cardboard box three or four feet long full of files. And I said, 'Mr. Hays, why don't you give me all that stuff?' He said, 'No. I can't give it to you. You got to give me something in return for it.' In other words, 'I got to get my son out of all this trouble.' I said, 'There's nothing I can do about your son.' " Hays then pressed Dees to drop the suit against *him*. Recalls Dees: "I said, 'Let's just give me them files and let me take them back with me.' "

As they talked, Dees leafed casually through the records. "I saw the [United Klans] constitution in there, all kinds of records we later used. . . . I just quickly read it. I had never seen one before." But Hays refused to let Dees take the records.

Soon after that meeting, Bennie Hays, 67, was tried and convicted of fraud and sentenced to three years in prison. His wife, Opal, was convicted and put on probation. Dees issued a deposition subpoena to Mrs. Hays and included a demand for all the Klan records. "We told her that if she did not bring those documents . . . she'd go to prison," says Dees. "And if she attempted to destroy any of those documents, she'd go to prison for destroying records. It would be contempt of court, since I already knew about them and knew they existed." She brought all the documents.

The records included the United Klans' constitution, which described in great detail the organization's military structure. The purpose of the local unit, the constitution declared, is to carry out the goal of the national organization: maintaining the God-given supremacy of the white race. Other documents instructed Klansmen on the operation of a local unit, including such specific details as the proper location of the sacred altar. Mrs. Hays handed over a program from the 1981 convention at United Klans of America headquarters in Tuscaloosa commemorating the organization's twentieth anniversary, autographed by all of Henry Hays's Klan heroes. Dees's adversary, John Mays, was listed as the United Klans' Imperial Klonsel.

480

DELVING INTO THE KLAN'S VIOLENT HISTORY

Not surprisingly, the Klan records made no reference to a policy that encouraged or condoned violence. "We [had] everything we needed to show about the corporation: its purpose and the chain of command, who was who, and that they did have national officials at the local level causing this to happen," Dees remembers. "But we still didn't have enough. You have to show how they carry out this goal. Do they use violence to carry out this goal or is it just a political group and they make speeches, burn crosses, and back candidates for office?" Shelton was unlikely to admit to a United Klans policy condoning violence to achieve its goals. Dees recognized that he'd have to establish the existence of such a policy through the Klan's history of violence.

Klanwatch director William Stanton pored through old newspaper clippings to identify incidents involving members of the United Klans of America. Then he and Dees reviewed relevant trial testimony, narrowing the scope of their search for possible witnesses. One name stood out: Gary Thomas Rowe, Jr.

In the 1960s Rowe was one of the FBI's key informants on Klan activities in the South. He gained national prominence after testifying against Klansmen involved in the 1965 murder of civil rights worker Viola Liuzzo of Detroit near Selma, Alabama. Following the trial, Rowe was placed in the federal witness protection program, given a new identity and a new residence. The Justice Department, unwilling to compromise its witness protection program, refused to help Dees locate Rowe.

"I can't really tell you how I found this guy because it will breach so many confidences," explains Dees. "We got in touch with him and I said, 'Hey look, man, we need your help, please give me a call.' " When Rowe called, Dees told him about the lynching. "I said this is a really bad business," says Dees. Rowe replied he'd had enough of the Klan, according to Dees. It was all history now, and he had put it behind him. But Dees spoke emotionally about the lives affected by the Klan and Shelton. Rowe's testimony, he explained, would be a critical link in establishing the United Klans' custom and practice of condoning violence. "The only way to stop this is for you to testify," said Dees. "We have to put this bunch out of business." Rowe agreed to a deposition.

Mays and Shelton refused to attend Rowe's deposition. Dees recalls Mays explaining, "I won't be in the same room with [Rowe]." Dees grabbed the opportunity. "If you get to take a deposition of somebody by yourself with no other lawyer in the room—that's like shooting ducks on the water. They ain't got much of a chance to get up and fly.''

Rowe turned out to be a gold mine on the United Klans' history of violence. In a conference room of the Law Center's headquarters, Rowe testified that Shelton had not only implicitly approved attacks on blacks but also personally led a bloody assault on Freedom Riders at the Birmingham bus station in 1961.

Rowe described a meeting between two Birmingham police officers and several Klansmen, including Shelton, in a Birmingham restaurant about three weeks before the Freedom Riders' attempt to integrate the bus terminal. Birmingham Police Lieutenant Tom Cook told the group that city officials would allow the Klan 15 minutes to ''beat them, kick them, burn them, kill them, I don't give a shit. We just don't care,'' recounted Rowe. Cook added, ''We don't ever want to see another nigger ride on the bus into Birmingham again.'' When the Freedom Riders' bus pulled into the Trailways bus station on Mother's Day 1961, there was not a policeman in sight. And it was Shelton, according to Rowe, who then directed the brutal attack that left a score of Freedom Riders injured and one man paralyzed for life.

Dees then asked Rowe about another infamous incident: the 1965 killing of Viola Liuzzo. In March of that year, Dr. Martin Luther King, Jr., and other black civil rights leaders led a march of 25,000 people from Selma to Montgomery to demonstrate support for the passage of the Voting Rights Act. Shelton, speaking at Rowe's local Klavern, told a group of Klansmen, including Rowe, ''Dammit, we had to go down there and get that shit taken care of. It was getting out of hand down there. If necessary, you know, just do what you have got to do.''

Later Rowe received a call from Robert Creel, the state Grand Dragon of the United Klans. Creel said they were going to take a ride: ''Tommy, this is probably going to be one of the greatest days of Klan history . . . one of the days you will always remember until the day you die.'' Rowe said he drove with three other Klansmen—Eugene Thomas, William Orville Eaton, and Collie Leroy Wilkins—to Montgomery, where the civil rights march had ended.

Meanwhile, Liuzzo, a 39-year-old volunteer and mother of five, had dropped off a group of marchers at Brown's Chapel in Selma and headed back to Montgomery accompanied by Leroy Moton, a black teenager who had carried an American flag during the march. At the edge of the city, Liuzzo pulled up to a stop light alongside the car carrying the Klan members.

Rowe recounted the incident in his deposition: "I believe Eaton was the one that said, 'Goddamn, look over there.' And Wilkins said, 'I'll be a sonofabitch, look at that. Let's take them.' " At the next red light they stopped again, and Thomas said, "You guys get down in back, get down in back." Rowe and Wilkins leaned over each other in the back seat to avoid being seen. "I was trying to see what the hell was going on," recalls Rowe. "I eased my eye up . . . and this black man was looking directly over at the car. I saw him, a big round-faced black man. And he had on a black furry-looking cap and a green sport coat and a white shirt and a tie."

The Klan members gave chase as the two cars approached a bridge. The two cars then raced across the bridge, their speeds climbing to 80 and 90 miles an hour. Then Thomas said to Wilkins, "This is it, let's do it." Thomas reached into the compartment between the seats, pulled out a pistol, and handed it to Wilkins. Wilkins shouted to Rowe, "When we get that motherfucker on up there and get him stopped somewhere, I'm going to get that sport coat for you." Rowe added, "I will always remember that. He said, 'It will just about fit you.' "

Gradually they gained on the car. As they passed, Wilkins rolled the window down. "We got pretty much even with the car and the lady just turned her head solid all the way around and looked at us," Rowe said. "I will never forget it in my lifetime, and her mouth flew open like she—in my heart I've always said she was saying, 'Oh, God,' or something like that . . . you could tell she was startled. At that point, Wilkins fired a shot. The first shot hit the glass but it didn't appear to penetrate it. . . . He fired three or four more shots.

"I saw a black man kind of fall over toward the dash of the car, kind of fell over on her shoulder and slumped down toward like in her lap over the wheel. At that point, she just kind of fell right down toward the wheel. . . . The car went straight as a board I bet you for five hundred foot. It didn't turn, it didn't stop, it went down the road. I said, 'Jesus goddamn Christ, look at that. Let's get out of here.' And Gene Thomas said, 'Goddamn, I don't believe it.' At that time the car just very casually . . . went and ran off the road into some bushes."

The four men were arrested the next day and charged with the murder of Liuzzo. Moton was uninjured. Rowe testified in the criminal trials against the three Klansmen, but juries in the state court acquitted them. They were then convicted in federal court of conspiracy to deprive citizens of their civil rights and given the maximum sentence of ten years in prison.

After a brief recess, Dees again pressed Rowe for details about the Klan's history of violence. He handed Rowe an old newspaper photograph of a bloody attack on a black man; Rowe identified it as a picture taken the day of the Freedom Rider beatings at the Birmingham bus station. As Rowe scanned the crowd of people in the picture, he quickly identified one of them—a balding man standing off to the side—as Robert Chambliss. A member of Rowe's United Klans unit, Chambliss was later convicted of the September 1963 bombing of Birmingham's Sixteenth Street Baptist Church. Four black girls attending Sunday school were killed in the explosion, their bodies found huddled together beneath the masonry debris. Chambliss died in prison in 1985.

Dees continued to prod Rowe. "How many people there do you see that were members of the United Klan?" Dees inquired. Rowe looked carefully at the photograph crowded with angry, lead-pipe-wielding men. "I see one, two, three, four, five, six, seven, eight, nine, ten, eleven, twelve, thirteen, fourteen—approximately fourteen or fifteen of them that I know for sure," Rowe answered.

SEARCH FOR A KLANSMAN IN HIDING

Dees felt he was on his way to establishing a pattern of violence followed by the Klan. Yet these incidents occurred two decades earlier. Dees worried that a jury might regard Rowe's experiences as nothing more than vestiges of another era, the Old South. They needed more recent evidence of Klan violence intended to accomplish the goals of the United Klans of America.

William Stanton had turned up another name: Randy Charles Ward. In April 1979, 13 members of the Childersburg, Alabama, unit of the United Klans were prosecuted by federal authorities for shooting into the homes of blacks, including that of state NAACP president Charles Woods. The shootings were intended to intimidate them from leading efforts to integrate the Childersburg police and fire departments. At the trial of the Klansmen, Ward, 22, had admitted firing a 12-gauge shotgun into Woods's home and then testified for the federal government against the other Klansmen. Ward's testimony led to the convictions of ten of the Klansmen. After being placed on five years' probation, Ward disappeared into the witness protection program.

Investigator Roy began tracking Ward, but with little success. Roy says he treats searches for a person in the witness protection program "like a missing persons case. It's like grabbing the end of a thread and pulling it in. Sometimes you get lucky and sometimes you just keep on pulling." But Ward's trail died in 1979. They had no clue as to his new identity. All they had was his former name, his date of birth, and his address in 1979. "We checked everything there is to check," Dees says. But the investigator kept coming up empty. "[Ward's] Social Security number ended, driver's license number ended—his trail just died," Dees says.

Roy then began a search for Ward's family. The Childersburg police offered no help. Confronting a lot of Klan sympathy in the area, Roy aroused only the curiosity and suspicion of the community. Ward's family had moved from Childersburg nearly ten years earlier, leaving no forwarding address. "They had gone into hiding," says Roy. Only after reviewing volumes of records in Childersburg and surrounding counties and making hundreds of telephone calls did Roy finally locate Ward's family.

Roy recalls that Ward's parents were "visibly upset" when he came to their door inquiring about their son. "They didn't know me from Adam's house cat," he says. But Roy sat down with them, telling them about the Donald case and explaining young Ward's importance to the action against the Klan. They sympathized but expressed concerns about their son's safety. He had started a new life after the trial, married, had a child. Roy asked only that Randy Ward call him. "They didn't want to call him from their house because they didn't want his number to appear on their phone bill," Roy says. "For years they had taken extensive measures to avoid a link." But the family, Roy believes, put a lot of pressure on Randy Ward to come forward. "They were real sound, hardworking people. They tried to weather the storm while he was young but now wanted him to do the right thing."

Several days later, Randy Ward called Roy. Ward listened in silence as Roy described in vivid detail the slaying of Michael Donald and its impact on Donald's family. "He was moved enough that, after I assured him how we'd handle it, he agreed to meet with us," Roy recalls. Ward spoke with remorse about his experience with the Klan. He showed a real "change of heart," remembers Roy. "It's not like when you were young and full of piss and vinegar." As Roy explains the transformation: "One day you don't have a job, no money, and you turn to these people and the next day you're giving orders. You really believe in them until you get in trouble. Then you're left in jail, your friends and colleagues have deserted you."

Ward flew to Birmingham and met Dees, Roy, and Stanton in the office of an attorney who had prosecuted the Childersburg case and gained Ward's trust. Although Ward still had serious reservations, the former prosecutor told him, "Just listen to these guys," recalls Dees. Dees showed Ward the grisly photographs of the lynching and talked about the victim's family. When quizzed by Dees, Ward told them that he got the approval of the United Klans Titan before shooting into the homes of blacks. Then Dees asked him if he would testify. "We felt here we needed a live witness," he says, and his more recent involvement would make him an extremely important witness. "Everybody always looks at the Klan [and says], 'Oh, yeah, that's what they used to do years ago, they don't do that now,' " Dees explains. "[Here] a year and a half before the [Donald] murder, they're doing the same thing. That made Gary Thomas Rowe's testimony believable."

Ward then startled Dees by adding that Shelton had visited the Childersburg unit only a month before the shootings. "[Shelton] told us a story about how he stopped the blacks in Birmingham in 1961 when the Freedom Riders came," Ward told them. And then Shelton added, according to Ward, "Sometimes you just got to get out there and stop them." Dees was stunned. Shelton was telling the local unit his war story, in effect encouraging them to commit violence to accomplish the Klan's goals. Explained Ward: "I was so revved up in this that I would have killed for Bobby Shelton."

After several hours of discussion, Dees persuaded Ward to appear and testify at the Donald trial.

"THEY GOT TO LIVE WITH THEMSELVES"

Dees downplays the difficulty of convincing former Klansmen, particularly those hidden within witness protection programs, to come forward and testify publicly about the Klan; even when, as in this case, they have nothing to gain and a great deal to risk by talking. He guides them as easily as a preacher hearing a sinner's repentant cries for salvation. "How did we get 'em to talk? I think it was just how you convince anybody to do anything: You show them the rightness of your cause. You try to give them the bigger picture of life in front of them. One day they're not going to be on this earth, and they're going to look back, and they're going to say, 'What did I do to help my fellowman? I did a lot of bad things in the

Klan and maybe this is an opportunity to do a little good.' They got to live with themselves. You talk to people about what life's all about.''

On February 9, 1987, an all-white jury was selected to hear the Donald case. The NAACP's class action was no longer at issue because the United Klans had consented a week earlier to a broad injunction barring harassment of blacks in Alabama. The only question remaining was whether seven members of unit 900 and the United Klans of America should be held liable in the death of Michael Donald.

In the first day of testimony, Dees called to the stand James "Tiger" Knowles: the man who had confessed to killing Michael Donald and bargained for a life sentence. Knowles, now 24 and under federal witness protection, entered the crowded federal courtroom surrounded by U.S. marshals and walked to the witness stand, skirting the counsel table where Beulah Mae Donald sat with her lawyers. A few feet away sat Shelton and five other Klansmen named in the suit.

Dees had interviewed Knowles before calling him and found a young man much changed since March 21, 1981. The bearded Knowles, wearing blue jeans and a plaid shirt, said he joined the United Klans of America at age 13 with the approval of his parents, also Klan members. Then he unemotionally described to the jury how he and Henry Hays "went out looking for a black person," ultimately abducting and killing Michael Donald. Finally, as Mrs. Donald wept softly, Knowles stepped down from the witness stand to demonstrate how he strangled Michael Donald.

Klan officials had persuaded him to go along with the slaying, Knowles testified. And it was Bennie Hays who had suggested the killing. "Mr. Hays is who I took orders from," he explained. (Hays repeatedly denied that he ever made any statement about killing a black.) "He took his orders from Mr. Shelton." Knowles said that he and Henry Hays selected a black at random for lynching "to get the message across—not just to the state of Alabama, but to the whole United States—that the Klan didn't want blacks on juries."

Dees then showed Knowles a drawing that appeared in a 1979 issue of the *Fiery Cross,* a United Klans newspaper, of a black man with a noose around his neck. The caption read, "White people should give blacks what they deserve." Stanton had discovered the drawing during a review of Klan literature maintained in the library of the Anti-Defamation League of B'nai B'rith in New York. Knowles admitted he had seen the drawing before the killing. When asked whether it had influenced his decision to hang a black person, Knowles replied, "Yes, it did."

But Shelton, editor and publisher of the newspaper, whom Dees had called to authenticate the Klan corporate documents, declared that he too objected to the drawing and that nothing in the United Klans' bylaws advocates violence to achieve the political goal of white supremacy. "I'm not ashamed to be a white person," he added.

Knowles admitted under cross-examination by Mays that he had never heard Shelton tell anyone to commit acts of violence, but countered that the instructions came through a paramilitary chain of command. "He instructed us to follow our leaders," Knowles said.

Later one of the Klan defendants, William O'Connor, testified that on the morning Donald's body was found hanging from a tree, Bennie Hays told him it was "a pretty sight or a pretty picture, something like that." Another witness testified he heard Hays say that "it would look nice on the news. It's gonna look good for the Klan." Defendant Bennie Hays, acting as his own attorney, denied making such statements and called both liars. "I never saw such a horrible sight," he said.

WOULD WARD SHOW UP IN COURT?

The following day Dees planned to read Rowe's deposition in court and then to call Randy Ward to the stand. Whether Ward would be there the next day to testify was always a question. "We had a very thin string tied to Randy he could have broken any time," recalls investigator Roy. They recognized that Ward had a real fear of the Klan and what they might do to him. "I have no doubt when he got to the stand, he was going to testify favorable for us," remembers Dees. "But there were some strong doubts I'd ever get him to testify in the first place. Several times we thought he'd go back to where he came from."

They could only count on his desire to try to remedy a past wrong and the relationship of trust they had tried to foster. During one of their meetings Ward wanted to see his parents and didn't have enough money to get there. "Life hadn't been good for him," Dees says. "I just said, 'Look, Joe [Roy], go rent the guy a car.' So Joe took him to the airport and rented him a car. Then Joe told him when he was ready to catch a plane back, drop [the car] at the airport, and stamp the card." Dees sensed Ward appreciated that trust.

When Dees returned to his hotel after the first day of testimony, Ward was there waiting for him.

After Rowe's deposition was read into the record, Ward was called. He had been in the U.S. marshal's office all morning. Now he strode to the witness stand surrounded by marshals and bodyguards hired by Dees. "We promised him all these things," says Dees. Although Ward was on the plaintiffs' list of potential witnesses, Mays had never asked to take his deposition. "They hated him and Gary Thomas Rowe because they were ratters," says Dees. "They thought nobody would believe 'em."

Ward talked of his involvement as an officer of the United Klans in intimidating blacks in Talladega County in 1978. "Everybody was fired up when Mr. Shelton came to town," Ward testified. "People would follow him through hell if they had to."

In closing arguments, Dees and Michael Figures stressed that the corporate United Klans should be liable for its members' actions, just as a commercial corporation is held liable for the actions of its employees. Dees told the jury that the highly complex, well-financed Klan is not a group of "good ol' boys." And he said that the conspiracy that began in the barn housing unit 900 was only the latest chapter in a long history of violence endorsed by the United Klans. "They wanted to leave their mark," Dees explained. So they added to the "trail of victims and bombings and killings of the United Klans that stretches across the Southeast."

Mays, who had called no witnesses, dismissed Dees's agency theory and argued that there had been no evidence that either Shelton or the United Klans organization was involved in the killing of Donald, a killing Mays called an atrocity. Neither the Klan nor any other political organization, he contended, should be held accountable for the misguided actions of its members. "It is a dangerous thing," he told the jury, to hold a political organization "like the . . . United Klans of America, the NAACP, the Black Panthers, the Right to Life Committee, and other political organizations which have strong views about certain things [liable] when their members go out and commit acts of violence."

When the defendants had a chance to give summations, Knowles appealed directly to the crowded courtroom. "I hope that people learn from my mistakes," he said tearfully. "I've lost my family. I've got people after me now. Everything I said is true." He turned to Michael Donald's mother, his voice cracking with emotion, and said, "I can't bring your son back. But I'm sorry for what happened. And God knows if I could trade places with him, I would." Then, sobbing, he pled to the jury, "I do hope that you find a judgment against me and everyone involved. Because we are guilty."

After deliberating four and a half hours, the jury returned a verdict against each of the Klansmen—and against the United Klans of America.

Klan groups "don't die overnight," explains Irwin Suall, an authority on the Klan and similar groups with the Anti-Defamation League of B'nai B'rith. But, he says, the Donald case has already caused an "erosion" in United Klans membership. "Their fear that they may be hit hard in their pocketbooks," he explains, may ultimately change the way the Klan does business.

EPILOGUE

Eight weeks after the jury's verdict, the United Klans of America reached a settlement with Beulah Mae Donald, and on May 7, 1987, turned over to her its headquarters outside Tuscaloosa, Alabama. As part of the settlement, United Klans waived its right to appeal. Donald sold the headquarters for about $55,000. She died on September 17, 1988.

Of the individual Klan members found liable, only two had property available to satisfy the judgments against them. William O'Connor's wages were garnisheed until he lost his job. Bennie Hays did not contest the lien against his house and ten acres of property.

After the murder case against Bennie Hays and Frank Cox ended in a mistrial in February 1988 when Hays had a seizure in court, the Mobile, Alabama, district attorney moved to sever the two defendants' cases so Cox could be tried without interference from Hays. On June 23, 1989, Cox was convicted of first-degree murder. He was sentenced to 99 years and is currently serving time in a federal penitentiary. Hays's trial is pending; no trial date has been set.

Tiger Knowles is in a federal penitentiary in the witness protection program. Henry Hays is in Alabama on death row. Witnesses Gary Thomas Rowe and Randy Ward have re-entered federal witness protection programs.

John Mays now handles criminal cases exclusively. He has not done work for United Klans of America since the Donald settlement. The Southern Poverty Law Center has not had any reports on United Klans or Robert Shelton since the Donald case, and last winter, John Paul Rogers, a United Klans grand dragon in Florida, said the group was defunct.

Morris Dees, Jr., is still executive director of the Southern Poverty Law Center, and Joseph Roy is still a Law Center investigator. Michael Figures, now with Mobile's Figures, Jackson & Harris, continues to represent the Donald estate, and still serves as an Alabama state senator.

Israel
v.
Ivan Demjanjuk

IVAN THE TERRIBLE'S TERRIBLE DEFENSE

BY

SUSAN ADAMS

A more even courtroom contest might have forestalled doubts about the justice of the conviction of a former Cleveland autoworker for Nazi war crimes.

There was something confusing, even absurd, about the scene in the Jerusalem courtroom on the morning of April 29, 1987. More than two months into the trial of alleged Nazi war criminal John Demjanjuk, his lawyers were openly clashing—with each other. As Israeli defense attorney Yoram Sheftel rose to make an objection, lead defense counsel Mark O'Connor ordered him to sit down and shut up. Jabbing a pencil in Sheftel's face, O'Connor hissed, ''Turkey, get in your Porsche and go back to Tel Aviv.''

This particular confrontation, in the middle of what was arguably the most controversial and significant Holocaust trial ever, was only a hint of the problems in the Demjanjuk defense team. O'Connor, a solo practitioner from Buffalo, New York, who had never tried a major case, and Sheftel, a second-tier Tel Aviv criminal defense lawyer with a history of antagonizing judges, were totally out of their league.

It is difficult to overstate the importance of these proceedings. Demjanjuk, a Ukrainian who had immigrated to the U.S. in 1952 and lived for nearly 30 years in relative obscurity in the Cleveland suburbs, was the first American citizen to be denaturalized and extradited to stand trial in Israel for Nazi war crimes. Unlike most such defendants, this defendant's identity was at issue; Demjanjuk insisted that he was not the sadistic death camp guard known as "Ivan the Terrible."

The crimes with which Demjanjuk was charged were unspeakable. Ivan the Terrible personally beat, tortured, then gassed many of the more than 850,000 Jews who perished at the Treblinka death camp. Worse, Ivan pursued his horrible task with brutal enthusiasm, crushing his victims' heads with a lead pipe before they reached the gas chambers, or slashing off their ears, arms, or women's breasts with his sword. On one occasion he ordered a prisoner to lie facedown on the ground and pull down his pants, then he took a wood drill and bored into the man's backside.

The law under which Demjanjuk was tried, the Nazis and Nazi Collaborators Law, is the only statute in Israel that carries the death penalty.

The Demjanjuk case has raised disturbing questions: Could Israeli judges objectively evaluate the testimony of Holocaust survivors? Should Israel have the right to try accused Nazis? The gravity of these issues emphasizes the need for due process and a strong, meticulous defense—which is not at all the defense Demjanjuk got.

Arguments between the defense lawyers were even more heated outside the courtroom, and as the trial wore on, it became clear that the defense team was fractured beyond repair. In June 1987, as the prosecution rested its case, Demjanjuk fired chief counsel O'Connor, leaving the case to Sheftel and O'Connor's American co-counsel, Cleveland criminal defense lawyer John Gill. Sheftel and Gill were soon joined by a well-regarded former prosecutor from Canada, Paul Chumak.

But the newly constituted team continued to mishandle the case, putting on amateurs as expert witnesses and preparing Demjanjuk so badly that he was unable to give convincing answers to questions put by his own lawyers. Evidence or arguments that might have worked in his favor were never brought forth in a persuasive manner.

In April 1988 the court found Demjanjuk guilty and sentenced him to death by hanging. Now 68 years old, he sits in a prison near Tel Aviv awaiting his last appeal to the Israeli Supreme Court. He is held under tight restrictions, barred from speaking to reporters. After 11 years of emotionally charged legal proceedings that included a U.S denaturalization trial, deportation and extradition hearings, numerous appeals, and four denials of cert by the U.S. Supreme Court, even Demjanjuk's own lawyers predict that he will hang.

His family continues to believe fervently, even desperately, in his innocence. They are quick to blame the most recent conviction on O'Connor, and on what they insist was a biased court. For his part, O'Connor, who responded to only a few questions in two telephone conversations, has repeatedly and publicly backed the fairness of the Israeli court and claimed that it was his "former assistants" who botched the case.

The three-judge panel's carefully crafted verdict—440 pages in Hebrew and 768 pages in English translation—is compelling. And the facts of the case—the identification of Demjanjuk's wartime photos by ten Holocaust survivors and one German SS man; the identity card issued at a training camp for Nazi guards that bears Demjanjuk's photo; and the defendant's lack of a credible alibi—are convincing.

Whether better counsel could have won acquittal for Demjanjuk is a question that will remain unanswered. But there is no doubt that better lawyers could have raised the quality, and thus the reliability, of the proceedings to a much higher plane.

How Demjanjuk came to rely on such ineffective counsel is a curious, and in the end a tragic, story for which no one is willing to bear the responsibility.

When he hired Mark O'Connor in 1983, Demjanjuk had already suffered a series of legal defeats and expended the energies of one set of lawyers. Relying on local Cleveland defense attorney John Martin of Oliver, Carson & Martin and on Martin's then-associate Spiros Gonakis, Demjanjuk had lost his citizenship in a 1981 Cleveland denaturalization trial and lost an appeal to the Sixth Circuit. Then his case was denied review by the U.S. Supreme Court.

Martin and Gonakis have never talked to the press about their representation of Demjanjuk. According to Demjanjuk's son-in-law, Edward Nishnic, after losing the denaturalization trial and appeals, the family decided it needed a lawyer with immigration experience. (Nishnic married Demjanjuk's daughter Irene in 1983; he and Demjanjuk's 23-year-old son, John, Jr., are now the family spokesmen.)

The family turned for advice to Edward O'Connor of Buffalo, who had testified on Demjanjuk's behalf in his denaturalization trial. Following World War II, O'Connor had served as one of three displaced persons commissioners appointed by the United States government to help European war refugees relocate in America.

According to the 1948 Displaced Persons Act, those who had fought for or assisted the Nazis were not eligible for aid by the commission. Demjanjuk (who later anglicized his first name, Ivan, to John) lied on his 1951 application for immigration to the U.S. about his whereabouts during the war. He wrote that from 1934 to 1943 he was in Sobibor, Poland, the site of a Nazi death camp. At his denaturalization trial, Demjanjuk claimed he had not in fact been in Sobibor but had picked the name of a Polish town at random because he feared repatriation to the U.S.S.R. O'Connor, virulently anti-Soviet, testified that such fears had led many Eastern European refugees to falsify their immigration forms.

When the Demjanjuks contacted him, O'Connor recommended his only son, Mark, then 40, an attractive Vietnam veteran and 1968 graduate of the State University of New York at Buffalo Law School who shared his father's contempt for the Soviet Union. According to Nishnic, Ed O'Connor told the family that he would assist his son, who, he claimed, was an experienced immigration lawyer. (The elder O'Connor died in 1985.)

The family dispatched Demjanjuk's eldest daughter, Lydia, then 33, to Buffalo, where Mark O'Connor was in solo practice. Lydia was charmed, and the family hired the young lawyer without checking his credentials.

In an early interview for this article, O'Connor claimed that as a result of his father's reputation, "my immigration practice was known. My international practice here in Buffalo was known in the Ukrainian community." Since that conversation in May O'Connor has not responded to repeated inquiries, including questions about his experience prior to taking on the Demjanjuk case.

It now seems that O'Connor had little if any experience as a trial lawyer or in immigration or international law. He is not a member of the American Immigration Lawyers Association, and Gordon Sacks, who served as the immigration judge for the Buffalo area from the mid-1970s through 1986, says he can't remember O'Connor ever coming before him. James Grable, Buffalo district counsel for the U.S. Immigration and Naturalization Service since 1976, also says he never practiced across from O'Connor.

A 1987 article on O'Connor in *The National Law Journal* reported that O'Connor represented the People's Republic of the Congo in a "sovereignty dispute" before the United Nations. But the published opinion in the 1978 case indicates that O'Connor defended the Congo's New York mission in a suit brought by a creditor who held a lien on the mission's mortgage and was trying to foreclose on the property. The suit was dismissed on procedural grounds.

As for trial experience, although the federal and state courts in Buffalo do not reference cases by lawyers' names, longtime staff attorneys in the offices of the Buffalo district attorney and U.S. attorney report that they know of no cases O'Connor tried prior to taking on the Demjanjuk case. And interviews with a half dozen trial lawyers active in the area reveal little knowledge of O'Connor before he started work for Demjanjuk.

Despite his apparent inexperience, the handsome and confident O'Connor won the family's trust. "We were of course dazzled by his verbosity and his appearance," says Nishnic, with a note of bitterness in his voice. "He is a very smooth operator."

For O'Connor, the case was a ticket to publicity and international recognition, but it must also have appealed to his anti-Soviet sentiments. Demjanjuk's family claimed that he was a victim of a Soviet frame-up. Following the war, the family asserts, the government of the U.S.S.R. paid a military pension to Demjanjuk's mother in the mistaken belief that Demjanjuk had been killed in action. In the early 1960s Demjanjuk's wife visited his mother in the Ukraine. It was then, the family contends, that the Soviets discovered Demjanjuk was living in the U.S. and plotted revenge. According to the Demjanjuks, the KGB forged a Nazi identity card and gave the bogus information to a left-leaning Ukrainian-American journalist, who passed it along to the INS.

O'Connor met co-counsel John Gill during the fallout from another controversial case involving an accused Nazi, Chicago-area resident Frank Walus. Walus had lost his citizenship in a 1978 Chicago denaturalization trial, but the decision was reversed in 1980 by the Seventh Circuit. The appeals court found that Holocaust survivors called as witnesses had falsely identified Walus.

When Demjanjuk lost his denaturalization case, Walus spoke in Cleveland on Demjanjuk's behalf. Walus criticized Nazi hunter Simon Wiesenthal, who then filed libel charges against Walus and *The Cleveland Plain Dealer,* which had published Walus's remarks. To handle the libel suit, Walus's lawyers from Chicago's Biggam, Cowan, Marquardt & Lunding looked in *Martindale-Hubbell* for a litigation firm with a non-Jewish name. According to former Biggam, Cowan associate William Barnett, Jr., they picked a small firm named Kelley & Gill. John Gill, a former fireman who handles mostly court-appointed cases, took the case.

Gill says that O'Connor contacted him and asked to join Walus's defense team. O'Connor managed to convince the Biggam, Cowan lawyers that he should work on the libel case, and he and Gill became co-counsel. Through their work on Walus's suit, O'Connor learned that Gill dabbled in document examination. O'Connor took Gill's hobby for expertise and asked him to work on the Demjanjuk case as a document expert.

If the Demjanjuks had observed their lawyers' work on the Walus libel case, they might have realized that O'Connor and Gill were less than expert. Their pleadings were riddled with weak arguments, mistakes in grammar and spelling, and incomprehensible sentences.

For example, in a memorandum opposing Wiesenthal's motion for attorneys' fees, Gill and O'Connor wrote, "We urge that the speed with which a final conclusion of this particular case is reached would not be changed by even one hour if the money sought by plaintiff's law firm was paid now or at some undertermined [sic] future date or even at all."

The case was resolved privately.

Over the next three years O'Connor, assisted by Gill, fought Demjanjuk's deportation and extradition in immigration court and in federal court. All the while O'Connor assured the family there was nothing to worry about.

There was an element of the case that seemed to favor the defense. The only piece of known documentary evidence against Demjanjuk is an identity card from a Nazi training camp, Trawniki, bearing Demjanjuk's name, a photograph, and a physical description. The Trawniki card also lists Demjanjuk's postings, and Treblinka is not among them. According to the card, Demjanjuk had spent the war first at Trawniki, then at a work farm called LG. Okzow, and finaly at the Sobibor death camp. The Nazis destroyed all the Treblinka records when they shut down the camp in late 1943, so there is no documentary evidence from the camp pertaining to Ivan the Terrible. When the card was first introduced as evidence in the U.S. proceedings, O'Connor never brought out the fact that the card doesn't list Treblinka. Instead he contended that the Trawniki card, which was in the custody of the KGB, was a forgery.

O'Connor based his defense of Demjanjuk on the Soviet conspiracy theory, presenting an array of farfetched witnesses—among them a Soviet labor camp survivor who came to court in full Cossack regalia. Since the man hadn't known Demjanjuk in Europe, immigration judge Adolph Angelilli ruled the witness had nothing to contribute and dismissed him. O'Connor's pleadings on behalf of Demjanjuk, like those in the Walus case, were full of grammatical and spelling errors and nonsensical arguments.

There were other signs that O'Connor was not up to his task. For one thing, he alienated several Ukrainian-American leaders who were a major source of financial support for his client.

The Demjanjuks had spent their life's savings on the denaturalization trial, says Nishnic, so they turned to the Ukrainian community for help. Many Ukrainians who fled Soviet domination share the Demjanjuks' belief that the Communist regime might take revenge by creating a false case against them. Also, the question of Ukrainian-Nazi collaboration is a sensitive one for most Ukrainian-Americans.

After he was retained, O'Connor spoke to congregations at Ukrainian churches in the U.S. and Canada. Money started pouring in. According to Nishnic, the family trusted O'Connor to keep track of the contributions, which the lawyer deposited in his own account. Although there is no reliable accounting of just how much O'Connor collected, Nishnic claims the sums were quite large, upwards of a half million dollars. (To date, Nishnic says, donations total more than $1.5 million.)

One of the largest contributors, Newark-based Americans for Human Rights in the Ukraine, gave O'Connor a quarter of a million dollars, according to its president, Bozhena Olshaniwsky. After donating more than $200,000, recalls Olshaniwsky, the group requested an accounting of how the money was being spent. According to Olshaniwsky, after several exchanges O'Connor balked and turned on the group and on her.

"[O'Connor] branded them KGB agents and cut them off," says Nishnic. "O'Connor told me personally that the Ukrainian community wants John Demjanjuk to hang so they can get the blood off their hands."

But the family continued to trust O'Connor. "Mark had convinced us that he is the only one that can save John's life," recalls Nishnic.

The day Demjanjuk was sent to Israel, February 27, 1986, the family was still under O'Connor's spell. "He told us he'd filed a motion with the marshals service," says Nishnic of the tense scene at New York's John F. Kennedy International Airport. "Even when Dad was sitting on the runway we thought someone was going to stop the thing." But U.S. Marshals Service associate legal counsel Joey Lazar says he is not aware of any such motion.

The plane took off. O'Connor and the family remained behind. Demjanjuk was without legal representation in Israel for two months until O'Connor arrived in April. Looking back, Demjanjuk's son, John, Jr., is angry that O'Connor didn't go sooner and that he advised the family not to visit. If it weren't for O'Connor, says John, Jr., "I would have been there on the first plane."

In contrast to Demjanjuk's inexperienced defense lawyers, the Israeli government put together a crack team of seven aggressive young prosecutors, chaired by State Attorney Yona Blatman, whose post is roughly equivalent to a cross between the U.S. solicitor general and a U.S. attorney. While Blatman, 59, was the senior member of the staff, the greatest share of the work, including most in-court examinations, fell to Michael Shaked, 43, a savvy senior assistant from the criminal division of the Jerusalem district attorney's office. Shaked's courtroom style was soft-spoken yet relentless, and according to a junior member of the prosecution team, he was extremely demanding of the staff.

Next in the line of responsibility was Michael Horowitz, a former police investigator who is now a senior assistant in the Tel Aviv district attorney's office. Horowitz, 37, speaks fluent English, Dutch, and German and is described by the junior staffer as "one of those geniuses who's so smart that he's impatient with normal people."

The rest of the team—Dafna Bainvol, Eliyahu Avraham, Gabriel Finder, and Eliyahu Gabai—were young, ambitious lawyers with top academic credentials. Three were American-trained.

After Demjanjuk was indicted in Israel in late September 1986, the pressure on O'Connor started to build. He needed to hire an Israeli co-counsel to advise him on Israeli procedure. Based on British common law, the Israeli legal system is similar to the American, but there is no constitution and no jury system. Demjanjuk's case would be heard before a panel of three judges, two from the district court level and one from the Supreme Court. Israeli judges take an active role in the proceedings, frequently putting questions to the witnesses and to the lawyers. The trappings of the court, too, are different. Counsel as well as judges wear formal black robes. And although there would be simultaneous translation into English for the American lawyers, and into Ukrainian for Demjanjuk, the official language of the court is Hebrew.

For four months O'Connor waffled and stalled on retaining Israeli co-counsel. For a short time in November O'Connor worked with a well-respected Israeli academic and former military judge and prosecutor, Gershon Orion, who volunteered to take the case at cost. But the two clashed, and Orion quit after ten days. Orion says he found O'Connor ill-prepared.

In January, a month before the trial began, O'Connor finally hired defense lawyer Yoram Sheftel. Sheftel had made headlines in 1981 by winning a Supreme Court case for notorious American organized crime figure Meyer Lansky after he was denied a visa by Israel. The two attorneys had met in mid-October while O'Connor was visiting Demjanjuk in prison, where Sheftel was seeing clients.

Sheftel, 39, drives one of the few Porsches in Israel and, when he's not in court, wears wild floral prints and four necklaces, including what he calls his "freak star of David," made of jade. A self-described former beatnik, he lives in a small Tel Aviv bachelor flat crowded with souvenirs of foreign travels: African warrior statues stand guard beside his television and Thai dolls decorate his shelves. His friends and clients, including the Demjanjuk family, know him as "Sheffy."

Sheftel's flamboyance doesn't always play well in the courtroom, where he defends mostly drug cases, robberies, and murders. Sheftel has had long-standing rifts with Tel Aviv's chief prosecutor, Aron Shadar, and with the chief judge on the Demjanjuk case, Supreme Court Justice Dov Levin.

A native Israeli, a fervent Zionist, and a veteran of four wars, Sheftel has had no problem standing up to charges that his representation of Demjanjuk was anti-Israeli or anti-Jewish. His outspokenness and commitment to Jewish survival often combine in statements like, "If there were six million Jews like Meyer Lansky there never would be a Holocaust in the world."

According to former prosecutor M. Dennis Gouldman, who as head of the international section of the state attorney's office was in charge of Israel's extradition request for Demjanjuk, one of Israel's motives in pursuing the case was the desire to communicate the horrors of Treblinka to the Israeli public. To make room for spectators, the proceedings were held at a convention center in a 300-seat theater normally used for film screenings. This setting, with lawyers, judges, and witnesses on a stage and spectators in the audience, emphasized the dramatic atmosphere. Closed circuit video screens outside the hall accommodated another 150 observers, and the trial aired daily on both radio and television. In regular attendance were many Holocaust survivors and their children.

Demjanjuk's bold entry into the hall the first day, February 16, puzzled many observers. Smiling and waving, the hefty, balding defendant called good morning, *"Boker tov,"* to the crowd, using Hebrew he had learned from the prison guards. As tension built over the next three weeks, Demjanjuk grew quiet, listening motionless through headphones to a Ukrainian translation of the proceedings.

The prosecution's first witness, Israeli Holocaust memorial chairman Yitzhak Arad, laid out the historical setting of Ivan the Terrible's crimes. In measured detail, Arad described Operation Reinhard, the Nazis' covert plan to exterminate the Jews of Europe. Treblinka was the largest and most efficient of four Polish death camps. Of the estimated 850,000 to 1.2 million Jews who entered Treblinka, only about 60 escaped death in a failed revolt in August 1943. Following the uprising the Nazis ran the gas chambers one more time, then shut the camp and plowed under the remains. Treblinka, testified Arad, became "perhaps the largest Jewish cemetery in the history of the world."

After Arad, the prosecution put on the crucial witnesses—five Treblinka survivors who had identified Demjanjuk. Ten survivors had fingered his wartime photo, but four had died since the beginning of the U.S. investigation in the mid-seventies. Another Israeli survivor who had testified in the Cleveland denaturalization trial, Sonia Lewkowicz, declined to take the stand.

The survivors' testimony on direct examination was wrenching. Unable to control their emotions, they broke down as they recalled Treblinka. All were certain that the Ivan the Terrible of their nightmares was sitting there in the courtroom. With tears in his eyes, Pinhas Epstein, 61, who had worked as a corpse carrier at Treblinka, declared that he could never forget the brutal guard. Pointing to Demjanjuk's photo, he cried, "This is Ivan as I remember him. . . . I dream about Ivan every night."

These witnesses would have challenged the most talented defense lawyers. The best strategy might have been not to cross-examine them at all, then later, during the defense case, to have presented expert witnesses on memory and identification. After all, the survivors were elderly, and their memories could have faded. One, Gustav Boraks, was even a little senile.

But O'Connor chose to cross-examine the survivors. Although he did bring out some inconsistencies in their testimony, his questions were often convoluted and rambling. Repeatedly the judges intervened to clarify questions or to press O'Connor to get to the point. "We have spent forty-five minutes in cross-examination and we are still on the same burial pit," chief judge Dov Levin said to O'Connor during the cross-examination of survivor Epstein. "This way we will never get anywhere."

Often O'Connor's inquiry seemed to feed the prosecution's case. It was on cross-examination, for example, that Epstein told the court how, when he watched news coverage of Demjanjuk's arrival at Ben-Gurion Airport, he had recognized the defendant's stride. "I recognized him among other things by his walk,'' said Epstein in response to a question from O'Connor. ''Just as in Treblinka.''

In one instance O'Connor, perhaps unwittingly, insulted survivor Eliyahu Rosenberg by asking whether the witness had ever ''wanted to help the victims.''

''In what way could I have helped them?'' Rosenberg answered, visibly shaken. ''By screaming, 'Don't go in the gas chambers'? They didn't want to go in there. Don't ask me questions of that nature, Mr. O'Connor, I implore you.'' Pointing to Demjanjuk, Rosenberg blurted, ''Ask him what he would have done to me.'' Then turning to the bench, Rosenberg shouted, ''I was never asked such a painful question in my life, even by the worst anti-Semite.''

Co-counsel Gill didn't fare much better. He angered the judges when he asked 72-year-old survivor Yehiel Reichman where the women prisoners hung up the guards' laundry. ''More than 800,000 people died in pits here. Is it necessary to know where they hung out the laundry?'' asked Judge Levin testily.

After the survivors' testimony ended March 11, the trial turned to more tedious matters. The Israeli police investigators who had conducted the photo identifications took the stand, as did the prison doctor who had examined Demjanjuk. Next came a dozen expert witnesses, eight of whom testified on the identity card's authenticity, followed by historians who refuted Demjanjuk's alibi. Demjanjuk claimed that he had been an inmate at a Nazi prisoner-of-war camp in Chelm, Poland, during the year that Ivan the Terrible was murdering Jews at Treblinka. But Israeli Holocaust historian Shmuel Krawkowski testified that Chelm was a transit camp where prisoners were held only a few weeks.

Although O'Connor dominated the defense, behind the scenes he was running into serious problems with his colleagues. For the most part Gill hesitated to step beyond the limited role of document expert and didn't confront O'Connor. But Sheftel did.

Sheftel says his ''first major row'' with O'Connor came during the trial's opening week. When he advised O'Connor that it was improper under Israeli rules to admit a piece of evidence, recalls Sheftel, O'Connor asked the court for a short recess and berated him. Sheftel conceded, but the court refused to admit the evidence. Later, Sheftel says, O'Connor threatened to fire him if he ever objected to O'Connor's orders again.

The following week, during O'Connor's cross-examination of survivor Rosenberg, Sheftel and O'Connor clashed in open court over the translation of the witness's 1947 statement that Ivan the Terrible had been killed in the uprising. There were two texts, in German and in Yiddish, that had to be translated into Hebrew, the court's official language. O'Connor does not speak German, Yiddish, or Hebrew, so the judges asked Sheftel and prosecutor Shaked, both of whom speak some German and Yiddish, to agree on the translation.

O'Connor exploded, jumping out of his chair and accusing Sheftel of collaborating with the prosecution behind his back. "Sit down and don't get up again," O'Connor shot at Sheftel. Judge Levin suggested that the defense lawyers decide on a unified strategy. "Mr. Sheftel will not rise again," replied O'Connor.

Nevertheless the court accepted the translation agreed upon by Sheftel and Shaked. Later, the court would decide that Rosenberg had not witnessed the death of Ivan and that he had merely been repeating an account he heard from others.

During the noon break, Sheftel says he confronted O'Connor and demanded an apology. O'Connor complied, but the split between O'Connor and Sheftel was beyond repair.

Demjanjuk's son, John, Jr., attended court daily. He sat directly behind his father and made sure that he understood the Ukrainian translation.

At first, says the younger Demjanjuk, he didn't know how to interpret the clashes between Sheftel and O'Connor. But then O'Connor started claiming that Sheftel was stealing materials and failing to translate important documents from Hebrew. "[O'Connor] was constantly trying to raise suspicions in my mind about what Sheffy's motives were," the young man recalls.

At the same time, Nishnic was getting reports that O'Connor's performance in court was poor. "Somebody that belongs to our church said they thought he was awful long-winded and didn't really seem to get along with the other attorneys," Nishnic recalls. Gill, says Nishnic, was also complaining about O'Connor.

Problems between the defense lawyers climaxed when the court recessed for Passover in mid-April. Sheftel claims that when he discovered that O'Connor had prepared no defense witnesses, O'Connor "threatened me that I would be fired if I let the family know." O'Connor also threatened to withhold money owed to him, says Sheftel.

By this time Nishnic had planned a trip to Israel to assess the situation firsthand. Apparently O'Connor decided to try to fend off Nishnic in the U.S. Nishnic says that on Monday, April 20, five days before he was due to arrive in Jerusalem, he learned that O'Connor was on his way to

Cleveland. Nishnic knew he didn't want to be alone with O'Connor, so he caught the first flight out and crossed O'Connor in midair.

When Nishnic arrived at his hotel in Jerusalem, he got a panicked call from his wife, Irene. O'Connor, she explained, had phoned Cleveland on his arrival in New York and had terrified Demjanjuk's wife, Vera, threatening that if she fired him, her husband would die.

"He was screaming and yelling and my mother-in-law almost had a heart attack," Nishnic says his wife told him. "He was screaming from the top of his lungs how we're out to kill John, how I had no business in Israel, how we're walking into the enemy's hands."

O'Connor flew back to Israel, catching up with Nishnic at the hotel. According to Nishnic, O'Connor launched into a long list of Sheftel's faults: He was a plant by the Mossad, the Israeli secret service; he had purposefully sabotaged the case; he had brainwashed Gill. "The guy was like a nightmare," recalls Nishnic. "He was like a nut."

Sheftel says that at this point he quietly decided that he would push O'Connor out of the case. He advised Nishnic and John, Jr., that they should institute a policy of majority rule. The family and the defendant agreed. If two lawyers agreed on a particular strategy, they would have their way.

O'Connor refused to comply. By late June, Sheftel and O'Connor were clashing daily, inside and outside the courtroom. In a June 25 Associated Press story O'Connor accused Sheftel of "intentionally destroying the defense. . . . [Sheftel] is an Israeli. He is Jewish. He is under tremendous negative pressure from the Israeli media for representing an alleged mass murderer," O'Connor told reporters. "He has reached a breaking point."

Sheftel's response was calculated. The public dispute was "an embarrassment," he remarked to the AP reporter. "We tried to keep it out of public view until Mr. O'Connor made it impossible."

In late June Sheftel and Gill both refused to continue if O'Connor stayed on the case. The family finally decided to fire O'Connor.

At the time the Demjanjuks thought they could bring in another U.S. lawyer. John Broadley, a partner in the Washington, D.C., office of Chicago's Jenner & Block, had been handling a Freedom of Information Act case Nishnic had instituted against the Justice Department. Broadley, a British-born transportation litigation specialist, had become fascinated with the case. Together with an associate, Broadley says he spent approximately $160,000 of lawyer time *pro bono* on the FOIA litigation, a portion of which he won. When members of the family started to consider firing O'Connor, they contacted Broadley about coming to Israel.

At the end of June, Gill and John, Jr., drafted a letter dismissing O'Connor. John, Jr., brought it to his father to sign. It was a difficult step for Demjanjuk, says Nishnic. "Mr. Demjanjuk looked on Mark O'Connor as a son," says Nishnic. "He looked on him as the great messiah." At the same time, says John, Jr., Demjanjuk trusted his family to advise him.

But O'Connor refused to accept his client's decision. Nishnic says O'Connor visited Demjanjuk in his cell. "He came to Dad and said, 'If you fire me, you're dead. I'm the only one that can save you.'"

O'Connor filed a series of letters with the court, accusing Sheftel of mishandling the case and plotting against him, and told reporters that the family was pressuring Demjanjuk to make decisions against his will.

The judges granted O'Connor's request for a hearing to determine whether his client understood what he was doing. In the proceeding on July 15, Demjanjuk was confused and indecisive. A second hearing was set, and this time Demjanjuk stuck to his decision. O'Connor was finally off the case.

Meantime, Broadley's firm had decided not to allow him to take the case. Jenner & Block managing partner Rodney Joslin concedes that many partners had strong feelings about the case, but he says financial rather than emotional considerations finally determined the firm's decision. The case had been tendered as a paying matter, says Joslin, and the firm's finance committee thought the Demjanjuks' funding problems were too great.

Without Broadley, the family started searching desperately for another lawyer. Through a Ukrainian organization in Toronto, Nishnic found a Canadian of Ukrainian descent, Paul Chumak, who was about to leave his post as assistant crown attorney (the equivalent of assistant district attorney in the U.S.). In 17 years as a prosecutor Chumak, 44, had earned a reputation as an energetic and diligent advocate. But he was starting from square one.

At the second hearing on O'Connor's dismissal, the court had turned down a defense motion for an extension. Severely handicapped, on July 27 the defense began presenting its case.

Demjanjuk was the first defense witness. Under Israeli law, if a defendant chooses to testify on his own behalf, he must testify first. According to Sheftel, Gill, Nishnic, and John, Jr., O'Connor had never prepared Demjanjuk to testify. Sheftel immediately assumed the job. He put together a 35-page summary of all Demjanjuk's past statements and spent more than 70 hours with the defendant, going over the document and drilling him on his alibi. Gill also put in some 20 hours with Demjanjuk.

When O'Connor was fired, Sheftel and Gill agreed that the American attorney would be officially designated lead counsel and examine Demjanjuk. They held to that plan despite the fact that Sheftel had spent more than three times as many hours with Demjanjuk. "I didn't want that anyone would have thought [I] was pushing O'Connor [out] because [I] wanted to become lead counsel," explains Sheftel. Sheftel and Gill also claim that Sheftel had to go to Europe to prepare witnesses.

For seven days Demjanjuk struggled on the stand. In his lackluster fashion, Gill led Demjanjuk through his youth in the Ukraine and the crucial years of 1942 and 1943. While Demjanjuk recalled many details about his youth, his description of the war years was sketchy.

Under tough questioning by prosecutors Blatman and Shaked, Demjanjuk could not explain why he recalled so few specifics about the POW camp where he claimed to have been imprisoned during the months that Ivan the Terrible was murdering Jews at Treblinka.

Over the years Demjanjuk had changed the details of his story many times. For example, Demjanjuk still bears a scar from a mysterious tattoo under his right armpit. Such tattoos were given to Waffen-SS combat soldiers. Demjanjuk contends that his was a blood-group tattoo he received while a prisoner of war in Graz, Austria, in 1944. In 1984 Demjanjuk testified that he had removed the tattoo shortly after the German capitulation in 1945. Later he told Israeli police that he had begun to scratch out the tattoo in Heuberg, Germany, where he claims to have been sent in the spring of 1944. In addition, in 1981 Demjanjuk had told U.S. authorities that it was snowing when he reached Heuberg. At trial he testified that he arrived in Heuberg in "spring, closer to summer, 1944."

Prosecutor Blatman pressed Demjanjuk on why, in his 1978 testimony to U.S. immigration officials, he failed three times to recall the name of the POW camp in Poland that constituted the most important part of his alibi.

When the prosecutors hammered away at these contradictions in Demjanjuk's prior testimony, the defendant became exasperated and defensive. Demjanjuk drew hisses from the crowd when he answered, "I would like to forget what happened during those years. But you are pressuring me to remember."

On redirect, Gill failed to elicit answers to any of the questions raised by the prosecutors. Instead he asked his client to repeat the subjects he knew best. The judges grew frustrated. "You're saying that at certain points, the accused told the truth," said Judge Levin to Gill during redirect. "So what? That's like asking someone if a light is on in the hall. If it is and he says yes, he's not lying."

During Demjanjuk's testimony, O'Connor attended court daily and took notes. Although he was officially off the case, he still had the ear of the media, and he started to make statements damaging to Demjanjuk. Asked about the claims that he hadn't prepared Demjanjuk in advance, O'Connor told Michele Lesie of *The Cleveland Plain Dealer*, "When a man tells the truth—if he has been handled properly on direct—he'll come out with flying colors. There's a difference between preparing a witness—and preparing him to lie."

After Demjanjuk, the defense put on two embarrassingly inexpert expert witnesses located by Gill. Their attempts to prove the Trawniki identity card a forgery were disastrous.

Edna Robertson, whom Gill had met through one of the document-examiner societies to which he belongs, came first. Robertson had testified as a document expert in more than 50 U.S. trials, but her qualifications were limited.

Robertson testified that stains on the card indicated that it was a forgery. In cross-examination, however, prosecutor Shaked brought out the fact that the witness was not a forensic chemist and charged that she had not properly tested the stains. Robertson disputed the authenticity of signatures on the Trawniki card—but she also found discrepancies in signatures taken from documents known to be genuine. On the last day of her cross-examination, the judges discredited Robertson's testimony. "We find your opinion a grave error, both in the eyes of the prosecution and the defense," said Judge Levin.

The next witness was worse. Anita Pritchard was presented by Gill as a psychologist and document examiner, but her qualifications consisted of a bachelor's degree from a correspondence college, a master's in human relations from the University of Oklahoma, and enrollment in a correspondence program for a doctorate in psychology. She had testified only once in court.

Pritchard was supposed to discredit the testimony of a police investigator and an anthropologist, who had superimposed current photographs and videotapes of Demjanjuk on the identity card photo to demonstrate that the man on the card had the same facial structure as Demjanjuk.

Gill says he had met Pritchard several years earlier at a conference where Pritchard had lectured on the differences between the right and left sides of the face. But he hadn't contacted her until after the prosecution put on their photo experts. At that time, Gill says, Pritchard wasn't willing to testify in the Demjanjuk case, but she reluctantly consented to appear when he contacted her again in June 1987. Gill never scrutinized Pritchard's credentials or her prepared testimony.

Pritchard fell apart under questioning by Shaked. On her second day on the stand, she took back everything she had said the day before. Shaked also got her to admit that she was not licensed to practice psychology, and that her experience with superimposing photos was self-taught.

Two nights after she finished testifying, Pritchard tried unsuccessfully to commit suicide by taking an overdose of pills and slitting her wrist.

Following Pritchard's testimony the court recessed so that Judge Zvi Tal could sit on a special judicial panel hearing the case of Mordechai Vanunu, an Israeli nuclear technician on trial for revealing defense secrets to *The Sunday Times* of London. While sitting on the Vanunu panel, Tal suffered a heart attack, and the court extended the recess.

During the break Chumak was able to find at least one credible document expert, Julius Grant, an Englishman who was one of the experts who discovered the fraud in the forged Hitler diaries in 1983. Willem Wagenaar, a Dutch memory expert, also agreed to testify, as did Nikolai Tolstoy of England, a relative of the Russian author and a well-regarded historian on the subject of forced repatriation by the Soviet Union.

But these witnesses did little for the defense. Grant said only that the card was "unlikely to be authentic." Wagenaar's statements about memory were likewise more speculative than conclusive. And while Tolstoy said it was, indeed, likely that Demjanjuk had lied on his immigration application because he feared being sent back to the Ukraine, Tolstoy was unable to corroborate the details of Demjanjuk's alibi.

There were more embarrassments for the defense. One of the best witnesses arranged by Gill, William Flynn, got caught in a dispute between the court and the defense and was then tripped up by the prosecutors' careful research. Flynn, the chief document examiner for the state of Arizona, is well known for having uncovered Mark Hofmann's forgeries of Mormon documents in the White Salamander case.

Under direct examination, Flynn claimed that the signature on the Trawniki card was not Demjanjuk's. Flynn had prepared forged samples of the other signatures on the card, plus a photo montage of his own face and a Nazi uniform, but the judges refused to admit these materials into evidence, reasoning that Flynn's talents as a forger were not relevant to the case. The defense then moved to have Flynn's testimony expunged and asked him to withdraw as a witness—a protest, Sheftel says, against the court's refusal to admit Flynn's documents.

When the prosecution asked for the right to cross-examine the witness, Flynn told the judges he was in a quandary, because he had a contract with the defense team, and they were asking him not to testify. Nishnic even threatened to sue Flynn if he testified. But the judges informed Flynn that he could be compelled to testify, and he agreed to continue.

The prosecutors then presented a tape recording of a conference in Palm Springs, California, at which Flynn had made statements that seemed to suggest he believed the Trawniki card was authentic. Flynn again protested, saying his employers had told him not to answer questions. The prosecution agreed to end Flynn's examination there, but argued that the witness had not allowed himself to be fully cross-examined.

Sheftel describes the Flynn incident as an example of the judges' bias against the defense.

When none of the defense witnesses could definitively pronounce the Trawniki card a forgery, Sheftel made an argument that seems absurd. Because the KGB is so expert at forging documents, he claimed, it was impossible to uncover the fraud. But the defense witnesses had already testified that the document was flawed, noting, for example, that the height given for Demjanjuk is off by five centimeters.

Closing arguments began in late January. The prosecution carefully pulled together all the details of its tightly constructed case and criticized the defense witnesses' lack of expertise.

The defense started out well, but then became caught up in points not related to the central question of Demjanjuk's identity. Sheftel dwelled on the notion of a Soviet plot against Demjanjuk and a U.S. effort to cover up the true facts of the case.

Twice over the course of the trial Sheftel had compared the proceedings to a "Moscow-style show trial" and accused the judges of bias. Now, during his summation, he heatedly charged both Israeli and U.S. investigators with transgressions ranging from ignorance of proper identification procedures to "deliberate forgery and a conspiracy to mislead the court." By the third day of Sheftel's summation, Levin grew impatient. "Would you please lower your voice," Levin requested. "We are getting something of a headache, not from the content but the volume."

But if Sheftel irritated the judges, Chumak—who had done little in court up to this point—angered them. In closing his portion of the summation, he compared the Demjanjuk case to the Dreyfus trial. The anti-Semitism that had convicted Alfred Dreyfus in nineteenth-century France was parallel to the "anti-Ukrainianism" behind the Soviet effort to frame Demjanjuk, Chumak asserted. The political aspects of Demjanjuk's trial might "exert psychological pressure" on the judges, suggested Chumak.

"To the Jewish people, the concept of Dreyfus has a very clear meaning, and your statement will be interpreted within that concept," responded Judge Levin. "Defend your reputation and withdraw the base contention you have just sounded. It cannot merit anyone and leaves a most distasteful atmosphere."

Chumak conceded his error. "I had no intentions of casting aspersions," he said.

By the time both sides rested their case, the trial had dragged on for a year. The judges took another two months to render their verdict.

On April 18, 1988, they pronounced Demjanjuk guilty on all counts: crimes against the Jewish people, crimes against humanity, war crimes, and crimes against persecuted people. The judges spent 12 hours reading selections from their lengthy and thorough decision. Midday, as the court's decision became clear, Demjanjuk's family quietly left the courtroom. Demjanjuk himself was not present. Complaining of a sore back, he watched the proceedings on closed circuit television in an anteroom.

As he was led away by guards that evening, Demjanjuk shouted to reporters, "I am very good. I'm not worried. I am an innocent man. I am sure I will win in appeal. . . . This is ridiculous what happened *hayom* ['today' in Hebrew]."

A week later the court reconvened for the last time. As the death sentence was pronounced, emotions that had been held in for more than a year broke loose. "Die, die, die," chanted a group of spectators. Some rose silently while others sang, "The people of Israel live." Demjanjuk sat stonily. Judge Levin called the court to order and advised the defense they had 45 days to file an appeal.

Since the verdict, the Demjanjuk defense has been in disarray. According to Nishnic, fund-raising has lagged, and the defense fund is $180,000 in debt. Gill has withdrawn, claiming he cannot afford to continue.

Sheftel worked alone on the written appeal, which he filed in June. The brief, 280 pages in English translation, repeats the arguments the defense made at trial and claims that the judges were biased and that slanted media coverage created a "lynch atmosphere." The appeal also charges that the judges violated an Israeli law restricting press coverage of trials by subscribing to a press-clipping service.

In a brief interview for this article, Chief Judge Levin explained that the court used the clipping service in order to protect the defense. "From time to time there were some articles which were not fair to the defense," said Levin. When the judges found such articles, he explained, they instructed the court liaison to reprimand the authors. "The defense complained that there was misconduct by the press," said Levin. "How can we know, how can we do something if we don't read the press?" On the issue of bias, Levin answered simply. "We are professional judges, in every case."

In September Sheftel recruited another Israeli lawyer to work on the appeal. Retired judge Dov Eitan, 53, served a total of 17 years on the Israeli bench, first as a magistrate and then as a district court judge in Jerusalem. Since December 1983, Eitan has worked as a criminal defense lawyer with the Jerusalem firm of Bar-On, Eitan and Company.

In December 1989 Sheftel, Chumak, and Eitan will argue the appeal before a new panel of five judges from the Israeli Supreme Court. Given the unequivocal tone of the verdict and the fact that the defense has yet to produce new witnesses or, for that matter, more convincing arguments, it is not likely that Demjanjuk will win. The president of Israel, Chaim Herzog, has the power to set aside the death sentence, but journalists and lawyers who followed the case in Israel predict that Herzog will let the verdict stand.

Even Sheftel is not optimistic. "There are substantially more chances the appeal will be rejected than that it will succeed," he says soberly. "Because of this, most likely Mr. Demjanjuk is going to be hanged."

Still, the family holds out hope. In April they made what appears to be a last-ditch legal effort in the U.S. Relying on 31-year-old Cleveland solo practitioner David Eisler, they filed suit in Cleveland federal district court, charging the U.S. attorney's office, the commissioner of the INS, the director of the Office of Special Investigation, and the attorney general with fraud in pursuing the case against Demjanjuk. The complaint alleges that the OSI fraudulently concealed evidence relating to the facts of the case and to the credibility of the survivor-witnesses. Judging from the shoddily composed complaint, it is unlikely the suit will go anywhere. The government has already moved to dismiss it.

In September, the defense suffered a publicity blow when one of Demjanjuk's longtime supporters, Cleveland travel agent Jerome Brentar, was dismissed from an ethnic advisory committee to Vice President Bush's presidential campaign. Jewish and Nazi-hunting organizations charged that Brentar was linked to anti-Semitic groups and subscribed to the revisionist theory of the Holocaust.

Could top-flight defense counsel have acquitted Demjanjuk? According to journalist Tom Segev, who wrote about the trial for the well-regarded Hebrew language daily *Ha'aretz,* the cult of the Holocaust survivor is so strong in Israel that it would have been impossible for even the best lawyer to convince these judges that they should doubt the survivors' testimony. "The major difficulty involved in a possible acquittal," explains Segev, "is to tell the eyewitnesses, 'Yes, we believe you are telling us the truth as you see it, but what you tell us is not enough.' . . . The judges would have to be intellectual giants," says Segev. "Given the various taboos which are still connected to the survivors of the Holocaust, one doesn't question Holocaust survivors."

But even so, Segev and several other close observers suggest that the defense might have won if it had taken another tack—a tack that was, in fact, suggested by the judges. While Sheftel was making his summation, Judge Levin asked whether the defendant would like to change his alibi and admit that the Trawniki card is real. Because the card has no posting for Treblinka, Demjanjuk could have used it as an alibi.

Harvard Law professor Alan Dershowitz, who attended portions of the trial and has written several articles about it, agrees that the "Sobibor defense" might have succeeded.

In retrospect, Demjanjuk had another alternative: in the two years between his denaturalization in 1981 and the Israelis' extradition request in 1983, he could have left the U.S. But Demjanjuk insists—and his family fervently believes—that he was an innocent prisoner of war during the Holocaust. If Demjanjuk had fled the U.S. or admitted that the identity card is real, he would have had to admit that he had collaborated with the Nazis. He would also have had to admit that he had lied.

Demjanjuk is, of course, the only man who really knows whether that is so. But a better defense would have given everyone else a much surer opinion.

EPILOGUE

John Demjanjuk is imprisoned in Israel pending his appeal before the Israeli Supreme Court. Because of two bizarre events and new evidence, the appeal is now scheduled to be argued in May 1990. In November 1988 the defense team's newest member, former judge Dov Eitan, plummeted to his death from the upper floor of a Jerusalem office tower. Eitan, 53, left no note and Israeli police declared the incident a suicide. Then, at Eitan's funeral, a Holocaust survivor threw acid in the face of defense attorney Yoram Sheftel. Sheftel has recovered and is handling the appeal.

In addition, the defense recently uncovered new evidence relating to the U.S. Justice Department's investigation of Demjanjuk, providing a further basis for postponement of his appeal.